The Cambridge Handbook of Visuospatial Thinking

nated display
ltivariate data
rint and form
sks involving
is a relatively
tanding of vi-
sent and pro-
to cognitive
ıre, medicine,
tics, and ani-
ɔad overview
y researchers
research and

'sychology at
d in the areas
and working
ıl *Psychology:*
the *Journal of*

t of Psychol-
llow of both
imental Psy-
ɔlished in the
comprehen-
ıychology and
as Associate

Cambridge
 king Memory:
Mechanisms of Active Maintenance and Executive Control.

The Cambridge Handbook of Visuospatial Thinking

Edited by

PRITI SHAH & AKIRA MIYAKE

 **CAMBRIDGE**
UNIVERSITY PRESS

CAMBRIDGE UNIVERSITY PRESS
Cambridge, New York, Melbourne, Madrid, Cape Town, Singapore, São Paulo

Cambridge University Press
40 West 20th Street, New York, NY 10011-4211, USA

www.cambridge.org
Information on this title: www.cambridge.org/9780521807104

First published 2005

Printed in the United States of America

A catalog record for this publication is available from the British Library.

Library of Congress Cataloging in Publication Data

The Cambridge handbook of visuospatial thinking / edited by
Priti Shah, Akira Miyake.
     p.   cm.
Includes bibliographical references and indexes.
ISBN 0-521-80710-7 (hardback) – ISBN 0-521-00173-0 (pbk.)
1. Mental representation.   2. Space perception.   3. Imagery
(Psychology)   4. Visualization.   5. Thought and thinking.
I. Shah, Priti, 1968–   II. Miyake, Akira, 1966–   III. Title.
BF316.6.C36   2005
152.14′2 – dc22   2004020365

ISBN-13   978-0-521-80710-4 hardback
ISBN-10   0-521-80710-7 hardback

ISBN-13   978-0-521-00173-1 paperback
ISBN-10   0-521-00173-0 paperback

Contents

List of Contributors

Marcia L. Collaer
Department of Psychology
Middlebury College
Middlebury, VT 05753
collaer@middlebury.edu

Sergio Della Sala
Department of Psychology, PPLS
University of Edinburgh
Edinburgh EH89JZ
Scotland, United Kingdom
sergio@staffmail.ed.ac.uk

Eric G. Freedman
Department of Psychology
University of Michigan, Flint
Flint, MI 48502-1950
freedman@umich.edu

Diane F. Halpern
Berger Institute for Work, Family,
  and Children
Claremont McKenna College
850 Columbia Ave.
Claremont, CA 91711-6400
Diane.Halpern
  @claremontmckenna.edu

Mary Hegarty
Department of Psychology
University of California, Santa
  Barbara
Santa Barbara, CA 93106
hegarty@psych.ucsb.edu

Friderike Heuer
Department of Psychology
Lewis & Clark College
615 SW Palatine Hill Rd.
Portland, OR 97219-7899
heuer@lclark.edu

Amy E. Learmonth
Department of Psychology
Rutgers University
152 Frelinghuysen Rd.
Piscataway, NJ 08854-8020
amyel@rci.rutgers.edu

Robert H. Logie
Department of Psychology, PPLS
University of Edinburgh
Edinburgh EH89JZ
Scotland, United Kingdom
rlogie@staffmail.ed.ac.uk

Richard E. Mayer
Department of Psychology
University of California, Santa
  Barbara
Santa Barbara, CA 93106
mayer@psych.ucsb.edu

Akira Miyake
Department of Psychology
University of Colorado at Boulder
345 UCB
Boulder, CO 80309-0345
akira.miyake@colorado.edu

Daniel R. Montello
Department of Geography
University of California, Santa
  Barbara
Santa Barbara, CA 93106
montello@geog.ucsb.edu

Nora S. Newcombe
Department of Psychology
Temple University
Philadelphia, PA 19122
newcombe@astro.ocis.temple.edu

Daniel Reisberg
Department of Psychology
Reed College
3203 SE Woodstock Blvd.
Portland, OR 97202
Daniel.Reisberg
  @directory.reed.edu

Mike Rinck
Maastricht University
Department of Medical, Clinical,
  and Experimental Psychology
Postbus 616
6200 MD Maastricht, NL
M.Rinck@DMKEP.unimaas.nl

Priti Shah
Department of Psychology
525 East University
University of Michigan
Ann Arbor, MI 48109–1109
priti@umich.edu

Holly A. Taylor
Department of Psychology
Paige Hall
Tufts University
Medford, MA 02155
htaylor@ tufts.edu

Barbara Tversky
Department of Psychology
Building 420
Jordan Hall
Stanford, CA 94305-2130
bt@psych.stanford.edu

Ioanna Vekiri
N. Plastira 103
Thessaloniki, 55132, Greece
aretsou@hol.gr

Michelle Vincow
Verizon Laboratories
18 Day St. #207
Somerville, MA 02144
mvincow@yahoo.com

David A. Waller
Department of Psychology
234 Benton Hall
Miami University
Oxford, OH 45056
wallerda@muohio.edu

Christopher D. Wickens
Beckman Institute
University of Illinois
405 N. Mathews
Urbana, IL 61801
cwickens@uiuc.edu

Michelle Yeh
Volpe National Transportation
  Systems Center
55 Broadway
Cambridge, MA 02142
yeh@volpe.dot.gov

Preface

Navigating across town, comprehending an animated display of the functioning of the human heart, viewing complex multivariate data on a business's website, reading an architectural blueprint, and forming a three-dimensional mental picture of a house are all tasks involving visuospatial thinking. As suggested by the breadth of this list of tasks, the field of visuospatial thinking is a relatively diverse interdisciplinary research enterprise. An understanding of visuospatial thinking – in particular, how people represent and process visual and spatial information – is relevant not only to the field of cognitive psychology but also to education, geography, architecture, medicine, design, computer science/artificial intelligence, semiotics, and animal cognition.

The goal of this handbook is to present a broad overview of the research on this topic that can be used by researchers interested in visuospatial thinking in both basic and applied or naturalistic contexts. The focus of this volume is higher-level visuospatial thinking, which involves the use of internal or external visual or spatial representations from visual imagery to diagrammatic reasoning. Our focus on higher-level visuospatial thinking contrasts with lower-level visuospatial cognition, such as object recognition, visual attention, and scene perception.

There are at least three reasons why we felt that there is a need for this handbook. First, historically, research on visuospatial thinking has been a relatively loosely connected enterprise, often with little interaction among researchers addressing related questions. For example, although there are similar issues involved in the processing of graphs, diagrams, and maps, little communication across these research areas exists, and few generic models or theories can provide a unified framework for the comprehension of various visual displays. Similarly, although research on visuospatial thinking at multiple levels (e.g., object recognition, scene perception, diagram comprehension) has been done, few models cut across these levels. This state of affairs in the visuospatial thinking domain is in stark contrast to the field of text comprehension, where a number of well-developed models that cut across different levels of analysis already exist. By bringing together different lines of related research in a single volume, we believe that this handbook will provide one step toward the development of a more unified subdiscipline of cognitive science, the field of higher-level visuospatial thinking.

Another closely related reason is that much research on visuospatial thinking is distributed across different disciplines and in many cases has been conducted in the context of applied problems. For example, cognitive psychologists examine the nature of limitations in visuospatial working memory and specify the nature of individual and group differences in visuospatial abilities in lab-based settings (e.g., Logie & Della Sala, Chapter 3; Hegarty & Waller, Chapter 4; Halpern & Collaer, Chapter 5). At the same time, similar questions are asked in more applied contexts. Medical researchers consider how limitations in spatial abilities may affect surgeons using virtual tools, and meteorologists consider how spatial abilities may influence the interpretation of interactive weather displays. In another example, the communication of three-dimensional information in two-dimensional format is critical for many situations (e.g., Wickens, Vincow, & Yeh, Chapter 10; Shah, Freedman, & Vekiri, Chapter 11; and Mayer, Chapter 12), but extensive research related to this topic has been conducted in rather disparate fields, including chemistry, architecture, multimedia instruction, and radiology. Because of the distributed nature of research on visuospatial thinking across different domains, it has been difficult for researchers to know what relevant work has been done on a certain topic and to keep up with the large body of available research. A researcher in an applied domain (e.g., someone interested in three-dimensional visuospatial thinking during surgery) may not be prepared to identify the different communities that have examined related questions. Our intention is to bring together the important research on visuospatial thinking in different contexts so that researchers in various disciplines can apply what has been learned in other subfields of visuospatial thinking to their own fields.

A third reason for editing a handbook on visuospatial thinking is that current technology requires new types of visuospatial thinking. Information technology, for example, requires people to comprehend and use animated, three-dimensional, and interactive displays and also to navigate through virtual as well as physical space. Along with such technological advances are numerous new empirical studies – yet again, these studies are frequently done within the context of specific fields without making much contact with related research in other disciplines. In this handbook, several examples of visuospatial thinking involving current technology from navigation through virtual space to the comprehension of complex multimedia representations are presented and discussed in some detail.

We decided against including a larger number of short chapters, as is frequently done in books with the word *handbook* in the title. We instead opted for providing in-depth reviews of central topics in higher-level visuospatial thinking so that readers may gain a strong foundation in each selected topic. This means that the information contained here does not cover all possible topics within research on visuospatial thinking, but many of the core topics are covered in a fairly comprehensive manner in each chapter. From our own experience, we have found handbooks that are somewhat selective but offer an in-depth coverage of major topics more useful than those that offer a comprehensive yet somewhat cursory treatment of many topics, and we hope that readers also see some benefits in our "selective, in-depth" approach.

The handbook can be loosely divided into four sections, beginning with a section with the basic cognitive mechanisms underlying visuospatial thought, such as visuospatial imagery and working memory. In Chapter 1, Barbara Tversky begins with a fundamental theoretical issue that applies to all the remaining chapters in the volume, the role of visuospatial representations in human thought. Specifically, in her tutorial overview chapter, she addresses such fundamental questions as, "What kinds of internal and external visuospatial representations do we use, how do they relate to one another, and for what are they useful?" In Chapter 2, Dan Reisberg and Friderike Heuer provide an up-to-date review of research on mental imagery. Their chapter also includes the latest research on the neural basis of mental imagery, including sections on neuroimaging studies and research on neuropsychological patients with mental imagery deficits. In Chapter 3, Robert Logie and Sergio Della Sala provide an in-depth discussion of one important building block of visuospatial thinking – visuospatial working memory – from the perspective of neuropsychological studies of disorders of visuospatial cognition, particularly those of hemispatial neglect.

The second section of the handbook focuses on individual and group differences in spatial abilities. We devote a few chapters to this topic because historically this topic has been a relatively large component of cognitive research on visuospatial thinking and has been of practical importance to most applied topics in visuospatial thinking. In Chapter 4, Mary Hegarty and David Waller review the research on individual differences in visuospatial thinking, including psychometric spatial abilities, navigational skill, mechanical reasoning abilities, and other visuospatial abilities. They also consider various relationships among spatial abilities (e.g., navigation skill and psychometric spatial skill), the relationship between spatial ability and other skills (e.g., mathematical ability and musical skills), and the effects of aging on visuospatial thinking. In Chapter 5, Diane Halpern and Marcia Collaer critically evaluate evidence for sex-related differences in visuospatial abilities in humans and other animals. In addition, they consider underlying explanations for sex-related differences, such as differences in brain laterality, hormones, and life experiences. Finally, in Chapter 6, Nora Newcombe and Amy Learmonth provide an in-depth, theoretically motivated account of the development of spatial skills. The authors' main focus is children's ability to represent and use knowledge about geographical space, such as their ability to remember spatial locations, imagine space from different perspectives, and navigate through space.

The third section of the handbook focuses on constructing and using visuospatial mental representations in the performance of complex everyday tasks, such as navigation, map reading, and the comprehension of verbal directions. In Chapter 7, Daniel Montello provides a comprehensive review of current views on the mechanisms and representations involved in human navigation. In Chapter 8, Holly Taylor discusses research on the comprehension and production of maps and other external representations of geographical space. Finally, Chapter 9, written by Mike Rinck, concerns the nature of processes and representations involved in the mental construction of spatial representations from verbal descriptions (e.g., reading a passage in which the main character moves from one location to another). Called *spatial situation models*, these representations serve as an interface between visuospatial thinking and language comprehension.

The final section of the handbook presents four exemplar applied contexts that have lately received a large amount of research attention. In Chapter 10, Chris Wickens, Michelle Vincow, and Michelle Yeh discuss two of these contexts: navigational displays (e.g., pilot navigation or head mounted displays) and information visualization displays. In their chapter, the authors emphasize the importance of various frames of reference and the difficulties of translating between frames of reference in the context of different tasks. In Chapter 11, Priti Shah, Eric Freedman, and Ioanna Vekiri describe research on the comprehension of graphs. They consider the display, content, task, and individual difference factors that influence the interpretation of quantitative data presented visually. Finally, in Chapter 12,

Richard Mayer examines the effects of visuospatial media on thinking and learning from an educational perspective and presents a model of multimedia comprehension and principles of multimedia.

As mentioned, this handbook is intended to serve as a resource for readers in the cognitive sciences as well as researchers in related disciplines who may have an applied interest in visuospatial cognition. In addition, we hope that this volume will be useful to advanced undergraduate and graduate students and other individuals who are interested in learning about the field of visuospatial thinking but do not have strong background knowledge in it.

To make this volume accessible to a broad, interdisciplinary audience as well as to novice student readers, we have implemented a number of features.

We asked chapter authors to define the technical terms that they used in their chapters, even when those terms were used in other chapters, so that each chapter can serve as an independent resource for the reader. Also, because handbook readers usually read a subset of chapters relevant to their interests rather than reading the entire book from cover to cover, we have deliberately maintained some level of redundancy across chapters so that readers would not have to refer to other chapters to comprehend the one they are reading. At the same time, we have included a number of cross-references in each chapter so that interested readers can learn more about the related topics by taking a look at other related chapters. Additionally, we solicited reviews of chapter drafts from graduate students. We explicitly asked these reviewers to identify any concepts or technical terms that were unclear to the reader and then asked the authors to revise their chapters accordingly. Each chapter was reviewed by experts in certain aspects of visuospatial thinking research so that the contents of each chapter are accurate and of interest to expert researchers in the field as well. Finally, we asked authors to provide a list of important further readings so that readers can use these chapters as a springboard for learning about different subfields of visuospatial thinking.

The field of visuospatial thinking is a diverse interdisciplinary research community. We hope that this handbook serves as a useful resource for researchers currently conducting research in visuospatial thinking as well as researchers new to the field and that it also provides a useful bridge between basic and applied research on visuospatial thinking.

Priti Shah and Akira Miyake

Acknowledgments

We would like to thank a number of people and agencies that have supported this book project.

First, we would like to acknowledge granting agencies that have supported our own work during the time we have been working on this book. Priti Shah was supported by grants from the Office of Naval Research (N00014-98-1-0812, N00014-98-1-0350, and N00014-02-1-0279). Akira Miyake was supported by grants from the National Institute of Mental Health (MH63207).

We owe a debt of gratitude to the two groups of reviewers who provided detailed feedback on the chapters contained in this handbook. One group of reviewers consisted of experts on certain aspects of visuospatial thinking. The other group of reviewers were graduate students. For each chapter, two graduate students, one from within the discipline of cognitive psychology and one from outside of cognitive psychology but in a field relevant to visuospatial cognition (e.g., education, information science), reviewed the chapters for readability, comprehensibility, and content. These reviewers were (in alphabetical order): Damian Betebenner, Kirsten Butcher, Leslie Cohen, David Collister, Elizabeth Davis, Patricia DeLucia, Mike Emerson, Naomi Friedman, Julie Heiser, Jeff Holmes, Alex Kauper, Steve Kosslyn, Kate Masarik, Joe Mikels, Beth Mulligan, Mitch Nathan, Naomi Norman, Danny Oppenheimer, David Pearson, Jim Pellegrino, John Reiser, Patricia Reuter-Lorenz, Matt Rossano, Gunnar Schrah, Julia Sluzenski, Jim Van Overschelde, Sashank Varma, Daniel Voyer, and Rolf Zwaan. Thanks to all.

We would also like to thank people who generously helped us at various stages of the book project, including Linda Anderson, Aysecan Boduroglu, Evelyn Craft-Robinson, and Rachel Orlowski at the University of Michigan and Michie Shaw and Andrew Wilson at TechBooks. We would particularly like to thank our editor at Cambridge University Press, Phil Laughlin, for his thorough and timely help and especially his patience.

In addition, Priti Shah gratefully acknowledges the support of her colleagues and students at the University of Michigan on this book project as well as on her research. Jim Hoeffner has provided much love and support during the entire editing process. He deserves a mountain of thanks (and a vacation) (or two). Finally, Kiran and Avani provided lots of joyful diversions.

Akira Miyake gratefully acknowledges the support of his colleagues at the University of Colorado, Boulder, where most of the editing of this handbook (as well as our previous book with Cambridge University Press, *Models of Working Memory: Mechanisms of Active Maintenance and Executive Control*) took place. He is extremely grateful for the encouragement that his Boulder colleagues, students, and friends provided on these book projects as well as his research. He would also like to thank the University of Toronto for providing necessary resources for completing the last stages of the handbook editing process.

1

Functional Significance of Visuospatial Representations

Barbara Tversky

ABSTRACT

Mental spaces are not unitary. Rather, people conceive of different spaces differently, depending on the functions they serve. Four such spaces are considered here. The space of the body subserves proprioception and action; it is divided by body parts, with perceptually salient and functionally significant parts more accessible than others. The space around the body subserves immediate perception and action; it is conceived of in three dimensions in terms of relations of objects to the six sides of the body: front/back, head/feet, left/right. The space of navigation subserves that; it is constructed in memory from multimodal pieces, typically as a plane. The reconstruction generates systematic errors. The space of external representations, of pictures, maps, charts, and diagrams, serves as cognitive aids to memory and information processing. To serve those ends, graphics schematize and may distort information.

INTRODUCTION: FOUR FUNCTIONAL SPACES

When physicists or surveyors exercise their trades, aspects of space are foreground, and the things in space background. Things are located in space by means of an extrinsic reference system, in terms of metric measurement. Within the reference system, aspects of the space, whether large or small, distal or proximal, for entities small or large, are uniform. Surveyors laying out a road, for example, need to know the exact distance from point A to point B, the exact curvature of the terrain, the exact locations of other objects, natural and built. In other words, they need first to measure aspects of the space as accurately as possible. For human cognition, the void of space is treated as background, and the things in space as foreground. They are located in space with respect to a reference frame or reference objects that vary with the role of the space in thought or behavior.

1

Which things, which references, which perspective depend on the function of those entities in context, on the task at hand. In human cognition, the spatial relations are typically qualitative, approximate, categorical, or topological rather than metric or analog. They may even be incoherent, that is, people may hold beliefs that cannot be reconciled in canonical three-dimensional space. Human directions to get from A to B, for example, are typically a string of actions at turning points, denoted by landmarks, as in "go down Main to the Post Office, take a right on Oak." The directions are given in terms of entities in the space, paths, and landmarks, and in approximate terms, right, left, straight (Denis, 1997; Tversky & Lee, 1998). In addition, for human cognition there are many spaces, differing in the roles they play in our lives. Those considered here are the space of the body, the space surrounding the body, the space of navigation, and the space of external representations, such as diagrams and graphs. These mental spaces do not seem to be simple internalizations of external spaces like images (e.g., Kosslyn, 1980, 1994b; Shepard, 1994; Shepard & Podgorny, 1978); rather, they are selective reconstructions, designed for certain ends.

What are the different functions that space serves us? The space of the body, the space around the body, the space of exploration, and a uniquely human space, the space of depictions, serve different functions in human activity and hence in human cognition. Things in space impinge on our bodies, and our bodies act and move in space. In order to interpret those impingements, we need knowledge of the receptive surfaces on the body. In order to coordinate those actions, we need knowledge of what the body can do and feedback on what the body has done. The space of the body has a perceptual side, the sensations from outside and inside the body, and a behavioral side, the actions the body performs. Proprioception tells one about the other. Representations of the space of the body allow us to know what the parts of our bodies can do, where they are, what is impinging on them, and, importantly, how to interpret the bodies of others. Actions of others may have consequences for ourselves, so we need to anticipate those by interpreting others' intentions. The space around the body is the space in which it is possible to act or see without changing places, by rotating in place. It includes the surrounding objects that might get acted on or need to be avoided. The space around the body represents the space that can immediately affect us and that we can immediately affect. Both these spaces are experienced volumetrically, although the space of the body is decomposed into its natural parts and the space around the body is decomposed into the six regions projecting from the six surfaces of the body. The space of navigation is the space of potential travel. It is too large to be seen at once, so it is pieced together from a variety of kinds of experiences: perceptual, from actual navigation, or cognitive, from maps or descriptions. In contrast to the space of the body and the space around the body, it is known primarily from memory, not from concurrent perception. It is typically conceived of as primarily flat. Finally, the space of external representations considered here is typically space on paper meant to represent an actual space, as in a map or architectural drawing, or to represent a metaphoric space, as in a diagram or graph. External representations are creations of people to aid cognition. They can be directly perceived, but they themselves are representations of something else. This is a capsule of what is yet to come.

THE SPACE OF THE BODY

Through our bodies, we perceive and act on the world around us and learn about the consequences of our actions. One way that we view and think about bodies is as objects. Common objects can be referred to at several levels of abstraction. What I am wearing on my feet can be called clothing or shoes or running shoes. What I am sitting on can be referred to as furniture or a chair or a desk chair. Despite those possibilities, there is a preferred level of reference, a most common way of talking in everyday speech, the level of shoe or chair, over a broad range of contexts. This level has been termed the *basic* level (Rosch, 1978). The basic level has a special status in many aspects of human cognition. Central to recognition and to categorization of objects at the basic level is contour or shape. Underlying shape for most objects are parts in the proper configuration (cf. Biederman, 1987; Hoffman & Richards, 1984; Tversky & Hemenway, 1984). Although objects have many features, parts constitute the features most diagnostic of the basic level of categorization. Many other cognitive tasks converge on the basic level. For example, it is the highest level for which people can form a general image; people report that forming images of shoes or chairs is not difficult, but forming single images of clothing or furniture is not possible. It is the highest level for which action patterns are similar. The same behaviors are appropriate to different kinds of shoes and different kinds of chairs, but not toward different pieces of clothing or furniture. The basic level is also the highest level for which a general image, one that encompasses the category, can be formed, the highest level for which action patterns are similar, the fastest level to identify, the earliest level acquired by children and introduced to language, and more (Rosch, 1978).

Thus, the basic level has a special status in perception, action, and language. Parts may be critical to the basic level because they form a link from perception or appearance of an object to its function. Parts that are perceptually salient tend to be functionally significant as well; moreover, the shapes of parts give clues to their functions (Tversky & Hemenway, 1984). Think of arms, legs, and backs of chairs, and of course, of people. What is especially intriguing for the parts of the human body is that the size of the brain representations are not proportional to the physical size of the parts themselves. The brain has twin representations of the body, on either side of the sensorimotor cortex, one for the sensory part, one for the motor part. In both cases, certain parts, like lips and hands, have larger than expected amounts of cortex devoted to them, and other parts, like backs, have smaller than expected amounts of cortex devoted to them.

Bodies are a privileged object for humans. Unlike other objects, they are experienced from inside as well as from outside. People determine the actions of their own bodies and those actions provide sensory feedback. Insider knowledge of the body seems to affect how bodies are perceived. Consider an interesting phenomenon in apparent motion. Apparent motion occurs when two similar integrative stimuli occur in rapid succession. Instead of perceiving two static images, people perceive a single image that is moving. Apparent motion is the basis for movies and for the lights on movie marquees. The motion is normally seen at the shortest path. However, when the shortest path for apparent motion violates the ways that bodies can move, a longer motion path is seen for intermediate interstimulus intervals (Heptulla-Chatterjee, Shiffrar, & Freyd, 1996). Thus, when a photo of an arm in front of the body and an arm behind the body are played in rapid succession (but not too rapid), viewers see the elbow jutting out rather than passing through the body. The shortest path is preferred for objects, even when it violates a physical property of the world, that one solid object cannot pass through another solid object, suggesting that knowledge of the body is privileged for perception. In other experiments, people were asked to judge whether two photos of humans in contorted positions of the body were the same or different. Observers were more accurate when they actually moved the limbs, arms or legs, whose positions were changed in the photos, provided the movements were random (Reed & Farah, 1995). Neuroscience literature also indicates privileged areas of the brain for representing the body; when those areas, primarily in parietal cortex, are damaged, there can be disruption of identification or location of body parts (e.g., Berlucchi & Aglioti, 1997; Gross & Graziano, 1995). Moreover, sections of the lateral occipital temporal cortex are selectively responsive to the sight of human bodies (Downing, Jiang, Shuman, & Kanwisher, 2001).

Insider knowledge of the body seems to affect mental representations of the space of the body as well, as revealed in the speed with which different body parts are identified. Despite diversity in languages, certain body parts are named across most of them: head, arm, hand, leg, foot, chest, and back (e.g., Andersen, 1978). These parts differ in many ways, including size, contour distinctiveness, and function. In detecting parts in imagery, size is critical; larger parts are verified faster than smaller ones (Kosslyn, 1980). In object recognition, parts that are distinct from their contours, parts that stick out, are critical (Biederman, 1987; Hoffman & Richards, 1984; Tversky & Hemenway, 1984). Finally, although the functional significance of parts is correlated with contour distinctiveness, the correlation is not perfect. Is one of these factors (size, perceptual salience, or functional significance) more critical to mental conceptions of the body than others? In a series of experiments, participants saw either the name of one of the frequently named body parts or a depiction of a side view of a body with one of the parts highlighted (Morrison & Tversky, 1997; Tversky, Morrison, & Zacks, 2002). They compared this to a depiction of a side view of a body with a part highlighted, responding same or different depending on whether the parts matched. Neither of the comparisons, name–body or body–body, revealed an advantage for large parts; on the contrary, large parts were slower to verify than small ones. For both comparisons, verification times were faster for parts that were high on contour distinctiveness and functional significance. Functional significance was roughly indicated by relative size in sensorimotor cortex. For body–body comparisons, verification times were more highly correlated with contour distinctiveness; these comparisons can be quickly made just on the basis of visual appearance, without processing the body as a body or the parts as actual parts. That is, the two pictures can be treated as meaningless visual stimuli for the comparison entailed. In contrast, for name–body comparisons, verification times were more highly correlated with functional significance. In order to compare a name with a depiction, at least some aspects of meaning must be activated. Names are powerful. In this case, it appears that names activate aspects of meaning of body parts that are closely tied to function.

People move the separate parts of their bodies in specific ways in order to accomplish the chores and enjoy the pleasures of life. They get up and dress, walk to work (or to their cars), pick up mail, open doors, purchase tickets, operate telephones, eat food, hug friends and family. The space of the body functions to achieve these ends. Different body parts are involved in different sorts of goals and functions, the feet and legs in navigating the world, the hands and arms in manipulating the objects that serve us. Mental representations of the space of the body reflect the functions of the body parts.

THE SPACE AROUND THE BODY

The space around the body is the arena for learning about the world and for taking actions and accomplishing goals in it. The proximal space from which the world can be perceived and in which action can readily be taken is a second natural delineation of space by function. One effective way to study the cognition of space, the space around the body and other spaces as well, is through narrative descriptions of space. When descriptions of space are limited and coherent, people are able to construct mental models of them (e.g., Ehrlich & Johnson-Laird, 1982; Franklin & Tversky, 1990; Glenberg, Meyer, & Lindem, 1987; Mani & Johnson-Laird, 1982; Morrow, Greenspan, & Bower, 1989; Rinck, Chapter 9; Rinck, Hahnel, Bower, & Glowalla, 1997; Taylor & Tversky, 1992b; Tversky, 1991). The mental spatial models are mental representations that preserve information about objects and the spatial relations among them and are updated as new information comes in. They allow rapid inferences of spatial elements, locations, distances, and relations from new viewpoints.

Narratives have been used to establish mental models of the space around the body (e.g., Bryant, Tversky, & Franklin, 1992; Franklin & Tversky, 1990; Franklin, Tversky, & Coon, 1992; Tversky, Kim, & Cohen, 1999). Participants studied narratives that addressed them as "you," and placed them in an environment such as a hotel lobby, a museum, or a barn, surrounded by objects at all six sides of their bodies, front, back, head, feet, left, and right. Thus, the narratives described the world from the point of view of the observer (you), in terms of directions from the observer. After learning the environment from narratives, participants were reoriented to face a new object, and probed with direction terms for the objects currently in those directions. Several theories predicting the relative times to retrieve objects at the various directions around the body were evaluated (Franklin & Tversky, 1990). The data did not fit the Equiavailability Theory, according to which all objects should be equally accessible because none is privileged in any way. The data also did not conform to a pattern predicted from an Imagery Theory, according to which observers would imagine themselves in a scene and then imagine themselves examining each direction for the relevant object; an imagery account predicts slower times to retrieve objects in back of the observer than to left and right, counter to the data. The pattern of retrieval times fit the Spatial Framework Theory best. According to this theory, people remember locations of objects around the body by constructing a mental spatial framework consisting of extensions of the axes of the body, head/feet, front/back, and left/right, and attaching the objects to them. Accessibility of directions depends on asymmetries of the body and asymmetries of the world. The only asymmetric axis of the world is the up/down axis created by gravity. Gravity of course has broad effects on the way the world appears and the way we can act in it. For the upright observer, this axis coincides with the asymmetric head/feet axis of the body. Times to retrieve objects at head and feet are in fact, fastest. The front/back axis is also asymmetric but does not coincide with any asymmetric axis of the world. The front/back axis separates the world that can be readily perceived and acted on from the world behind the back, difficult for both perception and action. Finally, the left/right axis lacks any salient asymmetries, and is, in fact, slowest.

The spatial situation can be varied in many ways: by altering the orientation of the observer (Franklin & Tversky, 1990), by adding more observers (Franklin et al., 1992), by putting the array in front of the observer instead of surrounding the observer (Bryant et al., 1992), by having the environment rotate around the observer instead of having the observer turn to reorient in the environment (Tversky et al., 1999). These variants in the situation lead to consequent variants in the retrieval times that can be accounted for by extensions of the Spatial Framework Theory. When the observer is described as reclining, and turning from side to front to back to side, no body axis correlates with gravity. Retrieval times in this case depend only on body asymmetries. The front/back axis of the body seems to be the most salient as it separates the world that can be readily perceived and manipulated from the world behind the back. Along this axis, front has a special status, as it is the direction of orientation, of better perception, of potential movement. In fact, for the reclining case, times to retrieve objects in front and back are faster than times to retrieve objects at head and feet, and times to front faster than those to back (Bryant et al., 1992; Franklin & Tversky, 1990). What about narratives describing two characters, for example, in different scenes? In that case, the viewpoints of each character in each scene are taken in turn; in other words, participants construct and use separate mental models for each situation, yielding the spatial framework pattern of data. However, when two characters are integrated into a single scene, participants seem to construct a single mental model that incorporates both characters, and take a single, oblique point of view on them and the objects surrounding them (Franklin et al., 1992). In this case, they do not take the point of view of either of the characters so their bodies are not aligned with any of them. Thus no area of space is privileged for the participant, and in fact, reaction times are the same for all directions for both characters. How about when narratives describe the environment as rotating rather than the observer as turning? In the case of the rotating environment, participants take twice as much time to reorient as when narratives describe the observer as reorienting. In the world we inhabit, people move, not environments, so although people can perform mental feats that the world does not, it takes longer to imagine impossible than possible, normal, mundane interactions with the world (Tversky et al., 1999).

Not only can the spatial situation be varied, the mode of acquisition can be varied; the space around the body can be acquired from narrative, from diagrams, from models, and from experience (Bryant & Tversky, 1999; Bryant, Tversky, & Lanca, 2001; Franklin & Tversky, 1990). As long as retrieval is from memory rather than perception, the Spatial Framework pattern of retrieval times obtains (Bryant et al., 2001). When responding is from perception, then patterns closer to the Imagery model obtain. This is because it in fact takes longer to look behind than to look left or right. Surprisingly, as participants learn the environments, they cease looking, so that although the information is available from perception, they respond from memory. As a consequence, the retrieval times come to correspond to the Spatial Framework model. Although diagrams and models are both external spatial representations of the scenes, they instill slightly different mental models (Bryant & Tversky, 1999). The models were foot-high dolls with depictions of objects hung in the appropriate directions around the doll. When learning from models, participants adopt the embedded point of view of the doll, and, just as from the original narratives, they imagine themselves reorienting in the scene. The diagrams depicted stick figures with circles at the appropriate directions from the body; the circles contained the names of the objects. When learning from diagrams, participants adopt an outside point of view and imagine the scene rotating in front of them, as in classic studies of mental rotation (e.g., Shepard & Cooper, 1982). We speculated that the three-dimensional models encouraged participants to take the internal viewpoint of the doll whereas the flat and flattened space of the diagram encouraged participants to treat the diagram as an object, in other words, to mentally manipulate the external representation instead of using it to induce an internal perspective. These perspectives, however, are flexible; when directed to do so, participants used the diagram to take an internal viewpoint or used the model to adopt an external one. The two perspectives and the mental transformations of them, viewing an object from outside versus viewing a surrounding environment from inside, appear in other analogous tasks, and are subserved by different neural substrates (e.g., Zacks, Rypma, Gabrieli, Tversky, & Glover, 1999). They reflect the two dominant perspectives people take on space, an external view, prototypically the view people have on objects that they observe and manipulate, and an internal view, prototypically the view people have on environments that they explore. One remarkable feature of human cognition is that it allows both viewpoints on both kinds of external realities.

The space around the body, that is, the space immediately surrounding us, the space that functions for direct perception and potential action, is conceptualized in three dimensions constructed out of the axes of the body or the world. Objects are localized within that framework and their relative locations are updated as the spatial situation changes. The mental spatial framework created out of the body axes underlies perspective-taking, allows updating across rotation and translation, and may act to establish allocentric or perspective-free representations of the world from egocentric experience.

THE SPACE OF NAVIGATION

The space of navigation serves to guide us as we walk, drive, fly about in the world. Constituents of the space of navigation include places, which may be buildings or parks or piazzas or rivers or mountains, as well as countries or planets or stars, on yet larger scales. Places are interrelated in terms of paths or directions in a reference frame. The space of navigation is too large to perceive from one place so it must be integrated from different pieces of information that are not immediately comparable. Like the space around the body, it can be acquired from descriptions and from diagrams, notably maps, as well as from direct experience. One remarkable feature of the human mind is the ability to conceive of spaces that are too large to be perceived from one place as integral wholes. In order to conceive of spaces of navigation as wholes, we need to paste, link, join, superimpose, or otherwise integrate separate pieces of information. In addition to being separate, that information may be in different formats or different scales or different perspectives; it may contain different objects, landmarks, paths, or other details. Linking disparate pieces of information can be accomplished through spatial inferences anchored in common reference objects, reference frames, and perspectives. The linkage is necessarily approximate, leading to consistent errors, as shall be seen in the section on cognitive maps (see also Montello, Chapter 7, for a more detailed discussion of navigation and Taylor, Chapter 8, for a more detailed discussion of cognitive maps as well as externally presented maps).

Places

Many navigable environments can be loosely schematized as landmarks and links, places and paths. Places that is, configurations of objects such as walls and furniture, buildings, streets, and trees, selectively activate regions of the parahippocampus, part of the network of brain structures activated in imagining travel. Not only is this area selectively active under viewing of scenes, but also patients with damage to this area experience severe difficulties acquiring spatial knowledge of new places (e.g., Aguirre & D'Esposito, 1999; Cave & Squire, 1991; De Renzi, 1982; Epstein & Kanwisher, 1998; Rosenbaum et al., 2000). The brain has areas selectively sensitive to only a small number of kinds of things, places, faces, objects, and bodies, suggesting both that these entities have special significance to human existence and that they are at least somewhat computationally distinct.

Perspective of Acquisition

Descriptions of the space of navigation locate places with respect to one another and a reference frame, from a perspective. They typically use one of two perspectives or a mixture of both (Taylor & Tversky, 1992a, 1996). In a *route* perspective, the narrative takes a changing point of view within an environment, addressing the reader or listener as "you," describing you navigating through an environment, locating landmarks relative to your changing position in terms of your left, right, front, and back. For example, "As you drive down Main Street, you will pass the bank on your right and the post office on your left. Turn right on Cedar, and the restaurant will be on your left." In a *survey* perspective, the narrative takes a stationary viewpoint above the environment, locating landmarks relative to each other in terms of an extrinsic frame of reference, typically, north-south-east-west. For example, "The bank is east of the post office and the restaurant is north of the post office." The components of a perspective, then, are a landmark to be located, a referent, a frame of reference, a viewpoint, and terms of reference. In both speech and writing, perspectives are often mixed, typically without signaling (e.g., Emmorey, Tversky, & Taylor, 2000; Taylor & Tversky, 1992a, 1996). When descriptions are read for the first time, switching perspective slows reading time as well as statement verification time (Lee & Tversky, submitted). However, when descriptions from either perspective are well learned, participants respond as fast and as accurately to inference statements from the read perspective as from the other perspective (Taylor and Tversky, 1992b). Moreover, maps constructed from reading either perspective are highly accurate. This suggests that both route and survey perspectives can instill mental representations of environments that are perspective-free, more abstract than either perspective, perhaps representations like architects' models, that allow the taking of different perspectives with ease.

There is a third linguistic perspective used to describe smaller environments, those that can be seen from a single viewpoint, such as a room from an entrance. This perspective has been termed a *gaze description* (Ehrich & Koster, 1983; Ullmer-Ehrich, 1982). In a gaze description, landmarks are described from the stationary viewpoint of an observer relative to each other in terms of the observer's left and right. For example, "The desk is left of the bed, and the bookcase is left of the desk." These three perspectives correspond to the three perspectives analyzed by Levinson (1996): gaze to relative, route to intrinsic, and survey to extrinsic. They also correspond to natural ways of acquiring environments, from a single external viewpoint, from traveling through the environment, and from viewing an environment from a height (Taylor & Tversky, 1996; Tversky, 1996). These distinct ways of perceiving and acquiring environments may account for the confluence of type of reference object, reference frame, and viewpoint in the three types of description.

When environments are more complex and acquired from experience, type of experience, notably, learning from experience versus learning from maps, can affect the mental representations established. In particular, some kinds of information are more accurate or accessible from some experiences than others. Those who learned an industrial campus from experience estimated route distances better than those who learned from a map (Thorndyke & Hayes-Roth, 1982). In learning a building, those who studied a map were better at imagining adjacent rooms that were not directly accessible by navigation than those who navigated the building (Taylor, Naylor, & Checile, 1999). The goals of participants, to learn the layout or to learn routes, had parallel effects on mental representations. This suggests that some of the effects of learning from navigation versus from maps may have to do with goals or expectations regarding the environment. Learning a route and studying a map appear to activate different areas of the brain as well (e.g., Aguirre & D'Esposito, 1997; Ghaem et al., 1997; Maguire, Frackowiak, & Frith, 1997). Similarly, acquiring a virtual environment from a route perspective yields relatively more activation in the navigation network pathways, that is, parietal, posterior cingulate, parahippocampal, hippocampal, and medial occipital gyrus, whereas acquiring a virtual environment from an overview perspective yields relatively more activation in ventral structures, such as ventral occipital and fusiform gyrus. The perspective-dependent pathways active at encoding were also active in recognition of the environments, and there were additional parallel effects of perspective of test stimuli (Shelton, Burrows, Tversky, & Gabrieli, 2000; Shelton, Tversky, & Gabrieli, 2001).

Cognitive Maps

The mental representations that we draw on to answer questions about directions and distances; to tell someone how to get from A to B; to make educated guesses about weather patterns, population migrations, and political spheres of influence; and to find our ways in the world differ from the prototypical map on paper. In contrast to maps on paper, mental maps appear to be fragmented, schematized, inconsistent, incomplete, and multimodal. This is an inevitable consequence of spatial knowledge acquired from different modalities, perspectives, and scales. *Cognitive collage*, then, is a more apt metaphor than *cognitive map* (Tversky, 1993). In contrast to libraries and map stores, our minds do not appear to contain a catalog of maps in varying scales and sizes that we can retrieve on demand. Evidence for this view comes from studies of systematic errors in memory and judgment (for reviews, see Tversky, 1993, 2000b, 2000c).

These systematic errors, some of which will be reviewed later, suggest that people remember the location of one spatial object relative to reference spatial entities in terms of an overall frame of reference from a particular perspective. Some evidence for each of these phenomena will be reviewed. Locations are indexed approximately, schematically, not metrically. Thus, the choice of reference objects, frames of reference, and perspective leads to systematic errors in their direction. As Talmy has observed, the ways language schematizes space reflect and reveal the ways the mind schematizes space (Talmy, 1983; Tversky & Lee, 1998). Spatial perception and memory are relative, not absolute. The location of one object is coded relative to the location of a reference object, ideally a prominent object in the environment, and also relative to a reference frame, such as the walls and ceiling of a building, large features of the surroundings such as rivers, lakes, and mountains, or the cardinal directions, north, south, east, or west.

Reference Objects

When asked the direction from Philadelphia to Rome, most people indicate that Philadelphia is north of Rome. Similarly, when asked the direction from Boston to Rio, most people indicate that Boston is east of Rio. Despite being in the majority, these informants are mistaken, but they are mistaken for good reason. People remember the locations and directions of spatial entities, continents in this case, but also cities, roads, and buildings, relative to each other, a heuristic related to perceptual grouping by proximity. In the case of Philadelphia and Rome, the United States and Europe serve as reference objects for each other; hence, they are grouped, and remembered as more aligned than they actually are. In actuality, Europe is for the most part north of the United States. In the case of Boston and Rio, North and South America are grouped and remembered as more aligned than they actually are; in actuality, South America lies mostly east of North America. Such errors of alignment have been found for artificial as well as real maps, for visual blobs as well as geographic entities (Tversky, 1981).

Landmarks are used to structure routes and organize neighborhoods. When asked where they live, people often say near the closest landmark they think their interlocutor will know (Shanon, 1983). Dramatic violations of metric assumptions are one consequence of encoding locations relative to landmarks. Distance estimates to a landmark from an ordinary building are reliably smaller than distance estimates from a landmark to an ordinary building (McNamara & Diwadkar, 1997; Sadalla, Boroughs, & Staplin, 1980).

Perspective of Judgment

Saul Steinberg delighted the readers of *The New Yorker* for many years with his maps that poked fun at egocentric views of the world. The New Yorker's view, for example, exaggerated the size and distances of the streets of Manhattan, and reduced the size and distances of remote areas. These whimsical maps turned out to presage an empirically documented phenomenon, that spaces near one's perspective loom larger and are estimated to be larger than spaces far from one's perspective. Unlike the cartoon maps, the research also showed that perspective is flexible; students located in Ann Arbor, Michigan, adopted a west coast perspective as easily as an east coast perspective and from either perspective, overestimated the near distances relative to the far ones (Holyoak & Mah, 1982).

Reference Frames

External reference frames, such as the walls of a room or the cardinal directions or large environmental features such as bodies of water or mountains, also serve to index locations and directions of spatial objects. Objects may also induce their own reference frame, usually constructed out of their axis of elongation or symmetry and the axis perpendicular to that. When asked to place a cutout of South America in a north-southeast-west reference frame, most people upright South America so that its natural axis of elongation is rotated in the mind toward the nearest axis of the world, the north-south axis. Similarly, when asked the direction from Stanford to Berkeley, most people incorrectly indicate that Stanford is west of Berkeley, when in fact, Stanford is slightly east of Berkeley. This is because the natural axis of elongation of the San Francisco Bay area is rotated in memory toward the closest environmental axis, the north-south axis. Rotation effects also appear for other environments, roads, artificial maps, and visual blobs (Tversky, 1981).

Reference frames other than the cardinal directions are used to anchor spatial entities. States are used to index the locations of cities so that, for example, most people mistakenly think that San Diego is west of Reno because for the most part, California lies west of Nevada (Stevens & Coupe, 1978). Geographic objects can also be indexed functionally. For example, buildings in Ann Arbor are grouped by town versus university although they are in fact interwoven. People erroneously underestimate distances within a functional grouping relative to distances between functional groupings (Hirtle & Jonides, 1985). Political groupings have a similar affect: Hebrew speakers underestimate distances between Hebrew-speaking settlements relative to Hebrew-speaking to between Hebrew-speaking and Arabic-speaking settlements; likewise, Arabic speakers underestimate distances between Arabic-speaking settlements relative to Arabic speaking settlements compared to between Arabic-speaking and Hebrew-speaking settlements (Portugali, 1993).

Why Systematic Errors?

The biases and errors in the space of navigation reviewed here are not the only ones that have been investigated; there are a variety of other fascinating errors of direction, location, and orientation (see Tversky, 1992, 2000b, 2000c, for reviews). The space of navigation serves a richness of functions in our lives, allowing us to find our ways to home and other destinations; to describe environments and routes to others; to make judgments of location, distance, and direction; and to make inferences about metereological, geographic, geological, and political events. Our knowledge of spaces too large to be seen from one place requires us to piece together disparate pieces of spatial information. Integrating disparate pieces of information can be accomplished through common objects, reference objects, reference frames, and perspectives. The integration is necessarily schematic, and the schematization inevitably leads to error.

Why would the mind or brain develop and use processes that are guaranteed to produce error? These systematic errors contrast with other spatial behaviors that are finely tuned and highly accurate, such as catching fly balls, playing the piano, or wending one's way through a crowd to some destination. Unlike the judgments and inferences and behaviors reviewed here, these highly accurate behaviors are situated in environments replete with cues and are highly practiced. The errors described here are often one-time or infrequent responses made in the abstract, not situated. They need to be performed in limited capacity working memory and are based on schematized mental representations constructed ad hoc for current purposes. In many cases, the errors induced by schematization are corrected in actual practice. A turn that is actually 60 degrees may be described ambiguously as a right turn or remembered incorrectly as 90 degrees but the schematization will not matter as the actual environment will disambiguate the vagueness of the expression and will not allow the error to be enacted (see Tversky, 2003, for development of these ideas about optimization and error).

In practice, actual navigation depends on far more than cognitive maps or collages, which are error-prone. Actual navigation is situated in environments that evoke memories not otherwise likely to be aroused. Actual navigation is motoric and invokes motor, proprioceptive, and vestibular responses that may not be otherwise accessible. Some of the intriguing findings are that motor responses may dominate visual ones in memory for locations (Shelton & McNamara, 2001), and motor responses are more critical for updating rotational than translational movement (Rieser, 1999). The interconnections between the cognitive and the sensorimotor in navigation are fascinating but beyond the purview of this chapter (see Golledge, 1999, for a recent collection of papers).

THE SPACE OF EXTERNAL REPRESENTATIONS

One distinctly human endeavor is the creation of external tools that serve cognition. Such inventions are ancient, going back to prehistory. Trail markers, tallies, calendars, and cave paintings have been found across the world, as have schematic maps in the sand, on petroglyphs, in portable wood carvings or constructions of bamboo and shells (e.g., Southworth & Southworth, 1982; Tversky, 2000a). Yet another ancient example of an external cognitive tool, invented independently by many cultures, is writing, whether ideographic, reflecting meaning, or phonetic, reflecting sound.

The space of external representations has a different status from the previous spaces; it is invented, created in order to enhance human cognition. It uses space and spatial relations to represent both inherently spatial relations, as in maps and architectural drawings, and metaphorically spatial relations, as in flow diagrams, organizational charts, and economic graphs. Interestingly, using space to represent space is ancient and ubiquitous, whereas using space to represent metaphoric space is modern. External cognitive tools function to extend the powers of the mind by offloading memory and computation (e.g., Donald, 1991; Kirsh, 1995). At the same time, they capitalize on human skills at spatial reasoning (e.g., Larkin & Simon, 1987). Several chapters in this volume consider in more detail specific types of external representations (Taylor, Chapter 8 [maps]; Wickens, Vincow, & Yeh, Chapter 10 [navigational aids]; Shah, Freedman, & Vekiri, Chapter 11 [graphs]; and Mayer, Chapter 12 [multimedia displays]).

External representations consist of elements and the spatial relations among them. Typically, elements in a diagram or other external representation are used to represent elements in the world. Thus a tally uses one undistinguished mark on paper or wood or bone to represent one element in the world. Typically, spatial relations in a diagram are used to represent relations among elements in the world. Distance in a map usually corresponds to distance in real space. A notable exception to this is mathematical notation, where elements such as + and − are used to represent relations or operations on elements.

Elements

In many cases, elements bear resemblance to what they represent. This is evident in ideographic languages such as Hittite, Sumerian, Egyptian, and Chinese, where, for example, a depiction of the sun or of a cow is used to represent the corresponding objects (e.g., Gelb, 1963). Not only resemblances, but figures of depiction are used to convey more abstract concepts, *synecdoche*, where a part stands for a whole, as in the horns of a ram for a ram, and *metonymy*, where a symbol or an association substitutes, as in a staff of office for a king. These figures of depiction appear in modern icons as well, where a trash can is for dumping files and a pair of scissors for cutting them. Obviously, these devices are used in descriptions as well as depictions, for example, when the U.S. government is referred to as the White House. The power of depictions to represent meanings iconically or metaphorically is nevertheless limited, and most languages developed devices for representing the sounds of words to increase the range of writing.

In many useful diagrams, similar elements appear with similar abstract meanings, geometric elements such as lines, crosses, blobs, and arrows. Their interpretations are context-dependent, as for many word meanings, such as line or relation or area or field. For these schematic elements, their meanings share senses that appear to be related to the mathematical or gestalt properties of the elements. Lines in tallies are undistinguished shapes that indicate objects whose specific characteristics are irrelevant. In other diagrams, notably maps and graphs, lines are one-dimensional paths that connect other entities, suggesting that they are related. Crosses are intersections of paths. Blobs or circles are two-dimensional areas whose exact shape is irrelevant or can be inferred from context. Thus, these elements schematize certain physical or semantic properties, omitting others. Like classifiers in spoken language, for example, roll or *sheet* of paper, they often abstract characteristics of shape. Three research projects illustrate the use of such schematic elements in graphs, diagrams, and maps, respectively.

Bars and Lines in Graphs. As noted, lines are paths that connect elements, thereby calling attention to an underlying dimension. Bars, by contrast, separate; they contain all the elements that share one feature and separate them from the elements that share other features. In graphs, then, lines should be more readily interpreted as trends and bars as discrete comparisons. Similarly, trend relationships should be more readily portrayed as lines and discrete relations as bars. In studies of graph interpretation and production, exactly this pattern was found (Zacks & Tversky, 1999). One group of participants was asked to interpret bar or line graphs of one of two relations: height of 10- and 12-year-olds, where the underlying variable, age, is continuous; or height of women and men, where the underlying variable, gender, is discrete. Participants were more likely to interpret line graphs as trends, even saying that as people get more male, they get taller. They were more likely to interpret bar graphs as discrete comparisons, as in 12-year-olds are taller than 10-year-olds. Mirror results were obtained for producing graphs from descriptions. Discrete descriptions yielded bar graphs and trend descriptions yielded line graphs, even when discordant with the underlying discrete or continuous variable, age or gender.

Arrows in Diagrams. Arrows are asymmetric paths, so they indicate an asymmetric relation, such as time or motion. Their interpretation seems to have a natural basis, both in the arrows sent to hunt game and in the arrows formed by water descending hills. As such, they are readily interpreted and used to indicate direction, in space, time, and causality. About half the participants sketching route maps to a popular fast food place put arrows on their maps to convey direction in space (Tversky & Lee, 1998). Diagrams of complex systems illustrate the power of arrows to affect mental representations of them. Participants were asked to describe diagrams of a bicycle pump, a car brake, or a pulley system (Heiser & Tversky, submitted). Half the diagrams had arrows and half did not. Participants who saw diagrams without arrows wrote structural descriptions of the systems; they described the system's parts and spatial relations. Participants who saw diagrams with arrows wrote functional descriptions; they described the sequence of operations performed by the systems and the outcomes of each operation or action. The arrows suggest the temporal sequence of operations. Apparently, the human mind jumps from temporal order to causal order in fractions of a second. As for graphs, production mirrored comprehension: given structural descriptions of the pump, brake, or pulleys, participants produced diagrams without arrows, but given functional descriptions, participants' diagrams included arrows.

Lines, Crosses, and Blobs in Route Maps. Route maps include a greater variety of schematic elements. Straight lines are produced and interpreted as more or less straight paths, and curved lines as more or less curvy paths. Crosses are produced and interpreted as intersections where the actual angle of intersection is not represented. Circular or rectangular shapes stand for landmarks of varying shapes and sizes. These uses are all the more surprising as maps offer the potential for analog representation, yet both producers and users of route maps seem satisfied with schematic, approximate, even categorical representation of paths, nodes, and landmarks (Tversky & Lee, 1998, 1999). Interestingly, the elements and distinctions made in route maps are the same as those made in route directions given in language, suggesting that the same conceptual structure underlies both and encouraging the possibility of automatic translation between them.

Relations

Spatial relations can be depicted at several levels of abstraction, capturing categorical, ordinal, interval, and ratio relations. Proximity in space is used to convey proximity on spatial and nonspatial relations. How close one person stands to another, for example, can reflect social distance, which in turn depends on both the relations between the individuals and the socio-cultural context. Categorical uses of space include separating the laundry belonging to different family members by separate piles and separating the letters belonging to different words by the spaces between words, a spatial device adopted by phonetic writing systems. Ordinal uses of space include listing groceries to be purchased in the order of the route taken through the store, listing presidents in historical order, or listing countries in order of geography, size, or alphabet. Hierarchical trees, such as those used in evolutionary or organizational charts, are also examples of ordinal spatial relations that convey other ordinal relations, such as time or power. In interval uses of space, the distance between elements as well as the order of elements is significant. Graphs, such as those plotting change in productivity, growth, crime rate, and more over time, are a common example. Note that in each of these cases, proximity in space is used to represent proximity on some nonspatial attribute. Space, then, is used metaphorically, similar to spatial metaphors in speech, such as the distance between their political positions is vast.

For both interval and ordinal mappings, direction of increases are often meaningful. In particular, the vertical direction, the only asymmetric direction in the world, one induced by gravity, is loaded with asymmetric associations (e.g., Clark, 1973; Lakoff & Johnson, 1980; Tversky, Kugelmass, & Winter, 1991). Both children and adults prefer to map concepts of quantity and preference from down to up rather than up to down. For the horizontal axis, they are indifferent as to whether increases in quantity or preference should go left to right or right to left, irrespective of whether they write right to left or left to right (Tversky et al., 1991). Almost all the diagrams of evolution and geological ages used in standard textbooks portrayed man or the present day at the top (Tversky, 1995a). The association of up with good, strong, and valuable appears in language as well, in both word and gesture. We say that someone's on top of the heap or has fallen into a depression. We give a high five or thumbs down.

The progression of levels of information mapped in external representations from categorical to ordinal to interval is mirrored in development. Four- and five-year-old children, speakers of a language written left-to-right as well as speakers of languages written right-to-left sometimes represent temporal, quantitative, and preference relations at only a categorical level; for example, breakfast, lunch, and dinner are separate events, not ordered on a time scale. Most young children, however, do represent these relations ordinally on paper, but not until the preteen years do children represent interval relations (Tversky et al., 1991).

Maps are often given as a quintessential example of ratio use of space, where not only intervals between points are meaningful, but also ratios of intervals; that is, zero is meaningful rather than arbitrary. And indeed, distance and direction between elements representing cities on a map are often meant to represent distance and direction between cities in the world. Yet not all maps, either ancient or modern, seem to intend to represent distance and direction metrically (Tversky, 2000a). Sketch maps drawn to aid a traveler to get from A to B typically shrink long distances with no turns (Tversky & Lee, 1998). Maps from many cultures portray historical and spiritual places, such as medieval Western maps that show the Garden of Eden and the continent of Asia at the top, with Europe left and Africa right at the bottom. Similar melanges of legend and geography appear in ancient New World and Asian maps (see wonderful collections in Harley & Woodward, 1987, 1992, and Woodward & Lewis, 1994, 1998). Tourist maps, ancient and modern, frequently mix perspectives, showing the system of roads from overview perspective with frontal views of tourist attractions superimposed. Such maps allow users both to navigate to the attractions and to recognize the attractions when they arrive. An exemplary contemporary map that has served as a model for graphic designers is the London Underground Map. It intentionally distorts metric information in the service of efficient representation of the major subway lines and their interconnections. Subway lines are represented as straight lines, oriented horizontally, vertically, or diagonally, not reflecting their actual paths. This map is efficient for navigating a subway system, but not for conveying distances and directions on the ground overhead. Even highway maps, which are meant to convey direction and distance accurately for drivers, distort certain information. If the scale of such maps were faithfully used, highways and railways wouldn't be apparent. Symbols for certain structures like rest stations and tourist attractions are also routinely added.

Maps, then, schematize and present the information important for the task at hand. Underground maps suit different purposes from road maps, which serve different purposes from topographic or tourist maps, and successful versions of each of these select and even distort certain information and omit other. Successful diagrams do the same. Schematic diagrams save information processing, but they also bias certain interpretations.

Distortions in Memory for External Representations

Like internal representations, external representations are organized around elements and spatial relations among them with respect to a reference frame. Just as there are systematic distortions in memory for maps and environments in the direction of other elements and reference frames, memory for external representations is distorted in the same directions (e.g., Pani, Jeffres, Shippey, & Schwartz, 1996; Schiano & Tversky, 1992; Tversky & Schiano, 1989; Shiffrar & Shepard, 1991). Distortions in memory for external representations, in particular graphs, also illustrate semantic factors in organizing external representations. In X-Y plots, the most common graph, the imaginary diagonal has a special status as it is the line where $X = Y$. The identity line serves as an implicit reference frame for lines in X-Y graphs. Participants viewed lines in axes that were interpreted either as X-Y plots or as shortcuts in maps. In memory, graph lines were distorted toward the 45-degree line but lines in maps were not (Schiano & Tversky, 1992; Tversky & Schiano, 1989). Lines that were given no meaningful interpretation showed yet a different pattern of distortion (Schiano & Tversky, 1992). These studies demonstrate the effects of meaning on selection of reference frame and consequent memory. Other distortions are general effects of perceptual organization, not dependent on the meaning assigned the stimuli. Symmetry exerts one such effect. Rivers on maps, curves on graphs, and nearly symmetric forms assigned no meaning are all remembered as more symmetric than they actually were (Freyd & Tversky, 1984; Tversky & Schiano, 1989). As usual, systematic distortions give insight into the way stimuli are organized, with both perceptual and conceptual factors operative.

Creating Graphic Representations

External representations constructed by people all over the world and throughout history as well as from laboratory studies on children and adults from different cultures demonstrate that external representations use elements and the spatial relations among them in meaningful, readily interpretable, cognitively natural ways. Maps, charts, and diagrams have been developed in communities of users, similar to spoken language. Also similar to spoken language, depictions are produced and used, leading to refinements and improvements in accuracy and efficiency (e.g., Clark, 1996; Engle, 1998; Schwartz, 1995). Elements in external representations use likenesses, figures of depictions, and schematic forms to stand for elements in the world. Proximity in the space of external representations is used to convey proximity in spatial as well as other relations at several levels of abstraction. These direct and figurative uses of elements and space render external representations easy to produce and easy to comprehend. This is not to say that diagrams are immediately comprehended; they may be incomplete, ambiguous, or difficult to interpret, yet on the whole, they are more directly related to meaning than, say, language. Diagrams schematize, but language schematizes even more so; diagrams retain some visual and spatial correspondences or metaphoric correspondences to the things they represent.

Many have proposed that graphics form a "visual language" (e.g., Horn, 1998). The visual language of graphics lacks the essential structural and combinatoric features of spoken languages, but it can be used to communicate. The components and principles of natural language form an insightful framework for analyzing properties of depictions. Following this analysis, elements of graphics compare to words of a language, the semantic level of structure, and the spatial relations between elements as a rudimentary syntax, expressing the relations among elements. Spatial relations readily convey proximity and grouping relations on spatial and other dimensions, but obviously, natural language can convey a far richer set of relations, including nesting, overlap, conditionals, and negation. The addition of other elements to simple spatial relations allows expression of many of these relations. Hierarchical trees express part-of and kind-of and other hierarchical relations. Venn diagrams show them as well, along with intersection and negation. Developing complete graphic systems for expressing complex logical relations that would allow logical inference has proved to be a challenge (e.g., Allwein & Barwise, 1996; Barwise & Etchemendy, 1995; Shin, 1995; Stenning & Oberlander, 1995). Some, like the present chapter, have analyzed how graphics communicate (e.g., Pinker, 1990; Winn, 1987). Others have proposed guidelines for creating graphic representations (e.g., Cleveland, 1985; Kosslyn, 1994a; Tufte, 1983, 1990, 1997).

Comprehending Graphic Representations

Still others have presented analyses of how graphics are comprehended (e.g., Carpenter & Shah, 1998; Larkin & Simon, 1987; Pinker, 1990; see also

Glasgow, Narayanan, & Chandrasekeran, 1995). For example, according to Carpenter and Shah (1998), graph comprehension entails three processes: pattern recognition, translation of visual features into conceptual relations, and determining referents of quantified concepts and associating them to functions. These processes occur in iterative cycles. Graph comprehension is easier when "simple pattern identification processes are substituted for complex cognitive processes" (p. 98). In the wild, comprehension and production of graphics work hand in hand in cycles so that created graphics get refined by a community of users, at the same time creating conventions within that community (e.g., Clark, 1996; Zacks & Tversky, 1999).

Three-dimensionality and animation present special challenges to graph comprehension. The availability and attractiveness of these techniques has enticed many, yet there is little support that they are beneficial to comprehension. Moreover, there is evidence that each presents difficulties for perception and comprehension, suggesting that they should not be adopted as a default but rather only under considered circumstances.

Three-dimensional graphics are often used gratuitously, to represent information that is only one- or two-dimensional (bar graphs are a common example), yet reading values from three-dimensional bar graphs is less accurate than reading values from traditional two-dimensional bar graphs (Zacks, Levy, Tversky, & Schiano, 1998). Moreover, three-dimensional displays are often perceptually unstable, reversing like Necker cubes, and parts of three-dimensional displays often occlude relevant information (Tversky, 1995b). Even when data are inherently three-dimensional, comprehending the conceptual interrelations of the variables is difficult (Shah & Carpenter, 1995).

Animation is increasingly used to convey conceptual information, such as weather patterns (Lowe, 1999), the sequence of operations of mechanical or biological systems (e.g., Palmiter & Elkerton, 1993) or the sequence of steps in an algorithm (e.g., Byrne, Catrambone, & Stasko, 2000). Many of these are exactly the situations where animations should be effective, namely, for conveying changes in spatial (or metaphorically spatial) relations over time. Nevertheless, there is no convincing evidence that animations improve learning or retention over static graphics that convey the same information (for a review and analysis, see Tversky, Morrison, & Betrancourt, 2002). The cases where animations were reported as superior have been cases where the proper controls have not been included or where interaction is involved for animations. Even more than three-dimensionality, animations can be difficult to perceive, especially when they portray parts moving in relation to one another. Generations of great painters depicted galloping legs of horses incorrectly, presumably because

the correct positions could not be ascertained from watching natural animations. Stop-gap photography allowed correction of those errors. Even
when a single path of motion is portrayed, it can be misinterpreted, as the
research on naïve physics showing incorrect perceptions of trajectories has
demonstrated (e.g., Kaiser, Proffitt, Whelan, & Hecht, 1992; Pani, Jeffres,
Shippey, & Schwartz,1996; Shiffrar & Shepard, 1991). Despite the lack of
support for animations to convey information about changes in parts or
states over time, there may be other cases where animations may be effective, for example, when used in real time for maintaining attention, as in
fill bars that indicate the percent of a file that has been downloaded or in
zooming in on details.

One lesson to be learned from the work on three-dimensionality and
animation is that realism per se is not necessarily an advantage in graphic
communication. Effective graphics schematize the information meant to be
conveyed so that it can be readily perceived and comprehended. Realism
can add detail that is irrelevant, and makes the relevant harder to discern.

EXTERNAL AND INTERNAL REPRESENTATIONS

External visuospatial representations bear many similarities to those that
reside in the mind. This is not surprising as external representations are
created by human minds to serve human purposes, many of the same purposes that internal representations serve. Of course, there are differences
as well. The constraints on internal representations, for example, working
memory capacity and long-term memory fallibility, are different from the
constraints on external representations, for example, construction ability
and the flatness of paper. Their functions differ somewhat as well. Yet both
internal and external representations are schematic, that is, they omit information, they add information, and they distort information. In so doing,
they facilitate their use by preprocessing the essential information and directing attention to it. The cost of schematization is the possibility of bias
and error, when the representations are used for other purposes. It is these
biases and errors that reveal the nature of the schematization.

MULTIPLE FUNCTIONAL SYSTEMS IN THE BRAIN

Prima facie evidence for the multiplicity of spaces in the mind comes from
the multiplicity of spaces in the brain. Many have been suggested, varying
in ways that are not comparable, among them, content, modality, reference
frame, and role in behavior. As the features distinguishing each space are

not comparable, they do not form a natural taxonomy. However, they do suggest the features of space that are important enough in human existence to be specially represented in the brain.

Space is multimodal, but for many researchers, vision is primary. The visual world captured by the retina is topographically mapped in the occipital cortex, the primary cortical projection area for the visual system. Yet even in the occipital cortex, there are many topographic maps, differing in degree of processing of the visual information. As visual information undergoes more processing, spatial topography becomes secondary and content becomes primary. There are regions in the occipital cortex and nearby that are differentially sensitive to different kinds of things, objects, faces, places, and bodies (e.g., Epstein & Kanwisher, 1998; Downing et al., 2001; Haxby et al., 2001). Some of the regions partial to kind of object retain an underlying topography. Significantly, areas representing the fovea overlap with areas sensitive to faces whereas areas representing the periphery have greater overlap with areas sensitive to places (Levy, Hasson, Avidan, Henler, & Malach, 2001).

After the occipital cortex, the visual pathways split into two major streams, one ventral to the temporal lobe and one dorsal to the parietal lobe. These have been termed the "what" and "where" systems by some researchers (Ungerleider & Mishkin, 1982), the "what" and "how" systems by others (Milner & Goodman, 1992), and object-centered versus viewer-centered by yet others (Turnbull, Denis, Mellet, Ghaem, & Carey, 2001). Damage to the ventral pathway results in difficulties in identifying objects whereas damage to the dorsal pathway leads to difficulties in locating objects in space, demonstrated in tasks that entail interactions with the objects. However conceived, the dorsal system seems to be responsible for aspects of objects and the ventral for relations of objects to surrounding space.

Farther upstream are regions underlying the integration of spatial information from more than one modality, for example, vision and touch. Neurons in the ventral premotor cortex and the putamen of macaque monkeys have receptive fields tied to parts of the body, notably parts of the face and arms. These neurons respond to both visual and tactile stimuli (Graziano & Gross, 1994; Gross & Graziano, 1995). Single cells in ventral premotor cortex of macaques respond when the monkey enacts a particular action, like grasping or tearing, and when the monkey views someone else performing that action (Rizzolatti, Fadiga, Fogassi, & Gallese, 2002). A variety of spatial reference systems are also built into the brain. Neurons in the temporal cortex of macaques are selectively responsive to different spatial reference systems, those of viewer, of object, and of goal (Jellema,

Baker, Oram, & Perrett, 2002). Other evidence suggests that objects and locations are represented in multiple reference systems. Recordings from rat hippocampus show that as they explore new environments, rats establish allocentric as well as egocentric representations of the space around them (O'Keefe & Nadel, 1978). Also illuminating are studies of patients with spatial neglect, who, due to brain damage, do not seem to be aware of half of their visual field, more commonly, the left half. Consistent with the single-cell recordings from macaques, a recent analysis of dozens of cases of neglect shows that the critical site for damage is right (Karnath, Ferber, & Himmelbach, 2001). Careful studies have shown that the neglect is not simply of the visual field; for example, it may be of the left half of an object in the right visual field. Nor is the neglect confined to the visual modality; it extends, for example, to touch. Such studies as well as work on intact people suggest that objects and locations are coded in terms of several reference systems simultaneously, for example, those that depend on the object, on the viewer, and on the environment (Behrmann & Tipper, 1999; Robertson & Rafal, in press).

All in all, the neuroscientific evidence shows that the brain codes many aspects of space, notably, the things in space, their spatial relations in multiple reference frames, and interactions with space and with things in space. Many of these form the basis for the functional spaces distinguished here. And many subserve functions other than spatial thinking, supporting the naturalness of thinking about other domains spatially. Moreover, some are directly linked to other senses or to action. Significantly, regions that subserve space may serve other functions as well, establishing a basis for thinking about space metaphorically.

IN CONCLUSION

From the moment of birth (and undoubtedly before), we are involved in space, and consequently, in spatial cognition. Sensations arrive on our bodies from various points in space; our actions take place in space and are constrained by it. These interactions occur at discernable levels, that of the space of the body, that of the space in reach or in sight around the body, that of the space of navigation too large to be apprehended at once, and that of the space of external representations, of graphics constructed to augment human cognition. Each mental space extracts and schematizes information useful for function in that space. So useful are these mental spaces that they subserve thinking in many other domains, those of emotion, interpersonal interaction, and scientific understanding (e.g., Lakoff & Johnson, 1980). We feel up or down, one nation's culture or language invades or penetrates another, inertia, pressure, and unemployment rise or fall. At its loftiest, the mind rests on the concrete.

ACKNOWLEDGMENT

Preparation of this chapter and some of the research reported were supported by Office of Naval Research, Grant Numbers NOOO14-PP-1-O649 and N000140110717 to Stanford University. Amy Shelton provided excellent information on the brain, for which I am grateful. I am also grateful to Priti Shah and several anonymous reviewers who graciously pointed to inclarities and infelicities. I hope I have succeeded in correcting them. Finally, I am most grateful to my wonderful collaborators.

Suggestions for Further Reading

On bodies, events, and brain:
Meltzoff, A., & Prinz, W. (Editors). *The imitative mind*. Cambridge: Cambridge University Press.

On cognitive maps:
Kitchin, R., & Freundschuh, S. M. (Editors). (2000). Levels and structure of cognitive mapping. In *Cognitive mapping: Past, present and future*. London: Routledge.

On navigation:
Golledge, R. (Editor). *Cognitive mapping and spatial behavior*. Baltimore: The Johns Hopkins Press.

On language and space:
Bloom, P., Peterson, M. P., Nadel, L., & Garrett, M. (Editors). *Language and space*. Cambridge, MA: MIT Press.

On metaphoric space
Gattis, M. (Editor). (2001). *Spatial schemas in abstract thought*. Cambridge, MA: MIT Press.

References

Aguirre, G. K., & D'Esposito, M. (1997). Environmental knowledge is subserved by separable dorsal/ventral neural areas. *Journal of Neuroscience, 17*, 2512–2518.
Aguirre, G. K., & D'Esposito, M. (1999). Topographical disorientation: A synthesis and taxonomy. *Brain, 122*, 1613–1628.
Allwein, G., & Barwise, J. (Eds.). (1996). *Logical reasoning with diagrams*. Oxford: Oxford University Press.
Andersen, E. S. (1978). Lexical universals in body-party terminology. In J. H. Greenberg (Ed.), *Universals of human language, Vol. 3* (pp. 335–368). Stanford, CA: Stanford University Press.

Barwise, J., & Etchemendy, J. (1995). Heterogeneous Logic. In J. Glasgow, N. H. Naryanan, & G. Chandrasekeran (Eds.), *Diagrammatic reasoning: Cognitive and computational perspectives*. Cambridge, MA: MIT Press.

Behrmann, M., & Tipper, S. P. (1999). Attention accesses multiple reference frames: Evidence from neglect. *Journal of Experimental Psychology: Human Perception and Performance, 25,* 83–101.

Berlucchi, G., & Aglioti, S. (1997). The body in the brain: Neural bases of corporeal awareness. *Trends in Neuroscience, 12,* 560–564.

Biederman, I. (1987). Recognition-by-components: A theory of human image understanding. *Psychological Review, 94,* 115–145.

Byrne, M. D., Catrambone, R., & Stasko, J. T. (2000). Evaluating animations as student aids in learning computer algorithms. *Computers & Education, 33,* 253–278.

Bryant, D. J., Tversky, B., & Franklin, N. (1992). Internal and external spatial frameworks for representing described scenes. *Journal of Memory and Language, 31,* 74–98.

Bryant, D. J., & Tversky, B. (1999). Mental representations of spatial relations from diagrams and models. *Journal of Experimental Psychology: Learning, Memory and Cognition, 25,* 137–156.

Bryant, D. J., Tversky, B., & Lanca, M. (2001). Retrieving spatial relations from observation and memory. In E. van der Zee & U. Nikanne (Eds.), *Conceptual structure and its interfaces with other modules of representation* (pp. 116–139). Oxford: Oxford University Press.

Carpenter, P. A., & Shah, P. (1998). A model of the perceptual and conceptual processes in graph comprehension. *Journal of Experimental Psychology: Applied, 4,* 75–100.

Cave, C. G., & Squire, L. R. (1991). Equivalent impairment of spatial and nonspatial memory following damage to the human hippocampus. *Hippocampus, 1,* 329–340.

Clark, H. H. (1973). Space, time, semantics, and the child. In T. E. Moore (Ed.), *Cognitive development and the acquisition of language* (pp. 27–63). New York: Academic Press.

Clark, H. H. (1996). Using language. Cambridge: Cambridge University Press.

Cleveland, W. S. (1985). *The elements of graphing data*. Monterey, CA: Wadsworth.

De Renzi, E. (1982). *Disorders of space exploration and cognition*. Chichester: John Wiley.

Denis, M. (1997). The description of routes: A cognitive approach to the production of spatial discourse. *Current Psychology of Cognition, 16,* 409–458.

Donald, M. (1991). *Origins of the modern mind*. Cambridge, MA: Harvard University Press.

Downing, P. A., Jiang, Y., Shuman, M., & Kanwisher, N. (2001). A cortical selection for visual processing of the human body. *Science, 293,* 2470–2473.

Ehrich, V., & Koster, C. (1983). Discourse organization and sentence form: The structure of room descriptions in Dutch. *Discourse Processes, 6,* 169–195.

Ehrlich, K., & Johnson-Laird, P. N. (1982). Spatial descriptions and referential 1 continuity, *Journal of Verbal Memory and Verbal Behavior, 21,* 296–306.

Emmorey, K., Tversky, B., & Taylor, H. A. (2000). Using space to describe space: Perspective in speech, sign, and gesture. *Journal of Spatial Cognition and Computation, 2,* 157–180.

Engle, R. A. (1998). Not channels but composite signals: Speech, gesture, diagrams and object demonstrations are integrated in multimodal explanations. In M. A. Gernsbacher & S. J. Derry (Eds.), *Proceedings of the Twentieth Annual Conference of the Cognitive Science Society*. Mahwah, NJ: Erlbaum.

Epstein, R., & Kanwisher, N. (1998). A cortical representation of the local visual environment. *Nature, 392*, 599–601.

Franklin, N., & Tversky, B. (1990). Searching imagined environments. *Journal of Experimental Psychology: General, 119*, 63–76.

Franklin, N., Tversky, B., & Coon, V. (1992). Switching points of view in spatial mental models acquired from text. *Memory and Cognition, 20*, 507–518.

Freyd, J., & Tversky, B. (1984). The force of symmetry in form perception. *American Journal of Psychology, 97*, 109–126.

Gelb, I. (1963). *A study of writing*. Second edition. Chicago: University of Chicago Press.

Ghaem, O., Mellet, E., Crivello, F., Tzourio, N., Mazoyer, B., Berthoz, A., & Denis, M. (1997). Mental navigation along memorized routes activates the hippocampus, precuneus, and insula. *NeuroReport, 8*, 739–744.

Glasgow, J., Narayanan, N. H., & Chandrasekaran, B. (1995). *Diagrammatic reasoning: Cognitive and computational perspectives*. Cambridge, MA: MIT Press.

Glenberg, A. M., Meyer, M., & Lindem, K. (1987). Mental models contribute to foregrounding during text comprehension. *Journal of Memory and Language, 26*, 69–83.

Golledge, R. G. (Ed.). (1999). *Wayfinding behavior: Cognitive mapping and other spatial processes*. Baltimore: The Johns Hopkins Press.

Graziano, M. S. A., & Gross, C. G. (1994). Mapping space with neurons. *Current Directions in Psychological Science, 3*, 164–167.

Gross, C. G., & Graziano, M. S. A. (1995). Multiple representations of space in the brain. *The Neuroscientist, 1*, 43–50.

Harley, J. B., & Woodward, D. (Eds.). (1987). *The history of cartography. Vol. 1: Cartography in prehistoric, ancient and medieval Europe and the Mediterranean*. Chicago: University of Chicago Press.

Harley, J. B., & Woodward, D. (Eds.). (1992). *The history of cartography. Vol. 2. Book One: Cartography in the traditional Islamic and South Asian Societies*. Chicago: University of Chicago Press.

Heiser, J., & Tversky, B. (submitted). Descriptions and depictions of complex systems: Structural and functional perspectives.

Heptulla-Chatterjee, S., Freyd, J., & Shiffrar, M. (1996). Configurational processing in the perception of apparent biological motion. *Journal of Experimental Psychology: Human Perception and Performance, 22*, 916–929.

Hirtle, S. C., & Jonides, J. (1985). Evidence of hierarchies in cognitive maps. *Memory and Cognition, 13*, 208–217.

Hoffman, D. D., & Richards, W. A. (1984). Parts of recognition. *Cognition, 18*, 65–96.

Holyoak, K. J., & Mah, W. A. (1982). Cognitive reference points in judgments of symbolic magnitude. *Cognitive Psychology, 14*, 328–352.

Horn, R. E. (1998). *Visual language*. Bainbridge Island, WA: MacroVu, Inc.

Jellema, T., Baker, C. I., Oram, M. W., & Perrett, D. I. (2002). Cell populations in the banks of the superior temporal sulcus of the macaque and imitation. In

A. Meltzoff & W. Prinz (Eds.), *The imitative mind: Evolution, development, and brain bases* (pp. 267–290). Cambridge: Cambridge University Press.

Kaiser, M. K., Proffitt, D. R., Whelan, S. M., & Hecht, H. (1992). Influence of animation on dynamical judgments. *Journal of Experimental Psychology: Human Perception and Performance, 18,* 669–690.

Karnath, H-O, Ferber, S., & Himmelbach, M. (2001). Spatial awareness is a function of the temporal not the posterior parietal lobe. *Nature, 411,* 950–953.

Kirsh, D. (1995). The intelligent use of space. *Artificial Intelligence, 73,* 31–68.

Kosslyn, S. M. (1980). *Image and mind.* Cambridge, MA: Harvard University Press.

Kosslyn, S. M. (1994a). *Elements of graph design.* New York: Freeman.

Kosslyn, S. M. (1994b). *Image and brain: The resolution of the imagery debate.* Cambridge, MA: MIT Press.

Lakoff, G., & Johnson, M. (1980). *Metaphors we live by.* Chicago: University of Chicago Press.

Larkin, J. H., & Simon, H. A. (1987). Why a diagram is (sometimes) worth ten thousand words. *Cognitive Science, 11,* 65–99.

Lee, P. U., & Tversky, B. (submitted). Switching perspective in spatial descriptions.

Levy, I., Hasson, U., Avidan, G., Henler, T., & Malach, R. (2001). Center-periphery organization of human object areas. *Nature Neuroscience, 4,* 533–539.

Levinson, S. (1996). *Frames of reference and Molyneux's question: Cross-linguistic evidence.* In P. Bloom, M. A. Peterson, L. Nadel, & M. Garrett (Eds.), *Space and language* (pp. 109–169). Cambridge, MA: MIT Press.

Lowe, R. K. (1999). Extracting information from an animation during complex visual processing. *European Journal of the Psychology of Education, 14,* 225–244.

McNamara, T. P., & Diwadkar, V. A. (1997). Symmetry and asymmetry of human spatial memory. *Cognitive Psychology, 34,* 160–190.

Maguire, E. A., Frackowiak, R. S. J., & Frith, C. D. (1997). Recalling routes around London: Activation of the right hippocampus in taxi drivers. *Journal of Neuroscience, 17,* 7103–7110.

Milner, A. D., & Goodale, M. A. (1995). *The visual brain in action.* Oxford: Oxford University Press.

Mani, K. & Johnson-Laird, P. N. (1982). The mental representation of spatial descriptions. *Memory and Cognition, 10,* 181–187.

Morrison, J. B., & Tversky, B. (1997). Body schemas. In M. G. Shafto and P. Langley (Eds.), *Proceedings of the Meetings of the Cognitive Science Society* (pp. 525–529). Mahwah, NJ: Erlbaum.

O'Keefe, J., & Nadel, L. (1978). *The hippocampus as a cognitive map.* Oxford: Oxford University Press.

Palmiter, S., & Elkerton, J. (1993). Animated demonstrations for learning procedural computer-based tasks. *Human-Computer Interaction, 8,* 193–216.

Pani, J. R., Jeffres, J. A., Shippey, G. T., & Schwartz, K. T. (1996). Imagining projective transformations: Aligned orientations in spatial organization. *Cognitive Psychology, 31,* 125–167.

Pinker, S. (1990). A theory of graph comprehension. In R. Freedle (Ed.), *Artificial intelligence and the future of testing* (pp. 73–126). Hillsdale, NJ: Erlbaum.

Portugali, Y. (1993). *Implicate relations: Society and space in the Israeli-Palestinian conflict.* The Netherlands: Kluwer.

Reed, C. L., & Farah, M. J. (1995). The psychological reality of the body schema: A test with normal participants. *Journal of Experimental Psychology: Human Perception and Performance, 21*, 334–343.

Rieser, J. J. (1999). Dynamic spatial orientation and the coupling of representation and action. In R. G. Golledge (Ed.). *Wayfinding behavior: Cognitive mapping and other spatial processes* (pp. 168–191). Baltimore: The Johns Hopkins Press.

Rinck, M., Hahnel, A., Bower, G. H., & Glowalla, U. (1997). The metrics of spatial situation models. *Journal of Experimental Psychology: Learning, Memory, and Cognition, 23*, 622–637.

Rizzolatti, G., Fadiga, L., Fogassi, L., & Gallese, V. (2002). From mirror neurons to imitation: Facts and speculations. In A. Meltzoff & W. Prinz (Eds.), *The imitative mind: Evolution, development, and brain bases* (pp. 247–266). Cambridge: Cambridge University Press.

Rock, I. (1973). *Orientation and form.* New York: Academic Press.

Rosch, E. (1978). Principles of categorization. In E. Rosch & B. B. Lloyd (Editors), *Cognition and categorization* (pp. 27–48). Hillsdale, NJ.

Rosenbaum, R. S., Priselac, S., Kohler, S., Black, S. E., Gao, F., Nadel, L., & Moscovitch, M. (2000). Remote spatial memory in an amnesic person with extensive bilateral hippocampal lesions. *Nature Neuroscience, 3*, 1044–1048.

Sadalla, E. K., Burroughs, W. J., & Staplin, L. J. (1980). Reference points in spatial cognition. *Journal of Experimental Psychology: Human Learning and Memory, 6*, 516–528.

Schiano, D., & Tversky, B. (1992). Structure and strategy in viewing simple graphs. *Memory and Cognition, 20*, 12–20.

Schwartz, D. L. (1995). The emergence of abstract representations in dyad problem solving. *The Journal of the Learning Sciences, 4*, 321–354.

Shah, P., & Carpenter, P. A. (1995). Conceptual limitations in comprehending line graphs. *Journal of Experimental Psychology: General, 124*, 43–61.

Shanon, B. (1983). Answers to where questions. *Discourse Processes, 6*, 319–352.

Shelton, A. L., Burrows, J. J., Tversky, B., & Gabrieli, J. D. E. (November, 2000). Effects of route and survey perspectives on brain activation during scene recognition. Paper presented at the Thirtieth Annual Meeting of the Society for Neurosciences, New Orleans.

Shelton, A. L., & McNamara, T. P. (2001). Visual memories from nonvisual experiences. *Psychological Science, 12*, 343–347.

Shelton, A. L., Tversky, B., & Gabrieli, J. B. E. (March, 2001). Switching between route and survey perspectives in spatial memory. Paper presented at meetings of Cognitive Neuroscience Society, New York.

Shepard, R. N. (1994). Perceptual-cognitive universals as reflections of the world. *Psychonomic Bulletin and Review, 1*, 2–28.

Shepard, R. N., & Cooper, L. (1982). *Mental images and their transformation.* Cambridge: MIT Press.

Shepard, R. N. & Podgorny, P. (1978). Cognitive processes that resemble perceptual processes. In W. K. Estes (Ed.), *Handbook of learning and cognitive processes, Vol. 5* (pp. 189–237). Hillsdale, NJ: Erlbaum.

Shiffrar, M. M. & Shepard, R. N. (1991). Comparison of cube rotations around axes inclined relative to the environment or to the cube. *Journal of Experimental Psychology: Human Perception and Performance, 17*, 44–54.

Shin, S.-J. (1995). *The logical status of diagrams*. Cambridge: Cambridge University Press.

Southworth, M., & Southworth, S. (1982). *Maps: A visual survey and design guide*. Boston: Little, Brown and Company.

Stenning, K., & Oberlander, J. (1995). A cognitive theory of graphical and linguistic reasoning: Logic and implementation. *Cognitive Science, 19*, 97–140.

Stevens, A., & Coupe, P. (1978). Distortions in judged spatial relations. *Cognitive Psychology, 10*, 422–437.

Talmy, L.: How language structures space. (1983). In H. L. Pick, Jr. & L. P. Acredolo (Eds.), *Spatial orientation: Theory, research and application* (pp. 225–282). Plenum, NY.

Taylor, H. A., Naylor, S. J., & Chechile, N. A. (1999). Goal-specific influences on the representation of spatial perspectives. *Memory and Cognition, 27*, 309–319.

Taylor, H. A., & Tversky, B. (1992a). Descriptions and depictions of environments. *Memory and Cognition, 20*, 483–496.

Taylor, H. A., & Tversky, B. (1992b). Spatial mental models derived from survey and route descriptions. *Journal of Memory and Language, 31*, 261–282.

Taylor, H. A., & Tversky, B. (1996). Perspective in spatial descriptions. *Journal of Memory and Language, 35*, 371–391.

Thorndyke, P., & Hayes-Roth, B. (1982). Differences in spatial knowledge acquired from maps and navigation. *Cognitive Psychology 14*, 560–89.

Tufte, E. R. (1983). *The visual display of quantitative information*. Cheshire, CT: Graphics Press.

Tufte, E. R. (1990). *Envisioning information*. Cheshire, CT: Graphics Press.

Tufte, E. R. (1997). *Visual explanations*. Cheshire, CT: Graphics Press.

Turnbull, O. H., Denis, M., Mellet, E., Ghaem, O., & Carey, D. P. (2001). The processing of visuospatial information: Neuropsychological and neuroimaging investigations. In M. Denis, R. H. Logie, C. Cornoldi, M. de Vega, & J. Englelkamp (Eds.), *Imagery, language and visuo-spatial thinking* (pp. 81–108). Hove, UK: Psychology Press.

Tversky, B. (1981). Distortions in memory for maps. *Cognitive Psychology, 13*, 407–433.

Tversky, B. (1996). Spatial perspective in descriptions. In P. Bloom, M. A. Peterson, L. Nadel, & M. Garrett (Eds.), *Language and space.* (pp. 463–491). Cambridge, MA: MIT Press.

Tversky, B. (1991). Spatial mental models. In G. H. Bower (Ed.), *The psychology of learning and motivation: Advances in research and theory*, Vol. 27 (pp. 109–145). New York: Academic Press.

Tversky, B. (1992). Distortions in cognitive maps. *Geoforum, 23*, 131–138.

Tversky, B. (1993). Cognitive maps, cognitive collages, and spatial mental models. In A. U. Frank & I. Campari (Eds.), *Spatial information theory: A theoretical basis for GIS* (pp. 14–24). Berlin: Springer-Verlag.

Tversky, B. (1995a). Cognitive origins of graphic conventions. In F. T. Marchese (Ed.), *Understanding images* (pp. 29–53). New York: Springer-Verlag.

Tversky, B. (1995b). Perception and cognition of 2D and 3D graphics. *Human factors in computing systems* (p. 175). New York: ACM.

Tversky, B. (2000a). Some ways that maps and diagrams communicate. In C. C. Freksa, W. Brauer, C. Habel, & K. F. Wender (Eds.). *Spatial cognition II: Integration abstract theories, empirical studies, formal models, and powerful applications* (pp. 72–79). Berlin: Springer.

Tversky, B. (2000b). Levels and structure of cognitive mapping. In R. Kitchin & S. M. Freundschuh (Eds.). *Cognitive mapping: Past, present and future* (pp. 24–43). London: Routledge.

Tversky, B. (2000c). Remembering spaces. In E. Tulving & F. I. M. Craik (Eds.), *Handbook of memory* (pp. 363–378). New York: Oxford University Press.

Tversky, B. (2001). Spatial schemas in depictions. In M. Gattis (Ed.), *Spatial schemas and abstract thought* (pp. 79–111). Cambridge, MA: MIT Press.

Tversky, B. (2003). Navigating by mind and by body. In C. Freksa, W. Brauer, C. Habel, & K. F. Wender (Eds.), *Spatial cognition III: Routes and navigation, human memory and learning, spatial representation and spatial reasoning* (pp. 1–10). Berlin: Springer-Verlag.

Tversky, B., & Hemenway, K. (1984). Objects, parts, and categories. *Journal of Experimental Psychology: General, 113*, 169–193.

Tversky, B., Kim, J., & Cohen, A. (1999). Mental models of spatial relations and transformations from language. In C. Habel & G. Rickheit (Eds.), *Mental models in discourse processing and reasoning* (pp. 239–258). Amsterdam: North-Holland.

Tversky, B., Kugelmass, S., & Winter, A. (1991). Cross-cultural and developmental trends in graphic productions. *Cognitive Psychology, 23*, 515–557.

Tversky, B., & Lee, P. U. (1998). How space structures language. In C. Freksa, C. Habel, & K. F. Wender (Eds.), *Spatial cognition: An interdisciplinary approach to representation and processing of spatial knowledge* (pp. 157–175). Berlin: Springer-Verlag.

Tversky, B., & Lee, P. U. (1999). Pictorial and verbal tools for conveying routes. In C. Freksa, & D. M. Mark (Eds.). *Spatial information theory: Cognitive and computational foundations of geographic information science* (pp. 51–64). Berlin: Springer.

Tversky, B., Morrison, J. B., & Betrancourt, M. (2002). Animation: Does it facilitate? *International Journal of Human-Computer Studies, 57*, 247–262.

Tversky, B. Morrison, J. B., & Zacks, J. (2002). On bodies and events. In A. Meltzoff & W. Prinz (Eds.), *The imitative mind* (pp. 221–232). Cambridge: Cambridge University Press.

Tversky, B., & Schiano, D. (1989). Perceptual and conceptual factors in distortions in memory for maps and graphs. *Journal of Experimental Psychology: General, 118*, 387–398.

Ullmer-Ehrich, V. (1982). The structure of living space descriptions. In R. J. Jarvella & W. Klein (Eds.), *Speech, place and action* (pp. 219–249). New York: Wiley.

Ungerleider, L. G., & Mishkin, M. (1982). Two cortical visual systems. In D. J. Ingle, M. A. Goodale, & R. J. W. Mansfield (Eds.). *Analysis of visual behavior.* Cambridge, MA: MIT Press.

Winn, W. D. (1987). Charts, graphs and diagrams in educational materials. In D. M. Willows & H. A. Haughton (Eds.), *The psychology of illustration.* New York: Springer-Verlag.

Woodward, D., & Lewis, G. M. (1994). *The history of cartography. Volume 2, Book 2: Cartography in the traditional East and Southeast Asian societies.* Chicago: University of Chicago Press.

Woodward, D., & Lewis, G. M. (1998). *The History of cartography. Volume 2, Book 3: Cartography in the traditional Africa, America, Arctic, Australian, and Pacific societies.* Chicago: University of Chicago Press.

Zacks, J., & Tversky, B. (1999). Bars and lines: A study of graphic communication. *Memory and Cognition, 27,* 1073–1079.

Zacks, J., Levy, E., Tversky, B., & Schiano, D. J. (1998). Reading bar graphs: Effects of depth cues and graphical context. *Journal of Experimental Psychology: Applied, 4,* 119–138.

Zacks, J., Rypma, B., Gabrieli, J. D. E., Tversky, B., & Glover, G. H. (1999). Imagined transformations of the body: An fMRI study. *Neuropsychologia, 37*(9), 1029–1040.

2

Visuospatial Images

Daniel Reisberg and Friderike Heuer

ABSTRACT

We review evidence indicating that mental images, like pictures and percepts, depict rather than describe the represented content, and that visual images rely heavily on the same neural substrate as actual vision. Given this shared substrate, it is perhaps unsurprising that images also show certain sensory effects (e.g., sensory aftereffects) often associated with relatively low-level processes in vision. We argue, though, that images (like percepts and unlike pictures) are organized depictions, perceived within a perceptual reference frame that governs how certain aspects of the form are understood, and we consider some of the implications of this reference frame for image function. Evidence is also presented for a distinction between visual and spatial images, each with its own functional profile and its own neural substrate. Finally, we consider differences from one individual to the next in the vividness of mental images. We argue that, despite the skepticism of many investigators, vividness self-reports are interpretable and meaningfully linked to performance in at least some imagery tasks.

INTRODUCTION

How many windows are there in your house or apartment? Who has bushier eyebrows, Tony Blair or George W. Bush? For most people, questions like these seem to elicit "mental pictures." You know what Blair and Bush look like, and you call a "picture" of each before your "mind's eye" in order to make the comparison. Likewise, you call to mind a "map" of your house or apartment, and count the windows by inspecting this map. Many people even trace the map in the air by moving their finger around, following the imagined map's contours.

Various practical problems also seem to evoke images. There you are in the store, trying on a new sweater. Will the sweater look good with your blue pants? To decide, you may try to visualize the blue of the pants, using your mind's eye to ask how they will look with the sweater. Similarly, imagine asking yourself, "Where did I leave my keys? Did I leave them on my desk?" To figure this out, you may try visualizing what your desk looked like when you left the office – were the keys in view?

These examples illustrate the common, everyday use of visual images as a basis for making decisions, or as an aid to remembering. However, these examples – and the commonsense terms in which we have described them – raise a number of concerns. There is, after all, no tiny eye somewhere deep in the brain, and so the phrase "mind's eye" cannot be taken literally. Likewise, mental "pictures" cannot be actual pictures – with no eye deep inside the brain, who or what would inspect such images? Therefore, we need to find an account of mental imagery that avoids these problematic notions.

In this chapter, we will explore what is known about mental imagery, and about visual imagery in particular. After this introduction, we review some of the (by now classic) findings that make it clear visual images do function in important ways as if they were mental pictures, and that the processes of imaging do resemble those used for actual seeing. We also present data showing that visual imagery relies heavily on brain areas ordinarily involved in visual perception, and this points the way toward a conception of visual imagery that avoids the problematic notions of a "mind's eye" and "mental pictures."

These commonalities between imagery and perception must, however, be placed alongside of some points of contrast between visual imagery and perception, and likewise, points of contrast between visual images and actual out-in-the-world pictures. Our next section, therefore, turns to these points of contrast, focusing on differences between the discoveries that can be made from (or about) mental images and those that can be made from (or about) actual pictures. The following section continues this broad theme, focusing on the question of just how "visual" visual images truly are. In particular, we explore the possibility that some tasks that might seem to rely on visual imagery may in fact rely on some other form of representation.

We then turn to another long-standing puzzle – the huge differences often observed in how different individuals describe the vividness of their visual imagery. Many authors have suggested that these self-reports cannot be taken seriously, but we will explore the possibility that these vividness reports do capture an important dimension of mental imagery, and are predictive of performance in some circumstances.

Finally, we tackle a point that flows out of the issues just mentioned. As we will see, the data draw our attention to the fact that visual imagery is, of course, not the only modality of imagery available to us. This fact – obvious as it is – proves useful in untangling a number of data patterns in the literature, but it also invites a further question: Can we extrapolate from what we know about visual imagery to make claims about these other modalities? This issue is briefly discussed in the chapter's closing section.

THE RESEMBLANCE BETWEEN IMAGES AND PICTURES, IMAGERY AND PERCEIVING

Chronometric Studies of Imagery

Introspectively, visual imagery certainly seems (for many people) to re-semble actual seeing: Imagers routinely report that their images resemble pictures, and that they read information off the image much as one reads information off of a picture. No wonder, then, that Shakespeare's Hamlet spoke of the "mind's eye," and of course this expression remains in com-mon use centuries after Shakespeare coined it.

Here as always, we need to be wary of these introspectively based self-reports, but, even so, many studies make it clear that – this time, at least – the self-reports do capture some essential properties of mental imagery. More precisely, the available data strongly indicate that mental images are qualitatively distinct from other forms of mental representation, and, moreover, that mental images truly do *depict* the represented content (much as a picture would), whereas other forms of representation seem instead to *describe* the represented content.

Depictions come in many forms (sculptures, photographs, line draw-ings, and blueprints are just a few examples), and this invites us to ask what exactly it is that distinguishes a depiction from a description. There is not a full consensus on this issue (for two somewhat different views, see Kosslyn, 1983; Rey, 1981), but several points do seem important: Both de-pictions and descriptions represent a content, but they do so in markedly different ways. Not only does a depiction represent its content, but the *parts* of the depiction also represent the *parts* of the same content. Thus, part of a picture of a mouse represents the mouse's head, part of the picture represents the mouse's tail, and so on. There is no such correspondence in a description. No part of the word "mouse" represents a particular bit of the mouse's anatomy. (The letter *m*, for example, is in no sense a representation of the left side of the mouse.)

Second, depictions (but not descriptions) represent how content would appear if viewed from a particular vantage point: A photograph, for example, shows what a scene would look like if viewed from a particular angle and a particular distance. A description of the scene, in contrast, might be entirely silent on these points.

Third, the relationship between a description and the content it represents is often arbitrary. There is nothing gray or furry about the word mouse, and other languages represent the same content with entirely different words. A depiction, on the other hand, represents its content by virtue of a relationship that can be roughly understood as one of resemblance, so that one can say that the depiction "looks like" the thing being represented. This is in some ways a complicated notion (cf. Rey, 1981; Fodor, 1981), but in any case hinges on the depiction preserving certain properties of the thing being represented. Thus, for example, points that are close together on the represented form (the mouse's eyes and its nose) should be functionally close together in the depiction. A point that is *between* two other points on the represented form should be between the relevant points on the depiction (and so, in the depiction, the representation of the mouse's neck should be between the bit showing the mouse's head and the bit showing the mouse's body). Similarly for the relationship of *alignment*; this, too, should be preserved in the depiction.

Finally, and as a consequence of points already mentioned, the pattern of what information is *prominent* within the image, and what information is less so, should depend on certain spatial properties, rather than considerations of importance. In a picture of a cat, for example, the cat's claws and whiskers might not be all that prominent, even though these are features strongly associated with cats. In contrast, the cat's head is likely to be quite prominent in the picture (simply because it is large and up front), even though a *description* of a cat might not even mention the head (because the presence of the head is self-evident and so not worth noting).

Numerous studies make it clear that, by any of these criteria, mental images function as depictions and not as descriptions. Thus, for example, participants are very fast in "locating" features within their image that would be quite prominent in the corresponding picture (such as a cat's head), and they are correspondingly slower in locating features within the image that would be small or hidden from view in a depiction, even if these features have a strong semantic association to the represented target (e.g., a cat's whiskers or claws). Importantly, this pattern of information availability reverses if participants are asked questions about the target object with no instruction to rely on a mental image. Thus, if participants are simply asked questions about cats, their responses are very quick for strongly associated features such as whiskers, and there is no relationship between response times and size or prominence (Kosslyn, 1976).

Similarly, mental images seem to be represented from a determinate viewing angle and distance – as a depiction must be. This is evident in the data just described, since "visibility from a specific perspective" and "occlusion" both seem to play a role in those data: Response times are short when participants are asked about the cat's head, for example, because the cat's head is prominent *from a particular viewing angle*. Likewise, response times are long when participants are asked about the cat's claws because these are occluded from view from most viewing angles. Thus the data just described make no sense unless we assume a representation that somehow specifies viewing angle and somehow respects occlusion. (For more on occlusion in imagery, however, see Keenan, 1983; Keenan & Moore, 1979; Kerr & Neisser, 1983; Neisser & Kerr, 1973.)

In addition, several studies have directly examined the role of viewing position in mental imagery, with tasks requiring (in some trials) that participants scrutinize details within the image, and (in other trials) that they make broader judgments about the image's larger-scale features (Kosslyn, 1983). The data show that participants can judge an image's fine details only if they "zoom in" for a closer look at the image; conversely, they can make judgments about large-scale features only if they zoom out for a broader view. These results make it clear that we can meaningfully speak of the image *having a viewing perspective*, as a depiction must.

The studies of zooming in on an image, or zooming back, also indicate that mental images functionally preserve distance relationships within the imaged scene. Thus the time needed for this zooming is a positive function of the "distance traveled" in the zoom; more precisely, the greater the imagined zoom needed for a particular trial, the slower the response. Similarly for the times needed to imagine scanning across an image: These times, too, depend closely on the distance traveled in the scan (Denis & Kosslyn, 1999; Kosslyn, Ball, & Reiser, 1978). Distance relationships are also crucial in the time needed to imagine an image rotating into a new position: These rotation times are a positive function (and, in many studies, a linear function) of the degree of rotation required (Shepard & Cooper, 1982). All of these results confirm that points that are close to each other in the depicted scene seem to be functionally close in the image, so that one can move swiftly from a point to any of its near neighbors; travel to more distant points requires more time.[1] Thus, images rather directly represent the spatial layout of the represented scene – exactly as one would expect for a depiction of that scene.

The "Imagery Debate" and the Limits of Chronometric Data

The studies just reviewed seem to provide a persuasive package of evidence, but in truth these studies have been controversial, with much of the controversy emerging from a theoretical debate prominent in the research literature across the late 1970s and early 1980s. That debate hinged on why the results of imagery experiments took the form they did. One position was that mental images are "displayed" on a specialized "analog medium" within the brain, much as a painting is displayed on a canvas or a computer image on a CRT monitor. According to this view, the results just surveyed are the inevitable consequence of the properties of this medium. By analogy, a painting will be limited by the size of its canvas and will reflect the surface texture of the canvas. In the same fashion, mental images necessarily inherit the properties of their display medium – including a limited extent, a certain grain size, and various other attributes all leading to the results we have already discussed. (For clear statements of this view, see Kosslyn, Pinker, Smith, & Shwartz, 1979; Kosslyn, 1981.)

An opposing view was that imagery does not require a specialized medium, but instead is realized through the same mechanisms as any other mental representation. From this perspective, the properties of mental images derive only from the fact that the participants' task in an imagery experiment is to "simulate" in their thoughts, as best they can, how an event would unfold if it were actually viewed. (Again, for a clear statement of this view, see Pylyshyn, 1981.) Thus, for example, because participants know that travel over longer distances requires longer times, they easily simulate this result in their imagery, thus producing the well-documented

---

[1] Note the distinction here between *functional proximity* and *physical proximity*. Physical proximity obviously refers to how close two points are to each other in physical (Euclidean) space. Functional proximity refers to how readily and how quickly one can move from one point to another. These two forms of proximity are often the same, but do not need to be. (With some forms of "travel," for example, points that are physically close may be functionally distant and vice versa.) In any case, the imagery data reviewed so far speak only to functional proximity – the ease of moving from one point to another – and not to physical proximity. Likewise, the data speak to *functional alignment* (the most quickly traveled path from Point A to Point B is through Point C), and not *physical alignment* (Point C is spatially between Points A and B). For more on these issues, see, for example, Reisberg (2001).

linear relation between scanning distance and scanning times (e.g., the result reported by Kosslyn et al., 1978).

According to this latter view, the results of imagery experiments are heavily influenced by participants' knowledge – often unconscious "tacit knowledge" – about how physical events unfold; this knowledge will guide how the participants seek to simulate these events in their imagination. In addition, the results will be heavily influenced by participants' understanding of the task set for them by the experimenters (e.g., whether their task is truly to simulate the relevant event, or to seek some other means of answering the experimenters' questions). For this reason, imagery experiments will be particularly susceptible to the effects of experimenter demand.

In fact, at least some of the chronometric results we have described can be interpreted in terms of experimenter demand (cf. Intons-Peterson & White, 1981; Intons-Peterson, 1983). Far worse, though, there is reason to believe that chronometric results cannot discriminate between the two broad hypotheses we have described – one cast in terms of an imagery medium, and one cast in terms of strategic simulation. Anderson (1978), for example, noted that any pattern in the data can be explained only by making claims about the nature of the image representation *and* the nature of the processes used to read or access that representation. As a consequence, any result apparently favoring one sort of representation can always be explained in terms of a different representation if one makes suitable changes in describing how the processes operate. (For related, and more modern, concerns about chronometric results, see, for example, Intons-Peterson, 1999; Richman, 1999.)

Clearly, then, there is more than one way to think about the chronometric results we have so far described. These results certainly seem to suggest a depictive, not descriptive, mode of representation, but it is unclear whether this is best understood as resulting from the use of an imagery medium, which would shape any representation using this medium, or as resulting from strategic simulation, guided by tacit knowledge. But if we cannot choose between these alternatives by appeal to response-time findings, how should we proceed? As is often the case, investigators have turned to other sorts of data and other investigative tools in hopes of resolving the issues. We turn next to one of those other sorts of data.

Images and the Brain

A number of neuroimaging studies have made it clear that, when participants are visualizing, activity levels are high in various parts of the occipital cortex; this brain area is, of course, crucially involved in visual perception (Behrmann, 2000; Farah, 1988, 1989; Ishai & Sagi, 1995; Kosslyn, 1994; Miyashita, 1995; Thompson & Kosslyn, 2000). Moreover, the exact pattern of brain activation during mental imagery depends to some extent on the type of image being maintained. For high-resolution, detailed imagery, Areas V1 and V2 (which we know to be spatially organized) are particularly active, and, remarkably, the amount of brain tissue showing activation increases as participants imagine larger and larger objects (Behrmann, 2000; Kosslyn et al., 1993; Kosslyn et al., 1999; Kosslyn & Thompson, 2003; Kosslyn, Thompson, Kim, & Alpert, 1995; Mellet et al., 2000). In a similar fashion, Area MT/MST, sensitive to motion in ordinary perception, is particularly activated when participants are asked to imagine movement patterns (Goebel, Khorram-Sefat, Muckli, Hacker, & Singer, 1998); brain areas that are especially active during the perception of faces are also highly activated when people are imagining faces (O'Craven & Kanwisher, 2000).

These data are by their very nature correlational, making interpretation difficult. Recent developments, however, provide a way to deal with this issue: The technique of *transcranial magnetic stimulation* (TMS) involves the creation of a series of strong magnetic pulses at a specific location on the scalp; this causes a temporary disruption in the small brain region directly underneath this scalp area. In this fashion, it is possible to disrupt Area V1 (primary visual cortex) in an otherwise normal brain. Not surprisingly, using TMS in this way causes problems in vision, but it also causes parallel problems in visual imagery, providing powerful argument that Area V1 is crucial both for the processing of visual information and for the creation and maintenance of visual images (Kosslyn et al., 1999).

Further confirmation for these claims comes from neuropsychological evidence, examining the impact of various forms of brain damage on mental imagery. In many cases, patients who have lost some aspect of their vision suffer parallel deficits in their imagery – just as we would expect if these two activities rely on overlapping neural areas. Thus, patients who (because of stroke) have lost the ability to perceive color often seem to lose the ability to imagine scenes in color; patients who lose the ability to perceive fine detail seem also to lose the ability to visualize fine detail, and so on. If (as a result of occipital damage) patients have a scotoma (blind spot) in a particular region of visual space, or some restriction on the *extent* of visual space, they are likely to have a corresponding limit on their visual imagery (DeRenzi & Spinnler, 1967; Farah, 1988, 1989; Farah, Soso, & Dasheiff, 1992; Kosslyn, 1994; Kosslyn & Thompson, 1999;

note, though, that we will return to some contrasting evidence in a later section).

As another striking example, researchers investigated the imagery of two patients who had developed unilateral neglect syndrome as a result of right-pariental damage caused by a stroke (Bisiach & Luzzatti, 1978; Bisiach, Luzzatti, & Perani, 1979). If these patients were shown a picture, they seemed to see only the right side of it; if asked to read a word, they only read the right half. The same pattern of neglect was evident in the patients' imagery, and they consistently neglected the right half of scenes they were imagining, just as they did with perceived scenes. (For some contrasting data, though, see Beschin, Basso, & Sala, 2000; Beschin, Cocchini, Della Sala, & Logie, 1997; Coslett, 1997.)

How should we think about all this? In ordinary perceiving, one begins with a stimulus, and derives from it an internal representation of that stimulus. This internal representation, often called a *percept*, obviously depicts the external stimulus, and so does show directly what many aspects of the stimulus look like. However, the percept is far more than a mere transcription or copy of the stimulus because the representation is organized and interpreted in ways the stimulus is not (more on this point below). For this reason, it is important to keep separate the stimulus, with which perception begins, and the percept, which we can think of, roughly, as the product of perceiving.

The percept is a depiction, but in no literal sense is it a "picture." Instead, the percept is a mental representation, resulting from earlier interpretive steps, and instantiated in the neural substrate. Thus, inspection of the percept does not require an "inner eye" useful for scanning some sort of picture. Instead, information is drawn from the percept through a set of processes (again: instantiated in the neural substrate) that can take this representation as their input, and use the information derived from this in subsequent processing and analysis.

Images may be thought of in roughly the same way, and, according to the evidence just reviewed, may be instantiated in the same neural substrate, and analyzed through roughly the same processes, as percepts. Images, of course, do not begin with a sensory input; when visualizing a scene, the scene is typically not before one's eyes! Therefore, many of the interpretive processes through which a percept is derived from a stimulus are likely to be irrelevant for imagery. Nonetheless, the representation achieved through perception (i.e., the percept) is likely to resemble in many ways the representation created through imagery. On this basis, then, images, just like percepts, would depict, with no need for appeals to "mental pictures"

or "inner eyes." And, because they are depictions, images can have all the
properties suggested by the chronometric results, with no need for any
"projection screen," deep within the brain, nor for any homunculus sitting
and viewing this screen.

These points obviously bear on issues raised in the last section, issues central to the so-called "Imagery Debate." More than two decades
ago, Kosslyn and others proposed that visual imagery relies on a special
"display medium," and that the properties of this medium govern many
aspects of imagery functioning. The neural evidence seems to confirm this
proposal. Apparently, both images and percepts are instantiated via patterns of activation in the brain's visual cortex, and we know that this cortex
is specialized in several ways that support and shape these depictions. Crucially, many areas of this cortex are topographically organized, with separate areas of cortex representing separate areas of space, and adjacent areas
of cortex typically representing adjacent (or nearby) areas of space. These
"visual maps" in the brain also have limited extent and limited resolution,
with the degree of resolution depending in an orderly way on a region's
anatomic position within the map. These are, as it turns out, properties
directly reflected in the functioning of both images and percepts.

In short, then, imagery does seem to rely on a distinct medium, and it is a
medium whose properties both serve and constrain the capacity for depicting a spatial layout. It is on this basis that at least some authors regard the
Imagery Debate as now settled (cf. Kosslyn, 1994; we will, however, need
to return to this theme later in the chapter, and add some complications to
this apparent resolution).

Sensory Effects in Imagery

If mental imagery relies heavily on the mechanisms of perception, then we
should expect to find interference between imagery and perception, with
use of either disrupting the other, on the assumption that the mechanisms
needed for each cannot be used for more than one task at a time. Closely
related, we might expect that imagery will show many of the functional
patterns observed in perception. Both of these predictions have been confirmed many times.

For example, Segal and Fusella (1971, 1970) asked their participants to
detect very faint signals – either dim visual stimuli or soft tones. Participants did this either while forming a visual image or while forming an
auditory imagery, and the results showed a selective interference pattern:
Auditory imagery made it difficult to detect faint auditory signals; visual

imagery made it more difficult to detect faint visual signals (also see Craver-Lemley, Arterberry, & Reeves, 1997; Craver-Lemley & Reeves, 1987, 1992; Farah & Smith, 1983; Johnson, 1982; Logie, 1986; Matthews, 1983).

In other studies, participants have been asked to image stimuli *related to* the one they are trying to perceive. In this case, imagery seems to produce a priming effect, with perception facilitated if participants have just been visualizing the target form in the appropriate position (Farah, 1985; Heil, Rösler, & Hennighausen, 1993; Ishai & Sagi, 1997; also see McDermott & Roediger, 1994).

In the same vein, a number of studies have documented various "sensory" effects in mental imagery. For example, participants in some studies have shown color aftereffects produced by imaged adapting stimuli; other studies have shown perceptual adaptation effects after participants spent some time imaging how the world would look through displacement prisms (Finke, 1989; for some critical evaluation of these data, see Harris, 1982; Intons-Peterson & White, 1981; Kolers, 1983; Kunen & May, 1981).

Likewise, consider studies of "two-point acuity" in imagery. In one study, participants were first shown two dots, then the dots were removed, but participants were asked to imagine that the dots were still present. The participants then moved their eyes away from the imaged dots' position, and, as they looked further and further away, they had to judge whether they could still "see" that the dots were indeed separate. In this way, "two-point acuity" was measured with imagined stimuli, and the data show a remarkable correspondence between participants' performance with these imagined dots and their performance with actually perceived dots (Finke & Kosslyn, 1980). In both cases, acuity fell off abruptly if the dots were not in the center of vision, and the decline in acuity was virtually the same in perception and in imagery. Moreover, in vision, acuity falls off more rapidly if participants look above or below the two dots, rather than to the left or right, and this pattern, too, was observed in the imagery condition. Thus, qualitatively and quantitatively, the imagery data match the perceptual data.

IMAGES ARE NOT PICTURES

Neutral Depictions, Organized Depictions

We have now surveyed a considerable quantity of evidence documenting the fact that images depict the represented content, and also considerable

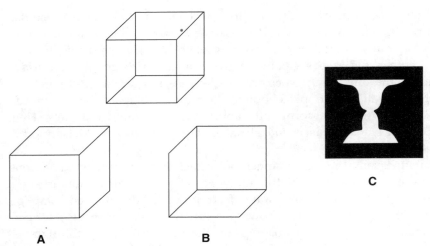

FIGURE 2.1. The drawing of the Necker cube (top) is a neutral depiction, indeterminate with regard to configuration in depth. Thus the cube is compatible with the construal shown in A, the construal shown in B, and many other construals as well. The *perception* of the cube, in contrast, is an organized depiction, somehow specifying configuration in depth. Thus the perception of the cube is not indeterminate but somehow specifies one configuration or another. Likewise, the drawing of the vase/profiles (C) is a neutral depiction, indeterminate as to whether it is vase or profiles. However, the *perception* of this form specifies a figure/ground organization and is thus vase (but not profiles) or profiles (but not vase).

evidence for a functional and biological overlap between the processes of imagery and those of perception. Further data, however, demand a refinement of these views, because we still need to ask *what sort of depiction* images provide. As we will see, the data suggest that images (like percepts, and unlike pictures) are *organized* depictions, and, as such, images have a duplex nature: They depict *and* they describe represented content.

As an entry to this issue, consider, for example, the Necker cube (Figure 2.1, top). The drawing of this cube – the stimulus itself – is infinitely ambiguous. It is compatible with the construal shown in Figure 2.1A, and also the construal shown in Figure 2.1B. For that matter, the drawing is compatible with any other three-dimensional construal that happens to have this particular two-dimensional projection. Put differently, the drawing itself is indeterminate with regard to three-dimensional interpretation; the drawing is neutral with regard to configuration in depth.

Our perception of the cube, in contrast, is not indeterminate; it is not neutral. Instead, we perceive the cube either as similar to Figure 2.1A or to

Figure 2.1B. Our perception, in other words, goes beyond the information given by specifying a configuration in depth.

The same point can be made for an endless series of other stimuli. Consider the classic vase/profiles figure (Figure 2.1C). The figure itself is not "vase-and-not-profiles," nor is it "profiles-and-not-vase." Instead, the figure itself is entirely neutral with regard to interpretation, and so it affords either interpretation. Our perception, though, lacks this equipotentiality. The perception somehow specifies that we are looking at the vase, and not the profiles, or that we are looking at profiles, and not the vase. This then turns out to have a variety of consequences – for how the dimensions of the figure are understood, for how attention is deployed across the figure, and for how (or whether) the figure will be remembered later on (e.g., Goldmeier, 1937/1972; Rock, 1983).

These points remind us about some essential properties of *percepts* (again: our mental representations of the stimulus world around us). Percepts are clearly depictions, and can therefore be thought of as akin to pictures in at least some regards. At the same time, though, percepts are rather different from pictures. The picture of the Necker cube is indeterminate regarding depth; the percept specifies depth. The picture of the vase/profiles is neutral regarding whether it is vase or profiles, but the percept specifies one or the other.

For convenience, let us call the sort of depiction that is in a picture a *neutral depiction*, and the sort that is in a percept an *organized depiction*. What does this difference consist of? One suggestion relies on terminology proposed by Peterson and her colleagues (e.g., Peterson, Kihlstrom, Rose, & Glisky, 1992): A percept exists within what Peterson et al. call a *perceptual reference frame* that specifies, on a small set of dimensions, how the percept is to be understood. The reference frame does not specify the referent of the form – does not tell what the representation is a representation *of*, but it does specify how the form is configured in depth, what the figure-ground relationships are, how the form is parsed, what its top and bottom are, where the form's "front" is (if it has one at all), and probably what its axes of symmetry are – a small set of perceptual specifications detailing how the form is organized, and governing subsequent processing of the form. In these terms, then, *organized depictions* (like percepts) are those accompanied by a perceptual reference frame, and shaped by that frame. *Neutral depictions* have no reference frame, and therefore are inherently ambiguous and in need of interpretation.

With this context, what sort of depictions are mental images – neutral depictions, like pictures, and so open to multiple construals, the way pictures

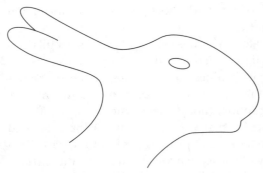

FIGURE 2.2. The duck/rabbit figure used by Chambers and Reisberg (1985).

seem to be? Or are they organized depictions, the way percepts are? One line of evidence on this point comes from a series of studies by Chambers and Reisberg (1985, 1992; Reisberg & Chambers, 1991). They led their participants to memorize some of the classic ambiguous figures, including the duck/rabbit (Figure 2.2). Participants were then asked to form a mental picture of the form and tried to reinterpret this imaged form, just as they had reinterpreted a series of training figures. The result was clear-cut: Zero participants were able to discover the duck in a rabbit image or the rabbit in a duck image. In sharp contrast, 100% of the participants were able, moments later, to draw a picture of the form they had just been imaging and to reverse the figure in their own drawings. This makes it clear, among other things, that participants did in fact remember the figure, had encoded it accurately, and fully understood their task.

The Chambers and Reisberg results have been controversial and other laboratories have not been able to replicate the zero rate of image-based reversals (Brandimonte & Gerbino, 1993; Hyman, 1993; Kaufman & Helstrup, 1993; Peterson et al., 1992; for some conjectures on why these other labs have observed nonzero reversal rates, see Reisberg, 1994). Even so, other laboratories have reliably replicated the finding that the reversal of mental images is difficult and quite rare, with 80% or 90% of the participants failing to reverse the image, even though reversal of the corresponding *picture* is extremely easy, with 100% of the participants succeeding in this reversal.

Image-Based Discovery

The results just cited are what we would expect if images are *organized depictions*. If images are understood within a perceptual reference frame, then they should be determinate with regard to the various appearance specifications mentioned earlier. They should, in other words, specify the form's figure/ground organization, specify the form's "front," and so on. One might say, therefore, that images, like percepts, are (in just these ways) "already interpreted," and thus resistant to reinterpretation.

At the same time, however, these results pose a puzzle for us. It is clear that imagery can be a rich source of new ideas and inventions; images can remind us and instruct us. This is easily documented in the laboratory (e.g., Anderson & Helstrup, 1993; Finke, 1990; Finke, Pinker, & Farah, 1989; Pinker & Finke, 1980), but is also evident in the broader history of ideas, which is, after all, filled with instances in which great discoveries in the arts, science, and technology were inspired by mental images of one sort or another (Miller, 1986; Shepard, 1988).

Given this grand potential for image-based discovery, why did Chambers and Reisberg's participants routinely fail to find a simple and obvious form in their images? The reason is simple: Whenever one examines a mental image, seeking some new perspective or some new idea, one is asking, in essence: *What does the depicted form resemble?* Thus, our understanding of image-based discovery must be built on an understanding of how people judge *resemblance*, and, crucially, we know that the pattern of resemblance depends both on stimulus geometry and also on the perceptual reference frame that is organizing that geometry (i.e., the specification of figure/ground, the assignment of orientation, and so on). This point has been well documented in perception (cf. Figure 2.3), and it seems highly

     a   *b*   *c*   *d*

FIGURE 2.3. For most people, C resembles D, but A does not resemble B. After all, C and D are both symmetrical, whereas A is, but B isn't. Likewise, C and D are both the same shape (diamonds), whereas A and B are different shapes. But, of course, all of these judgments depend on the *geometry as interpreted by the perceiver*, the geometry and its reference frame. This is revealed by the fact that A and C are identical except for a 45-degree rotation, and so are B and D. Thus the geometric relationship within the left pair is identical to that within the right pair. What distinguishes the pairs (and so what leads to a perception of resemblance in one pair only) is how that geometry is understood – and, in particular, how perception specifies the "top" of each form (Rock, 1975).

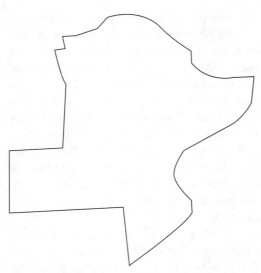

FIGURE 2.4. The test figure employed by Reisberg and Chambers (1991).

likely that it will apply to imagery as well. It follows from these premises, then, that discoveries will flow easily from an image only if the discovery is compatible with both the depicted geometry and also the reference frame. If the discovery is incompatible with either of these, then the image will not resemble the target form, and so for this reason will not call the target form to mind. Hence the sought-after discovery will be much more difficult, and much less frequent.

As an illustration of how all this matters, participants in one study were shown the shape shown in Figure 2.4. The participants memorized this "nonsense shape" just as they had a series of training figures, and then were asked to imagine the shape rotated 90 degrees clockwise. At this point, the participants were asked what familiar geographic form this figure resembled (Reisberg & Chambers, 1991).

What should we predict here? Participants initially perceived this form within a particular reference frame, probably one that identified the edge top-most in the drawing as being the form's top. When they imaged the form rotated into a new position, they presumably maintained this understanding about the form's top, and, as a result, their image depicted the proper geometry for Texas, but with the wrong reference frame (one that identified the state's eastern boundary as the shape's "top"). Because of this inappropriate reference frame, the mental image should not, in the participants' view of it, resemble Texas. (Again, recall that resemblance is governed both by the imaged geometry and the reference frame.) As a consequence, the image should not call Texas to mind, and so, on these grounds, we should predict that these participants would not recognize Texas in their image. This is precisely what the data showed. Exactly zero participants were able to recognize Texas in their own image.

Of course, one might object that this task was simply too difficult. Perhaps the Texas outline is too complicated to image properly. Or perhaps the participants weren't sufficiently familiar with Texas geography. Another study, however, rules out these possibilities. The hypothesis at issue suggests that participants' difficulty in this procedure lies solely in the fact that they were imaging the Texas form with the wrong reference frame – one that identified the eastern edge of Texas as the form's top. If this is correct, then the result should change if participants are led to the 'proper' reference frame, by means of suitable instruction.

In a follow-up study, Reisberg and Chambers again had participants encode the form shown in Figure 2.4, and then asked them (with the drawing removed from view) to form an image of the shape. This time, though, participants were told directly to think of the form as having a "new top," and, specifically, to think of the left side as the top. With this instruction, performance was vastly improved, and now a third of the participants recognized Texas in the imaged form, in contrast to the zero success rate in the earlier procedure. (For similar data also showing the effects of hints that change the imagers' reference frame, see Hyman, 1993; Peterson et al., 1992.)

These (and other findings) leave us with a reasonably consistent data pattern, and it seems useful to highlight two points within this pattern. First, it is important that participants *succeed* in image-based discovery in many contexts – for example, recognizing Texas in their image if the image is organized appropriately, finding the duck in a rabbit image if given a suitable hint. This is possible only because an image represents a form's geometry in a fashion that lets us judge what the imaged form looks like. This is presumably what images (in contrast to a purely descriptive mode of representation) are for. This is, in other words, presumably why we use images and why we evolved the capacity for imaging. More to the point, all of this reminds us once again that images *depict*.

At the same time, the fact that participants *fail* to recognize Texas (for example), when they understand the image in the wrong way, underscores the importance of the image's reference frame – a reference frame that somehow *describes* how the depiction is to be organized. When the frame is inappropriate, it can render image-based discoveries much less likely, and in some cases, it seems, rule them out altogether.

All of this implies that we need to distinguish two classes of image-based discovery, or, more accurately, two classes of discovery that one might hope to make, based on a mental image. First, there are discoveries compatible with both the imaged geometry and the reference frame. Examples would include discovering the state of Texas *once the northern edge of the state has been identified as the form's top*, or discovering the duck in the duck/rabbit form *once the left side of the form has been identified as the form's front*. Discoveries of this sort are relatively easy to make, and so quite common in many studies. These discoveries are also not dependent on further hints, either verbal hints or hints implicit in an example. In addition, evidence from Anderson and Helstrup (1993) suggests that participants are equally likely to make these discoveries from an image or from an actual out-in-the-world picture; in fact, in some cases, participants are more likely to make these discoveries with the image than with a picture, presumably because they can manipulate the image in a variety of ways that they cannot manipulate the picture.

Things are entirely different, though, for discoveries one might hope to make from an image that are compatible with the imaged geometry, but not with the reference frame. Examples would include discovering the state of Texas *with some edge other than the northern edge identified as top*, or discovering the duck in the duck/rabbit form *while still identifying the rabbit's face to be the form's front*. Discoveries of this sort are relatively infrequent and quite dependent on hints. Moreover, the hints that succeed tend to be precisely those that guide the person holding the image toward the proper reference frame, one that is compatible with the target shape. In addition, there seems to be an enormous benefit for discoveries in this category from picking up a pencil and actually drawing the imaged form. This was evident in Chambers and Reisberg's duck/rabbit studies, in which participants routinely succeeded in reversing the figure in their own drawing, even though they had failed to reverse their own images. Similar results, also showing a benefit of drawing the imaged form, have appeared in subsequent studies (e.g., Verstijnen, Hennessey, Leeuwen, Hamel, & Goldschmidt, 1998; Verstijnen, Leeuwen, Goldschmidt, Hamel, & Hennessey, 1998).

This distinction will surely be important for our understanding of why image-based discoveries seem to happen readily in some contexts, but only rarely in other contexts. In addition, this distinction also draws attention once again to the fact that mental images have a "duplex" quality, inasmuch as they contain both depictive information (representing the geometry of the imaged form) and also descriptive information (which stipulates how that geometry is organized). Work remains to be done to specify a formal account of how these two types of information are instantiated in a mental image, and, harkening back to an earlier section, to specify how both types of information are realized in the neural substrate of imagery. In the meantime, though, both aspects of imagery are plainly visible in how images function – and specifically in the apparent *limits* on that function.

We also note that these comments call us back once more to the Imagery Debate of the 1970s and 1980s. In an earlier section, we argued that the special medium side of the debate was correct on some crucial points. We now add that the other side of the debate was also right on some key issues: Pylyshyn (1981) argued consistently that, in important regards, images are rather different from pictures. Images, he argued, are "cognitively penetrated" in the sense that their representation includes (and is influenced by) our beliefs and knowledge about the imaged form. This point is certainly related to the argument offered here that images are organized (not neutral) depictions, and that (in the reference frame) they contain some amount of descriptive information. Perhaps, then, the Imagery Debate cast our theoretical options in terms that were too coarse. Images are neither wholly depictive nor wholly descriptive, neither pictures nor propositions. They are a hybrid representation, and their function is constrained by both their depictive and their descriptive aspects.

Imaged Synthesis

As we have just seen, the limits on image-based discovery can provide important insights into the nature of images, and underscore the fact that images are organized depictions, not neutral ones. Even with these limits, however, it is clear that image-based discovery does play a crucial role in problem solving, including problem solving that we would genuinely call creative. This point is, as we have noted, evident in the many historical cases in which discoveries have been apparently inspired or guided by imagery. In addition, the link between the terms "image" and "imagination" reflects the commonsense understanding that mental imagery is often crucial for endeavors we might consider imaginative or creative.

Despite these points, most research on mental imagery has focused on the role of images within rather constrained laboratory tasks. Indeed, not so many years ago, Finke (1993) lamented the "neglect" of "creative imagery" as a research topic, noting that "few studies have explicitly addressed the role that visualization plays in the creative process, at least from the perspective of modern cognitive psychology and cognitive science" (p. 255).

Fortunately, this neglect is now being corrected, thanks in part to paradigms developed by Finke and his coworkers. As a result, we are starting to assemble a reasonable understanding of how creative imagery is influenced by instructions, by the nature of the sought-after goal, and so on. Many of the relevant studies rely on a procedure often dubbed *imaged synthesis*, developed in an early study by Finke and Slayton (1988). In this procedure, participants are given a small number of elements – for example, a sphere, a wire, and a cone – and told to imagine combining these parts to make some object or device. Participants are allowed to vary the size, orientation, or position of the parts, and can think of the parts as made from any material they choose. This simple technique does yield inventions judged to be creative by independent evaluators. For example, Figure 2.5 shows a "hip exerciser" invented by one participant, constructed from a half-sphere, a wire, and a rectangular block. To use the exerciser, one attaches the wires to the walls on opposite sides of a room, stands on the half-sphere, and shifts one's weight back and forth. Of course, the creativity in view here is modest in comparison to (say) the great historical

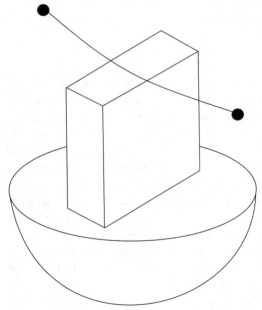

FIGURE 2.5. An example of an image-based creative invention; see text for details.

discoveries discussed by Miller (1986) or Shepard (1988). Nonetheless, this does seem a genuinely creative discovery, and stands as testimonial both to the power of imagery and also to the feasibility of studying creative imagery in laboratory settings.

VISUAL IMAGES AND SPATIAL IMAGES

Imagery and the Blind

We have now reviewed many lines of evidence arguing for close parallels between imagery and perception. People seem able to read information off of an image in much the same way that they read information from a visual scene. The neural mechanisms serving visual imagery seem to overlap considerably with those needed for visual perception. Many data patterns that characterize vision (e.g., a relationship between acuity and position in the visual field, or the aftereffects of visual adaptation) can also be documented in visual imagery.

At the same time, other results indicate points of contrast between imagery and perception, and these results, too, must be accommodated. For example, a number of studies have examined imagery in people blind since birth (Carpenter & Eisenberg, 1978; Kerr, 1983; Marmor & Zabeck, 1976; also see Vecchi, 1998; for related data, see Jonides, Kahn, & Rozin, 1975; Paivio & Okovita, 1971; Zimler & Keenan, 1983). In tests involving mental rotation or image scanning, these individuals yield data quite similar to those obtained with sighted research participants – with response times proportionate to the "distance" traveled, imaged "rotation times" dependent on angle of rotation, and so on. Likewise, people who are congenitally blind also show a memory advantage for materials that are more readily imaged; they also benefit from specific instructions to use imagery as an aid to memory.

It seems unlikely that the congenitally blind are using visual imagery to perform these tasks. Presumably, therefore, they have some other means of thinking about spatial layout and spatial relations. This "other means" might be represented in their minds in terms of a series of imagined movements, so that it is "body imagery" or "motion imagery" rather than visual imagery. Alternatively, perhaps spatial imagery is not tied to any sensory modality, but is part of their broader cognition about spatial arrangements and layout. (Reisberg & Logie, 1993, provide a discussion of motion-based imagery; for some explorations of motor imagery, and its relationship to actual movement, see Annett, 1995; Engelkamp, 1986, 1991; Ganis, Keenan,

Kosslyn, & Pascual-Leone, 2000; Jeannerod, 1995; Johnson, 2000; Logie, Engelkamp, Dehn, & Rudkin, 2001; Maruff et al., 1999; Parsons, 2001; Saltz & Donnenwerth-Nolan, 1981.)

These points are interesting on their own, but also invite a further question: Various imagery tasks, it seems, can be done by the blind without relying on a representation that is in some way visual. Is the same true for sighted participants? Do they also have recourse to a nonvisual mode of spatial representation when performing imagery tasks? If so, what adjustments does this demand in our theorizing about the relationship between mental imagery and perception? We will return to this issue after more of the relevant data are in view.

— Visual vs Spatial imagery.

Do Visual Tasks Interfere with Imagery?

As we have noted, many studies have documented *mutual interference* between imagery and perception, with participants less able to perceive while visualizing, and less able to visualize while observing a visual input. Other studies, however, yield a different result. Baddeley and Lieberman (1980) asked their participants to imagine a 4 × 4 matrix. Within the matrix, a particular cell was designated as the starting square, and, from this starting point, participants were instructed in how to fill this imagined matrix: "In the starting square, place a '1'; in the next square to the right, put a '2'; in the next square up, put a '3'," and so on. Then, after a short delay, the participants had to report back the "contents" of the matrix.

It seems likely that this task requires imagery, but imagery of what sort? In one condition, participants tried to remember these matrices while simultaneously doing a visual interference task. As they were hearing the sentences, they were shown a series of lights, some of which were bright and others dim; their task was to press a key whenever they saw a bright stimulus. In a second condition, participants had to remember the matrices while simultaneously doing a spatial interference task. They were required to move their hands in a particular spatial pattern, but were blindfolded so that they could not rely on vision in guiding their motion.

In this study, no interference was observed when participants were asked to memorize the matrices while doing the visual task. Interference was observed, though, when the matrix task was combined with spatial interference. Apparently, memorizing these matrices depends on some sort of spatial skills, and, correspondingly, it seems that the imagery relevant for this task is spatial, not visual, in nature. (For related evidence, see Logie & Marchetti, 1991; Morris, 1987; Quinn, 1988; Quinn & Ralston, 1986; Smyth &

Pendleton, 1989. For more on how visual imagery and imagery for movement might interact, see Kosslyn, 1994; Logie, 1995; Wexler, Kosslyn, & Berthoz, 1998.)

Notice, then, that the pattern of evidence here is mixed. In some studies, such as Baddeley and Lieberman's, concurrent visual activities do not interfere with performance of imagery tasks, although concurrent spatial activities do cause interference. Yet in other studies, concurrent visual activities cause interference. For example, Quinn and McConnell (1996) asked participants to use a visual mnemonic (a pegword system) to learn a word list. Interference was observed if participants did this task while looking at dynamic visual noise on a computer screen – a result indicating interference between an imagery-based task and a visual input (also see Quinn & McConnell, 1999; McConnell & Quinn, 2000).

Neuroscience Points of *Contrast* Between Imagery and Perception

Why is it that mental imagery tasks are sometimes disrupted by concurrent visual processing, and sometimes not? One suggestion is that we are seeing evidence here for different types of imagery. One type is indeed visual in important regards, and so is disrupted by simultaneous visual activity. The other type of imagery involves some sort of spatial representation, and thus is available to the congenitally blind (as well as to those with normal vision), and is disrupted by simultaneous spatial (not visual) activity.

This distinction between *visual imagery* and *spatial imagery* is also suggested by other sorts of evidence. For example, we have already noted the many reported cases in which brain damage has led to parallel damage in imaging and perceiving; these cases provide a powerful argument that these two activities overlap considerably in their neural substrates. However, there are also numerous exceptions to this data pattern – cases in which brain damage causes problems in imagery but not perception, or vice versa. For example, Goldenberg, Müllbacher, and Nowak (1995) describe a patient whose bilateral occipital lobe lesions have produced cortical blindness, but, despite this profound visual deficit, the patient does well on many (but not all) mental imagery tasks (also see Chatterjee & Southwood, 1995). Similarly, a number of investigators have documented cases of patients who do well on imagery tasks despite severe visual agnosia (Bartolomeo et al., 1998; Behrman, Moscovitch, & Winocur, 1994; Behrmann, Winocur, & Moscovitch, 1992; Jankowiak, Kinsbourne, Shalev, & Bachman, 1992; Servos & Goodale, 1995). Still other cases show the inverse pattern – with impaired imagery performance despite intact perception (see Farah, 1984, for a review).

How should we think about these results? It is important here to bear in mind that, while mental imagery overlaps with perception in its neural basis, the two are obviously not identical in their neural basis. We have already commented on the neuroimaging data that speak to this overlap, and, indeed, this overlap can be demonstrated in numerous ways, with many different forms of data (PET, fMRI, SPECT, ERP, etc.). However, we should be careful not to overstate this pattern: According to one cataloguing of the various brain sites involved in either imagery or perception, roughly two thirds of the sites are involved in both activities; the remainder are involved in one of these activities but not the other (Kosslyn & Thompson, 1999; Kosslyn, Thompson, & Alpert, 1997).

With this backdrop, the proposal to be considered is obvious: Damage to brain areas crucial for imagery *and* perception will produce parallel deficits; damage to brain areas needed for only one of these activities will produce deficits in only one domain. Moreover, to the extent that we can specify what aspects of imagery and of perception are supported by what brain areas, we should be able to make reasonably precise predictions about the impact of brain lesions at specific sites – including whether those lesions will disrupt perception, or imagery, or both. (As an impressive example of how this specification might unfold, see Kosslyn & Thompson, 1999.)

In addition, another consideration is also likely to be crucial, and brings us back to our current theme. We have already suggested that there are different types of mental imagery. Some imagery can truly be described as visual, and represents directly what a shape or layout *looks like.* Other imagery depicts spatial layout in some nonvisual fashion, perhaps in terms of body movements, mentally representing (for example) how one would move to explore certain layouts, or manipulate the layouts. (Consistent with this latter proposal, there are some fMRI data linking the "imagery task" of mental rotation to motor areas in the brain – see, for example, Ganis et al., 2000; Goldenberg, 1999; Richter et al., 2000.)

In a similar spirit, Kosslyn and Thompson (1999) offer the conjecture that there may be three types of mental imagery. They consider, first, spatial imagery, "mental representations of spatial relations, rather than that of shapes, textures or colors." Second, they propose the existence of "figural imagery," instantiated in the inferior temporal lobes, and providing "low-resolution topographic image(s) . . . generated from the activation of stored representations of shapes and other object properties." Finally, they consider "depictive imagery," relying on high-resolution representations instantiated in the medial occipital cortex.

Again, these distinctions lead to an obvious proposal. The imagery we have called "visual" and that Kosslyn and Thompson call "depictive" obviously overlaps with the processes of visual perception, both in its biological basis and in its pattern of functioning. Damage to the neural mechanisms crucial for perception, therefore, should produce parallel deficits in this form of imagery. The imagery we have called "spatial" does not have this overlap with perception, and so tasks drawing on this form of imagery are likely to be spared by damage to the visual system.

In summary, then, why does brain damage sometimes have precisely parallel effects on imagery and perception, but sometimes very different effects – disrupting one of these processes but not the other? We have offered a two-part explanation: First, visual imagery and perception overlap in their neural basis but are not identical, and, as a direct consequence of this, damage to the brain can disrupt brain sites needed for both of these activities, or one, or the other; this by itself guarantees some unevenness in the data pattern. Second and perhaps more interesting, we have discussed several reasons to distinguish visual and spatial tasks, and, with that, visual and spatial imagery. Only one of these (namely, visual imagery) relies on brain areas also crucial for visual perception, and so, on this basis, it is inevitable that we will find cases in which visual perception is disrupted but spatial imagery is spared, or vice versa. Parallel deficits between imagery and perception will only be expected for tasks requiring visual imagery.

Neuroscience Distinctions Between Visual and Spatial Imagery

The proposal just sketched also leads to another prediction: If visual imagery is distinct from spatial imagery, then we would expect to find neurological dissociations not just between perception and imagery, but also between the types of imagery. Consider the case of L.H., a brain-damaged individual studied by Farah, Hammond, Levine, and Calvanio (1988). L.H. suffered a brain lesion as the result of an automobile accident, but recovered reasonably well. After his recovery, however, he continued to have difficulties with a variety of visual tasks. In one test, the experimenter named a number of common objects (e.g., "football"), and L.H. had to report the color of each ("brown"). Control participants got 19 of 20 items correct; L.H. got only 10 correct. In another test, the experimenter named an animal (e.g., "kangaroo"), and L.H. had to indicate whether the animal had a long tail or short, relative to its body size. Again, control participants got 19 of 20 items correct on this test; L.H. got only 13 correct.

In contrast, L.H. does well in spatial tasks, including several of the classical imagery tasks such as image scanning or mental rotation. Indeed, on the Baddeley and Lieberman matrix task (described earlier), L.H. was correct on 18 of 20 items, virtually identical to the performance of control participants. Thus L.H. does quite well on tasks requiring spatial manipulations or memory for spatial positions, even though he does poorly on tasks requiring judgments about visual appearance or memory for visual appearance. This pattern fits well with the claim that visual imagery is indeed distinct from spatial imagery, and that these two forms of imagery are served by different brain regions and thus susceptible to different types of brain damage (see Logie and Della Sala, Chapter 3, for additional and extensive discussion of this dissociation).

In the same fashion, the distinction between visual and spatial imagery may allow us to resolve an apparent discrepancy in the neuroimaging data. A number of authors have reported that mental imagery tasks produce considerable activation in the primary visual cortex, Area 17. This is as one would expect if imagery does indeed involve mechanisms ordinarily used for actual vision. However, other authors have reported the opposite finding, with imagery producing no activation in the primary visual cortex (e.g., Mellet, Tzourio, Denis, & Mazoyer, 1995; Mellet et al., 1996). A number of proposals have been offered in hopes of explaining this data conflict, and one very promising proposal fits well with the argument we are developing here (after Kosslyn & Thompson, 1999, 2003): Studies not showing activation in Area 17 have relied on imagery tasks that required judgments about spatial positions (e.g., a task requiring image scanning). Studies showing activation in Area 17 have relied on tasks that required a higher-resolution depictive image. The suggestion, therefore, is that Area 17 is likely to be well-activated during tasks that require visual imagery, but not tasks requiring spatial imagery. This in turn provides further warrant for including this distinction within our theorizing.

Imagery and Reasoning

The distinction between visual and spatial imagery also turns out to be relevant to another research literature – namely, the literature exploring the ways in which imagery can influence *reasoning*. Take, for example, problems like this one: "Ann is taller than Beth. Cathy is shorter than Beth. Who is tallest?" It seems plausible that people would reason about this problem by forming a mental image of these three women, and then "inspecting" the image to learn who is tallest. If so, then performance should be improved if the problem is cast (as this example was) in concrete, easy-to-visualize terms, in comparison to similar problems phrased in abstract terms that are more difficult to visualize.

The literature on this point, however, is inconsistent, with some studies showing that imagery does facilitate this sort of reasoning, other studies showing no effect, and some studies showing that imagery *impedes* this sort of reasoning (for a review, see Knauff & Johnson-Laird, 2002). What underlies this pattern? Knauff and Johnson-Laird argue that the key lies in distinguishing different types of problems. Some reasoning problems, they note, hinge on visual relationships: "The dog is cleaner than the cat. The ape is dirtier than the cat. Does it follow that the dog is cleaner than the ape?" Other problems hinge on relationships that can be envisaged either visually or spatially ("The cat is above the dog. The dog is below the mouse . . ."). And still other problems involve relationships that are difficult to envisage either visually or spatially: "The ape is smarter than the cat. The cat is smarter than the dog. The bird is dumber than the dog. Does it follow that the bird is smarter than the ape?"

Knauff and Johnson-Laird explored participants' reasoning performance with different problems that had been categorized in these terms. Across three experiments, they found that visual relationships reliably impeded the process of reasoning by slowing it down; this is plausibly due to the distraction created by superfluous visual detail, or to the cognitive load created by participants' efforts toward maintaining the detail in their images. In addition, their data also show a trend toward spatial relationships *improving* performance by speeding up reasoning, although this effect was not reliable in their results.

This result (and related findings, reviewed by Knauff and Johnson-Laird; also Hegarty, 2004) thus makes two points pertinent to our discussion. First, their results obviously speak to the function of imagery, and the ways that it can (for better or for worse) influence performance on a variety of cognitive tasks. Second, their data also speak to the utility of the spatial-visual distinction, with that distinction serving in this case to clear up an otherwise inconsistent pattern in the literature.

Overall, then, it does seem that the distinction between visual and spatial imagery is well-motivated – providing clarity for several research literatures, and directly supported by a variety of results. Before moving on, though, we do note one historic irony here. The term "visuospatial" is commonly used as a description of a type of imagery, or a type of memory (cf. Logie's 1995 book, *Visuo-spatial Working Memory*). Similarly, various psychometric tests have been devised to assess an individual's abilities in "visuospatial tasks." Indeed, we smilingly note that the editors of the present volume followed this tradition by specifically requesting from us a chapter on "visuospatial imagery," and the title of the present chapter conforms to their request. The suggestion of the past few pages, however, is that this terminology risks confusion, blending together two forms of representation that may be distinct. Whether a change in terminology will avoid this confusion remains to be seen.

IMAGE VIVIDNESS

The Trouble with Vividness

Many historical accounts point to Galton's investigations as the first modern research on mental imagery (e.g., Galton, 1883). Galton asked his participants simply to describe the contents of their mental images, and he found that these descriptions varied enormously from one participant to the next. Some participants described images of photographic clarity, rich in detail, almost as if they were seeing the imaged scene, rather than visualizing it. Other participants, however, reported very sketchy images, or no images at all. They were certainly able to think about the scenes or objects Galton had named for them, but in no sense were they "seeing" these scenes. Their self-reports rarely included mention of color or size or viewing perspective; indeed, their reports were largely devoid of visual qualities. In recounting Galton's data, William James (1890, p. 57) concluded, "some people undoubtedly have no visual images at all worthy of the name."

Across the last century, researchers have often voiced considerable skepticism about these imagery self-reports. As one broad concern, and despite James' endorsement, perhaps all of Galton's participants had the same imagery capacity but some were cautious in how they chose to describe their imagery, whereas others were more extravagant. In this way, Galton's data might reveal differences in how people talk about their imagery, rather than differences in the imagery per se.

In addition, and more pressing, a number of studies have sought empirical correlates of these imagery self-reports, with the expectation that people who claim to have vivid imagery should have some corresponding performance advantage on tasks that require imagery. Conversely, people who report sparse (or no) imagery should be unable to imagine rotated objects, use imagery mnemonics, and so on. However, tests of these suggestions have routinely yielded null findings. Many studies have found no difference, for example, between vivid imagers and sparse imagers in their speed or accuracy of mental rotation, how quickly they scan across their images, or how effective their images are in supporting memory. Indeed, people who insist they have *no* imagery tend to do as well as everyone else on these tasks; individuals who boast of clear and detailed imagery show no corresponding processing advantage (e.g., Ernest, 1977; Katz, 1983; Kosslyn, Brunn, Cave, & Wallach, 1985; Marks, 1983; Reisberg, Culver, Heuer, & Fischman, 1986; Richardson, 1980). As it turns out, there are stable individual differences in the performance of all of these imagery tasks, but these differences are unrelated to self-reported vividness (Kosslyn et al., 1985; see also Hegarty & Waller, Chapter 4).

Rehabilitating the Vividness Notion

These findings have led many investigators to be skeptical about self-reports of image vividness. After all, it does seem plausible that different people might mean different things in claiming their images are "moderately vivid" or "very vivid," and this by itself could make it difficult (or even impossible) to compare one person's self-report to another's. And once this concern is raised, the numerous failures to link vividness reports to performance measures seem to provide ample reason for maintaining this skepticism.

Despite these negative assessments, some investigators have continued to explore the dimension of image vividness, both experimentally and as a predictor of performance on other tasks. Why this persistence, despite the discouraging results just described? In our view, the answer lies in the fact that Galton documented a truly striking phenomenon. It is, of course, easy for each of us to assume that our experience, and our perspective, is shared by all around us. Galton's observations, however, imply that at least one conspicuous aspect of our inner experience is not universally shared. Instead, others seem (if, for the moment, we take the vividness reports at face value) to have subjective experiences markedly different from our own.

Why, then, have measures of vividness – such as Marks's (1977) Vividness of Visual Imagery Questionnaire (VVIQ) – been so often unsuccessful as predictors of performance in imagery tasks? There are surely several reasons. First, it seems undeniable that the measurement of imagery vividness (via the VVIQ or any other instrument) is an uncertain matter at best, and, as we have noted, what one person considers a "moderately vivid" image may differ from what another considers "moderately vivid." This sort of concern obviously hinders any attempt at measurement.

Second, measures such as the VVIQ seek to quantify vividness with just a single number, in essence an assessment of "overall vividness." But is this appropriate? Perhaps performance in imagery tasks is instead influenced by some other dimension of vividness – for example, the proportion of the image that is fully elaborated, or the maximum vividness found anywhere within the image. This issue has been largely neglected by researchers, and clouds the interpretation of any vividness measures. (For more on this point, see Reisberg & Heuer, 1988.)

In addition – and perhaps most important – we must be careful in asking which imagery tasks *should be* correlated with vividness self-reports. Imagery tasks differ in the particular skills they require and in the aspects of imagery that they emphasize. For some tasks, for example, a high-resolution depiction is crucial; for others, it is irrelevant. For which tasks, then, should "vivid imagery" be particularly helpful? If we select the wrong tasks, then it would be entirely unsurprising if vividness reports were a poor predictor of performance.

In addition, we argued in previous sections that there are different types of mental imagery. Some tasks demand visual (or depictive) images; others require spatial images. Still other tasks can be supported through either form of representation. Is it possible that these distinctions are useful in understanding the relation between vividness self-reports and performance in imagery tasks? The next section pursues this issue.

Image Vividness and the Visual/Spatial Distinction

Researchers have employed many different instruments to measure image vividness. (Richardson, 1999, provides a recent review.) However, virtually all of these instruments include an explicit invitation to participants to *compare their imagery to actual vision*. For example, Marks's VVIQ repeatedly instructs participants to form a "mental picture" before their "mind's eye." The response scale for the VVIQ then offers, as one of its endpoints, a response indicating that the image is "perfectly clear and as vivid as *normal vision*" (italics added). And of the sixteen items that comprise the VVIQ, six explicitly mention color, perhaps the clearest case of a property that is essentially visual, not spatial. A seventh item on the test mentions a rainbow (and so invites participants to think about the rainbow's colors).

It seems plausible, therefore, that measures like the VVIQ are gauging the *visual* richness of mental imagery, and thus are influenced by the degree to which the mental image provides a high-resolution depiction of the colors, textures, and details of the represented scene. On this view, we should not expect these self-reports to be predictive of tasks relying on *spatial* imagery, because, for judgments of relative distances or position, the visual qualities provided by a "vivid image" are neither necessary nor helpful (cf. McKelvie, 1999). Thus, it is entirely sensible, from this perspective, that measures of vividness are uncorrelated with performance on imagined rotation tasks, or image scanning, or imagined folding – all tasks requiring spatial judgments or spatial manipulations, and so tasks probably relying on spatial imagery, not visual.

On this view, however, imagery vividness should be correlated with performance in tasks requiring *visual* imagery, and several results confirm this suggestion. For example, consider the two-point acuity experiment discussed earlier. This task requires little in the way of spatial judgments; instead, it requires someone to maintain a very high-resolution depiction and to make exact judgments about what this depiction would *look like.* This therefore seems likely to be a task drawing on visual, not spatial, imagery, and, indeed, performance in this task is related to imagery self-report. People who describe their imagery as vivid yield data in close correspondence to the perceptual data; people with less-vivid imagery do not show this close correspondence (Finke & Kosslyn, 1980).

Other studies have shown a lawful relationship between image vividness and color memory (e.g., Reisberg et al., 1986), consistent with the claim that judgments about color require a visual representation rather than a spatial one. Still other studies have shown a relationship between image vividness and memory for faces (Reisberg & Leak, 1987), another task that plausibly involves visual imagery.

Finally, at least some neuroscience evidence also accords with the claims being developed here. Farah and Peronnet (1989) measured event-related potentials (ERPs) while their participants were generating mental images. They found that the occipital ERPs were consistently larger for those participants who rated their images as particularly vivid. This is, of course, entirely consistent with our claim: Image vividness is an index of the quality of visual imagery, and this form of imagery is likely to be instantiated in the visual cortex. It is appropriate, therefore, that vivid imagery is associated with increased activity levels in the occipital lobe. (Also see Goldenberg, Podreka, & Steiner, 1990; Marks, 1990.)

How Does Vividness Influence Memory?

In short, then, we believe that many investigators have been too quick to dismiss self-reports of imagery vividness. There are, to be sure, many null findings associated with vividness measures, but, as noted, some of these findings may be attributed to methodological concerns, and other null findings may reflect a failure in previous studies to distinguish between visual and spatial tasks, visual and spatial imagery. Once this distinction is made, the data pattern becomes more orderly than it initially appears.

At the same time, we must not overstate our argument here. The available data on imagery vividness are messy, and even when systematic relationships are found, the direction of the relationship is sometimes positive and sometimes negative. For example, both Reisberg et al. (1986) and Reisberg and Leak (1987) found that participants with vivid imagery were reliably less accurate in their memory tasks. Similar data were reported by Eberman and McKelvie (2002), who found that those with vivid imagery were more likely to make errors about the source of a memory (whether they had read a particular bit of information, or heard it on an audiotape); this error arose only when participants were specifically instructed to form images of the event described in the audiotape or text. (For contrasting cases, though, with positive relations between imagery vividness and memory accuracy, see, for example, Riske, Wallace, & Allen, 2000; Walczyk & Taylor, 2000.) Thus work certainly remains to be done before we can claim to understand the nature of, and influences of, vivid imagery.

Even so, the available data are clear enough so that we must not shut the door on this avenue of research. This point seems all the more important in light of the fact that research into the nature of conscious experience has been flourishing in recent years, with contributions from psychologists, philosophers, and neuroscientists (Atkinson, Thomas, & Cleeremans, 2000, provide a recent review). It would be unfortunate indeed if the study of mental imagery were not part of this larger endeavor, inasmuch as imagery has largely been defined in many settings as a particular species of conscious experience. In fact, we urge the reader to look back at the opening paragraphs of this chapter: We began the chapter – as virtually every survey of imagery research does – with reference to a set of commonsense subjective experiences, and used these to anchor the phenomena of mental imagery. Clearly, therefore, we need to understand more about the conscious experience of imagery, and research into image vividness seems an important element of that understanding.

There may, in fact, be no danger here, since a stream of research on image vividness has continued over the last two or three decades, despite the neglect of this topic by many investigators. Baddeley and Andrade (2000), for example, explored experimentally a number of factors that might influence the vividness of images. They report that the vividness of visual images is diminished by a concurrent visual task (e.g., observing a flickering visual pattern) and that the vividness of auditory images is diminished by a concurrent auditory task (e.g., counting aloud to ten, over and over). Their participants also reported more vivid images for meaningful stimuli than nonsensical ones, and for static images in comparison to dynamic ones. These findings are interesting for many reasons, including the simple fact that the data do show regular patterns, buttressing the claim that vividness ratings are meaningful and interpretable.

McKelvie (1995) provides a recent review of studies exploring the relationship between image vividness (measured by the VVIQ) and performance on a variety of cognitive or perceptual tasks. Confirming the claim that VVIQ scores are, in fact, meaningful, McKelvie reports a mean correlation of .273 between imagery and performance measures. The relationship between vividness and tasks involving learning and memory was also positive, but somewhat weaker (mean correlation = .137).

Why is the relationship between vividness and memory weaker than the relationship between vividness and "cognitive task" performance? This may simply reflect the fact that some studies (as we have mentioned) report a negative relation between imagery and memory, and this obviously weakens the overall pattern.

As we mentioned earlier, it is not clear why some studies show this negative relationship between imagery and memory accuracy, while others show the opposite, and this plainly is an issue that needs further research. In the meantime, though, we can plausibly ask why a negative relationship, with "vivid imagers" showing less accurate memory, is *ever* observed. One suggestion derives from a line of research focused largely on memory issues rather than specifically on questions about imagery, and focused in particular on the sources of memory errors. This research has highlighted the fact that remembering is more than a matter of simply bringing the desired content into mind. In addition, one must become convinced that the memory is indeed a memory, and not just a passing fantasy or a thought merely associated with the retrieval cue. Similarly, if one decides that a remembered thought is a memory, one must still become convinced that it is a memory from the right source (and not, for example, a recollection of some event other than the target event). Only when these assessments (called reality monitoring and source monitoring) have been made does one take the memory seriously, and take action based on it.

Of course, the assessments just described will be more difficult if the false leads provided by memory are recalled (or imagined) in vivid and rich detail, especially sensory detail (cf. Thomas & Loftus, 2002; for discussion specifically of how vivid imagery might influence source memory, see Eberman & McKelvie, 2002). As a result, vivid imagery may sometimes be an obstacle to accurate memory, with vividly imagined fictions difficult to distinguish from accurate recollections. Consistent with this view, a number of studies have reported a statistical link between vivid imagery (measured by the VVIQ) and vulnerability to memory error (e.g., Tomes & Katz, 1997; Wilkinson & Hyman, 1998; Winograd, Peluso, & Glover, 1998; for some contrasting data, though, see Heaps & Nash, 1999; for other evidence illustrating how vivid imagery might disrupt performance, see Knauff & Johnson-Laird, 2002).

These last points, concerned with memory error, actually serve to highlight several themes. First, and most specifically, these points provide us a way to think about the fact that image vividness is sometimes negatively related to memory accuracy, and this in turn removes one bit of murkiness from the research literature on image vividness. Second, the growing number of studies that have documented this link between vividness and memory error provides all the more reason to believe that image vividness reports can be taken seriously – a central theme of this section. Third, and finally, this tie between image vividness and memory accuracy serves to remind us of a still larger theme: As we scrutinize the nature of mental imagery, it is all too easy to focus on tasks specifically designed to tap this imagery, and, as a result, we can lose track of the role of imagery in other mental tasks. As just noted, though, imagery interacts with memory and memory accuracy, and problem solving, and also the comprehension of text and many other areas as well. The contribution of imagery to these other domains remains an issue in need of further scrutiny.

IMAGERY IN OTHER MODALITIES

Finally, we wish to close with a brief further point. Our exploration of "visuospatial imagery" drew attention to the fact that there are (not surprisingly) different types of imagery, and our understanding of imagery will surely gain by a consideration of how these types of imagery are alike (functionally and biologically) and how they differ. In this chapter, we have distinguished between just two types, visual and spatial imagery, but we might well want to examine imagery in other modalities, including auditory imagery, imagery for smells and tastes, imagery for pain, and so on.

Some of the research needed for this consideration is already underway. In the domain of auditory images, for example, Halpern (1988, 1991) has argued that auditory images seem to be extended in time in the same way that visual images seem to be (functionally) extended in space; her research draws on the image-scanning task already used effectively in the study of visual imagery. Researchers have likewise shown that the neural mechanisms serving auditory imagery overlap with those of audition, again in parallel with the relevant research on visual imagery (e.g., Zatorre & Halpern, 1993; Zatorre, Halpern, Perry, Meyer, & Evans, 1996). Studies also indicate that auditory images are resistant to reinterpretation just as the visual image of, say, the duck-rabbit is (Reisberg, 1994; Reisberg, Smith, Baxter, & Sonenshine, 1989).

In these ways, auditory images seem indeed to have a profile analogous to that of visual images. At the same time, auditory images also have traits of their own. In particular, auditory images can often be supplemented by means of covert subvocalization, and this supplementing seems to extend the range of tasks that can be performed with ("enacted") auditory images (Reisberg, 1992, 1994; Smith, Wilson, & Reisberg, 1996) This in turn invites questions about the role of similar enactment in visual imagery, and this is an issue researchers are beginning to explore (e.g., Reisberg & Koch, 1995).

Our point here, however, is not to survey auditory imagery in detail. Instead, we mention these other findings simply to highlight the fact that many aspects of visual imagery will find parallels in other domains, whereas other aspects will not. Exploring these (possible) parallels seems certain to enrich our understanding of all modalities, and is surely a prospect that imagery researchers should welcome.

CONCLUSION

Where, then, does all of this leave us? There is no question that images, pictures, and percepts do have much in common. All three of these representations are *depictions*, preserving many aspects of the spatial layout of the represented object or scene, and showing, in a direct fashion, what the represented object or scene *looks like*. Moreover, many of the processes needed to transform or draw information from a mental image resemble those used in ordinary perception; these include processes needed for scanning across the image, or zooming in on the image, or locating details within the image.

Many of these shared properties are likely to derive from the fact that at least some mental imagery relies on the same neural mechanisms as actual vision. This is reflected in the well-documented overlap between the pattern of brain activation observed when a participant is imaging and the pattern during perception. It is also reflected in neuropsychological evidence, showing that brain damage often produces parallel deficits in imagery and in perception.

At the same time, however, the data also demand two important distinctions, qualifying our claims about imagery. First, we need to distinguish between neutral depictions (such as pictures) and organized depictions (such as images or percepts), with the latter apparently understood within a perceptual reference frame that specifies the form's perceptual organization. The fact that images are organized depictions is evident in several aspects of image functioning, including some apparent limits on image-based discovery. As a result, it may be misleading to think of images (as Shakespeare did) as mental pictures. Images (as depictions) are certainly picture-like, but (as organized depictions) they are not pictures.

Second, we also need to distinguish different types of images. Obviously, images of a friend's voice or the smell of cinnamon are different from visual images, and, as we briefly mentioned in the previous section, research is needed to explore these other modalities of imagery. Even within the "visuospatial" realm, however, we need to distinguish at least two types of images, which we have here called visual and spatial. This distinction can be made on many grounds. Visual images rely on much the same brain tissue as visual perception; spatial images do not. Visual images are likely to be disrupted by brain damage that disrupts visual perception; spatial images are not. Visual images are likely to suffer interference from concurrent visual tasks; spatial images suffer interference from concurrent spatial (or motoric) tasks. Visual images are unlikely to be available to the congenitally blind, whereas spatial images are available. Finally, estimates of imagery vividness are likely to be indexing the richness of visual images, not spatial, and so these estimates are likely to be predictive of performance in tasks relying on visual imagery, but not tasks relying on spatial imagery.

We hasten to add, however, that there are some loose ends in this picture. The evidence does indicate that images are organized depictions, not neutral ones, but it remains to be seen whether the perceptual reference frame crucial for an organized depiction is best understood as part of the image itself, or as a pattern of processing biases that guide how the image is interpreted. Further specification is also needed for what exactly is contained within the perceptual reference frame, and how the reference frame is established and how it can be altered. Similarly, the distinction between visual and spatial imagery is endorsed by many investigators, but we still need to sharpen this distinction and to explore what sorts of tasks rely on each sort of imagery. Finally, the evidence is certainly accumulating that reports of imagery vividness are interpretable and do have predictive value, but research on this topic is still greeted skeptically by many investigators.

In short, then, we have made enormous progress in our understanding of mental imagery, and visual imagery in particular. We have a substantial, well-replicated, and quantitatively precise set of data; we have an impressive convergence between cognitive and neuroscience investigations; we have a rich set of theoretical explanations with which to explain the available evidence. Nonetheless, work remains to be done, and we have tried in this chapter to highlight both the knowns and unknowns of mental imagery.

Suggestions for Further Reading

The following references will be useful for anyone wishing further information on the topics covered in this chapter.

For further discussion of the "Imagery Debate," see many of the papers in:
Block, N. (Editor). (1981). *Imagery*. Cambridge, MA: MIT Press.

For more contemporary treatments of these issues, see, for example:
Kosslyn, S. M. (1994). *Image and brain: The resolution of the imagery debate*. Cambridge, MA: MIT Press.
Pylyshyn, Z. (2001). Is the imagery debate over? If so, what was it about? In E. Dupoux (Ed.), *Language, brain, and cognitive development: Essays in honor of Jacques Mehler* (pp. 59–83). Cambridge, MA: MIT Press.

For more on the neural substrate of mental imagery, see:
Kosslyn, S. M., & Thompson, W. L. (1999). Shared mechanisms in visual imagery and visual perception: Insights from cognitive neuroscience. In M. S. Gazzaniga (Ed.), *The new cognitive neurosciences*. Cambridge, MA: MIT Press.
Thompson, W. L., & Kosslyn, S. M. (2000). Neural systems activated during visual mental imagery: A review and meta-analyses. In J. Mazziotta & A. Toga (Eds.), *Brain Mapping II: The applications*. New York: Academic Press.

For further discussion of image-based discovery, see the papers in:
Cornoldi, C., Logie, R. H., Brandimonte, M. A., Kaufmann, G., & Reisberg, D. (Eds.). (1996). *Stretching the imagination: Representation and transformation in mental imagery*. New York: Oxford University Press.

Finally, for readers wishing a slightly more elementary and more detailed presentation of the materials covered in this chapter, see:
Reisberg, D. (2001). *Cognition: Exploring the science of the mind* (2nd ed.). New York: W. W. Norton.

References

Anderson, J. R. (1978). Arguments concerning representations for mental imagery. *Psychological Review, 85*, 249–277.

Anderson, R. A., & Helstrup, T. (1993). Visual discovery in mind and on paper. *Memory and Cognition, 21*, 283–293.

Annett, J. (1995). Motor imagery: Perception or action? *Neuropsychologia, 33*(11), 1395–1417.

Atkinson, A. P., Thomas, M. S. C., & Cleeremans, A. (2000). Consciousness: Mapping the theoretical landscape. *Trends in Cognitive Science, 4*, 372–382.

Baddeley, A. D., & Andrade, J. (2000). Working memory and the vividness of imagery. *Journal of Experimental Psychology: General, 129*(1), 126–145.

Baddeley, A. D., & Lieberman, K. (1980). Spatial working memory. In R. Nickerson (Ed.), *Attention and performance* (pp. 521–539). Hillsdale, NJ: Erlbaum.

Bartolomeo, P., Bachoud-Levi, A. C., De Gelder, B., Denes, G., Dalla Barba, G., Brugieres, P., & Degos, J. D. (1998). Multiple-domain dissociation between impaired visual perception and preserved mental imagery in a patient with bilateral extrastriate lesions. *Neuropsychologia, 36*, 239–249.

Behrmann, M., Moscovitch, M., & Winocur, G. (1994). Intact visual imagery and impaired visual perception in a patient with visual agnosia. *Journal of Experimental Psychology: Human Perception and Performance, 20*, 1068–1087.

Behrmann, M. (2000). The mind's eye mapped onto the brain's matter. *Current Directions in Psychological Science, 9*, 50–54.

Behrmann, M., Winocur, G., & Moscovitch, M. (1992). Dissociation between mental imagery and object recognition in a brain-damaged patient. *Nature, 359*(6396), 636–637.

Beschin, N., Basso, A., & Sala, S. D. (2000). Perceiving left and imagining right: Dissociation in neglect. *Cortex, 36*, 401–414.

Beschin, N., Cocchini, G., Della Sala, S., & Logie, R. H. (1997). What the eyes perceive, the brain ignores: A case of pure unilateral representational neglect. *Cortex, 33*, 3–26.

Bisiach, E., & Luzzatti, C. (1978). Unilateral neglect of representational space. *Cortex, 14*, 129–133.

Bisiach, E., Luzzatti, C., & Perani, D. (1979). Unilateral neglect, representational schema, and consciousness. *Brain, 102*, 609–618.

Block, N. (Ed.). (1981). *Imagery*. Cambridge, MA: MIT Press.

Brandimonte, M. A., & Gerbino, W. (1993). Mental image reversal and verbal recoding: When ducks become rabbits. *Memory and Cognition, 21*, 23–33.

Carpenter, P. A., & Eisenberg, P. (1978). Mental rotation and the frame of reference in blind and sighted individuals. *Perception and Psychophysics, 23*, 117–124.

Chambers, D., & Reisberg, D. (1985). Can mental images be ambiguous? *Journal of Experimental Psychology: Human Perception and Performance, 11*, 317–328.

Chambers, D., & Reisberg, D. (1992). What an image depicts depends on what an image means. *Cognitive Psychology, 24*, 145–174.

Chatterjee, A., & Southwood, M. H. (1995). Cortical blindness and visual imagery. *Neurology, 45*, 2189–2195.

Cornoldi, C., Logie, R. H., Brandimonte, M. A., Kaufmann, G., & Reisberg, D. (Eds.). (1996). *Stretching the imagination: Representation and transformation in mental imagery*. New York: Oxford University Press.

Coslett, H. B. (1997). Neglect in vision and visual imagery: A double dissociation. *Brain, 120*(7), 1163–1171.

Craver-Lemley, C., Arterberry, M. E., & Reeves, A. (1997). Effects of imagery on vernier acuity under conditions of induced depth. *Journal of Experimental Psychology: Human Perception and Performance, 23*(1), 3–13.

Craver-Lemley, C., & Reeves, A. (1987). Visual imagery selectively reduces vernier acuity. *Perception, 16*(5), 599–614.

Craver-Lemley, C., & Reeves, A. (1992). How visual imagery interferes with vision. *Psychological Review, 99*, 633–649.

Denis, M., & Kosslyn, S. M. (1999). Scanning visual mental images: A window on the mind. *Cahiers de Psychologie Cognitive/Current Psychology of Cognition, 18*, 409–465.

DeRenzi, E., & Spinnler, H. (1967). Impaired performance on color tasks in patients with hemispheric lesions. *Cortex, 3*, 194–217.

Eberman, C., & McKelvie, S. J. (2002). Vividness of visual imagery and source memory for audio and text. *Applied Cognitive Psychology, 16*, 87–95.

Engelkamp, J. (1986). Motor programs as part of the meaning of verbal items. In I. Kurcz, E. Shugar, & J. H. Danks (Eds.), *Knowledge and language*. Amsterdam: North-Holland.

Engelkamp, J. (1991). Imagery and enactment in paired-associate learning. In R. H. Logie & M. Denis (Eds.), *Mental images in human cognition* (pp. 119–128). Amsterdam: Elsevier.

Ernest, C. (1977). Imagery ability and cognition: A critical review. *Journal of Mental Imagery, 2*, 181–216.

Farah, M. (1984). The neurological basis of mental imagery. *Cognition, 18*, 245–272.

Farah, M. (1985). Psychophysical evidence for a shared representational medium for mental images and percepts. *Journal of Experimental Psychology: General, 114*, 91–103.

Farah, M. (1988). Is visual imagery really visual? Overlooked evidence from neuropsychology. *Psychological Review, 95*, 307–317.

Farah, M. (1989). Mechanisms of imagery-perception interaction. *Journal of Experimental Psychology: Human Perception and Performance, 15*, 203–211.

Farah, M., & Smith, A. (1983). Perceptual interference and facilitation with auditory imagery. *Perception and Psychophysics, 33*, 475–478.

Farah, M. J., Hammond, K. M., Levine, D. N., & Calvanio, R. (1988). Visual and spatial mental imagery: Dissociable systems of representation. *Cognitive Psychology, 20*, 439–462.

Farah, M. J., & Peronnet, F. (1989). Event-related potentials in the study of mental imagery. *Journal of Psychophysiology, 3*, 99–109.

Farah, M. J., Soso, M., & Dasheiff, R. (1992). Visual angle of the mind's eye before and after unilateral occipital lobectomy. *Journal of Experimental Psychology: Human Perception and Performance, 18*, 241–246.

Finke, R. (1989). *Principles of mental imagery*. Cambridge, MA: MIT Press.

Finke, R. (1990). *Creative imagery: Discoveries and inventions in visualization.* Hillsdale, NJ: Erlbaum.

Finke, R. (1993). Mental imagery and creative discovery. In B. Roskos-Ewoldsen, M. J. Intons-Peterson, & R. Anderson (Eds.), *Imagery, creativity, and discovery* (pp. 255–285). New York: North-Holland.

Finke, R., & Kosslyn, S. (1980). Mental imagery acuity in the peripheral visual field. *Journal of Experimental Psychology: Human Perception and Performance, 6,* 126–139.

Finke, R., Pinker, S., & Farah, M. (1989). Reinterpreting visual patterns in mental imagery. *Cognitive Science, 13,* 51–78.

Finke, R., & Slayton, K. (1988). Explorations of creative visual synthesis in mental imagery. *Memory and Cognition, 16,* 252–257.

Fodor, J. A. (1981). Imagistic representation. In N. Block (Ed.), *Imagery* (pp. 63–86). Cambridge, MA: MIT Press.

Galton, F. (1883). *Inquiries into human faculty.* London: Dent.

Ganis, G., Keenan, J. P., Kosslyn, S. M., & Pascual-Leone, A. (2000). Transcranial magnetic stimulation of primary motor cortex affects mental rotation. *Cerebral Cortex, 10*(2), 175–180.

Goebel, R., Khorram-Sefat, D., Muckli, L., Hacker, H., & Singer, W. (1998). The constructive nature of vision: Direct evidence from functional magnetic resonance imaging studies of apparent motion and motion imagery. *European Journal of Neuroscience, 10*(5), 1563–1573.

Goldenberg, G. (1999). Mental scanning: A window on visual imagery? *Cahiers de Psychologie Cognitive, 18*(4), 522–526.

Goldenberg, G., Müllbacher, W., & Nowak, A. (1995). Imagery without perception – A case study of anosognosia for cortical blindness. *Neuropsychologia, 33,* 39–48.

Goldenberg, G., Podreka, I., & Steiner, M. (1990). The cerebral localization of visual imagery: Evidence from emission computerized tomography of cerebral blood flow. In P. J. Hampson & D. F. Marks (Eds.), *Imagery: Current developments. International library of psychology* (pp. 307–332). London, UK: Routledge.

Goldmeier, E. (1937/1972). Similarities in visually perceived forms. *Psychological Issues, 8,* (entire).

Halpern, A. (1988). Mental scanning in auditory imagery for songs. *Journal of Experimental Psychology: Learning, Memory and Cognition, 14,* 434–443.

Halpern, A. (1991). Musical aspects of auditory imagery. In D. Reisberg (Ed.), *Auditory imagery.* Hillsdale, NJ: Erlbaum.

Harris, J. (1982). The VVIQ and imagery-produced McCollough effects: An alternative analysis. *Perception and Psychophysics, 32,* 290–292.

Heaps, C., & Nash, M. (1999). Individual differences in imagination influation. *Psychonomic Bulletin and Review, 6,* 313–318.

Hegarty, M. (2004). Mechanical reasoning by mental simulation. *Trends in Cognitive Sciences. 8,* 280–285.

Heil, M., Rösler, F., & Hennighausen, E. (1993). Imagery-perception interaction depends on the shape of the image: A reply to Farah. *Journal of Experimental Psychology: Human Perception and Performance, 19,* 1313–1319.

Hyman, I. (1993). Imagery, reconstructive memory, and discovery. In B. Roskos-Ewoldsen, M. Intons-Peterson, & R. Anderson (Eds.), *Imagery, creativity and discovery: A cognitive approach* (pp. 99–122). Amsterdam: Elsevier.

Intons-Peterson, M. J. (1983). Imagery paradigms: How vulnerable are they to experimenters' expectations? *Journal of Experimental Psychology: Human Perception and Performance, 9*(3), 394–412.

Intons-Peterson, M. J. (1999). Comments and caveats about "scanning visual mental images." *Cahiers de Psychologie Cognitive, 18*(4), 534–540.

Intons-Peterson, M. J., & White, A. (1981). Experimenter naivete and imaginal judgments. *Journal of Experimental Psychology: Human Perception and Performance, 7,* 833–843.

Ishai, A., & Sagi, D. (1995). Common mechanisms of visual imagery and perception. *Science, 268,* 1772–1774.

Ishai, A., & Sagi, D. (1997). Visual imagery facilitates visual perception: Psychophysical evidence. *Journal of Cognitive Neuroscience, 9*(4), 476–489.

James, W. (1890). *The principles of psychology, vol. II.* New York: Dover Publications.

Jankowiak, J., Kinsbourne, M., Shalev, R. S., & Bachman, D. L. (1992). Preserved visual imagery and categorization in a case of associative visual agnosia. *Journal of Cognitive Neuroscience, 4,* 119–131.

Jeannerod, M. (1995). Mental imagery in the motor context. *Neuropsychologia, 33*(11), 1419–1432.

Johnson, P. (1982). The functional equivalence of imagery and movement. *Quarterly Journal of Experimental Psychology, 34a,* 349–365.

Johnson, S. H. (2000). Thinking ahead: The case for motor imagery in prospective judgements of prehension. *Cognition, 74,* 33–70.

Jonides, J., Kahn, R., & Rozin, P. (1975). Imagery instructions improve memory in blind subjects. *Bulletin of the Psychonomic Society, 5,* 424–426.

Katz, A. (1983). What does it mean to be a high imager? In J. Yuille (Ed.), *Imagery, memory and cognition.* Hillsdale, NJ: Erlbaum.

Kaufman, G., & Helstrup, T. (1993). Mental imagery: Fixed or multiple meanings? In B. Roskos-Ewoldsen, M. Intons-Peterson, & R. Anderson (Eds.), *Imagery, creativity and discovery: A cognitive approach* (pp. 123–150). Amsterdam: Elsevier.

Keenan, J. M. (1983). Qualifications and clarifications of images of concealed objects: A reply to Kerr and Neisser. *Journal of Experimental Psychology: Learning, Memory and Cognition, 9,* 222–230.

Keenan, J. M., & Moore, R. E. (1979). Memory for images of concealed objects: A reexamination of Neisser and Kerr. *Journal of Experimental Psychology: Human Learning and Memory, 5,* 374–385.

Kerr, N. H. (1983). The role of vision in "visual imagery" experiments: Evidence from the congenitally blind. *Journal of Experimental Psychology: General, 112,* 265–277.

Kerr, N. H., & Neisser, U. (1983). Mental images of concealed objects: New evidence. *Journal of Experimental Psychology: Learning, Memory and Cognition, 9,* 212–221.

Knauff, M., & Johnson-Laird, P. N. (2002). Visual imagery can impede reasoning. *Memory and Cognition, 30,* 363–371.

Kolers, P. (1983). Perception and representation. *Annual Review of Psychology, 34,* 129–166.

Kosslyn, S., Brunn, J., Cave, K., & Wallach, R. (1985). Individual differences in mental imagery ability: A computational analysis. *Cognition, 18,* 195–243.

Kosslyn, S. M. (1976). Can imagery be distinguished from other forms of internal representation? Evidence from studies of information retrieval times. *Memory and Cognition, 4,* 291–297.

Kosslyn, S. M. (1981). The medium and the message in mental imagery: A theory. *Psychological Review, 88,* 46–66.

Kosslyn, S. M. (1983). *Ghosts in the mind's machine.* New York: W. W. Norton.

Kosslyn, S. M. (1994). *Image and brain: The resolution of the imagery debate.* Cambridge, MA: MIT Press.

Kosslyn, S. M., Alpert, N. M., Thompson, L., Maljkovic, V., Weise, S., Chabris, C., Hamilton, S. E., Rauch, S. L., & Buonanno, F. S. (1993). Visual mental imagery activates topographically organized visual cortex: PET investigations. *Journal of Cognitive Neuroscience, 5,* 263–287.

Kosslyn, S. M., Ball, T. M., & Reiser, B. J. (1978). Visual images preserve metric spatial information: Evidence from studies of image scanning. *Journal of Experimental Psychology: Human Perception and Performance, 4,* 1–20.

Kosslyn, S. M., Pascual-Leone, A., Felician, O., Camposano, S., Keenan, J. P., Thompson, W. L., Ganis, G., Sukel, K. E., & Alpert, N. M. (1999). The role of area 17 in visual imagery: Convergent evidence from PET and rTMS. *Science, 284,* 167–170.

Kosslyn, S. M., Pinker, S., Smith, G. E., & Shwartz, S. P. (1979). On the demystification of mental imagery. *Behavioral and Brain Sciences, 2,* 535–581.

Kosslyn, S. M., & Thompson, W. L. (1999). Shared mechanisms in visual imagery and visual perception: Insights from cognitive neuroscience. In M. S. Gazzaniga (Ed.), *The new cognitive neurosciences.* Cambridge, MA: MIT Press.

Kosslyn, S. M., & Thompson, W. L. (2003). When is early visual cortex activated during visual mental imagery? *Psychological Bulletin, 129,* 723–746.

Kosslyn, S. M., Thompson, W. L., & Alpert, N. M. (1997). Neural systems shared by visual imagery and visual perception: A positron emission tomography study. *Neuroimage, 6(4),* 320–334.

Kosslyn, S. M., Thompson, W. L., Kim, I. J., & Alpert, N. M. (1995). Topographical representations of mental images in primary visual cortex. *Nature, 378(6556),* 496–498.

Kunen, S., & May, J. (1981). Imagery-induced McCollough effects: Real or imagined. *Perception and Psychophysics, 30,* 99–100.

Logie, R. (1986). Visuo-spatial processing in working memory. *Quarterly Journal of Experimental Psychology, 38A,* 229–247.

Logie, R. H. (1995). *Visuo-spatial working memory.* Hillsdale, NJ: Erlbaum.

Logie, R. H., Engelkamp, J., Dehn, D., & Rudkin, S. (2001). Actions, mental actions, and working memory. In M. Denis, C. Cornoldi, R. H. Logie, M. de Vega, & J. Engelkamp (Eds.), *Imagery, language, and visuo-spatial thinking.* Hove: The Psychology Press.

Logie, R. H., & Marchetti, C. (1991). Visuo-spatial working memory: Visual, spatial or central executive. In R. H. Logie & M. Denis (Eds.), *Mental images in human cognition* (pp. 105–115). Amsterdam: Elsevier.

Marks, D. (1977). Imagery and consciousness: A theoretical review from an individual differences perspectives. *Journal of Mental Imagery, 2,* 275–290.

Marks, D. (1983). Mental imagery and consciousness: A theoretical review. In A. Sheikh (Ed.), *Imagery: Current theory, research and application.* New York: John Wiley and Sons.

Marks, D. F. (1990). On the relationship between imagery, body, and mind. In P. J. Hampson & D. F. Marks (Eds.), *Imagery: Current developments. International library of psychology* (pp. 1–38). London, UK: Routledge.

Marmor, G. S., & Zabeck, L. A. (1976). Mental rotation by the blind: Does mental rotation depend on visual imagery? *Journal of Experimental Psychology: Human Perception and Performance, 2,* 515–521.

Maruff, P., Wilson, P. H., De Fazio, J., Cerritelli, B., Hedt, A., & Currie, J. (1999). Asymmetries between dominant and non-dominant hands in real and imagined motor task performance. *Neuropsychologia, 37*(3), 379–384.

Matthews, W. A. (1983). The effects of concurrent secondary tasks on the use of imagery in a free recall task. *Acta Psychologica, 53,* 231–241.

McConnell, J., & Quinn, J. G. (2000). Interference in visual working memory. *Quarterly Journal of Experimental Psychology: A Human Experimental Psychology, 53A*(1), 53–67.

McDermott, K., & Roediger, H. L. (1994). Effects of imagery on perceptual implicit memory tests. *Journal of Experimental Psychology: Learning, Memory and Cognition, 20,* 1379–1390.

McKelvie, S. (1995). The VVIQ as a psychometric test of individual differences in visual imagery vividness: A critical quantitative review and plea for direction. *Journal of Mental Imagery, 19,* 1–106.

McKelvie, S. J. (1999). Metric properties of visual images: Only a partial window on the mind. *Cahiers de Psychologie Cognitive, 18*(4), 556–563.

Mellet, E., Tzourio, N., Denis, M., & Mazoyer, B. (1995). A positron emission topography study of visual and mental spatial exploration. *Journal of Cognitive Neuroscience, 7,* 433–445.

Mellet, E., Tzourio, N., Crivello, F., Joliot, M., Denis, M., & Mazoyer, B. (1996). Functional anatomy of spatial mental imagery generated from verbal instructions. *Journal of Neuroscience, 16,* 6504–6512.

Mellet, E., Tzourio-Mazoyer, N., Bricogne, S., Mazoyer, B., Kosslyn, S. M., & Denis, M. (2000). Functional anatomy of high-resolution visual mental imagery. *Journal of Cognitive Neuroscience, 12*(1), 98–109.

Miller, A. (1986). *Imagery in scientific thought.* Cambridge, MA: MIT Press.

Miyashita, Y. (1995). How the brain creates imagery: Projection to primary visual cortex. *Science, 268,* 1719–1720.

Morris, N. (1987). Exploring the visuo-spatial scratch pad. *Quarterly Journal of Experimental Psychology, 39A,* 409–430.

Neisser, U., & Kerr, N. H. (1973). Spatial and mnemonic properties of visual images. *Cognitive Psychology, 5,* 138–150.

O'Craven, K., & Kanwisher, N. (2000). Mental imagery of faces and places activates corresponding stimulus-specific brain regions. *Journal of Cognitive Neuroscience, 12,* 1013–1023.

Paivio, A., & Okovita, H. W. (1971). Word imagery modalities and associative learning in blind and sighted subjects. *Journal of Verbal Learning and Verbal Behavior, 10,* 506–510.

Parsons, L. M. (2001). Integrating cognitive psychology, neurology and neuroimaging. *Acta Psychologica, 107*(1–3), 155–181.

Peterson, M., Kihlstrom, J., Rose, P., & Glisky, M. (1992). Mental images can be ambiguous: Reconstruals and reference-frame reversals. *Memory and Cognition, 20*, 107–123.

Pinker, S., & Finke, R. (1980). Emergent two-dimensional patterns in images in depth. *Journal of Experimental Psychology: Human Perception and Performance, 6*, 244–264.

Pylyshyn, Z. (1981). The imagery debate: Analogue media versus tacit knowledge. In N. Block (Ed.), *Imagery* (pp. 151–206). Cambridge, MA: MIT Press.

Pylyshyn, Z. (2001). Is the imagery debate over? If so, what was it about? In E. Dupoux (Ed.), *Language, brain, and cognitive development: Essays in honor of Jacques Mehler* (pp. 59–83). Cambridge, MA: MIT Press.

Quinn, J. G. (1988). Interference effects in the visuo-spatial sketchpad. In M. Denis, J. Engelkamp, & J. T. E. Richardson (Eds.), *Cognitive and neuropsychological approaches to mental imagery* (pp. 181–189). Dordrecht: Martinus Nijhoff.

Quinn, J. G., & McConnell, J. (1996). Irrelevant pictures in visual working memory. *Quarterly Journal of Experimental Psychology: A Human Experimental Psychology, 49A*(1), 200–215.

Quinn, J. G., & McConnell, J. (1999). Manipulation of interference in the passive visual store. *European Journal of Cognitive Psychology, 11*(3), 373–389.

Quinn, J. G., & Ralston, G. E. (1986). Movement and attention in visual working memory. *Quarterly Journal of Experimental Psychology, 38A*, 689–703.

Reisberg, D. (1994). The non-ambiguity of mental images. In C. Cornold, R. Logie, M. Brandimonte, G. Kaufmann, & D. Reisberg (Eds.), *Images and pictures: On perception and mental representation*. New York: Oxford University Press.

Reisberg, D. (2001). *Cognition: Exploring the science of the mind* (2nd ed.). New York: W. W. Norton.

Reisberg, D. (Ed.). (1992). *Auditory imagery*. Hillsdale, NJ: Erlbaum.

Reisberg, D., & Chambers, D. (1991). Neither pictures nor propositions: What can we learn from a mental image? *Canadian Journal of Psychology, 288*–302.

Reisberg, D., Culver, C., Heuer, F., & Fischman, D. (1986). Visual memory: When imagery vividness makes a difference. *Journal of Mental Imagery, 10*, 51–74.

Reisberg, D., & Heuer, F. (1988). Vividness, vagueness, and the quantification of visualizing. *Journal of Mental Imagery, 12*, 89–102.

Reisberg, D., & Koch, Z. (1995). *A role for motoric support in (so-called) visual imagery*. Paper presented at the annual meeting of the Psychonomic Society, Los Angeles, CA.

Reisberg, D., & Leak, S. (1987). Visual imagery and memory for appearance: Does Clark Gable or George C. Scott have bushier eyebrows? *Canadian Journal of Psychology, 41*, 521–526.

Reisberg, D., & Logie, R. (1993). The in's and out's of working memory: Escaping the boundaries on imagery function. In B. Roskos-Ewoldsen, M. Intons-Peterson, & R. Anderson (Eds.), *Imagery, creativity and discovery: A cognitive approach* (pp. 39–76). Amsterdam: Elsevier.

Reisberg, D., Smith, J. D., Baxter, D. A., & Sonenshine, M. (1989). "Enacted" auditory images are ambiguous; "Pure" auditory images are not. *Quarterly Journal of Experimental Psychology, 41A,* 619–641.

Rey, G. (1981). What are mental images? In N. Block (Ed.), *Readings in the philosophy of psychology* (Vol. 2, pp. 117–127). Cambridge, MA: Harvard University Press.

Richardson, J. (1980). *Mental imagery and human memory.* New York: St. Martin's Press.

Richardson, J. T. E. (1999). *Imagery.* East Sussex, UK: Psychology Press Ltd.

Richman, C. L. (1999). Don't cancel my reservations about mental travel. *Cahiers de Psychologie Cognitive, 18*(4), 574–579.

Richter, W., Somorjai, R., Summers, R., Jarmasz, M., Menon, R. S., Gati, J. S., et al. (2000). Motor area activity during mental rotation studied by time-resolved single-trial fMRI. *Journal of Cognitive Neuroscience, 12*(2), 310–320.

Riske, M. L., Wallace, B., & Allen, P. A. (2000). Imaging ability and eyewitness accuracy. *Journal of Mental Imagery, 24*(1–2), 137–148.

Rock, I. (1975). *An introduction to perception.* New York: Macmillan.

Rock, I. (1983). *The logic of perception.* Cambridge, MA: MIT Press.

Saltz, E., & Donnenwerth-Nolan, S. (1981). Does motoric imagery facilitate memory for sentences? A selective interference test. *Journal of Verbal Learning and Verbal Behavior, 20,* 322–332.

Segal, S., & Fusella, V. (1971). Effect of images in six sense modalities on detection of visual signal from noise. *Psychonomic Science, 24,* 55–56.

Segal, S. J., & Fusella, V. (1970). Influence of imaged pictures and sounds in detection of visual and auditory signals. *Journal of Experimental Psychology, 83,* 458–474.

Servos, P., & Goodale, M. A. (1995). Preserved visual imagery in visual form agnosia. *Neuropsychologia, 33*(11), 1383–1394.

Shepard, R. (1988). The imagination of the scientist. In K. Egan & D. Nadaner (Eds.), *Imagination and education* (pp. 153–185). New York: Teachers College Press.

Shepard, R. N., & Cooper, L. A. (1982). *Mental images and their transformations.* Cambridge, MA: MIT Press.

Smith, J. D., Wilson, M., & Reisberg, D. (1996). The role of subvocalization in auditory imagery. *Neuropsychologia, 33,* 1433–1454.

Smyth, M. M., & Pendleton, L. R. (1989). Working memory for movements. *Quarterly Journal of Experimental Psychology, 41A,* 235–250.

Thomas, A. K., & Loftus, E. F. (2002). Creating bizarre false memories through imagination. *Memory and Cognition, 30,* 423–431.

Thompson, W. L., & Kosslyn, S. M. (2000). Neural systems activated during visual mental imagery: A review and meta-analyses. In J. Mazziotta & A. Toga (Eds.), *Brain mapping II: The applications.* New York: Academic Press.

Tomes, J. L., & Katz, A. N. (1997). Habitual susceptibility to misinformation and individual differences in eyewitness testimony. *Applied Cognitive Psychology, 11,* 233–252.

Vecchi, T. (1998). Visuo-spatial imagery in congenitally totally blind people. *Memory, 6*(1), 91–102.

Verstijnen, I. M., Hennessey, J. M., Leeuwen, C. V., Hamel, R., & Goldschmidt, G. (1998). Sketching and creative discovery. *Design Studies, 19,* 519–546.

Verstijnen, I. M., Leeuwen, C. V., Goldschmidt, G., Hamel, R., & Hennessey, J. M. (1998). Creative discovery in imagery and perception: Combining is relatively easy, restructuring takes a sketch. *Acta Psychologica, 99*, 177–200.

Walczyk, J. J., & Taylor, R. W. (2000). Reverse-spelling, the VVIQ and mental imagery. *Journal of Mental Imagery, 24*(1–2), 177–188.

Wexler, M., Kosslyn, S. M., & Berthoz, A. (1998). Motor processes in mental rotation. *Cognition, 68*, 77–94.

Wilkinson, C., & Hyman, I. E., Jr. (1998). Individual differences related to two types of memory errors: Word lists may not generalize to autobiographical memory. *Applied Cognitive Psychology, 12*(Special Issue), S29–S46.

Winograd, E., Peluso, J. P., & Glover, T. A. (1998). Individual differences in susceptibility to memory illusions. *Applied Cognitive Psychology, 12*(Special Issue), S5–S28.

Zatorre, R. J., & Halpern, A. R. (1993). Effect of unilateral temporal-lobe excision on perception and imagery of songs. *Neuropsychologia, 31*(3), 221–232.

Zatorre, R. J., Halpern, A. R., Perry, D. W., Meyer, E., & Evans, A. C. (1996). Hearing in the mind's ear: A PET investigation of musical imagery and perception. *Journal of Cognitive Neuroscience, 8*(1), 29–46.

Zimler, J., & Keenan, J. M. (1983). Imagery in the congenitally blind: How visual are visual images? *Journal of Experimental Psychology: Learning, Memory and Cognition, 9*, 269–282.

3

Disorders of Visuospatial Working Memory

Robert H. Logie and Sergio Della Sala

ABSTRACT

In this chapter we argue that visuospatial working memory offers a useful theoretical construct, possibly open to further fractionation, that can account for a variety of symptoms shown by neuropsychological patients as well as for some important aspects of visuospatial cognition in the healthy brain. We discuss evidence that draws on studies of a range of impairments of visuospatial cognition that arise following focal brain damage in human adults, and specifically the condition known as unilateral spatial neglect, together with investigations of mental discovery and of immediate visuospatial memory in healthy adults. This evidence is incompatible with common assumptions about working memory as a temporary buffer between sensory input and long-term memory. It is also not consistent with assumptions that mental visual imagery and the processes of visual perception share broadly overlapping cognitive functions and/or neuroanatomical networks. It is proposed that visuospatial working memory can be viewed as part of a mental workspace in which visually presented material can be made available in an interpreted form together with other information in working memory derived from other sensory input or from the long-term store of knowledge.

DISSOCIABLE DISORDERS AND DISSOCIABLE COGNITIVE SYSTEMS

In 1883, Charcot and Bernard (Young & van de Wal, 1996) reported the case of an individual 'Monsieur X' who, following brain damage, had sudden onset of a clear deficit in forming visual images of objects, such as monuments and buildings, and of familiar people such as close relatives. He was also unable to use an imagery mnemonic that he had used prior to the brain damage for remembering and reciting poetry. This range of difficulties was accompanied by language and verbal memory functions

81

that appeared to be largely intact, as were his abilities to navigate in familiar environments. A few years later, Wilbrand (1887; Solms, Kaplan-Solms, & Brown, 1996) reported another patient 'Fräulein G' who suffered from an abrupt onset (most likely resulting from a stroke) of an inability to report details of locations or routes in her native city of Hamburg, Germany, nor could she navigate around this city in which she had lived for many years. Despite this debilitating impairment, she appeared to be able to generate vivid images of past events, and retained her high level of fluency in several languages acquired prior to the stroke. The limited formal testing carried out at the time allows only for an educated guess as to the nature of the problems faced by these patients. However, they do illustrate at least two apparently distinct forms of what might be considered to be deficits of visuospatial cognition. Also, the fact that these kinds of deficits can occur while leaving language and verbal functions largely intact suggests the language and visuospatial functions might be supported by rather different systems in the healthy brain. The theme for this chapter will be the nature of some of the cognitive deficits associated with impairments of visuospatial cognition, and what these disorders, together with evidence from studies of the healthy brain, suggest with regard to the organization and functioning of visuospatial working memory. We will address some of the cognitive impairments that have been studied or interpreted within the context of a visuospatial working memory system, with a particular focus on a syndrome known as *unilateral spatial neglect*.

Contributions to Theory from Neuropsychology

Neuropsychological evidence offers a great deal to the understanding of normal cognition. For example, it contributed very successfully in showing the clear differences between deficits of long-term memory shown by amnesic patients (Milner, 1965), and the deficits of verbal short-term memory (Warrington & Weiskrantz, 1970; Shallice & Warrington, 1970), as well as developing the concepts of implicit versus explicit memory (Schacter, 1987), and of episodic versus semantic memory (e.g., Shelton & Caramazza, 2001; Squire, 1987). Other examples come from the analysis of developmental and acquired disorders of reading, an endeavor that has had a major influence on understanding the organization of cognitive functions that support normal reading (e.g., Behrmann & Bub, 1992; Coltheart, Patterson, & Marshall, 1987). The study of brain-damaged individuals also has thrown light on processes of normal mathematical cognition (e.g., Butterworth, 1999; Dehaene, 1997; McCloskey, Sokol, & Goodman, 1986), and normal language processing (e.g., Caramazza & Hillis, 1991; Ellis & Young, 1996). Finally, there is substantive literature that has drawn on neuropsychology to investigate visual and spatial cognition in the healthy brain (e.g., Humphreys & Riddoch, 1987; Kosslyn, 1994; McCloskey & Rapp, 2000; Young, Newcombe, de Haan, Small, & Hay, 1993). In this chapter, we shall capitalize on the techniques and systematic investigations of both individual case studies and of groups of individuals who exhibit disorders of visuospatial working memory following damage to the brain as a result of stroke, head trauma, neurosurgery, or brain disease.

We began by describing two early case studies that demonstrate the nature of visuospatial impairments that can arise following brain damage. However, it was striking that the patients appeared to show quite contrasting patterns of spared and impaired abilities with one patient having difficulty in navigation while retaining an ability to recognize objects and landmarks, whereas the other showed the converse. This contrast is commonly referred to as a *neuropsychological double dissociation*, between patients. Such double dissociations have been reported in a wide variety of cognitive domains, and in general terms comprise an observation that one patient performs normally on task A, but performs pathologically poorly on task B, while a second patient performs pathologically poorly on task A, but performs normally on task B. Note that this is a contrast between patients, and is not a contrast across tasks. This means that the contrasting patterns cannot be explained in terms of the general cognitive demands of each task.

An Active and Current Memory in the Healthy Brain

Working memory, as discussed in this chapter, refers to the active processes of memory; generating new insights as well as offering an interpreted snapshot of the current state of our environment. It is a set of cognitive functions that are separate from the traces of past experience and accumulated knowledge in long-term memory. It is a system that can retrieve and manipulate the activated contents of long-term memory, allowing those contents to be reinterpreted. (For a more detailed discussion see Logie, 2003; for contrasting views of working memory see Miyake & Shah, 1999.) Working memory is a system that interacts only indirectly with perception. The environment and its interpretation within working memory might involve language, or it might involve the layout and identity of objects, or of a sequence of movements required to navigate through the environment and to interact with the objects we encounter. The two case studies with which we opened this chapter illustrate some of the dissociations that arise among the cognitive functions thought to be supported by visuospatial working memory. The fractionation of the system has been supported by converging evidence from neuropsychology and brain imaging as well as experimental studies with healthy volunteers.

FRACTIONATION OF VISUOSPATIAL WORKING MEMORY

Before discussing the detailed evidence for dissociations within visuospatial working memory, it is important to clarify what we mean by its visual as opposed to its spatial properties. By visual we refer to the visual appearance of an object or scene, its color, shape, contrast, size, visual texture, and the location of objects relative to one another with respect to a particular viewpoint in a static array. By spatial we refer to pathways or sequences of movements from one location to another in the scene, or the processes of change in the perceived relative locations of objects that occur when an observer moves (physically or in a mental image) from one viewpoint to another. There is some ambiguity in the literature as to the use of the word spatial, which sometimes is used to refer to relative locations or layouts of objects. In the description of neuropsychological impairments that we discuss, it should become clear that it is more useful to think of the term "spatial" as referring to the dynamic properties of a scene or representation (e.g., Logie, 1995; Pickering, 2001; Quinn & Ralston, 1986; Smyth & Pendleton, 1990).

Neuropsychological Dissociations Between Visual and Spatial Working Memory

The dissociation between visual and location/movement-based working memory gains support from the patterns of impairment observed in a number of individual case studies. Farah, Hammond, Levine, and Calvanio (1988) reported patient LH who, as a result of a closed head injury in an automobile accident, suffered damage in both temporal/occipital areas, in the right temporal lobe and in the right inferior frontal lobe. He performed well on tasks concerned with memory for locations and for pathways, such as letter rotation, 3-D form rotation, mental scanning, and recalling

LH & LE
→ visual deficit.

EP & MV.
→ spatial deficit.

a recently described pathway, but was severely impaired in his ability to remember colors and the relative size of objects and shapes of states in the map of the United States (further discussion of patient LH can be found in Reisberg & Heuer, Chapter 2). A similar case was reported more recently by Wilson, Baddeley, and Young (1999). Their patient, LE, was a professional sculptress, who, following systemic lupus erythematosus that resulted in diffuse damage to both the cortex and the white matter, was unable to generate visual images of possible sculptures and had a severe visual short-term memory deficit, including very poor performance on the Doors test (Baddeley, Emslie, & Nimmo-Smith, 1994), a recognition memory task among pictures of doors that are similar in appearance (see Figure 3.1), and on retention of black-and-white checkerboard patterns (Della Sala, Gray, Baddeley, & Wilson, 1997). However, she could draw complex figures that did not rely on memory, and performed within the normal range for Corsi block span (see upper part of Figure 3.2), a task that involves recalling a sequence of movements between blocks in a random array (Corsi, 1972; Milner, 1971).

Contrasting cases have been reported by Luzzatti, Vecchi, Agazzi, Cesa-Bianchi, and Vergani (1998), by Carlesimo, Perri, Turriziani, Tomaiuolo, and Caltagirone (2001), and by Hanley and Davies (1995). The Luzzatti et al. patient EP was affected by a slowly progressive deterioration of the brain and showed a focal atrophy of the anterior part of the right temporal lobe, including the hippocampus. Her performance was flawless on visual imagery tasks, such as making judgments about relative animal size, or the relative shapes or colors of objects. On the other hand, she was impaired on a range of topographical tasks such as describing from memory the relative locations of landmarks in her hometown. A similar pattern was reported for the Carlesimo et al. (2001) patient MV who had an ischemic lesion in the cortical area supplied by the pericallosal artery affecting a diffuse area of the right dorsolateral frontal cortex. The patient performed within the normal range on judging from memory, the shapes, colors, and sizes of objects and animals, but had pathologically poor performance on mental rotation tasks, on Corsi block span, and on immediate memory for an imagined path around a square matrix (Brooks, 1967). The Hanley and Davies patient, Mr. Smith, suffered from a right internal carotid artery stenosis. He was "terrible with maps" (p. 197) to the point that he was unable to find his way around his own house. He also had difficulties in getting dressed with a mismatch between orientation of the clothing (e.g., sleeves) and the position of his body parts. The patient reports were confirmed with formal testing in that his spatial

FIGURE 3.1. A black-and-white example of the Doors Test (Baddeley et al., 1994). In the original the stimuli are in color. It is a visual recognition test in which the participants attempt to memorize the features of a door (above) and later recognize it from a set of four similar doors (including the target and three distractors). Permission to reproduce this item has been kindly granted by Thames Valley Test Company, publisher of the "Doors and People" test.

Corsi Block Tapping Test

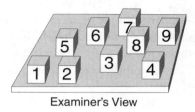

Examiner's View

Visual Patterns Test

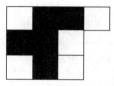

FIGURE 3.2. Top: The Corsi Block Tapping Test (Corsi, 1972). Bottom: An example of a matrix pattern of medium complexity as used in the Visual Patterns Test (Della Sala et al., 1997).

knowledge and ability to manipulate objects mentally were impaired. However, his ability to perceive and represent visual features of objects and scenes was intact. For example, he had no difficulty in comparing the colors or forms of objects, and had no difficulty in making mental size comparisons between objects and animals when presented with their names. He could readily identify the shapes of countries from silhouettes, but was unable to move these silhouettes into their correct relative geographical position. Finally, he performed very poorly on the Corsi blocks test, and on a series of mental rotation tasks.

The contrasting patterns shown in these patients echo dissociations that have been reported for patients with syndromes that are referred to as *topographical amnesia* and *landmark agnosia* (for a review, see Aguirre & D'Esposito, 1999). Patients with topographical amnesia appear unable to generate or remember routes around towns that were previously very familiar. This is despite having no difficulty in recognizing familiar buildings and other landmarks. Landmark agnosia is characterized by an inability to recognize familiar buildings, but with an apparently intact ability to remember, generate, and follow routes. One crucial point to note however is that in the literature describing such patients, the contrast is essentially between a perceptual impairment (landmark agnosia) and an impairment of a mental representation (topographical amnesia). Therefore it remains an area for investigation as to whether landmark agnosia might bear some similarities to the visual imagery disorders reported for patients LH (Farah et al., 1988) and LE (Wilson et al., 1999).

The idea that visual and spatial working memory, according to these definitions, comprise dissociable components of the cognitive system has been supported by a range of studies of healthy participants. For example, visual immediate memory appears to be unrelated to memory for a series of movements in both young children (e.g., Logie & Pearson, 1997; Pickering, Gathercole, Lloyd, & Hall, 2001) and in healthy adults (Della Sala, Gray, Baddeley, Allamano, & Wilson, 1999; Hecker & Mapperson, 1997; Logie & Marchetti, 1991; Tresch, Sinnamon, & Seamon, 1993).

The dissociation between visual and spatial working memory has been reported also in group studies of individuals with brain damage resulting from stroke or Alzheimer's disease (Della Sala et al., 1999; Grossi, Becker, Smith, & Trojano, 1993), in electrophysiological studies in healthy adults (Ruchkin, Johnson, Grafman, Canoune, & Ritter, 1997; MartinLoeches, 1997), and in studies of nonhuman primates (Goldman-Rakic, 1996; Meunier, Bachevalier, & Mishkin, 1997). Further discussion of this distinction, as well as implications of this distinction for research on imagery, can be found in Reisberg and Heuer, Chapter 2.

Dissociations in Perception and Dissociations in Working Memory

The separation in the representations held within working memory is often interpreted within the framework of the what and where dichotomy (Carlesimo et al., 2001; Pickering, 2001). This is a distinction between perceiving object identity and perceiving object location originally derived from single cell recording in studies of monkeys (Ungerleider & Mishkin, 1982). These studies demonstrated that monkeys attempting to identify an object rely on ventral/temporal pathways in the brain, whereas identifying the location of an object involves dorsal/parietal pathways. There are several problems with the apparently compelling link between the cognitive functions of visuospatial working memory and the neuroanatomical pathways associated with the what and the where of visual perception. One difficulty arises from the fact that the visual/location/movement distinction within working memory applies to the representation held and manipulated within working memory. It does not refer to the processes of perceiving and identifying an object and its current location. We argue next that the processes of perception and the operation of working memory are less closely linked than has been widely assumed. However, the ability to detect the location of objects and orient attention toward them appears to be a fundamental, built-in property of the perception and attention systems. It can be performed by infants who have very limited knowledge and experience of objects. In stark contrast, object identification requires prior experience with objects, their associated names, uses, and properties. However, the information held in working memory incorporates these characteristics from prior knowledge along with information about location, suggesting that a separation between what and where might be relevant for perception but might be less relevant for visuospatial working memory.

A further problem is that the concept of the so-called what and where pathways is overly simplistic at a neuroanatomical level. There are multiple connections and pathways involved following initial processing of sensory input within the primary visual cortex (e.g., Hof, Bouras, Constantinidis, & Morrison, 1990; Stein, 1992; Zeki & Shipp, 1988; Zeki cited in Della Sala, 1998). Moreover, the representations that we hold in working memory incorporate information from several sensory modalities (auditory, haptic, kinesthetic, and possibly even olfactory and gustatory) in addition to elements of prior knowledge not immediately available from the perceived scene.

The apparent similarity between the what–where distinction in perception and the visual–spatial distinction in working memory has been taken further in linking visual appearance and location information with activation patterns in brain imaging studies using PET and fMRI. For example, Jonides et al. (1993) tested two groups of participants on visual and location immediate memory tasks while undergoing functional brain imaging using PET. In the location task, volunteers were shown dots appearing briefly at random positions on a screen. After a short interval they were shown a visual cue and had to indicate whether or not the cue identified the location of one of the previously presented dots. In the visual task, participants were presented with unfamiliar shapes, and were later shown a second shape. The task was to indicate whether or not the initial and the comparison shape were identical. Both tasks were performed in a memory condition as described earlier, and in a perceptual condition, in which the target locations or shapes remained on the screen while the comparison took place. As with all neuroimaging studies, activation patterns are revealed by contrasting data obtained in different conditions. Subtracting out the brain activation patterns associated with the perceptual conditions in this study then reveals the patterns of activation associated with memory, but not with perception. Following this subtraction, Jonides et al. reported that there were clearly different neuroanatomical networks associated with memory for object shape, primarily in the left hemisphere, and memory for object location, primarily in the right hemisphere. Jonides and colleagues (e.g., see Smith & Jonides, 1995) interpreted these different activation patterns as reflecting the operation of the what and where pathways, and equated different components of working memory with particular sensory input channels. However, the Ungerleider and Mishkin (1982) what and where pathways were ventral and dorsal, respectively, and were not linked to the right or left hemisphere. In other words, in contrast to the interpretation within the original Jonides et al. paper, the what and where distinction in visual perception does not readily map onto systems in working memory that deal respectively with visual and locational properties of mental representations.

Subsequent studies using PET and fMRI (e.g., Courtney, Petit, Maisog, Ungerleider, & Haxby, 1998; Courtney, Ungerleider, Keil, & Haxby, 1996; Haxby, Petit, Ungerleider, & Courtney, 2000) using different stimuli, such as faces, have likewise shown a neuroanatomical segregation between memory for object identity (primarily ventral, prefrontal cortex), and memory for object location (primarily dorsal prefrontal cortex). However, it is striking that although the neuroanatomical correlates show dissociations that echo those found in behavioral data, the neuroanatomical sites that are activated appear to vary from study to study, possibly as a result of the use of rather different tasks that have rather different general cognitive demands. In other studies (e.g., Owen, Stern, Look, Tracey, Rosen, & Petrides, 1998; Owen, Herrod, Menon, Clark, Downey, & Carpenter, 1999; Petrides, 1996), the general cognitive demands of visual and location tasks were separately manipulated. The more demanding tasks appeared to be associated with the more dorsal areas, whereas the less demanding tasks were linked with activation in the more ventral areas. However, the same prefrontal areas in both hemispheres were associated with visual and location tasks when the overall task demands were equated. That is, the neuroanatomical segregation appears to be associated with task demand, and not with a contrast between object identity and object location. Tasks are described as visual or spatial, but as mentioned earlier, the term spatial is variously used to refer to location or to movements or to pathways that are held in a mental representation. Moreover, there is no guarantee that volunteers are using the cognitive resources that are assumed, and volunteers may adopt a range of cognitive strategies (e.g. Logie, Della Sala, Laiacona, Chalmers, & Wynn, 1996). Anderson (1978) argued further that a particular behavioral outcome in response to task demands might arise from a range of intervening cognitive processes, and different cognitive processes could give rise to the same behavioral outcome. This makes it extremely difficult to draw conclusions about cognitive processes solely on the basis of a single set of behavioral data. So too with brain imaging, it is the cognitive strategy adopted to perform the task that will determine the cognitive processes employed, and it is the cognitive processes employed that will influence the pattern of brain activation. As a result, we might not be able to draw firm conclusions about the areas of the brain that are involved in performing a given task unless we know which cognitive processes were used for meeting the task demands (e.g., Logie, Venneri, Della Sala, Redpath, & Marshall, 2003; Savage et al., 2001). In addition, brain imaging studies typically involve relatively small numbers of participants, and therefore individual variability in the strategy adopted for a task could have a very large impact on the averaged activation pattern across the group.

A further problem arises from the widespread technique of contrasting brain activation patterns across conditions. This is essentially a subtraction method in which activation associated with task A is contrasted with activation associated with tasks A and B together. The assumption is that the resulting patterns reflect the activation for task B, without the contaminating effect of task A. However, it might not be reasonable to assume the activation for task A does not change when task B is added (Bub, 2000; Frackowiak, Friston, Frith, Dolan, & Mazziotta, 1997). This approach has been referred to in the behavioral literature as *additive factors methodology*, and was originally proposed by Donders (1869/1969) as a means to interpret response time data. However, several of the problems with this methodology were recognized some considerable time ago, and the problems have been discussed recently in the context of brain imaging (e.g., Sartori & Umiltà, 2000). For example, there is no guarantee that the systems in the brain that are seen as theoretically or behaviorally distinct, are indeed independent in terms of neuroanatomical structures, pathways or systems. Nor can we assume that cognitive processes are linear and additive. The argument that cognition relies on parallel, distributed systems was made two decades ago (e.g., McClelland & Rumelhart, 1981). The brain clearly does operate with several functions in parallel, and there is unlikely to be a straightforward linear mapping between concepts derived from cognitive psychology and networks of neuronal structure or activity (e.g., D'Esposito, 2001; Henson, in press).

In summary, the brain imaging data are consistent with the notion that some aspects of visual and spatial working memory are separable, but it is important not to focus too literally on the specific neuroanatomical areas that appear to be active when people perform tasks that are thought to rely on these identified functions.

Nevertheless, it remains unclear as to precisely what a spatial or visual working memory system might comprise. For example, a requirement to retain locational or movement information might be simply more demanding of cognitive resources than is retention of the visual appearance of an object or shape. The visual/spatial distinction could then reflect a visual memory system coupled with an a-modal executive resource that supports retention of novel layouts and sequences of movements (Logie, Engelkamp, Dehn, & Rudkin, 2001).

It is worth noting too that different patients could perform poorly on a task for very different reasons. In addition to being open to the use of different strategies, most tests of cognitive function require several components of cognition for successful performance, and damage to any one component could disrupt overall performance on the tasks. For example, the Corsi blocks task is often assumed to assess a spatial working memory system. However, retaining a sequence of targeted movements requires memory for observed movement. It also might be crucial whether the target positions are coded relative to body position or relative to one another (e.g., Postma, Sterken, de Vries, & de Haan, 2000). Depending on the nature of the cognitive impairment following brain damage, performance could be poor because of deficits in any or all of the mentioned cognitive functions. Performance could also be poor because of the application of possible compensatory strategies that patients have developed as a result of their impairments. The compensatory strategy that they adopt may be suboptimal for the task concerned.

In other words, Corsi blocks cannot be a pure test of a spatial working memory system unless we consider that spatial working memory comprises visual and movement information, as well as retention of sequential information, and a decision process that is required as participants choose which block to touch next in the sequence.

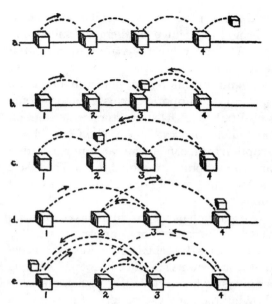

FIGURE 3.3. Cube Imitation Test as reported by Knox (1914). The examiner slowly and deliberately tapped the cubes with a smaller cube from left to right facing the person seeking immigration rights. The examinee was asked to repeat the sequence of movements performed by the examiner.

VISUOSPATIAL WORKING MEMORY AND THE CENTRAL EXECUTIVE

Some of the early systematic attempts to assess general intellectual ability were faced with the challenge of devising tasks that did not depend on knowledge of a particular language. This situation arose at Ellis Island in the United States, when psychologists were given the task of assessing the mental abilities of potential immigrants, many of whom did not have English as their native language. Knox (1914)[1] devised and reported a "cube imitation task" that was designed to assess the general intellectual abilities of "illiterate aliens." The Knox test (see Figure 3.3) was similar to the Corsi blocks test, except that the blocks were presented in a row rather than randomly arranged. The test involved imitating a series of taps on the blocks in the correct sequence as presented by the examiner. Clearly,

[1] We are grateful to John T. E. Richardson for drawing our attention to the work of Howard A. Knox.

what at that time was considered to be a property of general intelligence is now referred to as visuospatial cognition. However, there is a suggestion that temporary visual and spatial memory functions are important, but not sufficient for performance of a range of visuospatial working memory tasks, many of which appear to require additional support from executive resources (e.g., Salway & Logie, 1995). Support for this view has come from a series of experiments by Rudkin (2001) suggesting that retention and recall of sequences of movements in variations of the Corsi blocks task appear to be prone to disruption from concurrent random generation of numbers or from responding to randomly presented tones. These sets of data indicate that the Corsi blocks test might not be a pure measure of specifically visuospatial functions.

The involvement of executive control in visuospatial tasks also appears in some of the neuropsychology literature. For example, patient ELD (Hanley, Pearson, & Young, 1990) often is described in the literature as being an example of an individual who exhibits specifically spatial working memory deficits in the absence of visual imagery deficits, in contrast with patients (described earlier) showing the converse pattern of impairment and sparing (e.g., Farah et al., 1988; Wilson et al., 1999). However ELD showed difficulties with visual tasks (e.g., immediate memory for faces) and this was coupled with an intact ability to recall spatial information from long-term memory. More important for the present discussion is that ELD had deficits in using both imagery mnemonics and in using rote rehearsal for paired associate learning, and performed very poorly on the verbal version of the Brooks (1967) task involving the recall of a sequence of nonsense phrases. Performance on the spatial version of the Brooks task was even poorer, but as Salway and Logie (1995) have shown, it appears that the spatial version of the task involves rather more executive control than does the verbal version. These patterns of impairment suggest that ELD's difficulties might arise from a more general deficit of manipulating information in working memory rather than a specific problem with a spatial system. Therefore, manipulation and control of material within working memory are more readily viewed as executive rather than domain-specific functions.

Thus far, we have addressed the possibility that working memory is best viewed as a multiple component system, and that within such a system, there might be further fractionation between visual and spatial resources with performance on some spatial tasks requiring the use of executive functions. Next, we turn to the relationship between visuospatial working memory, and other parts of the cognitive system by exploring whether or not visuospatial working memory acts as a gateway between perception and long-term memory. We will then consider the impairments of different aspects of visuospatial working memory that arise from the phenomena of unilateral spatial neglect and of cortical blindness.

VISUOSPATIAL WORKING MEMORY: A WORKSPACE, NOT A GATEWAY

Working memory is often viewed as a form of transit lounge that acts to hold perceptual input on its way to long-term memory. This was the view in the widely cited model proposed by Atkinson and Shiffrin (1968), and still appears as an assumption in a wide range of contemporary, introductory textbooks as well as in some contemporary theory. However, a large body of evidence now points to the contents of working memory being interpreted rather than raw sensory images. This suggests that perceptual input activates prior knowledge and experiences in long-term memory, and it is the product of that activation which is held and manipulated within working memory. So, for example, if you now close your eyes and consider the objects that are in your immediate environment, those objects are identified – as a telephone, a cup, a calculator, a globe, a paperweight, a crystal clock – they are not raw sensory images comprising shades of color, contrast, texture, edges and contours. It is possible to manipulate these objects in your representation – imagine the cup containing the clock, the globe spinning, the telephone light flashing ominously. It is also possible to reach out and physically pick up and manipulate the objects without opening your eyes – physically reach out, pick up and spin the globe, or adjust the hands of the clock. We can perform the same mental operations on the contents of a representation retrieved from our knowledge base of past experience. We can represent mentally objects that are behind us in the immediate, familiar environment of an office, even if they have not been viewed recently. We can also represent and manipulate mentally the landmarks of a familiar square in our hometown, mentally restoring the towers and crenelations of an old Scottish castle, or rearranging the furniture in our living room. In other words, working memory cannot be considered a gateway between perceptual input and long-term memory, but more as a system for representing interpreted objects and scenes, allowing us to interact with and mentally manipulate those objects. Visuospatial working memory therefore gives us a representation of the environment on which we can act mentally or which we can enact physically.

FIGURE 3.4. Figure generated by a participant in "mental discovery" experiment by Barquero & Logie (1999). Volunteers were provided with the names of generic shapes and their task was to mentally manipulate the shapes and combine them in a recognizable object. In this example three letters of the alphabet (O, P, J) were combined to form a "man pushing a wheelbarrow."

The idea that visuospatial working memory is best viewed as a workspace rather than a gateway is supported by evidence from experimental psychology, for example, the area of mental discovery. One experimental method for investigation of this topic involves presenting healthy volunteers with the names of a small number of generic shapes, such as triangle, circle, rectangle. The volunteers are then required to mentally manipulate the shapes and combine them in such a way as to form a recognizable object. Figure 3.4 shows one example generated by a volunteer contributing to Experiment 2 reported by Barquero and Logie (1999). On the whole, the volunteers were quite good at generating drawings of recognizable objects and allocating labels for their mental constructions (see also Anderson & Helstrup, 1993; Finke & Slayton, 1988; Pearson, Logie, & Gilhooly, 1999). However, Barquero and Logie also showed that when volunteers were asked to perform the same task with the shapes of real objects, such as glass, pineapple, ax, then they had more difficulty in generating recognizable objects mentally, but their ability to reinterpret object shapes as being components of a completely different object improved if they were allowed to sketch their image on paper. These results suggest that healthy adults can use working memory to manipulate shapes and generate new discoveries. However, they also suggest that when people attempt to manipulate mentally the shapes of real objects, then it is difficult to divest the object identity from the object shape. When the shapes are drawn on paper, they can be reinterpreted via the perceptual system. That is, the meaning that arises from object identification through perception becomes part of the mental representation held in working memory. In sum, working memory can aid discovery, but it operates as a workspace, not just a temporary passive storage device. A major implication of working memory as a gateway is that it should accept as input raw sensory images that are devoid of the interpretation that can only come from the store of prior experience. The evidence here that the contents of working memory are interpreted, speaks to the idea that the material enters working memory from long-term memory, not directly from sensory input.

The original view of working memory as a gateway carries a second implication for the status of the information it holds, namely that there is no direct access route between sensory input and long-term memory. However, this runs into difficulty when attempting to account for the wide range of evidence for implicit processing of sensory input that arises from studies that we discuss in detail now, of patients with unilateral spatial neglect and with cortical blindness.

UNILATERAL SPATIAL NEGLECT

On September 25, 1919, U.S. President Woodrow Wilson suffered from a stroke while addressing an audience in Pueblo, Colorado (see Figure 3.5). As a result, he was affected by paralysis and loss of sensation on the left side of his body (L'Etang, 1995). In the following few days, it became clear that he also had a range of deficits that resulted in bizarre behavior. For example, his wife requested that any visitors be led to the right side of his bed or wheelchair. This was done to "ensure that he would not ignore people on his left side" (Weinstein, 1981, p, 357). In a detailed discussion of Wilson's impairments, Sigmund Freud (Freud & Bullitt, 1967) described the problem in psychoanalytic terms, as a rather strange form of neurosis. However, it seems much more likely that the deficits arose from a lesion in the parietal lobe of the right hemisphere. Indeed, Weinstein (1981) argued that Woodrow Wilson must have been suffering from what is now known as unilateral spatial neglect in addition to the physical paralysis.

FIGURE 3.5. Still from a video clip showing President Wilson after his major stroke. Taken from *Woodrow Wilson: Reluctant Warrior* produced by A&E Television Networks.

A key deficit in patients with unilateral spatial neglect is that they ignore one-half of extra personal space, most commonly the left, following a lesion in the right parietal lobe (for a review see Robertson & Halligan, 1999). An example CT scan is shown in Figure 3.6a. Thus, when asked to cross out items on a sheet in front of them, to copy a picture, or to indicate the center point of a line they will cross out items or reproduce only the right half of the picture, or show a significant bias in line bisection (see Figures 3.6b, 3.6c and 3.6d). When asked to describe their immediate environment, they will describe only the right half of the scene in front of them, and, in severe cases, will eat from only the right half of their plate. This deficit does not arise from failure of the visual sensory system, nor from a general intellectual impairment.

Implicit Processing in Neglect

Although such patients ignore information on their left side, they nevertheless appear to be affected implicitly by some of the ignored information. A now classic example is that of patient PS (Marshall & Halligan, 1988), who was shown a picture of two houses, one above the other. One of the houses looked perfectly symmetrical and normal, whereas the other house was

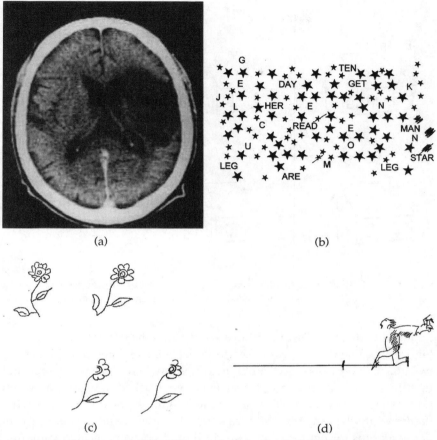

(a) (b)

(c) (d)

FIGURE 3.6. Clockwise: (a) The CT scan of neglect patient NL (Beschin et al., 1997) showing the typical right parietal lesion; (b) Performance on a cancellation task of patient RS affected by a very severe neglect (Beschin & Della Sala, 1999). The examiner crossed out two little stars in the middle and asked the patient to cross out all the other small stars. RS only succeeded in finding a few stimuli on the rightmost part of the array; (c) Performance on a copying task by a patient showing evidence of object-centered neglect (from our archives). This patient only copies the right half of each flower; (d) Line bisection performed by neglect patient FF (Cantagallo & Della Sala, 1998). The patient typically misplaced the center of the line (and later acknowledged his error by adding – in the right corner – a gracious figure tiptoeing toward the real center).

FIGURE 3.7. Left: Stimuli similar to those used in the burning house experiment (Marshall & Halligan, 1988). Right: What patients with neglect "perceive."

depicted with flames issuing from a window on the left of the picture (see Figure 3.7). The patient was asked to indicate if she detected whether the two houses were the same or different in any way, and consistently reported that the houses were identical. However, when asked to choose in which house she would prefer to live, she tended to choose the house without the flames while claiming that this was a complete guess, and not being aware of the reasons for her decision. This finding has been replicated, although not in all neglect patients reported, using the burning house stimuli as well as other material such as pictures of a whole banknote compared with one depicted as torn on the upper left corner, or a pair of wine glasses, one of which had a broken rim on the left (Bisiach & Rusconi, 1990; Cantagallo & Della Sala, 1998). It is notable that the effect is not simply a judgment that the two depicted stimuli are the same or different; the patients choose one in preference to the other. The fact that the phenomenon appears in some neglect patients demonstrates that the features on the left side of the stimuli are being perceived at a covert level, allowing sufficient activation of stored knowledge about the negative consequences of flames or broken glass to result in a rejection of the damaged item in the stimulus pair.

   Similar conclusions can be drawn from studies using pictures of chimeric animals (e.g., Buxbaum & Coslett, 1994; Vallar, Rusconi, & Bisiach, 1994; Young, Hellawell, & Welch, 1992). Such pictures comprise showing

FIGURE 3.8. Chimeric figures similar to those used by Vallar et al. (1994).

one-half of an animal joined to half of another animal. In the Vallar et al. (1994, Experiment 1) study, neglect patients were shown pairs of pictures. For one set of picture pairs, two identical animals were shown. For a second set of picture pairs, one picture depicted a normal animal, and the other picture depicted a chimeric-like figure (the front halves of two animals joined and facing in opposite directions, (see Figure 3.8). The task for the patients was to decide for each pair whether the pictures shown were the same or different. One patient in particular, case GS, is relevant for our discussions. In 100% of trials in which one picture showed a chimeric figure, GS indicated that the pictures appeared identical. However, Vallar et al. next presented the picture pairs along with a verbal cue that was the name of the animal depicted on the neglected (left) side, for example, the word sheep for the stimulus shown in Figure 3.8. Under these conditions, the patient's performance dramatically improved, responding correctly on 75% of the 'different' trials, but despite this she did not become aware of the chimeric nature of the stimuli.

Implicit processing of the unattended half of the space also has been observed in neglect patients with rather different experimental paradigms. When patient FF (Cantagallo & Della Sala, 1998) was presented with the drawing of a trombone with a rifle butt coming out from its left side, spontaneously, he reported that he was seeing a "trombone which *fired* notes." McGlinchey-Berroth, Milberg, Verfaellie, Alexander, and Kilduff (1993) showed that neglect patients improved their performance in a lexical decision task after they were primed by brief presentation of relevant pictures in their neglected field. All of these cases demonstrate that the information, while not available within working memory, was being processed by means of access to stored knowledge in long-term memory. These findings undermine the notion of working memory as a gateway to long-term memory (for further discussion, see Ellis et al., 1996).

In a series of recent experiments (Della Sala, Ellis, Logie, in preparation; Ellis, 2001), we demonstrated subliminal processing of semantic information in a neglect patient, GSt, and in a group of healthy volunteers. In one set of experiments, participants were presented with pictures of human figures, but with different characteristics depicted on the left and right side, and below each figure was shown a set of proverbs. Examples of the figures and proverbs are shown in Figure 3.9. The characteristic on the left side of each figure is a depiction of one of the proverbs. The task

(a)   (b)

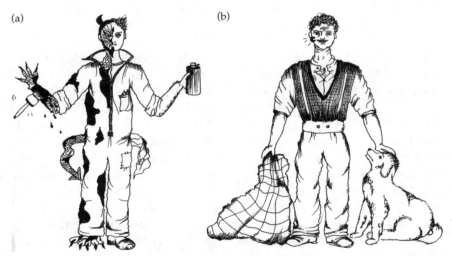

FIGURE 3.9. Examples of stimuli used by Ellis (2001) in the proverbs experiment; (a) A British proverb (The devil is not as black as he is painted); (b) A non-British proverb (Every fisherman with the great net has a spot).

was to identify which proverb was linked to any part of the figure shown. There were two sets of proverbs in the experiment. For one set, the target proverb was chosen to be well known to native English language speakers, and in particular to the participants in the study. In a contrasting set, the target proverb was semantically related to characteristics of the figure, but was unfamiliar, being an English translation of a Chinese or Russian proverb.

For the neglect patient, each figure was shown on paper and he was asked to describe the picture. He consistently omitted details on the left side of the figure for all 20 trials. While the figure was still present, he was then shown a set of six proverbs on paper, and the proverbs were read aloud to him twice, to ensure that there were no difficulties arising from neglect dyslexia. He was asked to indicate which of the proverbs seemed to be associated with the figure. He successfully identified the correct proverb on eight trials with the British proverbs, which is well above guessing levels. However for the non-British proverbs, he identified only four proverbs, which is essentially at chance (3.67). GSt was unable to give a rational basis for any of his choices, which were described as pure guesses. The fact that he could perform above chance suggests that the depicted information in the neglected field was accessing his stored knowledge of familiar proverbs. There would have been no stored information about the foreign proverbs, and these would have required more than simple automatic activation of prior knowledge for a correct response. This pattern then is consistent with that reported for patients in the burning house experiments.

An analogous finding arose in a series of follow-up experiments involving healthy volunteers. In one of these experiments, the same figures and contrasting proverb sets were used as for GSt. First, the figures and proverbs were presented together, but with only the nonrelevant half of the figure shown. For this experiment, the characteristics relevant to the target proverb were depicted on the left for half of the stimuli and on the right for the other half of the stimuli. This acted as a control condition to check for the impact of guessing, and the possibility that there were cues present on the nonrelevant side. Volunteers were at chance on selecting the correct item, with no difference between the British and non-British proverbs. This condition was contrasted with a manipulation in which the proverbs were presented on a computer screen along with the nonrelevant half of the figure. The relevant half was then shown subliminally followed by a pattern mask. Analogous with patient GSt, healthy elderly volunteers were above chance in selecting the correct British proverbs, but were at chance for the non-British proverbs.

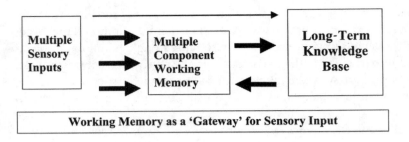

Working Memory as a 'Gateway' for Sensory Input

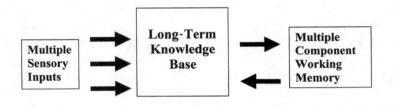

Working Memory as a 'Workspace' for Activated Prior Knowledge

FIGURE 3.10. Above: Flow of sensory input through working memory functioning as a gateway to the long-term store of knowledge and experiences. Below: The flow of sensory input directly activating stored knowledge, with the contents of working memory comprising some of the products of that activation.

Taken together, these data undermine the idea that sensory inputs are held within working memory en route to long-term memory. Rather, for those trials on which a correct response is generated, the stimuli activate stored knowledge in long-term memory at a level sufficient to constitute implicit processing, which in turn is sufficient to allow for selection of the correct item in the absence of conscious awareness of the reasons for doing so. The evidence for implicit processing of sensory input can only be handled by a gateway model of information processing by suggesting that there is some means for sensory input to circumvent the gateway and to gain direct access to working memory, resulting in an additional assumptions of either a leaky gateway, or a form of add-on fast track for some information. This leaky gateway concept is illustrated in the upper part of Figure 3.10. However, the data can be handled more readily by the idea that all sensory input feeds directly into long-term memory, and then only those inputs that result in activation above a threshold are transferred for retention and/or manipulation in working memory comprising a workspace that does not channel sensory input to long-term memory, as illustrated in the lower part of Figure 3.10.

A further implication of the gateway model is that damage to the transit function of the gateway should result in damage to the processing of sensory input. So, for example, should the visuospatial functions of working memory be damaged as a result of brain injury or disease, and if those visuospatial functions act as a gateway between sensory input and the store of prior knowledge, then the processing of sensory input should be impaired. However, as we discuss later in the chapter, patients that show visual or spatial representational and immediate memory impairments show no evidence of impairments in object identification or naming. This is rather more difficult for the gateway model to address, even with the additional direct route between sensory input and the store of knowledge.

Representational Neglect

Neglect is not confined to impairments in reporting details of extrapersonal space. It can also be demonstrated as an impairment of the mental representation of a scene, either recently perceived or drawn from more remote past experience (see Figure 3.11). A number of patients who have

FIGURE 3.11. Drawing of patient NL with pure representational neglect (Beschin et al., 1997) of a familiar landscape.

FIGURE 3.12. Piazza del Duomo test (Bisiach & Luzzatti, 1978). Patient with neglect will only consider details on the right side of their representational viewpoint.

been reported with perceptual neglect also present with representational neglect (e.g., Bartolomeo, D'Erme & Gainotti, 1994; Bisiach & Luzzatti, 1978), in which only half of the scene represented in a visual image can be reported. Bisiach and Luzzatti asked their two patients to describe from memory the Cathedral Square in Milan or the inside of a room in their home or workplace, and to do so from a particular viewpoint (e.g., with their back to the Cathedral). They successfully reported details that would have been on the right from that viewpoint, but reported very few, if any details on the left (see Figure 3.12). This was not simply because of a general memory problem or because there are few items to report from those locations, because when the patients were asked to describe the scene from the opposite viewpoint (i.e., facing the Cathedral from the other end of the square), they reported details now on their imagined right that had previously been omitted, but failed to report items now on their imagined left that had been reported successfully from the previous imagined viewpoint. Moreover, because these were reports from familiar locations that had been experienced prior to their brain damage, the impairments could not be interpreted as resulting from impoverished perceptual input as a result of perceptual neglect. Baddeley and Lieberman (1980) suggested that this pattern of impairments might reflect a deficit in the visuospatial system within working memory. This suggestion was reiterated by Bisiach (1993) in a general review of the patients who had been reported as showing both perceptual and representational neglect.

The concept of representational neglect as a deficit of visuospatial working memory arises again in more recent reports of patients who present with the representational deficit in the absence of any impairments in perceiving extrapersonal space (Beschin, Cocchini, Della Sala, & Logie, 1997; Coslett, 1997; Denis, Beschin, Logie, & Della Sala, 2002; Guariglia, Padovani, Pantano, & Pizzamiglio, 1993). One such case, patient NL (Beschin et al., 1997), presented with a persistent unilateral neglect limited to visual imagery, with no difficulty in reporting the contents of visually perceived scenes. His deficits appeared in tasks that required access to familiar scenes such as the Cathedral Square task (Bisiach & Luzzatti, 1978), or drawing from memory (see Figure 3.13), as well as in tasks that required the retention of spatial information over varying delays, of novel scenes or pictures. In one particular task, NL was first shown a printed matrix of sixteen squares arranged in four rows and four columns. The matrix was then removed, and NL was presented with the description of a path around the matrix starting in the second row and second column. He was asked to imagine the matrix and generate a visual image of the pathway as it was

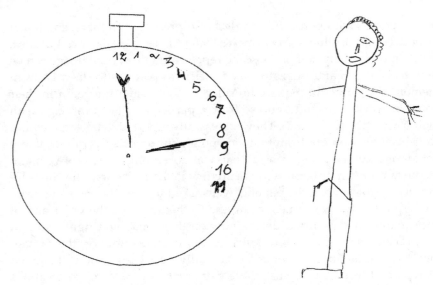

FIGURE 3.13. Left-sided omissions in representational tests showed by patient Mr. Piazza (Beschin et al., 2000). The patient omits the left side of the clock transposing all the details to the right side and ignores the eye and arm of the human figure on the left of his viewpoint.

being described. For example, in the first square put a 1, in the next square to the right put a 2, in the next square down put a 3, in the next square to the left put a 4 and so on. At the end of the sequence, he was to repeat the sequence of directions moved, based on his visual image. This task has been fairly widely used in studies of visuospatial working memory function in healthy adults (e.g., Brooks, 1967; Logie, Zucco, & Baddeley, 1990; Quinn & Ralston, 1986). Control subjects in the Beschin et al. study could recall sequences, on average, of around five items. NL's performance on this task was extremely poor, with correct recall of, on average, sequences of just two items. However, when NL was allowed to look at the blank matrix instead of holding it in an image, his performance was within the normal range. That is, the deficit appeared only when performance relied solely on maintaining and generating a visual image. This difficulty was removed when he could gain external stimulus support through his intact perceptual system.

    A particularly intriguing case of neglect was reported by Beschin, Basso, and Della Sala (2000). Their patient, Signor Piazza (fictitious name), suffered from two consecutive strokes, one in the right thalamus, and the other in the left parietal/occipital lobes. The left hemisphere stroke resulted in a severe perceptual neglect for material presented in the right hemispace, but with no problems in reporting information from memory of the right of previously experienced scenes. In contrast, the right hemisphere stroke resulted in a severe impairment of the patient's ability to report, from memory, details on the left side of a mental representation of a familiar scene, but his ability to perceive and identify objects presented on the left was intact. Moreover, when asked to recall the details of a picture presented either centrally or on the left, his performance was very poor. He could perceive from one hemispace without remembering what he perceived, and could image details in the other mental hemispace from stored information in long-term memory without being able to perceive (see Figure 3.14).

The gateway model of working memory would have great difficulty in accounting for the pattern of deficits found with patients, such as NL, who have normal perceptual input while having demonstrable impairment of their visuospatial working memory system. The model would have even more difficulty accounting for the pattern observed for Signor Piazza, since intact perception resulted in virtually no trace in working memory. The perceptual system does not appear to rely on working memory for intact function. Therefore, working memory, and visuospatial working memory in particular, is best seen as a workspace that holds and manipulates information that is interpreted. In other words, perception activates information in long-term memory, and it is the products of that activation that comprise the contents of working memory.

The pattern of impairment in these patients has an additional implication, namely that the processes of perception and the cognitive functions that support imagery appear to be less closely linked than is commonly assumed (see Denis & Kosslyn, 1999, for a discussion). Some further recent evidence for this conclusion has been reported by Denis, Beschin, Logie, and Della Sala (2002). In this group study, nine patients with representational neglect (eight of whom also had perceptual neglect), and healthy controls were asked to report the location of novel arrays of pictures of objects. In one, visual-perceptual condition, participants reported the items and their locations while they were in full view. In a second condition, the array of items was shown to the participant and then removed. The participant then had to report the items and their locations from memory. In a third condition, the experimenter read aloud a verbal description of the objects and their locations, but with no visual-perceptual input, and the participant was asked to recall the objects and positions. An example of such a description would be: "In front, on the left is a banana, to the right of the banana is an apple, behind the apple, on the right is a tomato, and to

FIGURE 3.14. Mr. Piazza (Beschin et al., 2000) would omit the right side of a house (top) when asked to copy it (middle) but its right side when asked to draw it from memory (bottom).

the left of the tomato is a lemon." A fourth control condition tested memory for a series of sentences that involved no locational information, for example, "The sugar is expensive, the flour is heavy, the coffee is foreign, the salt is damp." Participants were to recall the items and their properties.

The results showed that the patients did not differ from healthy control subjects in performance on recall of the nonlocational sentences. However, the patients consistently showed poorer reporting of items depicted or described on the left of the object array than on the right. It was of particular interest that the patients showed this evidence of neglect, even for the condition in which the layout was presented as an auditory verbal description involving no visual perceptual input. That is, the patients appeared to be attempting to form a visuospatial representation from the verbal description, although they were suffering from an impairment of their visuospatial representational system. Moreover, the one patient who had no perceptual neglect, suffering only from representational neglect, had close to ceiling performance for the perceptual condition, and showed poorer reporting from the left, only in the conditions involving memory following perception and memory following verbal description. That is, the patterns of performance clearly showed that the representational problems did not arise from any difficulties with the perceptual input, that the phenomena of perceptual neglect and of representational neglect are best viewed as different disorders, and that the representational system can be damaged quite separately from the perceptual system. This leads to the conclusion that the representational system and the perceptual system in the healthy brain might not overlap to any great extent.

PRESERVED REPRESENTATION IN VISUAL AGNOSIA AND
CORTICAL BLINDNESS

A possible caveat that might arise from basing our argument on neglect and associated disorders is that the impairments are lateralized, with only part of the visual field, or of the mental representation disrupted. However, dissociations also arise in patients for whom the damage is bilateral. For example, Madame D (Bartolomeo et al., 1998), was severely impaired in identifying visually presented objects, regardless of the visual hemifield, but showed no difficulty in a range of tasks that required visual imagery derived from previously stored knowledge. A similar dissociation was observed in patient DF (Servos & Goodale, 1995), who suffered from the sequelae of carbon monoxide poisoning, resulting in diffuse brain damage. She presented with a severe inability to discriminate objects as well as simple shapes or patterns. However, DF performed normally on a range of tasks requiring retrieval from long-term memory of the visual properties of objects, requiring the generation and scanning of mental images of objects from long-term memory, and requiring the drawing of objects from memory. With respect to this last task, she could clearly draw objects from memory but could not recognize these same objects from visual perception.

The pattern for DF contrasts sharply with the pattern of impairment and sparing in patient EP (Luzzatti, Vecchi, Agazzi, Cesa-Bianchi, & Vergani, 1998), who had no difficulty in identifying objects in her visual field, but was unable to undertake any form of mental processing on images in the absence of perceptual input.

Although several patients have been reported whose perceptual deficits have been accompanied by visual imagery, it is clear that a range of patients have presented with selective deficits, either showing visual agnosia with preserved visual imagery, or showing deficits of visual imagery with preserved object recognition (for reviews see Goldenberg, 1992, 1998).

An analogous dissociation between perception and imagery has been observed in patients affected by cortical blindness. This disorder is characterized by severe loss of vision resulting from damage to the primary visual cortex in the occipital lobe in both hemispheres (e.g., Anton, 1899; Della Sala & Spinnler, 1988; Joynt et al., 1985; see Cowey, in press, 2004, for a recent review). It has been commonly argued that patients with cortical blindness also show impairments of visual imagery (e.g., Policardi et al., 1996). However, several cases of cortically blind patients have been reported whose visual imagery was preserved (e.g., Chatterjee & Southwood, 1995; Goldenberg et al., 1995), which led to some authors questioning the role in visual imagery, of area V1 in the occipital cortex, thereby reopening the debate about the neuroanatomical substrates and the possible overlap between imagery and perception (Kleiser et al., 2001; Mellet et al., 1998).

CONCLUDING REMARKS

We have argued that visuospatial working memory offers a useful theoretical construct, possibly open to further fractionation, that can account for a variety of symptoms shown by neuropsychological patients as well as for some aspects of visuospatial cognition in the healthy brain. We have presented evidence that visuospatial working memory can be viewed as part of a mental workspace in which visually presented material can be made available in an interpreted form together with other information in working memory derived from other sensory input or from the long-term store of knowledge. For example, if we see pictures of vineyards, the interpretation that the pattern of shapes, texture, color on the glossy paper comprise a vineyard will become available within working memory. So too, the activation of associated phonological representations of the words such as grapes and wine together with the relevant articulatory codes can allow rehearsal and overt articulation of the words. Similarly, on hearing the words, the visual and spatial properties of the words grape or wine become available, allowing generation of a temporary representation of the visual form of the words that could then be written. Semantic information about wine, and possibly particular kinds of wine, could also be activated along with a representation of its distinctive odor and taste. Working memory could also draw on all of the available information to carry out further processing on the properties of the visual or phonological representations to allow spelling of the words, their segmentation, as well as imagining the actions associated with consumption of the beverage to which the words refer.

Future research in visuospatial working memory and its deficits might address the possible resolution of the ambiguity between neuroimaging and neuropsychology findings, the uncertainties with regards to cognitive demands of a range of tasks commonly used in clinical settings, as well as its theoretical development within the context of more general theories of cognition.

Suggestions for Further Reading

For further discussion of working memory see many of the chapters in:
Miyake, A., & Shah, P. (Eds.) (1999). *Models of working memory*. New York: Cambridge University Press.

For more detailed discussion of visuo-spatial working memory see:
Logie, R. H. (2003). Spatial and visual working memory: A mental workspace. In D. Irwin & B. Ross (Eds.), *Cognitive vision: The psychology of learning and motivation*, Vol. 42, pp. 37–78. San Diego, CA: Academic Press.

For more detail regarding the impact of brain damage on memory see:
Baddeley, A. D., Kopelman, M. D., & Wilson, B. A. (Eds.). (2002). *The handbook of memory disorders*. Chichester: Wiley.

For further discussion regarding the cognitive impairments associated with unilateral spatial neglect see:
Robertson, I. H., & Halligan, P. W. (1999). *Spatial neglect: A clinical handbook for diagnosis and treatment*. Hove, UK: Psychology Press.

References

Aguirre, G. K., & D'Esposito, M. D. (1999). Topographical disorientation: A synthesis and taxonomy. *Brain, 122,* 1613–1628.
Anderson, J. R. (1978). Arguments concerning representations for mental imagery. *Psychological Review, 85,* 249–277.

Anderson, R. A., & Helstrup, T. (1993). Visual discovery on mind and on paper. *Memory and Cognition*, *21*, 283–293.

Anton, G. (1899). Ueber die Selbstwahrnehmungen der Herderkrankungen des Gehirns durch den Kranken bei Rindenblindheit. *Archiv für Psychiatrie und Nervenkrankheiten*, *32*, 86–127.

Atkinson, R. C., & Shiffrin R. M. (1968). Human memory. A proposed system and its control processes. In K. W. Spence & J. T. Spence (Eds.), *The psychology of learning and motivation* (Vol. 2, pp. 89–105). New York: Academic Press.

Baddeley, A. D., Emslie, H., & Nimmo-Smith, I. (1994). *The doors and people test*. Bury St Edmunds, Suffolk, UK: Thames Valley Test Company.

Baddeley, A. D., & Lieberman, K. (1980). Spatial working memory. In R. S. Nickerson (Ed.), *Attention and performance* (pp. 521–539). Hillsdale, NJ: Lawrence Erlbaum Associates.

Barquero, B., & Logie, R. H. (1999). Imagery constraints on quantitative and qualitative aspects of mental synthesis. *European Journal of Cognitive Psychology*, *11*, 315–333.

Bartolomeo, P., D'Erme, P., & Gainotti, G. (1994). The relationship between visuospatial and representational neglect. *Neurology*, *44*, 1710–1714.

Bartolomeo, P., Bachoud-Lévi, A. C., de Gelder, B., Denes, G., Dalla Barba, G., Brugieres, P., & Degos, J. D. (1998). Multiple-domain dissociation between impaired visual perception and preserved mental imagery in a patient with bilateral extrastriate lesions. *Neuropsychologia*, *36*, 239–249.

Behrmann, M., & Bub, D. (1992). Surface dyslexia and dysgraphia: Dual routes, single lexicon. *Cognitive Neuropsychology*, *9*, 209–151.

Beschin, N., Basso, A., & Della Sala, S. (2000). Perceiving left and imaging right: Dissociation in neglect. *Cortex*, *36*, 401–414.

Beschin, N., Cocchini, G., Della Sala, S., & Logie, R. H. (1997). What the eyes perceive the brain ignores: A case of pure unilateral representational neglect. *Cortex*, *33*, 3–26.

Bisiach, E. (1993). Mental representation in unilateral neglect and related disorders: The twentieth Bartlett memorial lecture. *Quarterly Journal of Experimental Psychology*, *46A*, 435–461.

Bisiach, E., & Luzzatti, C. (1978). Unilateral neglect of representational space. *Cortex*, *14*, 129–133.

Bisiach, E., & Rusconi, M. L. (1990). Breakdown of perceptual awareness in unilateral neglect. *Cortex*, *26*, 643–649.

Brooks, L. R. (1967). The suppression of visualisation by reading. *Quarterly Journal of Experimental Psychology*, *19*, 289–299.

Bub, D. N. (2000). Methodological issues confronting PET and fMRI studies on cognitive function. *Cognitive Neuropsychology*, *17*, 467–484.

Butterworth, B. (1999). *The mathematical brain*. London: Macmillan.

Buxbaum, L. J., & Coslett, H. B. (1994). Neglect of chimeric figures: Two halves are better than a whole. *Neuropsychologia*, *32*, 275–288.

Cantagallo, A., & Della Sala, S. (1998). Preserved insight in an artist with extrapersonal neglect. *Cortex*, *34*, 163–189.

Caramazza, A., & Hillis, A. E. (1991). Lexical organisation of nouns and verbs in the brain. *Nature*, *349*, 788–790.

Carlesimo, G., Perri, R., Turriziani, P., Tomaiuolo, F., & Caltagirone, C. (2001). Remembering what but not where: Independence of spatial and visual working memory. *Cortex, 37*, 519–534.

Charcot, J-M., & Bernard, D. (1883). Un cas de suppression brusque et isolée de la vision mentale des signes et des objects (formes et couleurs). *Le Progrès Médicale, 11*, 568–571.

Chatterjee, A., & Southwood, M. H. (1995). Cortical blindness and visual imagery. *Neurology, 45*, 2189–2195.

Coltheart, M., Patterson, K., & Marshall, J. C. (Eds.). (1987). *Deep dyslexia.* London: Routledge & Kegan Paul.

Corsi, P. M. (1972). *Human memory and the medial temporal region of the brain.* Unpublished master's thesis. Montreal: McGill University.

Coslett, H. B. (1997). Neglect in vision and visual imagery: A double dissociation. *Brain, 120*, 1163–1171.

Courtney, S. M., Petit, L., Maisog, J. M., Ungerleider, L. G., & Haxby, J. V. (1998). An area specialized for spatial working memory in the human frontal cortex. *Science, 279*, 1347–1351.

Courtney, S. M., Ungerleider, L. G., Keil, K., & Haxby, J. V. (1996). Object and spatial visual working memory activates separate neural systems in human cortex. *Cerebral Cortex, 6*, 39–49.

Cowey, A. (2004). Fact, artefact and myth about blindsight. *Quarterly Journal of Experimental Psychology, 38A*, 577–609.

Dehaene, S. (1997). *The number sense: How the mind creates mathematics.* London: Penguin Press.

Della Sala, S. (1998). The visual brain in action by A. D. Milner & M. A. Goodale. Book review, *Neuropsychological Rehabilitation, 8*, 459–464.

Della Sala, S., Ellis, A. X. & Logie, R. H. Semantic Processing in the Semantic hemifild. Manuscript in preparation.

Della Sala, S., Gray, C., Baddeley, A., Allamano, N., & Wilson, L. (1999). Pattern span: A tool for unwelding visuospatial memory. *Neuropsychologia, 37*, 1189–1199.

Della Sala, S., Gray, C., Baddeley, A., & Wilson, L. (1997). *The visual patterns test: A new test of short-term visual recall.* Bury St Edmunds, Suffolk, UK: Thames Valley Test Company.

Della Sala, S., & Spinnler, H. (1988). Anton's (-Redich-Babinski's) syndrome associated with Dide-Botcazo's syndrome: A case report of denial of cortical blindness and amnesia. *Archives Suisses de Neurologie et de Psychiatrie, 139*, 5–15.

Denis, M., Beschin, N., Logie, R. H., & Della Sala, S. (2002). Visual perception and verbal descriptions as sources for generating mental representations: Evidence from representational neglect. *Cognitive Neuropsychology, 19*, 97–112.

Denis, M., & Kosslyn, S. M. (1999). Scanning visual mental images: A window on the mind. *Current Psychology of Cognition, 18*, 409–465.

D'Esposito, M. (2001). Functional neuroimaging of working memory. In R. Cabeza and A. Kingstoe (Eds.). *Handbook of functional neuroimaging of cognition,* (pp. 293–327). Cambridge, MA: MIT Press.

Donders, F. C. (1869/1969). On the speed of mental processes. *Acta Psychologica, 30*, 412–431.

Ellis, A. W., & Young, A. W. (1996). Producing spoken words. In A. W. Ellis & A. W. Young (Eds.), *Human cognitive neuropsychology: A textbook with readings*, (pp. 113–142). Hove, UK: Psychology Press.

Ellis, A. X. (2001). *Perception without awareness: A cognitive neuropsychological investigation of implicit visual information processing*. Unpublished doctoral dissertation, Aberdeen University, UK.

Ellis, A. X., Della Sala, S., & Logie, R. H. (1996). The Bailwick of visuospatial working memory: Evidence from unilateral spatial neglect. *Cognitive Brain Research, 3*, 71–78.

Farah, M. J., Hammond, K. M., Levine, D. N., & Calvanio, R. (1988). Visual and spatial mental imagery: Dissociable systems of representation. *Cognitive Psychology, 20*, 439–462.

Finke, R., & Slayton, K. (1988). Explorations of creative visual synthesis in mental imagery. *Memory and Cognition, 16*, 252–257.

Frackowiak, R. S. J., Friston, K. J., Frith, C. D., Dolan, R. J., & Mazziotta, J. C. (1997). *Human brain function*, Chapter 8, (pp. 141–159). San Diego: Academic Press.

Freud, S., & Bullitt, W. C. (1967). *Thomas Woodrow Wilson, twenty-eighth president of the United States: A psychological study*. London: Weidenfeld and Nicolson.

Goldenberg, G. (1992). Loss of visual imagery and loss of visual knowledge – A case study. *Neuropsychologia, 30*, 1081–1099.

Goldenberg, G. (1998). Is there a common substrate for visual recognition and visual imagery? *Neurocase, 4*, 141–147.

Goldenberg, G., Müllbacher, W. & Nowak, A. (1995). Imagery without perception – A case study of anosognosia for cortical blindness. *Neuropsychologia, 33*, 1373–1382.

Goldman-Rakic, P. S. (1996). The prefrontal landscape: Implications of functional architecture for understanding human mentation and the central executive. *Philosophical Transaction of the Royal Society of London, 351*, 1445–1453.

Grossi, D., Becker, J. T., Smith, C., & Trojano, L. (1993). Memory for visuospatial patterns in Alzheimer's disease. *Psychological Medicine, 23*, 63–70.

Guariglia, C., Padovani, A., Pantano, P., & Pizzamiglio, L. (1993). Unilateral neglect restricted to visual imagery. *Nature, 364*, 235–237.

Hanley, J. R., & Davies, A. D. M. (1995). Lost in your own house. In R. Campbell & M. A. Conway (Eds.), *Broken memories: Case studies in memory impairment*. (pp. 195–208). Oxford: Blackwell Publishers.

Hanley, J. R., Pearson, N. A., & Young, A, W. (1990). Impaired memory for new visual forms. *Brain, 113*, 1131–1148.

Haxby, J. V., Petit, L., Ungerleider, L. G., & Courtney, S. M. (2000). Distinguishing the functional roles of multiple regions in distributed neural systems for visual working memory. *Neuroimage, 11*, 145–156.

Hecker, R., & Mapperson, B. (1997). Dissociation of visual and spatial processing in working memory. *Neuropsychologia, 35*, 599–603.

Hanson, R. (in press). What can functional neuroimaging tell the experimental psychologist? *Quarterly Journal of Experimental Psychology* (A)

Hof, P. R., Bouras, C., Constantinidis, J., & Morrison J. H. (1990). Selective disconnection of specific visual association pathways in cases of Alzheimer's disease presenting with Balint's syndrome. *Journal of neuropathology and Experimental Neurology, 49*, 168–184.

Humphreys, G. W., & Riddoch, M. J. (1987). *To see but not to see: A case of visual agnosia.* Hove, UK: Lawrence Erlbaum Associates.

Jonides, J., Smith, E. E., Koeppe, R. A., Awh, E., Minoshima, S., & Mintum, M. A. (1993). Spatial working memory in humans as revealed by PET. *Nature, 363*, 623–225.

Joynt, R. J., Honch, G. W., Rubin, A. J., & Trudell, R. G. (1985). Occipital lobe syndromes. In P. J. Vinken, G. W. Bruyn, & H. L Klawans (Eds.), *Handbook of clinical neurology, Volume 1(45): Clinical neuropsychology.* Amsterdam: Elsevier.

Kleiser, R., Wittsack, J., Niedeggen, M., Goebel, R., & Stoerig, P. (2001). Is V1 necessary for conscious vision in areas of relative cortical blindness? *Neuroimage, 13*, 654–661.

Knox, H. A. (1914). A scale, based on the work at Ellis Island, for estimating mental defect. *Journal of the American Medical Association, 62*, 741–747.

Kosslyn, S. M. (1994). *Image and brain: The resolution of the imagery debate.* Cambridge, MA: MIT Press.

L'Etang, H. (1995). *Ailing leaders in power, 1914–1994.* London: The Royal Society of Medicine Press.

Logie, R. H. (1995). *Visuospatial working memory.* Hove, UK: Lawrence Erlbaum Associates.

Logie, R. H. (2003). Spatial and visual working memory: A mental workspace. In D. Irwin, & B Ross (Eds.), *Cognitive vision: The psychology of learning and motivation, Vol 42*, pp. 37–78. San Diego, CA: Academic Press.

Logie, R. H., Della Sala, S., Laiacona, M., Chalmers, P., & Wynn, V. (1996). Group aggregates and individual reliability: The case of verbal short-term memory. *Memory and Cognition, 24*, 305–321.

Logie, R. H., Engelkamp, J., Dehn, D., & Rudkin, S. (2001). Actions, mental actions, and working memory. In M. Denis, R. H. Logie, C. Cornoldi, J. Engelkamp, & M. De Vega (Eds.), *Imagery, language and visuospatial Thinking* (pp. 161–184). Hove, UK: Psychology Press.

Logie, R. H., & Marchetti, C. (1991). Visuospatial working memory: Visual, spatial or central executive? In R. H. Logie, & M. Denis (Eds.), *Mental images in human cognition* (pp. 105–115). Amsterdam: North Holland Press.

Logie, R. H., & Pearson, D. G. (1997). The inner eye and the inner scribe of visuospatial working memory: Evidence from developmental fractionation. *European Journal of Cognitive Psychology, 9*, 241–257.

Logie, R. H., Venneri, A., Della Sala, S., Redpath T., & Marshall, I. (2003). Cognitive strategies in brain imaging studies: The case of verbal working memory. *Brain and Cognition, 53*, 293–296.

Logie, R. H., Zucco, G., & Baddeley, A. D. (1990). Interference with visual short-term memory. *Acta Psychologica, 75*, 55–74.

Luzzatti, C., Vecchi, T., Agazzi, D., Cesa-Bianchi, M., & Vergani, C. (1998). A neurological dissociation between preserved visual and impaired spatial processing in mental imagery. *Cortex, 34*, 461–469.

Marshall, J. C., & Halligan, P. W. (1988). Blindsight and insight in visuospatial neglect. *Nature, 336*, 766–767.

MartinLoeches, M. (1997). Encoding into working memory of spatial location, color, and shape: Electrophysiological investigations. *International Journal of Neuroscience, 91*, 277–294.

McClelland, J. L., & Rumelhart, D. E. (1981). An interactive activation model of context effects in letter perception. Part 1. An account of basic findings. *Psychological Review, 88*, 375–407.

McCloskey, M., & Rapp, B. (2000). Attention-referenced visual representations: Evidence from impaired visual localisation. *Journal of Experimental Psychology: Human Perception and Performance, 26*, 917–933.

McCloskey, M., Sokol, S. M., & Goodman, R. A. (1986). Cognitive in verbal number production: Inferences from the performance of brain damaged subjects. *Journal of Experimental Psychology: General, 115*, 307–330.

McGlinchey-Berroth, R., Milberg, W. P., Verfaellie, M., Alexander, M., & Kilduff, P. T. (1993). Semantic priming in the neglected visual field: Evidence from lexical decision task. *Cognitive Neuropsychology, 10*, 79–108.

Mellet, E., Petit, L., Mazoyer, B., Denis, M., & Tzourio, N. (1998). Reopening the mental imagery debate: Lessons from functional anatomy. *Neuroimage, 8*, 129–139.

Meunier, M., Bachevalier, J., & Mishkin, M. (1997). Effects of orbital frontal and anterior cingulate lesions on object and spatial memory in rhesus monkeys. *Neuropsychologia, 7*, 999–1015.

Milner, B. (1965). Visually guided maze learning in man: Effect of bilateral hippocampal, bilateral frontal and unilateral cerebral lesions. *Neuropsychologia, 3*, 317–338.

Milner, B. (1971). Interhemispheric differences in the localization of psychological processes in man. *British Medical Bulletin, 27*, 272–277.

Miyake, A., & Shah, P. (1999). *Models of working memory.* New York: Cambridge University Press.

Owen, A. M., Stern, C. E., Look, R. B., Tracey, I., Rosen, B. R., & Petrides, M. (1998). Functional organization of spatial and nonspatial working memory processing within the human lateral frontal cortex. *Proceedings of the National Academy of Sciences, USA, 95*, 7721–7726.

Owen, A. M., Herrod, N. J., Menon, D. K., Clark, J. C., Downey, S., Carpenter, T. A. et al. (1999). Redefining the functional organisation of working memory processes within human lateral prefrontal cortex. *European Journal of Neuroscience, 11*, 567–574.

Pearson, D. G., Logie, R. H., & Gilhooly, K. J. (1999). Verbal representation and spatial manipulation during mental synthesis. *European Journal of Cognitive Psychology, 11*, 295–314.

Petrides, M. (1996). Specialized systems for the processing of mnemonic information within the primate frontal cortex. *Philosophical Transactions of the Royal Society of London, B – Biological Sciences, 351*, 1455–1461.

Pickering, S. J. (2001). Cognitive approaches to the fractionation of visuospatial working memory. *Cortex, 37*, 457–473.

Pickering, S. J., Gathercole, S. E., Lloyd, S., & Hall, M. (2001). Development of memory for pattern and path: Further evidence for the fractionation of visual and spatial short-term memory. *Quarterly Journal of Experimental Psychology, 54A*, 397–420.

Policardi, E., Perani, D., Zago, S., Grassi, F., & Ladavas, E. (1996). Failure to evoke visual images in a case of long-lasting cortical blindness. *Neurocase, 2,* 371–394.

Postma, A., Sterken, Y., de Vries, L., & de Haan, E. H. F. (2000). Spatial localization in patients with unilateral posterior left or right hemisphere lesions. *Experimental Brain Research, 134,* 220–227.

Quinn, J. G., & Ralston, G. E. (1986). Movement and attention in visual working memory. *The Quarterly Journal of Experimental Psychology, 38A,* 689–703.

Robertson, I. H. & Halligan, P. W. (1999). *Spatial neglect: A clinical handbook for diagnosis and treatment.* Hove, UK: Psychology Press.

Ruchkin, D. S., Johnson, R., Grafman, J., Canoune, H., & Ritter, W. (1997). Multiple visuospatial working memory buffers: Evidence from spatiotemporal patterns of brain activity. *Neuropsychologia, 35,* 195–209.

Rudkin, S. (2001). *Executive processes in visual and spatial working memory tasks,* Unpublished doctoral dissertation. University of Aberdeen, UK.

Salway, A. F. S., & Logie, R. H. (1995). Visuospatial working memory, movement control and executive demands. *British Journal of Psychology, 86,* 253–269.

Sartori, G., & Umiltà, C. (2000). How to avoid the fallacies of cognitive subtraction in brain imaging. *Brain and Language, 74,* 191–212.

Savage, C. R., Deckersbach, T., Heckers, S., Wagner, A. D., Schacter, D. L., & Alpert, N. M., et al. (2001). Prefrontal regions supporting spontaneous and directed application of verbal learning strategies: Evidence from PET. *Brain, 124,* 219–231.

Schacter, D. (1987). Implict memory: History and current status. *Journal of Experimental Psychology: Learning, Memory, and Cognition, 113,* 501–518.

Servos, P., & Goodale, M. A. (1995). Preserved visual imagery in visual form agnosia. *Neuropsychologia, 33,* 1383–1394.

Shallice, T., & Warrington, E. K. (1970). Independent functioning of verbal memory stores: A neuropsychological study. *Quarterly Journal of Experimental Psychology, 22,* 261–273.

Shelton, J. R., & Caramazza, A. (2001). The organisation of semantic memory. In B. Rapp (Ed.). *The handbook of cognitive neuropsychology* (pp. 423–443). Philadelphia: Psychology Press.

Smith, E. E., & Jonides, J. (1995). Working memory in humans: Neuropsychological evidence. In M. S. Gazzaniga (Ed.), *The cognitive neurosciences* (pp. 1009–1020). Cambridge, MA: MIT Press.

Smyth, M. M., & Pendleton, L. R. (1990). Space and movement in working memory. *Quarterly Journal of Experimental Psychology, 42A,* 291–304.

Solms, M., Kaplan-Solms, K., & Brown, J. W. (1996). Wilbrand's case of "mind-blindness." In C. Code, C-W. Wallesch, Y. Joanette, & A. R. Lecours (Eds.), *Classic cases in neuropsychology* (pp. 89–110). Hove, UK: Psychology Press.

Squire, L. R. (1987). *Memory and the brain.* New York: Oxford University Press.

Stein, J. F. (1992). The representation of egocentric space in the posterior parietal cortex. *Behavioral and Brain Sciences, 15,* 691–700.

Tresch, M. C., Sinnamon, H. M., & Seamon, J. G. (1993). Double dissociation of spatial and object visual memory: Evidence from selective interference in intact human subjects. *Neuropsychologia, 31,* 211–219.

Ungerleider, L. G., & Mishkin, M. (1982). Two cortical visual systems. In D. J. Ingle, R. J. W. Mansfield, & M. S. Goodale (Eds.), *The analysis of visual behavior* (pp. 549–586). Cambridge, MA: MIT Press.

Vallar, G., Rusconi, M. L., & Bisiach, E. (1994). Awareness of controlesional information in unilateral neglect: Effects of verbal cueing, tracing, and vestibular stimulation. In C. Umiltà & M. Moscovitch (Eds.), *Attention and performance XV* (pp. 377–391). Cambridge, MA: MIT Press.

Warrington, E. K., & Weiskrantz, L. R. (1970). Amnesic syndrome: Consolidation on retrieval? *Nature, 228*, 628–630.

Weinstein, E. A. (1981). *Woodrow Wilson: A medical and psychological biography.* Princeton, NJ: Princeton University Press.

Wilbrand, H. (1887). *Sie Seelenblindheit als Herderscheinung und ihre Beziehung zur Alexie und Agraphie.* Wiesbaden: Begmann.

Wilson, B., Baddeley, A. D., & Young, A. W. (1999). LE, a person who lost her 'mind's eye.' *Neurocase, 5*, 119–127.

Young, A. W., Hellawell, D. J., & Welch, J. (1992). Neglect and visual recognition. *Brain, 115*, 51–71.

Young, A. W., Newcombe, F., de Haan, E. H. F., Small, M., & Hay, D. C. (1993). Face perception after brain injury: Selective impairments affecting identity and expression. *Brain, 116*, 941–959.

Young, A. W., & van de Wal, C. (1996). Charcot's case of impaired imagery. In C. Code, C.-W. Wallesch, Y. Joanette, & A. R. Lecours (Eds.), *Classic cases in neuropsychology* (pp. 31–44). Hove, UK: Psychology Press.

Zeki, S., & Shipp, S. (1988). The functional logic of cortical connections. *Nature, 335*, 311–317.

4

Individual Differences in Spatial Abilities

Mary Hegarty and David A. Waller

ABSTRACT

This chapter reviews research on spatial abilities, which is concerned with individual differences in how people mentally represent and manipulate spatial information to perform cognitive tasks. We first review factor analytic studies of spatial abilities. This research tradition provided strong evidence that spatial ability is differentiated from general intelligence and that it is not a single, undifferentiated construct, but instead is composed of several somewhat separate abilities. We next review analyses of performance on spatial abilities tests by cognitive psychologists, which has shown that different spatial abilities may depend more or less on speed of processing, strategies, quality of spatial images, active maintenance of spatial information, and central executive processes. Third, we examine individual differences in large-scale or environmental spatial abilities such as wayfinding and navigation. Research on this topic has begun to characterize the factor structure of large-scale spatial abilities and these abilities' relation to more traditional measures of spatial abilities. Finally, we consider some of the functions of spatial ability in occupational and academic performance, including surgery, mechanical reasoning, and mathematical problem solving.

INTRODUCTION

The ability to represent and process spatial information is important for many common activities, such as finding our way to and from places in the environment, moving furniture, packing a suitcase, and catching a ball. It is also related to skilled performance in many occupations, such as car mechanic, airline pilot, and surgeon. It has been linked to academic success in mathematics and science. We are aware that people differ in spatial abilities. We know that some people have a better sense of direction than others, that not everyone is cut out to be a pilot, and that only some people are able to visualize the complex spatial relations between atoms in an organic compound. Do all of these activities rely on a single spatial ability or do they depend on different types of spatial ability? What are the essential differences in spatial representations and processes between people with more and less spatial ability? In this chapter we explore the different dimensions of spatial abilities, the cognitive processes that underlie these different abilities, and the functions of spatial abilities in everyday life and professional activities.

This chapter is different from most other chapters in this volume in that it explores the natural variation in performance among individuals, rather than variation due to experimental treatments. As Cronbach (1957) pointed out, experimental psychology and differential psychology (or correlational psychology) have been separate areas of research in the history of psychology. Because most research in cognitive psychology is experimental, it is worth considering why research on individual differences is important. First, a complete account of spatial cognition must account for the variance among people, as well as the central tendency, especially because individual differences in spatial abilities are so pervasive. Second, from a practical or applied perspective, understanding cognitive differences among people can inform decisions about whom to select or recruit for a job or training program. Third, by capitalizing on the natural variation among people, the study of individual differences can be an important strategy in basic research on spatial cognition. For example, if we are interested in the extent to which spatial representations and processes are important for a particular task, such as solving a mathematics problem, we can use the natural variation among individuals to identify those with more or less spatial ability and observe how they solve the problem. Unlike experimental methods, which tend to create discrete differences between experimental conditions, individual differences in ability vary continuously across the population and therefore allow us more precision in examining the relation between some spatial process and a criterion. We can also find natural variation in aspects of spatial cognition that are difficult to control experimentally, such as the speed of mental rotation. Finally, differences among individuals on some tasks might be large enough to make the effects of other variables (perhaps those manipulated by an experimentalist) difficult to detect. Research on individual differences can thus inform investigators about how to examine the effects that interest them by factoring out effects due to individual differences. A particularly powerful design is to combine the use of experimental methods and differential methods in the same study, in order to examine aptitude-treatment interactions (Cronbach, 1957).

In this chapter, we will review research on individual differences in spatial cognition from a somewhat historical perspective. We first review the factor analysis literature, which dominated early research in spatial abilities. The goals of this research movement were to develop measures of spatial ability, to establish its separability from general intelligence, and to examine the extent to which it is made up of different abilities. Next we consider research on the analysis of spatial abilities from the perspective of cognitive psychology. This research movement attempted to discover the basic perceptual and cognitive processes that differentiate people with high and low ability. Third, we examine individual differences in large-scale or environmental spatial abilities such as wayfinding and navigation. Until recently, this type of spatial ability has received relatively little research attention. Indeed, most of the individual differences literature has been dominated by analyses of paper-and-pencil tests, which measure spatial abilities at a smaller scale. Finally, we consider some of the functions of spatial ability in occupational and academic performance.

In this chapter, we will be concerned primarily with the measurement, classification, and characterization of spatial abilities. We will not discuss the underlying causes of differences in spatial ability, for example, the extent to which they can be trained or are based on innate factors. These issues are dealt with in some detail in the chapter on sex differences (Halpern & Collaer, Chapter 5).

THE FACTOR-ANALYTIC APPROACH TO VISUOSPATIAL ABILITIES

The scientific study of individual differences in visuospatial abilities began in the early 20th century as a result of widespread interest in predicting academic and vocational success through the use of standardized tests. Spatial testing emerged from early attempts to measure mechanical ability, typically in order to predict success in technical occupations. Because these abilities were generally assumed to require physical manipulation, many of these tests were based on performance on tasks that required assembly or manipulation of actual objects. Smith (1964) describes some of these early tests as consisting of "peg-boards, eye-boards, tests of tapping and aiming, tests of tweezer-dexterity, of wire-bending, tests involving the manipulation of nuts and bolts, and many others" (p. 41). As instruments such as Binet and Simon's *Scales of Intelligence* (1905) grew in popularity, ability tests began to shift their emphasis from physical manipulation to quantitatively scored multiple-choice questions that could be answered by means of paper-and-pencil tests. Paper-and-pencil assessments enabled testing in large groups, and as a result large data sets emerged that slowly began to clarify the structure of intelligence and the nature of visuospatial abilities (for a summary, see Smith, 1964). It took several decades to develop a consistent and powerful means of analysis as well as to overcome the prevailing bias to associate all aspects of intellectual ability with a single, general (typically verbal) intelligence. However, by 1939, Kelly (1928), Koussy (1935), Eysenck (1939), and Thurstone (1938) had all shown that spatial ability was distinct from verbal ability. These researchers made a primary distinction between verbal and spatial intelligence and noted that the latter accounted for a significant amount of variance in scores on large batteries of intellectual functioning. This conclusion is no longer disputed.

One of the most common methods used to describe the underlying structure of the intellect is called factor analysis. Factor analysis is a statistical technique that examines the patterns of correlations among a large number of variables (e.g., scores on many different paper-and-pencil tests). The technique attempts to reduce the information contained in many variables to a smaller number of constructs called factors. Mathematically, a factor is simply a weighted sum of each of the variables. Yet factors are typically conceptualized as representing an underlying ability. Tests that correlate highly with a given factor may be called markers for a factor and are said to load on that factor. Although generally helpful and very widely used, the factor-analytic approach has several limitations. For example, evidence for underlying mental factors can only be derived from testing batteries that include markers for that factor. This and other problems, discussed in length next, limit the effectiveness of factor analysis as a means of understanding the structure of the intellect. Yet much of the progress made toward understanding visuospatial ability arose from the factor-analytic tradition.

During the middle of the 20th century, research on individual differences in spatial abilities focused on determining the factor structure of spatial ability. Investigators such as Guilford and Lacey (1947), Zimmerman (1954), Thurstone (1950), and French (1951) all found that large batteries of spatial tests yielded evidence for several separable subcomponents of spatial ability. By the 1960s, many investigators no longer treated spatial ability as a unitary factor – rather, as an amalgam of several correlated factors. However, theorists differed on how best to characterize these factors. Some of these different characterizations, which we now discuss, are summarized in Table 4.1. Michael, Gulford, Fruchter, and Zimmerman (1957) published a review of then-existing literature, concluding that there

TABLE 4.1. *Summary of the spatial abilities factors identified in some of the primary studies using the factor-analytic approach, including representative spatial abilities tests cited by the authors as markers for each factor.*

Study	Factors identified	Tests cited as typical markers for each factor
Michael, Guilford, Fruchter, &	1. Spatial Visualization	- Paper Folding, Form Board (see Figure 4.1a)
Zimmerman, 1957	2. Spatial Relations and Orientation	- Cube Comparisons Test (see Figure 4.1b), Guilford–Zimmerman Spatial Orientation (see Figure 4.2), Card Rotations (see Figure 4.3a)
	3. Kinesthetic Imagery	- Hands test*
McGee, 1979b	1. Spatial Visualization	- Paper Folding
	2. Spatial Orientation	- Cube Comparisons, Guilford–Zimmerman Spatial Orientation
Lohman, 1988	1. Spatial Visualization	- Paper Folding, Form Board, Cube Comparisons
	2. Spatial Relations	- Card Rotations
	3. Spatial Orientation	- Guilford–Zimmerman Spatial Orientation
Carroll, 1993	1. Spatial Visualization	- Paper Folding, Form Board, Cube Comparisons, Guilford–Zimmerman Spatial Orientation
	2. Spatial Relations	- Card Rotations
	3. Closure Speed	- Snowy Pictures (see Figure 4.3b)
	4. Flexibility of Closure	- Hidden Figures (see Figure 4.3c)
	5. Perceptual Speed	- Identical Pictures (see Figure 4.3d)
	6. Visual Memory	- Silverman–Eals visual memory task (see Figure 4.4)

was consistent evidence for three factors of spatial ability: (a) *Spatial relations and orientation*, which was theorized to involve the ability to understand the arrangement of elements within a visual stimulus, primarily with respect to one's body frame of reference; (b) *Visualization*, which was thought to require the mental manipulation of objects; and

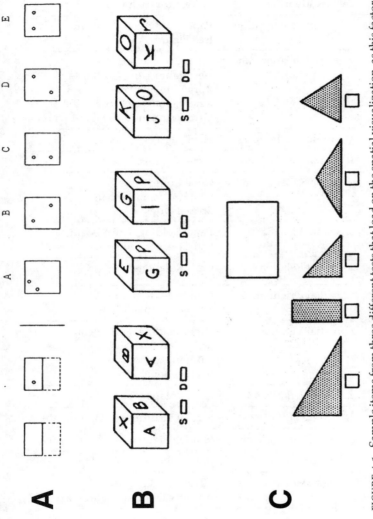

FIGURE 4.1. Sample items from three different tests that load on the spatial visualization, as this factor is described by Lohman (1988) and Carroll (1993). Because many different types of tests load on this factor, three representative examples are given: (a) Items on the Paper Folding test from Ekstrom et al. (1976, top) require examinees to choose which of the five alternatives (right) represents the appearance of the paper if it has been folded and punched as indicated on the left; (b) The middle panel illustrates three sample items from the Cube Comparisons test (Ekstrom et al., 1976). Examinees determine whether the two depicted cubes represent the same or different cubes; (c) The lower panel illustrates a sample item from the Form-Board test. Examinees determine which of the shapes on the bottom could be rearranged to complete the rectangle above them.

(c) *Kinesthetic imagery*, which was believed to be associated with left-right discrimination. Michael et al. admitted that none of these descriptions yielded perfectly clear-cut distinctions empirically, and despite many efforts to distinguish these factors, correlations among tests that served as markers for these factors were often very high (Borich & Bauman, 1972; Vincent & Allmandinger, 1971; Smith, 1964) – occasionally approaching the tests' own reliability (Roff, 1952).

Despite the shortcomings of the Michael et al. description of spatial ability, a strikingly similar model prevailed through the 1980s, primarily as a result of extensive summaries and reviews conducted by McGee (1979a) and Lohman (1979). McGee pointed out that much of the confusion and inconsistencies concerning the factor structure of spatial ability is due to inconsistent naming conventions among investigators. In his review, McGee concluded that most researchers have distinguished what he regarded as the same two fundamental dimensions of spatial ability (see Table 4.1). The strongest factor, spatial visualization (or VZ), was first defined by Guilford and Lacey (1947) and is typically described as an ability to manipulate, rotate, twist, or invert objects without reference to one's self. This ability is required for successful performance on tasks such as the Paper Folding test from the Ekstrom, French, Harman, and Dermen (1976) test battery (Figure 4.1a). For McGee, the second prominent dimension of spatial ability was spatial orientation (SO), which he characterized as "the comprehension of the arrangement of elements within a visual stimulus pattern and the aptitude to remain unconfused by the changing orientation in which a spatial configuration may be presented" (McGee, 1979b, p. 893). Spatial orientation is often conceived as an ability to imagine the appearance of objects from different orientations (perspectives) of the observer and has been described by Thurstone as the "ability to think about those spatial relations in which the body orientation of the observer is an essential part of the problem" (Thurstone, 1950, as reported in McGee, 1979a). A typical marker for this ability is the Guilford–Zimmerman (1948) Spatial Orientation test (Figure 4.2), which requires users to determine the change in position implied by two views from the prow of a boat. However, McGee's concept of spatial orientation was somewhat broader than that of Thurstone. For McGee, tests of mental rotation – which do not typically involve imagining a change in the body orientation of the observer – were considered as markers for SO. In another influential review, Lohman (1979) supported the existence of three major spatial abilities factors (Table 4.1). The first was spatial relations, which is defined by tests that require speeded performance of

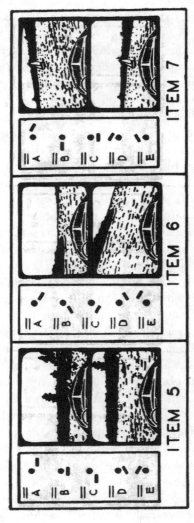

FIGURE 4.2. Three sample items from the Guilford–Zimmerman test of Spatial Orientation. Examinees determine which of five choices represents the change in orientation from the top to the bottom view of a boat's prow. Consulting Psychologists Press. Reprinted by permission.

simple (two-dimensional) mental rotation items (such as the Card Rotations test shown in Figure 4.3a). Lohman later referred to this factor as speeded rotation (Lohman, 1988). Lohman's second factor was spatial orientation, which he defined as the ability to imagine how a stimulus array will appear from another perspective – a more restricted definition than that of McGee, and similar to that of Thurstone (1950). Lohman agreed with McGee on the definition of his third factor, spatial visualization, but emphasized that it is defined by difficult spatial tasks that require a sequence of transformations of a spatial representation, and more complex stimuli. Examples of tests loading on the spatial visualization factor are the paper-folding test, form-board test, and mental rotation of three-dimensional figures, shown in Figure 4.1.

In the most extensive study to date, Carroll (1993) surveyed and reanalyzed more than 90 data sets that bear on the factor structure of visuospatial ability. Carroll examined the support for five visuospatial factors in the category that he referred to as "abilities in the domain of visual perception." These were visualization (VZ), spatial relations (SR), closure speed (CS), flexibility of closure (CF), and perceptual speed (P). A fifth factor, visual memory (MV) is described in a chapter of Carroll's book on abilities in the domain of learning and memory. It should be noted that Carroll's definition of visual-spatial abilities was somewhat broader than those of McGee (1979b) and Lohman (1979). For example, Lohman acknowledged the existence of closure speed, perceptual speed, and visual memory, but referred to them as minor factors that are not central to what is meant by "spatial ability."

Carroll found strong and consistent support for a spatial visualization factor that emphasizes "power in solving increasingly difficult problems involving spatial forms" (Carroll, 1993, p. 315). He also found support for closure speed (CS) and flexibility of closure (CF), both of which involve the ability to identify a stimulus (or part of a stimulus) that is either embedded in or obscured by visual noise. In general, tests of closure speed do not give the examinee information about the stimulus to be discovered. The target stimulus typically depicts a common object, and items are scored by the time to recognize these targets (see the sample item from the Snowy Pictures test in Figure 4.3b). Closure speed thus involves the ability to access representations quickly from long-term memory. On the other hand, tests of flexibility of closure tend to include the target stimulus (typically a geometric design), so that examinees know what to search for (see the sample item from the Hidden Figures tests in Figure 4.3c).

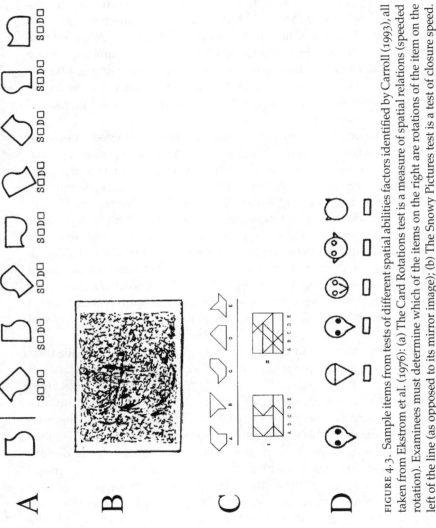

FIGURE 4.3. Sample items from tests of different spatial abilities factors identified by Carroll (1993), all taken from Ekstrom et al. (1976): (a) The Card Rotations test is a measure of spatial relations (speeded rotation). Examinees must determine which of the items on the right are rotations of the item on the left of the line (as opposed to its mirror image); (b) The Snowy Pictures test is a test of closure speed. Examinees must identify the object in the picture (in this case, an anchor); (c) The Hidden Figures test is a test of flexibility of closure. Examinees must determine which of the shapes, labeled A to E, is contained in each of the complex figures below; (d) The Identical Pictures test is a test of Perceptual Speed. Examinees must identify which of the pictures on the right is identical to the one on the left.

Flexibility of closure is thus more closely associated with the ability to hold a stimulus in working memory while attempting to identify it from a complex pattern.

Carroll also found evidence for a factor called perceptual speed (P), which was described by French (1951) as "speed in comparing figures or symbols, scanning to find figures or symbols, or carrying out other very simple tasks involving visual perception." Tasks that measure this factor often involve either matching two stimuli or searching a field for a target stimulus (see the sample item from the Identical Pictures test in Figure 4.3d). These tasks require virtually no mental transformations of stimuli and typically rely more on visual than spatial processing. Finally, Carroll recognized support for the existence of a visual memory factor, described by Ekstrom et al. (1976) as "the ability to remember the configuration, location, and orientation of figural material." Tests of visual memory generally require examinees to study a stimulus configuration for several minutes. These configurations can be either a maplike depiction of an environment, an array of objects, or a configuration of meaningless shapes. Examinees must then either recognize or recall the identity or the location of objects within the configuration (Figure 4.4). Visual-spatial memory has been of interest recently because Silverman and Eals (1992) have found significant gender differences favoring women on tests of spatial memory (see also Montello, Lovelace, Golledge, & Self, 1999). More recently, Robert and Ecuyer-Dab (2000) have shown that women's advantage in this task extends to memory of both stationary and repositioned objects.

A somewhat surprising result of Carroll's study is that he failed to find strong and consistent evidence for the separability of spatial relations from the spatial visualization factor; only 7 of the 94 data sets that he examined showed such a distinction. Spatial relations, associated with the ability to perform relatively simple mental transformations (typically rotations) quickly, was identified in 21 of the data sets reviewed by Carroll. Both Carroll and Lohman agree that a distinction between these two factors emerges only if several tests of each type appear in the testing battery. Despite this observation, the distinction between spatial relations and spatial visualization has remained important in the cognitive analysis of spatial test performance.

Carroll also failed to find consistent support for the separability of spatial orientation (SO) and spatial visualization (SV). Many investigators have supported the existence of spatial orientation (Guilford & Zimmerman,

FIGURE 4.4. A test of visual memory developed by Silverman & Eals (1992). After studying the picture on the left, examinees are shown one of the pictures on the right. In one condition (upper panel) examinees must put a cross through all the items that were not in the picture that they studied. In the other condition (lower panel) they must circle the items that were in the same place in the picture that they studied and put a cross through the items that have moved from their position in the studied picture. From J. H. Barkow, L. Cosmides, & J. Tooby (Eds.), *The adapted mind: Evolutionary psychology and the generation of culture* (pp. 357–358). Oxford: Oxford University Press. Reprinted by permission.

1948; McGee, 1979b; Thurstone, 1950) and it continues to appear prominently in descriptions of spatial ability. However, several studies have found that spatial orientation and spatial visualization are highly related (Borich & Bauman, 1972; Goldberg & Meredith, 1975; Vincent & Allmandinger, 1971), with markers correlating as highly as .75 (Roff, 1952). Although he generally supported the distinction of spatial orientation from spatial visualization, Lohman (1979) also concluded that "It is clear that the Guilford–Zimmerman Spatial Orientation and Spatial Visualization tests do not measure different factors." Finally, Carroll failed to find evidence for a factor known as spatial scanning, which was described by Ekstrom et al. (1976) as "speed in exploring visually a wide or complicated spatial field."

Evaluation of the Factor-Analytic Literature

The factor-analytic tradition has delineated several separable dimensions of visuospatial ability, and these abilities enable investigators to conceptualize the domain of spatial intelligence. Yet the factor analytic approach is not without its problems and limitations. Perhaps one weakness is the fact that most factor analytic studies of spatial ability have, until recently, generally employed *exploratory* factor analyses, the technique used to derive a relatively small set of factors from a large set of variables. Exploratory factor analysis can be used without any prior understanding of the interrelations among a set of variables. There are several variations of exploratory factor analysis techniques (and different methods of rotating solutions), and the use of different techniques can result in different conclusions being drawn. The choice of which technique to use is often based on subjective grounds. As a result, many different exploratory factor-analytic models have proliferated, each unable to disconfirm alternative models of spatial ability (Gustafsson, 1984; Sternberg, 1981). An increasingly popular approach that attempts to remedy some of these problems is called *confirmatory* factor analysis. This technique relies critically on prior specification of the underlying factor structure. In confirmatory factor analysis, the researcher begins with a hypothesized factor structure and then tests how plausible it is given the observed correlations among measures. Gustafsson (1984) has argued that this class of model allows a sharper analytic tool, capable of disconfirming theories in a way that exploratory analyses cannot. Later in the chapter, we will report some examples of recent research that has used this type of model.

Another shortcoming of the factor-analytic approach concerns the assumptions it makes in terms of strategies. Correlational analyses such as factor analysis not only assume that all examinees use the same strategy, but that a given examinee uses the same strategy on all items. Both of these assumptions are in general false (Barratt, 1953; Just & Carpenter, 1985; Lohman, 1988). That different strategies can be used to solve the same test item greatly confounds the correlational analyses of underlying mental processes. As we will see, research aimed at understanding strategies used on spatial ability tests has been enormously helpful in understanding the role of individual differences in spatial ability.

We have seen that, despite the widespread belief in the independent existence of SO, Carroll was unable to establish conclusive support for this factor. The confusion over the existence of spatial orientation highlights another problem with the factor analytic approach: Factor analyses are only able to describe the underlying structure of the variables that go into the analysis. If markers for a relevant or important factor are left out of a testing battery, the factor obviously cannot emerge from the analysis. Similarly, if a factor is poorly represented by too few or weak markers, then the recovered factor structure may not be very reliable.

Although Carroll's extensive reanalysis found little support for spatial orientation, this does not mean that such an ability does not exist – rather, it is possible that this ability has simply been poorly assessed historically. Theoretically, the critical distinction between spatial orientation and spatial visualization is that spatial orientation is related to the ability to imagine changing one's viewpoint (perspective), whereas spatial visualization involves imagining the movement of objects. Barratt (1953) and others have noted that test items putatively measuring spatial orientation can often be solved by imagining the stimulus moving rather than the imagining a change in the viewpoint of the observer. For example, although the Guilford–Zimmerman test of Spatial Orientation (Figure 4.2) is often thought to be a strong marker for SO, this test does not require adoption of alternate perspectives and most examinees do not do so (Barratt, 1953). It is thus possible that spatial orientation ability represents a separable spatial factor, but there have not been enough pure tests of this ability for it to be adequately measured and adopted into psychometric models of spatial ability.

Kozhevnikov and Hegarty (2001) have recently shown evidence of a perspective-taking ability that is distinct from spatial visualization. In their study, participants were shown a two-dimensional array of objects, and were asked to imagine themselves facing a particular direction within the array. They then indicated the direction to a target object from that perspective. Verbal reports from the participants indicated that the dominant strategy used to solve the test items was to imagine oneself reoriented with respect to the display (in a protocol study, only one out of eight participants reported rotating the array), suggesting that it is more effective than the Guilford–Zimmerman at measuring spatial orientation ability. This conclusion was also supported by systematic errors in which participants confused left/right as well as back/front pointing directions, suggesting that they encoded the locations of the objects with respect to body coordinates. A confirmatory factor analysis indicated that this measure of perspective taking is dissociable from measures of spatial visualization ability, while the Guilford–Zimmerman test is not (see also Hegarty & Waller, 2004).

If the factor analytic tradition has garnered only weak evidence for spatial orientation because of ineffective assessments of this ability, it has all but neglected assessing spatial abilities in at least two other relevant domains: dynamic spatial abilities, which are involved in reasoning about moving stimuli, and large-scale environmental spatial abilities, which are involved in acquiring knowledge as one moves around a large-scale environment. Much of this neglect stems from the fact that these factors can be difficult to assess by means of paper-and-pencil tests. We will discuss environmental spatial abilities in some detail later. For now, we focus briefly on what is known about dynamic spatial abilities.

Dynamic spatial abilities are those that are required to reason about moving stimuli. The advent of computer testing has led to renewed interest in the ability to reason about motion and the ability to integrate spatial information over time. Even before computer testing, though, Seibert (1970) reported an ability to "bridge small gaps in time and to merge intellectually . . . time-segmented fragments" and dubbed it serial integration (SI). This factor was revealed in tests in which the examinee identified a stimulus, parts of which were successively revealed and concealed over time. Gibson (1947) conducted similar tests on his "successive perception" ability using motion pictures as stimuli. More recently, Jones, Dunlap, and Bilodeau (1986) showed that performance on computer video games required different abilities from those assessed by paper-and-pencil tests. Similar conclusions were made by Hunt, Pellegrino, Frick, Farr, and Alderton (1988), who reported evidence for an ability to reason about moving stimuli (see also Fischer, Hickey, Pellegrino, & Law, 1994; Law et al., 1993).

Hunt et al. gave participants several traditional paper-and-pencil tests of spatial ability, several computer-administered tests of spatial ability involving static stimuli, and several computer-administered tests involving dynamic stimuli. The static computerized tests required participants to make perceptual comparisons of shapes quickly, to perform mental rotation, to image pieces combining to form a larger object (i.e., a form-board test), to add detail to mental images, and to compare folded and unfolded versions of cubes (i.e., surface development). The dynamic tests measured people's ability to remember and extrapolate movement trajectories, judge absolute and relative velocities, and combine judgments of velocity and path extrapolation. In one task, for example, participants watched a target move horizontally across the computer screen. Participants pressed a button to initiate the vertical motion of another object on the screen. The task required participants to time their response in order to make the object intersect the moving target. Hunt et al. found that, in general, the static computer-administered tests correlated more highly with the paper-and-pencil tests than with the computer-administered dynamic tests. This pattern of results, as well as results from confirmatory factor analyses, led them to conclude that the ability to reason about dynamic spatial relations represented a distinct factor of human spatial aptitude.

Despite the appeal of this conclusion, the precise characterization of performance differences on dynamic versus static tests is still an open question. For example, Larson (1996) has questioned the degree to which performance differences on dynamic versus static tasks are due to stimulus motion alone, and pointed out that most of the dynamic tasks used by Hunt et al. require entirely different mental operations than the static tasks require. When these operations are matched between static and dynamic stimuli, the difference between the two may be greatly reduced. Larson (1996) gave participants dynamic and static versions of a mental rotations task and found that performance on the two tasks correlated extremely highly. He concluded that more evidence is required to establish conclusively that there is a distinct visuospatial factor associated with the ability to reason about moving stimuli. Clearly, however, evidence for a dynamic spatial ability cannot be derived from tasks that require the same mental processes as static tests. The fact that Hunt et al. designed their tasks to encompass a broad range of mental processes and still found that these tasks correlate relatively highly with each other provides fairly compelling evidence for a general ability to reason about motion.

COGNITIVE ANALYSES OF PERFORMANCE ON SPATIAL ABILITIES TESTS

The factor-analytic tradition has generally focused on the discovery and description of the factors that underlie spatial ability. Perhaps more informative for cognitive psychologists is an analysis of the perceptual and cognitive processing demands made by these factors. Performance on tests of spatial abilities depends on execution of basic cognitive processes such as encoding a visual stimulus, constructing a visual image, retaining an image in working memory, transforming an image, and comparing a visual stimulus to an image in working memory. In recent years, cognitive psychologists have attempted to understand spatial abilities at a deeper level by analyzing the basic cognitive processes involved in solving items from tests of spatial abilities and examining the extent to which individual differences in these basic processes can be related to theories of imagery and working memory. These studies often combine the use of experimental methods with examination of individual differences to study aptitude-treatment interactions, as advocated by Cronbach (1957). For example, one method is known as the "componential approach" to understanding cognitive abilities (Sternberg, 1977). In this approach, researchers first conduct task analyses to identify the basic cognitive processes involved in performing items from psychometric tests. They then measure performance on the psychometric tests and on laboratory tests designed to isolate the constituent cognitive processes. By analyzing errors and reaction times on the laboratory tasks, researchers examine the extent to which individual differences in performance on the psychometric tests can be accounted for by speed and accuracy of the basic cognitive processes.

The Contribution of Speed of Processing

Tests of spatial ability usually involve items that must be solved within a time limit. Thus, the speed of basic cognitive processes is clearly a possible source of individual differences in test performance. Mumaw, Pellegrino, Kail, and Carter (1984) used a componential approach to study speed of processing in mental rotation tests. Their task analysis revealed that mental rotation involves processes of (1) encoding the stimuli, (2) rotation of one of the stimuli, (3) comparison of the rotated image to the other stimulus, and (4) executing a response. The researchers then assessed the performance of individuals on the Primary Mental Abilities (PMA) Space test (Thurstone, 1958), which is a test of spatial relations (speeded rotation), and also measured their speed and accuracy in laboratory mental rotation tasks involving alphanumeric characters and characters from the PMA test. For the laboratory mental rotation tasks, they calculated the intercept and slopes of the functions relating reaction time to rotation angle, arguing that the intercept represented the time to encode and compare the stimuli and to execute a response, whereas the slopes represented the time to mentally rotate the figures. Performance on the PMA was correlated with the slopes of the reaction time functions for both alphanumeric and PMA characters. It was also correlated with the intercept for PMA characters (but not alphanumeric characters) and was not correlated with accuracy on the mental rotation trials. Mumaw et al. concluded that individual differences in tests of spatial relations are largely due to differences in speed of mental rotation and speed of encoding and comparing unfamiliar stimuli. Differences in rate of rotation between high- and low-spatial individuals have also been reported in several other studies (Just & Carpenter, 1985; Pellegrino & Kail, 1982).

Although speed of processing can account for individual differences in simple spatial-relations tests, this is not the case for more complex tests that load on the spatial visualizations factor. These tests (e.g., paper-folding and form-board tests) typically require a sequence of spatial transformations and have relatively liberal time limits. To examine the effects of task complexity, Lohman (1988) constructed a faceted spatial test in which subjects had to retain, synthesize, rotate, and compare polygons. Items differed in the number of these basic processes that were required. For example, the simplest items merely required participants to maintain the representation of a polygon and match it against another, whereas more complex items involved synthesizing the representations of three different polygons and rotating the resulting representation. By varying the number of basic operations required by each item, and measuring reaction time on these items, Lohman could estimate the time taken for each basic operation. An important result of this study was that time to execute the basic processes was a poor predictor of the complexity of items that an individual could solve. Mumaw and Pellegrino (1984) reached the same conclusion in a study in which they varied the complexity of items in a form-board test.

To examine the relative contributions of speed and complexity to performance on a complex mental rotation task (rotation of three-dimensional shapes of the type used by Shepard & Metzler, 1971) Lohman (1986) constructed a task in which he varied the amount of presentation time (exposure) allowed for individual test items and the angle of rotation. Lohman then computed accuracy at these different levels of exposure and rotation, creating speed-accuracy curves for high- and low-spatial individuals. These curves showed that accuracy reached an asymptote at a lower level for low-spatial participants. That is, for any level of complexity (say a rotation of 120 degrees) there was a maximum level of accuracy reached by participants that did not increase with more time on the task. This level of accuracy was lower for low-spatial participants than high-spatial participants and the difference was greater for trials that required more rotation. Thus, for imagined rotation of three-dimensional figures, high- and low-spatial individuals differ in the complexity of items that they can rotate, and not merely in the speed of rotation.

In conclusion, componential analyses of spatial tests have identified a "speed – power" continuum along which tests can be placed (Lohman, 1988). Items on simpler tests, such as those loading on the perceptual speed or spatial relations factor, can be easily solved by most people. A speed limit must be imposed in order to observe individual differences, and consequently, these differences reflect speed of processing (Pellegrino

& Kail, 1982). In contrast, items loading on the spatial visualization factor, including three-dimensional rotation items, paper-folding and form-board tests are more complex, and cannot be solved by all individuals, even when given a liberal time limit. Differences in performance in these tests are characterized by differences in "power," or the complexity of items that a given individual can solve. It is generally assumed that these tests measure the ability to construct a high-quality representation of a novel stimulus, and to maintain the quality of that representation after transformations, such as stimulus rotation and synthesis (Lohman, 1979; Just & Carpenter, 1985; Mumaw & Pellegrino, 1984; Pellegrino & Kail, 1982).

On the other hand, research on cognitive aging (Salthouse, 1996) has suggested how individual differences in speed of processing might lead to the pattern of performance observed on power tests. Salthouse has noted that "power" tests involve a series of transformations, and the products of these transformations must be in memory at the same time to accomplish the task. Differences in speed of processing might lead to failure to complete the task because the products of early processes are no longer available by the time that later processes are completed. Salthouse has referred to this as the "simultaneity mechanism." This mechanism explains how differences in speed of processing might lead to an inability to solve items from complex spatial tasks such as form board and paper folding, even with a liberal time limit. Research reviewed earlier indicates that speed of elementary processing is not always correlated with accuracy in power tests, so speed is probably not the only factor accounting for individual differences in performance of these tests. Nevertheless, the possible contribution of the simultaneity mechanism needs to be more carefully examined in the individual differences literature.

The Contribution of Strategies

Because spatial visualization tests include more complex transformations, they are amenable to a range of strategies, and strategy differences can be another source of individual differences in performance. We already observed this in the discussion of performance on the Guilford–Zimmerman spatial orientations test for which Barratt (1953) found that the majority of individuals reported a mental rotation strategy rather than a true spatial orientation strategy.

Just and Carpenter (1985) used eye-fixation and verbal protocols to analyze individual differences in the Cube Comparisons test, shown in Figure 4.1b. They identified three strategies used to perform these items: a mental-rotation strategy, a perspective-taking strategy in which the solver imagines moving with respect to a fixed cube, and a strategy of comparing orientation-free descriptions of the cubes (e.g., the relative orientations of the letters on the right and left cubes). Most participants used a mental rotation strategy, but an important difference between high- and low-spatial individuals was that in using this strategy, low-spatial individuals rotated around axes that were orthogonal to the faces of the cubes. In contrast, high-spatial individuals rotated around noncanonical axes. Therefore, a trial that might involve two or more orthogonal rotations for a low-spatial individual could be accomplished in a single rotation by a high-spatial participant.

In addition to differences among individuals in solution strategy, individuals do not always use the same strategy to solve all items in a spatial visualization test. Kyllonen, Lohman, and Woltz (1984) modeled reaction times on Lohman's (1979) faceted spatial task (described earlier) and found that the reaction times for many participants were best fit by models assuming that they shifted strategies depending on practice and complexity of the item presented. Furthermore, the optimal strategies for solving complex spatial items did not necessarily require imaging a sequence of transformations to a figure. Rather, individuals sometimes depended on analytic strategies. For example, in the paper-folding test, they often applied the analytical principle that if the paper is folded down the middle before the hole is punched, the pattern of holes should be symmetrical around that fold. Kyllonen, Lohman, and Snow (1984) trained people to solve items on the paper-folding test using both visualization and analytical strategies. The effectiveness of this training depended on a complex interaction between the spatial and verbal aptitudes of the learner and characteristics of the problems. For example, for high-spatial individuals, the effectiveness of training depended on the difficulty of the problems (analytic training was preferable for the most difficult items whereas visualization training was preferable for other items). In the case of low-spatial individuals, this effectiveness depended on their verbal abilities (analytic training was more effective for high-verbal individuals, visualization training was more effective for those with low-verbal ability). Thus, it appears that to some extent spatial visualization tests measure the ability to choose the optimal strategy for solving a particular item, given one's abilities. The fact that spatial visualization items are often best solved by analytical strategies has been cited as an explanation of the fact that spatial visualization tests often load on the G factor, measuring general intelligence (Lohman, 1988).

Spatial Abilities and Working Memory

A major conclusion of cognitive research on spatial abilities, especially spatial visualization ability, is that high- and low-spatial individuals differ in the quality of the spatial representations that they construct and their ability to maintain this quality after transforming the representations in different ways (Carpenter & Just, 1986; Just & Carpenter, 1985; Lohman, 1988; Mumaw & Pellegrino 1984). Several difficulties experienced by low-spatial individuals suggest that they are less able to maintain a complex image after transforming it. For example, in the Cube-Comparisons task, individuals often "lose" information about the letter on one side of a cube after that side has been rotated "out of view" in their mental image (Just & Carpenter, 1985; Carpenter & Just, 1986). Similarly, when rotating Shepard-Metzler figures, low-spatial individuals often have to make several rotation attempts, suggesting that they lose information about a figure while attempting to rotate it (Carpenter & Just, 1986; Lohman, 1988). Individual differences in spatial visualization have therefore been modeled as differences in working memory resources for storage and processing of spatial information (Carpenter, Just, Keller, Eddy, & Thulborn, 1999; Just & Carpenter, 1985). In this view, a high-spatial individual might have more resources for storing and processing spatial information than a low-spatial individual.

Current theories conceptualize working memory as a system specialized for maintenance of information in an activated state as necessary for task performance, and for executive control of attentional resources in order to maintain task goals, inhibit distracting information, and schedule different subprocesses required to accomplish a complex task (Baddeley, 1986; Engle, Kane, & Tuholski, 1999; Miyake & Shah, 1999). These theories make a distinction between "short-term memory" tasks (such as digit span) that merely require the maintenance of information, and "working memory" tasks (such as the Reading Span Test, Daneman & Carpenter, 1980) that require storage in the face of competing processing requirements (Cowan, 1995). Furthermore, there is considerable evidence that maintenance of verbal and spatial information is carried out by different systems, which Baddeley (1986) referred to as the phonological loop and the visual-spatial sketchpad, respectively.

A number of recent studies have addressed the extent to which individual differences in spatial ability can be explained by differences in the functioning of working memory. Shah and Miyake (1996) examined the degree to which individual differences in spatial visualization can be accounted for in terms of differences in a spatial working memory system that is distinct from a verbal working memory system. They developed two tests of spatial working memory. The first, called the Arrow Span test, was a spatial "short-term memory" task that requires individuals to maintain spatial information (the direction of arrows) in working memory. The second, called the Rotation-Arrow Span, was a spatial "working memory" task that requires the maintenance of this information in the face of interference from an unrelated task (mental rotation). Both tasks were highly correlated with tests of spatial visualization. In contrast, spatial visualization tests had low correlations with a test of verbal working memory (the reading span test) and a test of verbal short-term memory (digit span). These results add support to the view that tests of spatial visualization rely on a spatial working memory system that is dissociable from verbal working memory. This conclusion was supported by a later study (Hegarty, Shah, & Miyake, 2000) showing that a spatial concurrent task (spatial tapping) interferes with performance on spatial abilities tests while a verbal concurrent task (articulatory suppression) does not.

Another issue, addressed by Miyake, Rettinger, Friedman, Shah, and Hegarty (2001) is the extent to which different spatial abilities factors can be explained by differential involvement of the storage and executive control components of the working memory system. The three factors examined by Miyake et al. (2001) were spatial visualization (SV), spatial relations (SR), and perceptual speed (P). The authors reasoned that tasks loading on all three factors seem to require the temporary maintenance of visuospatial information and thus should all involve the visuospatial component of working memory. In contrast, the three factors seem to differ in terms of the demand they place on the executive component of working memory. Tests of spatial visualization appear to be the most demanding of the executive component, because they require a sequence of internal spatial transformations to be performed on the stimulus, involving the management of task-specific goals and subgoals as well as the scheduling and coordination of different cognitive processes (Lohman, 1996; Marshalek, Lohman, & Snow, 1983). The spatial relations factor should involve the executive to a lesser extent. Although tasks that load on this factor also necessitate mental transformations, only a single transformation is needed for each item, and this requires less executive control. Finally, the visuospatial perceptual speed factor should require the least executive involvement because tasks that load on this factor merely require the maintenance of a visuospatial representation of a simple figure in memory and do not require any spatial transformation or extensive goal management.

Miyake et al. (2001) measured performance on tests of the three spatial factors and tests of spatial short-term memory (storage of spatial information), spatial working memory (storage and processing of spatial information), and executive working memory. First, confirmatory factor analysis of the working memory tasks did not indicate a clear distinction between spatial short-term memory and spatial working memory, so these tests were combined into a single visuospatial working memory factor, which was separable from the executive WM factor. Second, Miyake et al. examined the relation between the executive and spatial components of working memory and the three spatial ability factors (i.e., spatial visualization, spatial relations, and perceptual speed) using structural equation modeling. This is a multivariate technique that allows one to measure the degree of relation between latent variables, (i.e., the underlying factors of factor analysis), rather than that between manifest variables (i.e., individual tasks). In this particular study, structural equation modeling was used as a version of multiple regression analysis in which the predictor and dependent variables are all latent (as opposed to manifest) variables. By comparing the standardized coefficients for the paths from the executive and visuospatial WM and STM variables to the spatial ability factors, we evaluated our hypothesis regarding the contributions of executive and visuospatial aspects of working memory to spatial abilities. This analysis indicated that as predicted, the contribution of the executive variable was the strongest for the spatial visualization factor (.91) and the weakest for the perceptual speed factor (.43). The contribution of the visuospatial working memory factor was important across all three spatial ability factors.

These results suggest a close link between individual differences in spatial working memory and those in spatial abilities. They also shed new light on why the spatial ability subfactors (especially spatial visualization and spatial relations) are not completely independent and are usually correlated with one another. These factors are similar in as much as they rely on both executive control mechanisms and spatial storage. On the other hand, they can show some separability because the relative importance of these two components of working memory is different. Thus, depending on the difficulty levels of the psychometric tests or the ability levels of the test takers, it might not be always possible to clearly distinguish these factors.

Spatial Abilities and Mental Imagery

Analyses of the cognitive components of spatial ability often refer to mental imagery processes such as maintenance and transformation of mental images. There is also some overlap between the tasks included in the mental imagery literature and those on spatial abilities tests, the most prominent example being mental rotation. However, the psychological investigations of mental imagery and spatial abilities have generally been quite separate, with studies of imagery tending to use experimental methods rather than measuring individual differences. Consequently, there have been only a few attempts to study the relation between individual differences in spatial test performance and individual differences in imagery ability.

Historically, imagery ability has referred to differences in self-reported vividness of imagery. This tradition goes back to Galton's (1883) classic study in which he asked people to imagine their breakfast table on a given day and to rate the vividness of this image. Based on this tradition, researchers developed self-report measures such as the Questionnaire upon Mental Imagery (QMI) developed by Betts (1909) and the Vividness of Visual Imagery Questionnaire (VVIQ) developed by Marks (1973). In these measures, people read descriptions of perceptual experiences (scenes, etc.), constructed images of these experiences, and then rated the vividness of their mental images. This type of imagery ability has been consistently found to be unrelated to measures of spatial ability (Poltrock & Agnoli, 1986).

However, research in cognitive neuroscience and working memory suggests that there are different dimensions of imagery ability, some of which may be more closely related to spatial abilities (e.g., Kosslyn, 1995). In this literature, a distinction has been made between primarily visual imagery and primarily spatial imagery. Visual imagery refers to a representation of the visual appearance of an object, such as its shape, color, or brightness. A typical visual imagery task might be to state the color of an object that has a characteristic color that is not verbally associated with the object (e.g., a football). Spatial imagery refers to a representation of the spatial relationships between parts of an object, the location of objects in space or their movement, and is not limited to the visual modality (i.e., one could have an auditory or haptic spatial image). A typical spatial imagery task is mental rotation. For example, Farah, Hammond, Levine, and Calvanio (1988) demonstrated that following brain lesions, patients can be extremely impaired in tasks that require visual aspects of imagery yet show normal performance in tests of spatial imagery. In the working-memory literature, dual-task studies have also shown that visual imagery tasks are impaired by concurrently viewing irrelevant pictures but not by arm movements, whereas spatial imagery tasks are impaired by arm movements but not by irrelevant pictures (Logie, 1995).

Another conception of individual differences in imagery is based on Kosslyn's computational model of mental imagery (Kosslyn, 1980; Kosslyn & Schwartz, 1977). According to this theory, imagery takes place in a "visual buffer" with limited resolution and extent. The theory postulates several processing modules that are responsible for creating images from various sources, maintaining these images in memory, and transforming the images in various ways. For example, one module called PICTURE creates a visual image of an object from a long-term memory representation. Another called REGENERATE is responsible for refreshing images so that they remain activated in memory. A third called TRANSLATE moves part of an image relative to other parts.

Kosslyn, Brunn, Cave, and Wallach (1984) examined individual differences in the Vividness of Visual Imagery Questionaire (VVIQ), a test of spatial visualization (form board), and ten imagery tasks related to Kosslyn's (1980) theory of imagery. The imagery tasks included measures of the resolution of the visual buffer, ability to generate images from verbal descriptions, reorganization of mental images and transformation processes such as mental rotation. Kosslyn et al. (1984) first performed a task analysis of each imagery task to determine which of the processing modules in his theory of mental imagery (PICTURE, REGENERATE, etc.) were used in performing the task, and computed a measure of similarity between pairs of tasks based on the number of these processing modules that they shared. They then examined the extent to which task similarity (based on shared processing modules) was related to the correlations between pairs of tasks. The correlations between the tasks showed a large range, from $-.44$ to $.79$, indicating that the different imagery tasks did not measure a single undifferentiated ability, but instead measured a number of different abilities. The strength of these correlations was highly related to the number of processing modules that they shared according to the task analysis. Cluster analysis of the data suggested that the tasks could be grouped according to a small number of processing modules. One cluster of tasks primarily measured the ability to transform and find specific patterns in images, another primarily involved the ability to maintain images over time, and a third cluster primarily involved measures of image resolution.

We now turn to the question of the relation between different dimensions of imagery and spatial abilities. Although this question was not directly addressed by Kosslyn et al. (1984), one relevant result from that study was that the Form-Board test (a measure of spatial visualization) was included in the first cluster of tasks, which measured the ability to transform and find specific patterns in images. A study by Poltrock and Brown (1984) assessed the relation between imagery tasks and spatial visualization more directly. They administered nine imagery tasks of the type studied by Kosslyn (1980) and six tests of spatial visualization ability. Again the correlations between the imagery tasks were not high, suggesting that they reflected several different abilities, in contrast with measures of spatial visualization, which defined a single factor. In a regression model, the imagery tasks that were most predictive of spatial visualization were measures of speed and accuracy of image rotation, integration of image parts, and adding detail to images. These are strikingly similar to the measures of elementary processes proposed in cognitive-components studies of spatial ability (summarized by Pellegrino & Kail, 1982), suggesting that ability to accomplish these imagery processes might be the basis of individual differences in spatial abilities. In contrast, a self-report measure of image generation ability had a negative regression coefficient, indicating that the unique variance captured by that variable (the variance that it did not share with tests of imagery performance) was in fact negatively related to spatial visualization ability.

In related research, Kozhevnikov and colleagues studied the "visualizer-verbalizer" cognitive style, a measure of the extent to which people tend to use visual imagery versus nonvisual methods in cognitive tasks such as problem solving. Kozhevnikov, Hegarty, and Mayer (2002) identified two types of visualizers, those with high-spatial ability and those with low-spatial ability. Kozhevnikov and Kosslyn (2000) found that high-spatial visualizers are good at spatial imagery tasks such as mental rotation, but poor at visual imagery tasks such as interpreting degraded pictures, whereas low-spatial visualizers show the opposite pattern.

In summary, research on the relation between imagery and spatial abilities has suggested that there may be several different aspects of imagery ability that are differentially related to what is measured by spatial abilities tests. Although the components of mental imagery ability have been characterized in different ways, there seems to be consensus that the ability to construct vivid mental images (typically measured by self-report scales) is distinct from the ability to transform and detect patterns in images (measured by tests of performance). Vividness of mental imagery appears to be either unrelated or negatively related to measures of spatial ability, whereas ability to transform images accurately is positively related to spatial ability. Other aspects of imagery ability that may or may not be distinct from these are the ability to maintain images over time and resolution of the imagery buffer.

Evaluation of Cognitive Analyses of Spatial Abilities

Cognitive psychologists have studied individual differences in spatial abilities within several different research traditions: research on process analysis of spatial ability test performance, research on working memory, and research on mental imagery. We have seen that each of these research traditions has provided important insights into the nature of human spatial abilities. However, perhaps more striking is the degree of overlap between the concepts discussed in the different traditions. For example, research in mental imagery has been concerned with the maintenance and regeneration of images over time, which is clearly a working memory function. In addition, some of the cognitive components of spatial ability performance identified in the spatial abilities literature are strikingly similar to the processing modules identified in Kosslyn's theory of mental imagery. Furthermore, research on strategic variation in performance of spatial visualization tasks is consistent with results in the working memory tradition suggesting that executive processes are implicated in complex spatial visualization tasks.

An examination of any introductory textbook in cognitive psychology reveals that spatial abilities, spatial working memory, and visual-spatial imagery are largely treated as separate topics. The research reviewed in this section suggests that we can make more rapid progress in understanding these constructs if we combine insights from the different research traditions. For example, Kosslyn's theory of mental imagery might be used to specify the storage and processing demands made by different strategies for accomplishing spatial abilities tests. This analysis might provide information about the extent to which spatial tasks and strategies depend on image resolution, image maintenance, speed and accuracy of image transformations, and the interactions between these different factors (e.g., a tradeoff between resolution and speed of processing a mental image). It might also suggest when a task or strategy requires imagery processes to be augmented by other cognitive processes, such as goal maintenance. In this way, we might continue to develop a general theory of how individual differences in visual imagery and other cognitive processes account for individual differences in spatial cognitive tasks.

ENVIRONMENTAL SPATIAL ABILITIES

Informal observations suggest that people differ enormously in their abilities to find their way to places, to navigate efficiently, and to form accurate mental representations of large-scale environments such as buildings, campuses, or cities. We use the term *environmental spatial abilities* to refer collectively to abilities that require integrating spatial information over time and across the viewpoint changes associated with self-motion. Unlike abilities involving stimuli that can be apprehended from a single viewpoint (e.g., stimuli on a paper-and-pencil test), environmental knowledge is acquired over time, as a person explores or navigates an environment. As noted earlier, psychometricians have historically not assessed these abilities and as a result, the factor structure of environmental spatial abilities remains largely unexplored (for more general overview of environmental spatial skills, see Montello, Chapter 7 on navigation, and Taylor, Chapter 8 on understanding maps).

In 1975, Siegel and White synthesized much of the then-existing research on large-scale spatial knowledge acquisition and developed what is currently the dominant model of environmental knowledge. Their model posits a "main sequence" of representational changes that occur with more experience in an environment, from knowledge of landmarks, to knowledge of routes, and ultimately to knowledge of configurations. When viewed as an inevitable developmental sequence, the Siegel and White model has garnered much criticism (Colle & Reid, 1998; Foley & Cohen, 1984; Hanley & Levine, 1983; McDonald & Pellegrino, 1993; Montello, 1993; Schmitz, 1997). Yet as a description of different types of mental representations of space it remains very influential. Although Siegel and White did not directly address individual differences among adults, it is possible that these variations among people's ability to represent or process environmental information might be characterized by abilities to adopt mental representations of space with more or less sophistication or flexibility.

It is somewhat surprising, then, that of the few multivariate studies of environmental cognition, none has conclusively upheld the distinctions made by Siegel and White. In 1986, Lorenz and Neisser reported tentative evidence for three dimensions of environmental spatial abilities that appeared to be related to the distinctions made by Siegel and White: memory for landmarks, memory for routes, and awareness of geographical directions. However, Lorenz was unable to replicate these findings in a subsequent larger multivaritate study (Lorenz, 1988). Another large study by Allen, Kirasic, Dobson, Long, and Beck (1996) showed that environmental abilities (those required to learn a small model of a town) were distinguished primarily by the degree of metric knowledge required to perform various tasks. Allen et al.'s factor analysis of environmental spatial abilities revealed a "topological knowledge" factor requiring only relational judgments such as proximity and connectedness. Measures loading on this factor included scene recognition, scene sequencing, map placement, intraroute distance error, and route reversal, which reflect landmark and route knowledge. This factor was distinct from the "Euclidean" factors that represented the ability to judge metric distances and directions, which reflect knowledge of configuration.

More recently, Hegarty, Montello, Richardson, and Ishikawa (2004) have shown that separate environmental spatial abilities may be associated more with the medium through which an environment is learned (e.g., real world, video, computer-simulated), or the sensory inputs to that learning, than with the characteristics or processing demands of the task used to measure spatial knowledge. This finding makes clear the need to operationalize the domain of behaviors one wishes to account for, a point echoed by Allen (1999). It also calls into question the degree to which conclusions about the factor structure of real-world environmental spatial abilities can be assessed with tasks involving models or simulations of the environment (see also McDonald & Pellegrino, 1993). The current status of research on environmental spatial ability is not unlike that of visuospatial abilities with researchers in the early 20th century – there is probably too little empirical evidence to support unequivocal statements about the factor structure of this ability.

Although the factor structure of environmental spatial abilities remains poorly understood, investigators are beginning to understand better the relationship between environmental spatial abilities and those abilities measured by paper-and-pencil psychometric tests. On one hand, the processing demands of paper-and-pencil tests are clearly relevant to those required for acquiring large-scale environmental knowledge. Acquiring knowledge of the environment typically requires a person to encode visual stimuli and to compare mental images with visual stimuli. Likely, it also requires transformations of spatial information in memory. However, large-scale spatial abilities require more than this. They require the ability to integrate spatial information over time and across many views while using several sensory modalities. Environmental spatial abilities may also be tied more closely to processes associated with long-term than with short-term memory (Chase & Chi, 1981). Whereas items on psychometric tests are typically performed in seconds and place their demands almost exclusively on the capacity or processing power of working memory, environmental knowledge is typically acquired over days, weeks, or years (Moeser, 1988). This suggests that storage and retrieval processes in long-term memory may be relevant to understanding environmental spatial ability. Because of these differences, one might expect psychometric measures of spatial ability to be only mildly predictive of complex environmental abilities like wayfinding, navigation, and the ability to form a configural representation.

Early studies that focused on this relationship, however, tended to report significant associations between visuospatial abilities (as measured by psychometric tests) and environmental abilities. In one study, Thorndyke and Goldin (1983) selected twelve people who performed well on tests of procedural and survey knowledge of Los Angeles and compared them to a similar group of twelve who performed poorly on tests of their environmental knowledge. Among a host of other differences, the "good cognitive mappers" scored significantly higher on tests of spatial visualization, spatial orientation, and visual memory than the "poor cognitive mappers." Importantly, scores of verbal abilities were not different between the two groups, indicating that the spatial elements of the tests were critical components of their ability to distinguish between good and poor cognitive mappers. Thorndyke and Goldin concluded that paper-and-pencil tests of spatial abilities can be used effectively for the recruitment and selection of personnel for which cognitive mapping skill is important. These results have led some to believe that there is a significant relationship between spatial ability and environmental knowledge.

However, more recent studies that examine this issue closely generally find tenuous links between large- and small-scale abilities. Table 4.2 summarizes many of the studies that have compared performance on psychometric tests of spatial ability and performance in a large-scale environment. With very few exceptions, these studies have generally found very little correlation between the two types of abilities. Correlations as high as .5 were obtained by Walsh et al. (1981); however, these authors do not specify how many correlations they computed in order to arrive at the two sizable correlations that they report. Rovine and Weisman (1989) also obtained notable correlations (ca. .4) between an embedded figures test and various measures of wayfinding behavior. For all other studies, the correlation is closer to .2. In one particularly impressive study, Allen et al. (1996) used structural equations modeling to show that "higher-level" cognitive abilities such as spatial-sequential memory and perspective-taking skill mediate the relationship between laboratory assessments of spatial ability and real-world assessments of environmental knowledge, but that there is nearly no direct correlation between spatial ability and environmental knowledge. The weight of the evidence presented in Table 4.2 leads one to question whether performance on large-scale and small-scale tasks are substantively based on any common spatial abilities.

TABLE 4.2. *Summary of correlational studies of the relationship between spatial abilities and environmental knowledge in adults.*

Investigators (year)	Number of participants	Correlations reported	Range of correlations	Median correlation
Walsh, Krauss, & Regnier (1981)	31	2	.47 to .57	.52
Bryant (1982)	85	2	.26 to .39	.33
Goldin & Thorndyke (1982)	94	18	?? to .3	Not reported
Meld (1985/1986)	61	8	.03 to .24	.09
Pearson & Ialongo (1986)	353	8	.08 to .30	.18
Lorenz (1988) – (Study 1)	56	24	.01 to .34	.09
Lorenz (1988) – (Study 2)	109	15	.00 to .44	.10
Sholl (1988) – (Study 1)	28	4	.07 to .19	.14
Rovine & Weisman (1989)	45	18	.01 to .43	.21
Allen et al. (1996) – (Original sample)	100	42	.02 to .37	.16
Allen et al. (1996) – (Validation sample)	103	42	.00 to .41	.19
Juan-Espinosa et al. (2000)	111	4	.20 to .30	.27
Waller (2000)	151	9	.01 to .34	.20
Kirasic (2001)	240	30	.05 to .39	.22
Hegarty et al. (submitted)	221	12	.11 to .41	.26

Recently, however, Hegarty et al. (2004) have shown a closer relationship between paper-and-pencil assessments of spatial ability and measures of environmental spatial knowledge than previous research might suggest. These investigators gave participants a large battery of tests, including paper-and-pencil spatial tests, tests of general intelligence, and self-reported sense of direction. Subsequently, they measured participants' ability to learn the spatial characteristics of buildings experienced either in the real world, from a video, or from a desktop computer simulation. Although zero-order correlations between small-scale and environmental spatial abilities were generally only around .25, Hegarty et al. used structural equations modeling to show that when other relevant abilities were controlled for, and when error variance associated with specific tests was partialed out, the unique contribution of small-scale spatial ability to predicting environmental spatial ability was actually quite high (the path coefficient was .50). Hegarty et al. suggested three reasons for the stronger-than-expected relationship between paper-and-pencil and environmental abilities: (1) their measures of environmental spatial abilities represented ability to acquire knowledge of previously unfamiliar environments; (2) their measures of environmental spatial abilities were focused primarily on assessing configural knowledge – the most sophisticated form of environmental knowledge; and (3) their measures of small-scale spatial ability were broader than those typically used by other researchers, including measures of spatial working memory. These results suggest that the relationship between psychometrically assessed spatial abilities and environmental spatial abilities may be relatively strong when people are required to form a sophisticated spatial representation in a relatively short period of time.

If, in general, paper-and-pencil assessments of visuospatial ability are not highly predictive of abilities to learn and represent large real-world spaces, then they may be more closely related to abilities in an increasingly relevant domain: learning the spatial characteristics of computer-simulated ("virtual") environments. Recent findings tend to support a conclusion that psychometrically assessed spatial abilities are more closely associated with wayfinding and navigating in virtual environments than with similar activities in real-world environments (Hegarty et al. 2004; Juan-Espinosa, Abad, Colom, & Fernandez-Truchaud, 2000; Moffat, Hampson, & Hatzipantelis, 1998; Waller, 1999; see Wickens, Vincow, & Yeh, Chapter 10, for more general discussion of navigation in virtual environments). These studies are summarized in Table 4.3. Although correlations between visuospatial abilities and spatial knowledge of virtual environments rarely exceed .4, they are typically slightly higher than analogous relationships with abilities and knowledge of real environments. In one study, for example,

TABLE 4.3. *Summary of correlational studies of the relationship between spatial abilities and spatial knowledge acquisition in virtual environments.*

Investigators (year)	Number of participants	Correlations reported	Range of correlations	Median abs. correlation
Bailey (1994)	64	14	.04 to .36	.14
Moffat et al. (1998)	74	6	.34 to .62	.49
Waller (1999) – Darken (1996) data set	10	520	.00 to .81	.24
Juan-Espinosa et al. (2000)	111	2	.26 to .31	.29
Waller (2000)	151	9	.19 to .40	.28
Waller et al. (2001)	24	4	.05 to .16	.09
Hegarty et al. (submitted)	228	12	.17 to .45	.29

Waller (2000) gave people several tests of psychometrically assessed spatial ability, and then examined their ability to form an accurate representation of both a large real-world (campus) environment, and a room-sized maze that they learned in a desktop virtual environment. Performance on the paper-and-pencil tests was not significantly related to people's ability to estimate distances and directions in the real world; however, it did predict people's ability to do so in the virtual environment. Waller concluded that for many people, computer-simulated environments – particularly those portrayed in desktop systems – are probably perceived more as a small-scale stimulus with which they interact than as a large-scale environment in which they navigate. This may be because desktop displays do not involve the users' whole body in the same way that environmental learning does. Recent studies have shown that performance on spatial tasks is less accurate when vestibular and kinesthetic information is not present (Chance, Gaunet, Beall, & Loomis, 1998; Klatzky, Loomis, Beall, Chance, & Golledge, 1998). In the absence of these cue sources, the users of desktop virtual environments may need to rely more on the processes associated with small-scale visuospatial abilities.

FUNCTIONS OF SPATIAL ABILITIES

It is undeniable that visuospatial abilities are required for many common activities. A traveler packing a suitcase for a trip may need to perform an informal version of a form board task. Telling a lost traveler which direction to turn may involve the ability to imagine alternative perspectives. In order to keep track of the locations of his teammates and opponents, a basketball player needs the ability to reason about movement in the visual field. While spatial abilities are clearly involved in such activities, and this conclusion has been supported by correlations of spatial abilities tests with self-reports of such activities (Groth-Marnat & Teal, 2000; Lunneborg & Lunneborg, 1984, 1986), the degree to which individual differences in visuospatial abilities can account for differences in such behaviors is in general not well known.

Spatial ability is also important in predicting success in various occupations. This is probably not surprising because, as mentioned earlier, many tests of spatial ability were developed primarily for the purpose of personnel selection. It has also been strongly linked to academic success in mathematics and science. For example sex differences in mathematics performance are often associated with corresponding differences in spatial abilities (see Halpern & Collaer, Chapter 5). However, what is the basis for these associations? Do these occupations and academic disciplines require spatial ability per se, or are the associations based on other factors common to spatial abilities and occupational or academic success? In this section we first review some of the findings pertaining to the functions of spatial ability in occupational and academic success, based on predictive validity studies. We then explore more precisely the relation between spatial ability and complex cognition, based on recent work in cognitive psychology. In this research, cognitive psychologists analyze complex cognitive skills that characterize occupational and academic success and examine the contributions of spatial abilities to these skills. We will describe such studies in the domains of surgery, mechanical reasoning, and mathematics performance.

Spatial Abilities and Occupational Success

For most of the 20th century, the United States Armed Services have selected and classified personnel based on batteries of standardized tests that include assessments of visuospatial ability. During the middle of the 20th century, spatial tests were found to be especially predictive of success in aviation and piloting (Humphreys & Lubinski, 1996). Although the military's use of spatial testing for predicting success in piloting diminished during the latter half of the last century, subsequent experimental work has confirmed the association between spatial ability and piloting skill (Dror, Kosslyn, & Waag, 1993; Gordon & Leighty, 1988). Dror et al. (1993), for example, showed that pilots were faster than nonpilots at both mental rotation and at making precise distance judgments.

Spatial ability has also been linked to success in technical training programs and to job performance in occupations such as engineering drawing, shop mechanics, auto mechanics, drafting, and designing (Ghiselli, 1973; Likert & Quasha, 1970; McGee, 1979a). Ghiselli (1973) summarized much of the research on the associations between spatial ability, job proficiency, and success in training programs for a number of these occupations and found that validity coefficients were between .18 and .28 for job performance and between .35 and .46 for success in training programs. Although these correlations would not usually be classified as high, Ghiselli argued that they suggest moderate to substantial predictive validity, given that the criterion measures in most cases were supervisors' ratings, which typically have low reliability (in the .6 to .8 range). Furthermore, tests with low validity coefficients can be useful in applied settings, especially when used to select relatively few valid cases from a large pool of candidates (Hunt, 1995; Taylor & Russell, 1939). Until relatively recently, spatial tests were regarded as valuable for selection and classification only for occupations below the professional level (Humphreys & Lubinski, 1996). However, it is clear that spatial abilities are required for many professional occupations. As early as 1957, the United States Employment Service listed 84 professional occupations for which spatial abilities in the top 10 percent of the working population were required. These occupations included various types of engineers, scientists, draftsmen, designers, and medical doctors.

For one kind of medical doctor, the surgeon, spatial ability may be increasingly important. Performance in surgery is strongly dependent on spatial skills. Anatomical environments can be extremely complex, with intricate 3-D relationships between deformable structures that can vary from patient to patient. A good surgeon must be able to visualize relationships among tissues and organs that cannot be seen, as well as to construct 3-D mental models from 2-D images (X-ray, CT, and MRI images). Several studies have shown moderate to high correlations between standardized tests of spatial ability and performance ratings on a variety of surgical tasks in open surgery (Gibbons, Gudas, & Gibbons, 1983; Gibbons, Baker, & Skinner, 1986; Murdoch, Bainbridge, Fisher, & Webster, 1994; Schueneman, Pickelman, Hesslein, & Freeark, 1984).

While the advent of minimally invasive surgical techniques has improved the quality of care for patients, it has also brought new challenges to the surgeon. Minimally invasive surgery is performed through cannulas, typically 5–10 mm in diameter, inserted through the skin. Long thin instruments are then inserted through the cannula. This cannula creates a fulcrum and reduces the degrees of freedom of movement. The surgeon performs the operation by watching a video image from an endoscope inserted through one of the cannulas. This surgical situation gives rise to several obvious spatial problems. First, the surgeon must adapt to the changing orientations between camera and instruments. Second, the camera must be placed and tissue exposed so that key structures are not obscured and so that instruments will be effective with their limited degrees of freedom. Third, complex surgical procedures are carried out by a team of surgeons, (i.e., a camera operator and assistant in addition to the primary surgeon), and the team must be able to communicate spatial plans that depend on shared spatial representations of anatomy.

Tendick et al. (2000) describe a program of research to develop cognitive models of surgical skills and train these skills using VE simulations. One representative surgical skill studied by Tendick and his colleagues is the use of an angled laparoscope, that is, a scope that has the objective lens angled with respect to its axis. Angled laparoscopes are used in many surgical procedures because they expand the range of viewing directions for the surgeon. However, they are difficult to use. In order to view a particular part of the anatomy, users must use spatial reasoning to place the laparoscope in the correct location. Tendick et al. developed a VE simulation of an angled laparoscope. Learning rates of novices using this simulation for the first time were correlated .39 to .58 with different measures of spatial abilities (Eyal & Tendick, 2001).

Spatial Abilities and Mechanical Reasoning

As we have seen, the earliest spatial abilities tests were developed to measure mechanical reasoning and to predict performance in professions such as machine design, assembly, and repair (Smith, 1964). For many of these activities, the ability to infer the behavior of a mechanical system from a representation of the shape and connectivity of the components is critical. For example, a machine assembler must configure components correctly so that they will move together to achieve the desired effect. Similarly, someone who is repairing a mechanical system might have to first envision how the components should move in order to locate a faulty component that is, for example, jamming the system.

Hegarty (1992) used the term mental animation to refer to the ability to infer the behavior of a mechanical system from its configuration. A task analysis of the most popular test of mechanical reasoning (Bennett, 1969) revealed that a large proportion of items on this test involve mental animation (Hegarty & Sims, 1994). For example, Figure 4.5 shows a typical item from a test of mechanical comprehension. The item shows the configuration of components in pulley system. The task is to infer which direction the lower pulley will turn, given that the rope is being pulled.

Hegarty and her colleagues have studied the cognitive processes involved in solving mental animation items. First, Hegarty (1992) showed that whenever possible, people decompose the depicted mechanical system into components and infer the motion of these components piecemeal, in the order of the causal chain of events in the system. This conclusion was supported by error data, reaction time data, and measurement of eye fixations. Further research indicated that mental animation is highly correlated with spatial visualization ability (Hegarty & Sims, 1994; Hegarty & Steinhoff, 1997; Hegarty & Kozhevnikov, 1999) but not with verbal ability, and that it relies on spatial rather than verbal working memory (Sims & Hegarty 1997). As predicted, differences in performance between high- and low-spatial individuals were greater for items in which more mechanical

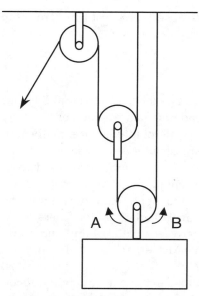

FIGURE 4.5. Item from a test of mental animation. Examinees are asked the following question: "When the rope is pulled, which direction (A or B) will the lower pulley turn?"

components had to be mentally animated. Low-spatial-individuals made more errors, but did not differ in their reaction times to solve problems.

Like tests of spatial visualization, mental animation appears to depend on both strategic differences among individuals and the ability to visualize complex spatial relationships. For example, one strategy that can be used on mental animation problems is to offload information onto the external display, for example by drawing an arrow on each mechanical component in a diagram as its direction of motion is inferred. This relieves people of the necessity of maintaining this information in working memory. Hegarty and Steinhoff (1997) found that when given the opportunity to make notes on diagrams, only some students did so. These students were able to use a strategy to compensate for limited spatial working memory resources and showed improved performance. Other students did not use this strategy and had poor performance. However, this strategy is not applicable to all mental animation problems because sometimes several components constrain each other's motions and therefore have to be mentally animated in parallel rather than serially (Hegarty & Kozhevnikov, 1999). Mental animation of problems that cannot be decomposed is particularly highly related to spatial ability, presumably because these problems are more dependent on spatial working memory resources.

Spatial Abilities and Mathematics

From almost the earliest days of intelligence testing, spatial ability has been considered to be closely related to academic achievement, particularly to success in mathematics. In addition to general intelligence, mathematical reasoning is typically thought to require abilities associated with visual imagery, as well as the ability to perceive, number, and space configurations, and to maintain these representations in memory (Hamley, 1935). Many investigators have assumed that spatial ability is more predictive of mathematical performance than is verbal ability. There is extensive research reporting correlations between spatial ability and mathematical performance (e.g., Battista, 1990; McGee, 1979b; Sherman, 1979; Smith, 1964). In a meta-analysis that included 75 studies, Friedman (1995) found that correlations between spatial and mathematical ability generally ranged between .3 and .45. Although moderate in size, these correlations suggest a substantial relationship between spatial and mathematical abilities. However, it is notable that Friedman's analyses showed a closer relationship between mathematical and verbal ability, with correlations in the .4 to .5 range.

Perhaps more interesting are findings that relate the specific processes required for success in mathematics with spatial ability. For example, recent research has studied the relation between people's cognitive style and how they represent problems in physics and mathematics. One important distinction from this literature is the visualizer-verbalizer cognitive style (Hegarty & Kozhevnikov, 1999; Kozhevnikov, Hegarty, & Mayer, 2002; Lean & Clements, 1981; Presmeg, 1992). This reflects the extent to which people use visual-spatial representations (images or diagrams) while solving problems that can be solved by either visual-spatial or more abstract analytical methods (Krutetskii, 1976). A puzzling result in the educational literature is that although spatial ability is correlated with performance in mathematics and physics, visualizers are not more successful at solving problems in these domains (Lean & Clements, 1981; Presmeg, 1992). Kozhevnikov, Hegarty, and Mayer (2002) showed that there are actually two types of visualizers; those with high-spatial ability and those with low-spatial ability. In one study conducted with elementary school students, high-spatial visualizers were more likely to construct diagrams or schematic spatial representations of the spatial relations between objects described in a problem, whereas low-spatial visualizers tended to construct pictorial images of the objects described in the problems (Hegarty & Kozhevnikov, 1999). For example, one problem described a man planting trees 5 meters apart on a path. Students were given the total length of the path and had to find the number of trees planted. High-spatial visualizers drew a diagram of the path, marking the position of trees on the path and the distance between them, whereas low-spatial visualizers reported a mental image of the man planting trees. Consequently, high-spatial visualizers were more successful in problem solving. In another study, Kozhevnikov, Hegarty, and Mayer (2002) presented college students with graphs of motion showing either the position, velocity, or acceleration of objects over time. Low-spatial visualizers tended to interpret the graphs as pictures, whereas high-spatial visualizers interpreted them correctly as abstract representations. These findings show that spatial ability is important for both constructing and comprehending abstract spatial representations in mathematical problem solving. Further discussion of the role of spatial thinking and mathematics can be found in Halpern and Collaer, Chapter 5.

CONCLUSIONS

The research that we have reviewed in this chapter has provided strong evidence that spatial ability is differentiated from general intelligence. It has also shown that spatial ability is not a single, undifferentiated construct, but instead is composed of several somewhat separate abilities, such as spatial visualization, flexibility of closure, spatial memory, and perceptual speed. These distinctions have evolved over decades of ongoing research. Unfortunately during much of the history of this research, the treatment of individual differences, the development of spatial abilities tests, and the design of factor analysis studies have not been systematic. Tests were developed primarily as predictors of real-world cognitive tasks and until recently, vitually all factor-analytic studies have been exploratory. As a result, research on the structure of spatial abilities has been largely atheoretical and has all but ignored individual differences in important aspects of spatial cognition, such as the processing of dynamic spatial displays and navigation in large-scale space. There is a need for a theoretical framework that outlines the space of different cognitive abilities associated with representing and processing spatial information. This framework would enable us to examine the status of current spatial abilities research, and the types of spatial abilities tests that need to be developed.

Research on the cognitive analysis of existing spatial tests can provide important input to this theoretical framework. Our review of this literature has shown that different spatial abilities may depend more or less on speed of processing, strategies, quality of spatial images, active maintenance of spatial information, and central executive processes. Cognitive research on spatial abilities has suffered from the fact that constructs such as working memory and imagery have typically been treated separately in the cognitive literature. Despite these constructs belonging to separate research traditions, we have seen that they are actually closely related to spatial processing. These constructs might be related in defining a theoretical framework for characterizing spatial abilities.

Most research on spatial ability to date has focused on tasks that require the mental manipulaton of small objects and that can be presented in paper-and-pencil tests. Research on large-scale spatial abilities is in its infancy. It is important that this relatively new research endeavor does not repeat the mistakes we have seen in the history of research on small-scale spatial abilities. For example, it is important to guide research by theory. This means considering up front what the dimensions are that define the space of large-scale spatial abilities and testing these models (see also Allen, 1999). Even more important is adherence to a set of principles and analytic methods that allow theories to be disconfirmed. Studies to date have suggested some of these dimensions, for example (1) a distinction between ability to learn a new environment versus wayfinding and navigation in a known environment, (2) a distinction between tasks that measure knowledge of landmarks versus routes or configurations, and (3) the nature of the processes and representations associated with different forms of learning.

Research on spatial ability has traditionally been very influenced by practical concerns, such as personnel selection, and there is a large body of literature showing strong relations between spatial abilities and various professions such as engineering, aircraft piloting, and surgery. Recent research has also begun to analyze complex tasks involved in these professions in terms of their demand on spatial skills. This is an important research direction that can elucidate how spatial information processing is involved in complex cognition and may be important in training complex spatial skills.

ACKNOWLEDGMENTS

This research was conducted while David Waller was at the University of California, Santa Barbara, and was supported by grants 9873432 and 9980122 from the National Science Foundation and N00014-96-10525 from the Office of Naval Research.

Suggestions for Further Readings

The following papers provide additional information on factor analytic studies of spatial ability.

This is an excellent historical introduction to spatial abilities testing and early factor analytic studies:

Smith, I. F. (1964). *Spatial ability: Its educational and social significance*. San Diego: Knapp.

Chapter 4: of this book presents a reanalysis of over 90 data sets that bear on the factor structure of spatial ability:

Carroll, J. (1993). *Human cognitive abilities: A survey of factor-analytical studies*. New York: Cambridge University Press.

This book also offers a thorough review of the factor analytic literature, and considers the environmental and biological determinants of individual differences in spatial abilities, with particular reference to those associated with sex differences:

McGee, M. G. (1979a). *Human spatial abilities: Sources of sex differences*. New York: Praeger.

The following papers offer excellent summaries of the literature on cognitive analyses of performance on spatial abilities tests. Lohman (1988) also summarizes some preliminary studies concerned with the training of spatial abilities:

Lohman, D. F. (1988). Spatial abilities as traits, processes, and knowledge. In R. J. Sternberg (Ed.), *Advances in the psychology of human intelligence* (pp. 181–248). Hillsdale, NJ: Erlbaum.

Pellegrino, J. W., & Kail, R. V. (1982). Process analyses of spatial aptitude. In R. J. Sternberg (Ed.), *Advances in the psychology of human intelligence* (Vol 1, pp. 311–365). Hillsdale, NJ: Erlbaum.

The following papers are good introductions to the study of environmental spatial cognition from individual differences and other perspectives:

Allen, G. L. (1999). Spatial abilities, cognitive maps and wayfinding: Bases for individual differences in spatial cognition and behavior. In R. G. Golledge (Ed.), *Wayfinding behavior: Cognitive mapping and other spatial processes* (pp. 46–80). Baltimore, MD: Johns Hopkins Press.

McDonald, T. P., & Pellegrino, J. W. (1993). Psychological perspectives on spatial cognition. In T. Garling & R. G. Golledge (Eds.), *Behavior and environment: Psychological and geographical approaches*. Amsterdam: Elsevier Science Publishers.

This short paper summarizes much of the literature on the relations of spatial abilities to performance in technical occupations and training programs:

Ghiselli, E. E. (1973). The validity of aptitude tests in personnel selection. *Personnel Psychology, 26*, 461–477.

References

Allen, G. L. (1999). Spatial abilities, cognitive maps and wayfinding: Bases for individual differences in spatial cognition and behavior. In R. G. Golledge (Ed.), *Wayfinding behavior: Cognitive mapping and other spatial processes* (pp. 46–80). Baltimore, MD: Johns Hopkins Press.

Allen, G. L., Kirasic, K., Dobson, S. H., Long, R. G., & Beck, S. (1996). Predicting environmental learning from spatial abilities: An indirect route. *Intelligence, 22*, 327–355.

Baddeley, A. D. (1986). *Working memory*. New York: Oxford University Press.

Bailey, J. H. (1994). Spatial knowledge acquisition in a virtual environment (Doctoral dissertation, University of Central Florida). *Dissertation Abstracts International, 55*(6-B), 2421.

Barratt, E. S. (1953). An analysis of verbal reports of solving spatial problems as an aid in defining spatial factors. *Journal of Psychology, 36*, 17–25.

Battista, M. T. (1990). Spatial visualization and gender differences in high school geometry. *Journal for Research in Mathematics Education, 21*, 47–60.

Bennett, C. K. (1969). *Bennett mechanical comprehension test*. San Antonio, TX: The Psychological Corporation.

Betts, G. H. (1909). *The distribution and functions of mental imagery*. New York: Columbia University Press.

Binet, A., & Simon, T. (1905). Methodes nouvelles put le diagnostic du niveau intellectuel des anormaux. *L'Annee' Psychologique, 11*, 191–244.

Borich, G. D., & Bauman, P. M. (1972). Convergent and discriminant validation of the French and Guilford–Zimmerman spatial orientation and spatial visualization factors. In *Proceedings of the Annual Convention of the American Psychological Association*. Vol. 7 (pt. 1) (pp. 9–10).

Bryant, K. J. (1982). Personality correlates of sense of direction and geographical orientation. *Journal of Personality and Social Psychology, 43*, 1318–1324.

Carpenter, P. A., & Just, M. A. (1986). Spatial ability: An information-processing approach to psychometrics. In R. J. Sternberg (Ed.), *Advances in the psychology of human intelligence* (Vol. 3, pp. 221–252). Hillsdale, NJ: Erlbaum.

Carpenter, P. A., Just, M. A., Keller, T. A., Eddy, W. F., & Thulborn, K. R. (1999). Graded functional activation in the visuospatial system with the amount of task demand. *Journal of Cognitive Neuroscience, 11*, 9–24.

Carroll, J. (1993). *Human cognitive abilities: A survey of factor-analytical studies*. New York: Cambridge University Press.

Chance, S. S., Gaunet, F., Beall, A. C., & Loomis, J. M. (1998). Locomotion mode affects the updating of objects encountered during travel: The contribution of vestibular and proprioceptive inputs to path integration. *Presence: Teleoperators and Virtual Environments, 7*(2), 168–17.

Chase, W. G., & Chi, M. T. H. (1981). Cognitive skill: Implications for spatial skill in large-scale environments. In J. H. Harvey (Ed.), *Cognition, social behavior, and the environment* (pp. 111–135). Hillsdale, NJ: Erlbaum.

Colle, H. A., & Reid, G. B. (1998). The room effect: Metric spatial knowledge of local and separated regions. *Presence: Teleoperators and Virtual Environments, 7*, 116–128.

Cowan, N. (1995). *Attention and memory: An integrated framework*. New York: Oxford University Press.

Cronbach, L. J. (1957). The two disciplines of scientific psychology. *American Psychologist, 12*, 671–684.

Daneman, M., & Carpenter, P. A. (1980). Individual differences in working memory and reading. *Journal of Verbal Learning and Verbal Behavior, 19*, 450–466.

Darken, R. P. (1996). Wayfinding in large-scale virtual worlds. Unpublished doctoral dissertation, George Washington University, Department of Electrical Engineering and Computer Science, Washington, DC.

Dror, I. E., Kosslyn, S. M., & Waag, W. L. (1993). Visual-spatial abilities of pilots. *Journal of Applied Psychology, 78*, 763–773.

Ekstrom, R. B., French, J. W., Harman, H. H., & Dermen, D. (1976). *Kit of Factor Referenced Cognitive Tests*. Princeton, NJ: Educational Testing Service.

El Koussy, A. A. H. (1935), An investigation into the factors involving the visual perception of space. *British Journal of Psychology, 20*, 92.

Engle, R. W., Kane, M. J., & Tuholski, S. W. (1999). Individual differences in working memory capacity and what they tell us about controlled attention, general fluid intelligence and functions of the prefrontal cortex. In A. Miyake & P. Shah (Eds.), *Models of working memory: Mechanisms of active maintenance and executive control* (pp. 102–134). New York: Cambridge University Press.

Eyal, R., & Tendick, F. (January, 2001). Spatial ability and learning the use of an angled laparoscope in a virtual environment. In J. D. Westwood et al., (Eds.), Medicine Meets Virtual Reality 2001, IOS Press, Amsterdam, pp. 146–152.

Eysenk, H. J. (1939). Review of "primary mental abilities" by L. L. Thurstone. *British Journal of Psychology, 9*, 270–275.

Farah, M. J., Hammond, K. M., Levine, D. N., & Calvanio, R. (1988). Visual and spatial memory: Dissociable systems of representation. *Cognitive Psychology, 20*, 439–462.

Fischer, S. C., Hickey, D. T., Pellegrino, J. W., & Law, D. J. (1994). Strategic processing in dynamic spatial reasoning tasks. *Learning and Individual Differences, 6*, 65–105.

Foley, J. E., & Cohen, A. J. (1984). Mental mapping of a megastructure. *Canadian Journal of Psychology, 38*, 440–453.

French, J. W. (1951). Description of aptitude and achievement tests in terms of rotated factors. *Psychometric Monograph, 5*.

Friedman, L. (1995). The space factor in mathematics: Gender differences. *Review of Educational Research, 65*, 22–50.

Galton, F. (1883). *Inquiries into human faculty and its development*. London: Macmillan.

Ghiselli, E. E. (1973). The validity of aptitude tests in personnel selection. *Personnel Psychology, 26*, 461–477.

Gibbons, R., Baker, R., & Skinner, D. (1986). Field articulation testing: A predictor of technical skills in surgical residents. *Journal of Surgical Research, 41*, 53–57.

Gibbons, R., Gudas, C., & Gibbons, S. (1983). A study of the relationship between flexibility of closure and surgical skill. *Journal of the American Podiatric Medical Association, 73*, 12–16.

Gibson, J. J. (1947). *Army air forces aviation psychology program, report no. 7: Motion picture testing and research*. Washington, DC: U.S. Government Printing Office.

Goldberg, J., & Meredith, W. (1975). A longitudinal study of spatial ability. *Behavior Genetics, 5*, 127–135.

Goldin, S. E., & Thorndyke, P. W. (1982). Simulating navigation for spatial knowledge acquisition. *Human Factors, 24*, 457–471.

Gordon, H. W., & Leighty, R. (1988). Importance of specialized cognitive function in the selection of military pilots. *Journal of Applied Psychology, 73*, 38–45.

Groth-Marnat, G., & Teal, M. (2000). Block design as a measure of everyday spatial ability: A study of ecological validity. *Perceptual and Motor Skills, 90*, 522–526.

Guilford, J. P., & Lacey, J. I. (1947). *Printed Classification Tests, A.A.F. Aviation Psychological Progress Research Report, No. 5*, Washington, DC: U.S. Government Printing Office.

Guilford, J. P., & Zimmerman, W. S. (1948). The Guilford-Zimmerman Aptitude Survey. *Journal of Applied Psychology, 32*, 24–34.

Gustafsson, J. E. (1984). A unifying model for the structure of intellectual abilities. *Intelligence, 8*, 179–203.

Hamley, H. R. (1935). *The testing of intelligence*. London: Evans.

Hanley, G. L., & Levine, M. (1983). Spatial problem solving: The integration of independently learned cognitive maps. *Memory and Cognition, 11*, 415–522.

Hegarty, M. (1992). Mental animation: Inferring motion from static diagrams of mechanical systems. *Journal of Experimental Psychology: Learning, Memory and Cognition, 18*, 1084–1102.

Hegarty, M. Montello, D. R., Richardson, A. E., Ishikawa T., & Lovelace, K. (2004). Spatial abilities at different scales: Individual differences in aptitude-test performance and Spatial-layout learning. Manuscript submitted for publication.

Hegarty M., & Kozhevnikov, M. (1999). Spatial abilities, working memory and mechanical reasoning. In J. Gero & B. Tversky (Eds.), *Visual and spatial reasoning in design*. Sydney, Australia: Key Centre of Design and Cognition.

Hegarty, M., Shah, P., & Miyake, A. (2000). Constraints on using the dual-task methodology to specify the degree of central executive involvement in cognitive tasks. *Memory and Cognition, 28*, 376–385.

Hegarty, M., & Sims, V. K. (1994). Individual differences in mental animation during mechanical reasoning. *Memory and Cognition, 22*, 411–430.

Hegarty, M., & Steinhoff, K. (1997). Individual differences in use of diagrams as external memory in mechanical reasoning. *Learning and Individual Differences, 9*, 19–42.

Hegarty, M., & Waller, D. (2004). A dissociation between mental Rotation and perspective-taking abilities. *Intelligence, 32*, 175–191.

Humphreys, L. G., & Lubinski, D. (1996). Assessing spatial visualization: An underappreciated ability for many school and work settings. In C. P. Benbow & D. Lubinski (Eds.), *Intellectual talent: Psychometric and social issues*, (pp. 116–140). Baltimore, MD: John Hopkins Press.

Hunt, E. (1995). *Will we be smart enough?* New York: Sage.

Hunt, E., Pellegrino, J. W., Frick, R. W., Farr, S. A., & Alderton, D. (1988). The ability to reason about movement in the visual field. *Intelligence, 12*, 77–100.

Jones, M. B., Dunlap, W. P., & Bilodeau, I. M. (1986). Comparison of video game and conventional test performance. *Simulation and Games, 17*, 435–446.

Juan-Espinosa, M., Abad, F. J., Colom, R., & Fernandez-Truchaud, M. (2000). Individual differences in large-spaces orientation: g and beyond? *Personality and Individual Differences, 29*, 85–98.

Just, M. A., & Carpenter, P. A. (1985). Cognitive coordinate systems: Accounts of mental rotation and individual differences in spatial ability. *Psychological Review, 92,* 137–172.

Kelly, T. L. (1928). *Crossroads in the mind of man.* Stanford: Stanford University Press.

Kirasic, K. C. (2001). Age differences in adults' spatial abilities, learning environmental layout, and wayfinding behavior. *Spatial Cognition and Computation, 2,* 117–134.

Klatzky, R. L., Loomis, J. M., Beall, A. C., Chance, S. S., & Golledge, R. G. (1998). Spatial updating of self-position and orientation during real, imagined, and virtual locomotion. *Psychological Science, 9,* 293–298.

Kosslyn, S. M. (1980). *Image and mind.* Cambridge, MA: Harvard University Press.

Kosslyn, S. M. (1995). Mental imagery. In S. M. Kosslyn & D. N. Osherson (Eds.), *Visual cognition: An invitation to cognitive science,* Vol. 2 (pp. 267–296), Cambridge, MA: MIT Press.

Kosslyn, S. M., Brunn, J., Cave, K. R., & Wallach, R. W. (1984). Individual differences in mental imagery ability: A computational analysis. In S. Pinker (Ed.), *Visual cognition* (pp. 195–244), Cambridge, MA: MIT Press.

Kosslyn, S. M., & Schwartz, S. P. (1977). A simulation of visual imagery, *Cognitive Science, 1,* 262–295.

El Koussy, A. A. H. (1935). An investigation in to the factors involving the visual perception of space. *British Journal of Psychology, 20,* 92.

Kozhevnikov, M., Hegarty, M. & Mayer (2002). Revising the visualizer/verbalizer dimension: Evidence for two types of visualizers. *Cognition and Instruction, 20,* 47–77.

Kozhevnikov, M., & Hegarty, M. (2001). A dissociation between object-manipulation spatial ability and spatial orientation abilities. *Memory and Cognition, 29,* 745–756.

Kozhevnikov, M., & Kosslyn, S. M. (2000). Revising cognitive style dimension: Evidence for two types of visualizers. *Abstracts of the Psychonomic Society, 5,* 242.

Krutetskii, V. A. (1976). *The psychology of mathematical abilities in schoolchildren.* Chicago: University of Chicago Press.

Kyllonen, P. C., Lohman, D. F., & Snow, R. E. (1984). Effects of aptitudes, strategy training and task facets on spatial task performance. *Journal of Educational Psychology, 74,* 130–145.

Kyllonen, P. C., Lohman, D. F., & Woltz, D. J. (1984). Componential modeling of alternative strategies for performing spatial tasks. *Journal of Educational Psychology, 6,* 1325–1345.

Larson, G. E. (1996). Mental rotation of static and dynamic figures. *Perception and Psychophysics, 58,* 153–159.

Law, D. J., Pellegrino, J. W., Mitchell, S. R., Fischer, S. C., McDonald, T. P., & Hunt, E. B. (1993). Perceptual and cognitive factors governing performance in comparative arrival-time judgments. *Journal of Experimental Psychology: Human Perception and Performance, 19,* 1183–1199.

Lean, C., & Clements, M. A. (1981). Spatial ability, visual imagery, and mathematical performance. *Educational Studies in Mathematics, 12,* 267–299.

Likert, R., & Quasha, W. H. (1970). *Revised Minnesota paper form board test*. New York: The Psychological Corporation.

Logie, R. H. (1995). *Visuospatial working memory*. Hove, UK: Erlbaum.

Lohman, D. F. (1979). Spatial ability: Review and re-analysis of the correlational literature. Tech. Rep. No. 8, Stanford University.

Lohman, D. F. (1986). The effect of speed-accuracy tradeoff on sex differences in mental rotation. *Perception and Psychophysics, 39*, 427–436.

Lohman, D. F. (1988). Spatial abilities as traits, processes, and knowledge. In R. J. Sternberg (Ed.), *Advances in the psychology of human intelligence* (pp. 181–248). Hillsdale, NJ: Erlbaum.

Lohman, D. F. (1996). Spatial ability and *g*. In I. Dennis & P. Tapsfield (Eds.), *Human abilities: Their nature and measurement* (pp. 97–116). Mahwah, NJ: Erlbaum.

Lorenz, C. A. (1988). The structure of the spatial domain: An analysis of individual differences. (Doctoral dissertation, Cornell University, 1988). *Dissertation Abstracts International, 49*(06 – B), 2400.

Lorenz, C. A., & Neisser, U. (1986). Ecological and psychometric dimensions of spatial ability Tech. Rep. No. 10, Emory Cognition Project, Emory University, Atlanta, GA.

Lunneborg, C. E., & Lunneborg, P. W. (1984). Contribution of sex-differentiated experiences to spatial and mechanical reasoning abilities. *Perceptual and Motor Skills, 59*, 107–113.

Lunneborg, C. E., & Lunneborg, P. W. (1986). Everyday spatial activities test for studying differential spatial experience and vocational behavior. *Journal of Vocational Behavior, 28*, 135–141.

Marks, D. F. (1973). Visual imagery differences and eye movements in the recall of pictures. *Perception and Psychophysics, 14*, 407–412.

Marshalek, B., Lohman, D. F., & Snow, R. E. (1983). The complexity continuum in the radex and hierarchical models of intelligence. *Intelligence, 7*, 107–127.

McDonald, T. P., & Pellegrino, J. W. (1993). Psychological perspectives on spatial cognition. In T. Garling & R. G. Golledge (Eds.), *Behavior and environment: Psychological and geographical approaches* (pp. 47–82). Amsterdam: Elsevier Science Publishers.

McGee, M. G. (1979a). *Human spatial abilities: Sources of sex differences*. New York: Praeger.

McGee, M. G. (1979b). Human spatial abilities: Psychometric studies and environmental, genetic, hormonal, and neurological influences. *Psychological Bulletin, 86*, 889–918.

Meld, A. (1985). Map- and route-learning strategies in spatial cognition: A comparison of survey and procedural knowledge. (Doctoral dissertation, University of Washington, 1986). *Dissertation Abstracts International, 46*(7-A), 1880.

Michael, W. B., Guilford, J. P., Fruchter, B., & Zimmerman, W. S. (1957). The description of spatial-visualization abilities. *Education and Psychological Measurement, 17*, 185–199.

Miyake, A., & Shah, P. (Eds.) (1999). *Models of working memory*. Cambridge: Cambridge University Press.

Miyake, A., Rettinger, D. A., Friedman, N. P., Shah, P., & Hegarty, M. (2001). Visuospatial working memory, executive functioning and spatial abilities. How are they related? *Journal of Experimental Psychology: General, 130,* 621–640.

Moeser, S. D. (1988). Cognitive mapping in a complex building. *Environment and Behavior, 20,* 21–49.

Moffat, S. D., Hampson, E., & Hatzipantelis, M. (1998). Navigation in a "virtual" maze: Sex differences and correlation with psychometric measures of spatial ability in humans. *Evolution and Human Behavior, 19,* 73–87.

Montello, D. R. (1993). Scale and multiple psychologies of space. In A. U. Frank & I. Campari (Eds.), *Spatial information theory: A theoretical basis for GIS* (pp. 312–321). Proceedings of COSIT '93. Berlin: Springer-Verlag.

Montello, D. R., Lovelace, K. L., Golledge, R. G., & Self, C. M. (1999). Sex-related differences and similarities in geographic and environmental spatial abilities. *Annals of the Association of American Geographers, 89,* 515–534.

Mumaw, R. J., & Pellegrino, J. W. (1984). Individual differences in complex spatial processing. *Journal of Educational Psychology, 76,* 920–939.

Mumaw, R. J., Pellegrino, J. W., Kail, R. V., & Carter, P. (1984). Different slopes for different folks: Process analysis of spatial aptitude. *Memory and Cognition, 12,* 515–521.

Murdoch, J. R., Bainbridge, L. C., Fisher, S. G., & Webster, M. H. C. (1994). Can a simple test of visual motor skill predict the performance of microsurgeons? *Journal of the Royal College of Surgeons, Edinburgh, 39,* 150–152.

Pearson, J. L., & Ialongo, N. S. (1986). The relationship between spatial ability and environmental knowledge. *Journal of Environmental Psychology, 6,* 299–304.

Pellegrino, J. W., & Kail, R. V. (1982). Process analyses of spatial aptitude. In R. J. Sternberg (Ed.), *Advances in the psychology of human intelligence* (Vol 1, pp. 311–365). Hillsdale, NJ: Erlbaum.

Poltrock, S. E., & Agnoli, F. (1986). Are spatial visualization ability and visual imagery ability equivalent? In R. J. Stenberg (Ed.), *Advances in the psychology of human intelligence* (pp. 255–296). Hillsdale, NJ: Erlbaum.

Poltrock, S. E., & Brown, P. (1984). Individual differences in visual imagery and spatial ability. *Intelligence, 8,* 93–138.

Presmeg, N. C. (1992). Prototypes, metaphors, metonymies, and imaginative rationality in high school mathematics. *Educational Studies in Mathematics, 23,* 595–610.

Robert, M., & Ecuyer-Dab, I. (November, 2000). *Do women excel in remembering the locations of both stationary and repositioned objects?* Poster session presented at the 41st annual meeting of the Psychonomics Society, New Orleans, LA.

Roff, M. (1952). A factorial study of tests in the perceptual area. *Psychometric Monograph No. 8.*

Rovine, M. J., & Weisman, G. D. (1989). Sketch-map variables as predictors of wayfinding performance. *Journal of Environmental Psychology, 9,* 217–232.

Salthouse, T. A. (1996). The processing-speed theory of adult age differences in cognition. *Psychological Review, 103,* 403–428.

Schmitz, S. (1997). Gender-related strategies in environmental development: Effects of anxiety on wayfinding in and representation of a three-dimensional maze. *Journal of Environmental Psychology, 17,* 215–228.

Schueneman, A., Pickelman, J., Hesslein, R., & Freeark, R. (1984). Neuropsychologic predictors of operative skill among general surgery residents. *Surgery, 96,* 288–295.

Seibert, W. F. (1970). The motion picture as a psychological testing medium: A look at cine-psychometrics. *Viewpoints, 46*(5), 91–102.

Shah, P., & Miyake, A. (1996). The separability of working memory resources for spatial thinking and language processing: An individual differences approach. *Journal of Experimental Psychology: General, 125,* 4–27.

Shepard, R. N., & Metzler, J. (1971). Mental rotation of three-dimensional objects. *Science, 171,* 701–703.

Sherman, J. (1979). Predicting mathematics performance in high school girls and boys. *Journal of Educational Psychology, 71,* 242–249.

Sholl, M. J. (1988). The relationship between sense of direction and mental geographic updating. *Intelligence, 12,* 299–314.

Siegel, A. W., & White, S. H. (1975). The development of spatial representations of large-scale spatial environments. In H. W. Reese (Ed.), *Advances in child development and behavior.* Vol. 10, pp. 9–55. New York: Academic Press.

Silverman, I., & Eals, M. (1992). Differences in spatial abilities: Evolutionary theory and data. In J. H. Barkow, L. Cosmides, & J. Tooby (Eds.), *The adapted mind: Evolutionary psychology and the generation of culture* (pp. 533–549). New York: Oxford University Press.

Sims, V. K., & Hegarty, M. (1997). Mental animation in the visual-spatial sketchpad: Evidence from dual-task studies. *Memory and Cognition, 25,* 321–332.

Smith, I. F. (1964). *Spatial ability: Its educational and social significance.* San Diego: Knapp.

Sternberg, R. J. (1977). *Intelligence, information processing and analogical reasoning.* Hillsdale, NJ: Erlbaum.

Sternberg, R. J. (1981). Nothing fails like success: The search for an intelligent paradigm for studying intelligence. *Journal of Educational Psychology, 73,* 142–155.

Taylor, H. C., & Russell, J. T. (1939). The relationship of validity coefficients to the practical effectiveness of tests in selection: Discussions and tables. *Journal of Applied Psychology, 23,* 565–578.

Tendick, F., Downes, M., Gogtekin, T., Cavusoglu, M. C., Feygin, D., Wu, X., Eyal, R., Hegarty, M., & Way, L. W. (2000). A virtual testbed for training laparoscopic surgical skills. *Presence, 9,* 236–255.

Thorndyke, P. W., & Goldin, S. E. (1983). Spatial learning and reasoning skill. In H. L. Pick & L. P. Acredolo (Eds.), *Spatial orientation: Theory, research, and application* (pp. 195–217). New York: Plenum.

Thurstone, L. L. (1938). *Primary mental abilities.* Chicago: University of Chicago Press.

Thurstone, L. L. (1950). *Some primary abilities in visual thinking* (Tech. Rep. No. 59). Chicago: University of Chicago, Psychometric Laboratory.

Thurstone, T. G. (1958). *Manual for the SRA primary mental abilities.* Chicago: Science Research Associates.

Vincent, W. J., & Allmandinger, M. F. (1971). Relationships among selected tests of spatial orientation ability. *Journal of Motor Behavior, 3*(3), 259–264.

Waller, D. (1999). An assessment of individual differences in spatial knowledge of real and virtual environments (Doctoral dissertation, University of Washington, 1999). *Dissertation Abstracts International, 60,* 1882B.

Waller, D. (2000). Individual differences in spatial learning from computer-simulated environments. *Journal of Experimental Psychology: Applied, 6,* 307–321.

Waller, D., Knapp, D., & Hunt, E. (2001). Spatial representations of virtual mazes: The role of visual fidelity and individual differences. *Human Factors, 43,* 147–158.

Walsh, D. A., Krauss, I. K., & Regnier, V. A. (1981). Spatial ability, environmental knowledge, and environmental use. In L. Liben, A. Patterson, & N. Newcombe (Eds.), *Spatial representation and behavior across the life span: Theory and application* (pp. 321–357). New York: Academic Press.

Zimmerman, W. S. (1954). Hypotheses concerning the nature of the spatial factors. *Educational and Psychological Measurement, 14,* 396–400.

5

Sex Differences in Visuospatial Abilities

More Than Meets the Eye

Diane F. Halpern and Marcia L. Collaer

ABSTRACT

Sex differences are found in a variety of tests of visuospatial abilities ranging from standardized paper-and-pencil or computerized tasks to tests of way-finding ability and geographical knowledge. The size of those differences and their direction vary (although most tasks favor males) depending on the type of skill being tested and the age and background of research participants. Sex differences may relate to differences in processing strategies, discrete underlying processes (e.g., working memory capacity), or expectations. Factors such as neural structure or function, sex hormone exposure, formal and informal learning experiences, and societal stereotypes appear to contribute jointly to these differences. Suggestions for further research include the design of better tests of visuospatial abilities, development of educational programs to enhance visuospatial performance, and a better understanding of the cognitive components that underlie visuospatial abilities, as well as the relationship of visuospatial abilities to mathematics and other cognitive skills.

INTRODUCTION

The ability to understand and mentally transform visuospatial information is central to the work of architects, chemists, dentists, designers, artists, engineers, decorators, mechanics, taxi drivers, and many other professions. All of these fields rely heavily on the ability to maintain a visual image while simultaneously deciding what it would look like if it were viewed from another perspective, moved to another location, or physically altered in some way. Like verbal and quantitative abilities, visuospatial abilities are needed for a broad range of cognitive tasks, but despite the importance of processing visuospatial information to many professions, surprisingly little is known about the cognitive components that comprise visuospatial abilities.

Visuospatial information processing involves an interplay of multiple cognitive processes, including visual and spatial sensation and perception, a limited capacity visuospatial working memory, and longer-term memories where visual and spatial information may be encoded in many ways. When we use the term "visuospatial," we are referring to information that is visual in nature (initiated by stimulation of the retina by light) and has spatial properties (involving the representation of space including relationships between objects within that space), and this information can either be sensed directly or generated from memory. For example, most people report that they can "see" the face of a loved one when his or her name is mentioned. The visual image of the face generated from memory corresponds in many ways to the direct visual perception, but is not identical. The imaged face may vary in details or clarity, depending on individual differences and the demands of a task. An imaged face, however, is spatial only in that the eyes are above the mouth and other within-face relations, but the entire face is not necessarily located within space, such as in front of a background object. Spatial representations can arise from stimulation of any sensory modality – audition or touch as well as vision. Images also can be "schematic," such as those times when a symbol is used as a place holder. For example, in understanding that "the boy is in front of the girl," the corresponding image does not have to depict any particular boy or girl, just provide some representation that maintains their spatial relationship. Thus, images can vary in the extent to which they convey spatial, visual, or schematic information.

A large body of research conducted over the last 25 years has revealed substantial sex differences for some, but not all, of the measures that reflect visuospatial information processing. Like verbal and quantitative abilities, the size and direction of the sex difference depends on the specific test or task that is used, or more precisely, the cognitive components that are needed to perform it. The many questions about sex differences in cognitive abilities are socially and politically sensitive because of the potential for misusing scientific results to fuel prejudice and discrimination. We note here that sex differences are found across a wide range of cognitive tasks, sometimes favoring females (e.g., there is a substantial female advantage in tests of writing and language fluency, many tests of learning and memory, and a smaller, but meaningful female advantage in mathematical computation) and sometimes favoring males (e.g., most of the visuospatial tasks considered in this chapter, as well as tests of quantitative problem solving) (Hyde, Fennema, & Lamon, 1990). Thus, cognitive sex differences vary in terms of which sex is superior and do not provide support for the idea that

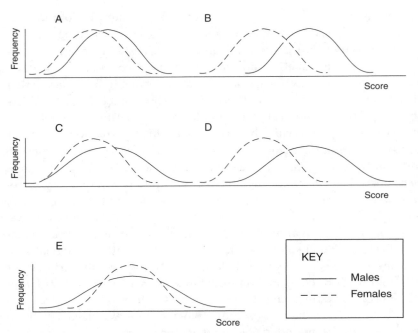

FIGURE 5.1. A graphic depiction of different ways in which two populations (females and males) can differ in the distribution of scores. In 5.1a and 5.1b, the male scores are, on average, higher than the female scores for these hypothetical data, showing differences in the amount by which the distributions overlap. 5.1c and 5.1d show the same mean differences, but the male distribution is drawn to reflect greater variability than the female distribution, with the result that there are more males in both tails of the distributions. Finally, 5.1e shows a situation in which both distributions have the same mean, but the males are more variable, so there are also more males in both tails of the distributions, even when the means are the same.

there is a "smarter" sex. (For a more detailed account of sex differences in cognitive abilities, including many areas that are not included in this chapter, see Halpern, 1997, 2000).

When a visuospatial task shows a sex difference favoring males, for example, it means that the average male outperforms the average female. In understanding data like these, it is important to consider the distance between the means for the distribution of female scores and the distribution of male scores. As shown in Figure 5.1a and 5.1b, when the means for the two distributions are close, we can expect many females to score above the "average" male; when the distributions are farther apart, we can expect fewer females to score above the average male.

These results do *not* support the idea that females cannot excel in visuospatial fields. Both males and females can show outstanding visuospatial skill, but more males than females achieve at high levels. In other words, a female with outstanding visuospatial ability will tend to find herself in the company of more males than females at her ability level. Throughout the chapter, bear in mind that the information pertains to group averages, and no one is average. In addition to the existence of mean differences, male and female performance can also differ in variance. Male scores tend to show greater variability (more "spread") than those of females (Hedges & Nowell, 1995), with a slightly higher percentage of males than females in both the upper and lower tails of the distribution. As a consequence, when combined with mean visuospatial differences favoring males, the tail ratio or ratio of males to females at extremely high ability levels, such as the top 1 to 5%, can strongly favor males, despite more modest differences in the middle of the distribution (Halpern, 2000). Figures 5.1c and 5.1d show how differences in the variance for males and females translate into more males at both the highest and lowest ends of the ability distribution. Finally, Figure 5.1e shows that even when the means for the female and male distributions are the same, males, being more variable, will have higher proportions in both the high and low ability extremes (i.e., the tails of the distribution).

Cognitive Components of Visuospatial Skills

In thinking about the component processes involved in visuospatial information processing, consider, for example, the many different combinations of retrieval from long-term memory, the generation, maintenance, transformation, and scanning of images, and the interplay among verbal, spatial, and pictorial cognitive codes that are needed to answer the following questions or perform the following tasks:

- Does the capital letter "f" have curved lines? The cognitive processes used in answering this question require the retrieval of information from long-term memory, the transformation of information about a letter from a verbal code to a spatial code, the generation of an image of the shape of the letter, a scan of the shape "looking for" curved lines, and then the execution of the appropriate response (e.g., answering "no").
- Does a novel, irregular shape that was just shown have five sides? The cognitive processes for this task would not require retrieval from

long-term memory, but would depend instead on the ability to maintain a shape in a visuospatial working memory long enough to scan its contours, count the sides, and execute a response.

- When will a ball that is seen moving across a computer screen "collide" with a line on the screen? In order to respond to a question like this one, judgments about the speed of the ball and its distance from the line need to be made and a response has to be timed to correspond to this calculation.

- What would a block look like when viewed from another angle? (See Hegarty & Waller, Figure 4.1B, this volume.) This is a perspective-taking task, which requires the ability to generate an image using knowledge about angles and "lines of sight" when objects are viewed from a different perspective.

- Draw a line to indicate where the water line will be in a tilted glass that is half full of water. This is the famous Water Level Task devised by the developmental psychologist Jean Piaget. In order to perform this task, knowledge that water remains horizontal regardless of the tilt of a glass must be retrieved from long-term memory, and then an approximately horizontal line must be drawn in the contours of the glass, ignoring the tilt cues that form the contours of the glass. An example of this task is shown in Figure 5.2.

- Find your way to a distant location using a map or find your way back from a distant place without a map. Way-finding tasks vary depending on whether they allow the use of a map, verbal directions, or memory of routes that were previously traversed.

- If a frog can climb 2 feet every hour, but slides back down 1 foot for every 2 feet it climbs, how long will it take the frog to climb out of a well that is 5 feet deep? This word problem requires the ability to derive a visuospatial representation from text, image the frog's progress up the well while converting progress to time. A detailed pictorial image of the frog is not useful, but a schematic representation is.

- After viewing an array of objects at various locations, other arrays are presented. Which objects were in the first array and where were they located? (See Hegarty & Waller, Figure 4.4, this volume.) This task requires visuospatial memory for objects and their locations. The nature of the memory system involved depends on the length of the interval between the two arrays – visuospatial working memory if the interval is less than approximately one minute; a longer-term memory for longer intervals.

FIGURE 5.2. An example of a Water Level Task. Participants are told that the glass containers are half filled with water and they are asked to draw a line indicating the top of the water level in the containers. As the containers are tilted to greater degrees, the line drawn increasingly departs from the horizontal. From D. F. Halpern, *Sex Differences in Cognitive Abilities*, 3rd ed. (2000). Mahwah, NJ: Erlbaum, p. 108. Reprinted with permission.

Paper-and-Pencil or Computerized Tasks That Show Sex Differences

What is surprising about this diverse set of visuospatial tasks is that when sex differences are found, they favor males. The only exception is the last example, which requires memory for objects and their location. There are, however, important differences among these tasks in the size of the differences between the sexes. Tasks that require disembedding figures that are "hidden" within the contours of a larger figure (Hidden Figures Test; see Hegarty & Waller, Chapter 4, Figure 4.3c) or simple transformation tasks that can be accomplished by keeping track of a distinctive feature, like imaging where a hole punch would be after a paper is folded a few times (Paper Folding Test; see Hegarty & Waller, Chapter 4, Figure 4.1a), show sex differences that are so small or fragile, they are essentially nonexistent, although when differences are found, they tend to favor males (Voyer, Voyer, & Bryden, 1995). Tasks like the Water Level Test and others that require ignoring nearby tilt cues show an effect size of approximately .5 standard deviations. (An effect size or d is the difference between group means expressed in terms of standard deviation [SD] units [d={male mean − female mean}/SD]. Thus, the mean for the male distribution is .5 standard deviation units above the mean for the female distribution.) The effect sizes for tasks that require the generation of an image vary depending on the complexity of the image to be generated and the nature of the task and range between .63 and .77 standard deviations (Loring-Meier & Halpern, 1999). Mental rotation tasks that require the maintenance of three-dimensional figural

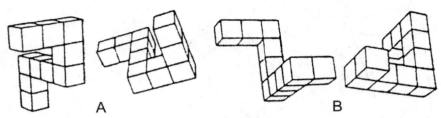

FIGURE 5.3. An example of a mental rotation task. Are the two figures the same except for their orientation? From D. F. Halpern, *Sex Differences in Cognitive Abilities*, 3rd ed. (2000). Mahwah, NJ: Erlbaum, p. 102. Reprinted with permission.

information in working memory while simultaneously transforming information show very large sex differences, somewhere between .9 to 1.0 standard deviations (Masters & Sanders, 1993; Nordvik & Amponsah, 1998). Differences that are probably as large as these or even larger are found in spatiotemporal tasks (judgments about moving objects), but there are not enough studies with spatiotemporal tasks to allow a reliable estimate of the effect size (Law, Pellegrino, & Hunt, 1993). An example of a mental rotation task is shown in Figure 5.3.

Way-Finding Tasks

A particularly meaningful visuospatial task is finding one's way through real space. A spate of studies conducted over the last few years offers insights into sex differences in how people find their way through complex environments (see Montello, Chapter 7, for a review of research on navigation and way-finding more generally, and Hegarty and Waller, Chapter 4, for additional discussion on the source of individual differences in way-finding). An important variable in way-finding tasks involves the use of maps (see Taylor, Chapter 8, for a review of research on the use of maps). In one study, participants were given a map that they were to use to give directions to a stranger (Brown, Lahar, & Mosley, 1998). Males were generally more accurate than females in the directions that they gave, and males were also more likely to use compass headings (North, South, East, West) when giving directions; females used landmarks more often when giving directions. This study, like many others, suggests that when females learn a route, either from a map or from direct experience, they tend to rely on landmarks to find their way, whereas, males are more likely to attend to and keep track of the compass direction in which they are traveling (Lawton, 1994). Similarly, when adults learned a route from a map, the males made fewer errors in getting to a destination, but the females had better recall for landmarks along the way (Galea & Kimura, 1993).

Psychological research in the 1950s was dominated by studies of the performance of rats in small mazes, and this continues to be an active area of research today. Earlier research with rats and other nonhuman animals reported large sex differences in maze performance (reviewed in Halpern, 1986). In what seems like a modern day variation on this earlier theme, researchers are now using virtual mazes to study human way-finding (Moffat, Hampson, & Hatzipantelis, 1998). Like the earlier work with nonhuman animals, there are very large sex differences favoring males in time needed to solve a maze (d = 1.57) and in the number of errors committed (d = 1.40). It is likely that these extremely large sex differences are related to a female preference for verbal strategies – a sequence of instructions (e.g., turn left at the light) – when navigating through real and "virtual" space, and a male preference for geometrical or Euclidian strategies involving compass directions and distances (e.g., head north for one mile, then turn west). Some mazes eliminate landmarks, consisting solely of walls, blind alleys, and choice points, so very large sex differences would be expected in maze-like situations where females cannot rely on their preferred navigational strategy. In many real-life circumstances, like navigating through a city, there is no obvious advantage to one strategy or the other because either a landmark strategy or Euclidian strategy will get people to their goal. However, if there is a detour or if there is a need to travel to new locations where the landmarks are unknown, then the Euclidian strategy will clearly be superior.

Some researchers have suggested that sex differences in way-finding relate to sex-related differences in brain activation. Functional magnetic resonance imaging (fMRI) was used to map neural activity as participants completed a three-dimensional virtual maze (Grön, Wunderlich, Spitzer, Tomczak, & Riepe, 2000). Males and females used many of the same brain areas during navigation (e.g., medial occipital gyri, parietal regions, and the "right hippocampus proper"), but also demonstrated some activational differences. Specifically, males showed enhanced activity of the left hippocampus (the hippocampus is an area involved in spatial mapping and the formation of certain types of memories), while females showed greater activity of the right parietal and prefrontal cortices (areas involved in visuospatial and attentional functions). These results may provide preliminary anatomical evidence for the neural underpinnings of the sex difference observed in human navigation.

The female superiority on tests of memory for objects and their locations (see Hegarty & Waller, Figure 4.4, this volume) can be understood as another example of the female preference to navigate using landmarks and, probably because females are attending more carefully to landmarks, they have better memory for them along a route. This conclusion is supported by a recent study in which a community sample of adults learned a walking route (Montello, Lovelace, Golledge, & Self, 1999). The researchers found that males made fewer "route-distance" errors and fewer directional errors; whereas, females made (marginally) fewer errors for landmarks. Of course, the fact that males and females tend to prefer and use different strategies in navigating through space does not mean that they cannot use a nonpreferred strategy. It is possible that females would benefit from training in how to use a geometrical or Euclidian strategy and understanding that it is a better strategy when detours are required or when landmarks are missing.

Long-Term Knowledge Acquired From Maps

A striking sex difference is found on tests of geography. Information about the locations of countries and other geographical markers is stored in long-term memory, with acquisition of the information almost always beginning with information in maps and other spatial arrays. Large sex differences in geographical knowledge could be due to many different factors, including difficulty for females in acquiring information from maps or globes, difficulty in storing or retrieving geographical information, use of inappropriate learning or recall strategies that affect accuracy and probability of recall, or just plain lack of interest in the subject matter. In fact, there is some evidence in support of all of these possibilities. In a review of large numbers of standardized tests, administered to (literally) millions of people, Willingham and Cole (1997) found a large sex difference favoring males on tests of what they labeled geopolitical topics – geography and political science. Females are less interested in these topics, so presumably are less motivated to learn geographical information and engage in fewer opportunities to learn about geography. Of course, the conclusions that females know less about geography than males because they are less interested in geography than males are derived from correlational data, so it remains possible that females are less interested in geography because they have less ability in these areas, rather than the reverse.

Dabbs, Chang, Strong, and Milun (1998) found that males not only had more knowledge about the world map, but males also used Euclidean coordinates more often than females when working with a map of the world. Thus, several studies suggest that there are important differences in the processes used by females and males when abstracting and using information from spatial arrays. Not surprisingly, females report more spatial anxiety with way-finding, which is a realistic emotion for many women who perform less well, on average, than men (Lawton, 1994).

Similarly, the finding that more females than males suffer from math anxiety has also been linked to sex differences in visuospatial skills (Tobias, 1993). One possible explanation for the male advantage on advanced tests of mathematics, such as the Scholastic Assessment Test in Mathematics (SAT) or the mathematics portion of the Graduate Record Examination, is that the sex differences found in these tests of mathematics are really reflections of the male advantage on many tests of visuospatial skills (Casey, Nuttall, Pezaris, & Benbow, 1995).

Visuospatial Skill and Mathematics

Certain visuospatial and mathematical abilities are related and visuospatial sex differences have been suggested to contribute to observed sex differences in mathematics performance (Hyde, Geiringer, & Yen, 1975; but also see Friedman, 1995). For example, Casey, Nuttall, Pezaris, and Benbow (1995) found that the sex difference on the Mathematics portion of the SAT-M was eliminated in several samples when the effects of mental rotation ability were statistically removed. This suggests that rotational skill may mediate certain high-level mathematical abilities, or at the least, that these two abilities tend to vary in unison. Linkage of mathematical and visuospatial skill has important consequences because high levels of both these skills are required for careers in fields such as the natural sciences and engineering (Hedges & Nowell, 1995; Lubinski & Benbow, 1992) in which females are typically underrepresented. However, the precise relationship between these variables is complex, varying with the specific visuospatial and mathematical measures considered (Tartre, 1990). In addition, these two variables appear to be more strongly linked in females than males (Friedman, 1995; Tartre, 1990), suggesting that females may be particularly hampered in mathematical domains if they have reduced visuospatial skill (additional discussion on the role of visuospatial thinking in mathematics and in other tasks can be found in Hegarty and Waller, Chapter 4).

Theoretical Perspectives

Sex differences in visuospatial tasks are among the largest effect sizes reported in the psychological literature. Cohen (1988) described effect sizes that are as large as those found in mental rotation tasks, for example, so large that statistical tests are not needed – they are obvious from a graph of the results. A central question for many psychologists and researchers in other fields is "How can we understand such large differences between females and males in their performance on tasks that require visuospatial processing?" To address possible answers to this question, we will discuss potential reasons for these differences, exploring how biological and experiential or social factors may contribute to them.

AN EVOLUTIONARY PERSPECTIVE

Proponents of evolutionary psychology, a currently popular branch of psychology that explains contemporary psychological phenomena by hypothesizing how the traits and behaviors that are common in modern societies could have been important in the evolution of the human species, have been particularly interested in studies of visuospatial cognition. Evolutionary psychologists posit that sex differences in visuospatial abilities reflect the division of labor in hunter-gatherer societies, where men traveled long distances to hunt animals and presumably developed a neuroarchitecture that supported spatial navigation. Women, on the other hand, gathered food closer to their home base and therefore developed brain structures and functions that supported memory for objects and their locations, because the location of the plants they gathered changed seasonally. The lone visuospatial task that shows an advantage for females is memory for objects and their locations, a finding that occurs consistently, even with different testing paradigms (Eals & Silverman, 1994; McBurney, Gaulin, Devineni, & Adams, 1997). In fact, females score higher than males on many measures that involve memory, including memory for personal information in general, or that includes location information (episodic memory), associative memory (recalling words in pairs), and a composite of memory tests, just to name a few examples (Herlitz, Nilsson, & Baeckman, 1997; Stumpf & Jackson, 1994).

Many cultures show similar patterns of visuospatial sex differences (Halpern, 2000; Nordvik & Amponsah, 1998), a finding that seems to support theories based on the principles of evolutionary psychology. Yet, other cross-cultural data appear to weaken evolutionary interpretations because the precise nature of sex differences varies by culture, even though the general pattern has been found in many countries around the world. For example, there are disproportionately more females among the highest achieving mathematicians in some Asian countries than in the West, and students in the United States routinely score well below those in many other industrialized countries in the world on international tests of mathematics, showing that culture is a critical factor in cognitive development (Stanley, 1990).

An inherent weakness in evolutionary explanations is that almost any set of findings can be interpreted as supporting the basic premises of evolutionary psychology because any post hoc explanation can be devised to show how an outcome could have been useful during evolution. James and Kimura (1997) modified research paradigms that showed that females had better memory for objects and their location to see if females would show better memory for location even when there were no objects at a location. An array of objects at various locations was shown for a brief period of time, after which a second array was shown, but this time, instead of adding new objects or taking objects away, some old objects were merely moved to new locations that were previously unoccupied. James and Kimura found that females and males performed equally well on this revision of the object array test. If females are not generally better at remembering objects and locations when the objects are moved to new locations, why should they show superior visuospatial ability in a similar task where objects are removed or added to an array? It is difficult to see how evolutionary theory could have predicted this result.

BIOLOGICAL FACTORS

This section explores how factors rooted in biology, specifically the "what-where" visual systems, hemispheric lateralization, and exposure to sex steroid hormones, may relate to visuospatial skill and to sex differences in those abilities. It is critical to realize that, although these factors are biological in nature, they are not fixed or immutable, but rather may be influenced by environmental and social inputs. For example, we consider hemispheric lateralization or specialization to be biological in nature because it represents a functional difference in the operation of the two cerebral

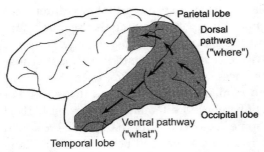

FIGURE 5.4. A schematic diagram of the pathways for the "what" (ventral) and "where" (dorsal) visual pathways in the human brain. Adapted from *Sensation and Perception*, 6th edition by Goldstein. © 2002. Reprinted with permission of Wadsworth, a division of Thomson Learning: www.thomsonrights.com. Fax 800 730 2215.

hemispheres; however, this characteristic is not necessarily predetermined, but could hypothetically be sensitive to a variety of influences, such as genetics, hormones, childhood play choices, and prior visuospatial experiences.

What–Where Systems

Neuroscientists who study the areas of the brain that are activated when people are engaged in different cognitive tasks have hypothesized that it is possible to separate "what," or object, information that would be encoded pictorially, from "where," or spatial location, information that would be encoded schematically (e.g., Brown & Kosslyn, 1995; Mishkin, Ungerleider, & Macko, 1983). A schematic diagram showing the visual pathways for "what" and "where" information is shown in Figure 5.4. This distinction is useful in thinking about sex differences in visuospatial abilities because, as this chapter details, it seems that females have superior object memory (memory for "what"), a type of memory that is especially well preserved with the use of verbal labels, and males have superior location and navigational skills (memory for the layout of space or the "where"), although the superior female performance on tests of object location seem to be an exception to this. When females need to navigate through space, they are more likely to use a relational scheme, where spatial information is encoded in the relations among objects, for example, "travel past the tall building on the left, make a right at the gas station." As noted, relational schemes utilize sequences of verbal instructions anchored by landmarks. With a relational scheme, it is possible to move successfully through space without ever considering compass headings or constructing a Euclidian map of the space. The possibility of visuospatial sex differences based on the neuroarchitecture of 'what–where' systems is speculative at this time, but it is an interesting question for future research. In addition, knowledge of what–where differences reinforces the idea that we need to consider how different styles of representation and strategy may influence visuospatial abilities, regardless of the fact that we are not sure whether representational and strategy differences are determined biologically or through experience.

Visuospatial Representation and Strategy

The relative independence of different types of visuospatial representation was confirmed in a study of successful and unsuccessful strategies in solving mathematical word problems (Hegarty & Kozhevnikov, 1999). The authors of this study differentiated between problem representations that were pictorial, largely "what"-based representations, encoding details of visual appearance, versus those that were schematic which largely encode spatial, or more "where"-based representations, and typically involve the use of a symbol in place of a detailed picture – for example, an image of an "X" to stand for a person or object named in the problem. Hegarty and Kozhevnikov found that the tendency to form pictorial images of the information in a mathematical word problem was negatively correlated with successful problem solving. By contrast, when an overall spatial schematic or map that maintained the geometric relationship among variables was formed, success at problem solving improved. This is an important finding because females perform poorer, on average, on advanced tests of mathematics, many of which involve abstract spatial information (Willingham & Cole, 1997). If the average poorer performance by females is caused, even in part, by the use of the same ineffective strategy that is depressing female scores on visuospatial tests, then performance in both areas might be improved by helping females use a more effective spatial/schematic strategy.

In fact, there is evidence that the poorer performance by females on both visuospatial tasks and advanced mathematical problems with a spatial component may have a common cause. Consider the well-replicated and large sex difference on mental rotation tasks. All subjects show an approximately linear increase in reaction times as a function of degree of rotation, when judging if a rotated figure is the same as a standard figure (Loring-Meier & Halpern, 1999). Reaction time also increases as a function of stimulus complexity, with more complex stimuli requiring longer reaction times than simpler ones (Loring-Meier & Halpern, 1999). In a study of the joint effects of complexity and angle of rotation, Bethell-Fox and Shepard (1988) found that, with repeated practice, the increase in reaction time that was attributable to stimulus complexity was substantially reduced, but only for subjects who used a holistic strategy to make their judgments. These subjects learned to perceive a complex stimulus as a single figure rather than a collection of contiguous parts. Subjects who used verbal strategies to perform the mental rotation task (e.g., matching a "pointy" feature on one side of the comparison figure to a similar feature on the standard), continued to respond more slowly to complex stimuli, even with repeated practice. Regardless of whether a holistic or verbal strategy was used, the relationship between reaction time and degree of rotation remained linear, showing that all subjects were performing some analogue to physical rotation when making their judgments. The conclusion from this study and others is that holistic/spatial strategies are more efficient in mental rotation tasks than analytic/verbal strategies. Numerous other studies have found that females are more likely to use analytic/verbal strategies than holistic strategies in mental rotation tasks, suggesting again that sex differences in the strategies used when processing visuospatial information are important in understanding why females usually perform more poorly than males on many visuospatial tasks (e.g., Clarkson-Smith & Halpern, 1983).

Hemispheric Lateralization of Function

Given established sex differences in visuospatial abilities, combined with an underlying assumption that cognitive skills derive from brain functioning, investigations of hemispheric lateralization are attempts to pinpoint one type of neural factor, which may contribute to these cognitive differences. For most individuals, the right and left cerebral hemispheres are asymmetrical (lateralized) for certain functions. Although there is overlap for some abilities, the left hemisphere is typically thought to be more specialized or dominant for verbal material and the right hemisphere for visuospatial or nonverbal material (Kolb & Wishaw, 1995). (The idea that some people are "right-brained" and others are "left-brained," although popular in the media, probably can be traced to this notion, but is a gross oversimplification and not justified by empirical findings.)

Hemispheric asymmetry, the degree to which a hemisphere specializes in a given function versus the degree to which it shares that function with the other hemisphere, may relate to the brain's ability to expertly carry out its cognitive functions. One prominent theory (Levy, 1971) proposes that differences in brain lateralization may contribute to sex differences in visuospatial and other cognitive abilities (see Voyer, 1996, for a description of alternatives to this). Levy's theory suggests that, when language is represented bilaterally, rather than being restricted to one (typically the left) hemisphere, certain language functions spill over into the more spatial right hemisphere and interfere with its optimal development or operation. Thus, the greater the degree of language lateralization, the greater is the resulting visuospatial skill. This theory can help to explain visuospatial sex differences only if females are more bilaterally organized (i.e., less lateralized) for language.

Considerable work and controversy has centered around the question of sex differences in lateralization. Measures of neural lateralization are not straightforward because they are not based on direct observations of neural functioning, but tend to be indirect estimates inferred from behavioral procedures (see Bryden, 1982, for a description of various methodologies). For example, dichotic listening procedures are often used to infer lateralization for auditory stimuli. In dichotic listening, two different language sounds (e.g., a consonant-vowel pair, such as "ba" vs. "da") are played simultaneously, one to each ear, and subjects report what they heard. Subjects tend to be more accurate in reporting verbal material played to the right ear than left ear. This right-ear advantage appears to result because, under the condition of simultaneous presentation conditions, material from each ear preferentially accesses the contralateral hemisphere. Thus, right-ear material presumably has direct access to the left, more verbal hemisphere, leading to more accurate perception and reporting (Bryden, 1982). Both sexes tend to show a right-ear advantage for auditory verbal material, but in studies where the sexes differ, males often show a greater degree of lateralization than females, suggesting that their language functions are more focally represented in the left hemisphere. In contrast, female language functions rely more heavily on contributions of both hemispheres (Hiscock, Inch, Jacek, Hiscock-Kalil, & Kalil, 1994).

To complicate this field of research, inconsistent and "difficult to interpret" results abound in the laterality literature, probably relating to methodological issues. Laterality findings can be influenced by age and handedness, by the strategy and overall accuracy of the subject, the allocation of attention, extraneous task demands, and procedural details, such as specific choice of stimuli and mode of presentation (Bryden, 1982). In addition, the size of the effect for sex in lateralization is extremely small (see Voyer, 1996) meaning that many studies, particularly with small samples, show no effect of sex. This combination of problems makes the field vulnerable to the "file drawer" problem (in which disconfirming studies fail to be published, giving the impression of an effect when one does not actually exist). Despite disagreements in the literature, however, reviews and meta-analyses suggest that the degree of asymmetry varies weakly by sex, with males generally showing slightly greater hemispheric specialization for visual as well as auditory information (Hiscock et al., 1994; Hiscock, Israelian, Inch, Jacek, & Hiscock-Kalil, 1995; McGlone, 1980; Voyer, 1996). This, in turn, suggests that the two hemispheres of females are more likely to share these specific duties. Lateralization differences, combined with the overall tendency for males to outperform females at visuospatial tasks, provides at least preliminary support for Levy's (1971) theory proposing that greater hemispheric specialization contributes to enhanced visuospatial abilities.

Sex Steroid Hormones

Gonadal hormones or sex steroids are hypothesized to influence a variety of cognitive processes, including visuospatial skill. These hormones are produced by the gonads, and to a lesser degree, the adrenals and include androgens, such as testosterone, estrogens, such as estradiol, and progestins, such as progesterone. All categories of hormones are produced in males and females; however, androgens predominate in males, and estrogens and progestins predominate in females. If hormones alter visuospatial ability, they could do so directly, by influencing the development or activity of specialized neural areas, or indirectly, through an effect on related cognitive skills or on life experiences. In humans, for example, hormones could alter visuospatial competency by predisposing a person to seek out (or avoid) certain activities, such as playing with toys that foster visuospatial development. In addition, given that nature and nurture are inseparable, hormones do not produce fixed, preprogrammed effects, but interact in a complex manner with environmental and experiential factors (Wallen, 1996).

Sex steroids are typically thought to produce two types of influences: Organizational effects, which are permanent and more likely to occur during early life (prenatal or early postnatal periods), and activational ones, which are transient and more likely to occur in adulthood. It is clear that sex steroids shape neural development in many species during prenatal or early postnatal life and alter a variety of reproductive and nonreproductive behaviors; the behavioral effects often are assumed to result from hormone action on the nervous system (Arnold & Gorski, 1984; Beatty, 1992). In addition, it should be noted that androgens, produced in large quantities in males, cause masculinization, but in many cases this masculinization occurs only after testosterone's conversion to other hormones, including estradiol, a potent estrogen. Thus, somewhat surprisingly, high levels of estradiol during early development cause masculinization (rather than feminization) of many characteristics (Arnold & Gorski, 1984).

We note here that brain architecture is also shaped by experience, so it cannot be assumed that differences in female and male brains result solely from hormonal action. The old nature-nurture dichotomy is surely wrong; nature and nurture are inseparable. A recent study that made front-page news in many major newspapers found that taxi cab drivers in London had enlarged portions of their right posterior hippocampus relative to a control group of adults whose employment required less use of spatial skills. The cab drivers showed a positive correlation between the size of the region of the hippocampus that is activated during recall of complex routes and the number of years they worked in this occupation (Maguire, Frackowiak, & Frith, 1997; Maguire et al., 2000). The finding that size of the hippocampus varied as a function of years spent driving taxis makes it likely that it was a lifetime of complex way-finding that caused the brain structure used in certain visuospatial tasks to increase in size, although other explanations also are possible.

Investigations of early hormone effects in humans can be difficult to interpret for several reasons. First, although hormone-behavior investigations are best conducted using measures that show clear sex differences, as these are most likely to be sensitive to hormone effects (Collaer & Hines, 1995), many studies fail to include these measures. Also, for ethical reasons, much of the research on potential hormonal influences in humans is nonexperimental or correlational because it can be unethical to manipulate hormones, particularly during early life. For these and other reasons, hormone manipulation studies in experimental animals (typically rodents) are often used to provide insight into the human situation. Both human and nonhuman studies will be discussed, beginning with studies in experimental animals. Research in experimental animals, although serving as the basis for much of what we know about humans, must be interpreted cautiously because they differ substantially from humans along biological, behavioral, and social dimensions. Confirmatory investigations in humans are required before generalizations can be made.

Rats do not complete paper-and-pencil visuospatial tasks. Instead, visuospatial research in rodents typically investigates spatial navigation, such as the ability to learn to solve a maze and remember the location of food rewards within an environment. When sex differences are found in maze tasks, males tend to be superior to females (Beatty, 1992), and relationships exist between maze performance, hormones, and brain characteristics, particularly within the hippocampus, an area mentioned earlier that plays a major role in spatial and learning functions (e.g., see Isgor & Sengelaub, 1998). The water maze and radial arm maze are two techniques used to study spatial sex differences in rodents. In both, an animal solves the maze in view of the surrounding room in order to reach a reward, and it uses certain aspects of the environment (e.g., room geometry, furniture, or decorations) to reach this desired endpoint. In a water maze, animals are placed into a large tank of opaque water from various starting points and must learn the location of a hidden platform that will allow them to escape the water. In a radial arm maze, animals travel out from a central platform along various arms or extensions to search for food, and depending on whether all arms of the maze are baited or only a fixed subset, this task can tap either visuospatial working memory alone[1] (remembering which of the arms have already been visited on that trial) or both working and longer term reference memory (learning and remembering the spatial position of the baited arms). Examples of the water maze and radial arm maze are shown in Figure 5.5.

Early-Life Hormone Exposure in Experimental Animals

In rats, early exposure to testosterone or its metabolites promotes better spatial skill and blocking testosterone can reverse the normal male advantage in maze performance, probably by altering aspects of brain development. Adult males with normal early hormone exposure and females treated prenatally with various masculinizing hormones (androgens or estradiol) performed faster at the end of water maze training than either normal females or males treated prenatally with an antiandrogen;

---

[1] There are at least two basic models of working memory (Becker & Morris, 1999). The type of working memory discussed in this section relates to memory for spatial information, is typically thought to involve hippocampal functioning, and appears to operate in both humans and experimental animals. This version of working memory, however, differs in fundamental ways from the type of working memory proposed by Baddeley (see Becker & Morris, 1999), which also operates in humans and is associated with the functioning of prefrontal cortex.

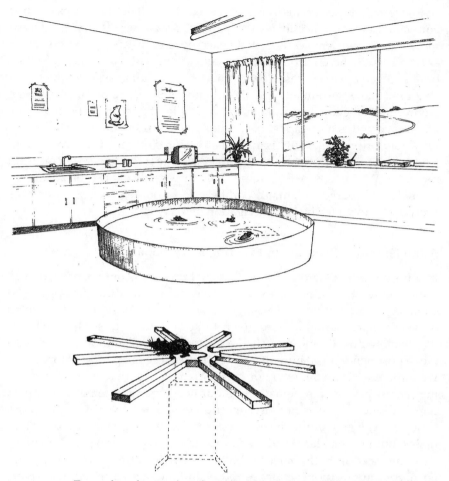

FIGURE 5.5. Examples of water (top figure) and radial arm (bottom) mazes. From: *Fundamentals of Human Neuropsychology* by Brian Kolb and Ian Q. Wishaw © 1980, 1985, 1990, 1996 by W.H. Freeman and Company. Used with permission.

additionally, regions of the hippocampus showed developmental differences as a function of sex and hormone treatment (Isgor & Sengelaub, 1998).

Similarly, in the radial maze, normal adult males as well as females treated neonatally with estradiol (and thus with "male-type" brains), made fewer errors during acquisition of a radial maze than did female controls or males that were deprived of sex steroids neonatally through castration (with "female-type" brains), although eventually all of the groups reached equivalent performance levels (Williams & Meck, 1991, p. 171). Interestingly, males and females encoded space differently and relied on different aspects of the environment for navigation. Animals with male-type brains solved the maze based on geometric or Euclidian aspects (the global shape) of the environment and those with female-type brains used both environmental geometry and landmarks. At least part of the normal male advantage in this maze appears to occur, not as a function of spatial memory superiority per se, but because of attentional or perceptual biases that lead males to encode space in a simpler way, making fewer demands on memory (Williams & Meck, 1991). This increased reliance on geometry by males compared to females parallels, to some degree, sex differences previously noted for human navigation or way-finding.

Adult Hormone Exposure in Experimental Animals

In adulthood, sex steroids often activate brain areas organized earlier in life. Long-term, continuous exposure to estradiol in adult rats appears to enhance certain aspects of learning and working memory. When *low* doses of steady-state estradiol were given to adult female rats whose ovaries had been removed (and thus, had a hormone status somewhat comparable to postmenopausal human females) for a sufficient period of time, they were more accurate in a version of the radial maze that measures working memory than were females without hormone replacement; however, reference memory was not affected (Luine, Richards, Wu, & Beck, 1998). Conversely, *high* chronic doses of estradiol enhanced spatial memory in males, but not females (Luine & Rodriguez, 1994). Thus, spatial memory was enhanced in both males and females by the administration of long-term, continuous (noncycling) estradiol, but the sexes differed in effective dose.

Briefer, cyclic exposure to estradiol, on the other hand, may impair spatial skill. Warren and Juraska (1997) studied water maze performance across the estrous cycle (similar to, but much shorter than, the human menstrual cycle) in female rats. They found that females in a high estradiol phase (proestrous) performed worse than those in a low estradiol phase (estrous) on the typical, spatial version of the Morris water maze, and they found opposing results (better performance by high-estradiol females) for a nonspatial or landmark-cued version of the water maze in which a ball was hung above the escape platform to mark its position. In contrast, estrous cycle fluctuations did not alter performance when rats were studied in a briefer water maze task, which included task pretraining (Berry, McMahan, & Gallagher, 1997). Thus, although brief, cyclic rises in estradiol may be detrimental to certain visuospatial abilities, the novelty or complexity of the spatial task may be important to consider.

Given evidence that estradiol affects visuospatial skill, might this reflect a direct action of the steroid on the brain? Estrogens are known to alter the density of dendritic spines and synaptic development in certain subregions of the brain, as well as influence the levels of certain neurotransmitters (see McEwen, Alves, Bulloch, & Weiland, 1998), all of which influence interneuronal communication, ultimately altering brain function. These synaptic and neurotransmitter alterations may influence spatial and other cognitive functions, but the exact nature of the brain-behavior relationship is not well understood.

In summary, steroids during early life or adulthood appear to influence certain aspects of visuospatial performance in rodents. However, the specific hormone (estradiol, androgen, or others, or their interactions), the size of the dose (high vs. low), timing (short vs. long term, or cyclic vs. continuous exposure) and the specific spatial ability under investigation (e.g., the degree to which the task indexes acquisition rate, spatial working memory or reference memory, or involves novelty) are all critical factors whose impact and interaction require further investigation.

Early-Life Hormone Exposure in Humans

Like other mammals, humans experience defined periods of hormone exposure. Testosterone is secreted phasically in males during periods of prenatal and early postnatal life, followed by a quiescent childhood period with very low production until puberty; estradiol secretion follows a similar pattern in females, although prenatal steroid secretion is generally lower for females than males (Bidlingmaier, Strom, Dorr, Eisenmenger, & Knorr, 1987; Hughes et al., 1999). If sex steroids organize the neurobehavioral development of humans, as they do other species, then people exposed to high, male-typical levels of androgens or estrogens during early development, regardless of genetic sex, would be predicted to show enhanced male-typical characteristics (including better performance on the subset of male-superior visuospatial tasks), and low levels of sex steroids would be associated with enhanced female-typical characteristics. Although hormone manipulations cannot be conducted experimentally in young humans, several endocrinological disorders provide relevant "experiments of nature" (see Collaer & Hines, 1995, for a review). Two methodological issues make interpretations of these studies challenging: First, the studies often use very small samples due to the rarity of the disorders; and second, their dependent measures often fail to show sex differences in the normal population and thus, may not be optimal for detecting potential hormone effects. Although a variety of endocrine populations exist, each making its own contributions to understanding, and posing its own set of interpretational challenges, this chapter will focus on just two: patients with congenital adrenal hyperplasia (CAH) and idiopathic hypogonadotropic hypogonadism (IHH), disorders marked by elevated versus deficient androgens, respectively.

Patients with CAH experience excessive androgens prenatally (and until postnatal treatment begins), but are raised in accord with their genetic sex. Studies of girls with CAH, in particular, are relevant to the question of whether sex steroids masculinize human cognition because their androgen levels are dramatically higher than those of normal females, whereas CAH males experience more typical male levels. If early androgens masculinize visuospatial abilities, CAH girls should show skills more like those of typical males.

In one study, a small sample of CAH girls showed enhanced and CAH boys showed reduced visuospatial ability (vs. control siblings) using a single visuospatial measure (the children's version of the Spatial Relations Test of the Primary Mental Abilities battery; Hampson, Rovet, & Altmann, 1998). In another study, CAH females outperformed control females on 3 of 5 visuospatial measures (Card Rotations, Mental Rotations, and Hidden Patterns, with a trend toward higher performance on Paper Folding, and no difference on Paper Form Board test, which generally shows a negligible sex difference), with no performance alterations in CAH males (Resnick, Berenbaum, Gottesman, & Bouchard, 1986). Interestingly, CAH girls also make toy choices more like those of normal boys (Berenbaum & Hines, 1992), raising the potential question of whether hormones shape abilities directly or by modifying life experiences (e.g., play activities) that may mediate cognitive development. However, not all studies have found visuospatial enhancements in CAH females, although these studies tended to use tasks with small or negligible sex differences (Baker & Ehrhardt, 1974) or patients with very mild CAH (McGuire, Ryan, & Omenn, 1975).

Males with IHH have deficient androgens because they lack normal brain regulation of testicular secretions. Although, in some cases, hypogonadism can occur later in life, individuals with congenital forms of IHH, who probably experience androgen deficits beginning at birth (Hier &

Crowley, 1982), are most interesting for organizational investigations and would be predicted to show reduced performance on male-superior visuospatial measures. Some studies have found impaired visuospatial abilities (Buchsbaum & Henkin, 1980; Hier & Crowley, 1982), or impaired visuospatial (as well as verbal) memory (Cappa et al., 1988). However, visuospatial impairments were not found in males who acquired hypogonadism after puberty (Hier & Crowley, 1982) or in a larger sample of males who acquired hypogonadism at a variety of ages (Alexander et al., 1998). Thus, visuospatial impairments may be more likely in adult males if their androgen deficiency began during early, as opposed to postpubertal or mixed, periods of life.

Adult Hormone Exposure in Humans

Menstrual Cycle. Do the "raging" hormones of the menstrual cycle influence visuospatial skill? In one series of studies, performance on sexually-differentiated visuospatial tasks was better during menstruation, when sex steroids were low, than during the preovulatory or midluteal phases when hormones (estrogen or estrogen plus progesterone) were higher (Kimura & Hampson, 1994). These effects were generally reversed (better performance when hormones were high) for tasks at which females typically excel (e.g., manual dexterity, verbal fluency). In other studies, women were worse at two- and three-dimensional mental rotation when hormones were high (e.g., midluteal phase), compared to lower hormone (e.g., menstrual) phases (McCormick & Teillon, 2001; Moody, 1997). The findings of visuospatial enhancement in humans during low phases of cycling hormones agree with rodent studies showing elevated maze performance during estrous (a low estradiol phase). Conversely, another study, using carefully selected sexually-differentiated tests and verifying ovulation, found no relationship to menstrual phase (Epting & Overman, 1998), and the authors speculate that either no menstrual effect exists (e.g., there is a file drawer problem) or that the young age of their participants (with perhaps less dramatic hormone changes) or the small number of participants may have obscured effects.

Normal Circulating Testosterone. Endogenous testosterone in normal young adults is suggested to show either a positive or curvilinear relationship with visuospatial abilities (i.e., increasing abilities with higher testosterone, or increasing ability to some optimal testosterone level but lower ability for higher testosterone, respectively). Visuospatial skill showed a curvilinear relationship with testosterone in right-handed males and females; this association was positive in females and negative in males (Gouchie & Kimura, 1991; Moffat & Hampson, 1996), suggesting an optimal level somewhere between the average female and male levels. Conversely, others have found positive relationships in normal males, such that higher testosterone males performed better (Christiansen & Knussmann, 1987; Errico, Parsons, Kling, & King, 1992), although these studies included some measures with very small (or unclear) sex differences. Other studies found no association between endogenous testosterone and sexually-differentiated visuospatial ability in normal young males (Alexander et al., 1998; Kampen & Sherwin, 1996).

This mixed picture of results suggests testosterone may play a role in visuospatial cognition, but it may be via estradiol, as some researchers have suggested (e.g., Nyborg, 1983). There are multiple hormones that vary cyclically and little is known about their joint effect on cognition. A clearer understanding will probably show that hormonal effects depend on many variables including the joint effects of many hormones, the age of the participant, and the test being used to assess visuospatial cognition.

Hormone Replacement. Steroids administered exogenously, as in the case of hormone treatment to remedy disease or normal aging, do not precisely mimic the magnitude and duration of endogenous sex steroids, and thus may produce different effects. Direct testosterone administration did not alter the visuospatial skills of young males with deficient adult sex steroids (in some cases, combined with early deficiency; Alexander et al., 1998; Hier & Crowley, 1982). However, testosterone administration to older males to combat age-related declines has produced more noticeable effects, including improved visuospatial (and verbal) memory (Cherrier, 1999), spatial working memory (Janowsky, Chavez, & Orwoll, 2000), and Block Design scores (Janowsky, Oviatt, & Orwoll, 1994).

An active area of research concerns estrogen replacement therapy in older adults, with most of the research conducted with women. The average expected life span has increased by several decades over the last 100 years in the United States and many industrialized countries. The result is the first large generation of old people, a segment of the population whose proportion is expected to rise even more dramatically over the next 50 years. Women are now living approximately one third of their lives after the onset of menopause, when estrogen output is severely curtailed. The number of age-associated dementias is also rising very rapidly, so the possibility that cognitive decline can be slowed or stopped in old age by administering hormones is being pursued with urgency.

There is also substantial evidence that visuospatial cognition declines at a faster rate than verbal cognition as people age. In a series of studies, Jenkins, Myerson, Joerding, and Hale (2000) found that older adults were slower than younger adults on all cognitive tasks, but the age-associated reduction in processing speed was greater for visuospatial tasks than verbal tasks. Older adults also exhibited smaller memory spans than younger adults, but the difference was greater for visuospatial memory than verbal memory. Finally, older adults had greater difficulty learning novel information than younger adults, but again this difference was greater when the novel information was visuospatial in nature than when it was verbal. Although these investigators did not analyze their data for sex differences, these results have obvious implications for understanding sex differences in cognitive abilities because visuospatial skills declined more quickly than verbal skills and females receive lower average scores than males on visuospatial tests across all ages. It is only a short leap to ask if any portion of the age-related loss in visuospatial abilities can be attributed to the precipitous decreases in steroidal hormones that occur at menopause for women and the more gradual decline that occurs for aging men.

The number of studies on the cognitive effects of estrogen replacement therapy is large and seems to be increasing at an exponential rate as researchers and practitioners race to find ways to preserve cognitive functioning before the great population bulge known as the post–World War II baby boom reaches old age. Not surprisingly, the results of these studies are not completely consistent, especially in light of the fact that different tests of cognitive abilities are used in different studies, dose size and method of administration vary within and across studies, the effects of unopposed estrogen and estrogen with progesterone are often mixed together, length of time on estrogen and baseline cognitive statuses vary, and ages often differ, just to name a few of the reasons why there are no clear-cut answers to the deceptively simple question of whether estrogen replacement therapy can maintain normal cognitive functions or delay or avoid cognitive decline in older adults. Few of the studies have focused exclusively on visuospatial abilities, although many have included some tests of these abilities in a larger battery of cognitive tests.

Evidence for a beneficial effect of estrogen in old age is clearest for verbal memory. Although there are many studies that have failed to find beneficial effects for hormone replacement in elderly women (e.g., Polo-Kantola, Portin, Polo, Helenius, Irjala, & Erkkola, 1998), there are a substantial number of studies that suggest that exogenous estrogen (pill, patch, cream, or other form) causes positive effects on the cognition of healthy older women and possibly women in early stages of Alzheimer's disease (e.g., Henderson, Paganini-Hill, Emanuel, Dunn, & Buckwalter, 1994; Wong, Liu, Fuh, Wang, Hsu, Wang, & Sheng, 1999). This conclusion is in accord with Sherwin's (1999) meta-analytic review of 16 prospective, placebo-controlled studies in humans, where she concludes that "Estrogen specifically maintains verbal memory in women and may prevent or forestall the deterioration in short- and long-term memory that occurs with normal aging. There is also evidence that estrogen decreases the incidence of Alzheimer disease or retards its onset or both" (p. 315). The results of these studies and others provide a strong causal link between levels of adult hormones and sex-typical patterns of cognitive performance.

Extrapolating from the findings that visuospatial abilities are depressed during high estrogen periods of the menstrual cycle for young women, it could be predicted that visuospatial skills would be depressed for older women who follow a regime of estrogen replacement. However, predictions about the effects of estrogen on visuospatial cognition in older adults need to consider the many different types of hormone-related outcomes that are reported in the research literature. For example, if hormone administration consists of continuous low doses instead of mimicking the cyclical pattern of low and high hormone concentrations that occurs normally in younger women, visuospatial abilities might be improved, as found in experimental work with rodents by Luine, Richards, Wu, and Beck (1998). There are not enough high quality studies (using double-blind, placebo-controlled, cross-over research designs) on the effect of exogenous hormones to determine how visuospatial abilities are affected. Given the rapid rate of research in the area of hormone replacement in older adults, we expect that investigators will be providing data on this question over the next several years.

LEARNING AND EXPERIENTIAL FACTORS

Like all cognitive skills, visuospatial information processing improves with instruction and practice. Watson and Kimura (1991) reported large sex differences, favoring males, in the ability to hit a moving or stationary target with a ball or other projectile (e.g., a dart thrown at a dartboard). However, boys are more likely to play sports that require aiming and, on average, receive more practice and training at these visual-motor tasks (National Collegiate Athletic Association, n.d.). Anticipating this criticism,

Watson and Kimura state that they controlled for experience with the task, often by selecting participants who report the same amount of experience in aiming at a target or some similar experiential variable. The underlying assumption is that both males and females improve at aiming tasks and other visuospatial tasks with practice, but males maintain their advantage, even when matched to females on experience.

As expected, numerous investigators have found an association between participation in visuospatial activities and visuospatial abilities (Newcombe, Bandura, & Taylor, 1983). However, the association between participating in visuospatial activities and ability level is correlational and does not permit a causal inference. It is possible that boys engage more in throwing sports because they are better at spatial skills or for a reason that is unrelated to cognition, such as boys' tendency to have greater upper body strength than girls. The same criticism can be made about a study that found that girls who play with traditional boys' toys tend to perform better on spatial tasks (Serbin & Sprafkin, 1986). It is possible that these girls are able to develop their spatial abilities by playing with traditional boys' toys, but it is also possible that the girls who chose boys' toys are the ones with better spatial abilities. These studies do not explain why boys engage in spatial activities and sports more often than girls do, illustrating the intractable problem of determining cause and effect from naturalistic studies. In a meta-analytic review of the literature that linked spatial activity participation with spatial ability, Baenninger and Newcombe (1989) concluded that there is a weak relationship and that the magnitude of the effect is the same for females as for males. Thus, according to these authors, both sexes benefit about equally from participation in spatial activities.

Training Effects

Everyone can improve their performance on visuospatial tasks with appropriate instruction. The key question in understanding sex differences in visuospatial skills is whether females benefit more from instruction than males do, either because they are generally lacking the same level of experience that males have or they are using inefficient strategies. The answer to this question depends on which visuospatial skill is being assessed and the nature of the training/educational experience. In a study of the effects of specific training on the Water Level Test, Vasta and Gaze (1996) found that training improved the performance of both females and males, so that by the end of their training, females performed at the same level as males when they had to draw the water level line in pictures of tilted bottles, but females continued to perform less well on a question that specifically asked about their understanding that water remains horizontal in tilted bottles.

Similarly, Ackerman, Kanfer, and Goff (1995) found that both males and females improved in a visuospatial-motor task (a plane simulator) with practice, but female performance matched male performance at the completion of the training only for some of the visuospatial subtasks assessed in their study. It is possible that a longer study would have yielded similar levels of proficiency for males and females for all of the visuospatial subtasks. Future research could employ a long-term training program to determine if female and male performance will converge for all visuospatial tasks, to identify the types of tasks that are most resistant to equal performance by females and males with prolonged practice and training, and to determine whether training on one specific type of task generalizes to other visuospatial skills.

It is comforting to note that adults who work at occupations that frequently involve partially filled liquid containers (e.g., bartenders) are more likely to perform accurately on the Water Level Test than those from other occupations (e.g., clerks; Vasta, Rosenberg, Knott, & Gaze, 1997). Earlier research suggested that experience with partially filled containers of liquids was detrimental to performance on the Water Level Test, but the earlier studies confounded age of participants with occupation to arrive at a faulty conclusion (Hecht & Proffitt, 1995).

Performance Factors

Many researchers have considered the possibility that females are equal to males in their ability to process visuospatial information, but some variable, unrelated to ability, is causing females to perform poorly. These are sometimes called "performance factors." One possibility is that females are more concerned with accuracy than males, so they are more cautious when taking visuospatial tests. According to this line of reasoning, female cautiousness results in slower responding, hence making it appear that females are less able. In an experiment designed to investigate this possibility, Goldstein, Haldane, and Mitchell (1990) used a paper-and-pencil measure of mental rotation and found the usual results that males completed more problems correctly in the allotted time limit. However, they went a step further and computed the number of the items correctly answered by females and males as a proportion of the number of items attempted. The proportional measure reduced the sex difference considerably because it did not penalize the females for completing fewer items. Conversely, in a study of visuospatial line judgment, males strongly and significantly outperformed females on the timed task (d = 0.85), as well as in proportional accuracy (d = 0.76; Collaer & Nelson, 2002). Some psychologists are highly critical of "corrections" for speed. They argue that it is the same as saying that someone who gets 9 problems correct out of 10 that were attempted in some time limit is performing at a higher level than someone who gets 89 correct in the same time limit, but attempted 100. Furthermore, when other researchers administered visuospatial tests, but eliminated all time limits, the size of the between-sex difference was unchanged (Masters, 1998; Resnick, 1993). Thus, it is unlikely that the large and consistent sex differences found across many decades of research are caused by performance factors that are unrelated to ability.

The Accuracy and Threat of Stereotypes

An exciting area of recent research has shown that stereotypes can affect performance on tests of cognitive abilities, without the conscious awareness of the person taking the test. In a clever set of experiments, Banaji and Hardin (1996) investigated reaction times to information that either was or was not consistent with a commonly held stereotype, such as the stereotype that females are poor in math or cannot be good engineers. They found that participants were slower in responding to simple questions about math and women that were inconsistent with stereotypes (being good at math is inconsistent with stereotypes about women) than to other types of questions that were either consistent with the stereotype or unrelated to a stereotype (e.g., being good at literature studies is consistent with stereotypes about women). Because differences in reaction times are typically in fractions of a second, the participants were unaware that they were taking longer to respond when the information they were processing was inconsistent with a stereotype. It did not matter if the participant endorsed the stereotype. In fact, most people report that they do not believe in stereotypes. Banaji and Hardin (1996) concluded that stereotypes operate like any other type of categorical information. Categories are fundamental to the way humans think, and categories or stereotypes operate automatically and without conscious awareness.

Steele (1997, 1998) and his colleagues have shown that negative stereotypes can decrease performance on cognitive tests when group membership is made salient (e.g., participants are asked to indicate their sex), the stereotype about one's group is negative (e.g., females are less able to use a map or spatial array than males), performance on the test is important to the individual (e.g., scores will be used to determine college admissions), and the test is difficult. According to Steele, the individual who is taking the test does not need to believe that the stereotype is true; all that is needed for stereotype threat to operate is a fear that one's performance will provide support for the negative stereotype. These are important studies, but this area of research, known as stereotype threat, is still new and there have been some statistically powerful studies in ecologically valid settings that have failed to find an effect for negative stereotypes. Stricker (1998) investigated the effect of stereotype threat by asking test-takers to indicate their sex and ethnicity either before taking a standardized mathematics test or after taking the same test. The underlying idea was that evidence of stereotype threat would be found if the female students who indicated their sex before taking the test had significantly lower scores than the female students who indicated their sex after taking the test. Stricker found no differences between the students who completed the demographic information before or after the test. A second study with another high-stakes test also failed to show a difference for students who completed the demographic information either before or after taking the test (Stricker & Ward, 1998).

It is difficult to make predictions about the role of stereotype threat on tests of visuospatial abilities because there are few high-stakes tests of these abilities (tests used to make important decisions about admissions to college or receipt of a scholarship), and the extent to which visuospatial abilities are part of our stereotypes about females and males is unknown. In one recent study with Turkish medical school students, Halpern and Tan (2001) found that, for these students, stereotypes about males and females did not include beliefs about differences in visuospatial abilities, but these same students showed the classic pattern of sex differences in a mental rotation test. Thus, it is not possible to make any strong conclusions about the way stereotype threat affects performance on tests of visuospatial abilities until additional studies are published and psychologists have a better understanding of the way in which stereotype threat operates.

Are Sex Differences in Visuospatial Abilities Disappearing?

There has been much interest in the possibility that sex differences in cognitive abilities, in general, and in visuospatial abilities, more specifically, are decreasing. This is an important question because one of the main tenets of the Women's Movement that began in the 1960s was that many, perhaps most or all, human sex differences not directly related to reproduction are created by sociocultural forces, with girls and boys receiving different messages about sex-role appropriate behaviors and different rewards. If the Women's Movement had its promised effect of providing equivalent learning opportunities for girls and boys, and if cognitive sex differences are primarily social in origin, then these sex differences should diminish and eventually disappear with changes toward a more sex-neutral society. Although some psychologists have reached this conclusion for certain cognitive tasks (Feingold, 1988; Hyde, Fennema, & Lamon, 1990), recent and more comprehensive meta-analyses do not support the notion that visuospatial sex differences are disappearing, especially for tests requiring mental rotation. Effect sizes are larger when the mental rotation task requires rotation in the depth plane (three dimensions) than when it requires rotation only in the picture plane (two dimensions). In Masters and Sanders's (1993) meta-analysis of mental rotation studies that required rotation in 3-D space, they concluded that sex differences have remained at approximately 0.9 standard deviation units for almost two decades. Voyer, Voyer, and Bryden's (1995) meta-analysis also supported the idea that sex differences are not generally declining: They aggregated effect sizes from studies that involved rotation in both the picture plane and studies that involved rotation in the depth plane and estimated the effect size in mental rotation studies at approximately .56 standard deviation units, but when rotation in depth was examined separately, the effect size was estimated at .94 standard deviation units. Resnick (1993) agreed that sex differences are not decreasing and estimated the effect size for mental rotation studies between .74 and .80 standard deviations. Finally, results from a recent study conducted in Norway, a country where sexual equality is highly prized, showed that sex differences in visuospatial tasks appear to be very similar in size to those found in the United States and many other countries over the last two decades (Nordvik & Amponsah, 1998). Of course, it is possible that sex differences will diminish over time in the future, but so far, we have no evidence that this is a likely trend.

DEVELOPMENT AND AGING: VISUOSPATIAL SEX DIFFERENCES ACROSS THE LIFE SPAN

Investigations of visuospatial abilities, as with most psychological research, often focus on college-aged students. Do other age groups show equivalent sex differences? Early work suggested that sex differences emerged at adolescence, potentially with puberty. More recent studies suggest a much earlier appearance, although the specific age at which girls and boys begin to differ may vary for different tasks. Clear sex differences have been found in preschoolers, probably as early as these skills can be assessed reliably, in spatial transformation (requiring either rotational or nonrotational operations; Levine, Huttenlocher, Taylor, & Langrock, 1999), and in the copying of a three-dimensional model using Legos (McGuinness & Morley, 1991). On a composite spatial score tapping a wide range of visuospatial abilities, the sexes began to differ around age 10 years (Johnson & Meade, 1987), and differences in mental rotation and spatial visualization have been found in children aged 9–13 years (Kerns & Berenbaum, 1991).

One question of interest is whether pubertal events, either biological or social, magnify sex differences. Although meta-analyses suggest that some visuospatial sex differences increase with age, at least through young adulthood, this increase may be apparent, rather than real, reflecting the use of tests that are inappropriate for younger children, the changing nature of tests used at different ages, or sample differences (e.g., participants over 18 years tend to be college students, and thus a more select sample, than younger, elementary school students; Linn & Petersen, 1985; Voyer, Voyer, & Bryden, 1995). Johnson and Meade (1987) found no increase in the magnitude of the male advantage between the ages of 10 and 18 years, and in a study of 9-year-olds, effect sizes for different types of visuospatial tasks (e.g., mental rotation, spatial perception, and visualization) were similar to those seen in adults (Vederhus & Krekling, 1996). Younger children, however, may show a different pattern. Four- to 6-year-olds demonstrated sex differences, but did not show the typical adult pattern of larger sex differences for items requiring mental rotation (Levine et al., 1999).

Another question is whether one's relative age of pubertal onset (early vs. late sexual maturation) relates to spatial skill. Males typically undergo puberty later than girls, and Waber (1976) has suggested that pubertal timing (as opposed to sex, per se) relates to patterns of functional brain lateralization and visuospatial ability. She found that late maturers, independent of sex, scored better on spatial versus verbal tasks and also showed greater hemispheric lateralization for verbal material, compared to early maturers. She interpreted these data in line with Levy's (1971) hypothesis (discussed earlier) that bilateral representation of language, thought to occur more often in females, interferes with optimal visuospatial development by encroaching on the more spatial domain of the right hemisphere. However, there have been a number of failures to replicate (as well as some confirmations of) the association between later pubertal timing and enhanced visuospatial ability, suggesting that such an effect may not exist or may be so small as to be unreliable (Geary & Gilger, 1989; Hassler, 1991; Newcombe & Dubas, 1992, Newcombe, Dubas, & Baenninger, 1989).

What happens to visuospatial skills beyond young adulthood? It is well established that visuospatial skills are more sensitive to the effects of aging than are verbal ones (Jenkins, Myerson, Joerding, & Hale, 2000). In fact, this same age-related decline occurs in nonhuman species, and its magnitude can vary by sex (e.g., Lacreuse, Herndon, Killiany, Rosene, & Moss, 1999). Do men and women show equivalent or differing rates of visuospatial decline? Meinz and Salthouse (1998) reviewed 25 studies to address this question and concluded that age did not erase the male advantage on a composite spatial score. The decline occurred at a roughly equivalent rate for both sexes. A similar pattern was observed for a composite score of working memory (reflecting memory for visuospatial as well as verbal material). Although a more fine-grained analysis of individual tasks may show some interactions between age and sex, there do not appear to be broad, general shifts.

Thus, visuospatial skills increase during childhood, peak in young adulthood, and decline with age. Differences between the sexes become apparent in early childhood (with some variations in the nature and magnitude of the difference during early childhood) and then stay roughly the same or increase slightly into adolescence or early adulthood and remain into old age.

WHAT WE KNOW ABOUT SEX DIFFERENCES IN VISUOSPATIAL COGNITION AND WHERE DO WE GO FROM HERE?

Visuospatial cognition is comprised of many component processes that include the retrieval of information from long-term memory, generation and maintenance of an image in a limited capacity visuospatial working memory, transformations in working memory, and all possible combinations with visual and spatial perception and verbal, visual, and spatial memory codes. Sex differences on many, but not all, visuospatial tasks are among the largest effect sizes found in psychology. Some portion of the sex difference may be due to sex-differentiated preferences for processing strategies when females and males perform complex visuospatial tasks. Females tend to use analytic or detail-oriented and verbal strategies, and males tend to use holistic and schematic strategies, which is probably the reason why females have better memory for landmarks along a route and males travel through complex environments more quickly and with fewer errors. There is evidence that these strategic differences also could be responsible for some portion of the sex difference found with mathematical problems containing spatial information.

Recent work on stereotype threat suggests that cognitive performance is depressed when negative stereotypes about one's own group are made salient for the relevant ability. We do not know if stereotype threat operates in ways that depress female performance on visuospatial tests because we do not know much about the stereotypes regarding visuospatial cognition. Steroidal hormones appear to play a role in visuospatial cognition, but given the wide variety of differences among tests (and the cognitive components of various visuospatial tests), we do not know the exact nature of the hormone-cognitive relationship. Simple relationships between hormone levels and types and visuospatial cognition seem unlikely. Sex differences in visuospatial abilities are found early in life and continue throughout the life span. Experience and training clearly are important variables in development of visuospatial abilities, with visuospatial activities and occupations potentially altering portions of the brain that underlie spatial cognition. Research regarding these topics is being conducted at a rapid rate, so we expect to have a much clearer understanding of the way in which brain characteristics, steroidal hormones, life experiences, social factors, and cognitive abilities influence each other in the next several years.

Visuospatial ability is important for success in many professions, but the development of these abilities has been largely ignored in education and training programs. There are few (e.g., Dental Admissions Test administered by the American Dental Association has sections with spatial tasks similar to paper folding and mental rotation) selection tests similar to the Scholastic Assessment Tests (SATs) or Graduate Record Examinations (GREs) for verbal and quantitative abilities that can be used to help individuals gauge their readiness for advanced work in fields where visuospatial information is a critical component, and there is no identifiable academic coursework or academic area where these abilities are developed explicitly, despite the fact that researchers have shown that visuospatial abilities can improve with instruction and practice (Humphreys, Lubinski, & Yao, 1993; Law, Pellegrino, & Hunt, 1993). We offer a stern caveat if such tests are developed. Given the large sex difference favoring males in most tests of visuospatial abilities, one likely outcome of a national testing program for visuospatial abilities would be to reduce even further the small number of women who enter advanced programs in mathematics, engineering, and the natural sciences, unless we couple these measures with programs that provide instruction in visuospatial information processing. This is especially critical because despite gains in the number of women in law and medical professions, the number of women in mathematics, science, and engineering has been declining over the last decade, at a time when the United States and other countries are facing a shortage of professionals in these fields (National Council for Research on Women, 2001). Additionally, there is a need to determine how well measures of visuospatial ability actually predict success in these areas, although a limited number of studies suggest that they do (e.g., Ackerman et al., 1995; Gordon & Leighty, 1988).

Visuospatial cognition is an exciting area of research because it offers the possibility of improving human performance in a wide range of areas and in expanding our knowledge of cognitive processes. We have identified a host of factors, some more social or experiential in origin (formal or informal training, performance factors, stereotypes, and cultural shifts) and others more biological ("what"-"where" neuroanatomy, hemispheric lateralization, and sex steroids) that appear capable of contributing to sex differences in visuospatial abilities. Each factor, in isolation, bears a complex relationship to visuospatial skill, often exerting its influence only on specific tasks or in specific contexts or individuals. The joint operation of a multivariate collection of factors, each of which may interact with others, presents an even more challenging set of opportunities for researchers. There is a pressing need for more research, and it seems that almost any researcher can find a question of interest to pursue, including individual differences, neuropsychology, hormones and behaviors, developmental processes, comparative psychology, education and training, and fairness issues in testing. Despite a massive research literature, we are still far from understanding the implications of large sex differences on many tests and tasks that assess visuospatial cognition.

Suggestions for Further Reading

For a comprehensive review of sex differences in cognitive abilities, including visuospatial ones:

Halpern, D. F. (2000). *Sex differences in cognitive abilities* (3rd ed.). Mahwah, NJ: Erlbaum.

Halpern. D. F., & Tan, U. (2001). Stereotypes and steroids: Using a psychobiosocial model to understand cognitive sex differences. *Brain and Cognition, 45,* 392–414.

For a meta-analytic review of sex differences in visuospatial skills and comparison of effect sizes across tasks:

Voyer, D., Voyer, S., & Bryden, M. P. (1995). Magnitude of sex differences in spatial abilities: A meta-analysis and consideration of critical variables. *Psychological Bulletin, 117,* 250–270.

For a review of sex differences on many different tests:
Willingham, W. W., & Cole, N. S. (1997). *Gender and fair assessment*. Hillsdale, NJ: Erlbaum.

References

Ackerman, P. L., Kanfer, R., & Goff, M. (1995). Cognitive and noncognitive determinants of complex skill acquisition. *Journal of Experimental Psychology: Applied, 1,* 270–304.

Alexander, G. M., Swerdloff, R. S., Wang, C., Davidson, T., McDonald, V., Steiner, B., & Hines, M. (1998). Androgen-Behavior correlations in hypogonadal men and eugonadal men: II. Cognitive abilities. *Hormones and Behavior, 33,* 85–94.

Arnold, A. P., & Gorski, R. A. (1984). Gonadal steroid induction of structural sex differences in the central nervous system. *Annual Review of Neuroscience, 7,* 413–442.

Baenninger, M., & Newcombe, N. (1989). The role of experience in spatial test performance: A meta-analysis. *Sex Roles, 20,* 327–344.

Baker, S. W., & Ehrhardt, A. A. (1974). Prenatal androgen, intelligence and cognitive sex differences. In R. C. Friedmanw, R. M. Richart, & R. L. Vande Wiele (Eds.), *Sex differences in behavior* (pp. 53–76). New York: Wiley.

Banaji, M. R., & Hardin, C. D. (1996). Automatic stereotyping. *Psychological Science, 7,* 136–141.

Beatty, W. W. (1992). Gonadal hormones and sex differences in nonreproductive behaviors. In A. A. Gerall, H. Moltz, & I. L. Ward (Eds.), *Sexual differentiation* (Vol. 11, pp. 85–128). New York: Plenum Press.

Becker, J. T., & Morris, R. G. (1999). Working memory(s). *Brain and Cognition, 41,* 1–8.

Berenbaum, S. A., & Hines, M. (1992). Early androgens are related to childhood sex-typed toy preferences. *Psychological Science, 3,* 203–206.

Berry, B., McMahan, R., & Gallagher, M. (1997). Spatial learning and memory at defined points of the estrous cycle: Effects on performance of a hippocampal-dependent task. *Behavioral Neuroscience, 111,* 267–274.

Bethell-Fox, C. E., & Shepard, R. N. (1988). Mental rotation: Effects of stimulus complexity and familiarity. *Journal of Experimental Psychology: Human Perception and Performance, 14,* 12–23.

Bidlingmaier, F., Strom, T. M., Dorr, H. G., Eisenmenger, W., & Knorr, D. (1987). Estrone and estradiol concentrations in human ovaries, testes, and adrenals during the first two years of life. *Journal of Clinical Endocrinology and Metabolism, 65,* 862–867.

Brown, H. D., & Kosslyn, S. M. (1995). Hemispheric differences in visual object processing: Structural versus allocation theories. In R. J. Davidson & K. Hugdahl (Eds.), *Brain Asymmetry* (pp. 77–97). Cambridge, MA: MIT Press.

Brown, L. N., Lahar, C. J., & Mosley, J. L. (1998). Age and gender-related differences in strategy use for route information: A "map-present" direction-giving paradigm. *Environment and Behavior, 30,* 123–143.

Bryden, M. P. (1982). *Laterality: Functional asymmetry in the intact brain*. New York: Academic Press.

Buchsbaum, M. S., & Henkin, R. I. (1980). Perceptual abnormalities in patients with chromatin negative gonadal dysgenesis and hypogonadotropic hypogonadism. *International Journal of Neuroscience, 11,* 201–209.

Cappa, S. F., Guariglia, C., Papagno, C., Pizzamiglio, L., Vallar, G., Zoccolotti, P., Ambrosi, B., & Santiemma, V. (1988). Patterns of lateralization and performance levels for verbal and spatial tasks in congenital androgen deficiency. *Behavioural Brain Research, 31,* 177–183.

Casey, M. B., Nuttall, R., Pezaris, E., & Benbow, C. P. (1995). The influence of spatial ability on gender differences in mathematics college entrance test scores across diverse samples. *Developmental Psychology, 31,* 697–705.

Cherrier, M. M. (1999). Androgens, ageing, behavior and cognition: Complex interactions and novel areas of inquiry. *New Zealand Journal of Psychology, 28,* 4–9.

Christiansen, K., & Knussmann, R. (1987). Sex hormones and cognitive functioning in men. *Neuropsychobiology, 18,* 27–36.

Clarkson-Smith, L., & Halpern, D. F. (1983). Can age-related deficits in spatial memory be attenuated through the use of verbal coding? *Experimental Aging Research, 9,* 179–184.

Cohen, J. (1988). *Statistical power analysis for the behavioral sciences.* Hillsdale, NJ: Erlbaum.

Collaer, M. L., & Hines, M. (1995). Human behavioral sex differences: A role for gonadal hormones during early development? *Psychological Bulletin, 118,* 55–107.

Collaer, M. L., & Nelson, J. D. (2002). Large visuospatial sex difference in line judgment: Possible role of attentional factors. *Brain and Cognition, 49,* 1–12.

Dabbs, J. M., Jr., Chang, E. L., Strong, R. A., & Milun, R. (1998). Spatial ability, navigation strategy, and geographic knowledge among men and women. *Evolution and Human Behavior, 19,* 89–98.

Eals, M., & Silverman, I. (1994). The hunter-gatherer theory of spatial sex differences: Proximate factors mediating the female advantage in recall of object arrays. *Ethology and Sociobiology, 15,* 95–105.

Epting, L. K., & Overman, W. H. (1998). Sex-sensitive tasks in men and women: A search for performance fluctuations across the menstrual cycle. *Behavioral Neuroscience, 112,* 1304–1317.

Errico, A. L., Parsons, O. A., Kling, O. R., & King, A. C. (1992). Investigation of the role of sex hormones in alcoholics' visuospatial deficits. *Neuropsychologia, 30,* 417–426.

Feingold, A. (1988). Cognitive gender differences are disappearing. *American Psychologist, 43,* 95–103.

Friedman, L. (1995). The space factor in mathematics: Gender differences. *Review of Educational Research, 65,* 22–50.

Galea, L. A. M., & Kimura, D. (1993). Sex differences in route learning. *Personality and Individual Differences, 14,* 53–65.

Geary, D. C., & Gilger, J. W. (1989). Age of sexual maturation and adult spatial ability. *Bulletin of the Psychonomic Society, 27,* 241–244.

Goldstein, D., Haldane, D., & Mitchell, C. (1990). Sex differences in visual-spatial ability: The role of performance factors. *Memory and Cognition, 18,* 546–550.

Goldstein, E. B. (2002). *Sensation and perception* (6th ed.). Pacific Grove, CA: Wadsworth.

Gouchie, C., & Kimura, D. (1991). The relation between testosterone levels and cognitive ability patterns. *Psychoneuroendocrinology, 16,* 323–334.

Gordon, H. W., & Leighty, R. (1988). Importance of specialized cognitive functions in the selection of military pilots. *Journal of Applied Psychology, 73,* 38–45.

Grön, G., Wunderlich, A. P., Spitzer, M., Tomczak, R., & Riepe, M. W. (2000). Brain activation during human navigation: Gender-different neural networks as substrate of performance. *Nature Neuroscience, 3,* 404–408.

Halpern, D. F. (1986). A different response to the question "Do sex differences in spatial abilities exist?" *American Psychologist, 41,* 1014–1015.

Halpern, D. F. (1997). Sex differences in intelligence: Implications for education. *American Psychologist, 52,* 1091–1102.

Halpern, D. F. (2000). *Sex differences in cognitive abilities* (3rd ed.). Mahwah, NJ: Erlbaum.

Halpern. D. F., & Tan, U. (2001). Stereotypes and steroids: Using a psychobiosocial model to understand cognitive sex differences. *Brain and Cognition, 45,* 392–414.

Hampson, E., Rovet, J. F., & Altmann, D. (1998). Spatial reasoning in children with congenital adrenal hyperplasia due to 21-hydroxylase deficiency. *Developmental Neuropsychology, 14,* 299–320.

Hassler, M. (1991). Maturation rate and spatial, verbal, and musical abilities: A seven-year-longitudinal study. *International Journal of Neuroscience, 58,* 183–198.

Hecht, H., & Proffitt, D. R. (1995). The price of expertise: The effects of expertise on the water-level task. *Psychological Science, 6,* 90–95.

Hedges, L. V., & Nowell, A. (1995). Sex differences in mental test scores, variability, and numbers of high-scoring individuals. *Science, 269,* 41–45.

Hegarty, M., & Kozhevnikov, M. (1999). Types of visual-spatial representations and mathematical problem solving. *Journal of Educational Psychology, 91,* 684–689.

Henderson, V. W., Paganini-Hill, A., Emanuel, C. K., Dunn, M. E., & Buckwalter, J. G. (1994). Estrogen replacement therapy in older women. Comparisons between Alzheimer's disease cases and nondemented control subjects. *Archives of Neurology, 51,* 896–900.

Herlitz, A., Nilsson, L-G., & Baeckman, L. (1997). Gender differences in episodic memory. *Memory and Cognition, 25,* 801–811.

Hier, D. B., & Crowley, W. F., Jr. (1982). Spatial ability in androgen-deficient men. *New England Journal of Medicine, 306,* 1202–1205.

Hiscock, M., Inch, R., Jacek, C., Hiscock-Kalil, C., & Kalil, K. M. (1994). Is there a sex difference in human laterality? I. An exhaustive survey of auditory laterality studies from six neuropsychology journals. *Journal of Clinical and Experimental Neuropsychology, 16,* 423–435.

Hiscock, M., Israelian, M., Inch, R., Jacek, C., & Hiscock-Kalil, C. (1995). Is there a sex difference in human laterality? II. An exhaustive survey of visual laterality studies from sex neuropsychology journals. *Journal of Clinical and Experimental Neuropsychology, 17,* 590–610.

Hughes, I. A., Coleman, N., Faisal Ahmed, S., Ng, K.-L., Cheng, A., Lim, H. N., & Hawkins, J. R. (1999). Sexual dimorphism in the neonatal gonad. *Acta Paediatrica Supplement, 428,* 23–30.

Humphreys, L. F., Lubinski, D., & Yao, G. (1993). Utility of predicting group membership and the role of spatial visualization in becoming an engineer, physical scientist, or artist. *Journal of Applied Psychology, 78*, 250–261.

Hyde, J. S., Fennema, E., & Lamon, S. J. (1990). Gender differences in mathematics performance: A meta-analysis. *Psychological Bulletin, 107*, 139–155.

Hyde, J. S., Geiringer, E. R., & Yen, W. M. (1975). On the empirical relation between spatial ability and sex differences in other aspects of cognitive performance. *Multivariate Behavioral Research, 10*, 289–309.

Isgor, C., & Sengelaub, D. R. (1998). Prenatal gonadal steroids affect adult spatial behavior, CA1 and CA3 pyramidal cell morphology in rats. *Hormones and Behavior, 34*, 183–198.

James, T. W., & Kimura, D. (1997). Sex differences in remembering the location of objects in an array: Location-shifts versus location-exchanges. *Evolution and Human Behavior, 18*, 155–163.

Janowsky, J. S., Chavez, B., & Orwoll, E. (2000). Sex steroids modify working memory. *Journal of Cognitive Neuroscience, 12*, 407–414.

Janowsky, J. S., Oviatt, S. K., & Orwoll, E. S. (1994). Testosterone influences spatial cognition in older men. *Behavioral Neuroscience, 108*, 325–332.

Jenkins, L., Myerson, J., Joerding, J. A., & Hale, S. (2000). Converging evidence that visuospatial cognition is more age-sensitive than verbal cognition. *Psychology and Aging, 15*, 157–175.

Johnson, E. S., & Meade, A. C. (1987). Developmental patterns of spatial ability: An early sex difference. *Child Development, 58*, 725–740.

Kampen, D. L., & Sherwin, B. B. (1996). Estradiol is related to visual memory in healthy young men. *Behavioral Neuroscience, 110*, 613–617.

Kerns, K. A., & Berenbaum, S. A. (1991). Sex differences in spatial ability in children. *Behavior Genetics, 21*, 383–396.

Kimura, D., & Hampson, E. (1994). Cognitive pattern in men and women is influenced by fluctuations in sex hormones. *Current Directions in Psychological Science, 3*, 57–61.

Kolb, B., & Whishaw, I. Q. (1995). *Fundamentals of human neuropsychology.* New York: Freeman & Co.

Lacreuse, A., Herndon, J. G., Killiany, R. J., Rosene, D. L., & Moss, M. B. (1999). Spatial cognition in rhesus monkeys: Male superiority declines with age. *Hormones and Behavior, 36*, 70–76.

Law, D., Pellegrino, J. W., & Hunt, E. B. (1993). Comparing the tortoise and the hare: Gender differences and experience in dynamic spatial reasoning tasks. *Psychological Science, 4*, 35–41.

Lawton, C. A. (1994). Gender differences in way-finding strategies: Relationship to spatial ability and spatial anxiety. *Sex Roles, 30*, 765–779.

Levine, S. C., Huttenlocher, J., Taylor, A., & Langrock, A. (1999). Early sex differences in spatial skill. *Developmental Psychology, 35*, 940–949.

Levy, J. (1971). Lateral specialization of the human brain: Behavioral manifestations and possible evolutionary basis. In J. A. Kiger (Ed.), *The biology of behavior* (pp. 159–180). Corvallis, OR: Oregon State University Press.

Linn, M. C., & Petersen, A. C. (1985). Emergence and characterization of sex differences in spatial ability: A meta-analysis. *Child Development, 56*, 1479–1498.

Loring-Meier, S., & Halpern, D. F. (1999). Sex differences in visual-spatial working memory: Components of cognitive processing. *Psychonomic Bulletin and Review, 6*, 464–471.

Lubinski, D., & Benbow, C. P. (1992). Gender differences in abilities and preferences among the gifted: Implications for the math-science pipeline. *Current Directions in Psychological Science, 1*, 61–66.

Luine, V. N., Richards, S. T., Wu, V. Y., & Beck, K. D. (1998). Estradiol enhances learning and memory in a spatial memory task and effects levels of monoaminergic neurotransmitters. *Hormones and Behavior, 34*, 149–162.

Luine, V. N., & Rodriguez, M. (1994). Effects of estradiol on radial arm maze performance of young and aged rats. *Behavioral and Neural Biology, 62*, 230–236.

Maguire, E. A., Frackowiak, R. S. J., & Frith, C. D. (1997). Recalling routes around London: Activation of the right hippocampus in taxi drivers. *Journal of Neuroscience, 17*, 7103–7110.

Maguire, E. A., Gadian, D. G., Johnsrude, I. S., Good, C. D., Ashburner, J., Frackowiak, R. S., & Frith, C. D. (2000). Navigation-related structural change in the hippocampi of taxi drivers. *Proceedings of the National Academy of Sciences, 97*, 4398–4403.

Masters, M. S. (1998). The gender difference on the Mental Rotations test is not due to performance factors. *Memory and Cognition, 26*, 444–448.

Masters, M. S., & Sanders, B. (1993). Is the gender difference in mental rotation disappearing? *Behavior Genetics, 23*, 337–341.

McBurney, D. H., Gaulin, S. J. C., Devineni, T., & Adams, C. (1997). Superior spatial memory of women: Stronger evidence for the gathering hypothesis. *Evolution and Human Behavior, 18*, 165–174.

McCormick, C. M., & Teillon, S. M. (2001). Menstrual cycle variation in spatial ability: Relation to salivary cortisol levels. *Hormones and Behavior, 39*, 29–38.

McEwen, B. S., Alves, S. E., Bulloch, K., & Weiland, N. G. (1998). Clinically relevant basic science studies of gender differences and sex hormone effects. *Psychopharmacology Bulletin, 34*, 251–259.

McGlone, J. (1980). Sex differences in human brain asymmetry: A critical survey. *The Behavioral and Brain Sciences, 3*, 215–263.

McGuinness, D., & Morley, C. (1991). Sex differences in the development of visuospatial ability in pre-school children. *Journal of Mental Imagery, 15*, 143–150.

McGuire, L. S., Ryan, K. O., & Omenn, G. S. (1975). Congenital adrenal hyperplasia. II. Cognitive and behavioral studies. *Behavior Genetics, 5*, 175–188.

Meinz, E. J., & Salthouse, T. A. (1998). Is age kinder to females than to males? *Psychonomic Bulletin and Review, 5*, 56–70.

Mishkin, M., Ungerleider, L. G., & Macko, K. A. (1983). Object vision and spatial vision: Two cortical pathways. *Trends in Neuroscience, 6*, 414–417.

Moffat, S. D., & Hampson, E. (1996). A curvilinear relationship between testosterone and spatial cognition in humans: Possible influence of hand preference. *Psychoneuroendocrinology, 21*, 323–337.

Moffat, S. D., Hampson, E., & Hatzipantelis, M. (1998). Navigation in a "virtual" maze: Sex differences and correlation with psychometric measures of spatial ability in humans. *Evolution and Human Behavior, 19*, 73–87.

Montello, D. R., Lovelace, K. L., Golledge, R. G., & Self, C. M. (1999). Sex-related differences and similarities in geographic and environmental spatial abilities. *Annals of the Association of American Geographers, 89,* 515–534.

Moody, M. S. (1997). Changes in scores on the mental rotations test during the menstrual cycle. *Perceptual and Motor Skills, 84,* 955–961.

National Collegiate Athletic Association (n.d.). Retrieved July 28, 2001, from http://www.gendercenter.org/sports.html

National Council for Research on Women. (2001). *Balancing the equation: Where are women and girls in science?* Washington, DC: Author.

Newcombe, N., Bandura, M., & Taylor, D. G. (1983). Sex differences in spatial ability and spatial activities. *Sex Roles, 9,* 377–386.

Newcombe, N., & Dubas, J. S. (1992). A longitudinal study of predictors of spatial ability in adolescent females. *Child Development, 63,* 37–46.

Newcombe, N., Dubas, J. S., & Baenninger, M. (1989). Associations of timing of puberty, spatial ability, and lateralization in adult women. *Child Development, 60,* 246–254.

Nordvik, H., & Amponsah, B. (1998). Gender differences in spatial abilities and spatial activity among university students in an egalitarian educational system. *Sex Roles, 38,* 1009–1023.

Nyborg, H. (1983). Spatial ability in men and women: Review and new theory. *Advances in Behaviour Research and Therapy, 5,* 89–140.

Polo-Kantola, P., Portin, R., Polo, O., Helenius, H., Irjala, K., & Erkkola, R. (1998). The effect of short-term estrogen replacement therapy on cognition: A random-ized, double-blind, cross-over trial in postmenopausal women. *Obstetrics and Gynecology, 91,* 459–466.

Resnick, S. M. (1993). Sex differences in mental rotations: An effect of time limits? *Brain and Cognition, 21,* 71–79.

Resnick, S. M., Berenbaum, S. A., Gottesman, I. I., & Bouchard, T. J., Jr. (1986). Early hormonal influences on cognitive functioning in congenital adrenal hyperplasia. *Developmental Psychology, 22,* 191–198.

Serbin, L. A., & Sprafkin, C. (1986). The salience of gender and the process of sex typing in middle childhood. *Child Development, 57,* 1188–1199.

Sherwin, B. B. (1999). Can estrogen keep you smart? Evidence from clinical studies. *Journal of Psychiatry and Neuroscience, 24,* 315–321.

Stanley, J. (1990, January 10). We need to know why women falter in math [Letter to the Editor]. *The Chronicle of Higher Education,* B4.

Steele, C. M. (1997). A threat in the air: How stereotypes shape intellectual identity and performance. *American Psychologist, 52,* 613–629.

Steele, C. M. (1998). Stereotyping and its threat are real. *American Psychologist, 53,* 680–681.

Stricker, L. J. (1998). *Inquiring about examinees' ethnicity and sex: Effects on AP Calculus AB Examination performance.* (Report No. 98, 2nd ed.). New York: The College Board.

Stricker, L. J., & Ward. W. C. (1998). *Inquiring about examinees' ethnicity and sex: Effects on computerized placement tests performance.* New York: The College Board.

Stumpf, H., & Jackson, D. N. (1994). Gender-related differences in cognitive abilities: Evidence from a medical school admissions testing program. *Personality and Individual Differences, 17*, 335–344.

Tartre, L. A. (1990). Spatial skills, gender, and mathematics. In E. Fennema & G. C. Leder (Eds.), *Mathematics and gender* (pp. 27–59). New York: Teachers College Press.

Tobias, S. (1993). *Overcoming math anxiety.* New York: W. W. Norton.

Vasta, R., & Gaze, C. E. (1996). Can spatial training erase the gender differences on the water-level task? *Psychology of Women, 20*, 549–567.

Vasta, R., Rosenberg, D., Knott, J. A., & Gaze, C. E. (1997). Experience and the water-level-task revisited: Does experience exact a price? *Psychological Science, 8*, 336–339.

Vederhus, L., & Krekling, S. (1996). Sex differences in visual spatial ability in 9-year-old children. *Intelligence, 23*, 33–43.

Voyer, D. (1996). On the magnitude of laterality effects and sex differences in functional lateralities. *Laterality, 1*, 51–83.

Voyer, D., Voyer, S., & Bryden, M. P. (1995). Magnitude of sex differences in spatial abilities: A meta-analysis and consideration of critical variables. *Psychological Bulletin, 117*, 250–270.

Waber, D. P. (1976). Sex differences in cognition: A function of maturation rate? *Science, 192*, 572–573.

Wallen, K. (1996). Nature needs nurture: The interaction of hormonal and social influences on the development of behavioral sex differences in rhesus monkeys. *Hormones and Behavior, 30*, 364–378.

Warren, S. G., & Juraska, J. M. (1997). Spatial and nonspatial learning across the rat estrous cycle. *Behavioral Neuroscience, 111*, 259–266.

Watson, N. V., & Kimura, D. (1991). Nontrivial sex differences in throwing and intercepting: Relation to psychometrically defined spatial functions. *Personality and Individual Differences, 12*, 375–385.

Williams, C. L., & Meck, W. H. (1991). The organizational effects of gonadal steroids on sexually dimorphic spatial ability. *Psychoneuroendocrinology, 16*, 155–176.

Willingham, W. W., & Cole, N. S. (1997). *Gender and fair assessment.* Hillsdale, NJ: Erlbaum.

Wong, W. J., Liu, H. C., Fuh, J. L., Wang, S. J., Hsu, L. C., Wang, P. N., & Sheng, W. Y. (1999). A double-blind, placebo-controlled study of tacrine in Chinese patients with Alzheimer's disease. *Dementia and Geriatric Cognitive Disorders, 10*, 289–294.

6

Development of Spatial Competence

Nora S. Newcombe and Amy E. Learmonth

ABSTRACT

This chapter discusses the development of visuospatial representation and thinking. Although development crosscuts all of the issues covered in other chapters in this handbook, it is typically (perhaps unfortunately) discussed separately within cognitive psychology. In this chapter, we offer a focused look at how the spatial abilities of the competent adult come about. Infants begin with certain spatial skills, as nativists have often stressed, and yet these skills change with development, as stressed by other theories including Vygotskyan, empiricist and interactionist approaches. Some important developmental changes include: the reweighting of initial spatial coding systems as the infant learns more about the world, the advent of place learning, and the acquisition of perspective taking and mental rotation. Children also begin to be able to use symbolic representations of space, including maps, models and linguistic descriptions, and they learn to think about space and to use spatial representations for thinking.

INTRODUCTION

Any of the chapters in this handbook could contain material on development. There are, after all, important developmental questions about visuospatial working memory (Logie & Della Sala, Chapter 3), visuospatial imagery (Reisberg & Heuer, Chapter 2), visuospatial abilities (Hegarty & Waller, Chapter 4), and indeed about all the other topics covered in this volume. In fact, one way to organize intellectual inquiry about topics in cognitive science in general would be to consider the issue of development as one facet of any question, along with such topics as cross-species capabilities, neurological substrates, and individual differences. In this way of proceeding, no account of working memory, or imagery, or any topic in cognitive science more broadly, would be considered complete without consideration of all of these facets of the problem. Each facet would provide information relevant for, and constraints on, the central questions in that field. Separate chapters on development would not be needed.

Historically, however, the study of development in infants and children has been pursued as a separate subfield from cognitive science, with its own journals, associations and conferences. Professional networking and organization frequently link the study of cognitive development more closely with the study of social development than with the study of cognitive phenomena. In addition, certain theoretical questions have concerned developmentalists more than other cognitive scientists, most notably issues surrounding the nature of the intertwined roles of innate abilities and environmental input in the development of knowledge. Because many researchers interested in visuospatial thinking may not have closely followed the literature on spatial development, the purpose of this chapter is to present a short overview of current thought and trends. More complete treatments are available elsewhere (Campos, Anderson, Barbu-Roth, Hubbard, Hertenstein, & Witherington, 2000; Newcombe & Huttenlocher, 2000).

A word about theoretical disputes in the field of spatial development is in order first. Much of the research on the development of spatial competence was initially guided by the writings of Piaget. According to Piaget, spatial understanding does not reach an adult level until a child is between nine and ten years old (Piaget & Inhelder, 1948/1967; Piaget, Inhelder, & Szeminska, 1960). Piaget characterized young children's spatial coding as topological rather than Euclidean or projective, without metric coding of distance, so that the spatial world at first consisted of objects related only by touching each other or not, being enclosed by one another or not, and being near to one another or farther away.[1] In fact, Piaget thought that, at first, infants had to begin spatial development by developing an understanding of the permanence of objects, that is, of the fact that an object always continues to exist and to take up space, even when it is not visible.

In addition, Piaget thought that infants and children had to develop out of a state of spatial egocentrism, one in which they believed that everyone's view of the world matched their own. In the subsequent developmental

---

[1] However, it is not clear how near-far coding fits with the claim of no metric coding (Newcombe, 1988). Near and far are essentially metric terms, although one nonmetric possibility for construing them involves a sensorimotor division of the world according to what is within grasping space, and what is not.

literature, the issue of egocentrism has been addressed in two rather different contexts. In infancy, the contrast has been between egocentric coding of location with respect to the infant's own body and motor movements, as opposed to allocentric coding of location, meaning coding in relation to external landmarks. In later childhood, egocentrism has referred to the response children sometimes display in perspective-taking tasks – saying that a person in another position will have the same view of a display as they do.

Each of these specific claims has been challenged by subsequent research, as we shall see. Doubts about the Piagetian framework have led, in broad overview, to three different approaches to spatial development. One school of thought is nativism, with associated claims of striking early ability and a modularity of functioning that is present at birth (Hermer & Spelke, 1994, 1996; Landau, Gleitman, & Spelke, 1981). Researchers in this tradition have contributed a great deal to our knowledge of infant competence, but have put too little stress on the importance of later development and the contributions of the environment to this process (Newcombe, 2002b). In addition, there is reason to doubt the specific modularity claim nativists have made with respect to the spatial domain, namely that children are born with a "geometric module." A second way to think about spatial development comes from Vygotskyan theories that emphasize the cultural embeddedness of spatial learning (e.g., Gauvain, 1993, 1995) and the role of spatial language in guiding and facilitating spatial thinking (Bowerman, 1996, 2000; Gentner & Ratterman, 1991). This kind of approach adds a great deal to our knowledge of spatial development, but it often focuses on cultural artifacts such as language, maps and models to the point that it loses sight of the fact that children actively explore their environment and receive feedback directly from their experiences regarding the adaptiveness of their spatial representations and spatial thought. Finally, there are interactionist theories that seek to integrate the insights of constructivism, nativism and Vygotskyan theory (Newcombe, 1998; Newcombe & Huttenlocher, 2000). The idea is, simply, that the goal of developmental psychology is to specify the early starting points for spatial development, the nature of subsequent development, and the ways in which environmental interactions, neural maturation and cultural guidance combine to contribute to these later developmental changes.

In order to describe the development of spatial competence, we must first consider what spatial competence is. As other chapters in this handbook have pointed out, spatial behavior is a fundamental aspect of adaptation for any mobile creature (see in particular the chapter on navigation,

Montello, Chapter 7). All organisms that move in an intentional and un-stereotyped way in their environments must have the means to encode their location with respect to the location of other objects. Most notably, they need to know where things are that they wish to avoid (such as preda-tors or physical dangers) and where things are that they wish to approach (food, home base, social partners). These are the abilities for which we may most expect to see commonalities with other mobile species. These are also the abilities for which we expect to see canalization of development, a term used in developmental psychology to indicate situations in which virtually all infants and young children, at least those without significant disabilities, go through essentially the same sequence of development at a similar pace. Canalization is common in species-typical behaviors with high adaptive value that have been the target of long periods of natural selection. Thus, we will first consider the development of the ability to encode location and navigate in the world.

We will next consider another aspect of human spatial competence, namely, the ability to think ahead about the consequences of spatial move-ment – to imagine what a scene will look like if viewed from another perspective and to imagine what objects will look like after they have been rotated, or transformed in some other way, such as being folded. The capac-ity for mental transformation of spatial relations seems likely to be linked to one of our species' distinctive adaptations, namely the ability to make and use tools. Whether or not such perspective-taking and mental trans-formation skills are uniquely human or are exhibited by other species is currently being studied.[2] We do know, however, that development of these skills in humans is clearly more protracted and more individually vari-able (i.e., less canalized) than the development of basic systems of spatial coding.

The remainder of the chapter concerns two kinds of spatial competence that are also likely unique to our species (although rudimentary aspects of them may be found in certain nonhuman primates, as shown by recent research by Kuhlmeier, Boysen, & Mukobi, 1999, and Kuhlmeier & Boysen, 2002). One such competence is the ability to communicate about space symbolically, both using visuospatial symbols such as maps and models and also through using language. A second, very interesting aspect of human spatial competence is the use of spatial representations and spatial thinking to attack nonspatial problems in reasoning and problem solving.

---

[2] Vauclair, Fagot, and Hopkins (1993) have found some behavioral evidence of mental rotation in baboons.

TABLE 6.1. *Four Systems of Spatial Coding.*

	Viewer-centered	**Environment-centered**
Simple	Response learning	Cue learning
Complex	Dead reckoning	Place learning

NATURE OF SPATIAL LOCATION CODING

As with a developmental analysis in any domain, understanding mature competence for the spatial coding allowing for navigation is the starting point for looking at development. The systems that adults use to navigate their environment can be divided into two broad types. *Viewer-centered systems* rely on the positioning and orientation of the viewer's body and code location with respect to the self. *Environment-centered systems* use location and direction information gained from objects in the environment. Each of these categories can be further divided into two systems, one simple and the other complex (Gallistel, 1990; Newcombe & Huttenlocher, 2000; Newcombe & Learmonth, 1999). An overview of this typology is shown in Table 6.1.

One kind of viewer-centered system is *response learning*, also called sensorimotor coding in the developmental literature. In response learning, a person learns to make a specific body movement in order to achieve a goal. For example, a worker at her desk hears the phone ring and reaches out to answer it without looking up. She is simply executing a set of scripted movements that result in the retrieval of the phone handset. As another example, consider someone who walks from the kitchen to his bedroom to get his watch from the bedside table, following a sequence of steps and turns that has become second nature. The drawback of this simple system is that it doesn't work if the phone is not in its usual position, or the watch was left in the living room. Nor does it succeed if the worker is not seated in her usual position, or the man curious about the time was in his study.

A more complex kind of viewer-centered spatial coding, and one that is much more flexible and useful, is *dead reckoning*, also called path integration. The dead reckoning system is used to get from one place to another by computation of changes in position over time (Gallistel, 1990; Goodridge & Taube, 1995). The dead reckoning system uses information from a variety of kinds of input to calculate changes in position, including vestibular, kinesthetic and proprioceptive information, as well as information from optic flow. So if people move to the other side of their desks or to another room of their house, they can still find the phone or the watch because their dead reckoning system allows for recomputation of the reach or walk needed to find these objects. The dead reckoning system allows one to navigate through a familiar place without light or with closed eyes. It is also the type of navigation that was used on ships before the advent of more sophisticated machinery for tracking location (Gallistel, 1990). Such a system works, although not perfectly – the accumulation of small errors can eventually lead to large mistakes in spatial localization.

A simple environment-centered system is *cue learning*. In cue learning, a person learns the association between a coincident landmark in the environment and the desired object or event. For example, a person need not know more than that the phone is on top of desk or the watch is on the bedside table in order to know where to find them, even if they are obscured in some way. This system only works, however, when the desired location is directly and completely specified by a single landmark. If someone were so foolish as to leave a watch somewhere on a large lawn, knowing simply that it is on the grass would not help a great deal to narrow the search for it.

The *place learning* system is the more complex of the environment-centered systems. Place learning informs us of our location in space relative to a landmark or set of landmarks, using information about distance and direction of the desired object from the landmarks. A landmark can be any distinguishable feature of the space, or even a part of a distinguishable feature, as long as it is fixed in place and unlikely to move. The information gained through place learning allows one to infer location by taking sightings of landmarks that occupy a known location and by using information about the distance and direction of a desired object from these distinct features of the environment. The knowledge that your watch was left two feet from the azalea in the direction of the large pine tree and about six feet from the porch door would help to locate the object so carelessly left on the lawn. Or a pirate might code a treasure chest as buried four paces from Skull Rock in the direction of the ocean, and six paces from the twisted palm.

There are two aspects of place learning that need a little further consideration. First, place learning is a parallel system to dead reckoning; they both can give an accurate picture of location and change in location. Normally, they agree. However, what happens in situations where the two systems are in conflict? The place learning system is usually preferred over the dead reckoning system. This is an adaptive choice because the dead reckoning system is subject to drift – errors in it concatenate, with an initial error followed by a second error leading to a total error likely larger than either of the two errors taken alone, and so on with the next error and the next. Thus, it needs to be reset periodically by the place learning system to function better after this has happened (Etienne, Teroni, Maurer, Portenier, & Saucy, 1985; Gallistel, 1990).

Second, place learning involves the coding of distance and direction. What happens when such metric information is uncertain, as might happen over time, or if coding was based on only very brief exposure? Huttenlocher, Hedges, and Duncan (1981) found that adults code landmarks in a hierarchical fashion. The actual location of an object in a continuous space is coded in fine-grained memory, but category information is also coded. For example, an object might be remembered as located in one of the quadrants of a circle, as studied by Huttenlocher et al., or in a sandy patch of ground. Category information influences the fine-grained estimations of location increasingly as there is uncertainty about the latter. Huttenlocher et al. propose a hierarchical coding model that explains their consistent finding that adults judge a location to be biased toward the center of a category. In the case of estimation of the location of points in a circle, as illustrated in Figure 6.1, people bias their estimates toward the center of gravity of the quadrant of the circle they remember the point as being within. Stated more generally, when estimates of locations are made, the fine-grained information is combined with category information, which

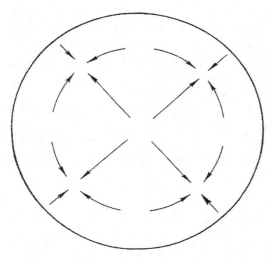

FIGURE 6.1. Schematic representation of bias for memory for locations in a circle. (From Huttenlocher, Newcombe, & Sandberg, 1994.)

leads to a bias toward the central value of the category, or the category prototype. Although this system introduces bias, it increases overall accuracy of a set of estimations by decreasing their variability (Huttenlocher, Hedges, & Duncan, 1991).

Newcombe, Huttenlocher, Sandberg, Lie, and Johnson (1999) evaluated predictions of this model of spatial coding for the existence of asymmetries in memory for the locations of points on a map. When people, even adults, are asked to estimate the distance from point A to point B, they frequently give an estimate different from their estimate of the distance from point B to point A. However, this seemingly illogical behavior is consistent with a coherent underlying spatial representation, if one allows for the different adjustments made toward a category prototype for points located in different sections of the category.

Over the past decade, behavioral research on the development and functioning of spatial coding systems has been increasingly synergistic with investigation of the neural bases of each of these spatial coding systems. It has long been known that place learning is associated with the hippocampus (O'Keefe & Nadel, 1978), based both on lesion data and single-cell recording techniques used with animals (e.g., Wilson & McNaughton, 1993) and on data from humans with brain damage (e.g., Bohbot, Allen, & Nadel, 2000). The parahippocampal area, perhaps particularly on the right side, also seems to be intimately involved in this kind of learning (Bohbot et al., 2000; Epstein & Kanwisher, 1998), as well as other areas with close connections to the hippocampus (Oswald & Good, 2000). Dead reckoning may be particularly dependent on posterior parietal cortex (Save & Moghaddam, 1996). Cue learning may involve the caudate nucleus (Maguire, Burgess, Donnett, Frackowiak, Frith, & O'Keefe, 1998; Packard & McGaugh, 1992; Redish, 1999). There has been less investigation of spatial memory using response learning except in short-term tasks where premotor areas seem to be involved (Graziano, Yap, & Gross, 1994). These facts help constrain and guide the fields of both behavioral and neural development, because our knowledge of behavioral change may provide ideas about neural function and our ideas about neural function may affect what we conclude from behavioral work.

DEVELOPMENT OF SPATIAL LOCATION CODING

The analysis of spatial coding in the previous section has delineated four ways of remembering spatial location, as well as a process of hierarchical coding that allows for adjustment of uncertain estimates using categorical information. This typology of spatial knowledge is quite different from Piaget's characterization of it as possibly topological, projective or Euclidean in nature, and it suggests a different set of developmental questions than he asked. We want to know to what extent these abilities are present at the start of life, to what extent they develop, and if they develop, when and how. We will therefore begin by looking at the evidence regarding each of the three coding systems that are present very early in life, namely response learning, dead reckoning, and cue learning. In the course of this discussion, we will discuss the changing reliance on the three coding systems, a reweighting that can explain some of the changes in spatial search behavior seen in infancy. In the context of this hypothesis of reweighting, we will be in a position to discuss the A not B error in infant search, first described by Piaget. We will then discuss place learning, which develops somewhat later than the other three systems, and the development of hierarchical coding. We will conclude this section on the development of spatial location coding with a critique of recent claims for the existence of a geometric module. The postulated module provides one of the strongest arguments currently extant for a nativist approach to the acquisition of spatial knowledge, so examining the issue carefully has important theoretical implications.

Before we begin, let us say a word about the importance of age in developmental psychology. At times, presentation of developmental research can seem focused almost exclusively on the descriptive task of deciding what capabilities infants and children can exhibit at what ages. However, ideally, this descriptive task is seen as subordinate to more interesting and important questions, such as characterizing the mechanisms of development (e.g., McClelland & Siegler, 2001; Siegler, 1996) and the nature of human competence. As we come to understand the descriptive facts, they influence theorizing and provide the database on which to test models and analytic theories that make specific predictions about new findings.

Development of Three Early Location Coding Systems

Piaget emphasized the role of response learning in infants' understanding of spatial location in his analysis of the overall stage of sensorimotor intelligence. His hypothesis was supported by a classic study of response learning (Acredolo, 1978). As illustrated in Figure 6.2, Acredolo trained infants to expect an interesting event to follow the sound of a centrally located buzzer in one of two windows – one to the infants' left and one to their right. Infants learned which way to turn. Once the response to the

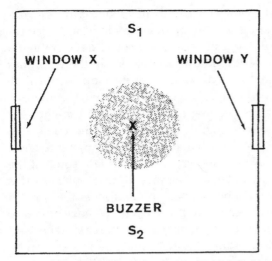

FIGURE 6.2. Experimental setting of Acredolo (1978). Child at S1 sees an interesting event at window X following a buzzer. After movement to S2, the question is where the child will look when the buzzer sounds.

correct window was established, the infants were rotated 180 degrees to the opposite side of the room, and researchers observed which window they now turned toward when the buzzer sounded. Infants of 6 and 11 months all made the incorrect response of anticipating the event at the same self-referenced place, that is, using response learning and making no adjustments for movement. At 16 months, the majority of the infants correctly adjusted for the movement. Bremner and Bryant (1977) obtained similar results. However, the paradigm used in these studies may underestimate babies' ability to use other coding systems, in various ways.

First, let us consider infants' ability to use dead reckoning. Landau and Spelke (1988) noted that the kind of motion Acredolo used was complex (involving both translation and rotation). Landau and Spelke found evidence of updating of response learning using dead reckoning in nine-month-old infants. They hid an object in one of two or three places (the number of hiding locations was constant for each individual infant, but varied between infants). The infant watched as the experimenter hid the object, then experienced one of three types of movement. In the rotation-only condition, the infant was moved 90 or 180 degrees around, but remained in the same place before being allowed to search for an object they had seen hidden. In the translation-only condition, the infant was moved to the right or left such that another hiding location occupied the same egocentric location as the correct location. In the rotation-plus-translation condition, as in the previous work, the infant was both moved laterally and rotated before being allowed to search. The results indicated that in both the rotation-only and the translation-only conditions, the infants could correct for their bodily movement and search in the right place. Performance in the combination condition was not as good, indicating that the complex movement was too much for the infant to correct for.

Other experiments have also indicated that infants have an ability to compensate for movement (i.e., to utilize dead reckoning), as long as that movement is within the infants' current motor repertoire. Self-produced movement is especially easy to take into account. For instance, by 6 months, infants do not make egocentric choices when the motion they are taken through is defined with respect to gravity – for instance, when they learn a location in a tilted position and are then tested when upright (Rieser, 1979). Rotations to the left and right of the sort that are produced by trunk movements while sitting can also be taken into account at this age (Lepecq & Lafaite, 1989; McKenzie, Day, & Ihsen, 1984).

Note, however, that to say that infants can use dead reckoning is not to claim that they have mature dead reckoning abilities. For instance, infants of 5 months have shown only a very crude ability to determine their direction of motion from optic flow information, as judged by experiments in which infants and adults look at displays that simulate optic flow during changes in direction. Adults can discriminate their direction of motion to within one degree of accuracy, but young infants discriminate only very large differences and do not look systematically at the focus of expansion in the displays (Gilmore & Rettke, 2003). There is also continued development over later childhood. For example, Rieser and Rider (1991) showed that adults were much better than 4-year-old children at locating objects after moving while blindfolded. The reason for the protracted nature of development of dead reckoning is unclear. Because movement in the world is very common, one might expect that the system would be tuned by environmental input fairly early.

So far, we have seen that infants may make use of dead reckoning as well as response learning, at least to some extent and in the right circumstances. Is there also evidence of cue learning in infancy? Acredolo (1978) suggested cue learning took some time to appear. In one condition of her study, infants were trained to look to one side for an event, as in the other conditions, but with the correct window marked by a large star. This availability of a landmark did not help the 6-month-olds, who still looked to the incorrect window. The 16-month-olds responded well even in the no-landmark condition and hence were not aided by landmarks. The 11-month-old group showed mixed results – about half the group followed the ego-centric rule of looking, and half used the landmark. Thus, this experiment found evidence of some cue learning only at 11 months.

Infants show evidence of cue learning as early as 6 months, however, under some conditions. In further exploration, Acredolo and Evans (1980) found that, when they added particularly salient cues (i.e., stripes and lights) that highlighted the correct window, even 6-month-old infants showed signs of making a choice based on something other than response learning. Six-month-old infants vacillated between the two sides, as if they were aware of the cue and able to use it, but were just not sure which system to rely on. Rieser (1979) also found evidence that 6-month-olds can use cue learning to locate objects, as long as they were not attracted to the ego-centrically defined choice and hence distracted. In another recent example of a study showing infants' early ability to use cue learning, McDonough (1999) found that at 7 months, infants can remember which of two distinctive containers holds a desired object, even after a delay of a minute that included distractions.

Additional evidence for the idea that response learning is a variable rather than a fixed tendency comes from two findings: choices based on response learning are less common when initial choices are not reinforced, and choices based on response learning are less common when infants are tested in environments in which they are emotionally secure (Acredolo, 1982). Thus, a variety of kinds of evidence suggest that response learning is not the only means infants have of coding spatial location, at least not by 5 or 6 months of age. Response learning, dead reckoning, and cue learning are all seen by then. However, the reliance infants place on these systems changes as they gain experience with the world and the consequences of action within it. Response learning comes to be regarded as less trustworthy, likely as experience shows that using it often results in failure. Piaget was correct in flagging a change, but he simply portrayed it as more absolute in nature than it appears to be.

A reweighting hypothesis of development (Newcombe & Huttenlocher, 2000) views the important mechanism of development as the analysis of which of the systems to use in which current situation. Early in life, the infant is not mobile, so both response learning and cue learning lead to the same response. As the infant grows and begins to move around more, response learning quickly becomes inaccurate. Once the infant is mobile, dead reckoning and both of the environment-centered systems are more accurate than response learning, so the weight assigned to each system changes in favor of the systems other than response learning. Evidence that crawling is important in the development of calibration of coding systems is summarized by Campos et al. (2000).

The A Not B Error

We have seen that there is evidence that response learning predominates at first, but that cue learning and dead reckoning can be seen in the situations that pull for them, and that they strengthen with age. How can these facts help to understand another kind of classic evidence for response learning (or sensorimotor coding), namely an error found in infants' spatial search between approximately 8 and 12 months, called the A not B error? The A not B error is observed on a task in which an infant sees a desired object hidden in the same location (A) repeatedly. The infant successfully searches that location (A) for the object. The infant then sees the object hidden in a new location (B), but continues to search for it at the first location (A). Thus, in this error, a child persists in searching for an object in the place it was usually found, even after seeing it hidden in a new location.

The effort to explain this phenomenon has led to a great deal of research into spatial understanding and search behavior. A number of accounts of the error and what it tells us about infant cognitive functioning currently exist. Diamond (1985) explored the issue of A not B errors in terms of the interaction of memory strength and inhibitory demands during the delay before search was allowed. She found that as infants got older they could tolerate longer and longer delays between hiding of the object in location B and search without making the A not B error. In her view, infants have a motor scheme that involves reaching for the object in location A, and must inhibit this reaching behavior given a memory of hiding at location B. If the memory decays, the ability to inhibit the previously reinforced response tends to win in a competition between the two tendencies. With development, both inhibition and memory increase. Other accounts of the A not B error have been proposed that use dynamic systems theory (Smith, Thelen, Titzer, & McLin, 1999) or insights and evidence taken from connectionist modeling (Munakata, McClelland, Johnson, & Siegler, 1997). However, none of these accounts has a detailed analysis of what kinds of spatial location memory are engaged by the task (Newcombe, 2001; Newcombe & Huttenlocher, 2000).

One important issue in theorizing about the A not B error has been evidence that the error is not seen in infants' looking responses, only in their grasping and manual search. Ahmed and Ruffman (1998) found that, with a series of hidings and appearances at location A, followed by hiding at location B, infants of 8- to 12-months looked longer at objects appearing at A than at B, indicating that they expected appearance at location B and viewed an object at A as unexpected. That is, they were not committing the A not B error. Similarly, but using a paradigm even more analogous to the standard A not B methodology, Hofstadter and Reznick (1996) found that, when looking to the hidden objects' location was all that was required of the infant, 7-month-olds did not make the A not B error. Intriguingly, however, they also found that 5-month-olds did make the A not B error in this situation.

One can supplement recent accounts of the A not B error, such as the dynamic systems theory advocated by Esther Thelen, Linda Smith, and their colleagues, with an analysis of spatial coding (see Thelen, Schoner, Scheier, & Smith, 2001, and commentary by Newcombe, 2001). In terms of our typology of spatial coding, the A not B situation faces infants with deciding whether to base their responses on one of five kinds of information that are available. Four are types of response learning (most frequent reach, most recent reach, most frequent look, most recent look) and one is a simple kind of place learning (distance from specified landmarks). Three of these pieces of information lead infants to make the wrong grasp (i.e., the most frequent reach, most recent reach, and most frequent look were all to Location A). Two kinds of information lead to the correct grasp (the most recent look and simple place learning). Succeeding in the A not B situation is a matter of weighting these alternatives correctly (Newcombe & Huttenlocher, 2000). Success in grasping comes later than success in looking because it requires ignoring information in the grasp system in favor of reliance on information regarding looking. This kind of account of development is interactionist because it postulates that early competencies are tuned and made adaptive by environmental input.

Development of Place Learning

So far, we have discussed the development of response learning, cue learning and dead reckoning. We have deferred examination of the fourth system, place learning, because it does not seem to be acquired in the first year of life, although components of it are present. Place learning requires the ability to code distance and direction, but also the ability to do so in relation to several landmarks at once. The first ability may be present early. Huttenlocher, Newcombe, and Sandberg (1994) showed that toddlers as young as sixteen months can successfully find an object hidden in a continuous space (such as a sandbox), illustrated in Figure 6.3, thus showing evidence of distance coding. In Figure 6.4, actual responses of toddlers

FIGURE 6.3. A child looking for a hidden object in a long rectangular sandbox, as in experiments conducted by Huttenlocher et al. (1994).

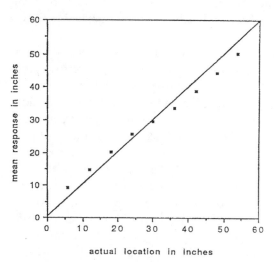

FIGURE 6.4. Average locations at which children searched for objects in Huttenlocher et al. (1994), Experiment 1, plotted against actual locations.

in searching for an object hidden in the sandbox are shown plotted against the actual hiding locations. One can see how close the data come to the diagonal line that would represent perfect performance. Newcombe, Huttenlocher, and Learmonth (1999) found coding of distance evident in looking time responses of 5-month-olds. Infants saw an object disappear and reappear in a sandbox several times. Then, on the experimental trial, the object disappeared as in all the other trials, but reappeared in a different location. Infants could apparently detect the change, because they looked longer when the object appeared in a different location from where it disappeared.

These studies show some ability to code distance in relation to the enclosing sandbox, but may not indicate the ability to code distance from discrete objects. There is some ambiguity as to the origins of this behavior. On the one hand, Lew, Bremner and Lefkovitch (2000) found that 9-month-olds were able to learn to look between two landmarks in order to see an interesting event, such as an experimenter playing a peekaboo game, in a fashion similar to the Acredolo paradigm. However, relational landmark use in this situation seems very simple – it is almost categorical, rather than metric, because one can succeed simply by using the relation "between." In an experiment requiring coding distance with respect to a landmark, Bushnell, McKenzie, Lawrence, and Connell (1995) studied 12-month-olds who searched for objects hidden under one of many small pillows covering the floor of a circular enclosure. A few of the pillows were colored differently than the others. The children could not use the location of colored cushions to guide search for objects hidden under unmarked cushions some distance away.

Whenever the ability to code distance from discrete objects as well as enclosing surfaces develops, this ability alone does not constitute place learning, which is defined as the coordinated use of several pieces of such information to uniquely determine a location. A watershed in the development of place learning may occur toward the end of the second year of life. As shown in Figure 6.5, children who were 16 to 20 months old could not use landmarks in a room to help to localize objects hidden in a sandbox after they had moved to the other side of the box, but children of 21 months and older did use distal landmarks, indicating that they have the ability to use the place learning system at its most powerful (Newcombe, Huttenlocher, Drummey, & Wiley, 1998). Mangan, Franklin, Tignor, Bolling, and Nadel (1994) and DeLoache and Brown (1983) have obtained similar results.

The place learning system is far from mature at 24 months, however. Children younger than 5 years or so do not do as well as older individuals in

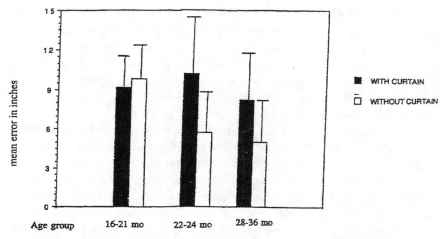

FIGURE 6.5. Average errors in searching for objects in the sandbox after moving around it, with and without being able to see distal landmarks, in Newcombe et al. (1998).

an eight-arm radial maze (Aadland, Beatty, & Maki, 1985; Foreman, Arber, & Savage, 1984). Children younger than about 7 years do not perform well in finding objects in large circular enclosures or open fields (Overman, Pate, Moore, & Peuster, 1996) or in using distal landmarks in a computer-generated arena (Laurence, Learmonth, Nadel, & Jacobs, in press).

Development of Hierarchical Coding

Hierarchical coding, in which fine-grained estimates of distances and angles are adjusted by categorical knowledge to compensate for uncertainty, is an adaptive system. The developmental question is when its components, learning of spatial categories and coding of distance and direction, are available, and whether they are hierarchically combined as soon as available or whether this mode of processing takes time to emerge. As we have seen, Newcombe, Huttenlocher, and Learmonth (1999) found that infants as young as 5 months old remember an object's location in terms of distance within the continuous enclosed space of a sandbox. Coding of spatial location in categorical terms is evident in experiments by Quinn (1994). Infants of 3 months group varying locations together as "above" or "below," at least so long as a perceptual referent is present to demarcate the categories (i.e., they are above or below a horizontal line) and when the locations are all marked in the same way (i.e., by a dot). More robust formation of spatial categories is evident by 6 months, when infants will form categories of above and below with respect to a wider frame of reference (i.e., no horizontal line is needed to form a boundary) and with respect to objects that vary in appearance as well as location (Quinn, Cummins, Kase, Martin, & Weissman, 1996). However, there is no evidence on whether or not category and fine-grained information are hierarchically combined in the first year of life.

We do know that hierarchical combination is evident by 16 months. When searching for objects hidden in a long sandbox, toddlers of this age show a bias in their searches toward the center of the box. This bias is evident in Figure 6.4 in the fact that children's responses at the left of the graph are above the diagonal line showing perfect responding, while children's responses at the right are below the line. A bias toward the center of the box appears even when children are located toward the sides of the box at hiding and at search. It also appears when they move laterally between hiding and search (Huttenlocher et al., 1994; Spencer, Smith, & Thelen, 2001). Thus, the biases in basically quite accurate searches do not reflect a perceptual process, or laziness. They are compatible with correction of a fine-grained estimate of location by a category prototype, in this case, the center of the box.

Early appearance of hierarchical combination does not, however, imply a mature ability. Several kinds of change occur over preschool and elementary school. First, as memory becomes more durable and hence uncertainty increases more slowly across delay (in a very systematic fashion for children of different ages – see Hund, Plumert, & Benney, 2002, and Schutte & Spencer, 2002), bias becomes less evident across the age range of 2 to 6 years (Schutte, 2001). Second, categories begin to be based on mentally created areas as well as perceptually given ones. For instance, in the sandbox, the prototype is initially the center of the box, but by 11 years or so, the box is mentally divided into right and left halves, with a prototype for each half (Huttenlocher et al., 1994; Schutte, 2001). In a model house, when people are asked to place objects at remembered locations after walls have been removed, category bias is evident for 11-year-olds and adults, but not earlier (Plumert & Hund, 2001). Third, by 10 years old, children become capable of hierarchical combination along two dimensions at once (Sandberg, Huttenlocher, & Newcombe, 1996).

There are many unanswered questions about the development of hierarchical coding. For instance, 11-year-olds seem like adults in many experiments, but they have also been found in several experiments to show less categorical bias than either younger children or adults (Hund, Plumert, &

Benney, 2002). However, it is already evident that, although the rudiments of hierarchical coding are present early, development continues across a wide age span. In fact, the age at which hierarchical coding seems mature is at least as late as that originally postulated by Piaget for the achievement of adult spatial competence. This fact suggests that the demonstrations of spatial abilities in infants and young children so exciting in recent decades may have distracted us from an essential insight that Piaget had regarding what tasks older children still find difficult. This is not to say that a hierarchical-coding account of development is fundamentally Piagetian, however, both because of the strength of the starting points seen for this line of development, and because the characterization of the nature of spatial representation is quite different.

A Geometric Module?

Historically, one argument favoring nativism has been demonstrations that infants possess surprising abilities that seem difficult to explain except as inherently preprogrammed. However, later-appearing abilities are consistent with nativism if they are seen as maturationally emergent, and even early-appearing abilities may depend on experience-expectant environmental input (Newcombe, 2002b). A stronger argument for the nativist approach comes from the idea of modularity of mind (Fodor, 1983). If certain abilities are isolated from other ones, developing along separate lines and dependent on specialized neural areas, it seems to many researchers that the brain/mind must have a great degree of specified architecture at birth (but see Elman et al., 1996). Modularity has been the focus of intense debate in a variety of domains of cognitive development (Karmiloff-Smith, 1992). In the spatial domain, Hermer and Spelke (1994, 1996) have claimed that children begin with a "geometric module" shared with other species. The geometric module processes information about the shape of enclosing spaces but does not utilize cue or landmark information.

Hermer and Spelke found that toddlers of 18 to 24 months, who we know can use landmarks under most circumstances, did not use landmarks when they were disoriented in a small rectangular room, and then asked to find an object they had seen hidden in one corner of the room before the disorientation. Toddlers preferred the correct corner and the opposite, geometrically congruent corner over the two other corners, but did not evidence a preference for the correct corner over the congruent corner even when a colored wall made possible the disambiguation of the two

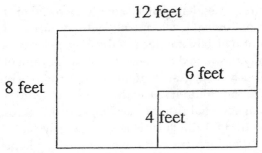

FIGURE 6.6. Relative room sizes used in studies by Hermer & Spelke (1996) and by Learmonth et al. (2001).

corners. Instead they divided their search between the correct and congruent corners. Hermer and Spelke explained this finding by claiming that
young children have an impenetrable geometric module for reorientation.
The impenetrable module would not allow the children to use the available
landmarks in combination with the geometric configuration of the room;
thus they could only use the geometric properties of the room to reorient.
In a rectangular room, geometry alone does not allow a distinction between
one corner and its opposite, congruent corner.

Learmonth, Newcombe, and Huttenlocher (2001) have, however, cast
doubt on this claim. They noted that Hermer and Spelke (1994, 1996) used
a room that was 4 by 6 feet (i.e., extremely small), and therefore conducted
the same experiment in a room that was 8 by 12 feet (four times the area
of the smaller room, but maintaining the same ratio of the longer and
shorter sides, as shown in Figure 6.6). They found that the children of 18 to
24 months did, indeed, use the colored wall to reorient, and chose correctly
between the two congruent corners. Learmonth, Nadel, and Newcombe
(2002) tested 4-year-old children in rooms of both sizes in a within-subjects
design. They found that, in the small room, they replicated the findings of
Hermer and Spelke (1994, 1996), while in the larger room, children could
use landmark information to distinguish between geometrically identical
corners.

These findings undermine the hypothesis of the impenetrable geometric module, because no sensible module would operate only in a very
restricted set of circumstances, such as small rooms. In fact, spatial cognition is generally considered to involve a large environment not a small
one, much larger in fact than the 8 by 12 feet rooms in which no evidence
was found of an impenetrable module. The findings do, however, raise
some questions. Why does the size of the space make a difference? And

why, in the small rooms, do children younger than 6 years of age ignore a landmark that would help them find a desired object (Hermer-Vazquez, Moffet, & Munkholm, 2001; Learmonth, Nadel & Newcombe, 2002)? As discussed at greater length by Newcombe (in press), the affordance of action in the larger space is a likely explanation for the better performance in the larger room. Action is known to enhance spatial attention and to be important in the retuning of hippocampal neurons (Lever, Wills, Cacucci, Burgess, & O'Keefe, 2002). Thus, action may be important for the combination of geometric and nongeometric information required to succeed in the rectangular-room studies. This approach can also explain the late success in the small room. Adaptive combination is, not surprisingly, more difficult for younger than for older children. An age difference is actually evident in the larger as well as in the smaller room – performance simply is above chance for toddlers in the larger room but at chance in the smaller room. Thus, there are no facts unique to development in the small room that need to be explained.

PERSPECTIVE TAKING AND MENTAL ROTATION

The development of perspective taking is a staple of introductory child development texts, few of which are complete without an illustration of Piaget and Inhelder's Three Mountains task (shown in Figure 6.7) or a similar display. These texts usually discuss findings suggesting that children are spatially egocentric until the age of 9 or 10 years. That is, when asked what an observer would see from another viewpoint, younger children pick the picture showing what they see from where they are.

In more up-to-date texts, this presentation may be modified by noting that some studies have shown earlier success in perspective-taking tasks. In fact, there is a voluminous literature on the development of perspective taking, with many studies focused on demonstrating earlier competence than Piaget postulated (see review by Newcombe, 1989). To cite some illustrative work, Borke (1975) showed that young children can do well on the Three Mountains task if they are asked to indicate what an observer would see by rotating a moveable display. Lempers, Flavell, and Flavell (1977) found that children as young as 2 years, asked to show an observer their drawing, held the paper up so that the picture faced the observer. Hughes and Donaldson (1979) showed preschoolers a display consisting of a mazelike arrangement of walls and open spaces. They positioned a policeman and a thief in various spots in this display, and asked when the policeman could spot the thief and when he could not. Children did well

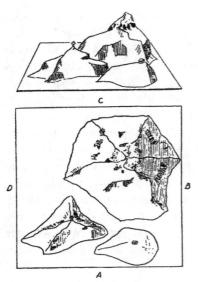

FIGURE 6.7. Apparatus used by Piaget and Inhelder (1948–1967) in the Three Mountains task.

on this task. Studies of this kind converged on the conclusion that young children can use a line-of-sight heuristic to infer what another observer can see (Yaniv & Shatz, 1990). Possession of such an heuristic undermines the claim of egocentrism, although it leaves open the possibility that children younger than 9 or 10 years have difficulty with the computation required to work out in detail what another observer would see of a complex display (i.e., how relations among objects, all of which remain visible, would be altered by observer movement).

There is a somewhat smaller literature on the development of mental rotation, but it follows a similar script. In this case, Piaget and Inhelder (1971) suggested a different age for the achievement of competence, tying it to the achievement of concrete operational skills at around the age of 7 or 8 years. However, analogous to the literature on perspective taking, papers appeared in the 1970s showing that younger children, as young as 4 years, could succeed on mental rotation tasks if presented engagingly and if children were not asked (as Piaget and Inhelder had) to indicate their predictions about the effects of mental rotation by drawing the outcomes (a difficult task). Marmor (1975, 1977) used a mental rotation paradigm involving bears with same or different arms raised, in which children had to indicate if a tilted bear was the same or different from a reference bear.

She examined the relation of reaction time to amount of rotation, finding that, as with adults, there was a linear relation between the two. More recently, there have been reports that, at least as indexed by looking time measures, babies of 4 to 6 months form expectations about what a rotating object moving behind an occluder will look like when it emerges (Hespos & Rochat, 1997; Rochat & Hespos, 1996).

Several questions can be raised about these literatures. One question has to do with the relation between perspective taking and mental rotation. Imagining walking around an object or a display seems formally similar to imagining the object or display rotating on its axis, and the "answer" (what one would see after the movement, whether of observer or of display) is identical. Yet mental rotation is sometimes easier than perspective taking (Huttenlocher & Presson, 1973) and sometimes harder (Huttenlocher & Presson, 1979). A second question is really a set of questions revolving around how to study development and whether the strategy of describing the abilities of children of different ages confronted with different tasks is a sensible method for coming to understand development. Researchers have debated how important is the question of age of emergence of competencies such as perspective taking and mental rotation, whether the age of emergence has been accurately estimated, and whether there is in fact any such thing as competence to estimate.

Let us look first at the relation of perspective taking and mental rotation. Huttenlocher and Presson (1973) found that children of 10 years or so were much more able to pick a picture showing the outcome of rotation of an array than they were to pick a picture showing the array after they had moved around it. They argued that the difference was linked to whether or not literally following the instructions leads to a conflict of frames of reference. With mental rotation, imaging movement of an array leaves one firmly planted in the reference frame of the perceptually present room. With perspective taking, imaging one's own movement transforms the reference frame and leads to a conflict between that imagined reference frame and the reference frame of the perceptually present room. This analysis leads to two predictions. First, physically moving around an array should make perspective taking much easier, and this is true (Huttenlocher & Presson, 1973; Shantz & Watson, 1971). Second, asking about what would be seen from another viewpoint should be much easier if one is not asked to choose among pictures. Asking a question such as "If you were over there, what object would be closest to you?" in fact allows for successful performance, both by older children (Huttenlocher & Presson, 1979) and even by children as young as 3 years (Newcombe & Huttenlocher, 1992).

Mental rotation is not always easier than perspective taking. In fact, with questions about the location of an object after rotation of an array used as a dependent measure, it becomes very difficult (Huttenlocher & Presson, 1979; Presson, 1982a; Simons & Wang, 1998; Wraga, Creem, & Proffitt, 2000). The reason for the difficulty of mental rotation with this kind of task is that the whole array needs to be rotated in order to answer a question about an individual element; people often approach such complex rotation tasks on a piecemeal basis (Just & Carpenter, 1985). Although there are other explanations of these effects and some debate about them (Simons & Wang, 1998; Wraga et al., 2000; see Newcombe, 2002a, for a fuller review), there is one bottom-line conclusion about what has been found. The complex pattern of differences between closely comparable spatial tasks suggests that what we call spatial cognition may be closely linked to perceptual-motor systems originally developed for actually acting in space. The neural machinery we use to move in the world is different from the neural machinery we use while stationary to interact with objects. There are, apparently, corresponding differences in our thought about these matters.

Now, let us turn our attention to the important issue of what developmental research on age of attainment of various competencies means. This issue is enormously complex and controversial. Chapman (1988) argued that most studies in the tradition of "children can succeed younger than Piaget thought" ignored the fact that, in changing the tasks, they changed the essential nature of what was assessed. For instance, he cited the case of Borke's (1975) use of a turntable to assess perspective taking. Use of this apparatus eliminates the need to represent and transform the internal relations among the elements of the display, which was what Piaget had wanted to assess. This argument is related to Thelen and Smith's (1994) case that there is no such entity as competence, but instead only the ability to cope with very specific situations defined by their task dynamics. These theorists go in opposite directions with their arguments: Chapman believes in the existence of competence and wants to hold to a rigorous definition of what performances constitute attainment, while Thelen and Smith believe that all, or preferably none, of the various abilities exhibited by humans of various ages deserve the name competence.

One way out of this impasse is to adopt the view that various definitions of competence are possible, and that such definitions can be usefully tied to ecological demands (Newcombe & Huttenlocher, 2000). Viewed in this way, findings that infants can walk early in life when given buoyancy by immersion in water is an interesting fact about the task dynamics of walking and its development, but not indicative of competence because humans generally locomote on dry land. The fact that adult humans cannot walk in environments with three times the Earth's gravity does not indicate they lack competence, because they are never called upon to do this task, at least not in the environment of adaptation. This perspective suggests that the descriptive task for developmental psychology is to study the sequence of abilities that unfold over time, and the determinants of that sequence and that progress. One implication is that early manifestations of components of an ability should not be ignored, but neither should they be regarded as the essence of a competence, with subsequent change no more than enrichment or refinement. With respect to perspective taking and mental rotation, this means that it is important to remember that children do, indeed, have difficulty with conflicting frames of reference until quite late in elementary school. Piaget did not characterize this difficulty quite correctly, but his essential observation has not been challenged by hundreds of subsequent papers on the topic.

EXTERNAL SYMBOLIC REPRESENTATIONS OF SPATIAL INFORMATION

We frequently want to find something that another person knows the location of, or to go somewhere we have never been, but that someone we know is familiar with. One of the most central of human adaptations is, of course, the ability to exchange information, thus eliminating the need to learn everything anew. Dealing with the spatial world is no exception. Being able to interpret models or maps that another person has made can save hours of wandering around a terrain, as when a relative of a dead pirate uses his treasure map to locate the gold bullion buried by Skull Rock. Being able to interpret verbal directions can be similarly helpful, as when someone says, "Looking for your watch? I saw it an hour ago lying in the grass by the azalea bush."

MAPS AND MODELS

Maps and models are spatial in nature and offer the viewer a spatial representation of the larger space complete with information about the relationship between objects in space. The task of understanding a map or model has several important elements. Most basically, in order to use a map or model, one must first understand that this is a small-scale representation of a larger space in which two types of correspondence obtain. First, the elements on the map correspond to elements in the world, and second, the relations among those elements hold on a larger scale in the world. Additionally, one must master other skills in order to use maps and models effectively, including interpreting arbitrary symbols such as a star standing for a city, orienting the map physically or mentally to align it with a space, and performing scale translations.

Models and maps both represent the spatial relations among objects in the world, but there are some differences. Models are usually three-dimensional in nature while maps are two-dimensional, models generally stand for smaller spaces than maps do, and the symbols models use are often small-scale replicas of the objects they represent rather than the arbitrary elements frequently used in maps (Newcombe & Huttenlocher, 2000). Although these generalizations do not always hold (consider whether a globe representing the world is a model or a map), it is useful to use these characteristics as a guide to understanding the two kinds of symbolizations. There has been separate developmental research on children's understanding in these two areas.

Models

DeLoache (1987, 1989, 1995) has studied the development of the ability to use models in detail. DeLoache reports a rapid change in the ability of children to use a model as a tool to find an object in the real space. Children in her studies (DeLoache, 1987, 1989) saw an object hidden in a specific place in the model, and were then asked to search for that object in the life-sized room represented in the model (or vice versa, but for simplicity's sake, we will describe the phenomena in unidirectional terms). DeLoache found that, despite the fact that the children could all retrieve the object in the place they had seen it hidden in the model, 2.5-year-olds could not use information from the model to guide their search for a larger version of the object in the life size space. However, 3-year-old children were able to use the model, at least as long as the model and the life-size space were very similar to each other. DeLoache (1995) argues that at around the third birthday children achieve a representational insight that allows them to see a model as a representation of the space.

This representational insight is not an all-or-none phenomenon. Even 3-year olds have difficulty with the task when the color of the objects in the model is different from those in the real space and even 2.5-year-olds can succeed when the size of the model room is not too much different from the size of the real room (DeLoache, Kolstad, & Anderson, 1991). Children of 2.5 years can also use pictures to guide their searches better than they can use models, perhaps because models are more a "thing in themselves" (DeLoache, 1991). Various interventions help children to achieve "representational insight" in situations they find difficult. Seeing a "shrinking machine" that was said to be able to miniaturize the real room helps (DeLoache, Miller, & Rosengren, 1997), as does a simple initial experience with systematic comparison of two model spaces (Loewenstein & Gentner, 2001).

Overall, the message of this research is that, between the ages of roughly 2 and 4 years, children become able to appreciate the idea that a small three-dimensional space can represent a larger one. This representational insight is an all-or-none phenomenon in particular situations, but its availability varies as a function of many variables, such as the similarity of the model to what is represented. Harking back to our discussion of competence, children of a certain age may seem either incompetent or competent, depending on just how one tests them. The best way to think about development seems, as before, to conceptualize it as starting from certain areas of restricted skill and as strengthening from these growing points, in part due to experience with success in the initially restricted situations. Eventually, competence is apparent enough in a variety of ecologically plausible settings that we count it as mature. However, even people possessing this "mature" competence may perform poorly in unusually challenging circumstances.

Maps

Maps might be more difficult for young children to understand than models, due to the fact that maps are usually two-dimensional, involve radical scale translation, and use noniconic elements to represent locations. However, two-dimensionality by itself may not be an issue (see the chapter on maps, Taylor, Chapter 8). Four-year-olds can understand schematic versions of the objects in the real world; if the map is made up of small-sized pictures of the target objects, 4-year-olds can use them (Uttal, 1994, 1996). By 6 years, children have no difficulty recognizing that there is a relationship between even arbitrary symbols on the map and objects in the real world: They can use a mark such as an X on a map to locate a ball (Presson, 1982b) and a blue dot to represent their starting point on the map (Sandberg & Huttenlocher, 2001). Even 3-year-olds have been found to be above chance in their ability to use relations such as "X marks the spot" (Dalke, 1998).

One should not overstress early competency, however. Five-year-olds have difficulty understanding the elements on a map in some cases (Liben & Yekel, 1996). The children in Liben and Yekel's (1996) study reported that the icons on the map were not a good enough representation of the items in the real world, pointing out deficiencies such as the fact that the tables didn't have legs.

Navigation Using Maps and Models

One important point of learning to use a map is to learn to use it to navigate in an unfamiliar space. This requires not only understanding that the map itself is a representation of a space in the real world. The child also has to understand the issues of scale difference and of the need to align the map with the space, either physically or mentally. The ability to scale distance in simple situations involving the location of a single object can be seen in some 3-year-olds and most 4-year-olds (Huttenlocher, Newcombe, & Vasilyeva, 1999). Preschoolers in these studies were able to use a point in a rectangle drawn on a piece of paper to locate an object hidden in a much larger rectangular sandbox. However, in more complicated situations involving a set of points, children as old as 5, 6, and 7 years show shrinking or expansion in their reproduction of layouts, even though they preserve relative location (Uttal, 1996).

The ability to align a map also shows a sequence of development extending from preschool into the school years, and even beyond (for problems that adults can have with alignment, see Levine, Jankovic, & Palij, 1982). Preschoolers can physically rotate a model in order to answer perspective-taking questions (Borke, 1975; Rosser, 1983). However, they show problems using rotated maps (Bluestein & Acredolo, 1979) or seeing correspondences between models that are aligned differently (Blades, 1991). By 6 years, children given aligned maps could preserve alignment information through corner turns (Sandberg & Huttenlocher, 2001), and by 8 years, children can deal with misaligned maps (Presson, 1982b).

Children use maps long before scaling and alignment abilities are fully in place, but only when the maps are in the necessary orientation and are very simple. Investigators have shown that 3- and 4-year-olds can benefit from the use of maps that have only a few, very identifiable icons and show a simple route (Uttal & Wellman, 1989). Six-year-olds are able to follow a route through an area using a map as long as they do not have to plan the route themselves (Cramer & Presson, 1995). The ability to use a map to plan a trip or to make inferences likely improves well into the elementary school years and beyond.

The fact that children learn to use maps slowly over the first decade or so casts doubt on an exclusively nativist approach to spatial development. If spatial understanding were firmly guided by preprogrammed understanding, cracking the code of mapping conventions should be no harder than learning a language, a process that is virtually complete by 3 or 4 years of age. Slow emergence is consistent with Piaget's argument that the ability to read a map required a shift from egocentric and topological space to the more mature Euclidean space at around 10 years old, but we have seen that there are other reasons to question the usefulness of this Piagetian typology of spatial representation. A sociocultural (Vygotskyan) perspective probably fits the facts best. This theory emphasizes the role of the adults around a child in guiding map understanding, by explanation and by providing scaffolding. This approach is appealing in that children do seem to benefit from practice and spatial instruction in other tasks (Baenninger & Newcombe, 1989; Huttenlocher, Levine, & Vevea, 1998). Recent investigation of how parents interpret graphic media in reading to their children points to the possible importance of parental input. What parents did was found to be correlated with spatial development (Szechter & Liben, 2004). In addition, Uttal (2000) has marshaled a great deal of evidence for the proposition that using maps transforms spatial understanding, rather than simply being a medium for communicating what is already known. This hypothesis is classically Vygotskyan.

LANGUAGE

It is not always possible to exchange spatial information using maps or models – for instance, when we are speaking on the telephone. Language can also be used to describe spatial location and spatial relations, although such encoding is not always easy. There are at least three reasons why talking about space can be a difficult process. First, spatial extent is a continuous dimension, but language usually expresses ideas categorically. Second, one can perceive several spatial relations simultaneously, but one can only talk about those relations one at a time. Third, speakers and listeners need to agree on spatial reference frames if they are to avoid ambiguity. For example, if a person is facing the side of a car, "in front of the car" could mean "between you and the car" or "in front of the car's headlights."

It seems, however, that people cope with these issues quite well. They can use categorical spatial coding to give meaning to categorical spatial terms, and they can use measurement language when they wish to be more precise about spatial extent (e.g., 38 feet NNW of the lighthouse). They use strategies, such as a mental tour, a bird's eye view, or hierarchical structuring, to organize their linguistic descriptions of a space (Linde & Labov, 1975; Plumert, Carswell, DeVet, & Ihrig, 1995; Plumert, Spalding, & Nichols-Whitehead, 2001; Shanon, 1984). They use other strategies to establish common frames of reference, such as assuming that an established frame will not shift in the middle of a conversation (Carlson-Radvansky & Jiang, 1998).

How do children attain this proficiency with spatial language? Children learn some spatial terms, such as "up" and "down," and "in," "on" and "under," in the years between 1 and 3 (Bloom, 1973; Nelson, 1974). This period is the same one that we have seen is important for the achievement of important elements of mature spatial coding. What then, is the relation between spatial language and spatial thought during development? It has widely been assumed that children's spatial concepts come first, and that, given these concepts, they seek the linguistic means of talking about them (e.g., Johnston, 1988).

More recently, however, the "cognition first" approach has been challenged (Bowerman, 1996, 2000) and it has been proposed that the language to which children are exposed guides what they notice about the spatial world. There are findings to support the "language guides acquisition" view. Children in Korean versus English language environments learn the very different spatial categories marked in their languages, at roughly the same pace (Choi & Bowerman, 1991). Very young children's comprehension is already affected by the spatial categories of languages whose words they are not yet producing (Choi, McDonough, Bowerman, & Mandler, 1999). When a native language uses an absolute system of spatial reference (in which, for instance, one says the equivalent of "the cup is north of the plate"), children learn to use this system at a surprisingly young age (Brown & Levinson, 2000).

Once a basic spatial vocabulary has been established, children still have a good deal to learn about spatial communication, mainly about the social understanding and cultural conventions that help to structure relationships between speakers and listeners. They do not communicate as efficiently as adults about spatial matters until around 8 to 10 years of age (e.g., Allen, Kirasic, & Beard, 1989; Gauvain & Rogoff, 1989). By then, they are proficient at such matters as choosing prominent landmarks for use in spatial description (Craton et al., 1990; Plumert, Ewert, & Spear, 1995), or at establishing common spatial reference frames (Taylor & Klein, 1994). One element in this developmental improvement may be the growth of spatial working memory (Ondracek & Allen, 2000). Another element may be parental scaffolding of children's spatial communication (Plumert

& Nichols-Whitehead, 1996). Parents use directive prompts (e.g., "Say whether it's beside the plant or closer to the teapot") to get their children to resolve ambiguity in spatial descriptions. Thus, the development of spatial communication is likely due to a mixture of the development of "basic hardware" and the acquisition of socially based information about what other listeners find easy to understand.

THINKING USING SPATIAL SYSTEMS

Spatial images and diagrams, both mental and worked out on paper, are often used in problem solving and creative thought (Gattis, 2001; Huttenlocher, 1968; Shepard, 1988; Tversky, 2000). That is, spatial competence may underlie more than simply specifically spatial behavior, but may also prove useful in thinking about nonspatial matters.

One good example of this idea is the solution of transitive reasoning problems. When people are told that, "Daniel is taller than Carl" and also that, "Carl is taller than Eric," they are able to conclude that "Daniel is taller than Eric." Huttenlocher (1968) proposed that the combination of the premise information into an integrated visuospatial representation was the basis for this ability. Clark (1969), however, argued for an alternative, linguistic account. Sternberg (1980) proposed that a combined spatial-linguistic model best accounted for the known phenomena about transitive reasoning. Recently, Hummel and Holyoak (2001) have presented a process model in which spatial representations are central. The model emphasizes the demands transitive reasoning place on working memory.

There has been considerable research interest in development of transitive reasoning. As with so many other topics in cognitive development, the origins of this interest were in Piagetian theory. Piaget thought that transitive reasoning was one of the hallmarks of the achievement of concrete operations at the age of around 7 or 8 years. Bryant and Trabasso (1972) argued, however, that children's difficulties with transitive reasoning were due to their difficulty in remembering the basic premises, not to their lack of understanding of logic. A counterargument to this memory hypothesis has focused on the fact that remembering the premises may itself be part of the reasoning process, not an autonomous prerequisite to reasoning. If memory involves placing the entities in order and forming an integrated spatial array, the encoding process itself assumes use of transitive reasoning (Chapman & Lindenberger, 1992a, 1992b; Halford & Kelly, 1984).

One possibility is that both long-term memory for premises and transitive reasoning requires working memory, as stressed in the Hummel-Holyoak model. In this account, development of either process depends on the development of working memory. In accord with this approach, investigators have found that performing concurrent tasks, which reduces the availability of working memory, reduces children's ability to perform transitive reasoning (Halford, Maybery, & Bain, 1986; Oakhill, 1984; Perner & Aebi, 1985). As we have seen before, the question of when children attain competence is not a simple one to answer. They appear to understand something about the structure of transitive reasoning arguments by the late preschool years, but, perhaps because of working memory limitations, they are unable to cope with many real-world situations in which transitive reasoning would be advantageous until later into the elementary school years.

A second example of how spatial thinking may facilitate thought about nonspatial matters comes from the use of graphs and diagrams to aid reasoning. Probably all readers of this volume are familiar with the way in which a well-constructed graph can focus one's thinking about data, or a diagram can clarify how an apparatus was set up or the sequence of events in an experiment. In the example of a diagram of an apparatus, one spatial structure is used to represent another. However, in the other examples, spatial concepts stand for nonspatial ones in a kind of analogical mapping. Gattis (2002) has investigated the ability of children in the early years of elementary school to understand and use simple graphs. The children had no prior exposure to graphical conventions, and yet they showed highly orderly analogical mappings similar to those shown by adults. This facility in the use of spatial reasoning suggests that graphs can be used to good effect in education and that qualitative instruction in their usefulness can begin early. Difficulties with graphs tend to occur when they are introduced later in a curriculum, in a quantitative and nonintuitive way.

SUMMARY

In this chapter, we have discussed the development of spatial competence considered as the development of several different abilities: spatial location coding using several different possible systems, hierarchical coding integrating various grains and types of coding, mental transformation of spatial information, external symbolization of spatial information using both visuospatial media and language, and the use of spatial systems for seemingly more abstract thought. We close by synthesizing this information, at both the descriptive and theoretical levels.

Table 6.2 provides a descriptive summary, which gives some of the rough age ranges that have been discerned for first appearance of an ability, its refinement, and the eventual attainment of what might be called mature competence (although we should remember that the average performance of adults in many spatial tasks is often error-prone and very amenable to improvement through practice and training). The table is, of course, based on currently available evidence, and many aspects of it remain to be investigated. For instance, hierarchical coding is listed as available at 16 months because we know that it is used by this age (Huttenlocher et al., 1994). However, younger children's hierarchical coding abilities have not been investigated, and it is possible that combination of information across levels may occur as early as 5 or 6 months, when the component skills of coding information both categorically and in a fine-grained way are known to be available.

At the theoretical level, the information summarized in this chapter and further distilled in Table 6.2 suggests the strengths and weaknesses of the existing theories of spatial development. Piagetian theory does not provide a very good typology for thinking about spatial representation, and Piaget obviously underestimated the abilities of infants and young children. On the other hand, attainment of spatial competence is not evident until as late in childhood as Piaget suggested, and some of the maturing abilities, such as the combination of hierarchical coding along two dimensions at once, are reminiscent of Piaget's thoughts about competence. Piaget's stress on the role of motor interaction with the physical world has also received substantial support. Nativist claims about geometric modules are questionable. On the other hand, the nativists' stress on searching for early ability in infants and toddlers has paid off in the rapid discovery of a wealth of information on what little children can do. Vygotskyan theories stress the impact of culture and adult instruction, and there is some evidence of such effects in the spatial domain, especially in the acquisition of external symbol systems such as maps and language. However, Vygotskyan theory seems ill equipped to deal with lines of spatial development that are not targets of direct instruction and that do not deal with cultural norms and artifacts, for example, the advent of hierarchical coding and place learning.

It is well known that models fit data better when they include more parameters, and hence it is perhaps inevitable that interactionist theories that combine constructivism, nativism, and Vygotskyan theory are more successful than any of these approaches is alone. However, integrative

TABLE 6.2. *Summary of Milestones in the Development of Spatial Competence.*

Age	Ability
Birth	Response learning dominant, i.e., infants of this age code spatial location chiefly, or possibly exclusively, in terms of actions that result in perceptual contact.
5–6 months	Response learning still dominant, but cue learning evident with salient landmarks or little competition and dead reckoning evident with simple actions that are already in the infant's repertoire. In addition, by this age, infants code spatial extent within an enclosing frame (i.e., a sandbox), and they group spatial locations into categories such as "above" and "below."
9 months	A not B errors are commonly observed in traditional paradigms, although such errors can also be seen earlier and later, for example, with shorter or longer delays.
16 months	By this age, and possibly earlier, children show hierarchical coding of location in which a fine-grained estimate is adjusted by knowledge of a spatial category, especially when the estimate is uncertain.
21 months	Children begin to show evidence of place learning, i.e., coding location in relation to distance and direction from external landmarks.
1–3 years	Children acquire basic spatial terms during this two-year period.
2–4 years	Children begin to show representational insight regarding models and maps during this period, gradually extending the range of circumstances in which they can see and use a symbolic relation to learn about space.
3–4 years	Children can succeed at mental rotation of objects in simple situations (e.g., imagining a teddy bear rotating in the plane) and also can take the perspective of other viewers (e.g., on the Three Mountains task) when they do not need to cope with conflicting frames of reference.
7 years	By this time, children show adult levels of performance on place learning tasks.
6–9 years	Map skills develop so that children can deal with complex maps, including many mapping conventions and perspectives. The ability to use maps in turn strengthens spatial thinking. Children also strengthen their spatial communication skills, in part as they are better able to understand what listeners need to know.
9–10 years	Children can succeed even at traditional perspective-taking tasks involving choosing among pictures showing different views of a display (a task requiring them to deal with conflicting frames of reference).
10–12 years	Children show mature hierarchical coding, in which they use the same categories as adults do to adjust their fine-grained estimates, and perform such adjustments along two dimensions at once.

approaches need not be banal. A world in which theory allows for the contribution of a wide variety of influences to development allows for the systematic and focused investigation of what develops when and how, given what kinds of necessary input. A detailed theory at this grain will be the best guide to understanding and intervention.

ACKNOWLEDGMENTS

Preparation of this chapter was supported by the National Science Foundation Grant No. BCS-9905098 to Temple University.

Suggestions for Further Reading

This article reviews research by the first author and other investigators that demonstrates the crucial role of action in spatial development and other lines of development in the first years of life:
Campos, J. J., Anderson, D. I., Barbu-Roth, M. A., Hubbard, E. M., Hertenstein, M. J., & Witherington, D. (2000). Travel broadens the mind. *Infancy, 1,* 149–219.

This essay considers the claim that infants have innately-specified spatial competence in more detail than is possible in the present chapter, and also considers parallel arguments and data from the domain of quantitative development:
Newcombe, N. S. (2002b). The nativist-empiricist controversy in the context of recent research on spatial and quantitative development. *Psychological Science, 13,* 395–401.

This book is an extensive treatment of all of the topics covered in the present chapter, and others that could not be addressed at all:
Newcombe, N. S., & Huttenlocher, J. (2000). *Making space: The development of spatial representation and reasoning.* Cambridge, MA: The MIT Press.

The part of this book that reviews research on spatial cognition in animals gives an invaluable comparative view of many of the same issues this chapter considers in development:
Shettleworth, S. (1998). *Cognition, evolution and behavior.* London: Oxford University Press.

This essay argues that map use has an important effect on the development of spatial cognition, and, in doing so, also provides a helpful guide to the extensive literature on children's map use:
Uttal, D. (2000). Seeing the big picture: Map use and the development of spatial cognition. *Developmental Science, 3,* 247–286.

References

Aadland, J., Beatty, W. W., & Maki, R. H. (1985). Spatial memory for children and adults assessed in the radial maze. *Developmental Psychobiology, 18,* 163–172.

Acredolo, L. P. (1978). Development of spatial orientation in infancy. *Developmental Psychology, 14,* 224–234.

Acredolo, L. P. (1982). The familiarity factor in spatial research. *New Directions for Child Development, 15,* 19–30.

Acredolo, L. P., & Evans, D. (1980). Developmental change in the effects of landmarks on infant spatial behavior. *Developmental Psychology, 16,* 312–318.

Ahmed, A., & Ruffman, T. (1998). Why do infants make A not B errors in a search task, yet show memory for the location of hidden objects in a nonsearch task? *Developmental Psychology, 34,* 441–453.

Allen, G. L., Kirasic, K. C., & Beard, R. L. (1989). Children's expressions of spatial knowledge. *Journal of Experimental Child Psychology, 48,* 114–130.

Baenninger, M., & Newcombe, N. (1989) The role of experience in spatial test performance: A meta-analysis. *Sex Roles, 20,* 327–344.

Blades, M. (1991). The development of the abilities required to understand spatial representations. In D. M. Mark & A. V. Frank (Eds.), *Cognitive and linguistic aspects of geographic space* (pp. 81–115). Dordrecht: Kluwer Academic Press.

Bloom, L. (1973). *One word at a time: The use of single word utterances before syntax.* The Hague: Mouton.

Bluestein, N., & Acredolo, L. (1979). Developmental changes in map-reading skills. *Child Development, 50,* 691–697.

Bohbot, V. D., Allen, J. J. B., & Nadel, L. (2000). Memory deficits characterized by patterns of lesion to the hippocampus and parahippocampal cortex. In H. E. Scharfman & M. P. Witter (Eds.), *The parahippocampal region: Implications for neurological and psychiatric diseases* (pp. 355–368). New York Academy of Sciences.

Borke, H. (1975). Piaget's mountains revisited: Changes in the egocentric landscape. *Developmental Psychology, 11,* 240–243.

Bowerman, M. (1996). Learning how to structure space for language: A cross-linguistic perspective. In P. Bloom, M. A. Peterson, L. Nadel, & M. F. Garrett (Eds.), *Language and space* (pp. 385–436). Cambridge, MA: The MIT Press.

Bowerman, M. (2000). Where do children's word meanings come from? Rethinking the role of cognition in early semantic development. In L. P. Nucci, G. B. Saxe, & E. Turiel (Eds.), *Culture, thought and development* (pp. 199–230). Mahwah, NJ: Lawrence Erlbaum Associates.

Bremner, J. G., & Bryant, P. E. (1977). Place versus responses as the basis of spatial errors made by young infants. *Journal of Experimental Child Psychology, 23,* 162–171.

Brown, P., & Levinson, S. C. (2000). Frames of spatial reference and their acquisition in Tenejapan Tzeltal. In L. P. Nucci, G. B. Saxe, & E. Turiel (Eds.), *Culture, thought, and development* (pp. 167–197). Mahwah, NJ: Lawrence Erlbaum, Associates.

Bryant, P. E., & Trabasso, T. (1972). Transitive inferences and memory in young children. *Nature, 232,* 456–458.

Bushnell, E. W., McKenzie, B. E., Lawrence, D. A., & Connell, S. (1995). The spatial coding strategies of one-year-old infants in a locomotor search task. *Child Development, 66,* 937–958.

Campos, J. J., Anderson, D. I., Barbu-Roth, M. A., Hubbard, E. M., Hertenstein, M. J., & Witherington, D. (2000). Travel broadens the mind. *Infancy, 1,* 149–219.

Carlson-Radvansky, L. A., & Jiang, Y. (1998). Inhibition accompanies reference-frame selection. *Psychological Science, 9*, 386–391.

Chapman, M. (1988). *Constructive evolution: Origins and development of Piaget's thought.* New York: Cambridge University Press.

Chapman, M., & Lindenberger, U. (1992a). How to detect reasoning-remembering dependence (and how not to). *Developmental Review, 12*, 187–198.

Chapman, M., & Lindenberger, U. (1992b). Transitivity judgments, memory for premises, and models of children's reasoning. *Developmental Review, 12*, 124–163.

Choi, S., & Bowerman, M. (1991). Learning to express motion events in English and Korean: The influence of language-specific lexication patterns. *Cognition, 41*, 83–121.

Choi, S., McDonough, L., Bowerman, M., & Mandler, J. M. (1999). Early sensitivity to language-specific spatial categories in English and Korean. *Cognitive Development, 14*, 241–268.

Clark, H. H. (1969). Linguistic processes in deductive reasoning. *Psychological Review, 76*, 387–404.

Cramer, L., & Presson, C. (1995). Planning routes around obstacles: Does type of map information matter? Poster presented at the Biennial Meeting of the Society for Research in Child Development, Indianapolis, IN.

Craton, L. G., Elicker, J., Plumert, J. M., & Pick, H. L., Jr. (1990). Children's use of frames of reference in communication of spatial location. *Child Development, 61*, 1528–1543.

Dalke, D. E. (1998). Charting the development of representational skills: When do children know that maps can lead and mislead? *Cognitive Development, 13*, 53–72.

DeLoache, J. S. (1987). Rapid change in the symbolic functioning of young children. *Science, 238*, 1556–1557.

DeLoache, J. S. (1989). Young children's understanding of the correspondence between a scale model and a larger space. *Cognitive Development, 4*, 121–139.

DeLoache, J. S. (1991). Young children's understanding of models. In R. Fivush & J. Hudson (Eds.), *Knowing and remembering in young children*, pp. 94–126. New York: Cambridge University Press.

DeLoache, J. S. (1995). Early understanding and use of symbols: The model model. *Current Directions in Psychological Science, 4*, 109–113.

DeLoache, J. S., & Brown, A. L. (1983). Very young children's memory for the location of objects in a large-scale environment. *Child Development, 54*, 888–897.

DeLoache, J. S., Kolstad, V., & Anderson, K. N. (1991). Physical similarity and young children's understanding of scale models. *Child Development, 62*, 111–126.

DeLoache, J. S., Miller, K. F., & Rosengren, K. S. (1997). The credible shrinking room: Very young children's performance with symbolic and nonsymbolic relations. *Psychological Science, 8*, 308–313.

Diamond, A. (1985). Development of the ability to use recall to guide, as indicated by infants' performance on AB. *Child Development, 56*, 868–883.

Elman, J., Bates, E., Johnson, M., Karmiloff-Smith, A., Parisi, D., & Plunkett, K. (1996). *Rethinking innateness: A connectionist perspective on development.* Cambridge, MA: The MIT Press.

Epstein, R., & Kanwisher, N. (1998). A cortical representation of the local visual environment. *Nature, 392*, 598–601.

Etienne, A. S., Teroni, E., Maurer, R., Portenier, V., & Saucy, F. (1985). Short-distance homing in a small mammal: The Role of exterceptive cues and path integration. *Experientia, 41*, 122–125.

Fodor, J. A. (1983). *Modularity of mind: An essay on faculty psychology.* Cambridge, MA: The MIT Press.

Foreman, N., Arber, M., & Savage, J. (1984). Spatial memory in preschool infants. *Developmental Psychobiology, 17*, 129–137.

Gallistel, C. R. (1990). *The organization of learning.* Cambridge, MA: The MIT Press.

Gattis, M. (Ed.) (2001). *Spatial schemas in abstract thought.* Cambridge, MA: The MIT Press.

Gattis, M. (2002). Structure mapping in spatial reasoning. *Cognitive Development, 17*, 1157–1183.

Gauvain, M. (1993). The development of spatial thinking in everyday activities. *Developmental Review, 13*, 92–121.

Gauvain, M. (1995). Thinking in niches: Sociocultural influences on cognitive development. *Human Development, 38*, 25–45.

Gauvain, M., & Rogoff, B. (1986). Influence of the goal on children's exploration and memory of large-scale space. *Developmental Psychology, 22*, 72–77.

Gauvain, M., & Rogoff, B. (1989). Ways of speaking about space: The development of children's skill in communicating spatial knowledge. *Cognitive Development, 4*, 295–307.

Gentner, D., & Rattermann, M. J. (1991). Language and the career of similarity. In S. A. Gelman & J. P. Byrnes (Eds.), *Perspectives on language and thought: Interrelations in development* (pp. 225–277). New York: Cambridge University Press.

Gilmore, R. O., & Rettke, H. (2003). Four-month-olds' discrimination of optic flow patterns depicting different directions of observer motion. *Infancy, 4*, 177–200.

Goodridge, J. P., & Taube, J. S., (1995). Preferential use of the landmark navigational system by head directions cells in rats. *Behavioral Neuroscience, 109*, 49–61.

Graziano, M. S. A., Yap, G. S., & Gross, C. G. (1994). Coding of visual space by premotor neurons. *Science, 266*, 1054–1057.

Halford, G. S., & Kelly, M. E. (1984). Why children have difficulty reasoning with three-term series problems. *Journal of Experimental Child Psychology, 38*, 42–63.

Halford, G. S., Maybery, M. T., & Bain, J. D. (1986). Capacity limitations in children's reasoning: A dual-task approach. *Child Development, 57*, 616–627.

Hermer, L., & Spelke, E. (1994). A geometric process for spatial reorientation in young children. *Nature, 370*, 57–59.

Hermer, L., & Spelke, E. (1996). Modularity and development: A case of spatial reorientation. *Cognition, 61*, 195–232.

Hermer-Vazquez, L., Moffet, A., & Munkholm, P. (2001). Language, space, and the development of cognitive flexibility in humans: The case of two spatial memory tasks. *Cognition, 79*, 263–299.

Hespos, S. J., & Rochat, P. (1997). Dynamic mental representation in infancy. *Cognition, 64*, 153–188.

Hofstadter, M., & Reznick, J. S. (1996). Response modality affects human infant delayed-response performance. *Child Development, 67,* 646–658.

Hughes, M., & Donaldson, M. (1979). The use of hiding games for studying the coordination of viewpoints. *Educational Review, 31,* 133–140.

Hummel, J. E., & Holyoak, K. J. (2001). A process model of human transitive inference. In M. Gattis (Ed.), *Spatial schemas and abstract thought* (pp. 279–305). Cambridge, MA: The MIT Press.

Hund, A. M., Plumert, J. M., & Benney, C. J. (2002). Experiencing nearby locations together in time: The role of spatiotemporal contiguity in children's memory for location. *Journal of Experimental Child Psychology, 82,* 200–225.

Huttenlocher, J. (1968). Constructing spatial images: A strategy in reasoning. *Psychological Review, 75,* 550–560.

Huttenlocher, J., Hedges, L. V., & Duncan, S. (1991). Categories and particulars: Prototype effects in estimation spatial location. *Psychological Review, 98,* 352–376.

Huttenlocher, J., Levine, S. C., & Vevea, J. (1998). Environmental effects on cognitive growth: Evidence from time period comparisons. *Child Development, 69,* 1012–1029.

Huttenlocher, J., Newcombe, N., & Sandberg, E. H. (1994). The coding of spatial location in young children. *Cognitive Psychology, 27,* 115–148.

Huttenlocher, J., Newcombe, N., & Vasilyeva, M. (1999). Spatial scaling in young children. *Psychological Science, 10,* 393–398.

Huttenlocher, J., & Presson, C. C. (1973). Mental rotation and the perspective problem. *Cognitive Psychology, 4,* 277–299.

Huttenlocher, J., & Presson, C. C. (1979). The coding and transformation of spatial information. *Cognitive Psychology, 11,* 375–394.

Johnston, J. R. (1988). Children's verbal representation of spatial location. In J. Stiles-Davis, M. Kritchevsky, & U. Bellugi (Eds.), *Spatial cognition: Brain bases and development* (pp. 195–205). Hillsdale, NJ: Lawrence Erlbaum Associates.

Just, M. A., & Carpenter, P. A. (1985). Cognitive coordinate systems: Accounts of mental rotation and individual differences in spatial ability. *Psychological Review, 92,* 137–171.

Karmiloff-Smith, A. (1992). *Beyond modularity: A developmental perspective on cognitive science.* Cambridge, MA: The MIT Press.

Kuhlmeier, V., & Boysen, S. (2002). Chimpanzees (Pan troglodytes) recognize spatial and object correspondences between a scale model and its referent. *Psychological Science, 13,* 60–63.

Kuhlmeier, V., Boysen, S., & Mukobi, K. (1999). Scale model comprehension by chimpanzees (Pan troglodytes). *Journal of Comparative Psychology, 113,* 396–402.

Landau, B., Gleitman, H., & Spelke, E. (1981). Spatial knowledge and geometric representation in a child blind from birth. *Science, 213,* 1275–1278.

Landau, B., & Spelke, E. (1988). Geometric complexity and object search in infancy. *Developmental Psychology, 24,* 512–521.

Laurence, H. E., Learmonth, A. E., Nadel, L., & Jacobs, W. J. (2003). Maturation of spatial navigation strategies: Convergent findings from computerized spatial environments and self-report. *Journal of Cognition and Development, 4,* 211–238.

Learmonth, A. E., Nadel, L., & Newcombe, N. (2002). Reorientation, landmark use and room size: Implications for modularity theory. *Psychological Science, 13,* 337–341.

Learmonth, A. E., Newcombe, N., & Huttenlocher, J. (2001). Disoriented toddlers can use both landmarks and geometry to reorient. *Journal of Experimental Child Psychology, 80,* 225–244.

Lempers, J. D., Flavell, E. R., & Flavell, J. H. (1977). The development in very young children of tacit knowledge concerning visual perception. *Genetic Psychology Monographs, 95,* 3–53.

Lepecq, J. C., & Lafaite, M. (1989). The early development of position constancy in a non-landmark environment. *British Journal of Developmental Psychology, 7,* 289–306.

Lever, C., Wills, T., Cacucci, F., Burgess, N., & O'Keefe, J. (2002). Long-term plasticity in hippocampal place-cell representation of environmental geometry. *Nature, 416,* 90–94.

Levine, M., Jankovic, I. N., & Palij, M. (1982). Principles of spatial problem solving. *Journal of Experimental Psychology: General, 111,* 157–175.

Lew, A. R., Bremner, J. G., & Lefkovitch, L. P. (2000). The development of relational landmark use in six- to twelve-month-old infants in a spatial orientation task. *Child Development, 71,* 1179–1190.

Liben, L. S., & Yekel, C. A. (1996). Preschoolers' understanding of plan and oblique maps: The role of geometric and representational correspondence. *Child Development, 67,* 2780–2796.

Linde, C., & Labov, W. (1975). Spatial networks as a site for the study of language and thought. *Language, 51,* 924–939.

Loewenstein, J., & Gentner, D. (2001). Spatial mapping in preschoolers: Close comparisons facilitate far mappings. *Journal of Cognition and Development, 2,* 189–219.

Maguire, E. A., Burgess, N., Donnett, J. G., Frackowiak R. S. J., Frith, C. D., & O'Keefe, J. (1998). Knowing where and getting there: A human navigation network. *Science, 280,* 921–924.

Mangan, P. A., Franklin, A., Tignor, T., Bolling, L., & Nadel, L. (1994). Development of spatial memory abilities in young children. *Society for Neuroscience Abstracts, 20,* 363.

Marmor, G. S. (1975). Development of kinetic images: When does a child first represent movement in mental images? *Cognitive Psychology, 7,* 548–559.

Marmor, G. S. (1977). Mental rotation and number conservation: Are they related? *Developmental Psychology, 13,* 320–325.

McClelland, J. L., & Siegler, R. S. (Eds.) (2001). *Mechanisms of cognitive development: Behavioral and neural perspectives.* Mahwah, NJ: Lawrence Erlbaum Associates.

McDonough, L. (1999). Early declarative memory for location. *British Journal of Developmental Psychology, 17,* 381–402.

McKenzie, B. E., Day, R. H., & Ihsen, E. (1984). Localization of events in space: Young infants are not always egocentric. *British Journal of Developmental Psychology, 2,* 1–9.

Munakata, Y., McClelland, J. L., Johnson, M. H., & Siegler, R. S. (1997). Rethinking infant knowledge: Toward an adaptive process account of successes and failures in object permanence tasks. *Psychological Review, 104,* 686–713.

Nelson, K. (1974). Concept, word, and sentence: Interrelations in acquisition and development. *Psychological Review, 81,* 267–285.

Newcombe, N. (1988). The paradox of proximity in early spatial representation. *British Journal of Developmental Psychology, 6,* 376–378.

Newcombe, N. (1989). Development of spatial perspective taking. In H. W. Reese (Ed.), *Advances in child development and behavior,* Vol. 22 (pp. 203–247). San Diego: Academic Press.

Newcombe, N. (1998). Defining the 'radical middle': Essay review of "A connectionist perspective on development." *Human Development, 41,* 210–214.

Newcombe, N. (2001). A spatial coding analysis of the A-not-B error: What IS "location at A"? *Brain and Behavioral Sciences, 24,* 57–58.

Newcombe, N. (2002a). Spatial cognition. In D. Medin (Ed.), Cognition Volume, *Stevens' Handbook of Experimental Psychology* (3rd ed.). New York: John Wiley.

Newcombe, N. (2002b). The nativist-empiricist controversy in the context of recent research in spatial and quantitative development. *Psychological Science, 13,* 395–401.

Newcombe, N. (in press). Evidence for and against a geometric module: The roles of language and action. In J. Rieser, J. Lockman, & C. Nelson (Eds.), *Action as an organizer of learning and development.*

Newcombe, N., & Huttenlocher, J. (1992). Children's early ability to solve perspective-taking problems. *Developmental Psychology, 28,* 635–643.

Newcombe, N., & Huttenlocher, J. (2000). *Making space: The development of spatial representation and reasoning.* Cambridge, MA: The MIT Press.

Newcombe, N., Huttenlocher, J., Drummey, A. B., & Wiley, J. (1998). The development of spacial location coding: Place learning and dead reckoning in the second and third years. *Cognitive Development, 13,* 185–200.

Newcombe, N., Huttenlocher, J., & Learmonth, A. (1999). Infants' coding of location in continuous space. *Infant Behavior and Development, 22,* 483–510.

Newcombe, N., Huttenlocher, J., Sandberg, E., Lie, U., & Johnson, S. (1999). What do misestimations and assymetries in spatial judgement indicate about spatial representation? *Journal of Experimental Psychology: Learning, Memory, and Cognition, 25,* 986–996.

Newcombe, N., & Learmonth, A. (1999). Change and continuity in early spatial development: Claiming the "radical middle." *Infant Behavior and Development, 22,* 457–474.

Oakhill, J. V. (1984). Why children have difficulty reasoning with three-term series problems. *British Journal of Developmental Psychology, 2,* 223–230.

O'Keefe, J., & Nadel, L. (1978). *The hippocampus as a cognitive map.* Oxford: Clarendon Press.

Ondracek, P. J., & Allen, G. L. (2000). Children's acquisition of spatial knowledge from verbal descriptions. *Spatial Cognition and Computation, 2,* 1–30.

Oswald, C. J. P., & Good, M. (2000). The effects of combined lesions of the subicular complex and the entorhinal cortex on two forms of spatial navigation in the water maze. *Behavioral Neuroscience, 114,* 211–217.

Overman, W. H., Pate, B. J., Moore, K., & Peuster, A. (1996). Ontogeny of place learning in children as measured in the Radial Arm maze, Morris Search Task, and Open Field Task. *Behavioral Neuroscience, 110,* 1205–1228.

Packard, M. G., & McGaugh, J. L. (1992). Double dissociation of fornix and caudate nucleus lesions on acquisition of two water maze tasks: Further evidence for multiple memory systems. *Journal of Neuroscience, 9*(5), 1465–1472.

Perner, J., & Aebi. J. (1985). Feedback-dependent encoding of length series. *British Journal of Developmental Psychology, 3,* 133–141.

Piaget, J., & Inhelder, B. (1948/1967). *The child's conception of space* (F. J. L. J. L. Lunzer, Trans.). New York: Norton.

Piaget, J., & Inhelder, B. (1971). *Mental imagery in the child; A study of the development of imaginal representation.* New York: Basic Books.

Piaget, J., Inhelder, B., & Szeminska, A. (1960). *The child's conception of geometry.* London: Routledge and Kegan Paul.

Plumert, J. M., Carswell, C., DeVet, K., & Ihrig, D. (1995). The content and organization of communication about object locations. *Journal of Memory and Language, 34,* 477–498.

Plumert, J. M., Ewert, K., & Spear, S. J. (1995). The early development of children's communication about nested spatial relations. *Child Development, 66,* 959–969.

Plumert, J. M., & Hund, A. M. (2001). The development of memory for location: What role do spatial prototypes play? *Child Development, 72,* 370–384.

Plumert, J. M., & Nichols-Whitehead, P. (1996). Parental scaffolding of young children's spatial communication. *Developmental Psychology, 32,* 523–532.

Plumert, J. M., Spalding, T. L., & Nichols-Whitehead, P. (2001). Preferences for ascending and descending hierarchical organization in spatial communication. *Memory and Cognition, 29,* 274–284.

Presson, C. C. (1982a). Strategies in spatial reasoning. *Journal of Experimental Psychology: Learning, Memory, and Cognition, 8,* 243–251.

Presson, C. C. (1982b). The development of map-reading skills. *Child Development, 53,* 196–199.

Quinn, P. C. (1994). The categorization of above and below spatial relations by young infants. *Child Development, 65,* 58–69.

Quinn, P. C., Cummins, M., Kase, J., Martin, E., & Weissman, S. (1996). Development of categorical representations for above and below spatial relations in 3- to 7-month-old infants. *Developmental Psychology, 32,* 942–950.

Redish, A. D. (1999). *Beyond the cognitive map: From place cells to episodic memory.* Cambridge, MA: The MIT Press.

Rieser, J. J. (1979). Spatial orientation in six-month-old infants. *Child Development, 50,* 1078–1087.

Rieser, J. J., & Rider, E. A. (1991). Young children's spatial orientation with respect to multiple targets when walking without vision. *Developmental Psychology, 27,* 97–107.

Rochat, P., & Hespos, S. J. (1996). Tracking and anticipation of invisible spatial transformation by 4- to 8-month-old infants. *Cognitive Development, 11,* 3–17.

Rosser, R. A. (1983). The emergence of spatial perspective-taking: An information-processing alternative to egocentrism. *Child Development, 54,* 660–668.

Sandberg, E. H., & Huttenlocher, J. (2001). Advanced spatial skills and advance planning: Components of 6-year-olds' navigational map use. *Journal of Cognition and Development, 2,* 51–70.

Sandberg, E. H., Huttenlocher, J., & Newcombe, N. (1996). The development of hierarchical representation of two-dimensional space. *Child Development, 67,* 721–739.

Save, E., & Moghaddam, M. (1996). Effects of lesions of the associative parietal cortex on the acquisition and use of spatial memory in egocentric and allocentric navigation tasks in the rat. *Behavioral Neuroscience, 110,* 74–85.

Schutte, A. R. (2001). Tests of a dynamic field theory of spatial memory: Longer-term memory for locations becomes more precise between 2 and 6 years. Paper presented at the Society for Research in Child Development, Minneapolis, MN.

Schutte, A. R., & Spencer, J. P. (2002). Generalizing the dynamic field theory of the A-not-B error beyond infancy: Three year-olds' delay- and experience-dependent location memory biases. *Child Development, 73,* 377–404.

Shanon, B. (1984). Room descriptions. *Discourse Processes, 7,* 225–255.

Shantz, C. U., & Watson, J. S. (1971). Spatial abilities and spatial egocentrism in the young child. *Child Development, 42,* 171–181.

Shepard, R. N. (1988). The imagination of the scientist. In K. Egan & D. Nadaner (Eds.), *Imagination and education* (pp. 153–185). New York: Teachers College Press.

Shettleworth, S. (1998). *Cognition, evolution and behavior.* London: Oxford University Press.

Siegler, R. S. (1996). *Emerging minds: The process of change in children's thinking.* New York: Oxford University Press.

Simons, D. J., & Wang, R. F. (1998). Perceiving real-world viewpoint changes. *Psychological Science, 9,* 315–320.

Smith, L. B., Thelen, E., Titzer, R., & McLin, D. (1999). Knowing in the context of acting: The task dynamics of the A-not-B error. *Psychological Review, 106,* 235–260.

Spencer, J. P., Smith, L. B., & Thelen, E. (2001). Tests of a dynamic systems account of the A-not-B error: The influence of prior experience on the spatial memory abilities of 2-year-olds. *Child Development, 72,* 1327–1346.

Sternberg, R. J. (1980). Representation and process in linear syllogistic reasoning. *Journal of Experimental Psychology: General, 109,* 119–159.

Szechter, L. E., & Liben, L. S. (2004). Parental guidance in preschoolers' understanding of spatial-graphic representations. *Child Development, 75,* 869–885.

Taylor, H. L., & Klein, A. G. (1994). *Referential communication of spatial location by children.* Paper presented at the 35th Annual Psychonomics Conference, St. Louis, MO.

Thelen, E., Schoner, G., Scheier, C., & Smith, L. B. (2001). The dynamics of embodiment: A field theory of perseverative reaching. *Behavioral and Brain Sciences, 24,* 1–86.

Thelen, E., & Smith, L. (1994). *A dynamic systems approach to the development of cognition and action.* Cambridge, MA: The MIT Press.

Tversky, B. (2000). Some ways that maps and diagrams communicate. In C. Freska, W. Brauer, C. Habel & K. F. Wender (Eds.), *Spatial cognition II: Integration, abstract theories, empirical studies, formal models, and powerful applications.* Berlin: Springer.

Uttal, D. H. (1994). Preschoolers' and adults' scale translations and reconstruction of spatial information acquired from maps. *British Journal of Developmental Psychology, 12,* 259–275.

Uttal, D. H. (1996). Angles and distances: Children's and adults' reconstruction and scaling of spatial configurations. *Child Development, 67,* 2763–2779.

Uttal, D. H. (2000). Seeing the big picture: Map use and the development of spatial cognition. *Developmental Science, 3,* 247–286.

Uttal, D. H., & Wellman, H. M. (1989). Young children's representation of spatial information acquires from maps. *Developmental Psychology, 25,* 128–138.

Vauclair, J., Fagot, J., & Hopkins, W. D. (1993). Rotation of mental images in baboons when the visual input is directed to the left cerebral hemispheres. *Psychological Science, 4,* 99–103.

Wilson, M. A., & McNaughton, B. L. (1993). Dynamics of the hippocampal ensemble code for space. *Science, 261,* 1055–1058.

Wraga, M., Creem, S., & Proffitt, D. (2000). Updating displays after imagined object and viewer rotations. *Journal of Experimental Psychology: Learning, Memory, and Cognition, 26,* 151–168.

Yaniv, I., & Shatz, M. (1990). Heuristics of reasoning and analogy in children's visual perspective-taking. *Child Development, 61,* 1491–1501.

7

Navigation

Daniel R. Montello

ABSTRACT

Navigation is coordinated and goal-directed movement through the environment by organisms or intelligent machines. It involves both planning and execution of movements. It may be understood to include the two components of locomotion and wayfinding. Locomotion is body movement coordinated to the local surrounds; wayfinding is planning and decision making coordinated to the distal as well as local surrounds. Several sensory modalities provide information for navigating, and a variety of cognitive systems are involved in processing information from the senses and from memory. Animals update their orientation – their knowledge of location and heading – as they move about. Combinations of landmark-based and dead-reckoning processes are used to update. Humans also use symbolic representations to maintain orientation, including language and cartographic maps. Factors have been identified that make orientation easier in some environments than others. Neuroscience has pointed to the role of certain brain structures in the maintenance of orientation and has uncovered evidence for neurons that fire preferentially in response to an animal's location or heading. Artificial intelligence researchers develop computer models that test theories of navigational cognition or just create competent robots.

INTRODUCTION

Few behavioral problems are more fundamental than getting from here to there. Humans and other mobile animals move about their environments in order to get to places with food, mates, shelter, margaritas, and other resources; they must also avoid threats and dangers such as predation, assault, exposure, and Hanson music blaring from a radio. Furthermore, animals must get from here to there efficiently; going far out of its way is no way to act for a creature with limited time, water, calories, and patience.

This coordinated and goal-directed movement of one's self (one's body) through the environment is *navigation*. Navigation is sometimes a highly technical activity carried out by specialists, or even groups of specialists (see Hutchins, 1995, for an analysis of navigation by teams of navy specialists and their high-tech equipment). However, it is by no means true that only ship captains, pilots, and explorers practice navigation. Virtually every one of us navigates many times a day, with no more technical assistance than the occasional sign or road map, if that. We go to work, we go to shop, we visit friends, we even find our way from the bedroom to the coffeepot each morning. Our main tools for navigating are our repertoires of cognitive abilities – our abilities to perceive, remember, and reason in space and place – and of motor abilities that use cognitive input to produce efficient movement.

In this chapter, I review concepts, theories, and empirical findings on cognitive aspects of navigation. The chapter is multidisciplinary, presenting work by psychologists in various subfields, geographers, linguists, anthropologists, neuroscientists, computer scientists, and others. I focus primarily on human navigation, but as a multidisciplinary topic, researchers study navigation in machines and nonhuman animals as well. Of course a chapter of this length cannot cover all work on navigation, so I provide citations to expanded treatments of particular work where appropriate. The chapter is organized into eight sections. I first discuss component skills in navigation, the proximally coordinated movement part called locomotion and the distally coordinated planning part called wayfinding. The next section discusses geographic orientation, knowing one's location and heading in the environment. Orientation involves reference systems that organize spatial knowledge. As we move, maintaining orientation is known as updating. A variety of sensory systems are involved in orientation, and attentional resources are required to different degrees for different tasks. The third section discusses the use of cartographic maps during navigation. Following that, I discuss characteristics of the external environment that facilitate or impede orientation while navigating. The fifth and sixth sections discuss neuroscience and artificial intelligence approaches, respectively. In conclusion, I consider the effects, both intended and unintended, of new technologies on human navigation. At the end, an annotated list provides suggestions for further reading.

COMPONENTS OF NAVIGATION: LOCOMOTION AND WAYFINDING

I propose that we consider navigation to consist of two components: locomotion and wayfinding. *Locomotion* is the movement of one's body around an environment, coordinated specifically to the local or proximal surrounds – the environment that is directly accessible to our sensory and motor systems at a given moment (or, at most, within a few moments). When we locomote, we solve behavioral problems such as identifying surfaces to stand on, avoiding obstacles and barriers, directing our movement toward perceptible landmarks, and going through openings without bumping into the sides.

There are various modes of locomotion. Unaided by machines, people of different ages (or different states of mind or body) roll, crawl, climb, slither, walk, hop, jog, or run. Aided by machines, there is the usual litany of planes, trains, and automobiles (and then some). Modes of locomotion are important because they determine much about the way we acquire and process information as we locomote. For one, modes differ in the degree to which they are active or passive. Most commonly, this distinction refers to whether the locomoting person controls his or her movement speed and heading. In this sense, active locomotion is self-directed. During self-directed locomotion, people attend to their surrounds and to their own movement, apparently leading to greater environmental learning (Feldman & Acredolo, 1979). They also send efferent commands to their muscles that may provide additional information for learning and orientation. A less common meaning of the active/passive distinction refers to whether the locomoting person is the source of the energy expended to make the body move. In this second sense, active locomotion is self-powered. Unaided by machines, locomotion is usually quite active. Using human-powered machines such as skates, rowboats, and bicycles is somewhat less active, and using machines with engines is particularly passive (the energy required to press a fuel pedal being minimal). Whether locomotion is self-powered is important because one's energy output may provide a heuristic basis for judgments of distance traveled (Montello, 1997); expending energy to move also affects one's arousal and attentional states.

In contrast to locomotion, *wayfinding* is the goal-directed and planned movement of one's body around an environment in an efficient way. Wayfinding requires a place goal, a destination we wish to reach. Frequently, this destination is not in the local surrounds. To a large extent, wayfinding is coordinated distally, beyond the local surrounds directly accessible to our sensory and motor systems at a given moment. Hence memory, stored internally in nervous systems and externally in artifacts such as maps, plays a critical role in wayfinding. When we wayfind, we solve behavioral problems involving explicit planning and decision making – problems such as choosing routes to take, moving toward distal landmarks, creating shortcuts, and scheduling trips and trip sequences.

The great majority of acts of navigation involve both locomotion and wayfinding components to varying degrees; the distinction is less "either/or" than "part-this/part-that." Evidence for the distinction's validity is provided by the simple fact that you can have one without the other. They are generally components of an integrated system of navigation that can be separated only conceptually, but they can sometimes be separated literally. One locomotes without wayfinding when pacing about the maternity ward. A passenger on a bus is locomoting without wayfinding, except when he or she makes decisions as to which bus to board and where to get off. Another example is provided by blind people, some of who can use a long cane or clicking sounds effectively to coordinate movement to the immediate surrounds but may have trouble maintaining orientation to distal goals. Conversely, the present framework includes trip planning at the kitchen table as part of navigation, even though actual movement is only imagined at that point. Effective wayfinding distinct from locomotion is also demonstrated by the Mars Rover autonomous vehicle – it stumbled badly when locomoting relative to nearby features (for example, confusing hills and holes, and falling into holes without any escape) but used its computer maps effectively for wayfinding.

Examples like these help us validate the distinction between locomotion and wayfinding, but they also help us define the semantic boundaries of the term navigation. In the extreme, being carried while sleeping clearly involves no component of wayfinding (on the part of the sleeper), but it also involves so little in the way of locomotion that we may consider it a boundary case for our definition of navigation – probably few researchers, if any, would call it navigation. Similarly, in the prototypical sense, trip planning in advance is only part of the act of navigation, which will also involve steering and acceleration when actually taking the trip. A planned trip that is never taken also provides a boundary case (the other boundary from being carried while asleep) for most researchers' definitions of navigation.

Knowledge Systems in Navigation

The distinction between locomotion and wayfinding has implications for our understanding of the psychology of navigation: "Locomotion is guided both perceptually by current sensory information and cognitively by previously acquired information" (Pick & Palmer, 1986, p. 135). The first form of guidance in this quote is what I am calling locomotion, the second is wayfinding. Locomotion and wayfinding differ greatly in the degree to which they involve perception/action versus memory/planning systems. These systems, in turn, rely differentially on nondeclarative or declarative knowledge and memory (Schacter & Tulving, 1994). *Nondeclarative* knowledge is know-how knowledge, and includes procedural skills and learned motor habits. Many locomotion skills require nondeclarative knowledge. A locomotory act like moving straight to a visible target is probably best understood as coordination of the ambulatory motor system to patterns of optic flow in the environment (Warren, Young, & Lee, 1986) rather than the activation of an internal representation of how the world looks when you move forward. Furthermore, such acts occur without awareness of how they occur – they are impenetrable (Frederickson & Bartlett, 1987). A person's visual-perception system may respond to the velocity or acceleration of changes in the proximal size of an object's image in the visual field (Kerzel, Heiko, & Kim, 1999), but this occurs completely outside of the person's awareness that it is the mechanism by which we avoid collisions. By the same token, impenetrable processes do not respond to conscious knowledge that might be relevant to their operation. That is why people flinch at cinematic depictions of collisions or falls, even when they are fully aware that they are viewing a film and no injury can possibly come to them. Characteristic of impenetrable processes, people are not able to explain how they perform locomotory tasks like walking without stumbling (they may speculate after the fact), if they even realize that it is a complex task worthy of explanation.

In contrast, *declarative* knowledge is know-that knowledge, and includes semantic knowledge of general facts and episodic knowledge of experienced events. It is consciously accessible or explicit knowledge, although it often becomes routinized to the degree that it does not claim much of a person's working-memory resources (more next). So quite unlike the example of walking to a visible target, a wayfinding act such as giving someone verbal directions clearly requires the activation of long-term knowledge representations (the *cognitive map*) into working memory in order to access one's knowledge of place layouts (Lovelace, Hegarty, & Montello, 1999). Except in unusual and perhaps contrived scenarios, there is no sense in which a person can do this simply by "tuning their perceptual system" to the local surrounds (as in Fajen & Warren, 2003), though that is typically an important part of the process. Similarly, wayfinding skills are also typically penetrable. People learn some wayfinding skills through direct instruction, and they can accurately report when they are applying the skills (as in a protocol analysis [Passini, 1992; Pick et al., 1995]).

It must be stressed that neither the declarative/nondeclarative nor the penetrable/impenetrable distinctions map perfectly onto the wayfinding/ locomotion distinction. Clear examples that support the validity of the mapping exist, as described earlier, but a few muddy cases and apparent contradictions exist too. Perceiving a surface of support for walking is typically a nondeclarative and impenetrable act, but quicksand appears to provide a surface of support when it does not. Some people use declarative knowledge to recognize quicksand for what it is and make the adaptive, and explicit, decision not to walk over it.

Perhaps the most interesting and important cases where the mapping of declarative/nondeclarative onto wayfinding/locomotion is problematic concern instances where *spatial inferences* are made in relatively immediate surrounds. Take the example of a person pointing directly to the start location after a short vision-restricted walk in a laboratory (e.g., Hazen, Lockman, & Pick, 1978; Loomis et al., 1993). Even though this is generally considered an inference because it involves a spatial judgment along a route not directly traveled, people can perform this inference quickly and easily, without awareness of how they are doing it (Rieser, Guth, & Hill, 1986). The inference appears to depend on the nondeclarative and impenetrable processing of information from nonvisual perception of movement in the local surrounds. Similarly, the desert ant can walk straight back to its nest after a circuitous outbound route (Figure 7.1), an act we would not want to attribute to explicit declarative knowledge. At some point, however, we might expect such journeys will become too long and/or complex for such implicit *path integration*, whether by ant or person (exactly when is not known). Declarative systems (in humans at least) may then be required to form internal or external maps of the journey as wayfinding components to navigation.

Metaphorical Navigation

A final comment about the meaning of navigation is in order. The concept of coordinated and goal-directed movement is an extremely flexible and general idea for the expression of meaning in many domains, including many that are not literally spatial. In other words, the concepts of navigation, journeying, getting lost, and so on are very useful metaphors (Johnson, 1987). We speak of "navigating" through a math problem, through a detective story, or through an emotional crisis. Many researchers are studying navigation in computer databases such as the World Wide Web (e.g., Kitchin, 1998). Others are exploring the use of landscape visualizations

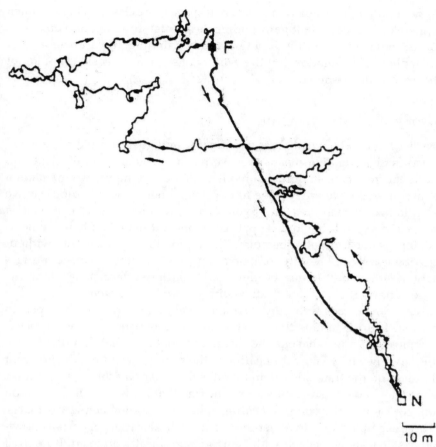

FIGURE 7.1. Direct route taken by desert ant back to its nest after a circuitous outbound trip (from Wehner, 1999).

as ways to metaphorically spatialize nonspatial information (Fabrikant, 2000). However one should be restrained in interpreting metaphors such as "traveling through cyberspace." Like all metaphors, application of the navigation metaphor has limitations. Real navigation involves real places or spaces on the earth, and real movement of the body. The earth's surface is approximately two-dimensional and Euclidean, often overlaid with path networks that modify travel geometry, covered with typical textures and landmark features, structured so as to afford particular types of actions, and so on. The cognitively relevant characteristics of cyberspace in its current form are quite different, although such systems may well become easier to use if redesigned to mimic real space more closely. There is much valuable research to be done extending the mental structures and processes of real navigation, both locomotion and wayfinding, to various forms of metaphorical navigation, but the validity of such an extension should not be uncritically assumed.

GEOGRAPHIC ORIENTATION

Earlier I defined navigation as coordinated and goal-directed movement. Successful navigation means that we reach our goal in an efficient and accident-free manner. To do so requires that as we move, we maintain a sense of where we are relative to our goal, where places and objects we should avoid are located, and so on. That is, we must maintain *orientation* as we move. All behavior (as opposed to uncoordinated body movement) requires some form of orientation: Putting food into your mouth without poking your cheek requires oriented movement. When we consider orientation with respect to our location on the earth's surface, as we do in the case of navigation, we are dealing with *geographic orientation*.

One can be geographically oriented to varying degrees, with respect to various features, and with respect to one or more scales of space or place. People may know what city they are in but not know their location within the city. They may know the bearing to their campsite but not their current location on the trail, other than that it is in the Appalachians; in contrast, they may know the direction along the trail that leads to their destination but not know which compass bearing or how many kilometers away that is. These examples serve to underline the point that a variety of partial knowledge states are associated with being geographically oriented. It rarely if ever makes sense to speak of being completely oriented because there is always some aspect of location or heading that a person does not know precisely. In other words, everyone is potentially *dis*oriented to some degree at all times! Of course, we can usually get to our destinations successfully without being completely oriented. However, in some situations, we fail to maintain adequate orientation, we get lost, and the consequences range from temporary nuisance to death. Behavioral science researchers have begun to apply their science to this problem (see contributions in Hill, 1999a).

Reference Systems

Geographic orientation always involves some mixture of knowing your location, and/or distances and directions to particular places or features.

However we are oriented, it is always relative to something, concrete or abstract. The system for defining orientation is called a *reference system*. A variety of taxonomies for reference systems have been proposed. Hart and Moore (1973) discussed three types: egocentric, fixed, and coordinated. *Egocentric* systems code location relative to one's body. In contrast to egocentric systems, both fixed and coordinated systems are *allocentric*: They code location relative to something outside of one's body, a feature or place in the environment. *Fixed* systems code location relative to a stable landmark, a recognizable and memorable feature. One's home is often used as the origin of a fixed system of reference. *Coordinated* systems code relative to abstract places defined by imaginary coordinate axes laid over large areas. Cardinal directions or latitude-longitude coordinates are examples of coordinated systems. The key distinction between fixed and coordinated systems is that fixed systems are tied to concrete and locally relevant features, natural or built. They are typically useful only over short distances and their continued usefulness depends on their continued existence (or at least continued memory of their existence). Coordinated systems are abstract and function over wide areas, often the entire earth (hence they are *geocentric*). Hart and Moore proposed, following Piaget (Piaget, Inhelder, & Szeminska, 1960), that there is a sequence in child development from egocentric to fixed to coordinated reference systems.

Levinson (1996) recently provided an overview of schemes for classifying reference systems from a variety of behavioral, cognitive, and neuroscience perspectives (e.g., "viewer-centered" versus "object-centered" in vision research [Tarr & Bülthoff, 1998]). As a linguist, however, Levinson's purpose was to explain reference systems in linguistic conceptual systems; absolute distance is apparently not relevant in any language to the closed-class linguistic expressions such as prepositions that reflect conceptual structure (L. Talmy, personal communication, September 22, 2001). So Levinson's typology focuses exclusively on directional reference. As a summary of the various schemes, Levinson proposed a classification of reference systems into relative, intrinsic, and absolute. *Relative* systems are essentially egocentric, as when an object is "to my left." *Intrinsic* systems code direction relative to the asymmetric shape of a feature in the environment; a house has a front door that allows us to speak of being "in front of the house." Finally, *absolute* systems code direction relative to global features that function over large areas or, like the coordinated systems of Hart and Moore, to abstract places defined by imaginary coordinate axes. The ocean provides an example in coastal areas; one may speak of "turning oceanside."

Compared to Hart and Moore's coordinated system, Levinson's absolute system better expresses an aspect of spatial reference that is fundamental to orientation relative to the earth's surface, whether by human or nonhuman animals. Animals orient themselves in terms of their heading[1] relative to the directional orientation of the global surrounds (McNaughton, Knierim, & Wilson, 1995). Whether a magnetic compass, the position of the sun, or the location of the ocean, anything that provides information about the orientation of the global surrounds may be said to provide an *azimuthal reference* (Loomis, Klatzky, Golledge, & Philbeck, 1999). Azimuthal reference captures the idea that the earth's surface is an unmoving and unchanging background for behavior (which at the spatiotemporal scale of animals, it largely is). A critical task for a mobile creature is to understand its movements against this background. Many animal species monitor celestial bodies, winds or currents, or magnetic fields in order to orient themselves to an azimuthal reference (Gallistel, 1990). Humans can and sometimes do monitor celestial bodies for the same reason, and of course, use compasses to monitor magnetism (the doubtful possibility of human magnetoreception is discussed next). Humans and other animals also use terrestrial features to orient to the azimuthal reference, when those terrestrial features are so large that they allow orientation over large portions of the animal's territory. Large bodies of water and large landform features like mountain chains often serve this function, when they are available. Such features might be termed *global landmarks*. And just as it is fundamental for an animal to align its internal cognitive map with the orientation of its surrounds, it is fundamental for a human animal to align its external cartographic map with the orientation of its surrounds – hence the common practice of turning maps while using them (Pick et al., 1995). I discuss this further in the section on using maps to navigate.

Updating During Navigation

Humans and other animals use a combination of two classes of processes to maintain orientation – to update knowledge of their location – as they

---

[1] Technically, *heading* is your facing direction, *course* is your movement direction, and *bearing* is the direction to a landmark relative to some reference direction (see Gallistel, 1990; Loomis et al., 1999). For a terrestrial animal, heading and course are the same unless the animal is not moving "forward," in the direction it is facing. Heading and course are often quite different for animals (or boats or planes) moving through air or water.

move about: landmark-based and dead-reckoning processes. *Landmark-based* processes (also called piloting, pilotage, or taking a fix) involve orientation by recognizing features in the world – landmarks. At minimum, landmark-based updating requires that we have an internal or external memory that allows the feature to be recognized. Recognizing a destination landmark in your local surrounds (i.e., in your sensory field) and moving towards it may be termed *beacon-following*, but most of the time there is more to landmark-based updating than just recognizing features in the local surrounds. Usually, we use recognized landmarks in the surrounds to orient ourselves (find our location and heading) on a map that includes the current location and the destination location, when the destination is not in fact visible (or otherwise sensible) from our current location. The map may be internal (cognitive) or external (cartographic). Psychologically, we recognize features in the local surrounds in order to key our current location to our location on a map, which in turn may be "read" to determine a route to our destination. Either way, whether recognized as a destination or as a key to the location of a destination, landmarks almost never function by directly saying "you are here" or "go this way" – visual memory (or that of other modalities) plays a critical role.

In contrast, *dead-reckoning*[2] updating does not involve the recognition of specific external features or landmarks. Instead, it involves keeping track of components of locomotion. Given knowledge of initial location, you can update your orientation by keeping track of the velocity and/or acceleration of your movement for a given period of time. Velocity and acceleration are vector quantities; dead reckoning thus combines knowledge of movement direction with knowledge of the rate of movement. Mathematically, this is equivalent to integrating velocity and/or acceleration with respect to time; hence *path integration* is often used synonymously for dead reckoning[3] (e.g., May & Klatzky, 2000). The psychological mechanism by which dead reckoning occurs is the subject of ongoing research (e.g., Loomis, Klatzky, Golledge, & Philbeck, 1999; McNaughton,

---

[2] The term *dead reckoning* is usually claimed to derive from *deduced reckoning* (e.g., Gallistel, 1990; Hutchins, 1995). Lewis (1994), however, states that "there is no warrant" for this etymology (note 1, p. 385). The etymology is neither supported nor refuted by the Oxford English Dictionary (2nd ed.). Support for Lewis's contention is provided by Pearsall and Trumble (1996), who include dead reckoning in their entry on the word *dead*, and give as definition 1 for the adverbial use of dead: "absolutely, exactly, completely" (p. 365).

[3] Some writers use the term *dead reckoning* to refer exclusively to velocity-based path integration; *inertial navigation* would refer to acceleration-based path integration (Loomis et al., 1999).

Chen, & Markus, 1991). Researchers have repeatedly shown that humans (e.g., Rieser, 1989) and other animals (e.g., Mittelstaedt & Mittelstaedt, 1980) dead reckon. An amazing example is the desert ant, studied extensively by Wehner (1996, 1999). Figure 7.1 shows the route a desert ant takes to return to its nest after a long and circuitous exploration for food. The research by Wehner and colleagues shows that the ant achieves this direct route by integrating its locomotion over time. By intentionally altering the pattern of polarized light falling upon the ants' eyes, these researchers demonstrated that this integration was based on an azimuthal frame set up by polarized sunlight.

However, by itself, dead reckoning does not provide a complete method of updating and navigation. Dead reckoning requires knowing a start location – it is not useful for establishing orientation relative to places other than that from which recent movement was initiated. Second, dead reckoning suffers from error accumulation. Any error in sensing or processing movement information accumulates over time; except for the unlikely situation where errors coincidentally cancel out, one's orientation becomes increasingly inaccurate over time when based solely on dead reckoning (see Loomis et al., 1993, for data on human dead-reckoning accuracy after walking short paths while blindfolded). Thus, an important research question is how dead reckoning combines with various strategies of landmark recognition to support updating and cognitive-map formation; Loomis et al. (1999) suggest that dead reckoning provides a glue for the formation of cognitive maps.

Sensory Systems for Updating

A variety of sensory and motor systems provide information for updating during locomotion (Howard & Templeton, 1966; Potegal, 1982). Humans recognize landmarks primarily visually, because vision is the most precise channel for spatial and pattern information, particularly at a distance, but landmark recognition may be based on audition, olfaction, radar or satellite signals, and so on. Movement information for dead reckoning is provided proprioceptively (via body senses), notably by the vestibular senses of the inner ear and the kinesthetic senses in the joints and muscles. In theory, motor efference to the limbs (centrally initiated neural commands to the musculature) could provide information for updating, though there is no evidence that it plays this role during whole-body locomotion. Such internally derived signals for dead reckoning are called *idiothetic*. However, external, or *allothetic*, signals play a large role here too. In particular, visual sensing of patterns of texture movement in dynamic optic arrays provides powerful input to our sense of orientation as we move about (Lee & Lishman, 1977), termed *visual kinesthesis* by Gibson (1966); it is important to distinguish this role of visual information from landmark recognition. Audition can contribute to dead reckoning as well (Loomis, Klatzky, Philbeck, & Golledge, 1998). Even magnetic sensing has been offered as a source of information for updating (Baker, 1989). However, this claim has never been reliably supported by direct evidence, and it has proved difficult to replicate in nonhumans (e.g., Kirschvink, Jones, & McFadden, 1985) let alone humans (Gould & Able, 1981).

In nonhuman species, the sensorimotor systems provide information via a variety of modalities and in different ways than that available to human travelers. These fascinating variations, including electrical sensitivity in eels and vision of incredible resolution in raptors, clearly take advantage of the unique ecological niches of different species (see Waterman, 1989). And it should not be forgotten that within the last several centuries, human navigators have made use of a variety of technologies that affect sensorimotor processing during locomotion – everything from lodestone compasses and quadrants to jets and satellites. I discuss new technologies for navigation further in the final section of the chapter.

Attentional Resources During Updating

Whether landmark or dead-reckoning based, updating processes vary in their demands on attentional resources (see Allen & Kirasic, 2003). As discussed earlier, some navigational acts require little attention – they do not use much working-memory capacity. Dead reckoning over relatively short distances is a good example; as cited earlier, Rieser et al. (1986) showed that people could update after short blindfolded walks very accurately and easily, without any awareness of having to think about the task. Other tasks, such as driving between home and work, become automatized over time, leaving attention for the radio, the cell phone, or daydreaming (at least during the majority of the time when active navigational decisions are not being made). Other updating processes, conversely, require working-memory capacity – they are controlled or effortful. Maintaining orientation over more than short distances in unfamiliar environments demands attention – one turns the radio off when nearing a destination in a city never visited before. Considerable attentional resources are needed when giving verbal navigation instructions – directions. Imagining a route and communicating it in words and gestures is generally not automatic, although the museum guard repeatedly pointing the way to the restroom demonstrates that even this can become automatized.

Updating procedures that can potentially be consciously and intentionally applied may be termed *explicit strategies*. Humans often update by using explicit strategies. The application of these strategies, particularly when they are first learned and applied, requires attentional resources. Common examples of strategies are making a point to memorize the number or color of the location of one's car in a parking lot, or simply paying attention. Other strategies include retracing your steps when lost, memorizing the sequence of right and left turns during a journey, verbalizing landmark names out loud, and walking to high points to improve visibility. An important strategy applied by many nautical navigators is *edge following*; when a destination lies along an edge like a coastline, intentionally head to one side of the destination and then follow the edge (hopefully down current) to your destination (Hutchins, 1995). Another method may be called *route* or *direction sampling* (Hill, 1999b). Starting from an established base location, a lost traveler can walk out in various directions for short distances, making sure to keep track of the base. In this way, new information is acquired without risking additional disorientation.

A good example of behavioral-science research on navigational strategies is provided by Cornell, Heth, and Rowat's (1992) research on the *look-back strategy*. Long recommended in wilderness manuals, the look-back strategy involves intentionally stopping, turning around, and memorizing the view behind you while traveling along a route. The strategy is based on the fact that routes often look different in either direction; upon returning from an excursion, the traveler sometimes does not recognize the view in the reverse direction and makes a wrong choice. An especially common version of this navigational error occurs when encountering a fork in the road during the return trip that was not evident during the original trip out (Yogi Berra's advice – that when you come to a fork in the road, you should take it – does not help much). Cornell et al. compared navigational performance by 6-, 12-, and 22-year-old subjects. Subjects took a walk on a college campus with an experimenter who instructed subjects in one of three strategy conditions: no strategy, retrace steps when route feels unfamiliar, or look back and notice view at various points along the walk. Subjects, particularly the 12- and 22-year-olds, stayed on route more and made more correct navigational choices in the look-back condition. This research demonstrated the efficacy of the look-back strategy, and showed it can be explicitly taught and applied effectively by preteens and adults.

The authors proposed that young children lack the metacognitive abilities to properly apply navigational strategies.

In general, wayfinding requires controlled, explicit strategies and working-memory processes when people are in unfamiliar places, including when they are lost. These are more accurately described as reasoning processes than perceptual processes. Passini (1992) provides a framework for understanding cognitive processes during such wayfinding situations. His framework, based on analysis of protocols collected from subjects navigating in public buildings, proposes that wayfinding is composed of three activities: knowledge storage and access (i.e., the cognitive map), decision making for planning actions, and decision execution to turn decisions into behaviors. Such a framework may be applied to understanding how we plan and execute trips, including multistop trips, wherein we organize travel to a series of destinations in an efficient manner (Gärling & Gärling, 1988).

NAVIGATION WITH CARTOGRAPHIC MAPS

Cartographic maps are the quintessential example of external spatial representations of the earth's surface upon which people navigate. There is a large literature on perceptual and cognitive aspects of maps and mapping (see Lloyd, 2000; MacEachren, 1995; Taylor, Chapter 8). There are many types of maps and many tasks for which maps are used. Navigation is but one such task, although among the most important one to most people. And a very important aspect of maps used for navigation is their orientation. To orient a map originally meant to place the east (the Orient) at the top of the map. Putting east at the top seems strange to some people but is no more inappropriate than designing maps with north at the top. The designed orientation of a map, with a particular direction toward the top, is essentially arbitrary, or at least based on rationales that may have no enduring logic. Convention is typically the strongest argument for a particular orientation.

Map orientation is not arbitrary when human psychology is taken into account, however (see also Wickens, Vincow, & Yeh, Chapter 10). Some map orientations make maps harder or easier to understand than others. When using maps to navigate, a large majority of people finds them easiest to use if the top direction of the map is the facing direction (heading) of the viewer. Thus, the "navigator" in the front passenger seat of the car frequently turns the road map as the car turns. This is "forward-up" or "track-up" alignment. If the map is not so oriented, the person navigates

FIGURE 7.2. Mounting the same YAH map in different orientations necessarily produces misaligned maps (from Levine et al., 1984).

less accurately and/or more slowly. For example, a person reading an "inverted" you-are-here (YAH) map, with her facing direction at the bottom of the map, might walk off in the opposite direction from her destination (see Figure 7.2). Such errors or extra time in using improperly oriented navigation maps are called *alignment effects*. Such effects are quite robust, as has been thoroughly documented by Levine and his colleagues (Levine, 1982; Levine, Marchon, & Hanley, 1984) and others (Warren, Rossano, & Wear, 1990). Find a misaligned YAH map and watch people use it – it will not be long before you are convinced of the disorienting power of such maps.

The name for the confusion might more accurately be *mis*alignment effect, because misalignment causes it. Navigation maps require an alignment or coordination of two directions. One is the direction a person is facing (or traveling) in the local surrounds. The other is the direction on the map toward its top. When these two directions are the same (are aligned), left and right on the map will match left and right in the local surrounds. It may also be easy to treat "forward" in the visual field as "up" on a map because the landscape does in fact "rise" in our visual fields as it stretches out in front of us (Shepard & Hurwitz, 1984). Maps can be misaligned with the surrounds to varying degrees (literally degrees – from 1 to 359 degrees). *Contraligned* maps are 180 degree out of alignment, with their top direction corresponding to straight backwards as the map is viewed.

In order to use a misaligned map properly, one must realize it is misaligned, figure out how it is misaligned, and fix the misalignment. There are a variety of ways a person might accomplish these tasks. For example, one can match the direction of a north arrow on the map with the local direction of north relative to one's heading. Or a person can match feature shapes, such as the outlines of buildings on the map and in the surrounds. On some maps, a YAH arrow can provide information about the proper alignment of the map – if it is pointing other than straight up, the map is misaligned. Once misalignment is recognized, a person can physically or mentally rotate the map or their orientation in the surrounds. When performed mentally, these tasks demand working memory and are easy to apply incorrectly, even for otherwise intelligent people. Levine et al. (1984) found misalignment errors even when the meaning and importance of the YAH arrow was stressed.

The occurrence of alignment effects in maps has practical implications for the design and operation of digital displays in navigation systems for cars or cell phones (Aretz & Wickens, 1992; McGranaghan, Mark, & Gould, 1987; Wickens et al., Chapter 10). Interestingly, a significant minority of people prefers navigation maps such as these to be aligned in a fixed orientation, such as "north-up" (Hickox & Wickens, 1999), probably because of the familiarity of looking at the map in a constant orientation. An interesting but unexplored possibility is that a fixed alignment may better facilitate using maps to acquire knowledge of spatial layout – to form cognitive maps. What differentiates people who prefer a fixed alignment from those who do not is also an important question for research. In any case, these considerations suggest that optimal design for vehicle navigation systems should allow both variable and fixed orientations, controllable by the driver.

For YAH maps, which cannot be picked up and turned, map orientation is clearly one of the most robust and straightforward human-factors issues to consider. However, there are a variety of other map-design issues that apply to navigation maps too, such as legend and symbol design. The degree of schematic abstraction in map design is another relevant issue. All maps are *schematic* to some degree, insofar as their depiction of reality is simplified or generalized; even the most detailed and accurate maps are schematic to some extent. Maps used for navigation need not communicate complete metric information about distances and directions. Particularly when the map is used to navigate on a constrained path network, such as a subway system, most navigators will only want to know the connections among network segments – the quantitative distance between stops may be irrelevant, for instance. In fact, since the London subway map of the 1930s first introduced this style of mapping (Ruggles & Armstrong, 1997), network navigation maps have often been designed in a highly schematic fashion. Such maps are sometimes called *topological* maps because they intend to communicate topological information such as line connectivity but not metric information such as distance. All pictures in our world are metric, however; they depict distances and directions even when that information is meant to be ignored. So does the navigator ignore the potentially misleading metric information? Evidence suggests that some navigators do overinterpret schematic map displays (Berendt, Rauh, & Barkowsky, 1998), possibly leading to the acquisition of distorted spatial knowledge. More research is needed on the effects of maps on wayfinding and spatial learning, and what information navigators actually need from maps.

THE PHYSICAL ENVIRONMENT IN NAVIGATION

Navigation occurs in physical environments. The visual and structural characteristics of those environments make it easier or harder to perform various navigation tasks. Flying through the air is different than walking over ground or sailing on the sea. Walking over prairie is different than walking over mountains or crawling through caves. With respect to cognition, these differences are trivially true for locomotion. Yes, it is easier to walk on firm ground than on muddy ground. Much more interesting are the ways that different environments afford different information for wayfinding tasks such as staying oriented to distant goals while moving about. Different information allows different wayfinding strategies, and it makes the strategies easier or harder to apply effectively.

There are many ways to conceptualize physical environments that might help us understand their role in navigation. Certainly, the distinctions suggested earlier are important: air versus water versus ground, flat ground versus mountainous ground, above ground versus underground. One distinction that encompasses a variety of relevant characteristics is that between built and natural environments. *Built* environments are created by humans; *natural* environments are created relatively freely of human agency. There are many intermediate cases, of course, and the very concept of "natural" is extremely complex and imperfect (e.g., Proctor, 1998). Nevertheless some useful generalizations can be made. Built environments have more regular patterns, like straight lines and right angles (although both are found in natural environments). In many built environments, for example, the road network consists entirely of rectilinear grids or symmetric radial patterns. Few buildings have corridor structures anywhere near the complexity of the average cave structure. The appearance of built and natural environments tends to be rather different, although not in any way that is easy to characterize generally. The presence of more curved, irregular, and asymmetric shapes in natural environments gives them a greater visual complexity in one sense, but at some point, this creates visual homogeneity as compared to the more minimalist character of built environments. Structures in built environments can vary capriciously in terms of color and height in ways that violate "natural logic"; in contrast, and unfortunately for the navigator, built environments sometimes capriciously lack variation. With respect to navigation, one of the most important differences between built and natural environments is that the first often come equipped with a semiotic labeling system that aids orientation – signs telling navigators where they are and where to go.

Weisman (1981) offers an interesting analysis of physical environmental characteristics that affect orientation during navigation (see also Gärling, Böök, & Lindberg, 1986). Although intended to apply to designed (i.e., built) environments, his factors apply nearly as well to natural environments. The four factors are: (1) differentiation, (2) visual access, (3) complexity of spatial layout, and (4) signage. *Differentiation* is the degree to which different parts of an environment look the same or different. Environments may be differentiated with respect to size, shape, color, architectural style, and so on. Generally, more differentiated environments are easier to wayfind in because the differentiated parts are more distinct and memorable – differentiation creates better landmarks (Appleyard, 1969; Lynch, 1960); at some point, however, differentiation could be taken to a disordered extreme that would be disorienting. Gladwin (1970) tells the fascinating story of the navigators of the Pulawat Islands of Micronesia (other South and West Pacific peoples have similar traditions). They are able to pick up a great deal of useful information from their watery environment, which is rich in differentiation to those trained to perceive it. This information allows technologically unaided boat trips of a hundred miles or more over open ocean, and includes air and water color, wave and swell patterns, sun and star patterns, and bird species identification.

The second factor of *visual access* (or *visibility*) is the degree to which different parts of an environment can be seen from various viewpoints. From which locations can navigators see their start locations, their destinations, and various landmarks along the way? Is the pattern of the environment, including its path structure, visible from a single viewpoint? Greater visual access obviously makes orientation easier. A promising approach to the systematic analysis of visual access is provided by *isovist theory* (Benedikt & Burnham, 1985); the *isovist* is the collected spatial extent of all views, or vistas, from a single location within an environment. A square room has a large and symmetric isovist (from its center) compared to that of a room of the same area broken up by dividing walls. And within the same environment, the isovist differs from different locations (Figure 7.3). Isovist theory, conceived by Hardy (1967) and named by Tandy (1967), was inspired by a planning concern for the visual appearance of the landscape and an appreciation of Gibson's (1950) ideas about the visual perception of texture gradients in the environment. The theory proposes that characteristics of isovists, such as size or shape, will help explain different psychological responses, such as ease of orientation and verbal description, in different places. In the disciplines of cartography and surveying, isovist analysis is known as *viewshed analysis* (see Llobera, 2003).

Weisman's (1981) third factor, *complexity of spatial layout*, is a heterogeneous notion that is difficult to express in formal terms. Exactly what constitutes a complex layout, in the sense that it makes orientation more confusing, is a question for research. A more articulated space, broken up into more different parts, is generally more complex, although the way the different parts are organized is critical. It is clear that certain patterns of path[4] networks are more or less complex in this sense; for example, oblique turns are more disorienting than orthogonal turns (Montello, 1991). What is difficult here, though, is that the overall shape or gestalt of a path layout can determine whether a particular element is disorienting (Weisman [1981] in fact focused on the "good form" of a layout's overall configuration). A curved street is understood better when it fits within a radial

---

4 I distinguish *paths*, linear physical features in the world upon which travel occurs (roads, trails), from *routes*, linear patterns of movement by a traveler. Routes of travel may occur on paths or across areas that contain no paths, like open fields.

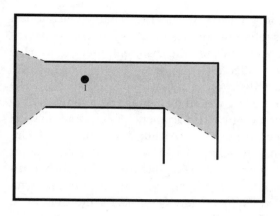

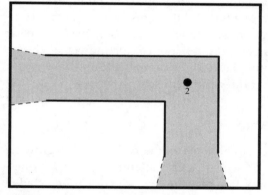

FIGURE 7.3. Two-dimensional isovists from two different locations (1 and 2) within the same hallway.

network pattern, as long as that radial pattern is in fact apprehended. A grid pattern may be disorienting if its axes do not run north-south and east-west – at least for those navigators who incorporate cardinal directions in their wayfinding. Layouts may be said to vary in their closeness to a good form – wayfinding is easier when the layout has an overall pattern that can be apprehended as a single simple shape. A square is easier than a rhombus; a circle is easier than a lopsided oval. People apparently try to understand layouts as good forms, and when the layout does not have such a form, disorientation can result (Tversky, 1992). A classic example is reported by Lynch (1960), who found that people were confused by the Boston Commons because they tended to assume it is a square when it is actually an irregular pentagon. I have heard that the Pentagon, headquarters of the U.S. military, was intentionally designed as a five-sided shape to disorient intruders. If they really wanted to disorient, they could have designed it with five sides but called it the "Square."

Finally, Weisman (1981) listed *signage* as a fourth factor that affects the legibility of environments. Earlier, I described signage as a semiotic system that aids orientation. The design and placement of signs and maps in the environment clearly affects orientation (Arthur & Passini, 1992). Unfortunately, as my discussion of misaligned YAH maps makes clear, signs can *disorient* too. Effective signage must be legible from a distance, must be clear and simple in design, must have enough but not too much information, and must be placed where the navigator needs information (at decision points, for instance). The challenge of designing comprehendible iconic symbols for signs is especially great; does an arrow pointing straight up mean go forward or go up one floor? With signs, as with layout complexity, many contextual factors influence effectiveness. A perfectly clear sign may be confusing if it is placed in a sea of competing visual clutter. And even the best designed and placed signs cannot entirely make up for poor characteristics of the other three physical-setting factors.

NEUROSCIENCE OF NAVIGATION

The neuroscience of navigation, in humans and nonhumans, is a growing area of research (Paillard, 1991). This research attempts to answer questions such as how spatial information relevant to navigation is encoded in nervous systems, which brain areas process navigation information, how sensory information for navigation is integrated in the nervous system, and how particular injuries or organic syndromes produce particular deficits in navigational behavior.

One of the earliest findings in this area concerned the involvement of the *hippocampus* in spatial learning during navigation. The hippocampus is a brain structure located within the temporal lobe, surrounded by the lateral ventricle, and connected to subcortical nuclei via the fornix and to the neocortex via the parahippocampal region (Eichenbaum, 1999). These anatomical connections point to the hippocampus as a final convergence location for outputs from many areas of the cerebral cortex, and a source of many divergent outputs to cortical and subcortical areas. These anatomical connections reflect the apparent role of the hippocampus as a major organizer of memory representations. Observations of rats with hippocampal lesions have revealed deficits in the ability to learn maze layouts

(Mizumori, 1994; O'Keefe & Nadel, 1978). Recordings of the activity of single brain cells in the hippocampi of rats as they navigate in mazes have revealed the existence of neurons that preferentially fire when the rat is in a particular location (O'Keefe, 1976). These *place cells* fire independently of the rat's heading, and even when stimulus features within the maze are modified, as long as extramaze features exist to define a location (O'Keefe & Conway, 1979). The extramaze cues are typically visually based, but can also be nonvisual. The location where the place cells fire is known as the *place field* (Mizumori, 1994).

However, spatial encoding is not unique to hippocampus cells; heading is coded by *head-direction cells* in structures with afferent and efferent connections to the hippocampus, and movement velocity appears to be coded in connected structures as well (Mizumori, 1994). Furthermore, the job of the hippocampus is not exclusively to process spatial information. It has long been known that hippocampal lesions in humans cause forms of amnesia for nonspatial information, and that nonhumans show some hippocampal-caused deficits in nonspatial learning (Eichenbaum, 1999). It is now generally recognized that the hippocampus serves to integrate information into flexible multimodal representations, organizing and encoding experience in relation to its spatiotemporal context. In humans, hippocampus lesions cause deficits in the ability to store episodic memories (Eichenbaum, 1999; Maguire, Burgess, Donnett, Frackowiak, Frith, & O'Keefe, 1998). Of course, this is not inconsistent with the idea that the hippocampus plays a central role in some aspects of spatial cognition; it just indicates that spatial cognition plays a central role in cognition more generally.

Findings of selective deficits and single-cell activity have led to several models of the role of the hippocampus and connected structures in spatial information processing during navigation and place learning. O'Keefe and Nadel (1978) proposed that the hippocampus is the site where an allocentric cognitive map of the environment is constructed and stored. More recently, McNaughton and his colleagues (e.g., McNaughton, Chen, & Markus, 1991; McNaughton et al., 1995) have developed and tested computational models of cortical-hippocampal interaction in which the hippocampus retains views of locations and their interrelations derived from movement. In other words, they have formally developed the idea that dead reckoning serves as a glue to integrate sensory experiences into memory representations of spatial layout, based on the maintenance of an azimuthal frame relating an organism's heading to the orientation of the external surrounds (see also Mizumori, 1994; Poucet, 1993).

TABLE 7.1. *Taxonomy of Topographic Disorientation Syndromes (from Aguirre &*
D'Esposito, 1999)

Disorder	Lesion Site	Proposed Impairment
Egocentric disorientation	Posterior parietal	Location of objects relative to self
Heading disorientation	Posterior cingulate	Heading relative to external environment
Landmark agnosia	Lingual gyrus	Appearance of salient environmental features
Anterograde disorientation	Parahippocampus	Creation of new representations of environments

Clinical studies of organic brain syndromes and injuries have shed light
on the neuroscience of navigation in humans (reviewed by Aguirre &
D'Esposito, 1999). Specific impairments in some aspect of navigational
ability following localized brain injuries are known as *topographical dis-*
orientation. Topographical disorientation refers particularly to physiologi-
cally caused deficits in wayfinding rather than locomotion: knowing which
way to head to get to a nonvisible landmark rather than being able to walk
straight to a beacon in the visual field, for example. Aguirre and D'Esposito
(1999) list four topographical disorientation syndromes that have been hypothesized to exist based on documentation of one or more clinical cases.
Reprinted in modified form in Table 7.1, their taxonomy includes egocentric disorientation, heading disorientation, landmark agnosia, and antero-
grade disorientation. The evidence is clearest for landmark agnosia, an inability to represent the appearance of salient features in the environment,
caused by lesions to the lingual gyrus. A couple of notable conclusions
from this work is that the role of the hippocampus in spatial learning is
not as clear in humans as in nonhumans, and that many nonhippocampal
structures play an important role in various aspects of spatial learning and
navigation.

Finally, brain imaging of awake and normally functioning humans is
beginning to increase our understanding of the neuroscience of navigation. Maguire et al. (1998), for example, reported positron emission tomography (PET) scans of humans while they navigated in a desktop virtual
town. The scans suggested different roles for right and left hemisphere
brain structures. Activity in both the right hippocampus and right inferior parietal cortex was associated with navigating to nonvisible landmarks. The authors interpreted this as consistent with the hippocampus's
role in forming allocentric maps and the inferior parietal cortex's role in

egocentric orientation. The left frontal cortex was active during responses to enforced detours, suggesting to the authors its role in planning and decision making, which are typical wayfinding acts, during navigation. Brain imaging techniques hold great promise for increasing our understanding of the neural substrates of cognition and behavior, including navigation. At this time, however, they are greatly limited by their restriction to use with nonmoving subjects. The relationship between navigation in real and virtual environments has yet to be conclusively established.

ARTIFICIAL INTELLIGENCE APPROACHES

An important body of cognitive work on navigation has been carried out by researchers in the field of artificial intelligence (AI). It is critical to keep in mind that AI researchers have varied goals. Some want to use computer simulations to test theories about how humans or other animals navigate. Others want to make a computer do something, regardless of whether it does it like an animal does it. A few researchers with this latter goal nonetheless believe they can learn something useful from looking at existing examples of successful navigating entities. They just don't worry about designing all aspects of their intelligent systems in realistic, animalistic, ways. Many researchers with the goal of making a navigating computer, a *robot*, are not concerned in the least with how animals do it. In such cases, the researcher only wants to make a system that works, regardless of whether it works like some animal. Thus, robots are frequently designed that take advantage of large memories and processing speeds, and powerful sensory-motor systems, that are quite unrealistic for an animal. No animal has a laser range-finder, for example.

AI research on navigation supports the value of distinguishing locomotion from wayfinding processes, as was mentioned earlier. Roboticists have typically focused on locomotion rather than wayfinding – their robots move down hallways or follow road patterns but often do not plan routes or give directions (e.g., Aloimonos, 1996). A telling example is provided by Brooks (e.g., 1991). For some time, he and his colleagues built robots that could locomote without internal representations of the external environment. He in fact attempted to make the scientific case that navigation did not require a cognitive map, but his evidence consisted of machines that could locomote (to an extent) but could not wayfind. In contrast, some AI workers other than roboticists have used computational models to test theories about how animals, including humans, navigate and learn spatial information (McDermott & Davis, 1984; Yeap, 1988). These

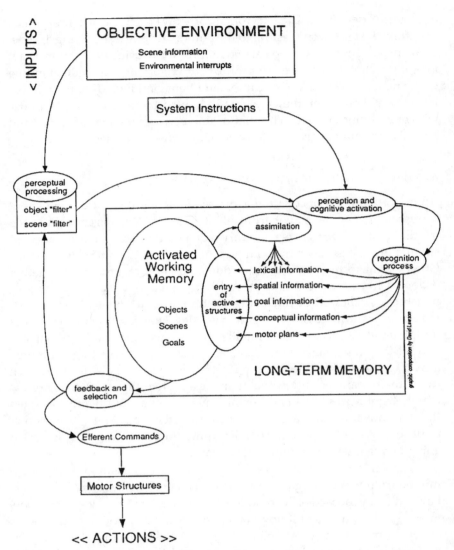

FIGURE 7.4. The NAVIGATOR model by Gopal et al. (1989), a computational-process model of navigation and spatial learning.

computational-process modelers typically focus on simulating wayfinding rather than locomotion – their models "reason" about choosing routes or heading in the direction of a goal, but they do not actually "go" anywhere. A good example is the NAVIGATOR model by Gopal, Klatzky, and Smith (1989), shown in Figure 7.4.

A complete computational simulation of animal navigation would clearly perform both locomotion and wayfinding tasks. Fortunately, the distinction between locomoting robots and wayfinding programs has been breaking down, in practice (M. E. Jefferies & W.-K. Yeap, personal communication, December 16, 1999). That is, researchers are more likely to create AI simulations that perform both locomotion and wayfinding.

The influential work of Kuipers and his colleagues is a case in point. He has done some of the earliest AI work on navigation that incorporates ideas about human navigation. It is worthwhile to consider his work in some detail, as it is the most comprehensive research program in AI that utilizes and develops organismic theories of navigation, and because it touches on nearly all of the issues that confront AI modelers working on navigation. Kuiper's TOUR model (1978) was a computational-process model of navigation and spatial learning. It has recently been clarified and extended more directly to locomotion tasks in his "Spatial Semantic Hierarchy" (SSH) (Kuipers, 2000). The SSH posits four distinct and somewhat separate representations or levels for knowledge of large-scale space derived from and supporting navigation; the four are simultaneously active in the cognitive map, according to Kuipers. The four levels are:

(1) *Control level* – This is grounded in sensorimotor interaction with the environment, and is best modeled in terms of partial differential equations that express control laws specifying continuous relations between sensory inputs and motor outputs.

(2) *Causal level* – This is egocentric like the control level, but discrete, consisting of *views* defined by sensory experiences and *actions* for moving from one view to the next. The views and actions are associated as schemas and are best modeled using first-order logic.

(3) *Topological level* – This includes a representation of the external world, but only qualitatively, including places, paths, regions and their connectivity, order, and containment. First-order logic is appropriate here too.

(4) *Metrical level* – This representation of the external world includes distance, direction, and shape, organized in a global allocentric reference system. This is modeled best by statistical estimation theory, such as Bayesian modeling.

Kuipers (2000) presents some evidence for the SSH from partial implementations on simulated and actual robots.

Other AI researchers have modeled navigation and spatial learning (Chown, Kaplan, & Kortenkamp, 1995; Yoshino, 1991). All of these

AI models share certain concerns or ideas. First, all posit multiple representations of space varying in the degree to which they depend on each other; as in Kuipers's SSH, some models suggest that different computational approaches or *ontologies* are most appropriate for different types of representations and different navigational tasks. All models include bottom-up processing from sensorimotor information, although as I suggest earlier, the models vary in the degree to which they explicitly model these bottom-up sensorimotor processes (they have to be modeled in a robot but may be assumed in a nonmoving program). All models posit the importance of landmarks, which are features or views in the space that are noticed as distinctive, remembered, and used to help organize spatial knowledge. In some way, all models concern themselves with the derivation of allocentric 3-D (or 2.5-D) maps from egocentric 2-D views of the world, including in some cases a distinction between local and global allocentric representations. Different models vary in the degree to which they posit metric knowledge of distances and directions in addition to topological knowledge; the metric knowledge is frequently modeled as being qualitative or fuzzy. The models all recognize the problem of integrating spatial information encoded in multiple systems of reference, and they generally employ some type of hierarchical representation structure such as graph trees to encode hierarchical spatial and thematic relations in the world. Taken together, these various properties of AI simulation models point to what may be their greatest contribution to the multidisciplinary understanding of navigation as a cognitive problem: The existence of partial, imprecise, and distorted knowledge enables the digital entity to deal robustly with uncertain and faulty information during navigational learning and problem solving.

SUMMARY AND CONCLUSIONS: THE FUTURE OF NAVIGATION

Navigation, coordinated and goal-directed movement through the environment, is a ubiquitous task performed by mobile animals. In prototypical form, it involves both planning and execution of movements. To navigate successfully, animals perform perceptual and cognitive operations on information from the body, from the environment, and, in the case of human beings, from symbolic sources such as maps, signs, or words. To understand navigation as a cognitive task, I organize it into the two components of locomotion and wayfinding. Locomotion refers to body movement coordinated to the local surrounds, and includes identifying surfaces of support, avoiding barriers, and other activities. Wayfinding refers to the planning and decision-making activities that allow goal-directed locomotion coordinated to the distal as well as local surrounds. Such activities include orienting to currently nonperceptible goals, giving verbal directions, and other activities.

Perhaps vision contributes the most navigational information under normal circumstances, at least for human beings, but a variety of other modalities such as vestibular sensing also play a part. Several other distinctions among psychological systems help us understand navigational behavior and information processing. Both perception/action and memory/ planning systems are involved, to different degrees in different navigational tasks. Both declarative and nondeclarative knowledge processes operate in navigational tasks as well. Locomotion tasks are more often cognitively impenetrable, and tend to demand less working-memory capacity, as compared to many wayfinding tasks. Penetrable wayfinding strategies can be intentionally acquired and applied.

Animals maintain a sense of location – they geographically orient. Animals can be oriented to varying degrees, with respect to various features, and with respect to different scales of space. Orientation requires a system of reference for defining location. A variety of reference systems are used by animals, particularly humans, but the system that orients the animal to the orientation of its global surrounds, an azimuthal system, is particularly fundamental to geographic orientation. Animals update their sense of orientation as they move about. To do this, they use a combination of landmark-based and dead-reckoning processes. Landmark-based processes involve the recognition of external features or scenes. Dead-reckoning processes involve attention to information about body movement (speed, direction) without recognition of specific landmarks.

People frequently use cartographic maps to navigate. The orientation of navigation maps has been shown to strongly affect how easily they are used. A forward-up alignment is typically, but not always, easiest to use. The difficulty of using maps that are misoriented relative to the surrounds is called an alignment effect. To use misaligned maps, the navigator must recognize they are misaligned and compensate appropriately. A variety of additional issues have implications for the design of cartographic displays used to navigate.

The structure and appearance of physical environments affects the ease of orienting within them. The distinction between built and natural environments helps account for some of the effects. In general, environments are easier to orient within when they have high differentiation, high visual access, and low complexity of spatial layout. The latter factor has an especially potent effect on orientation, although in ways that are often difficult to characterize a priori. Layout complexity depends in part on the situational context, and is a function of both local and more global geometric relations. Unique to environments that have at least partially been created by people, the quality of signage also affects orientation.

There is a growing body of literature on the neuroscience of navigation. This research includes studies of single-cell recordings of nonhumans (especially rats) performing navigation tasks, lesion studies in nonhumans, studies of organic syndromes in clinical patients that affect navigation in different ways (called topographical disorientation in this literature), and brain-imaging studies of normal adults performing navigation in simulated environments.

Finally, behavioral and computational scientists have investigated navigation as a problem for artificial intelligence. Some AI researchers use computational models to test theories of navigation by animals; others just want to make robots that work. Among the first group, several issues are recurring concerns: the existence of multiple representations of space, the relative contributions of bottom-up and top-down processes, the role of landmarks, the derivation of allocentric maps from egocentric views of the world, the relative roles of metric and nonmetric knowledge, and the application of multiple reference systems and hierarchical organization. Attention to these concerns allows AI models to address the robustness of navigation in the face of uncertain information.

There are important topic areas within the theme of navigation that could not be covered in any detail in this chapter, given its space limitations. There is a great deal of research on navigation by nonhuman animals (see Schöne, 1984; Wehner, Lehrer, & Harvey, 1996) that has only been touched on here. Focusing just on human navigation, questions about how and why individuals and the two sexes differ in their navigation styles and abilities is covered in Hegarty and Waller (Chapter 4), and Halpern and Collaer (Chapter 5), respectively. The development of navigational cognition throughout the life span, and ways that it differs as a function of age, are discussed in Hegarty and Waller (Chapter 4) and Newcombe and Learmonth (Chapter 6). Spatial knowledge acquisition (learning the cognitive map) often occurs during navigation and, as discussed in this chapter, produces knowledge that provides a basis for wayfinding behaviors. There is a great deal of research literature on spatial learning (Golledge, 1987; Montello, 1998; Thorndyke & Hayes-Roth, 1982) that is not reviewed in this chapter. And a complete discussion of higher-level cognition in navigation would include research on the verbal communication of navigational information (Allen, 1997). Finally, navigation in virtual environments is currently of great research interest (Ruddle, Payne, & Jones, 1997); this growing topic is considered in Wickens, Vincow, and Yeh (Chapter 10).

The advent of virtual-environments technology is but one example of the technological developments that are changing human navigation, including the cognitive processes that are part of navigation. Over the centuries, humans have developed a variety of new technologies to aid navigation. Recent developments will have effects on navigation, especially wayfinding, that are nothing short of revolutionary. A key technology is the satellite system for locating oneself on the earth's surface, known as the *Global Positioning System* (GPS). Inexpensive and portable access to this system is now available for automobile navigation systems, cell phones, and other types of personal navigation assistants. Particularly with recent improvements in the resolution of the satellite signal made available to civilians, people can accurately locate themselves most anywhere on the earth to within meters. Other navigational technologies include auditory signage for the visually impaired, and radio transmitters for tracking children or those suffering from Alzheimer's disease.

These technologies will clearly have a profound impact on how people stay oriented and make navigational decisions. Especially powerful is the way that digital information can be flexibly tailored to a specific situation in a way that rarely happened in the predigital age. Many, many hours of disorientation will be avoided; fear, anxiety, and frustration will be reduced; lives will be saved. However, one should not accept the advertisement hype that you will "never get lost again!" People will always get lost, and in some ways, they will get lost worse because of new technologies. Satellite systems fail sometimes, and they can be distorted or blocked by local obstructions. Electronic machines lose power or just plain break. Possessing the technology is going to lead to a false sense of security, which in turn will lead to an unprecedented lack of preparation and of practice in traditional navigation. Hikers will go out without appropriate prior planning or without good old paper maps or compasses. Who is going to bother with the look-back strategy when they can rely on a hand held satellite receiver tapping into millions of dollars of the latest technology? There are already documented cases of wilderness disorientation because of cell phone failure (E. H. Cornell & C. D. Heth, personal communications, July, 1999).

Even given accurately functioning technology, people will still be able to lose their way. Possessing a map or verbal directions, no matter how complete and accurate, has never guaranteed protection from disorientation, and it never will. Being provided with latitude-longitude coordinates certainly won't solve the problem. Making the map or the directions digital doesn't matter, and will in fact create more problems while the bugs in the databases and algorithms get worked out. There are a host of important and interesting new research questions that are created by new navigational technologies. How should navigational interfaces be designed (Streeter, Vitello, & Wonsiewicz, 1985), and how should people be trained to use them? However, many research questions will remain the same. New technologies do not obviate the need to decide what information should be given to navigators, and how it should be communicated. As long as people have to decide where to go and how to get there, navigation will remain one of the fundamental behavioral problems for human cognition.

ACKNOWLEDGMENTS

I thank the editors and three reviewers for comments that have increased the chapter's clarity. John Reiser suggested the interesting examples of blind navigation and the Mars Rover. An overview chapter such as this is an appropriate place to thank members of the UCSB spatial cognition community: Reg Golledge, Mary Hegarty, Jack Loomis, Helen Couclelis, Sara Fabrikant, and several graduate students and post-docs. I also thank the many contributions of mentors and colleagues at other institutions over the years. They have provided an intellectual milieu critical for the creation and refinement of ideas, but of course the poor ideas are all mine.

Suggestions for Further Reading

An insightful review and interpretation of literature on learning, particularly spatial learning in nonhumans, including behavioral, computational, and neuroscience work. Includes useful overview of basic concepts of navigation and spatial knowledge:
Gallistel, C. R. (1990). *The organization of learning*. Cambridge, MA: The MIT Press.

State-of-the-art edited collection by behavioral scientists working with humans and nonhumans. Provides overview of both wayfinding and locomotion:
Golledge, R. G. (Editor). (1999). *Wayfinding behavior: Cognitive mapping and other spatial processes*. Baltimore, MD: Johns Hopkins Press.

Explains situated cognition in an engaging manner, using a detailed explication of social and technical factors in nautical navigation as a demonstration case:
Hutchins, E. (1995). *Cognition in the wild*. Cambridge, MA: The MIT Press.

Comprehensive discussion of traditional navigation techniques by various peoples of the South and West Pacific islands. Both psychological and material issues considered:

Lewis, D. (1994). *We, the navigators: The ancient art of landfinding in the Pacific.* (2nd ed.). Honolulu: University of Hawaii Press.

Classic edited collection of human behavioral-science research on spatial cognition, development, and navigation:

Pick, H. L., & Acredolo, L. (1983). *Spatial orientation: Theory, research, and application.* New York: Plenum.

Edited special issue with many contributions by top researchers of nonhuman animal navigation. Organized around the theme that different mechanisms and structures operate at different scales of navigation:

Wehner, R., Lehrer, M., & Harvey, W. R. (Editors). (1996). Navigation: Migration and homing [Special issue]. *The Journal of Experimental Biology, 199*(1).

References

Aguirre, G. K., & D'Esposito, M. (1999). Topographical disorientation: A synthesis and taxonomy. *Brain, 122,* 1613–1628.

Allen, G. L. (1997). From knowledge to words to wayfinding: Issues in the production and comprehension of route directions. In S. C. Hirtle & A. U. Frank (Eds.), *Spatial information theory: A theoretical basis for GIS* (pp. 363–372). Berlin: Springer.

Allen, G. L., & Kirasic, K. C. (2003). Visual attention during route learning: A look at selection and engagement. In W. Kuhn, M. Worboys, & S. Timpf (Eds.), *Spatial information theory: Foundations of geographic information science* (pp. 390–398). Berlin: Springer.

Aloimonos, Y. (1996). *Visual navigation: From biological systems to unmanned ground vehicles.* Hillsdale, NJ: Lawrence Erlbaum Associates.

Appleyard, D. (1969). Why buildings are known. *Environment and Behavior, 1,* 131–156.

Aretz, A. J., & Wickens, C. D. (1992). The mental rotation of map displays. *Human Performance, 5,* 303–328.

Arthur, P., & Passini, R. (1992). *Wayfinding: People, signs, and architecture.* Toronto: McGraw-Hill Ryerson.

Baker, R. R. (1989). *Human navigation and magnetoreception.* Manchester: Manchester University Press.

Benedikt, M., & Burnham, C. A. (1985). Perceiving architectural space: From optic arrays to Isovists. In W. H. Warren & R. E. Shaw (Eds.), *Persistence and change: Proceedings of the First International Conference on Event Perception* (pp. 103–114). Hillsdale, NJ: Lawrence Erlbaum Associates.

Berendt, B., Rauh, R., & Barkowsky, T. (1998). Spatial thinking with geographic maps: An empirical study. In H. Czap, H. P. Ohly, & S. Pribbenow (Eds.), *Herausforderungen an die Wissensorganisation: Visualisierung, multimediale Dokumente, Internetstrukturen* (pp. 63–73). Würzburg: Ergon.

290 _Daniel R. Montello_

Brooks, R. A. (1991). Intelligence without representation. _Artificial Intelligence, 47,_ 139–159.

Chown, E., Kaplan, S., & Kortenkamp, D. (1995). Prototypes, location, and associative networks (PLAN): Toward a unified theory of cognitive mapping. _Cognitive Science, 19,_ 1–51.

Cornell, E. H., Heth, C. D., & Rowat, W. L. (1992). Wayfinding by children and adults: Response to instructions to use look-back and retrace strategies. _Developmental Psychology, 28,_ 328–336.

Eichenbaum, H. (1999). Hippocampus. In R. Wilson & F. Keil (Eds.), _The MIT encyclopedia of cognitive sciences._ Cambridge, MA: The MIT Press.

Fabrikant, S. I. (2000). Spatialized browsing in large data archives. _Transactions in GIS, 4,_ 65–78.

Fajen, B. R., & Warren, W. H. (2003). Behavioral dynamics of steering, obstacle avoidance, and route selection. _Journal of Experimental Psychology: Human Perception and Performance, 29,_ 343–362.

Feldman, A., & Acredolo, L. P. (1979). The effect of active versus passive exploration on memory for spatial location in children. _Child Development, 50,_ 698–704.

Frederickson, R. E., & Bartlett, J. C. (1987). Cognitive impenetrability of memory for orientation. _Journal of Experimental Psychology: Learning, Memory, and Cognition, 13,_ 269–277.

Gallistel, C. R. (1990). _The organization of learning._ Cambridge, MA: The MIT Press.

Gärling, T., Böök, A., & Lindberg, E. (1986). Spatial orientation and wayfinding in the designed environment: A conceptual analysis and some suggestions for postoccupancy evaluation. _Journal of Architectural Planning Resources, 3,_ 55–64.

Gärling, T., & Gärling, E. (1988). Distance minimization in downtown pedestrian shopping. _Environment and Planning A, 20,_ 547–554.

Gibson, J. J. (1950). _The perception of the visual world._ Boston: Houghton Mifflin.

Gibson, J. J. (1966). _The senses considered as perceptual systems._ Boston: Houghton Mifflin.

Gladwin, T. (1970). _East is a big bird._ Cambridge, MA: Harvard University Press.

Golledge, R. G. (1987). Environmental cognition. In D. Stokols & I. Altman (Eds.), _Handbook of environmental psychology_ (pp. 131–174). New York: Wiley.

Gopal, S., Klatzky, R., & Smith, T. R. (1989). NAVIGATOR: A psychologically based model of environmental learning through navigation. _Journal of Environmental Psychology, 9,_ 309–331.

Gould, J. L., & Able, K. P. (1981). Human homing: An elusive phenomenon. _Science, 212,_ 1061–1063.

Hardy, A. C. (1967). Landscape and human perception. In A. C. Murray (Ed.), _Methods of landscape analysis_ (Vol. October, pp. 3–8). London: Landscape Research Group.

Hart, R. A., & Moore, G. T. (1973). The development of spatial cognition: A review. In R. M. Downs & D. Stea (Eds.), _Image and environment_ (pp. 246–288). Chicago: Aldine.

Hazen, N. L., Lockman, J. J., & Pick, H. L., Jr. (1978). The development of children's representations of large-scale environments. _Child Development, 49,_ 623–636.

Hickox, J. C., & Wickens, C. D. (1999). Effects of elevation angle disparity, complexity, and feature type on relating out-of-cockpit field of view to an electronic cartographic map. *Journal of Experimental Psychology: Applied, 5*, 284–301.

Hill, K. A. (Ed.). (1999a). *Lost person behaviour*. Ottawa, Ontario: The National Search and Rescue Secretariat.

Hill, K. A. (1999b). The psychology of lost. In K. A. Hill (Ed.), *Lost person behaviour* (pp. 1–16). Ottawa, Ontario: The National Search and Rescue Secretariat.

Howard, I., & Templeton, W. B. (1966). *Human spatial orientation*. New York: Wiley.

Hutchins, E. (1995). *Cognition in the wild*. Cambridge, MA: The MIT Press.

Johnson, M. (1987). *The body in the mind: The bodily basis of meaning, imagination, and reason*. Chicago: The University of Chicago Press.

Kerzel, D., Heiko, H., & Kim, N.-G. (1999). Image velocity, not tau, explains arrival-time judgments from global optical flow. *Journal of Experimental Psychology: Human Perception and Performance, 25*, 1540–1555.

Kirschvink, J. L., Jones, D. S., & McFadden, B. J. (Eds.) (1985). *Magnetic biomineralization and magnetoreception in organisms*. New York: Plenum Press.

Kitchin, R. (1998). *Cyberspace: The world in the wires*. Chichester: Wiley.

Kuipers, B. (1978). Modeling spatial knowledge. *Cognitive Science, 2*, 129–153.

Kuipers, B. (2000). The Spatial Semantic Hierarchy. *Artificial Intelligence, 119*, 191–233.

Lee, D. N., & Lishman, R. (1977). Visual control of locomotion. *Scandinavian Journal of Psychology, 18*, 224–230.

Levine, M. (1982). You-are-here maps: Psychological considerations. *Environment and Behavior, 14*, 221–237.

Levine, M., Marchon, I., & Hanley, G. L. (1984). The placement and misplacement of you-are-here maps. *Environment and Behavior, 16*, 139–157.

Levinson, S. C. (1996). Frames of reference and Molyneux's question: Crosslinguistic evidence. In P. Bloom, M. A. Peterson, L. Nadel, & M. F. Garrett (Eds.), *Language and space* (pp. 109–169). Cambridge, MA: The MIT Press.

Lewis, D. (1994). *We, the navigators: The ancient art of landfinding in the Pacific* (2nd ed.). Honolulu: University of Hawaii Press.

Llobera, M. (2003). Extending GIS-based visual analysis: The concept of visualscapes. *International Journal of Geographical Information Science, 17*, 25–48.

Lloyd, R. (2000). Understanding and learning maps. In R. Kitchin, & S. Freundschuh (Eds.), *Cognitive mapping: Past, present, and future* (pp. 84–107). London: Routledge and Kegan Paul.

Loomis, J. M., Klatzky, R. L., Golledge, R. G., Cicinelli, J. G., Pellegrino, J. W., & Fry, P. A. (1993). Nonvisual navigation by blind and sighted: Assessment of path integration ability. *Journal of Experimental Psychology: General, 122*, 73–91.

Loomis, J. M., Klatzky, R. L., Golledge, R. G., & Philbeck, J. W. (1999). Human navigation by path integration. In R. G. Golledge (Ed.), *Wayfinding behavior: Cognitive mapping and other spatial processes* (pp. 125–151). Baltimore, MD: Johns Hopkins Press.

Loomis, J. M., Klatzky, R. L., Philbeck, J. W., & Golledge, R. G. (1998). Assessing auditory distance perception using perceptually directed action. *Perception & Psychophysics, 60*, 966–980.

Lovelace, K. L., Hegarty, M., & Montello, D. R. (1999). Elements of good route directions in familiar and unfamiliar environments. In C. Freksa & D. M. Mark (Eds.), *Spatial information theory: Cognitive and computational foundations of geographic information science* (pp. 65–82). Berlin: Springer.

Lynch, K. (1960). *The image of the city.* Cambridge, MA: The MIT Press.

MacEachren, A. M. (1995). *How maps work: Representation, visualization, and design.* New York: Guilford Press.

Maguire, E. A., Burgess, N., Donnett, J. G., Frackowiak, R. S. J., Frith, C. D., & O'Keefe, J. (1998). Knowing where and getting there: A human navigation network. *Science, 280,* 921–924.

May, M., & Klatzky, R. L. (2000). Path integration while ignoring irrelevant movement. *Journal of Experimental Psychology: Learning, Memory, and Cognition, 26,* 169–186.

McDermott, D., & Davis, E. (1984). Planning routes through uncertain territory. *Artificial Intelligence, 22,* 107–156.

McGranaghan, M., Mark, D. M., & Gould, M. D. (1987). Automated provision of navigation assistance to drivers. *The American Cartographer, 14,* 121–138.

McNaughton, B. L., Chen, L. L., & Markus, E. J. (1991). "Dead reckoning," landmark learning, and the sense of direction: A neurophysiological and computational hypothesis. *Journal of Cognitive Neuroscience, 3,* 190–202.

McNaughton, B. L., Knierim, J. J., & Wilson, M. A. (1995). Vector encoding and the vestibular foundations of spatial cognition: Neurophysiological and computational mechanisms. In M. S. Gazzaniga et al. (Eds.), *The cognitive neurosciences* (pp. 585–595). Cambridge, MA: The MIT Press.

Mittelstaedt, M. L., & Mittelstaedt, H. (1980). Homing by path integration in a mammal. *Naturwissenschaften, 67,* 566–567.

Mizumori, S. J. Y. (1994). Neural representations during spatial navigation. *Current Directions in Psychological Science, 3,* 125–129.

Montello, D. R. (1991). Spatial orientation and the angularity of urban routes: A field study. *Environment and Behavior, 23,* 47–69.

Montello, D. R. (1997). The perception and cognition of environmental distance: Direct sources of information. In S. C. Hirtle & A. U. Frank (Eds.), *Spatial information theory: A theoretical basis for GIS* (pp. 297–311). Berlin: Springer.

Montello, D. R. (1998). A new framework for understanding the acquisition of spatial knowledge in large-scale environments. In M. J. Egenhofer & R. G. Golledge (Eds.), *Spatial and temporal reasoning in geographic information systems* (pp. 143–154). New York: Oxford University Press.

O'Keefe, J. (1976). Place units in the hippocampus of the freely moving rat. *Experimental Neurology, 51,* 78–109.

O'Keefe, J., & Conway, D. H. (1979). Hippocampal place units in the freely moving rat: Why they fire where they fire. *Experimental Brain Research, 31,* 573–590.

O'Keefe, J., & Nadel, L. (1978). *The hippocampus as a cognitive map.* New York: Oxford University Press.

Paillard, J. (Ed.) (1991). *Brain and space.* Oxford: Oxford University Press.

Passini, R. (1992). *Wayfinding in architecture* (2nd ed.). New York: Van Nostrand Reinhold Company.

Pearsall, J., & Trumble, B. (Eds.) (1996). *The Oxford encyclopedic English dictionary* (3rd ed.). New York: Oxford University Press.

Piaget, J., Inhelder, B., & Szeminska, A. (1960). *The child's conception of geometry.* London: Routledge and Kegan Paul.

Pick, H. L., Heinrichs, M. R., Montello, D. R., Smith, K., Sullivan, C. N., & Thompson, W. B. (1995). Topographic map reading. In P. A. Hancock, J. M. Flach, J. Caird, & K. J. Vicente (Eds.), *Local applications of the ecological approach to human-machine systems, Vol. 2* (pp. 255–284). Hillsdale, NJ: Lawrence Erlbaum Associates.

Pick, H. L., & Palmer, C. F. (1986). Perception and representation in the guidance of spatially coordinated behavior. In M. G. Wade & H. T. A. Whiting (Eds.), *Motor development in children: Aspects of coordination and control* (pp. 135–145). Dordrecht: Martinus Nijhoff Publishers.

Potegal, M. (1982). Vestibular and neostriatal contributions to spatial orientation. In M. Potegal (Ed.), *Spatial abilities: Development and physiological foundations* (pp. 361–387). New York: Academic Press.

Poucet, B. (1993). Spatial cognitive maps in animals: New hypotheses on their structure and neural mechanisms. *Psychological Review, 100,* 163–182.

Proctor, J. D. (1998). The social construction of nature: Relativist accusations, pragmatist and critical realist responses. *Annals of the Association of American Geographers, 88,* 352–376.

Rieser, J. J. (1989). Access to knowledge of spatial structure at novel points of observation. *Journal of Experimental Psychology: Learning, Memory, and Cognition, 15,* 1157–1165.

Rieser, J. J., Guth, D. A., & Hill, E. W. (1986). Sensitivity to perspective structure while walking without vision. *Perception, 15,* 173–188.

Ruddle, R. A., Payne, S. J., & Jones, D. M. (1997). Navigating buildings in 'desk-top' virtual environments: Experimental investigations using extended navigational experience. *Journal of Experimental Psychology: Applied, 3,* 143–159.

Ruggles, A. J., & Armstrong, M. P. (1997). Toward a conceptual framework for the cartographic visualization of network information. *Cartographica, 34,* 33–48.

Schacter, D. L., & Tulving, E. (Eds.) (1994). *Memory systems 1994.* Cambridge, MA: The MIT Press.

Shepard, R. N., & Hurwitz, S. (1984). Upward direction, mental rotation, and discrimination of left and right turns in maps. *Cognition, 18,* 161–193.

Schöne, H. (1984). *Spatial orientation: The spatial control of behavior in animals and man* (translated from German, *Orientierung im Raum,* by Camilla Strausfeld). Princeton, NJ: Princeton University Press.

Streeter, L. A., Vitello, D., & Wonsiewicz, S. A. (1985). How to tell people where to go: Comparing navigational aids. *International Journal of Man/Machine Studies, 22,* 549–562.

Tandy, C. R. V. (1967). The isovist method of landscape survey. In A. C. Murray (Ed.), *Methods of landscape analysis* (Vol. October, pp. 9–10). London: Landscape Research Group.

Tarr, M. J., & Bülthoff, H. H. (Eds.) (1998). *Object recognition in man, monkey, and machine.* Cambridge, MA: The MIT Press.

Thorndyke, P. W., & Hayes-Roth, B. (1982). Differences in spatial knowledge acquired from maps and navigation. *Cognitive Psychology, 14,* 560–589.

Tversky, B. (1992). Distortions in cognitive maps. *Geoforum, 23*, 131–138.

Warren, D. H., Rossano, M. J., & Wear, T. D. (1990). Perception of map-environment correspondence: The roles of features and alignment. *Ecological Psychology, 2*, 131–150.

Warren, W. H., Young, D. S., & Lee, D. N. (1986). Visual control of step length during running over irregular terrain. *Journal of Experimental Psychology: Human Perception and Performance, 12*, 259–266.

Waterman, T. (1989). *Animal navigation*. New York: Scientific American Library.

Wehner, R. (1996). Middle-scale navigation: The insect case. *Journal of Experimental Biology, 199*, 125–127.

Wehner, R. (1999). Large-scale navigation: The insect case. In C. Freksa & D. M. Mark (Eds.), *Spatial information theory: Cognitive and computational foundations of geographic information science* (pp. 1–20). Berlin: Springer.

Wehner, R., Lehrer, M., & Harvey, W. R. (Editors). (1996). Navigation: Migration and homing [Special issue]. *The Journal of Experimental Biology, 199*(1).

Weisman, J. (1981). Evaluating architectural legibility: Way-finding in the built environment. *Environment and Behavior, 13*, 189–204.

Yeap, W. K. (1988). Towards a computational theory of cognitive maps. *Artificial Intelligence, 34*, 297–360.

Yoshino, R. (1991). A note on cognitive maps: An optimal spatial knowledge representation. *Journal of Mathematical Psychology, 35*, 371–393.

8

Mapping the Understanding of Understanding Maps

Holly A. Taylor

ABSTRACT

In some ways, maps are processed like any other visuospatial entity. However, because maps usually have a utilitarian function that results in comparison to an actual environment, processing of and memory for maps differs from that of other visuospatial forms. This chapter discusses comprehension and memory for maps, focusing on how perceptual information is understood conceptually. The cognitive map developed while learning a physical map has features similar to the actual environment, but also differs from it because of the cognitive processes used to form it. This chapter discusses those underlying processes and their effects on the resultant mental representation. Since the conceptual information takes the form of a mental or cognitive map, it is first important to understand some of the methodology used to study cognitive maps. This methodology allows for inferences about the nature and structure of cognitive maps and how they might be conceptualized. Further, the conceptualization of maps appears to be influenced by features of the individual, including cognitive goals, stage in development, and individual differences. These issues are discussed in the framework of conceptualizing map information.

INTRODUCTION

When you look at a map, what do you see? If looking at a standard street map, the first glance may look like any street map. There are roads, buildings, parks, and rivers. With a closer look, you begin to differentiate this map from others. The streets have different names in this city; the arrangement of the streets and buildings is different; there may be more parks than in another city. Since maps generally have a utilitarian function, you eventually hone in on the information you need from the map. This might involve finding a particular intersection, finding your current position, and then plotting a route between the two.

295

In actuality, a map consists of lines, shapes, dots, colors, and words. The same components can be seen in a corporate structure diagram, a data graph, or a line drawing depicting a grazing cow. Obviously, maps, diagrams, and line drawings have similarities, but they also have differences that affect how they are processed cognitively. Although the current chapter will address map processing, it is first important to show how map understanding may be similar to and different from processing of other visuospatial representations.

Differentiating Maps, Diagrams, and Figures

Maps, line drawings, and diagrams all represent something else, whether it be something concrete, like a grazing cow, or something abstract, like a corporate structure. To understand what is represented, perceptual information must be translated into conceptual information. All three visuospatial formats consist of component parts, thus the perceptual to conceptual conversion occurs on a local, component level and on an overall, global level. The relationship between the component parts leads to the global interpretation. The flexibility of the relationship between component parts differs, however, for these three representation types.

Figures 8.1 and 8.2 illustrate how component relationships help define depictions. Examine Figure 8.1A. Due to the arrangement of components or geons (Biederman, 1987), one may interpret the figure as a pig; this is the intention. The relative position of the components leads to this interpretation. Further, the interpretation goes beyond the individual components; there is a Gestalt. Rearrangement of the components necessarily leads to a different Gestalt, as illustrated in Figure 8.1B. Once the components are rearranged, the interpretation changes, in this case from a pig to a person, albeit a rather odd person. Although in this example, rearrangement of components leads to another object, more often rearranging components in a figure results in something completely uninterpretable.

Rearranging components of diagrams and maps does not necessarily lead to a global interpretation change. A rearranged map still looks like a map; a rearranged diagram still looks like a diagram. The accuracy of the map or diagram is compromised by such a rearrangement, but the basic interpretation can remain. This is illustrated in Figure 8.2. Both parts of this figure look like a map, but one is reasonably accurate and the other is completely fictitious. Figure 8.2A depicts part of a neighborhood near the Tufts University–Medford campus. Figure 8.2B has the same components, only rearranged. Although someone familiar with Tufts might say, "Well,

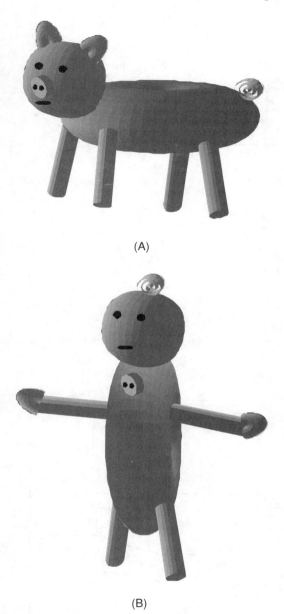

(A)

(B)

FIGURE 8.1. Same geons arranged into two configurations. 8.1A represents a pig. 8.1B represents a person.

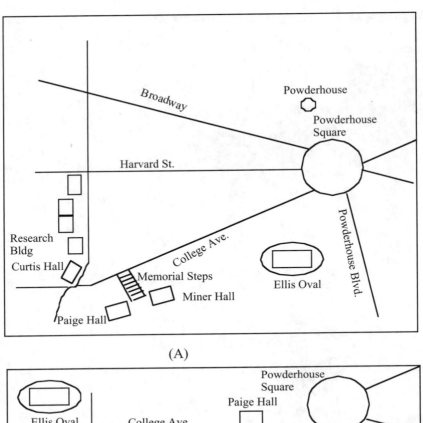

(A)

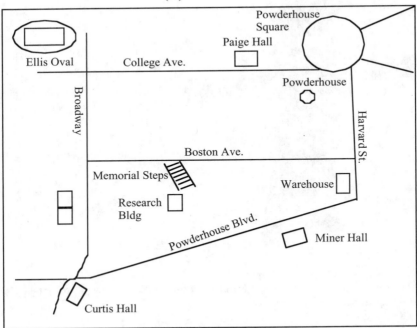

(B)

FIGURE 8.2. Same map components in two configurations. 8.2A represents a neighborhood near the Tufts University Medford campus. 8.2B represents a fictitious neighborhood.

Figure 8.2B bears some resemblance to the neighborhood near Tufts," it could never be used to find locations in this vicinity. Thus the map accuracy is compromised, but it is still seen as a map.

Even though the rearrangement of map and diagram components affects their accuracy more than their overall interpretation, maps differ from diagrams in what they represent (Winn, 1991). Maps depict a physical arrangement of locations in an environment. Diagrams tend to be more schematic and represent both concrete (e.g., circuit diagram) and abstract themes (e.g., corporate structure diagram). This is not to say that maps cannot be schematic – those used to depict subway systems are often just that. There is also evidence that individuals process maps differently from other diagrams, such as graphs. Tversky and Schiano (1989) presented similar depictions to participants and described them either as graphs or as maps. They found that participants remembered lines on graphs as being closer to an imaginary 45-degree line, but did not show the same memory distortion for lines on maps. The difference found between maps and graphs reflects conceptual differences between the two depiction types.

In many cases, individuals compare a map to the actual environment. Thus, location on a map is important. Location is not as important on other types of diagrams. For example, mirror images of a corporate structure diagram generally do not affect their accuracy. To compare a map to the environment actually requires two conversions, one from the perceptual information on the map to a conceptual understanding of what is represented and the second from this conceptual understanding to a perceptual match with the environment itself. Because a map can be compared to an actual environment, comprehending, remembering, and using maps requires a unique combination of cognitive processes.

The remainder of this chapter will focus on the processes involved in map learning, map memory, and map use. To understand these underlying processes one must first understand how they are studied. Thus, the chapter will first provide an overview of methodologies used to study map comprehension. It will go on to discuss how these methodologies inform our understanding of the conversion from perceptual to conceptual information and the possible outcomes of this conversion. Once perceptual information is conceptualized, the conceptualized pieces must be related together to understand the map as a whole. Thus, this chapter will cover issues of and difficulties with integrating individual landmarks into a unified cognitive map. Finally, characteristics of the map user come into play with conceptualization and integration in map comprehension. Two sections of this chapter will address these issues. The first will discuss how learning goals influence a user's map comprehension. The second will discuss how factors individual to the user affect the cognitive processes underlying map understanding.

METHODOLOGY FOR STUDYING MAP LEARNING

Cognitive or mental maps are internal entities. As such, they are subject to influences of the cognitive processes used to form them. These cognitive processes may result in differences between the mental map and the printed map. Because we cannot "see" the cognitive map, the methodologies for understanding their nature and content are important. Researchers in spatial cognition have employed a variety of methodologies, some more explicit, others more implicit, to try to glean the nature and content of mental maps. An understanding of the methodologies used to examine spatial representations provides a framework for interpreting research findings based on these methodologies.

The most explicit methodology asks an individual to sketch a map or make a model of a represented environment (Lynch, 1960). Sketch maps have strengths and weaknesses in terms of providing insights into cognitive representations. They have the advantage of resulting in a direct representation of an environment. In other words, through a sketch map one can directly see the properties of someone's mental map. They have the disadvantage of being influenced by an individual's drawing ability. Because drawing abilities vary widely, sketch maps can be difficult to quantify (Walsh, Krauss, & Regnier, 1981). Thus, other techniques have evolved to circumvent skill demands of map drawing, skills irrelevant to the internal spatial representation. Despite these problems, sketch maps still provide important data in understanding cognitive maps.

Other methodologies infer or interpolate an overall representation from pairwise judgments of map features. For example, a research participant may make Euclidean or route distance estimates between location pairs. Once all location pairs have been sampled, the data can be submitted to a multidimensional scaling (MDS) analysis (e.g., Shepard, 1980). MDS then provides a spatial representation of the individual's distance judgments that can be interpreted in a specified number of dimensions. Howard and Kerst (1981) submitted pairwise distance estimates to nonmetric MDS and found representations consistent with the originally learned maps, albeit distorted. Distortions were greater when participants made distance estimates from memory, compared to estimates made with an available map. Additive similarity tree analysis can be used similarly, although the output indicates how landmarks are clustered in memory better than the overall layout (Sattath & Tversky, 1977). Taylor and Tversky (1992a) used additive trees to represent information from sketch maps and verbal descriptions. Drawing order and order of mention in the description served as pairwise similarity data. Descriptions and depictions of an environment led to similar additive tree representations, indicating that both measures showed underlying landmark clusters in memory. Figure 8.3 shows simulated MDS and additive tree solutions of a data set based on Taylor and Tversky (1992a).

Since spatial memory can be compared to the actual environment, some methodologies examine accuracy of cognitive maps. Accuracy can be assessed from sketch maps, magnitude estimates, direction judgments, distance estimates, and rank ordering of location pairs based on proximity. Some of these measures are more cognitive in nature, such as distance judgment or rank order of locations. Other measures are more behaviorally based, requiring locomotive or orienting responses. Reiser (1989) had participants walk blindfolded between locations; other researchers have asked participants to orient or point to unseen locations (Farrell & Robertson, 1998; Sholl, 1987; Thorndyke & Hayes-Roth, 1982).

In most estimation tasks, individuals provide pairwise judgments of distance or direction. These judgments are then compared to the actual distances or directions in the environment. Estimation errors indicate distortions in memory. All of these methodologies purportedly provide an indication of mental representation accuracy, thus all should yield similar results. However, comparisons between tasks suggest that accuracy can also be a function of the task used to measure it (for a review, see Newcombe, 1985). The more familiar someone was with the response measure, the more accurate their mental representation appeared.

Other research has relied on implicit measures of spatial knowledge, primarily spatial priming. In these studies, participants see one location at a time and make some behavioral response to each. Behavioral responses have included deciding whether a location belongs in one region or another (McNamara, Halpin, & Hardy, 1992b), whether a location appeared on the map (Clayton & Habibi, 1991), or whether a place was correctly located (Naylor & Taylor, 1997). Priming lists are set up to examine effects of spatial proximity; adjacent location names in the list are either located near one another on the map or far from one another (e.g., Clayton & Habibi, 1991; Naylor & Taylor, 1997). If spatially near locations lead to faster responses than spatially far locations, this indicates spatial structure encoded in memory. Implicit measure, such as this, circumvent the possibility of strategic

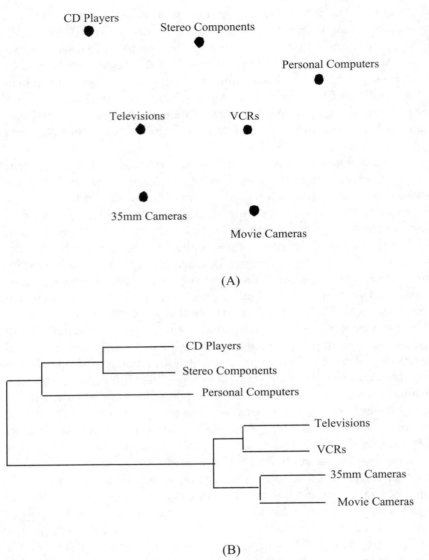

FIGURE 8.3. Simulated multidimensional solutions of map drawing data based on Taylor and Tversky (1992a). 8.3A illustrates a multidimensional scaling solution. 8.3B illustrates an additive tree solution.

processing that are inherent in the more direct measures where individuals explicitly recall spatial information. However, the implicit measures also provide a more abstract indication of spatial structure in memory.

Researchers can determine whether mental representations include separate location categories, either physical categories such as regions or conceptual categories (e.g., university buildings vs. town buildings), using the concept of *symbolic distance*. Symbolic distance effects occur when locations have some similarity, making them difficult to differentiate from one another. It is called "symbolic" distance because more similar locations result in a slowing of responses, whereas in true distance closer locations should yield faster responses. For example, people respond more slowly when asked whether a town is within a particular country if the town is near the border. Additionally, locations within a category are represented differently than those across categories. The distance between two locations within a region (or category) is generally underestimated while the distance between locations in different regions is generally overestimated.

In summary, various methods have been used to make apparent properties of an internal mental map. The more direct measures, particularly sketch maps, seem intuitively appealing because the spatial properties of the mental representation are given directly. However, these direct measures are subject to strategic processing and individual differences, such as drawing ability. Implicit measures, such as spatial priming or reliance on symbolic distance, circumvent noise introduced through strategic processing, but only provide abstract information about the mental representation. Because of these pros and cons, a successful approach to understanding how someone mentally represents a map would be to employ several measures in combination.

PERCEPTUAL TO CONCEPTUAL CONVERSION OF INFORMATION IN MAPS

Understanding Map Symbols

When someone reads a map, they interpret it as representing an environment (Taylor & Tversky, 1992a). Although this seems a statement of the obvious, the alternative is not so outlandish. Maps are an entity in and of themselves, like any other depiction. A Monet painting has greater value as a painting than as a representation of something from Monet's world. The prototypical use of a map, unlike a picture, is functional. Map readers use maps to learn the layout of an environment or to learn a route to a particular destination. The first step involved in understanding the relationship between a map and an environment is understanding the map itself and the meaning of its symbols.

Map symbols are successful when they correctly relate information to the user. Map symbols, however, vary from abstract to iconic, from geometric to pictorial, from arbitrary to purposeful. The transparency of the relationship between a symbol and its referent affects processing. The most effective map symbols should not need a legend (Robinson, Sale, Morrison, & Muehrcke, 1984), since attention needed to translate map symbols from a legend draws resources away from processing the map as a whole. MacEachren (1995) reviews map symbol categorization, including symbols varying in abstractness and other defining properties.

It is clear that map symbols range in abstractness, but how does this affect understanding? Greater symbol iconicity leads to greater interpretability and consequently faster search times (Florence & Geiselman, 1986). When individual landmarks are found faster, more time and mental resources can be spent in processing other aspects of the map. The clarity or iconicity of a map symbol, however, should not be assumed, just as the word meaning in a public opinion survey cannot be assumed (Schober & Conrad, 1997). A symbol (or word) with clear meaning for one person may be ambiguous for someone else. Age and/or experience can influence symbol interpretation.

Development of Symbol Comprehension

There is a developmental time course for understanding symbolic relations. Nine-month-old children treat pictures as objects, exploring them manually. By nineteen months, they understand that pictures can represent other objects (DeLoache, Pierroutsakos, Uttal, Rosengren, & Gottlieb, 1998). Despite having grasped these basic abstract relationships between pictures and their referents, children do not automatically comprehend other symbolic representations, such as those depicted on maps (DeLoache & Smith, 1999). DeLoache (1995) proposed a theory of symbol understanding in which several factors contribute to a child's symbolic understanding, including salience, iconicity, experience, and instructions. Salient symbols, or those that stand apart from other symbols, can be more easily identified. Iconic symbols can be easily matched to their referent in the environment. Scaffolding of knowledge through experience or instructions can also make the symbol–referent relationship more apparent. Additionally, the quality of the symbol is important, such that the more a symbol can be conceived of as an entity in and of itself, the more difficulty children have conceiving it as a symbol. DeLoache refers to this issue as *dual representation*, because the child must think of the symbol as both an object and as representing something else. As such, children have less difficulty locating a hidden object when they are shown its location in a photograph than when they are shown its location using a scale model (Marzolf & DeLoache, 1997). Children find the scale model too much like a dollhouse to also interpret it symbolically, overlooking the relationship between the scale model and its referent room.

Children appear to understand the representativeness of maps by early elementary ages. Blaut, McCleary, and Blaut (1970) found that children ages 5 to 7 successfully used maps in a simulation problem. Even in cases where maps were misaligned with the environment, children have demonstrated similar successes (Blades & Spencer, 1987, 1990). Sandberg and Huttenlocher (2001) found that 6-year-olds successfully used maps to plan routes. Further, the routes selected tended to be optimally efficient, showing the ability to consider alternate route options on the map. Blaut (1987) suggests that map learning is a basic ability children acquire during development.

Uttal and Wellman (1989) found evidence of integrative use of maps by younger, preschool children. They demonstrated that young children could learn a map outside the environment and then show near perfect performance based on their map knowledge. They further argued that preschoolers develop a strong functional representation from maps. In other words, they acquire knowledge about spatial layout sufficient to navigate through the layout. This is not to say that these young children have encoded accurate metric information about the environment from the map, but that they have a good representation of relative spatial information.

Although many animals clearly have extraordinary spatial memory (for a review, see Hauser, 2000), humans seem to be the only species that truly grasps the representative nature of maps. Premack and Premack (1983) attempted to train chimpanzees to understand maps. Although DeLoache found that young children could use scale models to find hidden objects, Premack and Premack (1983) found chimpanzees unable to use scale models for the same purpose. The chimpanzees could use an identical room to guide their behavior and with extensive training could use a canvas and reduced-sized furniture to locate hidden objects in a room. However, when the canvas was taken out of the actual room, most chimpanzees could no longer use it to guide their behavior and when it was rotated as little as 45 degrees, none of the chimpanzees succeeded.

Thus, although children must learn to understand symbol–referent relationships, they do succeed. When the symbol can also be interpreted as an object in and of itself, the role of the symbol as symbol is difficult for young children to grasp. With maps, there is good evidence that elementary aged and perhaps even preschool children can successfully interpret map symbols. This success is seen through accurate functional use of the maps. However, nonhuman primates do not seem to grasp the representative nature of maps that young children understand at a young age (see Newcombe & Learmonth, Chapter 6, for additional discussion of the development of symbolic competence).

Perceptual to Conceptual Processes and Their Consequences

The process of converting perceptual information to conceptual information from a map may not differ too much from other information-processing tasks. Salomon (1979) argued that how one learns from any medium depends on how the medium's symbol system interacts with cognitive processing. For example, Amlund, Gaffney, and Kulhavy (1985) found that map features presented as small drawings (e.g., a depiction of a house), as opposed to labeled points, were better learned, presumably because the drawings afforded dual encoding (Paivio, 1983). The small drawings could be encoded verbally and visuospatially.

In general, the nature of map features predict success in either remembering the map or using it for wayfinding. Maps include symbols of varying size, shape, color, and extent. These qualities make the map features subject to attentive and preattentive processing. Unusual features may preattentively *pop out* and thus be processed as distinct (Treisman & Gelade, 1980). Winn (1991) discusses *perceptual precedence* of map features, such that those with precedence receive early attentional resources. In other words, preattentive or pop-out features have a greater *perceptual precedence*. Perceptual precedence can also be defined in terms of the hierarchical organization of features. Although debated, there is evidence that individuals process the global layout prior to attending to detail (Navon, 1977). Further, Gestalt principles of perceptual organization can structure map processing. Features close together (*proximity*) (Pomerantz & Schwaitzberg, 1975) and similar in form or function (*similarity*) are remembered as belonging together spatially (Hirtle & Jonides, 1985).

The presence of boundary lines also affects the grouping of map components (Huttenlocher, Hedges, & Duncan, 1991; Newcombe, Huttenlocher, Sandberg, Lee, & Johnson, 1999; Taylor, 1961). Lloyd and Steinke (1986) examined whether individuals represent boundaries in cognitive maps. Since boundaries divide an area into regions, how consistently is regional information represented? Using a method of determining whether points fell inside or outside a region, Lloyd and Steinke (1986) determined region boundaries in a cognitive map using participant response times. As an example, people might be asked whether a city belongs in one of two adjacent states (North vs. South Carolina). A ridge of higher response times signals a region boundary based on the idea of a symbolic distance effect. Locations close to a regional boundary should require greater consideration in determining whether they belong to a region than locations far from the boundary. Participants showed fairly consistent regional boundaries, although the aggregate data led to a somewhat wide boundary. In other words, if asked about cities within states, results would show the state boundary line because response times near this state line would be longer. A comparison of the region assessment test to sketch maps showed comparable findings, although the region assessment test showed greater consistency. The increased consistency most likely resulted because individual differences in drawing ability did not affect the results.

On a smaller scale, Warren, Rossano, and Wear (1990) found that buildings with visually discriminable subsections were better remembered. Functional color coding leads to similar memory improvements. In their study, participants saw slides of buildings and had to mark the view of the photograph on the map. They made each judgment twice. Results showed that participants used salient building features to narrow the possible views. After identifying the salient building feature, the symbolic representation of that feature must be identified on the map. Highly distinguishable features and borders between building sections facilitated viewpoint identification.

Even without obvious boundary lines, individuals visually partition maps into sections (McNamara, Hardy, & Hirtle, 1989; Rossano & Hodgson, 1994). McNamara et al. (1989) showed participants a map without clusters or boundaries. Results indicated that people imposed their own regions on the map. Locations within a self-imposed region primed other locations, but locations across regions did not. Thorndyke and Stasz (1980) showed that this visual partitioning strategy is used by better map learners. Once the environment is partitioned into regions, people learn these sections in a global to local fashion (Rossano & Hodgson, 1994).

Within this global to local learning, map information appears to be organized hierarchically. Stevens and Coupe (1978) asked participants about the relative location of two cities. For example, they asked, "Which is further east Reno, Nevada, or San Diego, California?" Pairs were selected such that the relative location of the states (e.g., Nevada and California) predicted a different answer than the relative location of the cities. They found that participants answered primarily based on the states' relative locations, for example, incorrectly indicating that Reno is east of San Diego.

Hierarchical groupings are not limited to spatial location. Hirtle and Jonides (1985) found groupings based on function. Individuals remembered Ann Arbor, Michigan, town buildings as grouped together and University of Michigan buildings grouped together, even though the buildings are relatively interspersed. Maki, Maki, and Marsh (1977) provided some evidence that this type of conceptual grouping is specific to maps and not to other perceptual stimuli. They found a symbolic distance effect for judgments about relative spatial locations between states (previously learned information), showing slower response times for near state pairs. In contrast, they found the opposite effect for experimentally learned perceptual stimuli, with faster response times for near figure pairs. They argue that both the nature of the material and the extent to which it was encoded can influence performance.

The complexity of a representation also affects processing. Displays with higher density lead to longer search times (Florence & Geiselman, 1986). Wickens, Liang, Prevett, and Olmos (1996) examined complexity in the form of dimensionality. They presented participants with two- or three-dimensional map projections for simulated flight navigation. As in previous research (Wickens & Prevett, 1995) they found task-dependent effects of dimensionality. Three-dimensional maps could be used effectively for tracking paths, but two-dimensional maps better facilitated navigation. Even with tracking, the three-dimensional maps created some confusion, particularly with the vertical dimension. Three-dimensional maps are generally presented using a flat panel device, thus giving only two dimensions at a time. The third dimension must be interpolated. The ambiguity of three-dimensional displays was particularly detrimental for vertical tracking. In Wickens et al. (1996) lateral tracking performance did not differ between two- and three-dimensional maps, but three-dimensional maps led to significantly worse vertical tracking performance. When the vertical information is available but ambiguous, as with the three-dimensional maps, it is more detrimental than when it is not present, as with the two-dimensional maps. Display modifications enhancing vertical dimension interpretation improved vertical tracking (see Wickens, Vincow, & Yeh, Chapter 10, for additional discussion of this topic).

Like the three-dimensional aviation displays, topographic maps are considered complex because of the need to extract elevation information from contour lines. This three-dimensional interpretation requires attention to both the placement and curve of the line, and the associated height of the line relative to surrounding contours. Without both pieces of information, one cannot determine whether an area represents a hill or a valley. Attentional resources need to be devoted specifically to processing of the contour information for this information to be remembered (Kinnear & Wood, 1987).

Alignment, or more particularly misalignment, between map and environment also increases complexity and affects map comprehension. "You-are-here" maps that are contraligned with the environment frequently result in people heading in the wrong direction (Levine, Marchon, & Hanley, 1984). Rossano and Warren (1989b) went on to show that errors made with contraligned maps fell into predictable categories, based on the degree of misalignment. Map misalignment affects older adults even more so than younger ones (Aubrey, Li, & Dobbs, 1994; see also Montello, Chapter 7 and Wickens, Vincow, and Yah, Chapter 10 for additional discussion of alignment and "you-are-here" maps and Newcombe & Learmonth, Chapter 6, for discussion of children's use of them).

Two traditional electronic map-display approaches, track-up and north-up, differ in terms of alignment with the environment. Studies of these electronic maps show a trade-off in cognitive processing. Track-up maps keep the direction of travel moving toward to the top of the display and thus are always aligned with the environment. Each change in direction requires a reorientation of the map. North-up maps, in contrast, always have north at the top of the display. Thus, north-up maps are only aligned with the environment when the user is facing north. Aretz (1991) found that the track-up map's alignment with the pilot's ego-centered view led to faster and more accurate responses for immediate performance. However, since the track-up display continuously rotated, users had difficulty acquiring a complete cognitive map. The reverse was seen for north-up displays, where users developed better cognitive maps but showed performance decrements due to mental rotation costs. Similarly, Wickens et al. (1996) found that track-up maps better facilitated the determination of flight paths.

Although changing a map's orientation facilitates on-line path decisions, maps are generally kept in a single orientation when they are learned. As a consequence, map memory tends to be orientation specific (Evans & Pezdek, 1980; Levine, Jankovic, & Palij, 1982; Sholl, 1987). The consequence of an orientation-specific representation is faster and more accurate knowledge retrieval when aligned with the map orientation, usually north-up, but slower and less accurate responses when misaligned. These findings bring up interesting questions about spatial representations in general, answers to which are controversial. Does the idea of the *cognitive map*, first put forward by Tolman (1948), apply to all spatial situations? Presson, DeLange, and Hazelrigg (1989) suggest that different cognitive processes underlie different spatial situations. In particular, maps and paths are processed differently. McNamara and colleagues (Roskos-Ewoldson, McNamara, Shelton, & Carr, 1998; Shelton & McNamara, 1997), in contrast, argue that an orientation-dependent cognitive map develops regardless of whether the environment was learned from a map or from direct experience. Although direct experience provides different views of an environment, they argue that this results in several orientation specific representations rather than a more general orientation-free representation.

Distortions in Map Memory

The conversion of perceptual to conceptual information is not without error. Tversky (1981) finds systematic distortions in memory for maps. The first task in converting perceptual to conceptual information is segregating figure from ground on the map. As such, locations are remembered relative to other locations. In making the relative location comparisons, Tversky (1981) finds distortions that can be attributed to two cognitive heuristics, alignment and rotation. These heuristics are based on Gestalt theories of perceptual organization. The alignment heuristic results in a memory distortion where two landmarks are remembered as being more directly horizontally or vertically aligned with one another than they actually are. For example, when shown pictures with different relative alignments of North and South America, people incorrectly choose ones with good north-south alignment between the continents. The rotation heuristic is similar, but involves rotating a landmark to be more in line with a canonical frame, such as the border of a map or the north/south/east/west coordinate system. The rotation heuristic appears similar to findings showing that roads are schematized to perpendicular intersections (Moar & Bower, 1983; Tversky, 1981; Tversky & Schiano, 1989).

Other distortions in spatial memory correspond to distance and area. Tversky and Schiano (1989) showed that individuals impose symmetry onto their cognitive maps. Individuals were shown curves depicting rivers and remembered these curves as more symmetric than actually depicted.

They further showed that an accompanying description biasing toward either symmetry or asymmetry did bias memory. Map area can also be compressed in memory. Howard and Kerst (1981) found that, based on pairwise distance estimates, an original rectangular map was believed to be more of a square shape. Kerst and Howard (1978) found similar results related to both geographic area and distance.

It is clear that distortions arise from schematization and from the incorporation of prior knowledge. This relates to the asymmetry between perception and imagery (Intons-Peterson & McDaniel, 1990). Prior knowledge plays an especially strong role when the depicted region is familiar (Kulhavy & Stock, 1996). Tversky (Chapter 1) presents an additional discussion of distortions in cognitive maps.

INTEGRATING INDIVIDUAL LANDMARKS
INTO A COGNITIVE MAP

To be functionally appropriate in most everyday situations, maps must include sufficient detail. If the everyday situation involves navigating through an urban area, the map needs to be rather sizeable to show enough detail. Map makers accomplish this by printing on large sheets of paper that require folding for convenient storage. The frustration of such maps is apparent when attempting to refold them or when trying to relate fairly distant locations. With such a map, one cannot take in all the detail at once. To understand and mentally represent a large and/or detailed region, it requires integration of locations and spatial relations into a coherent whole. How is integration of spatial information accomplished?

Integrative learning takes time (Leiser, Tzelgov, & Henik, 1987; Shimron, 1978). Shimron (1978) examined the effect of limiting study time on map learning. He examined three aspects of the cognitive organization of map elements – coordinated position, shapes, and relative positions. *Coordinated position* refers to a landmark location with respect to the entire map. *Relative position* refers to landmark-to-landmark relations. Coordinated position should be the most difficult to learn, because multiple spatial relationships need to be considered. Indeed, Shimron (1978) found that time limits hindered most understanding of coordinated position. He suggests that map learning progresses from learning of local connections to integrating these connections into a more unified whole. Coordinated position involves this unified whole. Leiser et al. (1987) had participants learn either from a map or through simulated travel. In this case, simulated travel involved a close-up view of the map. Participants then "navigated" by moving to different locations on the map. A route planning test showed better performance by map learning participants, but only when map study time equaled time spent in simulated navigation.

In sum, the process of integrating map landmarks takes time and effort, particularly to understand how all the landmarks fit together as a whole. The features of maps, however, can facilitate learning coordinated position. Some aspects of maps can serve as a framework for relating other landmarks. These have been called an *interpretive framework* and will be discussed in more detail.

Interpretive Frameworks

Several researchers have suggested that people build up an interpretive framework for maps (Kulhavy, Schwartz, & Shaha, 1982; Kulhavy & Stock, 1996; Rossano & Morrison, 1996). The interpretive framework allows individual features to be situated within a larger spatial context (Kulhavy et al., 1982). For maps of urban areas, the street grid may serve as an interpretive framework. Kulhavy et al. (1982) examined how the presence of a street grid influenced map processing, both in terms of map features and their position. The interpretive framework could have one of two effects. It could capture attentional resources, detracting from processing of other map features or it could act as a scaffold to which other features are related, and consequently better remembered. Participants studied a map either with or without the street grid. In all other ways, the maps were identical. The presence of the street grid affected memory. When the grid was present, participants remembered fewer landmarks. However, of the landmarks remembered, participants placed them more accurately with the grid present. In other words, people used the interpretive framework to help locate landmarks. McNamara, Ratcliff, and McKoon (1984) added further credence to the use of roads as an interpretive framework. They found that cities close in route distance primed each other more than cities far in route distance, even after Euclidean distance had been equated.

When no interpretive framework is present, people try to impose one. In the Kulhavy et al. (1982) study, landmarks belonged to one of six conceptual categories based on function (e.g., education buildings). Participants studying the map without the grid tended to group landmarks conceptually.

Rossano and Morrison (1996) further applied the idea of interpretive frameworks to map learning. They used a campus map defined by a perimeter road. Using a pointing task, they showed that individuals located landmarks both near and external to the perimeter road better than internal landmarks. A map drawing task showed similar results. Taken together this research indicates that features serving as the map infrastructure do require attentional resources to learn, but also facilitate memory for landmark location.

Map Format and Integration

How might different map formats and presentation styles influence the encoding and integration of spatial information? Maps of large urban areas, to be manageable, generally come in one of two formats, a large chart map or an atlas. Both formats are widely used and both have advantages and disadvantages. Large charts depict the overall layout and certain necessary details, but are cumbersome to use. Atlases are more compact, but by depicting local sections on individual pages, the global layout cannot be seen. In sum, chart maps and atlases differ in the availability of overall layout information and consequently in the reliance on local information. However, do these formats affect how map information is remembered?

Taylor and Soraci (Taylor, 1999, 2000) examined map learning in situations approximating these two map formats. Participants learned a map one section at a time, either with overall layout information (chart map) or without it (atlas). For the chart map, overall layout information was gleaned from the placement of map sections in their spatially correct locations during learning. Participants in the atlas condition saw all map sections in the center of the screen. Figure 8.4 illustrates the learning conditions. Two recognition tasks assessed the mental representation people acquired from the map. One test assessed knowledge about the overall layout of map sections. The second test assessed knowledge about landmark-to-landmark relations.

If someone has a complete, integrated cognitive map, it represents both landmark-to-landmark relationships and overall layout information. Evidence of a well-integrated representation may be seen in overall better performance for one of the learning groups over the other. More subtle evidence of integration may instead be seen. This more subtle influence may show that learning via one map type leads to a representation less influenced by other map features or the learning situation itself. Our results supported this latter suggestion.

The nature of the two learning conditions brings up competing hypotheses. One hypothesis suggests that the availability of overall layout information will facilitate learning and integration (Navon, 1977). Rossano and Hodgson (1994) found that map learning progresses in a global to local

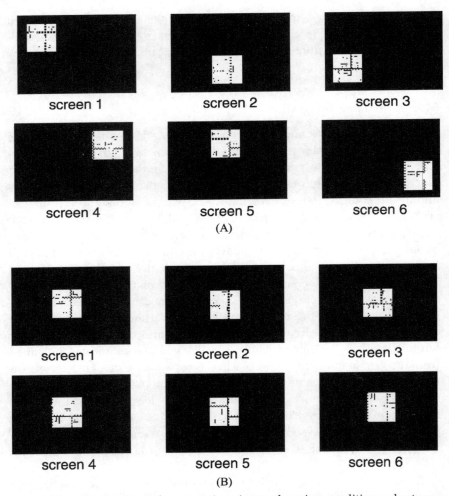

FIGURE 8.4. Presentation of map sections in two learning conditions, chart map and atlas. 8.4A represents the chart map presentation. 8.4B represents the atlas presentation.

fashion. A second hypothesis draws on ideas of generative-learning (e.g., Hirshman & Bjork, 1988; Slamecka & Graf, 1978; Soraci et al., 1994). Generative learning refers to the retention advantages that accrue when individuals actively encode information, as compared to the more passive encoding when information is simply provided. For example, one could be given the word pair *quick-fast* or could be asked to generate a synonymous word pair given the clue *quick-f*———. Those who generate the word pair themselves, even though generation of the word *fast* from the clue is fairly trivial, remember the word pair better. The generation effect is a robust phenomena that has been illustrated using a wide range of encoding rules, testing conditions, and stimulus types (e.g., Chechile & Soraci, 1999; Hirshman & Bjork, 1988; McDaniel, Waddill & Einstein, 1988; Slamecka & Graf, 1978; Soraci et al., 1999; Soraci et al., 1994; Wills, Soraci, Chechile, & Taylor, 2000). If generative-learning processes influence map learning, participants in the atlas condition should acquire a more integrated representation, because they must generate the overall layout. Further, atlas learners may more explicitly encode landmark-to-landmark relationships, since these relationships give the only clue about how the map pieces fit together.

Our findings (Taylor & Soraci, 1999) provided clues as to how people integrate information from maps, in general. Sectional maps, such as those simulated in our study, have regions of overlap. Depending on the size and shape of the region depicted by the map, some map sections will be central and some will be peripheral to the overall region. Participants located peripheral map sections better than central sections, making fewer errors and responding more quickly. Two possible explanations exist for this finding. Participants may have performed better on corner sections because the boundary of the map region serves as an additional landmark. Better memory for landmarks near boundaries has been shown in numerous studies (Huttenlocher et al., 1991; Newcombe et al., 1999; Rossano & Morrison, 1996; Taylor, 1961). Naylor and Taylor (1998) showed this boundary effect in map reproduction, in particular additional spatial boundaries enhanced map processing. Alternatively, participants may have performed more poorly on interior sections because these sections overlap more with other sections, a situation creating more opportunity for interference. We examined these hypotheses by determining which map sections people confused with one another and creating a confusion matrix from this information. The confusion matrix analysis supported the interference explanation. Confusions occurred primarily between adjacent sections, the primary alternative contexts for landmarks in overlap regions. Participants also better identified misplaced landmarks when they came from a distant section, as opposed to an adjacent section, showing a symbolic distance effect. This finding further supports the interference hypothesis.

These general findings related to integration were qualified by the learning condition results (atlas versus chart map). Chart map participants showed the differential effect of locating peripheral and central sections; the atlas participants did not. In other words, the atlas participants showed less interference with central sections. Similarly, chart map participants showed the symbolic distance effect when identifying misplaced landmarks; this effect was attenuated for atlas participants.

A follow-up study (Taylor, 2000) extended the results to another learning condition and to a recall test, in addition to the recognition tests. In this study, participants learned the map in one of three conditions – the same chart map and atlas conditions as used in the previous study and a full map condition. Study time was equated across learning conditions. Testing involved the same two recognition tasks used previously and also included a map drawing task. For this task, participants received a rectangular outline designating the map border and were asked to reproduce the map.

Results of the two recognition tests replicated the previous findings. Again, participants did not show overall differential performance based on learning condition. Their response pattern did differ, however. Atlas learners did not show an effect of peripheral versus central map sections, whereas chart map learners did. Participants who studied the whole map also did not show differential responses to map sections based on location. When identifying misplaced landmarks, chart map and whole map learners showed effects of landmark distance; atlas learners did not.

Performance on the recall/map drawing task did differ as a function of learning condition. Maps were scored for both identity and location information. Identity scoring included noting landmarks designated on the map, without regard for their spatial location. Location scoring involved noting the proportion of adjacent landmarks in the correct relative location. These two scoring methods showed similar results. Whole map learners drew the most accurate maps, followed by chart map learners, and finally atlas learners. Interestingly, an analysis examining the type of landmarks included showed that the atlas participants primarily left off the streets from the map. In other words, they did not build an interpretive framework for successful recall of the map (Kulhavy et al., 1982; Rossano & Morrison, 1996).

This research shows that when learning from a sectional map, the map structure influences the acquired cognitive map. Presumably, both proposed hypotheses play a role. The availability of layout information on a chart map afforded the opportunity for participants to attend to and encode the interpretive framework. The availability of this framework led to better recall of both landmark identity and location. The generative effort needed to piece the map together when the layout information was not available forced attention to landmark-to-landmark spatial relations, thus leading to less interference from external features of the map, such as map section locations and landmark distance, during recognition.

Influences of Time and Space on Map Integration

Learning the spatial location of landmarks cannot be divorced from learning them over time. Research on map learning frequently ignores potential temporal contributions to map comprehension. When looking at a map for the first time, you might visually scan the layout, focusing sequentially on individual landmarks. In the process of scanning in this way, two types of information contribute to building a mental representation, spatial and temporal. Spatial information includes the relative and coordinate locations of landmarks; temporal information involves the order the landmarks are examined. Either of these factors could structure one's mental representation, or they could work in combination. Adjacent spatial locations are usually experienced in a spatially and temporally contiguous manner, that is, adjacent locations are viewed in succession. Occasionally, experience with adjacent locations can be separated in time. In either of these cases, do individuals integrate locations based on the spatial structure or based on the temporal structure?

Clayton and Habibi (1991) suggest that people integrate map information using a temporal structure. In their study, individuals learned a fictitious map with spatial and temporal information either confounded or not confounded. The confounded order proceeded orderly from top to bottom and left to right, while the nonconfounded order appeared spatially random. Participants had to learn to criteria by recalling locations in temporal order. Recognition priming results showed spatial distance effects for the confounded learning order, but since spatial and temporal information was confounded, the true nature of the spatial distance effects cannot be attributed. Clayton and Habibi (1991) found temporal distance effects for the nonconfounded learning order. Based on this finding, they suggest that what has previously been interpreted as spatial structure in map memory may instead be temporal structure.

Other research has also found temporal memory effects, but not to the exclusion of spatial effects. McNamara et al. (1992b) found that both spatial and temporal information structured map memory. They found spatial and temporal priming for temporally and spatially proximal locations, suggesting an additive effect of these information types. In addition to recognition priming, they also used location judgments and distance estimation tasks, since these memory tasks have a clear spatial component. Both tasks showed spatial and temporal influences.

Although these findings indicate that both spatial and temporal information can be used to integrate individual map features into a more unified whole, they also ignore reasons why people may be learning a map. If people are learning a map simply to know what locations are within the map area, they need not pay attention to location information. Instead they can focus solely on landmark identity. In this case, list memorization is an efficient learning strategy. Indeed, Clayton, Habibi, and Bendele (1995) replicated Clayton and Habibi's (1991) results without using a map at all. After presenting the landmark names in a list format, participants showed temporal priming, just as they did when studying landmarks on a map. However, if people are learning a map to specifically know landmark locations, their learning strategy and consequently their memory representation may better reflect the spatial properties of the map. Naylor and Taylor (1997) and Curiel and Radvansky (1998) addressed this issue directly, examining how goal-directed learning changed the impact of either temporal or spatial information. In short, goals influenced learning and map memory. The details of these studies and general issues of goal influence on map learning will be discussed in detail later in this chapter.

Integration of Spatial and Nonspatial Information

Maps are frequently used in combination with other information. For example, an American history text may provide a map illustrating Sherman's march through the South during the Civil War. The map will be referred to in the accompanying text describing the battles fought during the march. In examples such as this, facts are associated with specific locations. Sometimes the facts are learned prior to knowing the actual locations, sometimes afterwards, and sometimes simultaneously. Results indicate that either of the two types of information, spatial and nonspatial, can facilitate learning of the other type.

McNamara, Halpin, and Hardy (1992a) had people learn environments either from a map (Experiments 1 and 3) or through actual experience with the environment (Experiment 2). In all cases, participants learned facts associated with locations, generally after they had learned the locations. With both ways of learning, map learning and direct experience, participants seemingly integrated spatial and nonspatial information. Evidence for this integration came from distance effects; nearby locations primed one another, leading to faster response times for nearby cities compared to distant cities. With map learning, they also found a fan effect for fact information. When asked to verify a fact about a particular location, participants had greater difficulty with any given fact when there were a greater number of facts associated with that location.

Others have examined how showing texts with maps facilitates learning of the map and learning of the text. Shimron (1978) had people either read stories associated with a map or had them copy the map while learning it. Results of map memory tasks favored the story group. Shimron (1978) concludes that the story information improved acquisition of the map information. Kulhavy and his colleagues (Abel & Kulhavy, 1989; Kulhavy, Stock, Verdi, Rittschof, & Savenye, 1993; Stock, Kulhavy, Peterson, & Hancock, 1995) have shown that the availability of a map when learning text about an area (e.g., historic description) facilitates learning of the text. Based on their findings in repeated studies, they present a theory (Kulhavy, Stock, & Caterino, 1994) based on dual coding (Paivio, 1983). The idea is also akin to ideas of working memory interference (Baddeley, 1992). Kulhavy et al. (1994) suggest that mentally encoded maps retain spatial information. Kosslyn, Ball, and Reiser (1978) support this contention by showing that mental scanning times increase as a function of physical distance. These information-rich images provide a computational advantage for textual working memory, because interference between the text and map does not occur. In other words, the information from the map and from the text is readily available. In their paper, Kulhavy et al. (1994) provided data supporting their theory from eight separate experiments.

GOAL-DIRECTED INFLUENCES ON MAP LEARNING

Maps are not learned in a vacuum. When someone examines a map, they usually have some intention, such as finding a particular route through an environment, determining the location of a specific landmark, or getting an overview of a new environment. Thus, in most naturalistic settings, map learning is a goal-directed activity.

Goals can influence learning in different ways. Goals guide attention and serve as anchors for selecting relevant stimuli (Britton, Meyer, Simpson, Holdredge, & Curry, 1979; LaBerge, 1995; Meyer, 1975). Goals also activate frameworks whereby new information can be interpreted. Individuals remember information related to learning goals more than goal-unrelated information (Anderson & Pichert, 1978). This finding may better reflect strategic retrieval since incorporating goals at retrieval also yields more goal-related information (Anderson & Pichert, 1978). In other words, goals can serve as an encoding framework and/or as a retrieval cue. In the map domain, Kinnear and Wood (1987) had participants study topographic contour maps. While learning, participants completed one of two tasks. One involved using the map contours; the other involved assessing distances on the map. Participants in the contour group later showed better recognition memory for the map. Since the foil maps for the recognition test resembled the studied map, participants' attention to the contours during learning allowed them to discriminate between studied and foil maps.

In research examining the nature of mental representations of maps, Rossano, Adams, Booker, and Middleton (1996) argue that for distance judgments, as distances increase, people rely more heavily on categorical as opposed to analogical information. Their results support this argument by showing greater difficulty when making distance discriminations as distance along an irrelevant axis increased. Thus, people switched to a more categorical or hierarchical approach with difficult distance discriminations, showing purposeful processing.

Goals and the Influence of Time and Space on Cognitive Maps

Naylor and Taylor (1997) specifically examined how a goal-directed learning task influences map memory. Participants had one of two tasks while learning the map of a building, either a spatially focused task or a temporally focused task. To show sufficient learning, participants had to reach criterion performance. During learning, a blank map was shown and room labels appeared one at a time, in a seemingly random spatial order. The presentation order, however, was the same on every learning trial. The spatial criterion test required participants to draw the map; the temporal criterion test required participants to list the locations in the order presented. Participants had to continue studying the map until they reached the criterion of two sequential, flawless performances. Memory was assessed using recognition priming, spatial priming, free-recall, and Euclidean distance estimations.

Memory results reflected the learning task. Participants who had a spatial learning criterion showed influences of spatial location on all memory tests, but no influences of temporal order. In contrast, participants who had a temporal learning criterion showed effects of temporal order on all memory tasks. Learning goal alone, however, does not fully explain what temporal learning participants acquired from the map. Memory tasks that required exhaustive memory search (free-recall) or retrieval of spatial information (spatial priming and Euclidean distance estimates) showed influences of spatial adjacency. The spatial properties of the map were learned, even when the criterion focused on presentation order. Although the spatial learning participants were exposed to the same presentation order, this information was not encoded. In a similar study, Curiel and Radvansky

(1998) observed temporal priming in their sequential learning group and spatial priming in their spatial learning group. Taken in combination, these results demonstrate that the reason for learning a map influences what is represented in memory.

Goals and Spatial Perspective in Cognitive Maps

The studies discussed previously suggest that goals focus attention on different aspects of an environment, thereby strengthening memory for the attended information. However, there are different ways to learn an environment, the most common being either from a map or through navigation (see Montello, Chapter 7, for an in-depth discussion of navigation). Goal effectiveness may vary depending on the information available or the need to process information beyond what is given. Maps and navigation differ in the information available. Configural information is readily available on a map, but must be integrated through extensive route knowledge with navigation. On maps, individual landmarks often lack distinction, because they are represented symbolically. Through navigation, the distinguishing characteristics of landmarks can be seen. Maps directly present relational information between all landmark pairs; relative location information is limited to local groupings during navigation. Evidence of superior memory for spatial after studying a map supports this difference (Thorndyke & Hayes-Roth, 1982).

This reasoning suggests that goals may influence map learning and navigation differently, because different information is more accessible through the two media. During navigation, route information is readily available, while configural information is not. Thus, providing a layout goal to a navigator may focus his or her attention on relative location information. This information can, in turn, be integrated into configural or survey knowledge. With maps, configural information is primary and route information secondary, although available. With both types of information available, a specific learning goal would focus attention on the associated information. A layout goal would emphasize configural information, which is already readily available. A route goal would focus attention on the secondary route information. However, how would this focus on route information affect overall map learning? It may draw attention away from the configural information. If this is the case, individuals studying a map with a route goal would have good route perspective knowledge, but poor survey perspective knowledge. Alternatively, the route goal may serve a more supplemental role, enhancing the available configural information with route

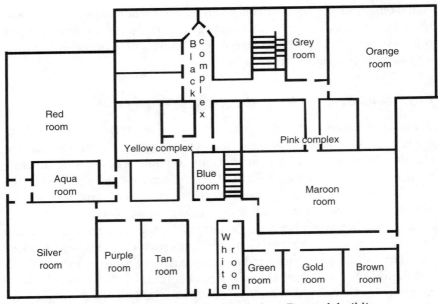

FIGURE 8.5. Map of the Tufts University Psychology Research building.

information. In this case, memory would have both survey and route perspective elements.

Taylor, Naylor, and Chechile (1999) specifically examined goal-directed spatial processing with both maps and navigation. Participants learned a building either from a map or through navigation (see map in Figure 8.5). Additionally, participants had one of two goals, either to learn the layout of the building or to learn routes between rooms. Participants studied for a minimum of 10 minutes and a maximum of 20. Leiser, Tzelgov, and Henik (1987) found that some differences in spatial memory based on simulated navigation and map study could be accounted for by study time differences. The minimum study time provided some equivalence between the two learning conditions. After studying, participants worked through a variety of memory tasks, some assessing route/navigation-based knowledge (e.g., route descriptions, route distance estimates) and some assessing survey/layout knowledge (e.g., configuration judgments, Euclidean distance estimates).

Results indicated that how participants learned the environment and why they learned it both affected memory. Overall, for tasks assessing route knowledge, participants performed better, on average, if they had a goal to learn routes between rooms or if they learned through navigation. Similarly, on tasks assessing layout knowledge, participants performed better either if they had a goal to learn the layout or if they studied a map.

Of the memory tests, the route distance estimates and the Euclidean distance estimates can be compared directly. Participants estimated route distance more accurately than Euclidean distance. Estimates also interacted with both learning medium (map, navigation) and goal (layout, route). For learning condition, participants who navigated gave more accurate route distance estimates, whereas map participants gave more accurate Euclidean distance estimates. For spatial goal, participants with a route goal made more accurate route distance estimates, whereas participants with a layout goal gave equally accurate estimates for both tasks.

Thus, understanding how individuals learn from maps cannot be completely divorced from why they are using the map. Someone pulling out a map to find a particular route through town will remember different things than someone pulling out the map to just get the "lay of the land."

INDIVIDUAL DIFFERENCES IN MAP PROCESSING

Map Conceptualization in the Haptic Domain

The conversion of perceptual to conceptual information does not always involve visual processing. Tactile maps present spatial information to the blind to help them orient within an environment. Tactile maps represent a spatial area using combinations of textures and shapes. Blind users haptically explore the textures to derive information about spatial layouts. Tactile maps successfully relate spatial information to users (Espinosa & Ochaita, 1998) and can be more efficient than learning through exploration. Blind children learn direction information more accurately from a tactile map than through actual exploration (Ungar, Blades, Spencer, & Morsley, 1994).

For best conceptual understanding of the features on a tactile map, Bentzen (1996) recommends constructing landmarks to enhance their tactile distinctiveness. Only landmarks from the same category should be represented using the same shape or texture. Similar to other information-processing skills, training on shape identification significantly improved identification of tactile map features (Berla & Butterfield, 1977), and additional noise in the form of textures detracted from identification (Berla & Murr, 1975). Although it is not known whether the cognitive processes involved in using tactile maps are shared with those necessary for using

visual maps (Golledge, 1991), there is some evidence of common underlying processes. For example, users of tactile maps develop orientation-
specific representations just as users of visual maps do (Rossano & Warren,
1989a).

Different Abilities and Development of Map Skills

For blind individuals, understanding the "big picture" or integrating information from a map is particularly challenging. As discussed earlier, tactile
maps represent information using predominantly raised shapes and different textures. Lederman and Klatzky (1987, 1990) found that people use a
number of distinctive movements when haptically exploring objects. Thus,
a map with a variety of textures and shapes would require a varied repertoire of exploratory movements, each of which activate different neurons
specialized for particular exploratory hand positions (Sakata & Iwamura,
1978). Haptic exploration includes such behaviors as line tracing and shape
recognition movements (Berla, Butterfield, & Murr, 1976). The way tactile
maps are explored leads to integration challenges. The movements used
depend on qualities of the objects. Similar to sectional maps, exploration
through tactile maps leads to small "snapshots" of landmark-to-landmark
relations. Through haptic exploration, the user can successively add these
local spatial relationships to their developing cognitive map. However,
blind users' success in integrating large-scale environments depicted with
tactile maps has been debated. Casey (1978) found that blind high school
students constructed maps that had small, disconnected groups of buildings. Presumably, Casey's (1978) blind students had learned their environment either through direct experience, verbal directions, or a combination
of these methods. In comparison, Espinosa and Ochaita (1998) showed
better practical route knowledge when blind participants studied a map
than when learning either through direct experience or verbal directions.
Thus, although blind students do not seem to construct maps from navigation experience very well, they benefit from using maps to explore the
environment.

Normal cognitive aging also seems to result in difficulty integrating spatial information into a unified cognitive map. Caplan and Lipman (1995)
examined different navigational aids in younger and older adults, proposing three factors that would make these aids more useful for older adults.
First, aids will be most effective when their use is obvious. Second, aids
will be more successful for individuals who have had previous success
with them. Third, aids will be most effective if they support age-related

cognitive deficits. They examined aids that were more or less maplike in younger and older men and women. They found an age by gender interaction. Age differences for men decreased as the aid became more maplike. In contrast, age differences for women increased as the aid became more maplike. Across the entire study, however, more maplike aids were more beneficial. Kirasic and Mathes (1990) also examined different aids (verbal description, verbal description with imagery, videotaped route, and map) for learning a new environment. They found that the map and the verbal directions led to the most efficient route finding.

Aging also affects use of maps during path finding. Aubrey and Dobbs (1989) had older and younger adults perform the Locomotor Maze test. For this test, participants receive a map depicting a path through nine locations. The locations were nine red disks on the floor arranged in a three-by-three matrix. Successive maps increase in difficulty with the addition of path segments. Participants walked the path depicted without turning the map, that is, without aligning it with their trajectory. Results showed younger and older adults performed similarly on simpler maps, but older adults made more errors and required more time at decision points with more complex maps. The researchers attribute this age-related decline in map use to difficulties in working memory and mental rotation. A follow-up study (Aubrey et al., 1994) compared a condition where participants could not turn the map to one where they could reorient the map. Results replicated the earlier study, showing decreased performance by older adults with more complex maps. Additionally, the misalignment (no turn) condition demonstrated that decision times increased as a function of the degree of misalignment.

Experience level with maps appears to play some role in map comprehension, although the results of expertise are mixed. Thorndyke and Stasz (1980) found strategy differences between good and bad map learners. However, whether people were good or bad map learners did not relate to their expertise level with maps. Experts and novices showed similar performance. Gilhooly, Wood, Kinnear, and Green (1988) partially replicated Thorndyke and Stasz's (1980) finding with respect to expertise, but also showed that expertise interacted with the type of map studied. For planimetric maps, no expertise differences emerged. However, for topographic maps depicting three-dimensional elevation, experts' performance superceded that of novices. Postigo and Pozo (1998) generally also failed to show expertise differences using a geographical map. College geography majors recalled map information no better than psychology majors, although college students generally remembered more than adolescents.

Lowe (2001), in contrast, found expertise differences with meteorological maps. Experts processed the maps more conceptually whereas novices relied on perceptual features.

CONCLUSIONS

When someone looks at a street map, they will see what they have always seen. Without close inspection, the standard street map of one urban area will be relatively indistinguishable from the map of another urban area. Researchers examining learning and memory from maps know that multiple cognitive processes underlie the ability to successfully use a map. Additionally, features of maps, the formats they are presented in, and individual's goals for using maps also affect how they are learned and remembered.

While research has addressed many issues involving map learning, we do not know everything about the processes involved. Most studies examining map learning use off-line measures after learning has taken place. There is a great need for more studies using on-line measurements. These studies could help elucidate the learning process and identify the nature of incomplete map representations. Learning from a map takes time, but the mental representation of the map begins when study begins. Thus, identifying the nature of intermediate map representations could help explain map learning in general.

The World Wide Web has brought more maps to more people. Many people now consult on-line maps when getting driving directions. In addition to providing directions, in map and verbal forms, these electronic sources allow people to manipulate the maps. How might the ability to manipulate a map influence learning from it? The most common manipulation allowed with these maps is zooming in and zooming out. By zooming in, people get finer detail about an area of interest. By zooming out, they get a broader perspective of where the area of interest fits within a larger area. How do these processes affect one's developing cognitive map? Are the same processes used to learn from a paper map evoked when learning from multimedia maps? Are additional processes needed with electronic maps? Because map systems on the World Wide Web are still developing, knowledge about the cognitive processing of maps should be incorporated into their design changes.

We know that people do not need a physical map to build a cognitive map. Montello (Chapter 7) reviews issues of cognitive mapping from navigation. People also build cognitive maps from verbal descriptions (Taylor & Tversky, 1992a, 1992b, 1996). Research has debated whether the cognitive maps acquired from these other sources are the same as those acquired from physical maps.

Maps may have similar features to other visuospatial displays. As such, when they are learned, some cognitive processes general to visuospatial processing are evoked. However, cognitive processes unique to map learning are also evoked. Understanding all of these processes and how they work together is the task for researchers interested in cognitive maps derived from physical maps. For now, researchers still struggle to disentangle the mystery of maps.

Suggestions for Further Reading

For a review and analysis of methodology used for understanding cognitive maps, see:

Newcombe, N. (1985). Methods for the study of spatial cognition. In R. Cohen (Ed.), *The development of spatial cognition*, (pp. 277–300). Hillsdale, NJ: Lawrence Erlbaum Associates.

For a discussion of different ways to structure maps and how those structures affect their use see:

MacEachren, A. M. (1995). *How maps work: Representation, visualization, and design.* New York: The Guilford Press.

For a discussion of general cognitive processes used in map learning see:

Rossano, M. J., & Morrison, T. T. (1996). Learning from maps: General processes and map-structure influences. *Cognition and Instruction, 14,* 109–137.

For a general discussion of cognitive maps and how they might be formed see:

Kulhavy, R. W., & Stock, W. A. (1996). How cognitive maps are learned and remembered. *Annals of the Association of American Geographers, 86,* 123–145.

For a review of the development of symbol comprehension in a spatial context see:

DeLoache, J. S., & Smith, C. M. (1999). Early symbolic representation. In I. E. Sigel (Ed.), *Development of mental representation: Theories and application* (pp. 61–86). Mahwah, NJ: Lawrence Erlbaum Associates.

References

Abel, R. R., & Kulhavy, R. W. (1989). Associating map features and related prose in memory. *Contemporary Educational Psychology, 14,* 33–48.

Amlund, J. T., Gaffney, J., & Kulhavy, R. W. (1985). Map feature content and text recall of good and poor readers. *Journal of Reading Behavior, 17*(4), 317–330.

Anderson, R. C., & Pichert, J. W. (1978). Recall of previously unrecallable information following a shift in perspective. *Journal of Verbal Learning and Verbal Behavior, 17,* 1–12.

Aretz, A. J. (1991). The design of electronic map displays. *Human Factors, 33,* 85–101.

Aubrey, J. B., & Dobbs, A. R. (1989). Age differences in extrapersonal orientation as measured by performance on the locomotor maze. *Canadian Journal of Aging, 8*, 333–342.

Aubrey, J. B., Li, K. Z. H., & Dobbs, A. R. (1994). Age differences in the interpretation of misaligned "You-are-here" maps. *Journal of Gerontology: Psychological Sciences, 49*, P29–P31.

Baddeley, A. (1992). Working memory. *Science, 255*, 556–559.

Bentzen, B. L. (1996). Choosing symbols for tactile maps. *Journal of Visual Impairments and Blindness, 90*, 157–159.

Berla, E. P., & Butterfield, L. H. (1977). Tactual distinctive features analysis: Training blind students in shape recognition and in locating shapes on a map. *Journal of Special Education, 11*, 335–346.

Berla, E. P., Butterfield, L. H., & Murr, M. J. (1976). Tactual reading of political maps by blind students: A videomatic behavioral analysis. *Journal of Special Education, 10*, 265–276.

Berla, E. P., & Murr, M. J. (1975). The effects of noise on the location of point symbols and tracking a line on a tactile pseudomap. *Journal of Special Education, 9*, 183–190.

Biederman, I. (1987). Recognition-by-components: A theory of human image understanding. *Psychological Review, 94*, 115–147.

Blades, M., & Spencer, C. (1987). The use of maps by 4 to 6-year-old children in a large-scale maze. *British Journal of Developmental Psychology, 5*, 19–24.

Blades, M., & Spencer, C. (1990). The development of 3- to 6-year-olds' map using ability: The relative importance of landmarks and map alignment. *Journal of Genetic Psychology, 151*, 181–194.

Blaut, J. M. (1987). Notes toward a theory of mapping behavior. *Children's Environments Quarterly, 4*, 27–34.

Blaut, J. M., McCleary, G. S., & Blaut, A. S. (1970). Environmental mapping in young children. *Environment and Behavior, 2*, 335–349.

Britton, B. K., Meyer, B. J. F., Simpson, R., Holdredge, T. S., & Curry, C. (1979). Effects of the organization of text on memory: Tests of two implications of a selective attention hypothesis. *Journal of Experimental Psychology: Human Learning and Memory, 5*, 496–506.

Caplan, L. J., & Lipman, P. D. (1995). Age and gender differences in effectiveness of map-like learning aids in memory for routes. *Journal of Gerontology: Psychological Sciences, 50B*, 126–133.

Casey, S. M. (1978). Cognitive mapping by the blind. *Journal of Visual Impairment and Blindness, 72*, 297–301.

Chechile, R. A., & Soraci, S. A. (1999). A multiple-process account of generation. *Memory, 7*, 483–508.

Clayton, K., & Habibi, A. (1991). Contributions of temporal contiguity to the spatial priming effect. *Journal of Experimental Psychology: Learning, Memory, and Cognition, 17*, 263–271.

Clayton, K., Habibi, A., & Bendele, M. S. (1995). Recognition priming effects following serial learning: Implications for episodic priming effects. *American Journal of Psychology, 108*, 547–561.

Curiel, J. M., & Radvansky, G. A. (1998). Mental organization of maps. *Journal of Experimental Psychology: Learning, Memory, and Cognition, 24*, 202–214.

DeLoache, J. S. (1995). Early understanding and use of symbols: The model model. *Current Directions in Psychological Science, 4*, 109–113.

DeLoache, J. S., Pierroutsakos, S. L., Uttal, D. H., Rosengren, K. S., & Gottlieb, A. (1998). Grasping the nature of pictures. *Psychological Science, 9*, 205–210.

DeLoache, J. S., & Smith, C. M. (1999). Early symbolic representation. In I. E. Sigel (Ed.), *Development of mental representation: Theories and application,* (pp. 61–86). Mahwah, NJ: Lawrence Erlbaum Associates.

Espinosa, M. A., & Ochaita, E. (1998). Using tactile maps to improve the practical spatial knowledge of adults who are blind. *Journal of Visual Impairment and Blindness, 92*, 338–345.

Evans, G. W., & Pezdek, K. (1980). Cognitive mapping: Knowledge of real-world distance and location information. *Journal of Experimental Psychology: Human Learning and Memory, 6*, 13–24.

Farrell, M. J., & Robertson, I. H. (1998). Mental rotation and automatic updating of body-centered spatial relationships. *Journal of Experimental Psychology: Learning, Memory, and Cognition, 24*, 227–233.

Florence, D., & Geiselman, R. (1986). Human performance evaluation of alternative graphic display symbologies. *Perceptual and Motor Skills, 63*, 399–406.

Gilhooly, K. J., Wood, M., Kinnear, P. R., & Green, C. (1988). Skill in map reading and memory for maps. *Quarterly Journal of Experimental Psychology: Human Experimental Psychology, 40*, 87–107.

Golledge, R. G. (1991). Tactual strip maps as navigational aids. *Journal of Visual Impairment and Blindness, 85*, 296–301.

Hauser, M. D. (2000). *Wild minds: What animals really think.* New York: Henry Holt and Company.

Hirshman, E., & Bjork, R. A. (1988). The generation effect: Support for a two-factor theory. *Journal of Experimental Psychology: Learning, Memory, and Cognition, 13*, 484–494.

Hirtle, S. C., & Jonides, J. (1985). Evidence of hierarchies in cognitive maps. *Memory and Cognition, 13*, 208–217.

Howard, J. H., & Kerst, S. M. (1981). Memory and perception of cartographic information for familiar and unfamiliar environments. *Human Factors, 23*, 495–503.

Huttenlocher, J., Hedges, L. V., & Duncan, S. (1991). Categories and particulars: Prototype effects in estimating spatial location. *Psychological Review, 98*, 352–376.

Intons-Peterson, M. L., & McDaniel, M. A. (1990). Symmetries and asymmetries between imagery and perception. In C. Cornoldi & A. McDaniel (Eds.), *Imagery and cognition* (pp. 47–76). New York: Springer-Verlag.

Kerst, S. M., & Howard, J. H. (1978). Memory psychophysics for visual area and length. *Memory and Cognition, 6*, 327–335.

Kinnear, P. R., & Wood, M. (1987). Memory for topographic contour maps. *British Journal of Psychology, 78*, 395–402.

Kirasic, K. C., & Mathes, E. A. (1990). Effects of different means of conveying environmental information on elderly adults' spatial cognition and behavior. *Environment and Behavior, 22*, 591–607.

Kosslyn, S. M., Ball, T. M., & Reiser, B. J. (1978). Visual images preserve metric spatial information: Evidence from studies of image scanning. *Journal of Experimental Psychology: Human Perception and Performance, 4*, 47–60.

Kulhavy, R. W., Schwartz, N. H., & Shaha, S. H. (1982). Interpretive frameworks and memory for map features. *The American Cartographer, 9*, 141–147.

Kulhavy, R. W., & Stock, W. A. (1996). How cognitive maps are learned and remembered. *Annals of the Association of American Geographers, 86*, 123–145.

Kulhavy, R. W., Stock, W. A., & Caterino, L. C. (1994). Reference maps as a framework for remembering text. In W. Schnotz & R. W. Kulhavy (Eds.), *Comprehension of graphics* (pp. 153–162). New York: North-Holland.

Kulhavy, R. W., Stock, W. A., Verdi, M. P., Rittschof, K. A., & Savenye, W. (1993). Why maps improve memory for text: The influence of structural information on working memory operations. *European Journal of Cognitive Psychology, 5*, 375–392.

LaBerge, D. (1995). *Attentional processing: The brain's art of mindfulness.* Cambridge, MA: Harvard University Press.

Lederman, S. J., & Klatzky, R. L. (1987). Hand movements: A window into haptic object recogntion. *Cognitive Psychology, 19*, 342–368.

Lederman, S. J., & Klatzky, R. L. (1990). Haptical classification of common objects: Knowledge-driven exploration. *Cognitive Psychology, 22*, 421–459.

Leiser, D., Tzelgov, J., & Henik, A. (1987). A comparison of map study methods: Simulated travel vs. conventional study. *Cahiers de Psychologie Cognitive, 7*, 317–334.

Levine, M., Jankovic, I. N., & Palij, M. (1982). Principles of spatial problem solving. *Journal of Experimental Psychology: General, 111*, 157–175.

Levine, M., Marchon, I., & Hanley, G. L. (1984). The placement and misplacement of you-are-here maps. *Environment and Behavior, 16*, 139–157.

Lloyd, R., & Steinke, T. (1986). The identification of regional boundaries on cognitive maps. *Professional Geographer, 38*, 149–159.

Lowe, R. K. (2001). Components of expertise in perception and interpretation of meteorological charts. In R. R. Hoffman & A. B. Markman (Eds.), *Interpreting remote sensing imagery: Human factors* (pp. 185–206). Boca Raton, FL: CRC Press.

Lynch, K. (1960). *The image of the city.* Cambridge, MA: MIT Press.

MacEachren, A. M. (1995). *How maps work: Representation, visualization, and design.* New York: The Guilford Press.

Maki, R. H., Maki, W. S., & Marsh, L. G. (1977). Processing locational and orientational information. *Memory and Cognition, 5*, 602–612.

Marzolf, D. P., & DeLoache, J. S. (1997). Search tasks as measures of cognitive development. In N. Foreman, R. Gillet (eds)., *A handbook of spatial research paradigms and methodologies: Vol. 1, Spatial cognition in the child and adult* (Vol. 1, pp. 131–152). Hove: Psychology Press.

McDaniel, M. A., Waddill, P. J., & Einstein, G. O. (1988). A contextual account of the generation effect: A three-factor theory. *Journal of Memory and Language, 27*, 521–536.

McNamara, T. P., Halpin, J. A., & Hardy, J. K. (1992a). The representation and integration in memory of spatial and nonspatial information. *Memory and Cognition, 20*, 519–532.

McNamara, T. P., Halpin, J. A., & Hardy, J. K. (1992b). Spatial and temporal contributions to the structure of spatial memory. *Journal of Experimental Psychology: Learning, Memory, and Cognition, 18*, 555–564.

McNamara, T. P., Hardy, J. K., & Hirtle, S. C. (1989). Subjective hierarchies in spatial memory. *Journal of Experimental Psychology: Learning, Memory, and Cognition, 15,* 211–227.

McNamara, T. P., Ratcliff, R., & McKoon, G. (1984). The mental representation of knowledge acquired from maps. *Journal of Experimental Psychology: Learning, Memory, and Cognition, 10,* 723–732.

Meyer, B. J. F. (1975). *The organization of prose and its effects on memory.* Amsterdam: North-Holland.

Moar, I., & Bower, G. H. (1983). Inconsistencies in spatial knowledge. *Memory and Cognition, 11,* 107–113.

Navon, D. (1977). Forest before trees: The precedence of global features in visual perception. *Cognitive Psychology, 9,* 353–383.

Naylor, S. J., & Taylor, H. A. (1997). *What is space without time? Spatial and temporal contributions to map memory.* Paper presented at the Psychonomic Society, Philadelphia, PA.

Naylor, S. J., & Taylor, H. A. (1998). [Spatial context effects in map learning]. Unpublished raw data.

Newcombe, N. (1985). Methods for the study of spatial cognition. In R. Cohen (Ed.), *The development of spatial cognition* (pp. 277–300). Hillsdale, NJ: Lawrence Erlbaum Associates.

Newcombe, N., Huttenlocher, J., Sandberg, E., Lee, E., & Johnson, S. (1999). What do misestimations and asymmetries in spatial judgement indicate about spatial representation? *Journal of Experimental Psychology: Learning, Memory, and Cognition, 25,* 986–996.

Paivio, A. (1983). The empirical case for dual coding. In J. C. Yuille (Ed.), *Imagery, memory, and cognition* (pp. 310–332). Hillsdale, NJ: Lawrence Erlbaum Associates.

Pomerantz, J. R., & Schwaitzberg, S. D. (1975). Grouping by proximity: Selective attention measures. *Perception and Psychophysics, 14,* 565–569.

Postigo, Y., & Pozo, J. I. (1998). The learning of a geographical map by experts and novices. *Educational Psychology, 18,* 65–80.

Premack, D., & Premack, A. J. (1983). *The mind of an ape.* New York: W. W. Norton.

Presson, C. C., DeLange, N., & Hazelrigg, M. D. (1989). Orientation specificity in spatial memory. What makes a path different from a map of a path? *Journal of Experimental Psychology: Learning, Memory, and Cognition, 15,* 887–897.

Reiser, J. J. (1989). Access to knowledge of spatial structure at novel points of observation. *Journal of Experimental Psychology: Learning, Memory, and Cognition, 15,* 1157–1165.

Robinson, A. H., Sale, R. D., Morrison, J. L., & Muehrcke, P. C. (1984). *Elements of cartography.* New York: Wiley.

Roskos-Ewoldson, B., McNamara, T. P., Shelton, A. L., & Carr, W. (1998). Mental representation of large and small spatial layouts are orientation dependent. *Journal of Experimental Psychology: Learning, Memory, and Cognition, 24,* 215–226.

Rossano, M. J., Adams, G. E., Booker, J. C., & Middleton, S. E. (1996). Semantic and visual factors affecting the representation of map information. *Perception, 25,* 677–700.

Rossano, M. J., & Hodgson, S. L. (1994). The process of learning from small-scale maps. *Applied Cognitive Psychology, 8,* 565–582.

Rossano, M. J., & Morrison, T. T. (1996). Learning from maps: General processes and map-structure influences. *Cognition and Instruction, 14,* 109–137.

Rossano, M. J., & Warren, D. H. (1989a). The importance of alignment in blind subjects' use of tactual maps. *Perception, 18,* 805–816.

Rossano, M. J., & Warren, D. H. (1989b). Misaligned maps lead to predictable errors. *Perception, 18,* 215–229.

Sakata, H., & Iwamura, Y. (1978). Cortical processing of tactile information in the first somatosensory and parietal assocation areas in the monkey. In G. Gordon (Ed.), *Active touch* (pp. 55–72). Elmsford, NY: Pergamon.

Salomon, G. (1979). *Interaction of media, cognition, and learning.* San Francisco: Jossey Bass.

Sandberg, E. H., & Huttenlocher, J. (2001). Advanced spatial skills and advance planning: Components of 6-year-olds' navigational map use. *Journal of Cognition and Development, Special Issue: 2,* 51–70.

Sattath, S., & Tversky, A. (1977). Additive similarity trees. *Psychometrika, 42,* 319–345.

Schober, M. F., & Conrad, F. G. (1997). Does conversational interviewing reduce survey measurement error? *Public Opinion Quarterly, 61,* 576–602.

Shelton, A. L., & McNamara, T. P. (1997). Multiple views of spatial memory. *Psychonomic Bulletin and Review, 4,* 102–106.

Shepard, R. N. (1980). Multidimensional scaling, tree-fitting, and clustering. *Science, 210,* 390–398.

Shimron, J. (1978). Learning positional information from maps. *The American Cartographer, 5,* 9–19.

Sholl, M. J. (1987). Cognitive maps as orienting schemata. *Journal of Experimental Psychology: Learning, Memory, and Cognition, 13,* 615–628.

Slamecka, N. J., & Graf, P. (1978). The generation effect: Delineation of a phenomenon. *Journal of Experimental Psychology: Human Learning and Memory, 4,* 592–604.

Soraci, S. A., Carlin, M. T., Chechile, R. A., Franks, J. J., Wills, T. W., & Watanabe, T. (1999). Cuing and encoding variability in generative processing. *Journal of Memory and Language, 41,* 541–559.

Soraci, S. A., Jr., Franks, J. J., Bransford, J. D., Chechile, R. A., Belli, R. F., Carr, M., & Carlin, M. T. (1994). Incongruous item generation effects: A multiple-cue perspective. *Journal of Experimental Psychology: Learning, Memory, and Cognition, 20,* 1–12.

Stevens, A., & Coupe, P. (1978). Distortions in judged spatial relations. *Cognitive Psychology, 10,* 422–437.

Stock, W. A., Kulhavy, R. W., Peterson, S. E., & Hancock, T. E. (1995). Mental representations of maps and verbal descriptions: Evidence they may affect text memory differently. *Contemporary Educational Psychology, 20,* 237–256.

Taylor, H. A. (2000). The role of map format on integration into a cognitive map. *GIScience 2000 Abstracts, 1,* 86–87.

Taylor, H. A., Naylor, S. J., & Chechile, N. A. (1999). Goal-specific influences on the representation of spatial perspective. *Memory and Cognition, 27,* 309–319.

Taylor, H. A., & Soraci, S. A. (1999). Seeing the map through the landmarks: Integrating information from maps. *Paper presented at the Annual Meeting of the Society for Applied Research in Memory and Cognition*, Boulder, CO.

Taylor, H. A., & Tversky, B. (1992a). Descriptions and depictions of environments. *Memory and Cognition, 20,* 483–496.

Taylor, H. A., & Tversky, B. (1992b). Spatial mental models derived from survey and route descriptions. *Journal of Memory and Language, 31,* 261–292.

Taylor, H. A., & Tversky, B. (1996). Perspective in spatial descriptions. *Journal of Memory and Language, 35,* 371–391.

Taylor, M. M. (1961). Effect of anchoring and distance perception on the reproduction of forms. *Perception and Motor Skills, 12,* 203–230.

Thorndyke, P. W., & Hayes-Roth, B. (1982). Differences in spatial knowledge acquired from maps and navigation. *Cognitive Psychology, 14,* 560–589.

Thorndyke, P. W., & Stasz, C. (1980). Inidividual differences in procedures for knowledge acquisition from maps. *Cognitive Psychology, 12,* 137–175.

Tolman, E. C. (1948). Cognitive maps in rats and men. *Psychological Review, 55,* 189–208.

Treisman, A., & Gelade, G. (1980). A feature integration theory of attention. *Cognitive Psychology, 12,* 97–136.

Tversky, B. (1981). Distortions in memory for maps. *Cognitive Psychology, 13,* 407–433.

Tversky, B., & Schiano, D. J. (1989). Perceptual and conceptual factors in distortions in memory for graphs and maps. *Journal of Experimental Psychology: General, 118,* 387–398.

Ungar, S., Blades, M., Spencer, C., & Morsley, K. (1994). Can visually impaired children use tactile maps to estimate directions? *Journal of Visual Impairment and Blindness, 88,* 221–233.

Uttal, D. H., & Wellman, H. M. (1989). Young children's representation of spatial information acquired from maps. *Developmental Psychology, 25,* 128–138.

Walsh, D. A., Krauss, I. K., & Regnier, V. A. (1981). Spatial ability, environmental knowledge, and environmental use: The elderly. In L. S. Liben, A. H. Patterson, & N. Newcombe (Eds.), *Spatial representation and behavior across the life span* (pp. 321–357). New York: Academic Press.

Warren, D. H., Rossano, M. J., & Wear, T. D. (1990). Perception of map-environment correspondence: The roles of features and alignment. *Ecological Psychology, 2,* 131–150.

Wickens, C. D., Liang, C., Prevett, T., & Olmos, O. (1996). Electronic maps for terminal area navigation: Effects of frame of reference and dimensionality. *The International Journal of Aviation Psychology, 6,* 241–271.

Wickens, C. D., & Prevett, T. (1995). Exploring the dimensions of egocentricity in aircraft navigation displays: Influences on local guidance and global situation awareness. *Journal of Experimental Psychology: Applied, 1,* 110–135.

Wills, T. W., Soraci, S. A., Chechile, R. A., & Taylor, H. A. (2000). "Aha" effects in the generation of pictures. *Memory and Cognition, 28,* 939–948.

Winn, W. D. (1991). Learning from maps and diagrams. *Educational Psychology Review, 3,* 211–247.

9

Spatial Situation Models

Mike Rinck

ABSTRACT

In this chapter, I review empirical and theoretical work on spatial situation models created from texts. Deep comprehension of a text involves the construction of a model representing the situation described in the text. One particular type of information represented in this situation model is spatial information, therefore the term *spatial situation model*. The empirical evidence reviewed in this chapter is organized around three research questions: First, do readers create spatial situation models during reading? I review a large body of evidence suggesting that they do. Second, what is the nature of spatial situation models? To answer this question, I describe empirical studies that explored the role of spatial information, the metrics and neuropsychological correlates of spatial situation models, individual differences in constructing these models, and models created from instructional texts. In addition, theoretical views of spatial situation models are reviewed. Third, what are the limitations of spatial situation models? In answering this question, I review a number of studies that challenge the assumption that spatial information is an important dimension of situation models. Finally, I discuss the possible future of multidimensional situation models and spatial situation models.

WHAT ARE SPATIAL SITUATION MODELS?

Imagine reading the latest Harry Potter novel, a travel guide for visiting Paris, or instructions for assembling a piece of furniture. What does it take to understand these very different types of texts? Among other things, all of them require comprehension of some important spatial information: Is Harry inside or outside of Hogwarts at a given moment, which direction do you have to take to get from Notre Dame to the Eiffel Tower, and do you have to attach the small board to the left side or to the right side of the large board? In all cases, you somehow have to correctly represent critical spatial aspects of the situation described by the text. More generally speaking, during the comprehension of texts, comprehenders build multilevel representations of the information conveyed (e.g., Gernsbacher, 1990; Glenberg & Langston, 1992; Graesser, Singer, & Trabasso, 1994; Johnson-Laird, 1983; Kintsch, 1988, 1998; van Dijk & Kintsch, 1983; Zwaan, Langston, & Graesser, 1995). They process the wording of the text and represent it as what has been called the surface structure. The most striking feature of the surface structure is that it is very short-lived: We usually forget the exact wording of a text very quickly. Readers are also assumed to build a representation of the text itself (the text base), containing the meaning of what was stated in the text, independently of the exact wording. Finally, and most importantly, readers represent the state of affairs described by the text, that is, they take the text as a starting point to create a mental microworld consistent with the text and with their knowledge of the described topic. This level of representation is the *situation model* (van Dijk & Kintsch, 1983) or *mental model* (Johnson-Laird, 1983). Situation models are the level of text representation corresponding to deep understanding, and serve to integrate the information stated in a text with the reader's prior knowledge. Thus, they are an amalgamation of information given by the text and information added by the reader. In short, situation models are tantamount to comprehension and they "represent what the text is about, not the text itself" (Glenberg, Meyer, & Lindem, 1987, p. 70). This definition captures the way the term situation model has been used in the literature, ever since it was introduced by van Dijk and Kintsch in 1983.

In contrast, the term mental model has been used to denote concepts in several different areas of research, including deductive reasoning (Johnson-Laird, 1983), dynamic systems (Gentner & Stevens, 1983), and text comprehension (Glenberg et al., 1987). With regard to deductive reasoning, Johnson-Laird (1983) suggested that people do not reason about syllogisms by following general rules of logic. Syllogisms are three-sentence problems consisting of two premises and a conclusion, and the task is to indicate if the conclusion follows correctly from the premises. For instance, a categorical syllogism might contain the premises "All the circles are striped" and "Some of the striped objects have bold borders," followed by the conclusion "Some of the circles have bold borders." Is this conclusion correct? According to Johnson-Laird (1983), people try to answer this question by applying a very specific and concrete interpretation to the problem. They create a specific model of the situation that satisfies the conditions specified by the premises, the mental model. For instance, Figure 9.1a illustrates what a person might have imagined as an interpretation of the two premises: a

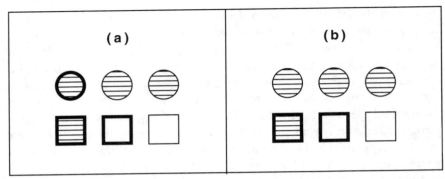

FIGURE 9.1. Two mental models that both satisfy the premises "All the circles are striped" and "Some of the striped objects have bold borders."

number of objects, some of them are circles and others are squares, some of them are striped and others are clear, some of them have bold borders and others do not. This model is then inspected to determine whether the conclusion is true, concluding that it is. This strategy makes efficient use of our mental resources (e.g., working memory capacity) and it may work fine. It often fails, however, if there is more than one model that satisfies the premises. For instance, the model depicted in Figure 9.1b is also a valid interpretation of the premises. For this model, however, the conclusion is not true, therefore, it has to be rejected in general. In case of premises that allow for multiple interpretations (such as the previous example), people tend to overlook alternative models and their relation to the conclusion. This leads to characteristic errors, and the mental models approach to deductive reasoning has been quite successful in predicting many of the errors that humans make (see Byrne & Johnson-Laird, 1989; Johnson-Laird & Byrne, 1991).

With regard to dynamic systems, it has been suggested that humans usually do not fully understand technical devices they have to operate (computers, cars, TV sets, etc.) and other systems they have to live with (the solar system, legislature, social relations, etc.). Instead, people use simplified and internalized mental models to explain the behavior of systems and the systems' reactions to interventions (Gentner & Stevens, 1983; Norman, 1998). These models are often quite useful in predicting the system's behavior at a level sufficient for effectively dealing with it. For instance, do you know exactly how the thermostat on your heating system works? Probably not, but you will have a mental model of it that you use to adjust the thermostat. Consulting your model, you should be able to answer the following question (taken from Norman, 1998): If you want to heat up your cold room as quickly as possible, should you turn up the thermostat to the desired temperature, or would it be faster to turn it all the way up to maximum, then turn it down once the desired temperature is reached? The answer to this question depends on the particular mental model of thermostats you have. If your model of thermostats is similar to your model of faucets (i.e., a valve model), the answer would be to set it to maximum. After all, opening the faucet as far as possible fills up your bathtub more quickly. Alternatively, your thermostat model might resemble a switch that controls the heater that can only be on or off (i.e., an on-off switch model). In this case, the answer would be that it does not matter, because both ways, the heater will run with its invariant intensity until the desired temperature is reached. This model has the additional advantage of being correct, at least at the level discussed here (the model may be incorrect in the way it represents how thermostats measure room temperature and react to it).

Only with regard to text comprehension may mental models and situation models be considered equivalent. However, even within text comprehension, distinctions between mental models and situation models may be made, with situation models being considered mental models of specific situations rather than of general states (see Zwaan, 2003). Because of these ambiguities of the term mental model, I will use the more precise term situation model throughout this chapter.

In addition to mental models, other concepts also have to be distinguished from situation models. Most importantly, situation models are different from *schemas* and *scripts*. Loosely speaking, schemas are mental representations of the properties that concepts generally have, for instance, what a dentist's office usually looks like. Scripts are a specific type of schema; they represent stereotypical sequences of events, for instance, the events typically involved in visiting a dentist. Situation models, on the other hand, are *specific* and *episodic*. For instance, a situation model would represent the specific visit to the dentist described in a text. Schemas and scripts are used to create situation models by supplying prior knowledge needed to deal with gaps or uncertainties in the text: Missing information is being inferred by filling in the most likely information stored in the corresponding schema or script (see the studies by Dutke, 1993, 1994, described next). Situation models also have to be distinguished from *mental images*. The latter are thought to be a specific type of analog or at least quasianalog mental representations. Analog here means that mental images preserve much of the information available in visible images, for instance information about size and distance. Thus, they are sometimes considered images in the head, although most mental imagery researchers would try to avoid equating mental images with perceptual images. In any case, it is an open question whether situation models may be equated with mental images, or whether situation models may be thought of as analog representations that are similar to mental images and created from text. I will get back to this question when I discuss theoretical views of spatial situation models.

Many different aspects of a situation are hypothesized to be represented in situation models, for instance, spatial, temporal, and causal relations as well as the protagonists' goals and emotions (Zwaan, Langston, & Graesser, 1995; Zwaan, Magliano, & Graesser, 1995; Zwaan & Radvansky, 1998; Zwaan, Radvansky, Hilliard, & Curiel, 1998). Thus, situation models are multidimensional by definition. Despite the multidimensionality of situation models, however, most experimental studies have addressed only single dimensions. Among these, spatial relations are the type of information examined most often, whereas other aspects of situation models have received relatively little attention. Spatial relations represented in situation models would include such information as the present location of the protagonist, important objects and actors, the appearance of the locations, and the movement path or goal of the protagonist. The reasons for the emphasis on spatial information are theoretical as well as practical: First, correctly representing spatial relations described in a text is often critical to understanding the text. Second, spatial relations described in a text can vary independently of the surface characteristics of the text. For instance, two objects may be located close to each other in the situation that a text describes even though there is a large amount of text between the descriptions of the two objects, creating a large surface distance. Or the reverse may be achieved by mentioning two entities in the same sentence even though they are located far from each other ("The Golden Gate Bridge is in San Francisco and the Eiffel Tower is in Paris"). Thus, with spatial relations, it is particularly easy to vary aspects of the situation model independently of text characteristics, making isolated experimental variations feasible.

The term *spatial situation model* (Morrow, 1994) has been coined to describe the representation of spatial information in situation models constructed from texts, and for the sake of simplicity, I will use it throughout this chapter. Strictly speaking, however, it is incorrect because there is no such thing as a model representing only spatial aspects of the situation described by a text. In this chapter, I will review empirical and theoretical work on spatial situation models conducted in the past two decades. Naturally, this chapter owes much to earlier reviews, most importantly to the ones by Dutke (1998); Graesser, Millis, and Zwaan (1997);

Morrow (1994); Rinck (2000); and Zwaan and Radvansky (1998). Each of these reviews will make an excellent complement to this chapter, particularly for readers interested in nonspatial dimensions of situation models. In my review, I will focus on what we know about spatial situation models from research investigating text comprehension. Spatial models constructed from nonverbal materials such as maps, graphs, or diagrams are covered by Chapters 8, 10, 11, and 12 of this handbook. Moreover, I will touch some topics only briefly because they are described in more detail in other chapters. Among these are spatial frameworks (Tversky, Chapter 1), individual differences in working memory capacity (Logie and Dela Sala, Chapter 3), and age-related differences in text comprehension (Newcombe and Learmonth, Chapter 6). Moreover, my description of the current state of affairs regarding spatial situation models will focus on narrative texts, that is, novels, stories, fairy tales, and other types of fiction. This is because there is not much research on spatial situation models using instructional texts (e.g., assembly instructions, textbooks, manuals), and much of the more general research on instructional texts is covered in other chapters of this volume.

RESEARCH IN SPATIAL SITUATION MODELS

In this main part of the chapter, I will try to review, summarize, and evaluate the most important results of 20 years of research on spatial situation models. The review will be organized around three research questions: Are spatial situation models created during reading, what is the nature of spatial situation models, and what are their limitations as a theoretical construct? Necessarily, this organization is theoretical rather than chronological. For instance, many researchers have explored the nature of spatial situation models while others were still accumulating evidence for their existence. Also, some of the limitations of spatial situation models have been known before some of the recent studies on their nature were conducted. Moreover, some studies are relevant to more than one of the three research questions. In these cases, I have tried to describe the studies where they seem most appropriate.

Question 1: Do Readers Create Spatial Situation Models During Reading?

This question has been answered in the affirmative using a number of different approaches and experimental paradigms. The dependent variables used to demonstrate the creation of spatial situation models may be divided into what have been labeled off-line measures and on-line measures. Off-line measures are collected after reading, thus, they measure completed situation models rather than the process of creating them. The most popular dependent variable is memory performance, usually in a recognition test, in which participants have to indicate whether a given word, phrase, or statement occurred in the text just read. In contrast, on-line measures are used to investigate situation models in progress, that is, the process of creating and updating situation models. The most popular on-line measures are reading times of words, phrases, and sentences as well as reaction times to test probes presented during reading.

Off-Line Measures of Spatial Situation Models. The importance of spatial situation models for remembering spatial descriptions was demonstrated long before the terms spatial situation model or mental model were introduced. In a study now considered classical, Bransford, Barclay, and Franks (1972) had their participants listen to sentences describing spatial arrangements of objects such as A1 or B1. In a later recognition test, these sentences as well as slightly changed sentences such as A2 and B2 were presented to the participants.

A1. Three turtles rested *on* a floating log, and a fish swam beneath *them*.
A2. Three turtles rested *on* a floating log, and a fish swam beneath *it*.
B1. Three turtles rested *beside* a floating log, and a fish swam beneath *them*.
B2. Three turtles rested *beside* a floating log, and a fish swam beneath *it*.

In the recognition test, participants who had heard sentence A1 often believed they had heard sentence A2, whereas sentences B1 and B2 were rarely confused. These differences cannot be explained by differences in the surface structure of the sentences because A1 and A2 as well as B1 and B2 differ only with respect to the pronouns "them" and "it." Moreover, the differences between A1 and A2 and between B1 and B2 are also equivalent at the text base level. Instead, the critical difference is related to the spatial layout of the objects. Sentences A1 and A2 describe essentially the same spatial situation, whereas sentences B1 and B2 describe different spatial situations. Thus, it seems safe to assume that people created spatial situation models of the layouts described by the study sentences (despite instructions that favored verbatim memorization!), stored them in memory, and based their recognition decisions on these models. The results reported by

Bransford et al. (1972) have recently been replicated in my own laboratory (Rinck, Hähnel, & Becker, 2001), although the effects were considerably smaller than in the original study.

A number of other studies have also used a memory-based approach to demonstrate the construction of spatial situation models during text comprehension. Some of these studies used texts as plain as the ones introduced by Bransford et al. (1972), that is, simple descriptions of object arrangements. For instance, Mani and Johnson-Laird (1982) presented short texts to their participants that described the two-dimensional spatial layout of five objects (A is behind B, A is to the left of C, etc.). In the following, I will refer to this paradigm as the *object layout task*. The layout descriptions were either determinate (describing exactly one spatial arrangement of the objects) or indeterminate (allowing for several different arrangements). For instance, the description "A is to the left of B and C is to the left of B" would be indeterminate because it is congruent with both the A-C-B arrangement and the C-A-B arrangement. In a later recognition test, Mani and Johnson-Laird (1982) found that people relied on a text base representation of indeterminate descriptions, whereas they favored the construction and storage in memory of a spatial situation model for determinate descriptions. This *cross-over effect* suggests that spatial situation models will be constructed, but only if the text describes a unique spatial situation. If readers realize that several different situations are consistent with the text, they will represent the meaning of the text itself rather than one of the several possible situations. Unfortunately, it has been difficult to replicate the cross-over effect, leading Payne (1993) to suggest that people retain a record of the mental operations used to construct the spatial model, instead of the model itself. However, later research (Baguley & Payne, 2000) indicated that a hybrid account may be most appropriate: People remember information about both the spatial model and the processes used to construct it. Another important variable may be found in individual differences in the participants' spatial abilities, as Dutke (1999) suggested (see following discussion).

The object layout task employed by Mani and Johnson-Laird (1982) and by Ehrlich and Johnson-Laird (1982) may be the only one that warrants the assumption that readers create situation models that are purely spatial. In this task, participants may ignore the meaning of the objects and focus on their relative locations instead. Using the same task, however, Dutke (1993, 1994) showed that readers will make use of the objects' meaning in order to create a situation model by integrating information from the text with prior knowledge. As in the Mani and Johnson-Laird (1982) study,

Dutke (1993, 1994) presented determinate and indeterminate descriptions of objects arrangements to his participants. In addition, half of the texts described unpredictable, nonschematic arrangements (e.g., tools spread out on a work bench), whereas the other half described schematic, and therefore predictable, arrangements (e.g., plate, knife, fork, spoon, and glass laid out on a table for a meal). Dutke found that for schematic arrangements, people constructed spatial situation models even for indeterminate descriptions. Obviously, they were able to use their world knowledge to fill in schematic object positions left open by indeterminate descriptions.

People can also use spatial situation models to reduce or even prevent interference during memory retrieval. This was demonstrated by Radvansky and his colleagues in a series of studies (e.g., Radvansky, Spieler, & Zacks, 1993; Radvansky & Zacks, 1991). In these experiments, participants first memorized a series of interrelated spatial statements about objects in locations, such as "The potted palm is in the hotel." Taken together, these statements described locations that contained only one object and locations with many objects. Likewise, some objects occurred only once whereas others occurred multiple times. For the number of objects, Radvansky and his colleagues observed a *fan effect* (Anderson, 1974) in a later recognition test: If an object occurred in several locations, it took participants longer to recognize any single statement containing the object. In contrast, having many objects in a location did not yield longer recognition times than having only one object in that location. This lack of interference is explained by the construction of an integrated spatial situation model created for each location: No matter how many objects are placed in a location, it is always the same single situation model that will be activated during memory retrieval. In contrast, associating an object with several locations will yield the activation of several models during retrieval, thereby creating interference.

On-Line Measures of Spatial Situation Models. All studies described so far used an off-line measure of text comprehension, namely memory performance, usually in a recognition test. In contrast, the following studies employed on-line measures to demonstrate the construction of spatial situation models, usually using reading times. In an early study employing the object layout task, Ehrlich and Johnson-Laird (1982) used descriptions of object arrangements similar to those of Mani and Johnson-Laird (1982). Each of these three-sentence texts described the arrangement of four objects. Half of the descriptions were continuous, that is, subsequent sentences always referred to objects that were already mentioned in the previous sentences and spatially adjacent to the new objects. For discontinuous descriptions, subsequent sentences did not always refer to previously mentioned or spatially close objects. This difference caused corresponding differences in reading time: Readers took longer to read discontinuous sentences than continuous ones, reflecting the additional effort needed to keep separate submodels in mind before being able to integrate them into a coherent spatial situation model.

One may object to the studies described so far because they employed rather short and dull materials instead of narrative texts such as novels or fairy tales. Therefore, the remainder of this chapter will focus on longer and (possibly) more interesting texts, most of them narratives. It should be pointed out, however, that the results reviewed so far are impressive exactly because of the unstructured and nonnarrative nature of the materials. They indicate that people do not need narrative structure to create spatial situation models. Instead, they organize the information themselves, creating spatial situation models spontaneously even in the absence of instructions or linguistic cues.

O'Brien and Albrecht (1992) introduced what I will refer to as the *inconsistency paradigm*. They presented short narratives to find out if readers monitor spatial information during reading and use it to create a coherent situation model. Each of their texts could contain a sentence that was spatially inconsistent with some information given earlier in the text. One of their texts started this way: "As Kim stood inside the health club she felt a little sluggish. Workouts always made her feel better. Today she was particularly looking forward to the exercise class because it had been a long, hard day at work. Her boss had just been fired and she had to fill in for him on top of her own work. She decided to go outside and stretch her legs a little." In a second version of the text, the word "inside" in the first sentence was replaced by "outside," making the sixth sentence spatially inconsistent with the situation model created so far: You cannot go outside if you are outside already. If readers monitor spatial information during reading and create a spatial situation model, they should notice the inconsistency and try to resolve it during the process of updating the situation model. Indeed, O'Brien and Albrecht (1992) found that readers took longer to read the sixth sentence if it was spatially inconsistent with earlier information. Similar results were observed by de Vega (1995); Haenggi, Gernsbacher, and Bolliger (1994); and Rinck and Hähnel (2000).

Zwaan and his colleagues (e.g., Zwaan, Langston, & Graesser, 1995; Zwaan, Magliano, & Graesser, 1995) investigated a more subtle aspect of spatial information processing, namely spatial discontinuities. A sentence would be considered spatially discontinuous if it introduced a new location in a story or described how a protagonist moved to a new place. Zwaan and his colleagues used published short stories instead of experimental passages, and for each sentence of the stories, they determined whether it described an event that was continuous or discontinuous with the previous events on five dimensions: space, time, protagonist, causation, and intentionality. In one study (Zwaan, Magliano, & Graesser, 1995), they collected reading times for each sentence and used a multiple regression technique to determine whether discontinuities on each individual situational dimension were related to increases in reading time. They found that spatial discontinuities were indeed associated with increases in reading times, suggesting that readers monitor spatial information during reading and incorporate it into the situation model. The increase in reading time was strongest, however, during rereading rather than first reading of the texts, and the other dimensions yielded more reliable increases. Thus, Zwaan et al. concluded that the spatial dimension of situation models is probably less important than others. I will come back to this argument later.

Taken together, the experimental evidence reviewed so far suggests that readers do indeed construct spatial situation models, as revealed by on-line measures such as reading times as well as off-line measures such as recognition scores. Readers seem to create spatial situation models spontaneously in the absence of instructions to do so, for plain descriptions of object layouts as well as for narrative texts, although spatial information might not be the most important type of information contained in narratives. It seems safe to conclude that situation models are well established as a third level of representation besides the surface representation and the text base. Therefore, the studies reviewed in the next section went one step further by presupposing the construction of spatial situation models to examine their effects on text comprehension.

Question 2: What Is the Nature of Spatial Situation Models?

Foregrounding and the Spatial Gradient of Accessibility in Situation Models. Many studies of spatial situation models have examined a phenomenon called foregrounding (Glenberg et al., 1987) or focusing of attention (Rinck & Bower, 1995), showing that spatial models guide readers' allocation of attention during text comprehension. In general, readers focus attention on the protagonist and on his or her location and movements, yielding a narrative Here-and-Now point centered around the protagonist (see Morrow, 1994). One consequence of the reader's focusing of attention around the Here-and-Now of the protagonist affects a process called *anaphor resolution*. Anaphors are linguistic expressions that may only be understood by relating them to previous information. Pronouns are prominent anaphors: To understand a pronoun, one has to find out what the pronoun refers to (Morrow, 1985). In general, foregrounding of concepts brings them into working memory, so they are easily available when one has to process a pronoun. Focus in language is used to resolve the referent of pronominal forms as in "John broke the window. It cut him." We know that the "him" refers to John, and the "it" to the broken glass of the window because these elements are in the foreground. The effect of focus can also be seen in ambiguous expressions such as "John walked past the car up the road into the house. The windows were dirty." What windows are being talked about? Morrow (1985) carried out a number of experiments in which people invariably used a principle of proximity to the protagonist to resolve what object is being referred to. Thus, if the protagonist is now at the house and we say "The windows were dirty," readers take that to be the windows of the house. If the text instead said something like "John was walking past the car toward the house. The windows were dirty," the windows would be those of the car.

As another result of foregrounding in spatial situation models, an effect of spatial distance on accessibility arises, that is, known objects spatially close to the protagonist become more primed and more accessible in memory than spatially distant objects. This effect has been referred to as the *spatial gradient of accessibility* or *spatial distance effect*. In an early study, Glenberg et al. (1987) demonstrated how spatial distance in situation models contributes to readers' comprehension of texts. Their participants read short narratives in which the protagonist moved from one place to another, taking a critical object with him or her (the *spatially associated* condition) or leaving it behind (*spatially dissociated*). A sample text in the associated condition reads: "Warren spent the afternoon shopping at the store. He picked up his bag and went to look at some scarves. He had been shopping all day. He thought it was getting too heavy to carry." In the dissociated condition, "picked up" was replaced by "put down," creating only minimal changes at the surface level and at the text base level. At the situation model level, however, the difference was important because the critical object (in this case, the bag) was spatially close to the focus of attention (the protagonist, Warren) in the associated condition and spatially distant from it in the dissociated condition. Glenberg et al. (1987) used two different ways of measuring how this manipulation of spatial distance in the situation model affected accessibility of the critical object in memory. In

Exps. 1 and 2, they presented a recognition test word instead of the final sentence and the participants had to indicate whether the word had
appeared in the text. If the name of the critical object was presented, participants' recognition latencies were shorter in the associated than in the
dissociated condition. In Exp. 3, Glenberg et al. used a less obtrusive measure of accessibility, namely reading time of the final sentence. All texts
were presented sentence by sentence in a self-paced manner, and reading
time of the final sentence containing the anaphoric reference to the critical object (by means of the pronoun "it") was measured. Comprehending
the final sentence involves updating of the situation model by adding a
new piece of information to it (e.g., the bag is getting too heavy). Reading
times comparable to the previously collected recognition latencies were
observed: References to the critical objects were understood more quickly
if the objects were spatially associated with the protagonist rather than
spatially dissociated, suggesting that the spatial aspects of situation models guide readers' allocation of attention during reading. Similar results
were also reported by Glenberg and Mathew (1992); Kaup (1994); and by
Müsseler, Hielscher, and Rickheit (1995). Thus, it seems safe to accept the
interpretation put forward by Glenberg et al. (1987): Readers create spatial situation models and use them to foreground entities that are spatially
close to the focus of attention. It may be objected, however, that Glenberg
et al. (1987) examined only a very rough variation of spatial distance in situation models: The critical object was either very close to the protagonist or
somewhere far away from the protagonist. Thus, it remained questionable
whether more gradual differences in spatial distance would cause gradual
differences in accessibility. This question was extensively investigated in
a number of studies on updating of spatial situation models using an experimental paradigm that was introduced by Morrow and his colleagues
(Morrow, Greenspan, & Bower, 1987; Morrow, Bower, & Greenspan, 1989)
and later modified by Gordon Bower and myself (Rinck & Bower, 1995).
In the following, I will refer to this paradigm as the *map-and-narrative task*.

In the experiments employing the map-and-narrative task, participants
first memorized the layout of a building with many rooms, each containing a number of critical objects. A sample layout taken from Rinck and
Bower (1995) is depicted in Figure 9.2. This procedure served to supply
participants with the prior knowledge necessary to create spatial situation
models during the second part of the experiment. In this part, participants
read a series of brief narratives, each one describing a new protagonist's
activities in that building. The narratives contained critical *motion sentences*

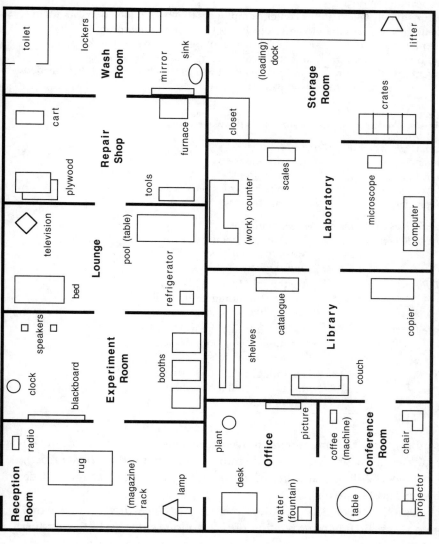

FIGURE 9.2. Sample layout from Rinck and Bower (1995). Anaphora resolution and the focus of attention in situation models. *Journal of Memory and Language, 34,* 110–131. Reprinted with permission from Academic Press.

TABLE 9.1. *Part of Sample Narrative from Rinck and Bower (1995).*

Wilbur wasn't so sure he wanted to be head of the center anymore.

He had just been informed that the board of directors would be making a surprise inspection tomorrow.

He immediately called all the center's employees together in the library and told them they had less than twenty-four hours to clean up the center.

He explained about the visit and said that all of their jobs were at stake.

He told everyone to spread out and clean and organize every room.

He went into the laboratory and made sure it was being cleaned, and then headed off to supervise the rest of the workers.

Critical Motion Sentence:
Wilbur walked from the laboratory into the wash room.

Alternatives of Object Test Probe:
Location Room:	mirrors – lockers
Path Room:	crates – lifter
Source Room:	computer – scales
Other Room:	couch – copier

Alternatives of Anaphoric Target Sentence:
Location Room:	He thought that the toilet in the wash room still looked like an awful mess.
Path Room:	He thought that the loading dock in the storage room still looked like a mess.
Source Room:	He thought that the work counter in the laboratory still looked like a mess.
Other Room:	He thought that the shelves in the library still looked like an awful mess.

describing how the protagonist moved from one room (the *source room*) through an unmentioned *path room* into another room (the *location room*), for instance, "Wilbur walked from the laboratory into the wash room" (see Table 9.1 and Figure 9.2).

Accessibility of objects in readers' memory was measured on-line in one of two ways directly after reading of the motion sentence. In the studies by Morrow et al. (1987, 1989), reading was interrupted and a test probe was presented instead of the next sentence. The test probes consisted of pairs of previously studied objects. For each of these object pairs, subjects had to decide whether the two objects were located in the same room or in different rooms. The observed decision times revealed a spatial distance effect: Accessibility of objects was higher if the spatial distance between the objects and the subjects' current focus of attention was shorter. Usually, attention was focused on the current location of the protagonist of the narrative. Objects located in the same room as the protagonist (e.g., mirror-lockers) were easier to access than objects from the unmentioned path room (e.g., crates-lifter) that the protagonist had just passed through. These path room objects were in turn more accessible than objects in the source room from which the protagonist had commenced his movement (e.g., computer-scales), or objects in some other room not recently visited in the building (e.g., couch-copier).

Morrow et al. (1989) also asked what is more important in determining the focus of attention: the physical location of the main character or his mental location? Where the protagonist is actually located or where he is thinking about? To answer this question, they had participants read stories containing sentences of the type "The protagonist was in Room A think-ing about [doing something] in Room B." The "something being done" mentioned only neutral topics (e.g., cleaning the floor, painting the walls) and never mentioned a specific object memorized in that room. Following such a sentence, the accessibility of objects in Room A and in Room B was probed. Morrow et al. (1989) found that participants were faster to retrieve information about objects in the room where the protagonist's mental fo-cus was (Room B) than in the room where he or she was physically located (Room A). This indicates a very flexible spatial focus of attention: It moves to what the main character is thinking about; that is, readers are in some sense simulating his or her thoughts.

One could object to the map-and-narrative task employed by Morrow and his colleagues because it involves interrupting participants as they read a story and asking them about the current location of the protagonist and various objects. Such a task might make readers concentrate unduly on the locations of things. Therefore, we devised a different technique to measure the accessibility of objects represented in the spatial situation model (Rinck & Bower, 1995). This task is unobtrusive and consists solely of having participants read the text at their own rate. With this technique, people also learn a spatial layout (see Figure 9.2), and then read narratives containing motion sentences such as the one used earlier: "Wilbur walked from the laboratory into the wash room." After each motion sentence, a critical "think about" sentence is inserted, which contains an anaphoric noun phrase referring to one of the objects learned previously. An example of these anaphoric target sentences would read "He thought that the toilet in the wash room still looked like an awful mess" (see Table 9.1). In this case, the anaphoric noun phrase refers to an object in the location room, that is, the room the protagonist is located in right now. Slightly different versions of the anaphoric target sentences referred to objects in the path room, the source room, or some other room (see Table 9.1). With this method, we found a spatial gradient in the reading times of these sentences: Anaphora resolution, and therefore reading of the anaphoric sentence, was faster if the sentence referred to an object in the location room, next fastest for an object in the path room, next fastest for an object in the source room, and slowest for an object in some other room in the building (Rinck & Bower, 1995).

Subsequent research has shown that this spatial gradient of accessibility is a surprisingly robust phenomenon. It was observed repeatedly in studies in which participants learned a building layout before reading the narratives (e.g., Bower & Rinck, 1999; Bower & Rinck, 2001; Haenggi et al., 1994; Haenggi, Kintsch, & Gernsbacher, 1995; Morrow et al., 1987, 1989; Morrow, Leirer, Altieri, & Fitzsimmons, 1994; Morrow, Stine-Morrow, Leirer, Andrassy, & Kahn, 1997; Rinck & Bower, 1995; Rinck & Bower, 2000; Rinck, Hähnel, Bower, & Glowalla, 1997; Wilson, Rinck, McNamara, Bower, & Morrow, 1993), as well as in studies in which the layout was learned from a verbal description (Rinck, Williams, Bower, & Becker, 1996, Exp. 1), or when there was no prior learning procedure as in the experiment by Traill and Bower described next. Moreover, in one study (Rinck et al., 1996), we systematically varied a number of factors that might influence the spatial gradient: the way the relevant spatial information was acquired (studying a text vs. a layout), the spatial scenario (a research center vs. a day care center), the direction of spatial distance (backward vs. forward on the protagonist's route), the language used (English vs. German), the manner in which the accessibility of objects was probed (object pair test probes vs. anaphoric sentences), the existence of prior knowledge about the objects (objects learned as part of the scenario vs. unknown objects), and the participants' task (reading narratives vs. imagining their own movements). Despite these variations, we observed a spatial gradient in all three experiments, indicating that the effects of spatial situation models may be generalized to a variety of experimental paradigms and cognitive tasks.

Control experiments also ruled out a number of alternative explanations of the spatial distance effect. First, one might object that higher accessibility of objects in the location room compared to objects in the source room is due to recency of mention rather than spatial distance in the situation model. In motion sentences of the type "The protagonist went from the source room into the location room," the location room is mentioned more recently (closer to the probe test) than the source room. However, the same pattern of results was observed when the order of mention was reversed using motion sentences such as "The protagonist went into the location room from the source room" (Morrow et al., 1987, Exp. 2). In fact, the spatial gradient of accessibility appears even if the location room is not mentioned at all. In one experiment, we observed similar distance effects when access was probed after motion sentences such as "Then he walked into the next room" (Rinck, Bower, & Wolf, 1998). So not even mentioning the location room, just implying it in the situation model, yielded exactly the same differences in accessibility. Second, differences in accessibility observed in these experiments could not be explained by surprising anaphoric references or by the order in which the rooms of the building were studied during the learning phase of the experiments (Rinck & Bower, 1995).

Another objection that is often raised against the map-and-narrative task is that the results may be due to the rather artificial map learning procedure. People usually learn about spatial environments by experiencing them directly rather than by memorizing a map. The objection seems unjustified, however. First, the same distance effects occurred after people learned about the relevant spatial information from studying a text describing the building (Rinck et al., 1996). These distance effects also arose when the texts and questions referred to a well-known spatial environment that people did not have to memorize at all. In an unpublished study by Saskia Traill and Gordon Bower, participants read stories about salesmen who traveled to various cities around the United States of America. For instance, a sentence in one story described how the main character drove his car from Miami to New York City. Following such motion sentences participants read anaphoric sentences designed to measure the accessibility of the source city (Miami), the location city (New York), or an unmentioned intermediate path city (Baltimore). As before, a spatial gradient of accessibility occurred in reading times, indicating that the location city was more available than the path city, which in turn was more available than the source city.

The latter results highlight one of the most impressive aspects of the spatial gradient of accessibility: Objects from the unmentioned path room may be more accessible than objects from the source room, even though only the source room is being explicitly mentioned in the motion sentence directly before accessibility is probed. This result suggests that spatial distance in situation models may be a more important cause of accessibility than surface characteristics of the text such as explicit mentioning. It should be noted, however, that in many of the studies mentioned earlier, the difference between path room and source room fell in the expected direction but was not statistically significant. In these studies, objects in the location room were more accessible than objects in any other room, with no differences between the latter. This pattern of results has been termed a *location effect*, in contrast to the gradual distance effect. In fact, the relation between path room and source room accessibility may be taken as an index of the relative strength of the surface representation compared to the situation model. The deeper readers process the texts, the stronger the advantage of the path room will be. If readers focus on surface characteristics instead, accessibility of source room objects may be as high as that of location room objects (Pigenet, 1997).

The Relation of Spatial Information to Other Information in Situation Models. As mentioned earlier, situation models created from narratives will not be purely spatial. In addition to spatial relations, other important aspects of the situation will be represented in the model, such as causal and temporal relations, people and objects, and the protagonists' goals and emotions. Recently, a number of studies have started to investigate how the spatial dimension of situation models is related to these other dimensions. In one series of experiments, Zwaan and his colleagues (Zwaan, Langston, & Graesser, 1995; Zwaan, Magliano, & Graesser, 1995, Zwaan et al., 1998) used the regressional approach described earlier to examine discontinuities in space, time, protagonists, intentional and causal relations. The inconsistency paradigm was employed by Haenggi et al. (1994) to compare spatial inconsistencies to emotional ones. Friedman and Miyake (2000) pitted the spatial dimension of situation models against the causal one. Their participants read texts varying in spatial and causal demands while responding to on-line test probes related to spatial or causal information. In another study, Andrea Hähnel and I (Hähnel & Rinck, 1999) examined the way readers focus their attention strategically on spatial and temporal information. This study differs from other ones described here because it did not measure automatic processes of foregrounding or focusing of attention. Instead, participants learned from the narrative that the protagonist had to focus deliberately on spatial, temporal, or both types of information in order to decide among different alternatives (e.g., different vacation trips). In recent series of experiments, my colleagues and I have employed the map-and-narrative task to compare the spatial gradient of accessibility to other gradients. In one study (Rinck et al., 1998), we varied spatial distance in the situation model independently of surface distance. The latter was varied by probing the accessibility of objects in rooms that the protagonist had or had not visited earlier. We (Rinck & Bower, 2000) also pitted spatial distance in the situation model against two types of temporal distance, namely story time distance and discourse time distance. Discourse time refers to real time passing "outside" a narrative during text comprehension, whereas story time refers to fictitious time passing (by description) "inside" the narrative. In another study (Bower & Rinck, 2001), we combined the spatial gradient of accessibility with the fan effect (see previous discussion) by varying the number of objects located in each room independently of the spatial distance between the objects and the protagonist. Finally, we (Bower & Rinck, 1999) varied spatial distance independently of goal relevance by probing the accessibility of objects that were either close to or far from the protagonist, and either relevant or irrelevant to the protagonist's current goal.

Surprisingly, almost all of the studies mentioned in the previous paragraph have one curious result in common: Most of them yielded additive effects of the spatial variable and the other variables. Spatial discontinuities, spatial inconsistencies, and spatial distance in the situation model hardly ever interacted with emotional, temporal, goal-related, causal, or other types of information represented in the situation model. Thus, a fairly large amount of experimental results obtained with very different paradigms converge on the same conclusion: The spatial dimension of situation models seems independent of other dimensions. This result is somewhat counterintuitive, at least as far as goal-related information is concerned. We conducted our experiments on spatial distance and goal relevance of objects (Bower & Rinck, 1999) expecting to find that objects spatially close to the protagonist are more accessible than distant ones because they have a higher probability of being involved in the goals and actions of the protagonist. Instead, we found that spatial proximity of an object increased its accessibility in addition to any increase caused by its goal relevance. Zwaan, van den Broek, Truitt, and Sundermeier (1996), however, found an interaction involving the spatial dimension. In their study, objects were more accessible if their locations were of potential causal relevance for later events: For instance, a pushpin that was lying on the floor, so the barefoot protagonist might step on it, was more accessible than a pushpin safely stored in a box. Thus, at least for the spatial and the causal dimension of situation models, the possibility of an interaction remains plausible. Further research will be needed to determine if spatial information is indeed represented independently of other information.

The Metrics of Spatial Situation Models. Speaking of spatial distance effects, one might ask exactly what type of spatial distance is represented in spatial situation models. Is it metric, Euclidean distance "as the crow flies"? In this case, the spatial situation model would reflect the metrics of the real world, such as distance being measurable on a ratio scale (e.g., in feet or meters). Alternatively, situation model distance might be categorical in nature, that is, divisions of a given distance into discrete units (e.g., rooms) between an object and the focus of attention would be represented. In this case, the number of rooms contained in a given distance rather than the size of the rooms would determine the spatial gradient of accessibility. The distinction between Euclidean distance and categorical distance lies at the heart of a deep theoretical controversy: Are spatial situation models analog representations, similar to mental images? Or should one think of them as more parsimonious and rather coarse representations? Before discussing this topic in more detail, I will review the empirical evidence related to it.

Although many authors have explicitly or implicitly assumed that situation models represent Euclidean distance, there are reasons to doubt this assumption. First, representing only categorical distance would be more parsimonious and much easier than representing fine-grained information such as Euclidean distance. Second, there is little empirical evidence for the representation of Euclidean distance. Most studies in this area confounded categorical and Euclidean distance. Moreover, an early study that tried to find direct evidence for Euclidean distance failed (Morrow et al., 1987). In this experiment, no distance effect on the accessibility of objects located in the situation model occurred at all, presumably because the experiment was not designed as a strong test of the situation model metrics. To supply such a test, we used the map-and-narrative task and constructed maps in which the two types of distance were unconfounded (Rinck et al., 1997). These maps contained paths leading through single path rooms that were either short or long, and paths through two path rooms that were either short or long. In this way, Euclidean distance (length of the path rooms) and categorical distance (number of path rooms) of different paths were varied orthogonally in the map. As in previous experiments, after memorizing the map, participants read stories containing motion sentences implying that the protagonist walked through a path room (or rooms) of one of these four kinds. A first surprising finding was that reading time for a motion sentence was longer when the implied path led through two rooms compared to one room. The size of the intermediate room (or rooms), that is, Euclidean distance traveled by the protagonist, had no effect on reading times at all. After each motion sentence, people read an anaphoric sentence that referred to an object in the part of the path room that was near to the protagonist or far away from him or her. Reading times of these anaphoric sentences yielded a similar finding. Metric distance between the object referred to and the protagonist had no effect whatsoever on anaphor reading times. Rather, reading times varied solely with categorical distance: References to an object that was one room away from the protagonist were understood more readily than reference to an object that was two rooms away regardless of the Euclidean distances involved. Thus, reading and anaphor look-up times were determined by categorical segments of space (i.e., rooms), not Euclidean metric distance. Paradoxically, in this situation people had acquired all the necessary metric information from studying the map, and they used the information to complete two other tasks: They were able to respond to interspersed test probes asking which of two objects was closer to the current location of the protagonist, and they could draw (after the experiment) a correctly scaled map of the building. However, they seemed not to use this metric knowledge during reading.

In a closely related series of experiments that employed a variation of the object layout task, Langston, Kramer, and Glenberg (1998) provided evidence that their participants constructed spatial situation models from descriptions of spatial arrangements. They failed, however, to find evidence for Euclidean distance being represented in the situation models. These authors had their participants read (or listen to) texts that described the object-by-object construction of a spatial layout, for instance, the arrangement of objects in an aquarium. According to the text, a recently mentioned critical object ended up adjacent to a previously introduced target object or farther away from it. Importantly, the amount of spatial distance between the critical object and the target object was never described explicitly. Langston et al. (1998) reasoned that – assuming that situation models represent Euclidean distances – the target object should be more accessible in memory and noticed by the participants if it is close to the focus of attention, that is, the critical object. However, in a series of seven experiments, they failed to find consistent support for this noticing hypothesis, which provides indirect evidence against the representation of Euclidean distance in situation models.

Taken together, the few studies that directly addressed this topic suggest that the metrics of spatial situation models might be rather simple, reflecting the use of categorical distance rather than Euclidean distance during reading. Despite the null effects of Euclidean distance on accessibility, however, it would be premature to conclude that the metrics of spatial situation models are generally restricted to an ordinal level. Often, the information supplied by the text and the reader's prior knowledge will be too inefficiently specified to construct situation models precise enough to reflect the Euclidean metric of the world. In some cases, however, both text and prior knowledge will supply sufficient information and the reader's goals will warrant the construction of detailed spatial situation models reflecting Euclidean distance. For instance, texts like the ones used by Rinck et al. (1997) or Langston et al. (1998) might specify the Euclidean distances involved (e.g., by having the room sizes measured by a decorator) and the readers might be motivated to represent this information by expecting comprehension questions regarding it. These cases may be rather rare, however. In general, the results reviewed in this section suggest that humans are remarkably flexible and adaptive in how they represent, retrieve, and use their knowledge, in this case knowledge about spatial distance.

Theoretical Views of Spatial Situation Models. The nature of the memory representation for a spatial situation model is a topic of intense interest and debate among cognitive scientists in general, and text comprehension researchers in particular. In general, two classes of models have been proposed to explain how situation models are constructed, updated, and represented in memory: imagelike, analog representations versus abstract representations such as associative networks and connectionist models. Proponents of analog perceptual symbol systems include Barsalou (1999), Glenberg (1997), and Paivio (1990). They propose that the basic elements of a spatial representation are analog percepts of regions and subregions of space and percepts of the included objects and their locations. Following this view, the representation of a map or building layout such as the ones used by Morrow and his colleagues would be like an analog, metric image. During narrative reading, this analog image would be called into service to represent the situation referenced by the texts. The sentences of the text would then be considered as instructions to run a mental simulation of the characters' actions within this situation model. Focus on the protagonist and foregrounding of objects spatially close to the protagonist might then be represented as a spotlight of intense activation of subregions within the overall image, perhaps by zooming into those regions and enlarging the objects contained therein (see Barsalou, 1999; Kosslyn, 1980).

An alternative view of how spatial information – and therefore spatial situation models – is represented in memory employs more symbolic and amodal representations, namely associative networks and connectionist procedures (Anderson & Bower, 1973; Bower & Rinck, 2001; Haenggi et al., 1995; Kintsch, 1988, 1998; Hirtle & Jonides, 1985; Langston & Trabasso, 1998; Langston, Trabasso, & Magliano, 1998; McNamara, 1991; McNamara, Hardy, & Hirtle, 1989: Stevens & Coupe, 1978). According to this view, the building map just mentioned would be represented as a hierarchical structure of the perceptual elements and concepts encoding the map of the building, with links between elements reflecting their geometric relationships. For the building maps used in the map-and-narrative tasks, this hierarchy would encode the rooms of the building in spatial relationships to one another, with connecting doors between some adjacent rooms, and with links to the objects contained in each room. We have recently shown how a model of this type may be used to explain the spatial gradient of accessibility and other spatial effects observed in many experiments (Bower & Rinck, 2001). Figure 9.3 sketches a fragment of the kind of hierarchy we used to represent participants' long-term memory of the laboratory building depicted in Figure 9.2. Symbols in Figure 9.3 represent perceptual objects (building, rooms, objects), and links between symbols represent a labeled spatial relationship (e.g., "contains," "north-of," "connecting door") between the nodes. These links can be used to retrieve some idea (symbol) from another idea (symbol) when it is activated by an internal or external cue.

Readers will use this memory structure when they later read brief stories describing events occurring in the building. When the reader processes a sentence such as "Wilbur walked from the laboratory into the wash room," the sentence is entered into his or her working memory; in turn, the concepts in the proposition transmit activation to the corresponding elements in the memory structure (e.g., the dashed lines going to the room symbols in Figure 9.3). Additionally, the reader will spontaneously draw some direct, low-level inferences warranted by the motion sentence, specifically, the protagonist's path and current location. In the present case, these inferences would be that "Wilbur walked through the storage rooms" and "Wilbur is now located in the wash room." These inferences will cause further activation to spread to the symbols representing the actor's path and present location. It is this inferred, second source of activation that accounts for the distance gradient of priming, that is, greater priming of the current location and some drop-off in priming for the path and source room. This activation on a connected node is presumed to accumulate rapidly once a concept is entered into working memory; it is also presumed to fade away quickly as time passes without that concept being used. This differential activation of propositions and inferences in working memory and their associated symbolic elements in long-term memory corresponds to

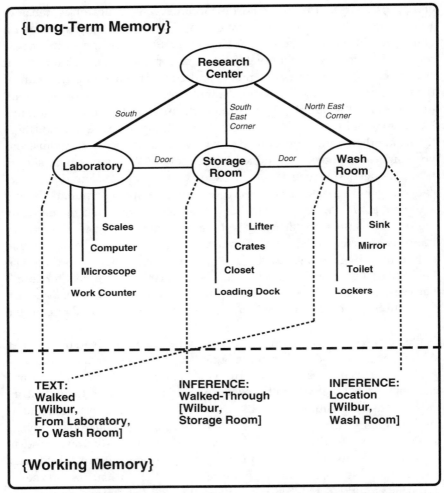

FIGURE 9.3. Part of a hierarchical associative network encoding spatial information acquired from a map such as the one shown in Figure 9.2 (adapted from Bower & Rinck, 2001). See text for explanations.

the notions of focus of attention or foregrounding within the situation model.

Which position describes the nature of spatial situation models more appropriately, the analog view or the symbolic one? To summarize, I believe that the empirical data currently available do not allow a definite answer, but that the data may be explained using more parsimonious nonanalog representations, and that the question may not be the most useful one, anyway. First, hardly any of the experiments reported in the literature and reviewed here was designed to distinguish between analog and symbolic representations of spatial situation models. Instead, most researchers seemed to subscribe to one view or the other, failing to notice that the results could also be explained by the alternative view. The only studies that might be considered directly relevant to this question are the ones on the metrics of spatial situation models described earlier. These studies are very scarce, however, and the one by Rinck et al. (1997) has not been replicated yet, so it would be premature to draw strong conclusions from them. Despite this lack of decisive data, however, I would like to argue that the available data allow at least one conclusion: All of the effects observed so far may be explained by nonanalog representations such as the ones contained in the models proposed by Bower and Rinck (2001), Haenggi et al. (1995), or Kintsch (1988, 1998). Thus, there seems no need to assume that readers create complex and detailed analog representations, if simpler and more parsimonious nonanalog ones suffice. This is most obvious for the extreme case of imagelike analog representations ("movies in the head"). Although people are capable of constructing detailed mental images from texts (for reviews of the literature on mental imagery, see Reisberg & Heuer, Chapter 2, or Denis & Kosslyn, 1999), it is quite unlikely that they will go through this effortful and time-consuming process regularly during reading. Thus, several researchers have pointed out differences between situation models and mental images (Bryant & Tversky, 1995; Denis, 1996; Johnson-Laird, 1996). Recently, we have added yet another difference (Rinck, Denis, & Bower, 2001): In this study, participants were asked to imagine themselves walking through a building. The architecture of the building was learned from a map, and the rooms were varied as in the Rinck et al. (1997) study. Thus, the imagined walks from a source room to a location room led through one or two path rooms, which were either short or long, thereby varying categorical distance and Euclidean distance independently of each other. Please remember that in the narrative reading situation studied in the earlier experiments (Rinck et al., 1997), reading times of motion sentences and reaction times to subsequent test probes had revealed spatial distance effects of categorical distance (number of rooms) without any effects of Euclidean distance (size of rooms). This was quite different in the recent mental imagery study (Rinck et al., 2001), in which Euclidean distance affected both dependent variables: It took participants longer to imagine motions through long rooms compared to short ones, and they took longer to retrieve objects from memory if Euclidean distance between the objects and the current focus of attention increased. The fact that Euclidean distance affected reading times and reaction times in the mental imagery task, but not in the narrative reading task, speaks strongly against equating spatial situation models and mental images. Moreover, Zwaan and Radvansky (1998) mention another convincing argument against the regular creation of detailed mental images during reading:

> ... and it takes participants at least 3 s to construct an elaborate image of, for example, a canary. Below the 3-s threshold, only rudimentary images may be formed (Marschark & Cornoldi, 1991). Given that normal word reading times are at least 10 times faster, it seems unlikely that readers typically generate detailed visual images during comprehension. (p. 178)

Finally, trying to determine the analog, imagelike versus nonanalog representation of situation models in memory may not be the most fruitful research question after all. Pursuing this question presupposes a premise that is likely to be unwarranted, namely that situation models are represented in a single format. In contrast to this assumption, the available data suggest that readers are very flexible in the way they create and update spatial situation models and represent them in memory. Depending on many factors such as reading goals and instructions, readers might limit their representational efforts to a rough, symbolic representation, or invest the cognitive resources needed to form a detailed, imagelike representation of the described spatial relations. In addition to these variable within-person factors, more stable individual differences in verbal and spatial abilities as well as motivation will determine the construction of spatial situation models. In fact, these individual differences will not only affect the level of detail represented in the model, they will also determine if a situation model is created at all. In the next section, I will review some of the individual differences relevant to spatial situation models. Moreover, for situations involving several texts or different media, there is no need to assume the same level of detail in their representations. This is certainly true of the map-and-narrative task, in which a distinction must be made between the way spatial information is represented in the memory representation of the map and the way it is represented in the situation model created during reading. It might well be that the map is represented analogically, for instance, as a perceptual image, whereas the situation model is symbolic, and not nearly so detailed because it integrates visual information from the map with verbal information derived from the text.

In closing this section, I would like to reiterate what situation models were originally supposed to be: They were incorporated into theories of text comprehension because it became obvious that readers do not primarily construct a representation of the text itself, but a representation of the situation described by the text, enriched by the readers' prior knowledge (for instance, see the evolution of the concept from van Dijk & Kintsch, 1983, to Kintsch, 1988). Thus, situation models in general, and also spatial situation models in particular, are defined by their contents rather than by their representational format. I am convinced that this is still the best way to think about situation models. Confusing this definition with questions regarding the representational format will hurt the concept of situation models both empirically and theoretically: On the empirical level, failures to find evidence for analog representations might erroneously be taken as evidence against the validity of situation models. Something similar seems to have happened to the concept of mental models as suggested by Johnson-Laird (1983). On the theoretical level, it would be inconsistent and confusing to define two representational levels of text comprehension by their contents (the surface level and the text base), whereas the situation model would be defined by its format. Thus, although future research might very well concentrate on the possibly analog nature of situation models, I believe that it would be wise to consider it a fascinating feature rather than a defining characteristic.

Individual Differences in Creating Spatial Situation Models. As mentioned earlier, readers obviously do not always construct spatial situation models when reading texts. If they do depends on several requirements, which are related to the text, to the instructions, to the readers' goals, and to their abilities. Morrow (1994) lists a number of the requirements that must be met before the construction of a situation model may be expected to occur. He suggests that readers will only be able to construct situation models if the text provides enough information, if they have sufficient prior knowledge about the situation described by the text, if the way the text organizes the information matches the way the readers' prior knowledge is organized, and if the construction of situation models serves the readers' goals. The first prerequisite was demonstrated by Mani and Johnson-Laird (1982) who showed that readers did not construct spatial situation models for indeterminate descriptions of spatial arrangements. The second requirement is illustrated by studies comparing experts to novices (see Morrow, 1994). These studies revealed that experts are often able to create situation models from difficult texts, whereas novices are not. The results reported by Dutke

(1993, 1994) suggest the same conclusion: People can use prior knowledge about schematic object arrangements to create spatial situation models even for indeterminate descriptions. The third prerequisite is related to experts as well: Their advantage in creating situation models diminishes if the text does not organize the information in a way compatible with the experts' organization. For instance, Coughlin and Patel (1987) showed that experienced physicians usually recall case descriptions better than medical students. This advantage disappears, however, if the descriptions are scrambled rather than organized in terms of the usual temporal structure of the disease. Finally, the fourth requirement was demonstrated impressively by Foertsch and Gernsbacher (1994). They directed the goals of their participants by giving them different types of comprehension questions following reading of the very same texts. The results showed that the participants worked very effectively by drawing only those inferences that they knew would be probed later on. Most importantly, they did not create inferences necessary for the construction of a situation model, if the comprehension questions referred only to information represented on the surface level or the text base level.

In addition to these situational variables, a number of more stable factors related to readers' individual differences have also been suggested to explain differences in the construction of spatial situation models from texts. Age is one of these factors, and it was investigated intensively by Morrow and his colleagues (e.g., Morrow, Leirer, & Altieri, 1992; Morrow et al., 1994, 1997). Their studies revealed that older and younger readers followed similar strategies in creating and updating spatial situation models, for instance, by focusing attention on the protagonist of a narrative. However, older readers' updating processes were generally slower than those of the younger ones, as indicated by probe reaction times and reading times. This disadvantage of the older readers increased with increasing difficulty of updating, for instance, when spatial distance between a probed object and the focus of attention increased. This finding suggests that older readers shifted their focus of attention more slowly as they updated their spatial situation model. Interestingly, Morrow, Altieri, and Leirer (1992) found that older readers' expertise may be able to make up for their age-related declines in cognitive capacity. In their research with younger and older pilots and nonpilots, aviation experience helped older pilots to process aviation-related information efficiently despite their age. Although this research is highly relevant, its quasiexperimental nature leaves an important question unanswered: What exactly is it that declines in age to produce age-related differences? Morrow and his colleagues administered a number of tests to answer this question, and their older participants usually differed from the younger ones in verbal abilities as well as visuospatial abilities.

Obviously, one would expect verbal abilities and visuospatial abilities to be crucial for the construction of spatial situation models. Indeed, differences in these abilities have been investigated most often. For instance, Long, Oppy, and Seely (1997) compared participants with low versus high reading skills (as measured by the verbal portion of the Scholastic Aptitude Test) with regard to their comprehension of two-sentence narratives. Long et al. (1997) found that readers with high reading skills made more of those inferences that are necessary for a coherent situation model than less-skilled readers, whereas the two groups did not differ with regard to inferences at the text base level. Individual differences in visuospatial abilities have also been investigated in a number of studies. These differences are described in detail in Hegarty and Waller (Chapter 4) and Halpern and Collaer (Chapter 5), therefore, I will only summarize some of the most important studies related to text comprehension rather than describing them in detail. In one of the few studies examining both verbal and visuospatial abilities, Haenggi et al. (1995) gave their participants a reading comprehension test as well as tests of two-dimensional and three-dimensional spatial imagery abilities. Afterwards, their participants completed the learning phase of the map-and-narrative task by studying either a map or a list of rooms and objects. They then read narratives and replied to test probes as in the studies by Morrow et al. (1987, 1989). Haenggi et al. (1995) found that reaction times to the test probes correlated with reading ability after both types of learning media. Three-dimensional spatial imagery ability was the best predictor of reaction times after studying a map, whereas two-dimensional ability was the best predictor after studying a list. Thus, differences in visuospatial abilities interacted with learning from different media as a prerequisite for creating a spatial situation model, rather than with updating of the model during reading. The latter result is compatible with the results reported by de Vega (1994) who did not find qualitative differences between readers with high versus low visuospatial abilities. Instead, he reported an overall difference, that is, high-ability participants produced faster reaction times and lower error rates than low-ability participants in all experimental conditions.

The results reported by de Vega (1994) illustrate one of the problems associated with individual differences in the construction of spatial situation models: Differences in verbal or visuospatial abilities are rarely associated with qualitative differences in processing. Instead, they often produce highly predictable, and therefore potentially trivial, main effects.

An interesting exception was recently reported by Dutke (1999). He used the object layout task introduced by Mani and Johnson-Laird (1982) to investigate the *cross-over effect* in more detail. According to this effect, readers will construct a spatial situation model of an object layout from a determinate description of the layout, whereas they will limit themselves to a representation of the text if they receive only indeterminate descriptions. However, Dutke (1999) showed that this effect occurred only for participants low in visuospatial abilities, whereas high-ability participants were able to create a spatial situation model in both situations. Dutke (1999) suggested that this differential effect may explain why some previous studies failed to replicate the cross-over effect: Most participants in these studies were undergraduate students who, on average, are high in visuospatial abilities.

So far, I have been deliberately vague about what the general term visuospatial ability is supposed to mean. The reason for this vagueness may be found in a second problem affecting research on individual differences in visuospatial abilities: The results have been interpreted in a variety of theoretical frameworks. For instance, some authors speak of *visuospatial capacity* (e.g., Denis & Cocude, 1997; Denis & Kosslyn, 1999), whereas others use the terms *spatial imagery ability* (Haenggi et al., 1994, 1995), *spatial ability* (Morrow et al., 1994), or *spatial visualization ability* (Morrow, Leirer, & Altieri, 1992). Yet others argue for the role of visuospatial working memory in particular (Logie & Della Sala, Chapter 3, or Shah & Miyake, 1996). Of course, all of these constructs are similar and more or less correlated. In fact, some of them showed correlations as high as $r = .68$ (see Shah & Miyake, 1996, Exp. 2). Therefore, it is quite uncertain what exactly we are dealing with in correlational studies of the relationship between visuospatial abilities and text comprehension. A fair amount of additional research will be necessary to clarify these issues.

Until a consensus can be reached, I personally favor studies of visuospatial working memory, mostly for methodological reasons. Unlike the other approaches, these studies may employ two complementary methodologies, thereby validating the empirical results and the concept of visuospatial working memory. One of these methods follows a correlational approach, whereas the other is experimental in nature. Using the correlational approach, one may measure people's spatial working memory span as well as their verbal span. A verbal span test has been available since 1980, when Daneman and Carpenter introduced their reading span task, which was later improved upon by Waters and Caplan (1996) who suggested a *sentence span task*. In addition, Shah and Miyake (1996) have developed a spatial span task that is formally equivalent to the sentence span task. Thus, readers' spatial and verbal working memory spans may be measured in highly comparable ways, and both may be correlated with indicators of text comprehension. Using the experimental approach, one may vary the type of secondary task that is given to participants while they read texts. For instance, secondary tasks may be verbal, spatial, or both in nature. In a yet unpublished study, I found that a spatial secondary task (keeping dot patterns in working memory) did indeed affect the creation and updating of spatial situation models in ways different from a verbal task (keeping consonant strings in working memory). A similar approach was chosen by Pazzaglia and Cornoldi (1999), when they examined the effects of four different secondary tasks (verbal, visual, spatial-sequential, or spatial-simultaneous) on the recall of abstract, visual, and spatial texts. Finally, in an elegant study by Friedman and Miyake (2000), both the experimental and the correlational approach were used. As mentioned previously, they had their participants read narratives that varied in spatial and causal demands while responding to on-line test probes related to spatial or causal information. Spatial demands were manipulated by letting the narratives take place in a building with a simple layout (one floor) or a complex layout (two floors). Causal demands were varied by deleting causally relevant sentences, thereby creating the need for demanding causal inferences. In addition, the participants' verbal working memory capacity and their spatial capacity were measured using the verbal span task and the spatial span task, respectively. Friedman and Miyake (2000) found highly similar effects when they compared both approaches: Performance with spatial test probes was affected by spatial, but not causal, demands, and performance with causal probes was influenced by causal, but not spatial, demands. Likewise, spatial probe performance was correlated with spatial working memory span, and causal probe performance was correlated with verbal working memory span.

To summarize, future research will have to determine if the experimental approach varying secondary tasks or text demands and the correlational approach using span tasks do indeed yield comparable results. The correlational approach tries to measure general limitations of people's visuospatial working memory, whereas the experimental approach varies working memory loads within these limits. Therefore, one might expect to find more differences between the approaches than existing studies have revealed so far.

The Neuropsychology of Spatial Situation Models. Much of the recent research on the neuropsychological basis of spatial situation models has focused on two questions: Do processes of deep text comprehension such as the construction and updating of situation models involve brain areas other than the traditional left-hemispheric areas of Broca and Wernecke? And does the construction of spatial situation models involve areas that are known to be active in other spatial tasks, for instance, in spatial imagery? Although this line of research is still in its infancy, recent neuroimaging studies using Positron-Emission Tomography (PET) or functional Magnetic Resonance Imaging (fMRI) suggest that the answer to both questions is yes.

For instance, Robertson, Gernsbacher, Guidotti, Robertson, Irwin, Mock, and Campana (2000) used a simple manipulation to address the first question. They presented a list of sentences to their subjects during fMRI. By using only indefinite articles in the sentences (e.g., *a* grandmother, *a* child, . . .) the sentences made up an unconnected list. By using definite articles instead (*the* grandmother, *the* child, . . .), the same sentences became similar to connected discourse. Robertson et al. (2000) found that comprehending connected sentences, compared to unrelated ones, created more neural activity in the frontal lobe of the right than the left hemisphere. Moreover, increased right-hemispheric activity has also been reported in other discourse comprehension tasks, for instance, in evaluating how well each sentence fits into an ongoing narrative (Robertson, Gernsbacher, & Guidotti, 1999). Other studies have shown that right-hemispheric areas are activated during the integration of information in comprehension of discourse (e.g., Fletcher, Happe, Frith, Baker, Dolan, Frackowiak, & Frith, 1995; St. George, Kutas, Martinez, & Sereno, 1999). These neuroimaging studies are augmented by evidence from brain lesion studies. For instance, Romani and Martin (1999) studied a patient who suffered from a left-frontal hematoma, yielding severe problems in memory for isolated words. Despite these problems, the patients' comprehension of and memory for stories was normal.

Regarding the second question, several studies have related patterns of brain activity observed during comprehension of spatial information to patterns known to occur during other spatial processing tasks. For instance, Mellet and his colleagues studied the construction of mental images from verbal input. Mellet, Tzourio, Crivello, Joliot, Denis, and Mazoyer (1996) found that creating three-dimensional mental images from verbal information (spatial prepositions) produced activation in brain areas also known to be involved in the processing of real visible stimuli. Mellet, Tzourio-Mazoyer, Bricogne, Mazoyer, Kosslyn, and Denis (2000) found that during an imagery task, creating mental images from verbal descriptions activated the same areas as creating them from pictures. Likewise, Carpenter, Just,

Keller, Eddy, and Thulborn (1999) reported that comprehending sentences that contain spatial information activated brain regions that would also be active during spatial tasks such as mental rotation.

Admittedly, many of the existing PET and fMRI studies suffer from technical constraints that do not allow for experimental designs as elaborated, controlled, and counterbalanced as one would expect of the behavioral experiments described earlier. Moreover, the tasks and materials are often anything but naturalistic. Therefore, it seems wise to conclude that during text comprehension and situation model construction, readers may activate right-hemispheric brain regions usually used in other spatial tasks. Whether they do so regularly during everyday text comprehension will have to be determined by many additional studies. Given the rapid expansion of neuropsychological research, we may expect numerous interesting findings from these studies.

Spatial Situation Models Created From Instructional Text. As I mentioned earlier, there are not many studies that addressed the construction of spatial situation models from instructional texts such as textbooks, instructions, or manuals. One might argue that many of the studies reviewed earlier did present expository rather than narrative texts, for instance, the object layout descriptions used by Mani and Johnson-Laird (1982) or Ehrlich and Johnson-Laird (1982). Indeed, the descriptions studied by the participants of these studies lack all the characteristics of narratives, such as protagonists with goals, actions, and emotions. Moreover, the participants read the descriptions in order to learn the layout of the objects. However, I hesitate to call these texts instructional because they did not contain any information that the participants might find useful outside the scope of the experiment. Therefore, the remainder of this part will focus on research with instructional texts that did contain potentially useful information. Much of this instructional research has employed texts in combination with illustrations, diagrams, or graphs. Within this research tradition, interest has focused mainly on the nontextual components accompanying the text. Although this line of research is clearly relevant to the creation and updating of spatial situation models, I will review it only briefly here because much of it is described in detail in Wickens, Vincow, and Yeh, Chapter 10; Shah, Freedman, and Vekiri, Chapter 11; and Mayer, Chapter 12 of this volume. The reasons for the lack of spatial situation model research with purely textual materials are not entirely clear to me, but I suspect that several factors contribute to it. First, researchers in text comprehension have traditionally been more interested in narratives, whereas many instructional psychologists investigating learning from instructional texts have not yet applied the concept of situation models to their work. I will try to do that in this part of the chapter. Second, even though much of the research exploring learning from instructional texts might be interpreted in terms of situation model theories, it did not address spatial relations. Instead, more abstract relations are often at the core of what readers have to comprehend when studying an instructional text. Finally, and possibly most importantly, it may be difficult to investigate situation models constructed from instructional texts because in many cases, readers will not be able to create them. We often read textbooks, instructions, manuals, or other materials to learn about a new knowledge domain, bringing very little prior knowledge with us. Moreover, in the attempt to apply what we read, we often have to experience that we did not fully understand the text, despite careful and repeated reading. Thus, the essential requirements for the construction of situation models are often not met: Deep comprehension based on text information combined with prior knowledge.

Despite these factors conspiring against the creation of spatial situation models from instructional text, there is evidence that they do indeed exist. To support this claim, I will briefly describe two types of instructions not covered in other chapters of this book: assembly instructions and spatial navigation instructions. Both of them differ from narrative texts in at least two important aspects: They are primarily intended to elicit actions on the side of the reader, and the reader's level of comprehension may be measured directly by observing the actions (e.g., the reader's success in assembling the object described by the instructions).

If you have ever tried to assemble a piece of furniture that came in many pieces tightly packed in a cardboard box, you probably know how important helpful *assembly instructions* are. Generally, these will be included in the box, and most probably, the instructional text will be accompanied by diagrams and illustrations (in fact, sometimes there are only diagrams and no text at all). Therefore, research on the comprehension of assembly instructions has focused on the use of diagrams included in these instructions. It is assumed that diagrams contained in assembly instructions serve at least two purposes: They facilitate the construction of a situation model of the current assembly step, and they improve mapping of the model to the object under construction (see Novick & Morse, 2000). Marcus, Cooper, and Sweller (1996) compared the effectiveness of purely textual instructions to purely diagrammatic ones. In three experiments, the participants received instructions for the connection and spatial layout of electronic resistors in parallel or in series, either by reading a text or by studying a diagram. All connection problems involved the same number of connections, but the parallel problems forced the participants to consider more possible connection points between resistors than did the series problems. Thus, the parallel problems should be more difficult because they put a heavier working memory load on the participants, at least when they receive textual instructions. With diagrammatic instructions, Marcus et al. (1996) expected no difference between parallel and series problems because the diagram showed all possible connection points, therefore, they did not have to be held in working memory. In fact, this pattern of results was observed in three experiments, indicating that diagrams were particularly helpful in more complicated assembly situations. Novick and Morse (2000) went a step further by comparing as series of step-by-step diagrams to a single final-state diagram. Their participants tried to create origami objects from instructions that consisted of text only, text plus final-state diagram, or text plus step-by-step diagrams (the last of which was identical to the final-state diagram). The quality of the instructions and the spatial situation models created from them was asserted by comparing the objects folded by the participants to the intended objects. Not surprisingly, Novick and Morse (2000) found that the text-only instructions yielded the poorest results, whereas the instructions including step-by-step diagrams were most effective. The final-state diagram was just as helpful as the step-by-step diagrams, however, when it was possible to extract the individual assembly steps from the final diagram. Again, the results were interpreted in terms of diagrams reducing the load on working memory during the assembly process.

Glenberg and Robertson (1999) examined the effectiveness of pictorial information accompanying instructional text in more detail. They chose a *spatial navigation* task in which the participants learned how to use a compass and a map when trying to locate objects (mountains) in the environment. Although the experiment was conducted in the laboratory, it allowed for a realistic test of the participants' ability to locate the objects by means of a compass and a map. Four groups of participants received different types of instructions after a verbal pretest: One group simply listened to the audiotrack of a videotape describing, in detail, the critical parts of a compass (e.g., direction of travel arrows) and the critical parts of a map (e.g., the compass rose). The second group did the same, and afterwards read the written version of the audiotrack. The third group saw the videotape including the audiotrack together with pictures of the compass and the map. The fourth group saw the videotape, too. In addition, when an object or an operation was introduced, an actor's hands showed the object or the operation. According to Glenberg and Robertson (1999), these conditions differ in the ease of indexing they allow, that is, how easy it is to relate terms and names contained in the text to parts of real objects and to actions performed with these objects. The fourth condition allows for easiest indexing because it is supplied by the actor's hands. The third condition allows for self-indexing by imagining the actions. In contrast, the purely textual conditions make indexing very difficult. Afterwards receiving the instructions, all participants took a verbal posttest and a behavioral test: They tried to locate mountains using a compass and a map. Results of the verbal posttest suggested that the four groups of participants had learned equivalent amounts of abstract knowledge. In the behavioral test, however, the fourth group outperformed the other groups in several performance measures: They read and followed new directions faster, referred to background information less frequently, and performed the test using the compass and map more accurately. Glenberg and Robertson interpret these results to indicate that instructions in general, and illustrated ones in particular, are only helpful if they allow indexing, that is, if they allow readers to identify the real-world referents of objects and actions mentioned in the instructions. Slightly rephrased, this means that instructions have to allow for the construction of a situation model.

Route directions are a particular type of spatial navigation instructions that probably every reader of this chapter has given and received many times in his or her life. Moreover, as recipients of route directions, most of us have experienced that these directions differ greatly in content and quality, sometimes causing frustration instead of successful navigation to the goal location. Despite the importance of route directions for everyday life, however, only a few studies have addressed their construction and comprehension. Early studies of route directions attempted to compare the mental representations derived from descriptions written from a route perspective as compared to descriptions from a survey perspective. For instance, Perrig and Kintsch (1985) described the layout of a small town by mentioning the local attractions, either as they were encountered along a possible route through the town or as they were viewed from a bird's eye perspective. They found that the linearly organized route description yielded a more coherent representation of the text base, but not a better situation model. A similar conclusion was reported by Taylor and Tversky (1992). Their participants also read descriptions of spatial scenarios (e.g., a city or a zoo) written from a route perspective or from a survey perspective; other participants received a map. Taylor and Tversky found that the two types of verbal descriptions yielded different representations of the text, but similar situation models. Moreover, these models were also comparable to the model created from studying the map. The functional quality of different route directions was empirically tested by Denis, Pazzaglia,

Cornoldi, and Bertolo (1999). They first had inhabitants of the city of Venice, Italy, describe possible (foot-)ways from predefined starting points to goal points in Venice. The quality of these naturally occurring descriptions was then rated by other inhabitants. Good and poor descriptions were selected according to these ratings. In addition, Denis et al. (1999) created short "skeletal" descriptions that contained only those components, that were judged to be important by a majority of the judges (for a detailed description of the procedure used to create skeletal descriptions, see Daniel & Denis, 1998). The functional quality of good, poor, and skeletal descriptions was examined by a behavioral test: New participants, who did not know Venice, were asked to navigate through the city using the descriptions. This test yielded clear-cut results: Both the good descriptions and the skeletal ones yielded fewer direction errors, fewer hesitations, and fewer requests for assistance than the bad descriptions. There was no systematic difference between good descriptions and skeletal descriptions. Thus, one may conclude that short descriptions containing only the most important information (e.g., landmarks and directions of turns) were sufficient for the creation of a correct spatial model and its application during navigation. The question of what exactly makes good descriptions and skeletal descriptions superior to poor ones may be tentatively answered by referring to Allen (2000). Allen created good route directions by applying general principles of communication: He found that wayfinding was more successful if route directions were given in the correct temporal-spatial order, if they concentrated on information related to choice points, and if they employed delimiters that were well known to most recipients.

To summarize, the few studies reviewed here suggest that readers do indeed create spatial situation models from instructional texts, if the readers' knowledge and the features of the texts allow for it. Given the possible lack of previous knowledge on the readers' side and the more abstract contents of instructional texts compared to narrative texts, it is hardly surprising that the construction and updating of spatial situation models from instructional texts is more difficult. However, the studies reviewed here also suggest some remedies to this problem. Among them, the use of appropriate diagrams and pictures as well as the correct spatial-temporal structuring of texts have been identified.

Question 3: What Are the Limitations of Spatial Situation Models?

After showing that spatial situation models exist and after identifying at least some of their critical features, the logical – not necessarily chronological – next step would be to identify possible limitations of their importance and usefulness for explaining text comprehension. Several attempts to do just this at differing levels of generality have been reported: Some authors questioned the significance of situation models in general, whereas others dealt specifically with the spatial aspect of situation models. The general critiques (e.g., McKoon & Ratcliff, 1992) will not be described here because others have already reviewed the extensive evidence for the validity of situation models (e.g., Graesser et al., 1994; Zwaan & Radvansky, 1998). Other, more specific studies examined the significance of spatial information represented in situation models, and compared it to other aspects such as temporal, causal, or emotional information. From these studies, two rather disappointing conclusions may be drawn: Spatial aspects of a described situation are not necessarily represented in the situation model, and other aspects of the situation may be more important and monitored more closely than spatial aspects.

The first conclusion seems at odds with all the studies reviewed in this chapter. However, these studies merely showed that readers are able to construct fairly detailed spatial situation models from the materials used in these particular experiments. If they would do the same in more natural reading situations, such as reading a novel at home for pleasure, is a completely different question. Creating detailed spatial situation models may be an ability used in particular situations rather than a habitual behavior occurring regularly during reading. In fact, some authors have criticized the materials and instructions in experiments employing the object layout task for placing undue emphasis on spatial relations while ignoring others. Most prominently, Zwaan and van Oostendorp (1993, 1994) have argued for the use of literary texts such as short stories and novels instead of the artificial text segments used in previous studies. Their participants read the opening pages of a mystery novel, and they failed to make spatial inferences necessary for the construction of a spatial situation model, if instructed to read "as they normally would read a mystery novel." If they were explicitly instructed to "construct a mental map of the situation," they made more spatial inferences but they also read more slowly. Similarly, Hakala (1999) found that readers did not make spatial inferences to update locations while reading naturalistic texts unless they were instructed to pay attention to spatial details (but see Levine & Klin, 2001, for a recent demonstration of counterevidence to this claim). Zwaan and van Oostendorp (1993, 1994) also suggested that spatial information might be monitored more closely and encoded in memory more reliably if it was causally relevant. This suggestion was confirmed by Zwaan et al. (1996, see previous discussion). The map-and-narrative task has also been criticized, namely for supplying readers with an artificially high level of prior spatial knowledge. Accordingly, Zwaan et al. (1998) found that spatial disconti-nuities contained in narratives yielded increases in reading times if partic-ipants had studied a map of the spatial scenario before reading. Without prior map learning, no increases due to spatial discontinuities occurred. In a related study employing the map-and-narrative task, we (Rinck, Wolf, & Hasebrook, 2000) observed a spatial distance effect (higher accessibility of objects in the location room compared to objects in an adjacent room) only if the text recently mentioned the current location of the protagonist. Incidentally, the latter requirement was regularly met in previous stud-ies using the map-and-narrative task because accessibility of rooms and objects was always tested directly after a motion sentence, which focused readers' attention on the changing location of the protagonist.

The second conclusion regarding the relative importance of spatial in-formation compared to other dimensions of situation models follows from studies investigating the multidimensionality of situation models (e.g., Zwaan, Langston, & Graesser, 1995; Zwaan, Magliano, & Graesser, 1995, Zwaan et al., 1998). In the studies by Zwaan and his colleagues, discon-tinuities in the space, time, protagonist, causation, and intentionality di-mensions of situation models were examined simultaneously. It turned out that spatial discontinuities yielded the weakest effects, which were not al-ways statistically significant. Accordingly, Zwaan et al. concluded that the spatial dimension of situation models is probably less important than the other dimensions. A similar conclusion may be reached from recent results observed by Andrea Hähnel and myself (Rinck & Hähnel, 2000). We used the inconsistency paradigm to study spatial, temporal, emotional, causal, and goal-related inconsistencies in a single experiment. Of all five dimen-sions, spatial inconsistencies yielded the weakest effect, whereas temporal and emotional inconsistencies yielded the strongest. Finally, both Rinck and Weber (2001) and Scott Rich and Taylor (2000) observed that location shifts yielded weaker effects on narrative comprehension than character shifts, concluding that the spatial aspects of a situation are less important to the situation model than the characters involved in the situation.

CONCLUDING REMARKS: THE FUTURE OF SPATIAL SITUATION MODELS

Is there a future for spatial situation models in research and theories of text comprehension? I believe not, if we are thinking about purely spatial models. These might have been appropriate as representations of the materials used in early studies (e.g., Ehrlich & Johnson-Laird, 1982; Mani & Johnson-Laird, 1982). For more complex and ecologically valid texts, however, it does not seem appropriate to think of models that represent only a single dimension of the described situation. Instead, as Zwaan and Radvansky (1998) stated, "The time has now come for researchers to begin to take the multidimensionality of situation models seriously" (p. 162). As for the spatial dimension of situation models, this might be achieved by examining it in conjunction with temporal, causal, emotional, goal-related, and other information contained in texts. The studies by Zwaan and his colleagues mentioned earlier (Zwaan, Langston, & Graesser, 1995; Zwaan, Magliano, & Graesser, 1995, Zwaan et al., 1998) come closest to this goal. The regressional approach used in these studies should be augmented by experimental studies in which several dimensions are varied independently of each other (e.g., with regard to their continuity). Hopefully, these studies will be able to combine experimental control with more natural materials than have been used so far. Using naturalistic materials, a number of different research questions seem worthwhile to me. Despite the fact that were are now looking back on 20 years of research in situation models, our answers to these questions are still surprisingly vague. For instance, how do the different dimensions of situation models interact in text comprehension? Which factors determine the varying importance of the different dimensions? How can we explain that people differ remarkably in their ability and willingness to construct situation models? What are the neuropsychological processes underlying the processing of different dimensions? How can we extend the concept of situation models successfully to expository texts? In short, how do different people with different goals process different dimensions of a situation described in different types of texts? I am sure that the answers to these complex questions will also address spatial information, however, not as a separate and particularly important type of information, but as one among many aspects of the situations described by texts or other media.

ACKNOWLEDGMENT

Preparation of this chapter was supported by Grant No. Ri 600/3–3 from the German Research Foundation (DFG). I would like to thank the many students and colleagues who collaborated with me in the studies mentioned here: Eni Becker, Guido Becker, Gordon Bower, Christine Brückner, Angie Dratler, Thomas Ellwart, Liane Erzigkeit, Gudrun Glowalla, Ulrich

Glowalla, Erin Graves, Winfried Hacker, Andrea Hähnel, Ulrich Herzberg, Jennifer Johnson, Sabine Köpke, Alfred Kohnert, Timothy McNamara, Daniel Morrow, Marlies Pistorius-Harzer, Pepper Williams, Anthony Wagner, Stephanie Wilson, and Karin Wolf. I am also grateful to Rolf Zwaan and two anonymous reviewers for helpful comments on an earlier version of the chapter. Correspondence should be addressed to Mike Rinck, Dresden University of Technology, D-01062 Dresden, FR Germany, by e-mail to <rinck@rcs.urz.tu-dresden.de>, or by fax to +49-351-463-33522.

Suggestions for Further Reading

Readers interested in dimensions of situation models not covered by this chapter should consult, for a most comprehensive and fairly current review of situation models, including spatial ones:
Zwaan, R. A., & Radvansky, G. A. (1998). Situation models in language comprehension and memory. *Psychological Bulletin, 123,* 162–185.

A more general review of discourse comprehension is presented in:
Graesser, A. C., Millis, K. K., & Zwaan, R. A. (1997). Discourse comprehension. *Annual Review of Psychology, 48,* 163–189.

For a comprehensive overview of the processes involved in all levels of language comprehension, see:
Gernsbacher, M. A. (Editor). (1994). *Handbook of psycholinguistics.* San Diego, CA: Academic Press.

For an elaborated theoretical model of text comprehension, I suggest Kintsch's 1988 article or his 1998 book:
Kintsch, W. (1988). The role of knowledge in discourse comprehension: A construction-integration model. *Psychological Review, 95,* 163–182.
Kintsch, W. (1998). *Comprehension.* New York: Cambridge University Press.

An introduction to mental models and their role in syllogistic reasoning may be found in:
Johnson-Laird, P. N. (1983). *Mental models.* Cambridge: Cambridge University Press.

Finally, an interesting and insightful roundtable discussion by leading experts in the field, who outline their views of spatial situation models, imagery, and visuospatial cognition is contained in:
de Vega, M., Intons-Peterson, M. J., Johnson-Laird, P. N., Denis, M., & Marschark, M. (1996). *Models of visuospatial cognition.* Oxford: Oxford University Press.

References

Allen, G. L. (2000). Principles and practices for communicating route knowledge. *Applied Cognitive Psychology, 14,* 333–359.

Anderson, J. R. (1974). Retrieval of propositional information from long-term memory. *Cognitive Psychology, 6,* 451–474.

Anderson, J. R., & Bower, G. H. (1973). *Human associative memory.* Washington, DC: Winston.

Baguley, T., & Payne, S. J. (2000). Long-term memory for spatial and temporal mental models includes construction processes and model structure. *Quarterly Journal of Experimental Psychology, 53A,* 479–512.

Barsalou, L. W. (1999). Perceptual symbol systems. *Behavioral and Brain Sciences, 22,* 577–660.

Bower, G. H., & Rinck, M. (1999). Goals as generators of activation in narrative understanding. In S. R. Goldman, A. C. Graesser, & P. van den Broek (Eds.), *Narrative comprehension, causality, and coherence: Essays in honor of Tom Trabasso* (pp. 111–134). Mahwah, NJ: Erlbaum.

Bower, G. H., & Rinck, M. (2001). Selecting one among many referents in spatial situation models. *Journal of Experimental Psychology: Learning, Memory, and Cognition, 27,* 81–98.

Bransford, J. D., Barclay, J. R., & Franks, J. J. (1972). Sentence memory: A constructive versus interpretive approach. Cognitive Psychology, 3, 193–209.

Bryant, D. J., & Tversky, B. (1995, November). *Acquiring spatial relations from models and diagrams.* Paper presented at the 36th Annual Meeting of the Psychonomic Society, Los Angeles, CA.

Byrne, R. M. J., & Johnson-Laird, P. N. (1989). Spatial reasoning. *Journal of Memory and Language, 28,* 564–575.

Carpenter, P. A., Just, M. A., Keller, T. A., Eddy, W. F., & Thulborn, K. R. (1999). Time course of fMRI activation in language and spatial networks during sentence comprehension. *NeuroImage, 10,* 216–224.

Coughlin, L. D., & Patel, V. L. (1987). Processing critical information by physicians and medical students. *Journal of Medical Information, 62,* 818–828.

Daneman, M., & Carpenter, P. A. (1980). Individual differences in working memory. *Journal of Verbal Learning and Verbal Behavior, 19,* 450–466.

Daniel, M.-P., & Denis, M. (1998). Spatial descriptions as navigational aids: A cognitive analysis of route directions. *Kognitionswissenschaft, 7,* 45–52.

Denis, M. (1996). Imagery and the description of spatial configurations. In M. de Vega, M. J. Intons-Peterson, P. N. Johnson-Laird, M. Denis, & M. Marschark (Eds.), *Models of visuospatial cognition* (pp. 128–197). Oxford: Oxford University Press.

Denis, M., & Cocude, M. (1997). On the metric properties of visual images generated from verbal descriptions: Evidence for the robustness of the mental scanning effect. *European Journal of Cognitive Psychology, 9,* 353–379.

Denis, M., & Kosslyn, S. M. (1999). Scanning visual mental images: A window to the mind. *Cahiers die Psychologie Cognitive/Current Psychology of Cognition, 18,* 409–465.

Denis, M., Pazzaglia, F., Cornoldi, C., & Bertolo, L. (1999). Spatial discourse and navigation: An analysis of route directions in the city of Venice. *Applied Cognitive Psychology, 13,* 145–174.

de Vega, M. (1994). Characters and their perspectives in narratives describing spatial environments. *Psychological Research, 56,* 116–126.

de Vega, M. (1995). Backward updating of mental models during continuous reading of narratives. *Journal of Experimental Psychology: Learning, Memory, and Cognition, 21,* 373–385.

Dutke, S. (1993). Mentale Modelle beim Erinnern sprachlich beschriebener räumlicher Anordnungen: Zur Interaktion von Gedächtnisschemata und Textrepräsentation [Mental models in memory for verbal descriptions of spatial arrangements: The interaction of memory schemata and text representation]. *Zeitschrift für experimentelle und angewandte Psychologie, 40,* 44–71.

Dutke, S. (1994). Mentale Modelle beim Erinnern sprachlich beschriebener räumlicher Anordnungen: Zeitliche Aspekte der Modellkonstruktion und - nutzung [Mental models in memory for verbal descriptions of spatial arrangements: Temporal aspects of model construction and use]. *Zeitschrift für experimentelle und angewandte Psychologie, 41,* 523–548.

Dutke, S. (1998). Zur Konstruktion von Sachverhaltsrepräsentationen beim Verstehen von Texten: 15 Jahre nach Johnson-Lairds Mental Models [Toward the construction of situational representations in comprehending texts: Fifteen years after Johnson-Laird's mental models]. *Zeitschrift für Experimentelle Psychologie, 45,* 42–59.

Dutke, S. (1999). Der Crossover-Effekt von propositionaler Textrepräsentation und mentalem Modell: Zur Rolle interindividueller Fähigkeitsunterschiede [The cross-over effect of the propositional text representation and the mental model: Towards the role of individual differences in spatial imagery ability]. *Zeitschrift für Experimentelle Psychologie, 46,* 164–176.

Ehrlich, K., & Johnson-Laird, P. N. (1982). Spatial description and referential continuity. *Journal of Verbal Learning and Verbal Behavior, 21,* 296–306.

Fletcher, P. C., Happe, F., Frith, U., Baker, S. C., Dolan, R. J., Frackowiak, R. S. J., & Frith, C. D. (1995). Other minds in the brain: A functional imaging study of "theory of mind" in story comprehension. *Cognition, 57,* 109–128.

Foertsch, J., & Gernsbacher, M. A. (1994). In search of complete comprehension: Getting "minimalists" to work. *Discourse Processes, 18,* 271–296.

Friedman, N. P., & Miyake, A. (2000). Differential roles for visuospatial and verbal working memory in situation model construction. *Journal of Experimental Psychology: General, 129,* 61–83.

Gentner, D., & Stevens, A. (1983). *Mental models.* Hillsdale, NJ: Erlbaum.

Gernsbacher, M. A. (1990). *Language comprehension as structure building.* Hillsdale, NJ: Erlbaum.

Gernsbacher, M. A. (Ed.). (1994). *Handbook of psycholinguistics.* San Diego: Academic Press.

Glenberg, A. M. (1997). What memory is for. *Behavioral and Brain Sciences, 20,* 1–55.

Glenberg, A. M., & Langston, W. E. (1992). Comprehension of illustrated text: Pictures help to build mental models. *Journal of Memory and Language, 31,* 129–151.

Glenberg, A. M., Meyer, M., & Lindem, K. (1987). Mental models contribute to foregrounding during text comprehension. *Journal of Memory and Language, 26,* 69–83.

Glenberg, A. M., & Mathew, S. (1992). When minimalism is not enough: Mental models in reading, Part II. *psycoloquy.92.3.64.reading inference-2.1.glenberg-mathew.*

Glenberg, A. M., & Robertson, D. A. (1999). Indexical understanding of instructions. *Discourse Processes, 28*, 1–26.

Graesser, A. C., Millis, K. K., & Zwaan, R. A. (1997). Discourse comprehension. *Annual Review of Psychology, 48*, 163–189.

Graesser, A. C., Singer, M., & Trabasso, T. (1994). Constructing inferences during narrative text comprehension. *Psychological Review, 101*, 371–395.

Hähnel, A., & Rinck, M. (1999). Strategische Fokussierung der Aufmerksamkeit beim Lesen narrativer Texte [Strategic focusing of attention during narrative reading]. *Zeitschrift für experimentelle Psychologie, 46*, 177–192.

Haenggi, D., Gernsbacher, M. A., & Bolliger, C. A. (1994). Individual differences in situation-based inferencing during narrative text comprehension. In H. van Oostendorp & R. A. Zwaan (Eds.), *Naturalistic text comprehension* (pp. 79–96). Norwood, NJ: Ablex.

Haenggi, D., Kintsch, W., & Gernsbacher, M. A. (1995). Spatial situation models and text comprehension. *Discourse Processes, 19*, 173–199.

Hakala, C. (1999). Accessibility of spatial information in a situation model. *Discourse Processes, 27*, 261–280.

Hirtle, S. C., & Jonides, J. (1985). Evidence of hierarchies in cognitive maps. *Memory & Cognition, 13*, 208–217.

Johnson-Laird, P. N. (1983). *Mental models*. Cambridge: Cambridge University Press.

Johnson-Laird, P. N. (1996). Images, models, and propositional representations. In M. de Vega, M. J. Intons-Peterson, P. N. Johnson-Laird, M. Denis, & M. Marschark (Eds.), *Models of visuospatial cognition* (pp. 90–127). Oxford: Oxford University Press.

Johnson-Laird, P. N., & Byrne, R. M. J. (1991). *Deduction*. Hove, UK: Erlbaum.

Kaup, B. (1994). *Zur Resolution pluraler Anaphern beim Textverstehen: Effekte funktionaler und räumlicher Distanz im mentalen Modell [Resolution of plural anaphors during text comprehension: Effects of functional and spatial distance in mental models]*. Diplomarbeit. TU Berlin.

Kintsch, W. (1988). The role of knowledge in discourse comprehension: A construction-integration model. *Psychological Review, 95*, 163–182.

Kintsch, W. (1998). *Comprehension*. New York: Cambridge University Press.

Kosslyn, S. M. (1980). *Image and mind*. Cambridge, MA: Harvard University Press.

Langston, M. C., & Trabasso, T. (1998). Modeling causal integration and availability of information during comprehension of narrative texts. In H. van Oostendorp & S. Goldman (Eds.), *The construction of mental representations during reading* (pp. 29–69). Mahwah, NJ: Erlbaum.

Langston, M. C., Trabasso, T., & Magliano, J. P. (1998). A connectionist model of narrative comprehension. In A. Ram & K. Moorman (Eds.). *Computational models of reading and understanding*. Cambridge, MA: MIT Press.

Langston, W., Kramer, D. C., & Glenberg, A. M. (1998). The representation of space in mental models derived from text. *Memory & Cognition, 26*, 247–262.

Levine, W. H., & Klin, C. M. (2001). Tracking of spatial information in narratives. *Memory & Cognition, 29*, 327–335.

Long, D. L., Oppy, B. J., & Seely, M. R. (1997). Individual differences in readers' sentence- and text-level representations. *Journal of Memory and Language, 36*, 129–145.

Mani, K., & Johnson-Laird, P. N. (1982). The mental representation of spatial descriptions. *Memory & Cognition, 10*, 181–187.

Marcus, N., Cooper, M., & Sweller, J. (1996). Understanding instructions. *Journal of Educational Psychology, 88*, 49–63.

Marschark, M., & Cornoldi, C. (1991). Imagery and verbal memory. In C. Cornoldi & M. A. McDaniel (Eds.), *Imagery and cognition* (pp. 41–56). New York: Springer.

McKoon, G., & Ratcliff, R. A. (1992). Inference during reading. *Psychological Review, 99*, 440–466.

McNamara, T. P. (1991). Memory's view of space. In G. H. Bower (Ed.), *The psychology of learning and motivation.* (Vol. 27, pp. 147–186). San Diego: Academic Press.

McNamara, T. P., Hardy, J. K., & Hirtle, S. C. (1989). Subjective hierarchies in spatial memory. *Journal of Experimental Psychology: Learning, Memory, and Cognition. 15*, 211–227.

Mellet, E., Tzourio, N., Crivello, F., Joliot, M., Denis, M., & Mazoyer, B. (1996). Functional anatomy of spatial mental imagery generated from verbal instruction. *Journal of Neuroscience, 16*, 6504–6512.

Mellet, E., Tzourio-Mazoyer, N., Bricogne, S., Mazoyer, B., Kosslyn, S. M., & Denis, M. (2000). Functional anatomy of high-resolution visual mental imagery. *Journal of Cognitive Neuroscience, 12*, 98–109.

Morrow, D. G. (1985). Prominent characters and events organize narrative understanding. *Journal of Memory and Language, 24*, 304–319.

Morrow, D. G. (1994). Spatial models created from text. In H. van Oostendorp & R. A. Zwaan (Eds.), *Naturalistic text comprehension* (pp. 57–78). Norwood, NJ: Ablex.

Morrow, D. G., Bower, G. H., & Greenspan, S. L. (1989). Updating situation models during narrative comprehension. *Journal of Memory and Language, 28*, 292–312.

Morrow, D. G., Greenspan, S. L., & Bower, G. H. (1987). Accessibility and situation models in narrative comprehension. *Journal of Memory and Language, 26*, 165–187.

Morrow, D. G., Altieri, P., & Leirer, V. (1992). Aging, narrative organization, presentation mode, and referent choice strategies. *Experimental Aging Research, 18*, 75–84.

Morrow, D. G., Leirer, V. O., & Altieri, P. A. (1992). Aging, expertise, and narrative processing. *Psychology and Aging, 7*, 376–388.

Morrow, D. G., Leirer, V. O., Altieri, P., & Fitzsimmons, C. (1994). Age differences in creating spatial models from narratives. *Language and Cognitive Processes, 9*, 203–220.

Morrow, D. G., Stine-Morrow, E. A. L., Leirer, V. O., Andrassy, J. M., & Kahn, J. (1997). The role of reader age and focus of attention in creating situation models from narratives. *Journal of Gerontology: Psychological Sciences, 52B*, 73–80.

Müsseler, J., Hielscher, M., & Rickheit, G. (1995). Focusing in spatial mental models. In G. Rickheit & C. Habel (Eds.), *Focus and coherence in discourse processing* (pp. 35–74). Berlin: de Gruyter.

Norman, D. A. (1998). *The design of everyday things*. Cambridge, MA: MIT Press.

Novick, L. R., & Morse, D. L. (2000). Folding a fish, making a mushroom: The role of diagrams in executing assembly procedures. *Memory & Cognition, 28*, 1242–1256.

O'Brien, E. J., & Albrecht, J. E. (1992). Comprehension strategies in the development of a mental model. *Journal of Experimental Psychology: Learning, Memory, and Cognition, 18*, 777–784.

Paivio, A. (1990). *Mental representations.* New York: Oxford University Press.

Payne, S. J. (1993). Memory for mental models of spatial descriptions: An episodic construction trace account. *Memory & Cognition, 21*, 591–603.

Pazzaglia, F., & Cornoldi, C. (1999). The role of distinct components of visuospatial working memory in the processing of texts. *Memory, 7*, 19–41.

Perrig, W., & Kintsch, W. (1985). Propositional and situational representations of text. *Journal of Memory and Language, 24*, 503–518.

Pigenet, Y. (1997, December). Spatial mental models: Variations on the Morrow and Bower paradigm. *Notes et Documents LIMSI No. 97–20.* LIMSI-CNRS, Orsay, France.

Radvansky, G. A., Spieler, D. H., & Zacks, R. T. (1993). Mental model organization. *Journal of Experimental Psychology: Learning, Memory, and Cognition, 19*, 95–114.

Radvansky, G. A., & Zacks, R. T. (1991). Mental models and the fan effect. *Journal of Experimental Psychology: Learning, Memory, and Cognition, 17*, 940–953.

Rinck, M. (2000). Situationsmodelle und das Verstehen von Erzähltexten: Befunde und Probleme [Situation models and narrative comprehension: Findings and problems]. *Psychologische Rundschau, 51*, 115–122.

Rinck, M., & Bower, G. H. (1995). Anaphora resolution and the focus of attention in situation models. *Journal of Memory and Language, 34*, 110–131.

Rinck, M., & Bower, G. H. (2000). Temporal and spatial distance in situation models. *Memory & Cognition, 28*, 1310–1320.

Rinck, M., Bower, G. H., & Wolf, K. (1998). Distance effects in surface structures and situation models. *Scientific Studies of Reading, 2*, 221–246.

Rinck, M., Denis, M., & Bower, G. H. (2001, April). *The metrics of spatial distance represented in mental images and situation models.* Paper presented at the Eighth European Workshop on Imagery and Cognition, St. Malo, France.

Rinck, M., & Hähnel, A. (2000). *Processing of spatial, temporal, emotional, causal, and goal-related inconsistencies in narratives.* Unpublished Manuscript, Dresden University of Technology.

Rinck, M., Hähnel, A., & Becker, G. (2001). Using temporal information to construct, update, and retrieve situation models of narratives. *Journal of Experimental Psychology: Learning, Memory, and Cognition, 27*, 67–80.

Rinck, M., Hähnel, A., Bower, G. H., & Glowalla, U. (1997). The metrics of spatial situation models. *Journal of Experimental Psychology: Learning, Memory, and Cognition, 23*, 622–637.

Rinck, M., & Weber, U. (2001). *Dimensions of situation models: An experimental test of the event-indexing model.* Paper presented at the 42nd Meeting of the Psychonomic Society, Orlando, Florida.

Rinck, M., Williams, P., Bower, G. H., & Becker, E. S. (1996). Spatial situation models and narrative understanding: Some generalizations and extensions. *Discourse Processes, 21*, 23–55.

Rinck, M., Wolf, K., & Hasebrook, J. (2000). Updating of spatial changes in situation models. *Proceedings of the Tenth Annual Meeting of the Society for Text and Discourse.* Université Lumière Lyon 2, France.

Robertson, D. A., Gernsbacher, M. A., Guidotti, S. J., Robertson, R. W., Irwin, W., Mock, B. J., & Campana, M. J. (2000). Functional neuroanatomy of the cognitive process of mapping during discourse comprehension. *Psychological Science, 11,* 255–260.

Robertson, D. A., Gernsbacher, M. A., & Guidotti, S. J. (1999, April). *FMRI investigation of the comprehension of written versus picture narratives.* Paper presented at the Annual Meeting of the Cognitive Neuroscience Society, Washington, DC.

Romani, C., & Martin, R. (1999). A deficit in the short-term retention of lexical-semantic information: Forgetting words but remembering a story. *Journal of Experimental Psychology: General, 128,* 56–77.

St. George, M., Kutas, M., Martinez, A., & Sereno, M. I., (1999). Semantic integration in reading: Engagement of the right hemisphere during discourse processing. *Brain, 122,* 1317–1325.

Scott Rich, S., & Taylor, H. A. (2000). Not all narrative shifts function equally. *Memory & Cognition, 28,* 1257–1266.

Shah, P., & Miyake, A. (1996). The separability of working memory resources for spatial thinking and language processing: An individual differences approach. *Journal of Experimental Psychology: General, 125,* 1–24.

Stevens, A., & Coupe, P. (1978). Distortions in judged spatial relations. *Cognitive Psychology, 10,* 422–437.

Taylor, H. A., & Tversky, B. (1992). Spatial mental models derived from survey and route descriptions. *Journal of Memory and Language, 31,* 261–292.

van Dijk, T. A., & Kintsch, W. (1983). *Strategies of discourse comprehension.* New York: Academic Press.

Waters, G. S., & Caplan, D. (1996). The measurement of verbal working memory capacity and its relation to reading comprehension. *Quarterly Journal of Experimental Psychology, 49A,* 51–79.

Wilson, S. G., Rinck, M., McNamara, T. P., Bower, G. H., & Morrow, D. G. (1993). Mental models and narrative comprehension: Some qualifications. *Journal of Memory and Language, 32,* 141–154.

Zwaan, R. A. (2003). Situation model: Psychological. In D. Herman, M. Jahn, & M. L. Ryan, (Eds.). *Routledge encyclopedia of narrative theory* (pp. 14137–14141). London: Routledge.

Zwaan, R. A., Langston, M. C., & Graesser, A. C. (1995). The construction of situation models in narrative comprehension: An event-indexing model. *Psychological Science, 6,* 292–297.

Zwaan, R. A., Magliano, J. P., & Graesser, A. C. (1995). Dimensions of situation model construction in narrative comprehension. *Journal of Experimental Psychology: Learning, Memory, and Cognition, 21,* 386–397.

Zwaan, R. A., & Radvansky, G. A. (1998). Situation models in language comprehension and memory. *Psychological Bulletin, 123,* 162–185.

Zwaan, R. A., Radvansky, G. A., Hilliard, A. E., & Curiel, J. M. (1998). Constructing multidimensional situation models during reading. *Scientific Studies of Reading, 2,* 199–220.

Zwaan, R. A., van den Broek, P., Truitt, T. P., & Sundermeier, B. (1996). Causal coherence and the accessibility of object locations in narrative comprehension. *Abstracts of the Psychonomic Society, 1,* 50.

Zwaan, R. A., & van Oostendorp, H. (1993). Do readers construct spatial representations during naturalistic story comprehension? *Discourse Processes, 16,* 125–143.

Zwaan, R. A., & van Oostendorp, H. (1994). Spatial information and naturalistic story comprehension. In H. van Oostendorp & R. A. Zwaan (Eds.), *Naturalistic text comprehension* (pp. 97–114). Norwood, NJ: Ablex.

10

Design Applications of Visual Spatial Thinking
The Importance of Frame of Reference

Christopher D. Wickens, Michelle Vincow,
and Michelle Yeh

ABSTRACT

When humans perform tasks involving spatial cognition and visual spatial thinking, like navigation, vehicle control, manual manipulation, or understanding of
the structure of data, they must often deal with displays and controls of the work
environment that are represented in different frames of reference. Such thinking
is challenged by the need to perform transformations between these different reference frames. The frame of reference can be defined by three axes of translation
and three axes of orientation, each with either static or dynamic properties. In
this chapter we describe important human performance limitations that constrain
visual–spatial thinking, as these are related to mental rotation and transformations of location. We describe how these limits have important implications for
the design of different displays that support the user of three-dimensional spatial
information, and support the user's understanding of three-dimensional motion.
Finally, we describe the implications of visual spatial thinking to two particular
applications: helmet-mounted displays and information visualization.

INTRODUCTION

Many systems with which people interact involve movement in space.
These include the simple movement of a pointer on the blackboard (or
mouse on a computer screen), the rotation of a steering wheel by a driver,
the careful channeling of a probe down a blood vessel by the endoscopic
surgeon, and the navigation of a spacecraft through space, or a simulated
craft through electronic space in a video game.

In all of these (and many other) applications, movement must be defined
in terms of some *spatial coordinate system*. This is often a Euclidian system
(e.g., X, Y, Z coordinates in 3-D space), but it may also involve an angular
coordinate system (e.g., azimuth angle, elevation angle, and length of a

vector). It may indeed involve a combination of these systems, such as that used in specifying an aircraft's movement involving three dimensions of location (XYZ) and three dimensions of angular orientation (pitch, roll, yaw). The specification of a systems' parameters within its own coordinate space defines that systems' *frame of reference*.

In many systems, the operator needs to *transform* the coordinate system from one frame of reference to another, and these transformations will be the focus of much of the discussion in the current chapter. An example might be the transformation between the rotational motion of a steering wheel (an angular coordinate system) and the location of the vehicle on the highway (a two-dimensional Euclidian system). Another example might be the mental transformation necessary to move a pointer on a horizontal overhead projector, and see the results of that movement on a vertical projector screen: the transformation between two two-dimensional Euclidian systems. A third example is when someone asks you to point to the west. Here you must translate between your own body frame of reference (orienting your hand, relative to your trunk), and a world frame.

Although there are a wide variety of coordinate systems that can define different reference frames (see Howard, 1986, 1993, for example), this chapter will focus on the following six:

- A world frame, defined in terms of the cardinal directions (N, S, E, W), and "up" and "down."
- An ego frame, defined in terms of the orientation of the trunk (left, right, front, back) or location of the observer.
- A head frame, defined in terms of the orientation of the head, which may sometimes be different from that of the ego–trunk (as when I turn my head off-axis).
- A vehicle frame, typically associated with the orientation of travel of a car, plane, or boat.
- A display frame, defining the orientation and movement of information on a display.
- A control frame, defining the orientation and movement of the control.

Because each frame of reference can be defined in terms of three degrees of location and three degrees of orientation, and because there are so many possible frames to consider in system interaction, it is easy to see how the description of the relation between frames can be one of overwhelming complexity. As an example of such complexity consider the situation of an astronaut (ego frame), who must control a joystick (control frame) to move and orient a robotic arm (vehicle frame) to a particular moving rotating object as viewed on a display (display frame), or relative to the earth's surface (world frame).

A key thesis of this chapter is that the mental transformations necessary to align or compare frames of reference are cognitively demanding, some more so than others. These demands are reflected in increased time, increased likelihood of errors, and increased mental workload, and so it is of interest for the system designer to understand what factors increase these demands. In many high-risk systems, such as vehicle control or medical operations, the premium is on reducing errors more than reducing time or workload (although these aspects are often correlated), because, for example, the movement of a control in the wrong direction is often more damaging than a delay in that movement.

In the following chapter we first present a generic analysis of spatial tasks, and of frames of reference. We then describe the relevance of these analyses to tasks involving mental rotation, 3-D displays, immersive displays, head-mounted displays, and information visualization.

TASK ANALYSIS

From the perspective of the applied psychologist or human factors engineer, who must design interfaces to support visual spatial tasks, it is critical to understand the task that must be accomplished by the frame of reference transformation. Such an understanding may be supported by a cognitive task analysis (Schraagen, Chipman, & Shalin, 2000), which generally reveals both the goals of the particular task, as well as the information necessary to support task performance.

There are, of course, a wealth of different tasks characterizing a diversity of activities; some involve action (transforming a control movement to a display movement) and others involve judgment (comparing a map image with a real-world view). It is possible to distill these tasks down to a relatively small set of "primitives" that capture the information-processing demands of such visual spatial thinking in applied environments (McCormick, Wickens, Banks, & Yeh, 1998). These include:

1. Where am I (or an icon controlled by me, such as a cursor. We refer to this as the *ego/icon*)? This question can be defined in terms of location and orientation.
2. Where do I want to go (in terms of location and orientation)?
3. How do I control (e.g., walk, move a wheel or joystick) in order to achieve the goal specified in (2)?
4. What is the array of space that I am observing and operating on?

Sometimes these task components may be carried out in isolation. For example the scientist observing an array of data may simply be interested in understanding its structural properties (task 4; see Shah, Freedman, & Vekiri, Chapter 11, for further discussion of this task), or the lost traveler in a city may simply be trying to identify the intersection where she stands (task 1; see Montello, Chapter 7, and Taylor, Chapter 8, for further discussion of such tasks). Often, however, tasks consist of groups of these primitives. Answering the question in task 1 for example (where am I?), may often depend on asking questions in task 4 (e.g., what is the landmark that I am looking at?). Much of navigation in everyday life requires simultaneous performance of tasks 1, 2, and 3.

The designer's goal then will be to consider the task (goals), the information provided, and then configure a system of displays and controls that will not impose the requirement of extensive transformations between frames of reference by the human operator. When these transformations are small or nonexistent, task performance meets the desired criteria of speed, accuracy, and automaticity. An example might be moving a finger to touch a target on a computer touch screen (Simon, 1969). When the transformations are large, performance is vulnerable, as when, one is driving southward with a north-up map, or when the controller of a model plane or unmanned air vehicle is trying to direct the plane as it flies toward him.

For several reasons it may be difficult or unwise for the designer to configure an interface such that all transformations between a control and display frame of reference can be avoided (i.e., as in a light pen, or a rotating track-up map). First, sometimes a given interface may need to support more than one task, and each task may require a different form of cognitive activity, and therefore possibly a different frame of reference. For example, a single map may need to support moment-to-moment navigation ("Which way do I turn at an intersection?"), as well as long-range planning; and for various reasons it may be confusing or cumbersome to provide multiple displays, each optimally suited for a particular task. Second, interfaces that may be designed to minimize transformations between frames of reference may be expensive, or involve highly vulnerable and fragile technology. Such is the case with many virtual reality systems that are designed to present information in a fully ego frame of reference. Third, sometimes optimizing the frame of reference for a task may spawn other costs unrelated to the transformation between frames of reference. We refer to these as spawned costs. As we see next for example, presenting information in a fully egocentric frame of reference can create unwanted attentional tunneling, and 3-D displays impose spawned costs of ambiguity.

As a consequence of the fact that designers cannot always optimize the frame of reference for a control or a display (or minimize the transformations between reference frames), it becomes important to establish the degree of human performance cost for such transformations. We discuss these costs next, in the context of a series of real-world design issues. First, however, we present a taxonomy of frames of reference that can be used as a framework for discussing the research.

REPRESENTING FRAMES OF REFERENCE

A frame of reference describes the spatial location and orientation of some entity. If the entity is in motion, the frame of reference describes the changes in location and motion. In the following, we shall first describe the frame of reference of either the user, or something directly controlled by the user, the ego/icon frame of reference. The most general description of the frame of reference is in terms of the matrix shown in Figure 10.1a in which we represent the six parameters necessary to characterize the static state of the ego/icon: its 3-D location (X, Y, Z) and its 3-D orientation, which here we represent as pitch, roll, and yaw (or azimuth). We can also use these same six terms to characterize the motion of the ego/icon, a critically important representation because it is typically the goal of an interface to support the movement or change in state of the ego/icon. On the right, in (b) we show only a two-dimensional representation of this description, ignoring, for simplicity, the Z axis of state (which would extend above or below the page), and ignoring the two axes of orientation motion (pitch and roll) that would involve movement in the Z axis. The static state is

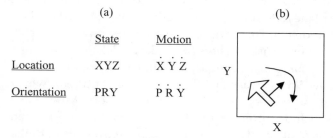

FIGURE 10.1. Representation of frame of reference; (a) Combinations of state and motion of location and orientation, each along three axes (X, Y, Z = spatial locations, P, R, Y = pitch, roll, and yaw); (b) Simplified two-dimensional representation of the degrees of freedom in frame of reference. The large white arrow depicts static location and orientation. The small black arrows depict linear and rotational motion.

represented by the direction and location of the white arrow. Motion is represented by the thin black arrows.

As a more concrete example, one may consider a user (the ego), or the user's viewpoint that can be located at any point in a 3-D room, defined by the coordinates X, Y, and Z, and can be translating in any direction within those three dimensions. Independent of this location specification, the viewpoint may be oriented in a particular direction (for example, an axis of viewing), which can be defined in terms of its pitch (forward rotation of the head relative to horizontal), its roll (sideways orientation of the head relative to the horizontal), and yaw (azimuth or compass heading). Finally, any momentary orientation along these three axes may be coupled with a momentary rotation motion around them.

This representation provides for tremendous complexity in systems that do not have constraints in their dimensions, allowing $3 \times 3 \times 3 \times 3 = 81$ unique descriptions or degrees of freedom of a reference frame, and, potentially $81 \times 81 = 6,561$ possible combinations of a pair of reference frames (e.g., a control–display relation). Fortunately, in most systems that are designed, many of these degrees of freedom are essentially frozen or have constraining links between them, simplifying the description. For example, a computer cursor generally has no orientation, and furthermore is often constrained to move on a 2-D screen. Thus, it can be defined by just four states (X, Y, location, and motion). Ground vehicles are constrained to operate in two dimensions of location and translation, and further constraints of vehicle dynamics generally couple orientation (yaw or heading) with dynamic position: forward movement is in the direction of heading. Although aircraft operate in three dimensions rather than two, similar constraints between orientation and location that are inherent in the flight dynamics of aircraft also simplify the description of frame of reference. For example, as the plane rolls, it will change its heading, and as it pitches, it will change its altitude (Z). The learning of these constraints represents an important source of expertise of pilots (Bellenkes, Wickens, & Kramer, 1997). However, just as complexity is reduced by the constraints inherent in most physical systems, it is increased by the number of entities for which a frame of reference can be specified in system interaction. As we have noted, these entities include ego/icon, the desired target state of ego/icon in the world, the control of ego/icon, the display that represents both the ego/icon and the target, and sometimes a separate representation for the trunk of the ego (person) and the head orientation. Any or all of these may show varying degrees of correspondence on the 81 attributes defining the frame of reference.

The challenging human factors issues of these spatial representations emerge when we begin to consider the varying degrees of misalignment between the frame of reference of controlled and displayed entities. In a simple computer interface when a cursor is directly controlled by a light pen on the screen, there is no transformation between control and display. When the cursor is controlled by a mouse, there is a spatial (location) transformation, because the mouse pad does not overlay the display screen. If the mouse pad rests on a horizontal surface, this will produce an added orientation transformation of motion between control and display (i.e., forward (Z) movement of the mouse maps to an upward (Y) movement of the cursor). In the following pages, we discuss three general aspects of these frame of reference transformations: of orientation, of location, and of motion, before we go into an in-depth treatment of two specific applications.

MENTAL ROTATION

Lateral Mental Rotation: Fixed Versus Rotating Maps

The transformation of mental rotation has received extensive research in both basic (e.g., Shepard & Metzler, 1971; Cooper & Shepard, 1973) and more applied domains (Aretz, 1991; Wickens, Liang, Prevett, & Olmos, 1996; Gugerty & Brooks, 2001; Levine, 1982; Warren, Rossano, & Wear, 1990; Eley, 1988). It is a transformation that is directly relevant to two tasks carried out by users in navigation systems: image comparison and travel. In the image comparison task, originally developed by Shepard and his colleagues (e.g., Shepard & Metzler, 1971; Cooper & Shepard, 1973), the user views two images and determines if they are identical given that one is rotated into the same frame of reference as the other. Such transformations take time, cause errors, and impose mental resource demands. In the world outside the laboratory, image comparison has a frequent manifestation in map–world comparison tasks, in which the user compares a forward view of what is actually seen (an ego-reference), with a map view (world reference), to determine if these are congruent; see Figure 10.2. (Aretz & Wickens, 1992; Goldberg, Maceachren, & Korval, 1992; Wickens, 1999; Schreiber, Wickens, Renner, Alton, & Hickox, 1998). The finding that there is an increasing cost in confirming the identity of the two viewpoints ("where I think I am on the map, is what I see in the world") as the compass orientation of the map is increasingly misaligned with the forward view orientation, is consistent with the findings from basic laboratory research

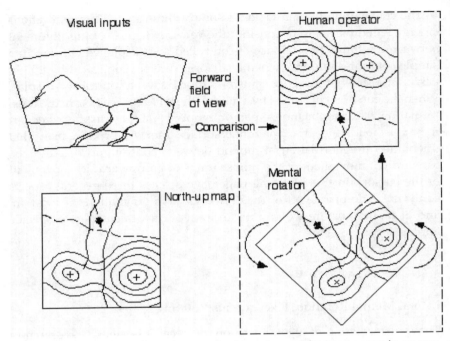

FIGURE 10.2. The mental rotation required to compare the image seen in an ego-referenced forward field of view (top left) with a world-referenced north-up map (bottom left) when the aircraft is heading south. The map image is mentally rotated (right) to bring it into congruence with the forward field of view.

(see Taylor, Chapter 8, for a review). Such findings have been applied nicely to the design of you-are-here maps by Levine (1982). He notes the costs that result when the direction in the world that a viewer faces when reading a map, is misaligned with the direction depicted as directly "up" on the vertically oriented map (or the direction that would be forward, if the map were rotated forward to a horizontal surface. We consider in the next section, the relatively "trivial" cost of this second form of map rotation from a vertical to a horizontal plane).

   In the travel task, the user executes some form of control to move a vehicle (or cursor: the ego/icon) in the direction depicted by the map. Here again, to the extent that the frame of reference defining the axis of control is misaligned with the axis of display, such that some form of mental rotation must take place, there is typically a cost, either in the time to choose which way to turn at a particular turn point (Shepard & Hurwitz, 1984), or in the error measured when tracking a desired target course for the controlled vehicle or cursor to follow (Aretz, 1991; Wickens, Liang, Prevett, & Olmos, 1996; Macedo, Kaber, Endsley, Powanusorm, & Myung, 1998). (To provide an intuitive example of such costs, try to rapidly position a cursor on a screen using a mouse that you have rotated 90 degrees on the mouse pad., so that left–right movement of the mouse corresponds to up–down movement of the cursor). A major design implication of these mental rotation costs, for both image comparison tasks and travel control tasks, is that a display map should be rotated as heading changes, so that the momentary direction of heading always corresponds to the upward (or forward) orientation of the map (Olmos, Liang, & Wickens, 1997). This map representation stands in contrast to a fixed map, which is typically positioned in a north-up orientation. With such a map, mental rotation problems will result whenever the orientation of the vehicle or viewpoint is substantially different from north.

Three important features modulate the magnitude of the mental rotation costs of a fixed north-up map, costs that prescribe a map should rotate so that the direction of travel is always "up" on the map. First, unlike simple mental rotation, it does not appear that the cost of axis disparity is linear, but rather follows a more geometric function such that small offsets impose only very minor costs, and the linear function only operates beyond offsets of around 45 degrees (Wickens, 1999; Gugerty & Brooks, 2001; Macedo et al., 1998). Practically, this means that maps need not rotate continuously with the direction of travel, or may be rotated slightly more slowly than changes in the actual ego-orientation or movement, as long as the offset is never greater than 45 degrees. Releasing this constraint for instant continuous map rotation can greatly reduce the technological requirements of image generation for continuously rotating complex maps, when the change in orientation of the traveler is also rapid.

Second, in travel control tasks, some degree of misalignment is far more tolerable if the control itself is constrained to move easily along only the cardinal (e.g., left–right) egocentric axes. For example in the automobile, the steering wheel can only rotate to the left or the right, and a typical computer "slider" will be constrained along a single linear path. However a mouse can move with equal ease along an infinite number of orientation paths, so that the mental rotation costs resulting when a mouse is rotated will be more serious at small angles of misalignment than is the case with driving, or with control with a single axis joystick that is constrained to move in a linear path. In the experiment of Macedo et al. (1998) in which such constraints were lacking, tracking error increased twenty fold in the most degrading (90° rotation) condition.

Third, it appears that verbal or categorical strategies can sometimes mediate these mental rotation costs. In particular, when there is 180-degree misalignment, mental rotation costs are not always as great as would be predicted by the linear function originally observed by Shepard and his colleagues in simple laboratory-based mental rotation studies (Aretz, 1991; Gugerty & Brooks, 2001). Users may be able to apply a direct ("left is right and right is left") strategy when the axes of the two frames of reference (either a map and a forward view, or a map and a control) are in direct opposition through a 180-degree rotation. It appears that the magnitude of this categorical reversal strategy is much greater in control tasks than in image comparison tasks. Indeed Macedo et al. (1998) found that the tracking error created by 180-degree misalignment was much lower (3.8 units) than that produced by 90-degree misalignment (21.6 units), and much closer to the aligned 0-degree value of 0.8 units.

Although we have focused our discussion of mental rotation on image comparison and travel control tasks, it should be noted that the issue of the horizontal, yaw, or azimuth frame of reference also pertains to a broader class of communications tasks, in which a variety of operators, using different maps, must coordinate. Consider, for example, the airborne forest fire commander who is directing aircraft on which way to fly (Delzell & Battiste, 1993). She will typically refer to a fixed north-up map, and can most easily communicate with other aircraft in terms of world-referenced terms ("fly north," or "fly heading 090 degrees"), whereas the pilots occupying individual aircraft in a variety of orientations will more easily deal with commands (particularly turning commands) that are presented in their own ego-referenced frame (e.g., "turn left," rather than "turn south"). In this case, designers of procedures for such operations will need to choose if it is better for the commander to engage in mental rotation and issue specific ego-referenced commands, or for individual pilots to engage in mental rotation in translating those commands. Finally, although rotating maps improve judgments of left–right, some evidence suggests that learning about the spatial properties of an environment can benefit from a fixed (north-up) map (Aretz, 1991), because of its consistency of representation over time, which is lacking in the rotating map.

Vertical Mental Rotation: 2-D Versus 3-D Displays

When users compare a rotating track-up 2-D map with a forward view, they must still engage in an additional transformation in which the map, viewed from a top-down orientation, is mentally rotated to envision a view corresponding to the horizontal forward view (Figure 10.2). This is the analogous vertical transformation to that between control and display frames, when a mouse is moved on a horizontal surface, to control a cursor on a vertical screen. The envisioning process by which the plan view is imagined in its 3-D forward view probably corresponds to something other than mental rotation, or at least it is mental rotation of a qualitatively different form than that of lateral rotation (Niall, 1997). In particular, in map-view image comparison tasks, it appears that the cost of the transformation in image comparison tasks is quite nonlinear, with small angle differences between the images to be compared imposing very small costs, and costs growing substantially only when rotation angles are well beyond 45 degrees (Schreiber, Wickens, Renner, Alton, & Hickox, 1998; Hickox & Wickens, 1999; Goldberg, Maceachren, & Korval, 1992).

This finding of nonlinearity has both a theoretical foundation and a number of important map design implications. From a theoretical perspective, the fundamental reason why the vertical transformation involved in envisioning may be less demanding than those in lateral rotation appears to be related to differences in the asymmetry of the three axes of space involved in mental rotation, and hence the asymmetrical marking of their endpoints (Franklin & Tversky, 1990). Shepard and Hurwitz (1984) note that the vertical axis is clearly marked by gravitational forces, such that "up" has a very different meaning from "down." Correspondingly, the fore-aft axis (or longitudinal axis) is asymmetrical both because our eyes look forward not backward, and our locomotion system is designed to move forward better than backward. As a consequence, it is easy to associate the two marked endpoints of these two asymmetrical axes, and the "forward is up" pairing has a strong association. Thus, mental rotation through the 90-degree forward axis (pivoting around the lateral axis) is relatively easy, and as a result it makes little difference whether a rotated map or display screen is mounted vertically or horizontally. (This is why it is so easy to move a mouse on a horizontal surface, to control a cursor on a vertical screen). In contrast there is only a very weak asymmetry between left and right. Confusions along this lateral axis are easy to occur, and therefore mental rotation is more likely to be required to bring two aligned frames into congruence when this axis is rotated. Furthermore, because neither left nor right are clearly marked, the association of these lateral end points with "up" or "forward" is far more arbitrary, and invites confusion. Note too that as long as the "forward-up" association is maintained, then there is never confusion about the otherwise confusing left–right mapping between, for example, a forward view and a vertically mounted rotating map.

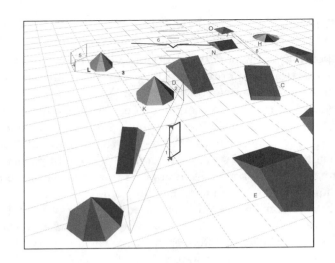

(a)

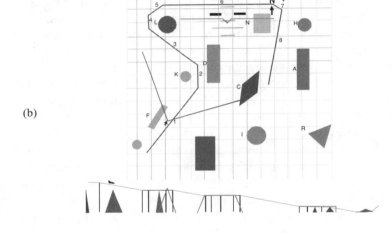

(b)

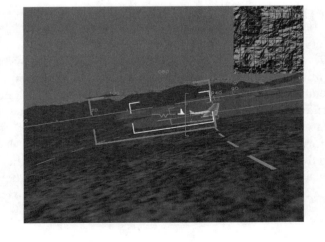

(c)

There are a number of practical implications imposed by the modest cost of 3-D mental rotation in the vertical plane. For reasons described next, these costs appear to be more profound in image comparison tasks than in control tasks. In particular, when people are navigating in a 3-D environment, and must compare their location and orientation implicitly signaled in a forward egocentric view with one represented on a map (Figure 10.2), then there is an advantage if the map view also adopts somewhat of a forward-looking representation (i.e., provides some degree of map rotation forward, from the vertical God's eye perspective that is typical of most "2-D maps"; Hickox & Wickens, 1999), as shown in Figure 10.3a. We have found for example that the advantage for pilots using a 3-D electronic map (Figure 10.3a) relative to a 2-D plan view (Figure 10.3b) is considerably greater when pilots are flying with a visual view of the terrain in front of the aircraft (i.e., when there are two images to be compared; Olmos, Liang, & Wickens, 1997), than when they are flying "in the clouds," and are only required to align the map image frame with the control frame (i.e., a control task) (Wickens & Prevett, 1995; Wickens et al., 1996).

The advantage of the 3-D display view in comparing the 3-D worldview is an example of what Roscoe (1968) describes as the *principle of pictorial realism*.

The fact that the cost of vertical mental rotation is distinctly nonlinear, and that small transformations (less than 45 degrees) require disproportionately less time than larger transformations has a second implication: For tasks that may require evaluation of the represented space from all vertical angles (e.g., a 0-degree forward view for identifying or comparing landmark images, and a vertical −90-degree view for route planning), then a fixed 45-degree view can be considered to be optimal because neither of these two transformations (from 45 degrees to 0 degrees or to 90 degrees) will be great enough to impose any serious costs (Hickox & Wickens, 1999; Wickens, 1999).

FIGURE 10.3. (a) Figure 10.3a depicts a 3-D exocentric display of electronic map for aircraft navigation, sometimes referred to as a tethered display. The pilot's own aircraft symbol is shown from above and behind, near the center of the display. The pilot of the aircraft, shown in Figure 10.3a with the ground shadow "dropline" and the small predictor line extending forward, must fly the aircraft along the path to the airport. (b) Figure 10.3b shows a 2-D map view upper, and a 2-D profile view lower. (c) Figure 10.3c is an immersed fully egocentric 3-D display. The rectangular tunnel represents the same flight path depicted by the lines in Figures 10.3a and 10.3b.

Spawned Costs of 3-D Displays

In spite of their natural advantages in reducing transformations in 3-D navigational tasks, 3-D maps do have limitations that are less related to their
frame of reference than to other spawned costs as described earlier. The
two most serious costs are those of *line of sight ambiguity* and of a *favored orientation.* Both of these costs are task dependent. The line of sight ambiguity
cost relates to the difficulty of resolving differences in perceived position
along the viewing axis of a display (Gregory, 1977; McGreevy & Ellis, 1986).
Even when depth cues are carefully incorporated into a 3-D display, such
costs are still encountered. As shown in Figure 10.4, which depicts a 3-D
display construction, these costs prevent users from establishing precisely
how far away a displayed representation is from them; and ambiguity of
how far away something is will, in turn, lead to corresponding ambiguity

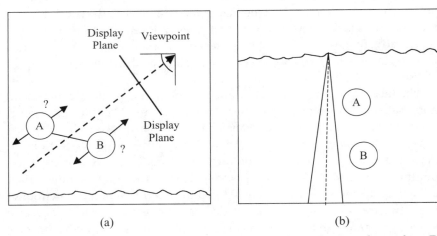

(a)   (b)

FIGURE 10.4. The spawned cost of 3-D ambiguity; (a) A side view shows the 3-D
display viewpoint, the line of sight viewing axis (dashed line), and two objects,
A and B. Their location along the viewing axis will be ambiguous to the viewer,
as reflected by the "?". This ambiguity will be amplified if fewer depth cues are
available in the display; (b) The actual appearance of the 3-D display shows a road
and distant mountains on the horizon, as it would be seen from the viewpoint
in (a) projected onto the display plane. A and B are ambiguous in their distance
from the observer and therefore their position in space. As a consequence, the
orientation and length of the vector between A and B are also ambiguous; as a
consequence of this ambiguity, the velocity of any object moving along this vector
will be ambiguous as well. If the vector is assumed to be longer, the velocity will be
assumed to be greater. Slant underestimation makes A perceived as higher, relative
to B, than it actually is.

of its absolute distance above or below the viewing axis. Correspondingly these costs will degrade the user's knowledge of the orientation of any vector in 3-D space (i.e., the spatial relation between two points lying along the vector); and ambiguity of this vector orientation knowledge will create a corresponding ambiguity of knowledge of the direction and speed of motion along such a vector. Thus, in Figure 10.4b, if we imagine that A and B are aircraft, it will be hard to determine if they are at the same altitude; and if A and B represent points along a flight path of a single aircraft, it's hard to determine if this path is parallel to the ground.

In addition to this ambiguity, a phenomenon called *slant underestimation* characterizes the view in Figure 10.4 (Perrone & Wenderoth, 1993; Alexander & Wickens, 2003). This is a bias to perceive the orientation of the vector A–B as more closely parallel to the display plane (i.e., an underestimation of the horizontal slant) than is the true case. This perception of a steeper slope (less slant away from the viewer) will be amplified if there are fewer depth cues in the display (Wickens, Todd, & Seidler, 1989; McGreevy & Ellis, 1986).

Although such ambiguity and resolution problems concerning the vertical position of objects may also be encountered in a 2-D viewpoint (i.e., a plan view map), the problems here are typically addressed by artificial design solutions: for example, contour lines for terrain maps, digital data tags for air traffic control displays, or as seen in Figure 10.3b, an alternative solution in the 2-D viewpoint is to provide a *coplanar display*, in which two 2-D views are presented along orthogonal axes, and precise estimation of location along each of these axes (or within each of the depicted planes) can be obtained. A triplanar display is an extension in which views are presented along three orthogonal axes (Andre, Wickens, Moorman, & Boechelli, 1991).

A fairly extensive body of applied research has compared coplanar viewpoints with 3-D (perspective) viewpoints, and has allowed the general conclusion to be drawn that, where precise estimation of location or vector orientation is required (such as in an air traffic controller's task of conflict prediction, or that of precisely positioning the end of a robotic arm), the coplanar viewpoint is superior (e.g., St. John, Cowen, Smallman, & Oonk, 2001; see Wickens, 2000, 2003, for a review). However, this superiority is gone when ambiguity is eliminated (e.g., by constraining all items to lie along a horizontal surface, or to move along the orthogonal axes), or where the task requires less precise location, but requires more general image perception of shape and configuration (as in the navigational image comparison tasks described earlier). Now the advantages of a 3-D view dominate, and the costs of visual scanning between the two orthogonal views in a coplanar display also begin to dominate.

The second spawned cost is the favored orientation cost of a 3-D display of space. This relates to the fact that any 3-D display must be oriented in some particular azimuth (heading or yaw) axis, giving this viewing direction a sort of primacy or greater importance relative to its 180-degree counterpart (behind). In natural vision, for example, our eyes give primacy to what is straight ahead, total neglect of what is behind, and degraded coverage of what is off to the side (because of the low acuity of peripheral vision). The 3-D displays, to an extent that depends on their geometric field of view and viewpoint location, will provide this primacy of certain information, and corresponding neglect of other information. We discuss this important issue more in the following section on location transformation.

LOCATIONAL TRANSFORMATIONS OF VIEWPOINT

Egocentric Versus Exocentric Displays

Figure 10.5 presents a schematic representation of three different frames of reference with which the ego/icon can be presented on a display. The example chosen is the representation of a pilot's aircraft in 3-D space. The 3-D exocentric, and the coplanar (two plane) view on the left (Figures 10.5a and 10.5b) have been considered already in the context of rotational transformations (Figures 10.3a and 10.3b, respectively). The 3-D viewpoint on the right in Figure 10.5c, however, differs from that in Figure 10.5a because of a locational transformation. In Figure 10.5a, the viewpoint is transformed behind and above ego/icon. In Figure 10.5c the viewpoint is not transformed at all relative to the pilot's eyes in the aircraft. Therefore, we refer to the viewpoint in Figure 10.5c as an egocentric or immersed 3-D viewpoint, in contrast to the exocentric or tethered viewpoint in Figure 10.5a. A more realistic example of the egocentric 3-D viewpoint is shown in Figure 10.3c; the flight path "tunnel in the sky" (e.g., Fadden et al., 2001).

The 3-D egocentric viewpoint shown in Figure 10.5c is a natural one, identical to the viewpoint of our eyes. Hence, it is not surprising that research has found it to support very effective navigational control or tracking through 3-D environments (Wickens & Prevett, 1995; Haskell & Wickens, 1993; McCormick et al., 1998; Barfield, Rosenberg, & Furness, 1995; Olmos, Wickens, & Chudy, 2000), when compared with a viewpoint that translates the location, relative to the ego/icon that is being controlled

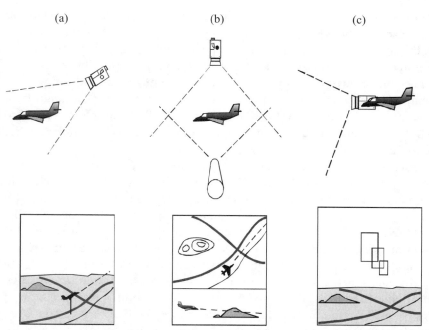

FIGURE 10.5. Three different frames of reference with which flight path and hazard information can be presented to the pilot. Each panel represents the viewpoint of a camera or image generator relative to the pilot. At the bottom is a schematic rendering of the view the pilot would see: (a) 3-D exocentric or "tethered" viewpoint. The view is rendered as if there is a tether linking the aircraft to the viewpoint at a constant distance behind and above; (b) 2-D coplanar view, showing a top down lateral view, and a vertical profile view. In the current rendering the profile is a side view. However, it could also be rendered as a view from behind; (c) 3-D immersed or egocentric view.

(Figures 10.3a and 10.5a). The source of the advantages of the fully immersed egocentric display appear to be threefold (Doherty & Wickens, 2000). First, it is a natural view, avoiding any transformations relative to the axis of control. Second, it presents objects or targets ahead of the controlled ego/icon with larger visual angle (because they are closer than in the exocentric view). Hence, as the space is traversed, relative movement of those objects is greater and can be more easily perceived; as a result the depth perception cue of motion parallax is very salient, and the control necessary to avoid or seek those objects can often be more effectively exercised. Third, the direction or orientation of those objects from the ego/icon is directly signaled by the direct viewpoint into the display. An object "above" you in space will always be above your forward path on the display. In contrast, with an exocentric viewpoint, the direction between ego/icon and any object in the environment is ambiguous for reasons discussed earlier in the context of Figure 10.4. That is, the location of ego/icon AND the location of any target elsewhere in space are both perceptually ambiguous. Hence the orientation of the vector between them will also be ambiguous, an ambiguity proportional to the sum of the variance of the ambiguity of each of its endpoints (ego/icon and the target). For example, it is hard to tell if the summit of the mountain K in Figure 10.3a, is above or below the altitude of the aircraft.

Such penalties for the 3-D exocentric viewpoint of Figures 10.5a and 10.3a, displaced in location, might suggest that it should be avoided in both control tasks (where the egocentric viewpoint of Figures 10.5c and 10.3c is superior) and in spatial judgment tasks (where the coplanar display of Figures 10.5b and 10.3b is superior because of the absence of line-of-sight ambiguity). Yet the 3-D exocentric viewpoint preserves one critical advantage over both of the other two viewpoints in terms of its ability to support *situation awareness*, or a general understanding of the relative location and dynamic behavior of objects in the volume of space around ego/icon (Garland & Endsley, 2000; Durso, 1999; Banbury & Tremblay, 2004). Such advantages are revealed by separate contrasts of the exocentric display with the egocentric display and with the coplanar display in turn. As noted previously, the favorable contrast with the coplanar display, results because the exocentric 3-D display requires less vertical mental rotation to perceive the 3-D structure of an environment (Hickox & Wickens, 1999) and avoids the mentally demanding integration of information across the two views of the coplanar display (St. John, Cowen, Smallman, & Oonk, 2001). The favorable contrast with the egocentric display results in part because the immersed viewpoint of the egocentric display presents a highly favored orientation, excluding from view all information beyond a specified viewing angle from this orientation – the field of view of the display. Hence dynamic, changing information outside of this view will not be seen. This is sometimes described as a *keyhole cost* of 3-D displays (Woods, 1984; Wickens, 2003). (Look at Figure 10.3c, and consider the pilot, with an egocentric traffic display, who may be unaware of an aircraft on a collision course, outside of this field of view.)

Of course, immersed displays may be designed with panning features to compensate for this tunnel vision, so that the viewpoint can be scanned, just as the head can rotate to look at objects behind and above the observer. However, such panning takes effort (and may therefore not be adequately

TABLE 10.1. *Costs and Benefits of Different Display Perspectives (from Wickens, 2003).*

	3-D		2-D
	Immersed	Tethered	Coplanar
1. Cost of Scanning	Low	Low	High[1]
2. Cost of Cognitive Integration Across Planes (Axis Pairs)	Low	Low	High[1]
3. Principle of Pictorial Realism	Confirmed[2]	Confirmed[2]	Violated
4. Line of Sight Ambiguity	Cost[3]	Double cost[3]	
5. Keyhole View	Cost[4]		

[1] Increased with greater physical separation between lateral and vertical display panels.
[2] Less benefit at higher altitudes.
[3] Cost is decreased with more depth cues.
[4] Cost is decreased with larger geometric field of view.

done; Wickens, Thomas, & Young, 2000). Furthermore, dynamic changes that take place out of the field of view may not be noted even if the changed element is viewed both before and after the change occurs but not at the moment of change (Rensink, 2002; Simons, 2000; Wickens & Rose, 2001). Finally, gathering information about the 3-D structure of the environment by mentally integrating multiple narrow views over time (panning the immersed display) is far more difficult, demanding of spatial working memory, and less accurate, than is ascertaining that structure from a single 3-D exocentric view, encompassing a wider range of 3-D space on one screen (Rudmann & McConkie, 1999). While the 3-D exocentric viewpoint will also exclude some aspects of a 3-D environment from view since it also has a favored orientation, the amount of exclusion can be reduced by increasing the length of the "tether" that links the viewpoint to the ego/icon (Wickens & Prevett, 1995; see Figure 10.5a).

In conclusion, a contrast between the three viewpoints, as shown in Figures 10.3 and 10.5, reveals different costs and benefits associated with each. Table 10.1 provides a summary of these differences. The selection of a single viewpoint for the user should depend on the relative importance of rapid and accurate travel and object avoidance (the immersed viewpoint is best), precise judgments of the relative location and distance of things (the coplanar viewpoint is best), the general understanding of 3-D structure (the 3-D exocentric viewpoint is best, the coplanar display is poorest), and the awareness of dynamic changes in the broad environment (the immersed viewpoint is poorest). Such a framework has provided useful guidance for the choice of display viewpoints in the cockpit and in other 3-D environments (Wickens, 2000, 2003).

Locational Transformations of Viewpoint 2: Dual Maps

A logical solution to the trade-off of weaknesses among the three viewpoints, described previously, is to incorporate multiple viewpoints or dual maps at a single workstation, allowing the user to employ each as he or she sees appropriate for the task at hand (Ruddle, Payne, & Jones, 1999; Olmos et al., 2000; Thomas & Wickens, 2000). (Alternatively, display interaction can be employed for the user to call up different viewpoints on a multifunction display.) Such a solution may partially address the problems described earlier, but may not fully eliminate them. For example, research has revealed that an immersed viewpoint is such a highly compelling one that it may attract attention away from other viewpoints that contain more relevant information (Olmos et al., 2000).

A particular challenge is imposed when different viewpoints present close, related, or overlapping regions of space. Here it is often difficult for the viewer to mentally integrate the two in order to understand how information in one viewpoint relates to that in the other, without becoming disoriented as attention is switched between the two. In order to address this mental integration problem, human factors engineers have adopted the principle of *visual momentum* (Woods, 1984; Wickens, 1993), borrowed from film editors who have crafted a series of techniques to prevent the movie viewer from becoming disoriented as the movie cuts from one scene to the next (Hochberg & Brooks, 1978). When applied to graphic displays of space, a typical feature of many of these visual momentum techniques is to highlight a common element in both (or all) display viewpoints, as illustrated in Figure 10.6. For example, if two maps depict overlapping areas, the region of overlap should be highlighted on both, shown by the shaded corners in Figure 10.6a. If both a rotating 3-D view (Figure 10.3a) and a fixed, large-scale map are placed side by side, a prominent indicator of north should be positioned on the rotating map, and a prominent indicator of the momentary direction of view (or heading) should be depicted on the north-up map. Aretz (1991) has further developed this concept by actually depicting the width and orientation of the geometric field of view from an immersed display as a wedge positioned on a small-scale 2-D plan view map as shown in Figure 10.6b. The actual appearance of such a wedge can be seen in Figure 10.3b. Incorporating such visual momentum

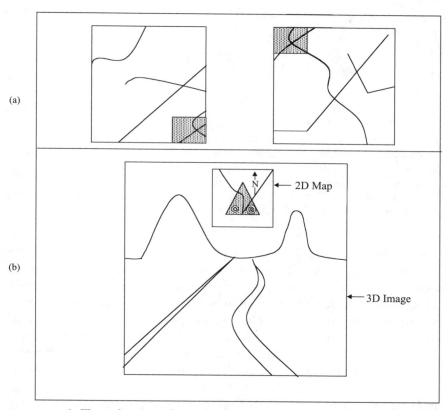

FIGURE 10.6. The techniques of visual momentum to assist visual–spatial thinking with dual maps: (a) The map on the left overlaps in its lower right corner, with the region in the upper left corner of the map on the right. Visual momentum highlights the region of overlap (shaded) between the two maps; (b) The shaded "wedge" in the upper small-scale north-up 2-D inset map depicts the region of space with two mountains and two roads viewed in the more local south-oriented 3-D image shown below, which characterizes an immersed view.

tools improves various aspects of dual map performance (Olmos et al., 2000; Aretz, 1991).

DYNAMIC DISPLAYS: WHICH FRAME MOVES?

Much of our previous discussion has focused on the location and orientation of reference frames. Display designers are sometimes confronted with the issue of how to depict motion of a dynamic element within a display. One issue is whether the display frame should represent the stable world

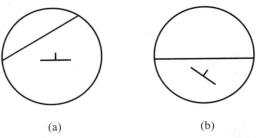

(a)   (b)

FIGURE 10.7. The aircraft attitude directional indicator, the pilot's most important instrument. The long line represents the horizon. The inverted "T" represents the aircraft (the ego/icon). Both indicators depict an aircraft looking forward along the direction of travel, pitched downward and banked rightward: (a) The inside-out, moving-horizon display typical of most aircraft cockpits; (b) The outside-in, moving aircraft display, conforming to the principle of the moving part.

within which the element's movement takes place (the display frame is the world frame), or present the world, moving around the fixed element in the display that represents the ego/icon (the display frame is the ego frame). This contrast defines the distinction between world-referenced and ego-referenced displays, respectively. This design issue has been highlighted in an ongoing debate over the design of the aircraft attitude directional indicator (ADI), the most important instrument for manual (i.e., nonauto-mated) aircraft flight control. The display shown in Figure 10.7 presents the aircraft (inverted "T") along with a horizon (long line). Both renderings in Figure 10.7 depict an aircraft banked to the right, and pitched down-ward (i.e., angling below the horizon). As shown in Figure 10.7a, the con-ventional design of this indicator has been as an ego-referenced moving horizon display. As an aircraft banks and pitches, the horizon rotates and translates vertically in the opposite direction, depicting the precise view a pilot would have inside the aircraft, looking at the real horizon out the window (assuming the pilot's head is aligned with the airplane; Previc & Ercoline, 1999). As such, the moving horizon display is sometimes called an *inside-out* display.

Researchers have argued, however, that this inside-out display violates the *principle of the moving part* (Roscoe, 1968, 2002). This principle asserts that the moving element on a display should correspond to (and move in the same direction as) the user's mental model of what moves in the real world. Put simply in the case of the ADI, the pilot's mental model is of an aircraft moving through and rotating within a fixed world frame of reference, not a world moving around a fixed aircraft frame (Johnson &

Roscoe, 1972). Hence, a more compatible design according to the principle of the moving part is that of a moving aircraft, with a fixed horizon (an "outside-in," world-referenced display) shown in Figure 10.7b. Indeed, research has shown that there are fewer confusions of motion when pilots fly with the outside-in display (Kovalenko, 1991; Roscoe, Corl, & Jensen, 1981; Previc & Ercoline, 1999). For example, if a pilot with an inside-out, moving-horizon display suddenly perceives a leftward rotation of the horizon as shown in Figure 10.7a (e.g., caused by turbulence, and indicating a right bank of the aircraft), this motion may momentarily be mistaken for a leftward rotation of the aircraft, since the pilot expects the moving element in the display to be the aircraft. Instinctively applying an erroneous rightward correction (in response to this incorrect perception) the pilot will then increase the right bank, perhaps putting the aircraft into a dangerous stall; that is, literally "sliding" out of the air (Roscoe, 2002).

Why then do not all displays show a moving icon against a fixed representation of the world in order to conform to the principle of the moving part such as the design of the Russian MIG fighter? The answer is that other principles may favor presenting an ego-referenced frame. In our discussion of mental rotation, we noted the desirability of using a rotating map (ego-frame) in order to avoid mental rotation, in spite of the fact that this violates the principle of the moving part (because a right turn of the vehicle will trigger a left rotation of the map). In addressing such conflicting principles, the designer should consider the speed of motion with which changes take place on the display (a speed often inversely related to the inertia of the controlled system). If speed is rapid, and motion is directly perceived, then it becomes more important to conform to the principle of the moving part. Such is the case in the ADI, since an aircraft may rotate rapidly around the long axis of its fusilage. However, if change is slow, such as the heading direction of a large aircraft or its position on that map, then the accuracy of motion perception becomes relatively less important for the tasks, compared to the perception of position and orientation. Hence an inside-out frame of reference may be relatively more acceptable. In this case, adherence to the principle of the moving part can be deemphasized, and other factors can be taken into consideration.

There are many additional issues of depicting motion within varying frames of reference for which space does not allow full coverage. As one example, we consider one of these issues briefly, related to how controlled motion of objects in the world should be depicted on a display. Consider the situation depicted in Figure 10.8 of an operator controlling a robot arm

Imagined Display

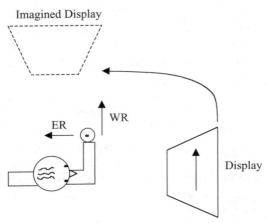

FIGURE 10.8. Display out of alignment with control. The operator must move the control in the direction of the arrow shown on the display to his right (WR = control movement in a world-referenced frame; ER = control movement in an ego-referenced frame). The ER appears to be the most natural way of associating movement in the display frame with that in the control frame, as the operator appears to imagine the display is viewed straight ahead, as shown by the dashed box.

in the world. The operator is looking to the right at a display. How should the control move in order to move the displayed object (the robot arm) in the direction shown by the arrow: forward (in a world-referenced frame designated by WR) or leftward (in an ego-referenced frame designated by ER)? Here again, evidence suggests that the ego frame is dominant. In other words, people imagine that the display (the dashed box) and the neck are rotated to the most natural forward position as defined by the trunk; and then assume an alignment of display-control motion that is consistent with that imagined rotation (Worringham & Beringer, 1989; Previc, 1998; Cohen, Otakeno, Previc, & Ercoline, 2001). In other words, they will want to move the control to the left in order to move the displayed ego/icon to the left relative to its display frame. We might label this the *trunk dominance principle* because the orientation of the trunk dominates the orientation of the head when the two are out of alignment.

HEAD-MOUNTED DISPLAYS

In Figure 10.8, we presented a display oriented for the user to see while looking to the right. If such a display were mounted rigidly to the head instead of a fixed location, it would be visible wherever the viewer was

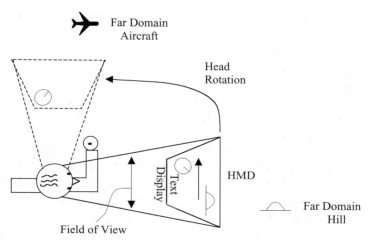

FIGURE 10.9. A head-mounted display (HMD). The operator is viewed from above, and the HMD is rendered as viewed by the operator, with the head rotated right (solid lines) or looking forward (dashed lines). Two objects, an aircraft ahead and a hill to the right of the viewer, can be seen in the far domain. The hill is represented in the database generating the HMD imagery and is thus presented as world-referenced imagery on the HMD. The aircraft is not, so the far domain aircraft is not represented on the HMD. The words "text display" represent vehicle-referenced imagery, and the small round dial gauge represents screen-referenced imagery.

looking. This concept, the *head-mounted display* or HMD (Melzer & Moffitt, 1997; Wickens & Rose, 2001; Yeh & Wickens, 1997) is illustrated schematically in Figure 10.9. Here the solid lines connecting the display to the user's head represent this rigid mounting. The dashed lines now correspond to the HMD when the user looks forward. The HMD is sometimes referred to as a wearable computer, which refers to the display of a computer that can be viewed as a user walks and looks around. Also, in many military environments it describes a helmet-mounted display. Designers of HMDs must consider two general human factors issues that we shall address next: (1) What is the advantage (or cost) of presenting information on an HMD rather than on a conventional fixed display (or a handheld display)? (2) How should the imagery on the HMD be presented? It turns out that the answer to the second question depends a lot on both the task and the frame of reference with which the imagery is presented, and so we shall focus on three different frames of reference for presenting HMD information. It further turns out that the decision to use an HMD to present information (and the choice of a particular frame of reference) also generates certain spawned costs, analogous to those encountered in the previous section, when choosing a 3-D display.

Frames of Reference in HMDs

The simplest frame of reference for an HMD is described as *screen referenced*. Here information is presented at a location on the screen, independent of the momentary head orientation. This is represented by the round dial gauge in Figure 10.9, although screen-referenced information could also be lines of text or spatial graphics such as a map. The advantage of screen-referenced symbology is that it can be viewed no matter how the head is turned. For example, screen referencing would allow a maintenance technician to view instructions continuously while searching for a physical component on a piece of equipment (Ockerman & Pritchett, 1998).

In contrast, *world-referenced* imagery on an HMD is depicted at a location such that it occupies a given orientation (azimuth and elevation) in the world relative to the observer. Thus the hill, shown to the right of the observer in Figure 10.9, will appear on the HMD as he looks right, but will vanish from the display as the head rotates forward. (Just as the real hill in the far domain would also vanish from direct view.) The range across which world-referenced imagery remains on the HMD as the head rotates depends on the field of view of the HMD, which is typically in the order of 30–60 degrees. The ability of the technology to display world-referenced imagery depends on an accurate and rapid head-tracking device that can measure head rotation, and rotate the imagery in the opposite direction, so that it is always aligned with some world-referenced fixed coordinate in the far domain.

The advantages of world-referenced imagery are twofold, as illustrated with the two different classes of HMD visibility: opaque and translucent. In the *opaque* HMD (the far domain is not visible), world-referenced imagery can create a *virtual reality*, essentially reconstructing a synthetic rendering of almost any environment desired (Durlach & Mavor, 1995; Barfield et al., 1995; Sherman & Craig, 2003). As documented elsewhere (e.g., Rolland, Biocca, Barlow, & Kancerla, 1995), virtual reality systems have numerous advantages in certain kinds of training tasks. In the *translucent* or see-through HMD, world-referenced imagery is overlaid on its real-world counterparts, often providing a better visual representation of those counterparts when visibility of the far domain is degraded (e.g., helping the pilot identify the location of a runway in haze). Such imagery may also be used to augment the reality of the far domain, for example, outlining the region of a tumor for the surgeon who is viewing an image of the human body or providing a text label for an overlaid geographical element. Hence such imagery is sometimes given the name of *augmented reality* (Milgram & Colquhoun, 1999).

The third frame of reference that can be adopted for an HMD in some applications is a *vehicle frame* of reference (Herdman, Johannsdottir, Armstrong, Jarmasz, LeFevre, & Lichacz, 2000). That is, the HMD would draw imagery to appear at a fixed location relative to the vehicle, independent of the direction of vehicle heading. In this regard, an HMD may be said to replace (or overlay) standard vehicle instruments, but it could also be designed to present new information that does not exist in those instruments (e.g., a text display that could always be seen whenever the operator rotated his head in a particular orientation). Given that the trunk is normally aligned with the vehicle, then a concept that is nearly equivalent to the vehicle frame is the trunk or ego-reference frame, in which imagery is presented at a constant orientation, relative to the trunk. In Figure 10.9, vehicle-referenced information is represented by the words "text display," which would always be seen if the head is oriented rightward and a little bit downward. (In Figure 10.9, the head is not rotated downward enough to see the word "display.") In contrast to screen-referenced imagery, which is always visible on an HMD, vehicle- (or ego-) referenced imagery is always accessible, since a simple head turn can always bring it into view at a consistent location. The advantage of such imagery over screen-referenced imagery is that it will not continuously obstruct the view of the far domain.

The costs and benefits of each of these frames of reference, relative to each other, and relative to a more stable head-down display, depend on the task. In the following discussion we introduce a slightly different task taxonomy than that used for spatial operations at the beginning of the chapter, using instead a more generic information-processing taxonomy, as this proves to be quite useful in distinguishing the costs and benefits of different frames of reference. We also note that many of the attentional issues relevant to HMD design are equally relevant to the design of head-up displays in vehicles (Newman, 1995; Weintraub & Ensing, 1992; Fadden, Ververs, & Wickens, 2001; Wickens, Ververs, & Fadden, 2004), which are typically translucent displays mounted forward of the observer. Indeed, the dashed display in Figure 10.9 could represent either a head-up display, or an HMD-oriented forward. Some of the conclusions described next, are based on the findings from the more prevalent head-up display research.

Task Performance Effects with HMDs

Accessing Information. As noted earlier, a key advantage of screen-referenced HMD imagery is its ability to be accessed and seen in a dynamic environment in which the body and head are constantly moving, independent of head orientation. Such an advantage will diminish to the extent that the operator remains at a fixed workstation, oriented head forward. Information access becomes slightly more difficult with vehicle-referenced imagery, since the head must turn to one particular orientation relative to the trunk in order to find it. However, that orientation is always consistent. In this regard the information-access costs of vehicle-referenced HMD imagery are exactly the same as those of vehicle-*mounted* imagery. Information access is more difficult still with world-referenced imagery because circumstances could arise when that imagery is directly behind the trunk orientation (i.e., when traveling away from the relevant location in the world).

Dividing Attention. The frame of reference also affects, to some extent, the ability to divide attention between the HMD imagery and the far domain (Yeh, Wickens, & Seagull, 1999). In a target search task, for example, the user can process world-referenced imagery while searching for far domain targets, such as the aircraft visible in the forward view of Figure 10.9. The search for relatively salient targets benefits from an HMD with world-referenced imagery, relative to a head-down display (Yeh et al., 1999; although the search for nonsalient targets may suffer as we discuss next).

Information Integration and Attention Guidance. Many HMD applications, particularly in military aircraft, are designed to guide the user's attention to a particular orientation in the far domain (i.e., world-referenced). This is accomplished by some sort of target cueing, such as an arrow pointing directly to the target (Yeh et al., 1999; Yeh, Merlo, Wickens, & Brandenburg, 2003). As noted previously, world-referenced imagery will also aid the user in integrating information on a display with spatial locations in the far domain, perhaps by overlaying relevant information over the far domain locations (an identification marker), or outlines of the far domain object, such as the hill overlay shown in the bottom right of Figure 10.9. In head-up displays, such overlays (e.g., a runway overlay on the real runway) are referred to as *conformal imagery* (Weintraub & Ensing, 1992), and offer particular benefits for tasks requiring the division of attention between near and far (Wickens & Long, 1995; Fadden et al., 2001; Foyle, Andre, McCann, Wenzel, Begault, & Battiste, 1996) by appearing to link the two domains together as the viewpoint is moved.

Focusing Attention. Any task pertaining exclusively to imagery in one domain or the other, and therefore requiring attention to be focused on that imagery, may suffer to the extent that visual information in one domain overlays (or is overlaid by) information in the other, creating clutter. Such overlay will always be present with screen-referenced imagery, and will be more disruptive of the focus of attention if the amount of screen-referenced imagery on the HMD is greater or as the salience of a far-domain target decreases (Yeh et al., 2003). The disruption may involve difficulty in reading the display because of background clutter, or difficulty in seeing small far domain images because of the overlaying imagery clutter (Wickens & Long, 1995; Fadden et al., 2001). These overlay problems will be diminished with vehicle referencing because the overlay will only exist at one small direction of view. It will also be diminished with world referencing, because here the function of overlay is typically to provide a redundant representation of the far domain, and so overlay will not obscure anything in the far domain that is not already present in the HMD imagery itself; see the mountain in Figure 10.9.

Maintaining Situation Awareness. In many respects, a world-referenced HMD is like an immersed 3-D display, whether it is translucent or opaque. Indeed, an opaque, world-referenced HMD that is used to create virtual reality is closely related to what is termed desktop VR, in which the viewing direction and location is altered by manipulation of some manual control device instead of head movement because, the view screen remains at a fixed location directly in front of the user. Thus the challenges of world-referenced HMDs for situation awareness mimic, to some extent, the same challenges of immersed 3-D displays, discussed in Section 5; namely those of attentional tunneling, a favored viewpoint, and a keyhole view of the 3-D world, which may inhibit noticing dynamic changes in regions other than that captured by the momentary forward view. Such problems will be far less serious if the entire domain to be monitored is visible at one head orientation (e.g., with screen-referenced imagery).

Creating Reality. Again, paralleling the effects of 3-D immersive displays, it is apparent that world-referenced imagery on an HMD will present a more realistic image, sense of immersion, or presence in the environment, and there are many training tasks in which this is a desirable feature (e.g., Pausch, Shackelford, & Proffitt, 1993; Pausch, Proffitt, & Williams, 1997; Sherman & Craig, 2003). This will be particularly true if the training involves some direct perceptual motor interaction with the environment, such as the rehearsal of a surgical procedure. However, the distinction between creating reality and maintaining situation awareness is an important one that designers must keep in mind. More reality does not necessarily create better situation awareness.

Spawned Costs of HMDs

HMDs with any sort of imagery generate certain spawned costs. For example, the limited field of view of an HMD may restrict peripheral vision of the far domain and this, as well as the overlap of visual imagery discussed earlier, can inhibit the search for uncued targets in the far domain (the small aircraft in Figure 10.9; Yeh et al., 1999, 2003). If HMDs are mounted to helmets that are heavy, this can also create fatigue and constrain the amount of head movement (Seagull & Gopher, 1997; Yeh et al., 1999), thus further inhibiting search. When world-referenced imagery is employed, care must be taken to ensure that the image generation, contingent on head tracking, is rapid. Otherwise there will be a lag in image drawing as the head is rotated rapidly, a lag that can disrupt perceptual motor performance and be a substantial source of motion sickness (Dudfield, Hardiman, & Selcon, 1995). Finally, it appears that world-referenced imagery on an HMD tends to lead users to greater trust or reliance on that imagery than when it is either screen-referenced or presented head down, when such imagery is used to direct attention (Yeh et al., 1999; Yeh & Wickens, 2001; Yeh et al., 2003). For example, an "intelligent cue" that guides the user to look for a particular target may be incorrect, either guiding attention to nothing, or to something that looks similar to, but is different from, that target. When such a breakdown in automation occurs, research indicates that the world-referenced HMD cueing produces a greater focus on, reliance on, or overtrust in the cue, than is the case with other frames of reference, or locations (head down) of the cueing guidance.

Conclusion

In conclusion, HMD performance effects are complex and not always easily predictable because of the number of different factors that are involved, many of which are not discussed here (see Melzer & Moffitt, 1997; National Research Council, 1997; Durlach & Mavor, 1995; Barfield et al., 1995; Yeh & Wickens, 1997, for further reading). From the perspective of the present chapter, a critical aspect appears to be the frame of reference available, which, coupled with a careful task analysis, can provide the designer with some guidance of how to represent both spatial and nonspatial information.

INFORMATION SPACE

The previous material in this chapter has focused on the representation of real space, defined by physical attributes and locations. In this final section, we address some similar issues in *information space* where entities, objects, or as we refer to them here, *nodes*, are not rigidly fixed in location; nor are movements within this space governed by the laws of physics. Instead, information space can be said to emerge inherently from the relationships between the nodes in the space, and graphically rendered movement can be accomplished as rapidly as the imagery can be updated. The creation and structure of that space is primarily the responsibility of the designer of the interface with which the space is represented and used. There is, however, an inherent spatial structure in most information databases underlying the space for the designer to draw on. This structure is defined, in part, by the distance between nodes, and such distance is in turn defined by the degree of relatedness (number of shared features, or closeness along a dimension) between nodes.

Figure 10.10 shows four qualitatively different kinds of information space structures, adopted from Durding, Becker, and Gould (1977). Figure 10.10a defines a classic hierarchical menu structure, such as an index, genealogical tree, company organization, or computer file structure. Similarity is defined in terms of relatedness, so all nodes within a given category are more related to each other ("closer") than nodes in different categories. Correspondingly, nodes that are one generation apart (e.g., joystick–control in Figure 10.10a) are more related than those that are two (joystick–interface) or three generations apart. Figure 10.10b defines a *network* of information nodes, which may represent for example a link diagram of eye scans between instruments, or a communication network of who talks to whom. Frequent communications between nodes (Bill–Debbie) define a close relationship, and so also do nodes that are separated by fewer links (Karen–Amy versus Karen–Bill). In many information databases, the strength of links may be determined by the number of shared features between nodes: for example, the number of shared keywords between articles in a bibliographical database.

Figure 10.10c presents a *matrix organization*, in which nodes are ordered along some external variable, such as chronology or topic type. This ordering scale may (or may not) define a scale of relatedness that is meaningful to the user, such as chronology (nodes that have similar dates are more likely to be more closely related). Finally, Figure 10.10d represents a true Euclidian space. This can describe real space (e.g., suppose the three

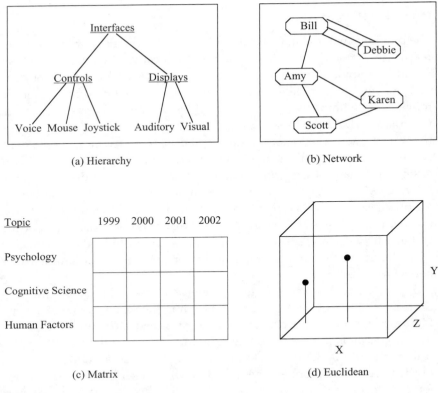

(a) Hierarchy

(b) Network

(c) Matrix

(d) Euclidean

Space

FIGURE 10.10. Information spaces.

dimensions are dimensions of the atmosphere in which temperature samples are taken), or a more conceptual space, such as three dimensions of economic health of a company (Wickens, Merwin, & Lin, 1994). It is important to note that equivalent data can sometimes be represented in the different formats shown here. For example, psychologists using factor analysis determine the degree of relatedness between different dimensions in network form (Figure 10.10b), but programs can then create from these data, a Euclidian structure (Figure 10.10d) that best captures these relations in terms of two or three dimensions.

Within each type of space, one can then describe both perceptual/cognitive activities of "searching" and "understanding," as well as action-related activities of "traveling" or "navigating," from node to node (or place to place). In addition to the form of representation of the information structure, and how this structure is rendered on a display, the second critical variable in information space is the task that a user is expected to carry out within the space (Vincow & Wickens, 1998). Here we describe a task analysis that is related to, but not identical to, that described at the beginning of the chapter. According to this analysis, the user may wish to:

(1) retrieve an entity (information about a node) whose identity is known. An example is the need to find a phone number of a person whose name is known precisely.

(2) retrieve information about a node whose existence is known, but the precise identity is not known. An example is locating a reference about a topic, a reference that you know exists, but whose author you cannot recall.

(3) compare nodes (in pairs or larger groups), that share some common task-related feature. An example might be a pilot, needing to make an emergency landing, who needs to compare information about the landing capabilities of the aircraft, and the runway length of the nearest airports (Seidler & Wickens, 1992; Wickens & Seidler, 1997).

(4) understand the overall structure of the database. This is often the task of the scientist or data analyst, who is looking to find patterns within a set of data observations (nodes) (Bederson & Schneiderman, 2003).

For each of these tasks (and particularly for the first three), the "ego/icon" as defined earlier in the chapter, can be simply described as the momentary focus of attention or point of regard within the database. It is a node or set of nodes about which detailed information is to be extracted. The designer of information systems must then be sensitive to the nature of the tasks that users must perform. If, for example, the only tasks required are those of known retrieval (task 1), then there is little need to present an information space at all, as more symbolic representations of the information can suffice. A simple alphabetically ordered list (e.g., the phone book), or a keyword retrieval system (directory assistance) is adequate. For task 2, lists and keyword retrievals are again often adequate; but a keyword retrieval will typically offer multiple options, leaving the user to recognize the needed option. A spatial visualization of all data in the database can support task 2 because the user can "find" the set of possible items; they are all in one place (close together in the space), and so the search for the desired item is rapid. It is for task 3 (comparison) and particularly task 4 (understanding) that simple keyword retrieval mechanisms are either awkward (task 3) or inappropriate (task 4) and therefore such tasks can generally be better served by a visual–spatial representation of the information. Such a representation may be passive and static, as for example, a static depiction of a menu structure that can support a user in choosing the correct node to access. Alternatively, the representation may be active and dynamic, allowing the user to navigate through it, visit different nodes, zoom in, zoom out, or view the entire space from different orientations.

Once a designer chooses to create an information space, there are naturally a host of human factor issues that must be addressed, many of which go well beyond the focus of this chapter. We consider here two important ones that reflect issues addressed earlier, the dimensionality of the information representation, and its frame of reference. In the context of information visualization, these two issues are closely intertwined.

Dimensionality

The primary reason for presenting a three-dimensional representation of information is if that information is inherently defined by three dimensions (Figure 10.10d). If it is not (e.g., Figure 10.10c), then two-dimensional representations are fine. There is no reason, for example, to present a simple graph of Y as a function of X, as a 3-D graph. If, however, the information does have three inherent dimensions (e.g., an X–Y relation as a function of time, or the evolving two-dimensional matrix structure of a company as it changes over time), then two further conditions may suggest the desirability of a three-dimensional representation: (a) The database is very densely populated, so that one can only see the overall structure (task 4), and easily find things in it (tasks 2 and 3), if all three dimensions are represented simultaneously. (b) The data involve simultaneous changes or correlations across all three dimensions, which can only be easily understood (task 4) by seeing their integrated representation (Wickens, Merwin, & Lin, 1994). In contrast to the 3-D representations, there are certainly plenty of alternatives to presenting three (or higher) dimensional data in 2-D (plan view) form, and these alternatives gain in their advantages to the extent that neither of these conditions apply. For example, the designer can present different pairs of dimension in coplanar form (see Figure 10.3c), can present different 2-D slices along the third dimension side by side, can allow the user to control the level of the third dimension that is represented (e.g., a computer slider that moves forward and backward in time; North, Shneiderman, & Plaisant, 1996; Wainer & Velleman, 2001), or represent that third dimension in some nonspatial form, such as color or gray scale (Merwin, Vincow, &

Wickens, 1994). Indeed research studies comparing 2-D versus 3-D representations of information spaces have not found consistent advantages of one over the other (Poblete, 1995; Risden, Czerwinski, Munzner, & Cook, 2000; Modjeska, 2000; Wickens et al., 1994). Such research suggests that the relative advantage depends on the task, on the extent to which multiple 2-D renderings support rapid access of (or movement along) the third dimension, and the degree of *egocentricity* of representing the point of interest in the 3-D view. This last issue relates directly to the frame of reference question, to which we now turn.

Frame of Reference

As we noted earlier, ego/icon in information space can best be thought of as the location and orientation of a point of interest. It is appropriate then to think of the frame of reference as defined by the extent to which this point of interest is highlighted – a local "zoom in" view of the space – versus not; a more global, wide-angle view of the space. In the terms described in Figure 10.5, it is apparent that the immersed display, by prominently highlighting the region just in front of the viewer, provides a local view, whereas the more exocentric display provides the global view (Figure 10.11). When

FIGURE 10.11. (a) Egocentric (increased) view of 3-D library database; (b) Exocentric view of the same database (from Vincow & Wickens, 1998).

(b)

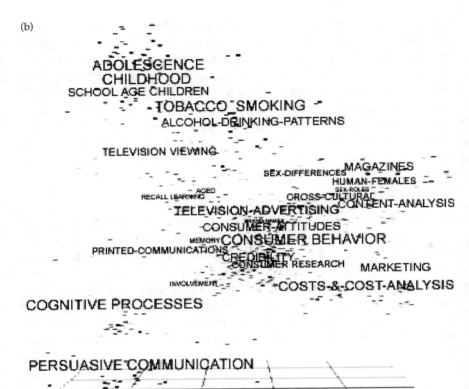

FIGURE 10.11 *continued.*

immersed and exocentric displays of information space are compared (Vincow & Wickens, 1998; McCormick et al., 1998), it is not surprising that more exocentric views support a better understanding of the structure of the information space. They also allow more rapid location of items within the space because the greater amount of the space represented on a single screen allows that search can be carried out through eye movements alone, rather than through manual manipulation of the viewpoint location and orientation (McCormick et al., 1998). Furthermore, an immersed view, with its keyhole view of the information space, can lead to the phenomenon of getting lost if navigation through the space is required (Modjeska, 2000; Snowberry, Parkinson, & Sisson, 1983).

As a consequence of the keyhole problems, comparative evaluations of immersed versus exocentric displays of information space have revealed few advantages for the immersed display. Its sole advantage would appear to be the greater visual resolution of information near the point of regard. However, in rendering information spaces electronically, there would appear to be other better solutions; for example, allowing a pop-up window next to the point of regard that can provide its specific detailed information at whatever level of detail is necessary.

SUMMARY AND CONCLUSIONS

In conclusion, we have seen how any representation of space, whether real or synthetic (as in information space) that also involves a user of that space, must inherently define at least two frames of reference: an ego-frame representing the momentary location and orientation of the user, and a world frame in which the space is represented. In designing interfaces to aid the user's interaction with the space, some or all of the six dimensions of each frame, and the possibility of added frames (related to head, display, control, or vehicle) must be considered. Most importantly, the tasks required of the user must be explicitly considered since these tasks impose varying kinds of transformations between reference frames, and these transformations in turn vary in their difficulty. Designing a system to minimize the number or degree of difficult transformations is good, but in real-world environments, such a design may spawn additional costs to performance. The optimal design must consider all of these factors.

ACKNOWLEDGMENT

This paper was written while the first author was supported by Contract No. NASA NAG 2-1535 from NASA Ames Research Center. Dr. David Foyle was the scientific technical monitor. Many of the ideas reported in the chapter derived from that support.

Suggestions for Further Reading

For a review of research on pictorial communication in virtual and real environments, see this edited volume:

Ellis, S., Kaiser, M., & Grunwald, D. A. (Editors). (1993). *Pictorial communications in virtual and real environments*. London: Taylor & Francis.

For a more extensive discussion of aviation displays, see:

Wickens, C. D. (2003). Aviation displays. In P. Tsang & M. Vidulich (Eds.), *Principles and practices of aviation psychology* (pp. 147–199). Mahwah, NJ: Lawrence Erlbaum Associates.

References

Alexander, A. L., & Wickens, C. D. (2003). The effects of spatial awareness biases on maneuver choice in a cockpit display of traffic information. *Proceedings of the 12th International Symposium on Aviation Psychology.* Dayton, OH.

Andre, A., Wickens, C. D., Moorman, L., & Boechelli, M. (1991). Display formatting techniques for improving situation awareness in the aircraft cockpit. *International Journal of Aviation Psychology, 11,* pp 205–218.

Aretz, A. J. (1991). The design of electronic map displays. *Human Factors, 33,* 85–101.

Aretz, A. J., & Wickens, C. D. (1992). The mental rotation of map displays. *Human Factors, 5,* 303–328.

Banbury, S. & Tremblay, S. (2004). A cognitive approach to situation awareness. Brookfield, VT: Ashgate.

Barfield, W., Rosenberg, C., & Furness, T. A. I. (1995). Situation awareness as a function of frame of reference, computer-graphics eyepoint elevation, and geometric field of view. *International Journal of Aviation Psychology, 5*(3), 233–256.

Bederson, B. & Schneiderman, B. (2003). *The craft of information visualization.* Elsevier.

Bellenkes, A. H., Wickens, C. D., & Kramer, A. F. (1997). Visual scanning and pilot expertise: The role of attentional flexibility and mental model development. *Aviation, Space, and Environmental Medicine, 68*(7), 569–579.

Cohen, D., Otakeno, S., Previc, F. H., & Ercoline, W. R. (2001). Effect of "inside-out" and "outside-in" attitude displays on off-axis tracking in pilots and nonpilots. *Aviation, Space, & Environmental Medicine, 72*(3), 170–176.

Cooper, L. A., & Shepard, R. N. (1973). The time required to prepare for a rotated stimulus. *Memory and Cognition, 1,* 246–250.

Delzell, S., & Battiste, V. (1993). Navigational demands of low-level helicopter flight. In R. S. Jensen & D. Meumlister (Eds.), *Proceedings of the 7th International Symposium on Aviation Psychology* (pp. 838–842). Columbus: Ohio State University.

Doherty, S., & Wickens, C. D. (2000). *An analysis of the immersed perspective flight path display benefit: Benefit of preview, prediction, and frame of reference* (Tech. Rep. ARL-00-5/NASA-00-1). Savoy: University of Illinois, Aviation Research Lab.

Dudfield, H. J., Hardiman, T. D., & Selcon, S. J. (1995). Human factors issues in the design of helmet-mounted displays. In R. J. Lewandowski, W. Stephens, & L. A. Haworth (Eds.), *Proceedings of the International Society for Optical Engineers (SPIE): Helmet- and Head-mounted Displays and Symbology Design Requirements II* (pp. 214–225). Bellingham, WA: SPIE.

Durding, B. M., Becker, C. A., & Gould, J. D. (1977). Data organization. *Human Factors, 19,* 1–14.

Durlach, N. I., & Mavor, A. (1995). *Virtual reality: Scientific and technological challenges.* Washington, DC: National Academy Press.

Durso, F. T. (1999). Situation awareness. In F. Durso (Ed.), *Handbook of applied cognition.* New York: John Wiley.

Eley, M. G. (1988). Determining the shapes of land surfaces from topographic maps. *Ergonomics, 31,* 355–376.

Ellis, S., Kaiser, M., & Grumwald, D. A. (Eds.). (1993). *Pictorial communications in virtual and real environments.* London: Taylor & Francis.

Fadden, S., Ververs, P. M., & Wickens, C. D. (2001). Pathway HUDS: Are they viable? *Human Factors, 43*(2), 173–193.

Foyle, D. C., Andre, A. D., McCann, R. S., Wenzel, E. M., Begault, D. R., & Battiste, V. (1996). Taxiway navigation and situation awareness (T-NASA) system: Problem, design philosophy, and description of an integrated display suite for low-visibility airport surface operations. *SAE Transactions: Journal of Aerospace, 105*, 1411–1418.

Franklin, N., & Tversky, B. (1990). Searching imagined environments. *Journal of Experimental Psychology: General, 119*, 63–76.

Garland, D., & Endsley, M. (2000). *Situation awareness analysis and measurement.* Mahwah, NJ: Lawrence Erlbaum Associates.

Goldberg, J. H., Maceachren, A. M., & Korval, X. P. (1992). Image transformations in terrain map comparison. *Cartographica, 29*, 46–59.

Gregory, R. L. (1977). *Eye and brain.* London: Weidenfeld and Nicolson.

Gugerty, L., & Brooks, J. (2001). Seeing where you are heading: Integrating environmental and egocentric reference frames in cardinal direction judgments. *Journal of Experimental Psychology: Applied, 7* (3), 251–266.

Haskell, I. D., & Wickens, C. D. (1993). Two- and three-dimensional displays for aviation: A theoretical and empirical comparison. *The International Journal of Aviation Psychology, 3*, 87–109.

Herdman, C. M., Johannsdottir, K. R., Armstrong, J., Jarmasz, J., LeFevre, J. A., & Lichacz, F. (2000). Mixed-up but flyable: HMDs with aircraft- and head-referenced symbology. *EPCE, 3.*

Hickox, J. C., & Wickens, C. D. (1999). Effects of elevation angle disparity, complexity, and feature type on relating out-of-cockpit field of view to an electronic cartographic map. *Journal of Experimental Psychology: Applied, 5*(3), 284–301.

Hochberg, J., & Brooks, V. (1978). Film cutting and visual momentum. In J. W. Senders, D. F. Fisher, & R. A. Monty (Eds.), *Eye movements and the higher psychological functions.* Hillsdale, NJ: Erlbaum.

Howard, I. P. (1986). The perception of posture, self-motion, and the visual vertical. In K. R. Boff, L. Kaufman, & J. P. Thomas (Eds.), *Handbook of perception and performance (Vol. 1)* (pp. 18-2–18-62). New York: Wiley.

Howard, I. P. (1993). Spatial vision within egocentric and exocentric frames of reference. In S. R. Ellis, M. Kaiser, & A. J. Grunwald (Eds.), *Pictorial communication in virtual and real environments* (pp. 338–357). London: Taylor & Francis.

Johnson, S. L., & Roscoe, S. N. (1972). What moves the airplane or the world? *Human Factors, 14*, 107–129.

Kovalenko, P. A. (1991). Psychological aspects of pilot spatial orientation. *ICAO Journal, 46*, 18–23.

Levine, M. (1982). You-are-here maps: Psychological considerations. *Environment and Behavior, 14*, 221–237.

Macedo, J. A., Kaber, D. B., Endsley, M. R., Powanusorm, P., & Myung, S. (1998). The effect of automated compensation for incongruent axes on teleoperator performance. *Human Factors, 40*(4), 541–553.

McCormick, E., Wickens, C. D., Banks, R., & Yeh, M. (1998). Frame of reference effects on scientific visualization subtasks. *Human Factors, 40*(3), 443–451.

McGreevy, M. W., & Ellis, S. R. (1986). The effect of perspective geometry on judged direction in spatial information instruments. *Human Factors, 28*, 439–456.

Melzer, J. E., & Moffitt, K. (Eds.) (1997). *Head-mounted displays: Designing for the user.* New York: McGraw-Hill.

Merwin, D., Vincow, M., & Wickens, C. D. (1994). Visual analysis of scientific data: Comparison of 3-D-topographic, color and gray scale displays in a feature detection task. *Proceedings of the 38th Annual Meeting of the Human Factors and Ergonomics Society* (pp. 240–244). Santa Monica, CA: Human Factors Society.

Milgram, P., & Colquhoun, H. (1999). A taxonomy of real and virtual world display integration. In Y. Ohta & H. Tamura (Eds.), *Mixed reality – merging real and virtual worlds.* Ohmsha (Tokyo) and Springer-Verlag (Berlin) (pp. 1–25).

Modjeska, D. K. (2000). *Hierarchical data visualization in desktop virtual reality.* Unpublished doctoral dissertation. University of Toronto.

National Research Council. (1997). *Tactical display for soldiers: Human factors considerations.* Washington DC: National Academy Press.

Newman, R. L. (1995). *Head-up displays: Designing the way ahead.* Brookfield, VT: Avebury.

Niall, K. K. (1997). "Mental rotation," pictured rotation and tandem rotation in depth. *Acta Psychologica, 95*, 31–83.

North, C., Shneiderman, B., & Plaisant, C. (1996). User-controlled overviews of an image library: A case study of the visible human. *Proceedings of ACM Digital Libraries '96 Conference.* ACM Press.

Ockerman, J. J., & Pritchett, A. R. (1998). Preliminary study of wearable computers for aircraft inspection. In G. Boy, C. Graeber, & J. M. Robert (Eds.), *HCI-Aero '98: International Conference on Human-Computer Interaction in Aeronautics.*

Olmos, O., Liang, C. C., & Wickens, C. D. (1997). Electronic map evaluation in simulated visual meteorological conditions. *International Journal of Aviation Psychology, 7*, 37–66.

Olmos, O., Wickens, C. D., & Chudy, A. (2000). Tactical displays for combat awareness: An examination of dimensionality and frame of reference concepts and the application of cognitive engineering. *The International Journal of Aviation Psychology, 10*(3), 247–271.

Pausch, R., Proffitt, D., & Williams, G. (1997, August). Quantifying immersion in virtual reality. *ACM SIGGRAPH '97 Conference Proceedings, Computer Graphics.*

Pausch, R., Shackelford, M. A., & Proffitt, D. (1993). A user study comparing head-mounted and stationary displays. *IEEE Symposium on Research Frontiers in Virtual Reality.* Los Alamitos, CA: IEEE.

Perrone, J. A., & Wenderoth, P. (1993). Visual slant underestimation. In S. R. Ellis, M. Kaiser, & A. J. Grunwald (Eds.), *Pictorial communication in virtual and real environments.* London: Taylor & Francis.

Poblete, F. P. (1995). *The use of information visualization to enhance awareness of hierarchical structure.* Unpublished thesis, master's, University of Toronto, Canada.

Previc, F. H. (1998). The neuropsychology of 3-D space. *Psychological Bulletin, 124*, 123–164.

Previc, F. H., & Ercoline, W. R. (1999). The "outside-in" attitude display concept revisited. *IJAP, 9*(4), 377–401.

Rensink, R. A. (2002). Change detection. *Annual Review of Psychology, 5*, 245–277.

Risden, K., Czerwinski, M. P., Munzner, T., & Cook, D. B. (2000). An initial examination of ease of use for 2-D and 3-D information visualizations of web content. *International Journal of Human-Computer Studies, 53*, 695–714.

Rolland, J. P., Biocca, F. A., Barlow, T., & Kancerla, A. (1995). Quantification of adaptation to virtual-eye location in see-through head-mounted displays. *1995 IEEE Virtual Reality International Symposium* (pp. 56–66). Los Alamitos, CA: IEEE.

Roscoe, S. N. (1968). Airborne displays for flight and navigation. *Human Factors, 10*, 321–332.

Roscoe, S. N. (2002). Ergavionics: Designing the job of flying an airplane. *International Journal of Aviation Psychology, 12*(4), 331–339.

Roscoe, S. N., Corl, L., & Jensen, R. S. (1981). Flight display dynamics revisited. *Human Factors, 23*, 341–353.

Rudmann, D. S., & McConkie, G. W. (1999). Eye movements in human-computer interaction. *Proceedings of the 3rd Annual FedLab Symposium, Advanced Displays and Interactive Displays Consortium* (pp. 91–95).

Ruddle, R., Payne, S. J., & Jones, D. M. (1999). The effects of maps on navigation and search strategies in very large-scale virtual environments. *Journal of Experimental Psychology: Applied, 5*, 54–75.

Schraagen, J. M., Chipman, S., & Shalin, V. (2000). *Cognitive task analysis.* Mahwah, NJ: Lawrence Erlbaum Associates.

Schreiber, B. T., Wickens, C. D., Renner, G. J., Alton, J., & Hickox, J. C. (1998). Navigational checking using 3-D maps: The influence of elevation angle, azimuth, and foreshortening. *Human Factors, 40*(2), 209–223.

Seagull, F. J., & Gopher, D. (1997). Training head movement in visual scanning: An embedded approach to the development of piloting skills with helmet-mounted displays. *Journal of Experimental Psychology: Applied, 3*(3), 163–180.

Seidler, K. S., & Wickens, C. D. (1992). Distance and organization in multifunction displays. *Human Factors, 34*(5), 555–569.

Shepard, R. N., & Hurwitz, S. (1984). Upward direction, mental rotation, and discrimination of left and right turns in maps. *Cognition, 18*, 161–193.

Shepard, S., & Metzler, D. (1971). Mental rotation of three-dimensional objects. *Science, 171*, 701–703.

Sherman, W. R., & Craig, A. B. (2003). *Understanding virtual reality.* San Francisco, CA: Morgan Kaufman.

Simon, J. R., (1969). Reaction toward the source of stimulus. *Journal of Experimental Psychology, 81*, 174–176.

Simons, D. J. (2000). Current approaches to change blindness. *Visual Cognition, 7*(1/2/3), 1–15.

Snowberry, K., Parkinson, S. R., & Sisson, N. (1983). Computer display menus. *Ergonomics, 26*(7), 699–712.

St. John, M., Cowen, M. B., Smallman, H. S., & Oonk, H. M. (2001). The use of 2-D and 3-D displays for shape-understanding versus relative-position tasks. *Human Factors, 43*(1), 79–98.

Thomas, L. C., & Wickens, C. D. (2000). *Effects of display frames of reference on spatial judgments and change detection* (Tech. Rep. ARL-00-14/FED-LAB-00-4). Savoy: University of Illinois, Aviation Research Lab.

Vincow, M. A., & Wickens, C. D. (1998). Frame of reference and navigation through document visualizations: Flying through information space. *Proceedings of the 42nd Annual Meeting of the Human Factors and Ergonomics Society* (pp. 511–515). Santa Monica, CA: Human Factors and Ergonomics Society.

Wainer, H., & Velleman, P. S. (2001). Statistical graphics: Mapping the pathways of science. *Annual Review of Psychology, 52*, 305–335.

Warren, D. H., Rossano, M. J., & Wear, T. D. (1990). Perception of map-environment correspondence: The roles of features and alignment. *Ecological Psychology, 2*, 131–150.

Weintraub, D. J., & Ensing, M. J. (1992). *Human factors issues in head-up display design: The book of HUD* (SOAR CSERIAC State of the Art Report 92-2). Dayton, OH: Crew System Ergonomics Information Analysis Center, Wright Patterson AFB.

Wickens, C. D. (1993). Cognitive factors in display design. *Journal of the Washington Academy of Sciences, 83(4)*, 179–201.

Wickens, C. D. (1999). Frames of reference for navigation. In D. Gopher & A. Koriat (Eds.), *Attention and performance, Vol. 16* (pp. 113–144). Cambridge, MA: MIT Press.

Wickens, C. D. (2000). Human factors in vector map design: The importance of task-display dependence. *Journal of Navigation, 53(1)*, 54–67.

Wickens, C. D. (2003). Aviation displays. In P. Tsang & M. Vidulich (Eds.), *Principles and practices of aviation psychology* (pp. 147–199). Mahwah, NJ: Lawrence Erlbaum Associates.

Wickens, C. D., Liang, C. C., Prevett, T. T., & Olmos, O. (1996). Egocentric and exocentric displays for terminal area navigation. *International Journal of Aviation Psychology, 6*, 241–271.

Wickens, C. D., & Long, J. (1995). Object versus space-based models of visual attention: Implications for the design of head-up displays. *Journal of Experimental Psychology: Applied, 1(3)*, 179–193.

Wickens, C. D., Merwin, D. H., & Lin, E. (1994). Implications of graphics enhancements for the visualization of scientific data: Dimensional integrality, stereopsis, motion, and mesh. *Human Factors, 36*, 44–61.

Wickens, C. D., & Prevett, T. T. (1995). Exploring the dimensions of egocentricity in aircraft navigation displays: Influences on local guidance and global situation awareness. *Journal of Experimental Psychology: Applied, 1*, 110–135.

Wickens, C. D., & Rose, P. N. (2001). *Human factors handbook for displays: Summary of findings from the Army Research Lab's Advanced Displays and Interactive Displays Federated Laboratory*. Adelphi, MD: Army Research Laboratory.

Wickens, C. D., & Seidler, K. S. (1997). Information access in a dual-task context: Testing a model of optimal strategy selection. *Journal of Experimental Psychology: Applied, 3(3)*, 196–215.

Wickens, C. D., Thomas, L. C., & Young, R. (2000). Frames of reference for the display of battlefield information: Judgment-display dependencies. *Human Factors, 42(4)*, 660–675.

Wickens, C. D., Todd, S., & Seidler, K. (1989). *Three-dimensional displays: Perception, implementation, and applications* (Tech. Rep. ARL-89-11/CSERIAC-89-1). Savoy: University of Illinois, Aviation Research Laboratory (also CSERIAC SOAR

89–001, Crew System Ergonomics Information Analysis Center, Wright-Patterson AFB, OH, December).

Wickens, C. D., Ververs, P. M., & Fadden, S. (2004). Head-up displays. In D. Harris (Ed.), *Human factors for civil flight deck design*. Brookfield, VT: Ashgate.

Woods, D. D. (1984). Visual momentum: A concept to improve the cognitive coupling of person and computer. *International Journal of Man-Machine Studies, 21,* 229–244.

Worringham, C. J., & Beringer, D. B. (1989). Operator orientation and compatibility in visual-motor task performance. *Ergonomics, 32*(4), 387–399.

Yeh, M., Merlo, J., Wickens, C. D., & Brandenburg, D. L. (2003). Head-up vs. head-down: The costs of imprecision, unreliability, and visual clutter on cue effectiveness for display signaling. *Human Factors, 45*(4), (pp. 390–407).

Yeh, M., & Wickens, C. D. (1997). Performance issues in helmet-mounted displays (Tech. Rep. No. ARL-97-9/Army Fed Lab 97-1). Savoy: University of Illinois, Aviation Research Lab.

Yeh, M., & Wickens, C. D. (2001). Display signaling in augmented reality: Effects of cue reliability and image realism on attention allocation and trust calibration. *Human Factors, 43,* 355–365.

Yeh, M., Wickens, C. D., & Seagull, F. J. (1999). Target cueing in visual search: The effects of conformality and display location on the allocation of visual attention. *Human Factors, 41*(4), 524–542.

11

The Comprehension of Quantitative Information in Graphical Displays

Priti Shah, Eric G. Freedman, and Ioanna Vekiri

ABSTRACT

This chapter describes current psychological research on graph comprehension. We describe current models of graph comprehension, including both detailed computational and mathematical models as well as general process models. In the next sections, we describe the influence of display characteristics (e.g., line graph vs. bar graph, color vs. black and white), data complexity, and task on graph interpretation. Finally, we describe the effect of individual differences and developmental factors. Specifically, we consider how graphical literacy skills, content knowledge, visuospatial abilities, and working memory influence the interpretation of graphs. Finally, we discuss practical implications of this review and provide directions for future research.

INTRODUCTION

Vividly obvious and memorable at their best, graphs make complex information visually salient. A classic example of a graph of this type is one of Napoleon and his army's march to Russia and back, shown in Figure 11.1. In this graph, the thick line represents the path of his soldiers going to Russia, and the width of the line represents the size of the army. The thin path depicts the return voyage. The decimation of Napoleon's army is visually salient and perhaps even shocking. Occasionally, the poor design of a graph or difficulty in extracting important information from a graph can lead to tragic consequences. Indeed, the decision to launch the space shuttle *Challenger* has been blamed on the use of displays that obscured the relationship between temperature and O-ring failures (Oestermeier & Hesse, 2000; Tufte, 1997).

As these examples illustrate, graphs are frequently used for practical purposes, from making historical information accessible and memorable

426

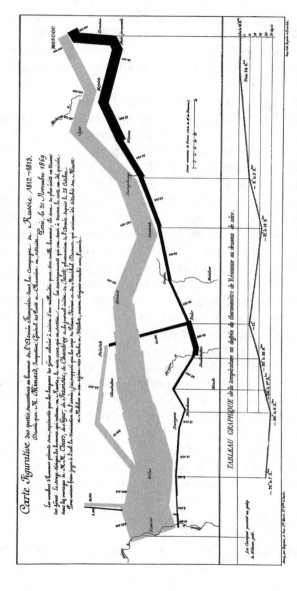

FIGURE 11.1. Napoleon's march to Russia. Reprinted with permission. Edward R. Tufte, *The Visual Display of Quantitative Information* (Cheshire, CT: Graphics Press, 1983).

to helping decision-makers comprehend relevant data. In science and social science, experts are often so dependent on graphs that they may be unable to do their work without them (Tabachneck-Schijf, Leonardo, & Simon, 1997). Indeed, use of graphs of quantitative data may be a central, possibly defining, feature of science. There is nearly a perfect correlation between the use of graphical displays and the "hardness" of a scientific discipline, both in scientific journals and textbooks (Smith, Best, Stubbs, Johnston, & Archibald, 2000).

Because graphical displays play a prominent role in the current Information Age and poor graph design or the inaccurate interpretation of data can lead to serious problems such as the _Challenger_ disaster, the study of cognitive and perceptual aspects of graph comprehension has been a thriving multidisciplinary enterprise. Each discipline considers the cognitive aspects of graphical displays with slightly different goals in mind. Cognitive psychological work aims to understand the cognitive and perceptual processes in graph interpretation and the influence of various display, task, and personal characteristic factors on these processes (including developmental factors). The goal of educational research has been on the errors that students make and the teaching of graphical literacy skills. Research in business and medicine has examined how graphs might influence people's decisions (to buy something, to choose a medical treatment, and so on). The goal of human factors and design research has been to guide the design of graphs. Finally, computer science research has sought to develop automated data display systems and novel information visualization tools, based in part on cognitive models of graph interpretation.

The goal of this review is to provide an integrative and evaluative review of this broad range of research, pointing out new questions and unresolved issues. We begin by characterizing graphs and describing general models of graph comprehension. We then outline research on the factors that influence graph comprehension: characteristics of the display (e.g., format, use of color), task (e.g., scientific visualization, read a point), data (e.g., complexity), and user (e.g., prior knowledge about content, scientific literacy).

GRAPHS AND VISUOSPATIAL COGNITION

Graphs are a unique form of visuospatial depictions that represent quantitative information via an analogy between quantitative scales and visual or spatial dimensions, such as length, color, or area (Bertin, 1983; Hegarty, Carpenter, & Just, 1991; Pinker, 1990). Graphs form a large part of a class of schematic diagrams (such as flow charts and Venn diagrams) that are based on *rational imagery*, meaning that information presented is systematically related to the graphic representation (Bertin, 1983). The relation is neither arbitrary, as is the relation between words and concepts, nor a first-order isomorphism, as is the relation between pictures and their referents (Winn, 1987). Because graphs fall on the middle of this continuum, along with other kinds of external displays considered in this volume such as maps (see Taylor, Chapter 8), navigational displays (see Wickens, Chapter 12), and diagrams (see Mayer, Chapter 12; Rinck, Chapter 9), many of the psychological and design issues that arise are quite similar to those in other chapters. At the same time, since graphs represent quantitative data, some of the psychological and design issues are quite different. In the conclusion, we highlight some of the common themes, as well as differences, between graphs and other external visuospatial representations.

MODELS OF GRAPH COMPREHENSION

One major goal in graph research has been to characterize the cognitive and perceptual processes in graph interpretation. For applied purposes, models of graph comprehension make predictions about how different factors influence the interpretation process and the subsequent understanding and accuracy of information encoded and remembered and, thus, provide guidelines about how best to display data.

There are two major classes of models of graph interpretation. First, a number of models provide detailed descriptions of simple graph interpretation tasks or subtasks, such as the ability to retrieve simple facts from a graph or the ability to discriminate between two proportions (e.g., Lohse, 1993; Meyer, 2000; Hollands & Dyre, 2000; Simkin & Hastie, 1986). Typically, these models emphasize perceptual processes, are mathematical or computational, and make predictions about the time necessary to retrieve specific facts from different kinds of displays and the accuracy of the retrieval process. However, these models do not address how people form general interpretations of data, perform open-ended tasks, or consider factors such as viewers' prior knowledge or content of graphs. A second class of models and task analyses focuses on more general process analyses (Bertin, 1983; Carpenter & Shah, 1998; Freedman & Shah, 2002; Pinker, 1990; Shah, 2001; Tabachneck-Schijf, Leonardo, & Simon, 1997) but is less precise in its predictions about specific processes or time and accuracy in performing tasks. Next, we briefly describe the major current models of graph comprehension and identify what these models imply about the influence of visual features of a graph, the type of data, task, prior knowledge, and other factors on graph interpretation.

Detailed Computational and Mathematical Models of Individual Fact Retrieval Tasks

One approach to modeling graph interpretation is to analyze the subcomponent perceptual processes. The *Understanding Cognitive Information Engineering* or UCIE (Lohse, 1993) model analyzes the processes of answering simple, fact-retrieval questions about line graphs (such as "What was the per capita income of France in 1969?") by combining a task analysis of individual perceptual and motor processes necessary to answer a question and estimates of the time to perform each step based on previous research. The UCIE model is based on a production-system architecture commonly used in human–computer interaction research (Card, Moran, & Newell, 1983). According to the UCIE model, the major factors that influence the time to interpret a graph include data complexity, the discriminability of visual features, and viewers' tasks. Working memory limitations also play a role because, when demand exceeds capacity, viewers may have to re-encode information. This model has been verified using eye fixations and reaction times and is perhaps the most detailed model of the entire process of graph comprehension, but it differs from other models in that it focuses entirely on perceptual processes and a limited range of tasks and types of graphs. Despite the seeming success of this model, one problem is that the reaction time predictions may hold because the test cases involve graphs that dramatically vary in visual and data complexity.

A related model is the visual search model (VSM) developed by Meyer (2000). According to the model, viewers sequentially scan each data point until the relevant item is found. Although this model is also fairly good in terms of predicting the time for simple data extraction tasks (Meyer, 2000), graph comprehension often involves the recognition of configuration or patterns, and many tasks do not depend on point comparisons. Indeed, the VSM cannot predict performance for identifying trends in data (Meyer, 1997).

A third, detailed information-processing analyses of relatively simple fact-retrieval tasks (Simkin & Hastie, 1986) also addresses a wider range of formats than Lohse's model and identifies some graph-specific subprocesses involved in encoding and discrimination tasks. These elementary perceptual processes include *anchoring, scanning,* and *superimposition* of the visual features. According to this model, the time to make a particular discrimination judgment (e.g., proportion A is greater than proportion B) is based on the minimum number of these elementary processes.

A final model specifies the magnitude and source of the biases involved in making proportion judgments (Hollands & Dyre, 2000; Spence, 1990). Making proportion judgments is relevant for graph comprehension (e.g., comprehension of pie charts). Depending on the specific stimuli, people underestimate some proportions and overestimate other proportions. Intriguingly, the over- and underestimation patterns are cyclical so that overestimation and underestimation of proportions alternate. In a two-cycle pattern, for example, people overestimate proportions less than .25, underestimate proportions between .25 and .5, overestimate proportions between .5 and .75, and underestimate proportions between .75 and 1.0 (Spence & Krizel, 1994; Spence, 1990). Hollands and Dyre propose a cyclical power model of proportion judgments based on Stevens's power law in which the number of cycles is dependent on the number of reference points, and the magnitude and direction of the bias is based on the Stevens's exponent.

General Process Models and Task Analyses

In addition to more detailed models of specific fact-retrieval tasks and discrimination and comparison processes that emphasize the low-level perceptual processes, a number of more general models emphasize the interaction of visual displays, expertise/prior knowledge, and task. In a classic book, Bertin (1983) proposed the generic task analysis of graph comprehension at this level. Three major component processes are required to comprehend a graph. First, viewers must encode the visual array and identify the important visual features (such as a straight line slanting downwards). Second, viewers must identify the quantitative facts or relations that those features represent (such as a decreasing linear relationship between x and y). Finally, viewers must relate those quantitative relations to the graphic variables depicted (such as population vs. year).

Pinker (1990) proposed a more elaborate version of this task analysis (see Figure 11.2). According to Pinker's model, viewers interpret a graph by first translating the encoded sensory image (called the *visual array* by Pinker) to a structural description of the relevant visual features of the graph, such as the bars or lines. The visual description is constrained by properties of the visual system (such as gestalt laws), processing constraints

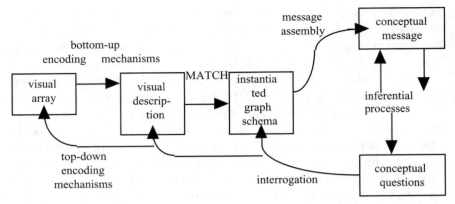

FIGURE 11.2. Pinker's proposed model of graph comprehension (adapted from Pinker, 1990, p. 104). Used with permission.

(such as working memory capacity), and the graph schema (a viewer's prior knowledge about graphs, such as the fact that there is an x–axis and a y–axis, that straight lines mean linear relationships, etc). For example, in viewing a line graph with two lines, the viewer may form a description, such as "two parallel lines increasing linearly with the dotted line above the solid line with age on the x–axis, height on the y–axis, and dotted lines representing boys and solid lines representing girls." Next, the visual description is translated into the conceptual message (a description of the quantitative information that is depicted) further aided by the knowledge in the graph schema. Thus, in this example, the viewer converts the visual description to "as children get older they get taller linearly and boys are slightly taller than girls at all ages." Finally, the viewer uses the conceptual message to answer questions about the quantitative information depicted in the graphs. Thus, if the question was "At age 8, who is taller, boys or girls?" the viewer can use the conceptual message to answer "boys."

In addition to models that account for either the perceptual or conceptual levels of graph comprehension, two approaches begin to attempt to integrate these levels. A production-system-based model that attempts to integrate these approaches was developed by Tabachneck-Schijf and her colleagues (Tabachneck-Schijf, Leonardo, & Simon, 1997). One advance of this model is that it considers what kinds of knowledge expert graph viewers have and how expertise influences the interpretation process. According to their model, experts (in this case, economics) have fairly elaborate graph schemas that associate fairly complex conceptual information with visual features of a display. Thus, graphs are especially useful for experts to reduce the complexity of the data comprehension process.

We have proposed an interactive model of graph comprehension (Freedman & Shah, 2002; Shah, 2001; Shah, Hoeffner, Gergle, Shellhammer, & Anderson, 2000) that attempts to integrate the two approaches and is preliminarily implemented computationally within the construction–integration framework of comprehension (Kintsch, 1988). According to our model, graph comprehension is represented as a sequential, constraint-satisfaction process in which characteristics of the visual display, a viewer's prior knowledge and expectations about the data, and his or her graphical literacy skills influence a viewer's interpretation of a data set. Bottom-up visual characteristics, such as the similarity of lines in a line graph or the proximity of bars in a bar graph (Carpenter & Shah, 1998; Shah, Freedman, Watkins, Rahman, & Miyake, 2004; Shah, Mayer, & Hegarty, 1999), influence the *visual chunks* that are encoded. Following Pinker (1990), a skilled graph viewer automatically forms a link between these visual chunks (the shape of the line) and the interpretation of the data. Eye fixation and reaction time data suggest that the extraction of individual visual chunks and their interpretation is sequential (Carpenter & Shah, 1998; Katz, Xi, Kim, & Cheng, 2002). When a perceiver lacks relevant graph skills or the display does not explicitly represent information that must then be inferred, comprehension is effortful.

Our model differs from Pinker in that, as visual chunks are activated, prior knowledge and expectations are also activated and have a top-down influence on what interpretations are formed. Thus, this model predicts that viewers are more likely to make inferences (such as identifying an overall trend in a line graph with multiple lines) when they have expectations about such a trend, as we have found in several empirical studies (Shah et al., 2004; Shah & Shellhammer, 1999). Indeed, the model also explains why, when viewers' prior knowledge is strong but they have little knowledge about links between graphic features and quantitative referents, they make errors in which viewers' interpretations are based on expectations rather than the data (Shah, 2001).

Common Themes From the Models

One main theme is a distinction between perceptual and conceptual processes. The first class of models focuses entirely on the perceptual processes that are relevant for many simple, fact-retrieval tasks. This set of models considers how the visual display features of a graph, such as discriminability of colors, the data complexity, and the viewer's task, together predict how quickly and accurately viewers are able to retrieve information from a graphical display.

The second class of models highlight the fact that graph comprehension can involve both perceptual and conceptual processes. These models suggest that visual features interact with viewers' prior knowledge about content and graph-reading expertise to predict when simple perceptual retrieval processes are sufficient to interpret a graph. Specifically, when a viewer has relevant information to make a link between visual features and meaning, perceptual processes are used; in such cases, interpretation is relatively fast and error-free. If visual features do not automatically evoke a relationship, either because the relationships are not visually integrated in a graph or because the graph viewer does not have the prior knowledge required to make an interpretation, information must be retrieved by complex inferential processes (Cheng, Cupit, & Shadbolt, 2001; Cleveland, 1993; Kosslyn, 1989, 1994; Larkin & Simon, 1987; Maichle, 1994; Pinker, 1990; Shah et al., 1999; Stenning & Oberlander, 1995). Thus, these models incorporate two additional factors that predict the viewers' interpretations of data: a graph viewer's prior knowledge about the content of the graph and their knowledge about graphs per se.

Together, these models predict that five factors play a role in predicting how viewers interpret graphs, how long it takes them, and viewers' subsequent interpretations/representations of data: the display characteristics (bar graph or line graph, animated or static), the data complexity, the viewer's task, the viewer's prior knowledge about content, and the viewer's graph-reading expertise and knowledge about graphs. In the following sections, we review the data associated with these factors.

DISPLAY CHARACTERISTICS

Visual display characteristics, such as format and color, influence both the low-level perceptual aspects of graph comprehension as well as the high-level cognitive processes. Furthermore, most of the research addresses how visual characteristics of a display influence graph comprehension. The research in this area ranges from the interpretation of different kinds of tangible line graphs for the blind (Aldrich & Parkin, 1987) to the use of color in meteorological displays (Hoffman, Detweiler, & Lipton, 1993) for more than 70 years (Croxton & Stryker, 1927). Thus, we begin with a discussion of the factors that influence graph comprehension with the major conclusions from the research on visual characteristics.

Abstract Characteristics

Quantitative values can be represented by a number of visual dimensions in a visual display, such as color, darkness, length, area, and so on. Several theoretical and empirical analyses suggest that for most tasks, spatial dimensions (and especially length) are the best dimensions for representing quantity, as compared to visual dimensions (such as color or shading) (Tversky, 2001; Kubovy, 1981; Cleveland & McGill, 1984, 1985). One argument (Tversky, 2001) is that spatial extent and other spatial dimensions are more natural representations of quantity because more of something physical is typically longer, further, higher, or bigger.

A theoretical division of different visual dimensions based on Kubovy's (1981) analysis specifically favors the use of spatial extent for representing quantitative information (Pinker, 1990). In this analysis, the two spatial (x–y) dimensions and time are called indispensable attributes (of two-dimensional visual information), whereas other attributes, such as color, lightness, or texture, are called dispensable attributes and considered less important. Pinker claims that indispensable dimensions are better than dispensable dimensions for representing quantitative information because attention is more selective for spatial position information and that spatial attributes are automatically encoded relationally.

Finally, psychophysical studies also support a rank-order in which spatial extent is perceived more accurately and affords finer discriminations and more linear mappings to quantitative information than other dimensions (Cleveland & McGill, 1984, 1985). Results of this classic work suggest that position and length comparisons are most accurate, and color and pattern density comparisons are least accurate, as shown in Table 11.1.

TABLE 11.1. *Rank Ordering of Visual Dimensions used to Represent Quantitative Information Most Accurate to Least Accurate (adapted from Cleveland & McGill, 1984).*

Rank	Visual Dimension
1	Position along a common scale
2	Position along nonaligned scales
3	Length, Direction, Angle (tie)
4	Area
5	Volume, Curvature (tie)
6	Shading, Color Saturation (tie)

Specific Characteristics of the Display

Tables Versus Graphs. Although tables are technically not graphs, one important question is whether tables or graphs are better suited for representing quantitative information, and under what circumstances (Schaubroeck & Muralidhar, 1991, 1992). One major finding is that a table allows people to get single point values most accurately and quickly (Guthrie, Weber, & Kimmerly, 1993; Meyer, 2000). When information is needed to be integrated, for example for detecting trends, tables require greater serial processing than graphical displays, and graphical displays are superior to tables (Carey & White, 1991; Greaney & MacRae, 1997; Legge, Gu, & Luebker, 1989; Te'eni, 1989; Tuttle & Kershaw, 1998). Similarly, when participants predicted the outcome based on trends depicted in the data, graphs are superior to tables (Meyer et al., 1999). Finally, viewers are somewhat more likely to remember information presented in graphs compared to in tables (Umanath, Scamell, & Das, 1990) and prefer graphs over tables (Carey & White, 1991; Te'eni, 1989).

Line Graphs and Bar Graphs. Viewers are more likely to describe x–y trends (e.g., as x increases, y decreases) when viewing line graphs (Carswell, Emery, & Lonon, 1993; Shah et al., 1999; Zacks & Tversky, 1999), and are more accurate in retrieving x–y trend information from line graphs than from bar graphs (Carswell & Wickens, 1987). Strikingly, even when two discrete data points are plotted in a line graph, viewers often describe the data as continuous. For example, a graph reader may interpret a line that connects two data points representing male and female height as, "The more male a person is, the taller he or she is" (Zacks & Tversky, 1999). This emphasis on the x–y trends can lead to incomplete interpretations when the data are complex (for example, multiple lines on a display representing a third variable). In one study, viewers focused entirely on the x–y trends and therefore were frequently unable to recognize the same data plotted when another variable was on the x–axis, such as in Figures 3a and 3b (Shah & Carpenter, 1995).

While line graphs emphasize x–y trends, bar graphs emphasize discrete comparisons (Carswell & Wickens, 1987; Shah et al., 1999; Zacks & Tversky, 1999). Furthermore, bar graphs of multivariate data appear to be less biasing than line graphs (Shah & Shellhammer, 1999). For example, viewers were more biased in their descriptions of the line graphs like the one in Figures 11.3a and 11.3b and focused on x–y relations, but described all

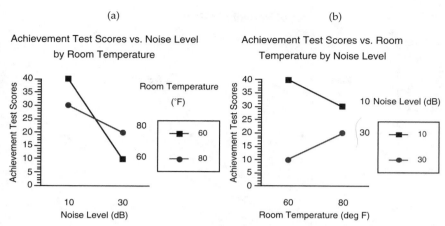

FIGURE 11.3. Figure 11.3a and 11.3b depict line graphs of the same data. However, the variable plotted on the x–axis is different in the two graphs. Viewers typically describe these two graphs differently and do not recognize them to be the same data.

three variables equally in bar graphs like the one in Figure 11.4 (Shah & Shellhammer, 1999).

Line graphs may also be especially susceptible to certain visual illusions when depicting three-variable data. Specifically, viewers assume

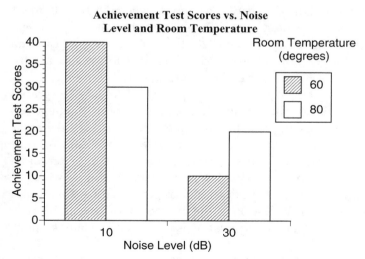

FIGURE 11.4. This graph is a bar graph of the line graphs in Figure 11.3. Viewers are less biased in their descriptions of bar graphs.

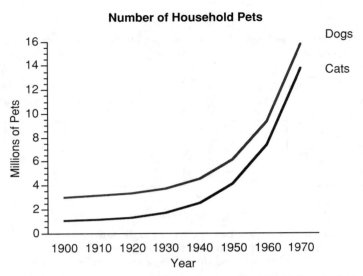

FIGURE 11.5. An example of a line–distance illusion. Although the two lines appear to converge, the distance between them is constant throughout the graph. This illusion may lead to the erroneous conclusion that the number of cats as household pets is increasing faster than the number of dogs.

that the distance between two lines is the shortest distance between them, rather than the vertical distance between them (Cleveland & McGill, 1984). The subsequent interpretation error is demonstrated by the graph in Figure 11.5, in which the relative difference between the number of cats and dogs as household pets appears to decrease from 1900 to 1960. In fact, the distance between the two lines is constant throughout the graph.

In summary, line graphs are good for depicting x–y trends, bar graphs for discrete comparisons. Thus, no graph format is necessarily better overall than any other format. Instead, there is an interaction of task and graphic format, called the *proximity compatibility principle* by Carswell and Wickens (1987). Integrated, objectlike displays (e.g., a line graph) were better for integrative tasks, whereas more separable formats (e.g., bar graphs) were better for less integrative or synthetic tasks such as point reading (Carswell & Wickens, 1987). Further discussion of the interaction of task and format and the role of task in graph interpretation is presented in a later section.

Depicting Proportional Data: Divided Bar Charts and Pie Charts. While bar graphs and line graphs are typically used for presenting metric information about absolute scales, divided bar charts and pie charts are frequently used for the presentation of proportion data. In general, pie charts are more accurate for making part/whole judgments than divided bar graphs, because divided bar graphs often require adding up information from different parts of the bar (Hollands & Spence, 1998; Simkin & Hastie, 1986; Spence & Lewandowsky, 1991). However, divided bar charts may be better when absolute values as well as proportions are important to communicate (Kosslyn, 1989).

Contour Plots. Contour plots (isotherms when referring to temperature) are sometimes used to represent three-variable data (Bertin, 1983), and, before the advent of recent dynamic, three-dimensional software, considered to be one of the best ways to perceive three-dimensionality. Contour plots are created by joining all points of a particular value (Bertin, 1983). Contour plots may be used in conjunction with other visual dimensions to represent additional variables. Contour plots have been studied as geographical displays by geographers and educators who find that when interpreted three-dimensionally, contour plots help subjects answer questions about traversing landscapes (Eley, 1981, 1983). This finding suggests that it might be possible to extract relationship information, particularly of different cross-sections, of data. The ability to interpret the three-dimensionality of a contour plot is affected by the ways in which contours are displayed. For example, the perception of the height and depth of the surface may be affected by the types of lines drawn on the graph (Bertin, 1983). In addition, certain colors are more likely to be interpreted as higher or lower (Phillips, 1982).

Three-Dimensional Displays. Three-dimensional displays (depicting multivariate data) and animations depicting quantitative information are becoming more common. However, there has been relatively little research on these types of displays. Three-dimensional displays were better than two-dimensional displays when the questions required integrating information across all three dimensions (Wickens, Merwin, & Lin, 1994). Another study (briefly described in Shah, 2001) examined the interpretation of three-dimensional wireframe graphs, an example of which is in Figure 11.6a (next to a line graph depicting the same data in Figure 11.6b). In this study, viewers were more likely to describe the relationships between all three variables when viewing wireframe graphs than when viewing line graphs (in which they focused on the x–y trends). Despite the potential benefits of three-dimensional displays, the use of three-dimensional linear perspective drawings can degrade or occlude information

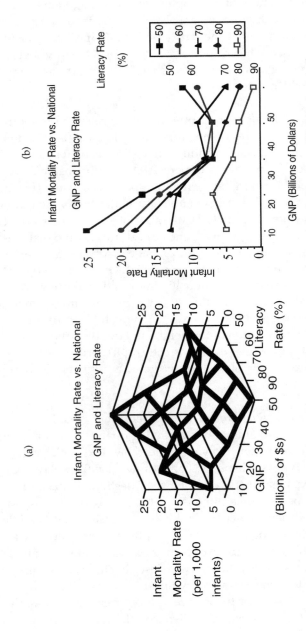

FIGURE 11.6. An example of a wireframe graph (Figure 11.6a) and a line graph (Figure 11.6b) that depicts the same data.

(Merwin, Vincow, & Wickens, 1994). In our study, viewers were inaccurate on tasks requiring reading individual data points in bar graphs, and had trouble identifying general trends such as, "As x increases, y increases" (Shah, 2001). Further discussion of the use of three-dimensionality in displays can be found in Tversky (Chapter 1) and Wickens, Vincow, and Yeh (Chapter 10).

Specialized Displays. Several types of displays are used by relatively restricted populations. In this section, we briefly discuss the visual features issues important for these specialized displays.

One type of commonly used visual display in contexts in which people are dealing with very high-dimensional data are picture graphs that depict different aspects of an n-dimensional data set as a function of different visual features on a picture. Consider the Chernoff faces shown in Figure 11.7 (Chernoff, 1973). In this typical use of faces, the dimensions of a multidimensional data set of demographic variables (such as literacy rates, average temperature, and population) were translated into visual dimensions such as the size and curvature of the mouth, the size and shape of the head, and so on. Theoretically, a viewer extremely familiar with a particular mapping between the features in these Chernoff faces

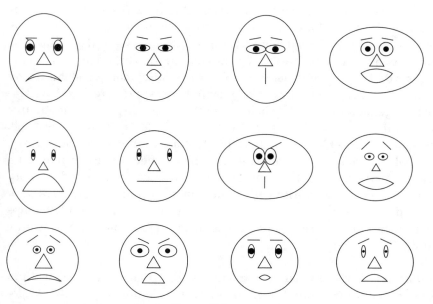

FIGURE 11.7. An example of a Chernoff figure.

and different demographic variables might be able to interpret this display. However, performance on making judgments from Chernoff faces has been found to be less accurate and slower for Chernoff faces than other types of graphs (Umanath & Vessey, 1994). One explanation for the difficulty of Chernoff faces is that viewers may be unable to keep track of the referents to the variables (Gower & Digby, 1981) and therefore cannot easily compare the different graphic objects as a function of one or more variables. Two suggestions for alleviating this difficulty are presenting only the minimal number of variables necessary to express a particular point in one graph, and providing viewers with captions or descriptions that help them identify the important quantitative features and their referents (Mittal, Roth, Moore, Mattis, & Carenini, 1995). In any case, the use of arbitrary visual dimensions in graphs that depict higher-dimensional data, such as Chernoff faces, glyphs (Anderson, 1960), and stars, ships, castles, and trees (Kleiner & Hartigan, 1981), likely increases the difficulty of interpreting such displays (Fienberg, 1979).

Another commonly used specialized display is a statistical, or thematic, map that represents qualitative or quantitative data organized by geographic areas (see Lewandowsky & Behrens, 1999, for a more thorough review). There are various types of statistical maps, depending on which visual dimensions, such as color, size, or symbols, are used to show quantitative or categorical information (MacEachren, 1994). Chloropleth maps use variations of color or texture to represent quantity of some variable; symbol maps use symbols that vary in size; numerals or data maps use numbers; and value-by-area cartograms use through the relative size of the regions they represent to depict numbers. Statistical maps benefit learning of quantitative geographical data, perhaps because they are encoded as intact images and as such they help integrate geographical and quantitative information (Kulhavy, Stock, & Kealy, 1993; Rittschof & Kulhavy, 1998; Rittschof, Stock et al., 1994). Specifically, for simple fact memory tasks, symbol and chloropletch maps lead to better memory about map data than numeric tables, but cartograms lead to worse encoding and memory (Rittschof et al., 1998). Although symbol maps facilitate the extraction of individual data values, they are less advantageous than chloropleth maps when their purpose is to recognize overall data trends and patterns (Dunn, 1988).

Animation. Use of animation implicitly assumes that it is an ideal medium for communicating complex multivariate information, especially temporal information (for example, quantitative trends over time). This research suggests that there are some potential benefits to animation. For example, motion cues can help people perceive the three-dimensional structure of graphs (Becker, Cleveland, & Wilks, 1988). In addition, animation may help viewers identify clusters of data and outliers or keep track of variable names. However, users have difficulty comprehending animated relationships and trends (Huber, 1987; Marchak & Marchak, 1991; Stuetzle, 1987). In general, the perception of animation is often difficult and error-prone (Hegarty, Quilici, Narayanan, Holmquist, & Moreno, 1999; Morrison, Tversky, & Betrancourt, 2000). Indeed, a review of dozens of studies comparing animated displays to informationally equivalent static diagrams failed to find any benefit of animations for conceptual information (Tversky, Morrison, & Betrancourt, 2002). In general, more research on the role of animation for graphs of quantitative information is needed before strong conclusions can be drawn. Readers interested in animation should also consult Tversky (Chapter 1) and Mayer (Chapter 12); both chapters discuss the role of animation more generally.

Other Perceptual Features

In addition to global decisions about the general format, a graph designer has the choice of a number of additional visual features, the most common of which include color, size, and aspect ratio (ratio of length to width).

Color. Color can either represent quantitative information (e.g., the closer to red the greater the debt, or the deeper the color saturation the higher the population) or to mark variables (e.g., the red bars represent girls and the blue bars represent boys; Brockmann, 1991; Cleveland & McGill, 1985; Hoffman et al., 1993). In general, color does not accurately represent precise quantitative information (Cleveland & McGill, 1985). Color can be misleading when representing metric information. For example, certain colors are more likely to be interpreted as higher or lower in displays such as contour plots, influencing how well viewers are able to imagine these plots three-dimensionally (Phillips, 1982). In some cases, color might be viewed as categorical, rather than continuous (Phillips, 1982). When color is used, a combination of hue, brightness, and saturation should be used to represent quantitative information; these factors together lead to better performance than the use of hue alone (Spence, Kutlesa, Rose, 1999). In addition, viewers are more accurate when color is used to represent linear data than nonlinear data (Spence et al., 1999).

Because color is often interpreted as categorical, very different colors can be helpful for tasks that require categorical judgments (Lewandowsky & Spence, 1989). Indeed, people are more accurate at data extraction tasks when color is used in pie charts, bar graphs, and tables (Hoadley, 1990). People are also better at identifying clusters in scatterplots when color is used (Ware & Beatty, 1988).

Another potential benefit of color is related to the process by which viewers map graph features to the correct (or incorrect) variables associated with them (Bertin, 1983; Pinker, 1990). In a recent study examining viewers' eye fixations as they interpreted graphs, viewers must continuously reexamine the labels to refresh their memory (Carpenter & Shah, 1998). Furthermore, several graph design handbooks suggest that keeping track of graphic referents imposes demands on working memory (Fisher, 1982; Kosslyn, 1994; Schmid, 1983). For example, it may be difficult for a viewer to keep track of the fact that a line with triangles represents the number of days the temperature was above 90 degrees across several years, and a line with circles represents the number of days that the temperature was below 32 degrees. If those dimensions are represented with a meaningful color, such as red for hot days and blue for cold days, it might help viewers keep track of variable names (Brockmann, 1991). Of course, use of semantically related features is highly dependent on assumptions shared by the graphic designer and graph reader. For example, green means *profitable* for financial managers but *infected* for health-care workers (Brockmann, 1991). In summary, color can provide helpful cues, especially with respect to helping viewers keep track of quantitative referents, but color is inadequate as the only source of precise quantitative information.

Unlike regular graphs, color is commonly used in statistical maps and there is significant work on this topic. Consistently, viewers were more successful in identifying data trends and clusters when they used monochrome as opposed to multiple-hue, multiple-texture, or symbol maps, regardless of the color of the monochrome map (Lewandowsky, Herrmann, Behrens, Li, Pickle, & Jobe, 1993; Mersey, 1990). In addition, monochrome maps required shorter eye-fixations on the legend as compared to the multiple-hue and multiple-texture maps (Antes & Chang, 1990). These results suggest that using a color scheme that associates higher values with increasingly saturated colors may decrease the amount of processing when readers have to compare and integrate data. When different hues or texture density are associated with different magnitudes in an arbitrary manner, viewers have to maintain in working memory or recheck the color key in order to translate the colors on the map. In elementary tasks whose purpose is the extraction of data values about single locations, monochrome maps lose their advantage over multiple-hue or symbol maps (Hastie, Hammerle, Kerwin, Croner, & Herrmann, 1996; Mersey, 1990). Thus, multiple-hue or symbol maps may make it easier for viewers to discriminate and translate the different colors or symbols into specific numerical values or categories.

Legend (or Key) Versus Labels. Another choice is the use of a legend or key, or to directly label graph features (such as lines and bars) according to their referents. Because legends or keys require that graph readers keep referents in memory, legends pose special demands on working memory (see, for example, Figure 11.8b). Thus, the conventional wisdom is that graph designers should avoid the use of legends (except when labels would lead to too much visual clutter; Kosslyn, 1994) and instead label graph features directly with their referents (as in Figure 11.8a). In fact, the use of labels rather than legends reduces the time to retrieve information from a graph (Milroy & Poulton, 1978; Shah et al., 2004). However, research on viewers' verbal descriptions while they interpret line graphs suggests that legends may help viewers appropriately group conditions in multivariate data (Shah et al., 2004).

The "Third" Dimension. One commonly used perceptual characteristic is the use of a third "spatial" dimension in a two-variable graph that does not convey additional information, such as the use of three-dimensional bars in a bar graph (see Figure 11.9). Such graphs are commonly used in the media (Spence, 1990; Tufte, 1983) and are also fairly common in textbooks. Generally, the a priori advice is that additional, noninformative features are not helpful and often distracting. Tufte (1983) even labeled an added third dimension as an example of *chart junk* and recommended keeping it to a minimum. As predicted by Tufte, the accuracy of interpreting three-dimensional bar graphs and pie charts is slightly lower than for two-dimensional equivalents (Fischer, 2000; Siegrist, 1996; Zacks, Levy, Tversky, & Schiano, 1998). In the context of statistical maps, people are less accurate when three-dimensional symbols (e.g., cubes, spheres) are used because it is difficult for them to compare the sizes of the various symbols with the legend of the map than when two-dimensional symbols are used (Heino, 1995).

Despite the somewhat lower accuracy of three-dimensional displays compared to two-dimensional displays, viewers express preference for these displays (Levy, Zacks, Tversky, & Schiano, 1996), and it is likely that viewers spend more time attending to visually appealing displays.

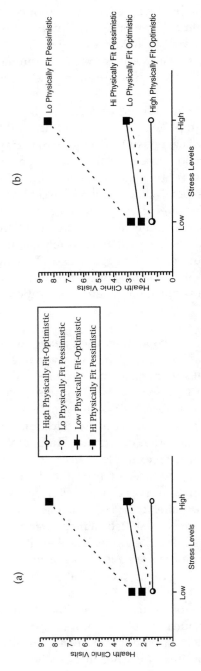

FIGURE 11.8. Figures 11.8a and 11.8b show the same data plotted with a legend and with labels. Viewers are faster at answering search-based questions when lines are labeled, but are sometimes better at grouping and making inferences from data when legends are used.

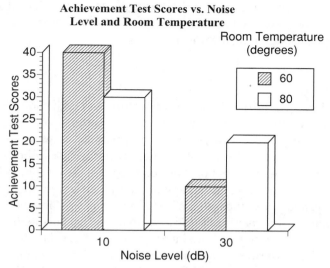

FIGURE 11.9. A three-dimensional bar graph.

Furthermore, some studies have found little difference in the accuracy or speed of making comparison judgments (Carswell, Frankenberger, & Bernhard, 1991; Spence, 1990), at least from memory (Zacks et al., 1998). Thus, the choice of using a noninformative third dimension depends on the trade-off between accuracy and visual interest (see Tversky, Chapter 1, for additional discussion).

Graph Size, Aspect Ratio, and Scale. Graphic features such as the graph size (and correspondingly the data density) set, the aspect ratio of a graph, and the scale (e.g., logarithmic or linear) change the type of information that is perceived (Cleveland, 1993). For example, viewers often mentally exaggerate the magnitude of correlations in scatterplots when the data appear to be dense (Cleveland, Diaconis, & McGill, 1982; Lauer & Post, 1989). This exaggeration occurs when the perceived density of the graph is increased either by the addition of data points, or by the reduction of the size of a graph. Similarly, the of a graph can have an influence on the patterns that viewers identify. Cleveland (1993) argues that viewers can most easily detect cyclical patterns when an aspect ratio that makes the curve closest to 45 degrees is used. Finally, the type of scale used changes the kind of information one can detect. For example, plotted functions that conform to the underlying logarithmic scale are linear and deviations from such linearity are more easily detected than deviations from the original logarithmic function (Cleveland, 1993). Of course, the interpretation of such a graph requires the viewer to have knowledge about what a deviation from normality implies about a logarithmic function.

DATA COMPLEXITY

In today's Information Age, the existence of vast quantities of data and the availability of fast and abundant computing power are creating a need for systems that support the retrieval, analysis, and interpretation of information. In many areas such as medicine and business (Klimberg & Cohen, 1999), the complexity of the information has required the development of new visualization tools that take advantage of interactivity, animation, three-dimensionality, and color. Indeed, there is a now fairly established field of computer science, *information visualization*, whose focus is the development of tools for presenting and interacting with complex data (see Card, Mackinlay, & Schneiderman, 1999, for many of the seminal papers in this field). Unfortunately, most research on graph interpretation has focused on relatively sparse, simple data sets. It is possible that models of simple graph comprehension may not scale up to account for more complex data sets and may not provide useful guidelines for the development of new information visualization tools (Meyer, Shamo, & Gopher, 1999; Shah & Freedman, 2002; Trafton, 2002). Thus, a new body of research has begun to examine how complexity influences the cognitive processes in the interpretation of data (Carpenter & Shah, 1998; Katz et al., 2002; Trafton, & Trickett, 2001).

There are a number of dimensions of complexity that researchers have noted, and the interpretation process might influence these dimensions differently. Thus, it is difficult to define complexity as a whole (Jarvenpaa, Dickson, & DeSanctis, 1985) and a number of taxonomies of data complexity have been proposed. Data can be complex in terms of the complexity of relationships, as in the data regularity (i.e., noise and consistency) or the complexity of the quantitative relations depicted (e.g., a monotonic relationship between two variables is less complex than a nonmonotonic relationship). Data can also be complex in terms of amount, as in the number of data points and the number of dimensions or variables (Meyer, Shinar, & Leiser, 1997, discuss the first three types). In addition, Tan (1994) distinguishes between three types of complexity: the number of elements on the x–axis component, the number of elements along the y–axis component, and the number of x–y pairings (called the entity component). A second complication is that there may be a distinction between data complexity and perceived psychological complexity (Tan, 1994). Vessey (1991) defines complexity cognitively in terms of the number of mental transformations needed to produce an appropriate response rather than in terms of the data per set.

Much of the research on data complexity has simply demonstrated that increased data complexity increases the time and errors on simple fact-retrieval tasks (Gillan, 1995; Greaney & MacRae, 1997; Meyer, Shinar, & Leiser, 1997). However, there is an interaction with both the type of format (complexity has a bigger influence on some formats than others), the nature of the complexity (sheer data volume or more complex relations), and specific type of task. For very simple tasks (e.g., reading the value of a specific data point), complexity influences time only when it influences the search requirements, as suggested by Lohse's (1993) model of graph comprehension. Increases in data complexity reduced performance on tables and bar graphs but not on line graphs (Meyer, Shinar, & Leiser, 1997; Tan, 1994). Similarly, Hollands and Spence (1998) found that increasing the number of components produced a relatively greater increase in the time to judge proportions in bar graphs than in pie charts. In each of these cases, complexity in some formats led to increased search steps, whereas in other formats it did not.

Complexity, in terms of the nature of the underlying relationships, but not in terms of sheer number of data points, influenced the time to perform more open-ended graph comprehension tasks (Carswell, Emery, & Lonon, 1993; Carswell & Ramsey, 1997; Carpenter & Shah, 1998). For example, in a study that examined viewers' eye-fixations as they interpreted line graphs, we found a linear relationship between the number of total gazes on a display and gazes on axes and labels with the number of distinct quantitative relations, but not with total number of data points (Carpenter & Shah, 1998). Complexity also influences the type of interpretations viewers give to data. For example, increasing the number of trend reversals in line graphs produced an increase in statements about local details and fewer statements about the global content. By contrast, increasing the number of data points produced the opposite pattern of interpretations (Carswell, Emery, & Lonon, 1993).

The work outlined here focuses on the influence of data complexity on the time to identify and comprehend quantitative relationships. However, there are a number of additional factors that typically correlate with data complexity. Dealing with complex data frequently coincides with complex tasks (e.g., making decisions or explaining data) rather than fact retrieval (Attali & Goldschmidt, 1996). Complex data also involve the extensive use of prior knowledge and viewers with data interpretation skills (experts use complex data, not novices). Finally, complex data are often presented via specialized displays that sometimes incorporate animation and interactivity. A more complete understanding of the interpretation of complex data necessitates further research that incorporates these factors.

TASK DEMANDS

The goal of a graph user can vary substantially (Meyer, Shinar, & Leiser, 1997). Consider a graph that depicts a relatively complex data set (such as the relationship between crime, poverty, and population density in different parts of the world). The casual reader might seek to identify "What country has the highest crime rate?" A scientist's goal might be to make comparisons among variables (Gelman, Pasarica, & Dodhia, 2002). Thus, they might ask, "How does the relationship between crime and population density differ in developed and developing nations?" A scientist's goal may be to also understand causal mechanisms underlying the data or to test a theory. Accordingly, they might check "If poverty is a contributor to crime, and population density is more highly correlated with poverty in developed nations than developing nations, then population density should correlate with crime in developed nations more than in developing nations." A statistician may use the graph to judge whether the data set violates normality assumptions or contains outliers (Cleveland, 1993; Donoho, Donoho, & Gasko, 1988; Wickens & Merwin, 1992). A graph viewer might be using graphical information in the context of decision making. For example, one might use a graph to make a business or purchase decision (Kleinmuntz & Schkade, 1993; Schkade & Kleinmuntz, 1994), a medical decision (Elting, Martin, Cantor, & Rubenstein, 1999), or a risk decision (Stone, Yates, & Parker, 1997; Stone, Sieck, Bull, Yates, Parks, & Rush, 2003). People also use graphical information during problem solving, for example, using quantitative data about different cities to identify a solution for economic problems in a particular inner city. Finally, graphical displays may also serve social purposes. For instance, a politician or business executive may want to convince the viewer of his or her perspective. Nevertheless, in most laboratory studies, the extraction of predefined information from the graphical display is clearly specified. In natural contexts, the viewer may not have explicit goals or the goals may not be exogenously defined (Trafton & Trickett, 2001). Thus, the differences in task specificity may be a key difference between laboratory-based graph comprehension and real-world graph comprehension.

Much research on the role of a viewer's task in graph comprehension has focused on comparing a relatively small subset of the types of tasks outlined here, such as fact retrieval and comprehension. The task demands reflect the particular outcome or response produced as a function of comprehending a graph. Performance is commonly assumed to be contingent on the congruence between task demands and the graphical format (Bennett & Flach, 1992; Jarvenpaa, 1989; Sparrow, 1989; Tan & Benbesat, 1990; Wickens & Carswell, 1995). The type of task determines the viewer's goals and the necessary component processes (Attali & Goldschmidt, 1996; Simkin & Hastie, 1986). As previously reviewed, different graphical formats facilitate retrieval of different facts and quantitative relationships (e.g., Shah et al., 1999; Simkin & Hastie, 1986; Zacks & Tversky, 1999). Congruence is determined by the degree to which task demands elicit the component processes that can be readily applied to a particular graphical format (Kennedy, Te'eni, & Treleaven 1998; Jarvenpaa, 1989). For example, selecting among alternative choices may require a component process of comparing values. Depending on the way in which the data is displayed, comparing values may be facilitated by the use of a bar graph.

One principle guiding the choice of format to be compatible with the task is the "proximity compatibility principle" (Wickens & Carswell, 1995) or "representational compatibility" (Sparrow, 1989). According to this principle, the effectiveness of a particular graphical presentation depends on the degree that the display contains the relevant information for the task demands. The perceptual proximity principle holds that if various information channels should be processed together, this information should be placed close together in physical space or they should share the same physical dimensions (e.g., color). Thus, line graphs are better than bar graphs for highlighting x–y trends (Wickens & Carswell, 1995; Zacks & Tversky, 1999). More generally, configural displays, in which the multiple dimensions are represented within a single figure, such as Chernoff faces, are better than separate displays like bar graphs when the task requires integrating multiple dimensions (Bennett & Flach, 1992). And, when information needs to be integrated over multiple displays, integral displays are more effective than nonintegrated displays (Jones, Wickens, & Deutsch, 1990). However, when task requirements necessitate selective or focused attention (e.g., extract a particular value), then perceptual proximity is relatively less important (Goettl, Wickens, & Kramer, 1991; Jones, Wickens, & Deutsch, 1990). Carswell, Emery, and Lonon (1993) have found that participants adjusted their spontaneous interpretive strategies depending on the complexity of the data. As complexity increased, people switched from making global interpretations of the overall pattern to local, point-by-point interpretations. Carswell et al. also found that increases in the size of the data sets resulted in a shift from local to global interpretations. Thus, when there are no explicit task demands, individuals are able to adjust the component process to meet the situational demands imposed by the particular type of graph.

Such conclusions about the interaction of task and format are applicable to some complex cognitive tasks in which comprehension of data is a component such as decision making and problem solving. Decision-makers are affected by graph format and the organization of information in graphs (Jarvenpaa, 1989, 1990; Kleinmuntz & Schkade, 1993; Schkade & Kleinmuntz, 1994). Thus, when bar graphs are organized around alternative choices, viewers extracted information about alternatives, but when graphs were organized around attributes, viewers extracted information about attributes. Even expert decision makers may not be able to overcome effects of format. In one study, research physicians making decisions about whether or not to stop clinical trials were dramatically influenced by the format of the data (Elting, Martin, Cantor, & Rubenstein, 1999). In that study, participants were more likely to notice likely differences in treatment groups when viewing data presented in an iconic format in which cases were represented by individual boxes that were colored or marked depending on outcomes, then pie charts, divided bar graphs, and tables.

Above and beyond the perceptual and cognitive factors that affect comprehension, it is quite likely that social cognitive factors influence decision making. For instance, viewers are more likely to engage in risk avoidance when risk information was presented in graphic format than numerically (Stone, Yates, & Parker, 1997). In a medical context, decision makers were less influenced by anecdotes of individual experiences with prostate cancer treatments and more influenced by statistical data when making decisions about prostate cancer treatments when the data were presented graphically rather than numerically (Fagerlin, Wang, & Ubel, 2004). It is not clear what mechanisms underlie these effects of graphics. One possibility is that graphs make salient some information, such as risks (Stone et al., 2003). An alternative possibility is, given the correlation between the use of graphs and the hard sciences cited earlier (e.g., Smith, Best, Stubbs, Johnston, & Archibald, 2000), that people find graphically presented information to be more valid or scientific. Or, viewers might make inferences about the confidence or expertise of the data presenter.

Many contexts require that the viewer go beyond the information literally depicted in the graphic to make predictions. In general, people are better able to make predictions about graphically presented information than numerical information (DeSanctis & Jarvenpaa, 1989). For example, when making a forecast regarding future values, participants were more accurate when they made a graphical response than when they made a numerical estimate (Carey & White, 1991). Similarly, Meyer et al. (1999) found a clear advantage of graphs over tables when subjects predicted the outcome based on trends depicted in the data.

Another more complex context in which graphs are used is problem solving. (Cheng, Cupit, & Shadbolt, 2001; Scaife & Rogers, 1996; Tabachneck-Schijf, Leonardo, & Simon, 1997; Trafton et al., 2000). For example, graphs are used by weather forecasters in the context of making forecasts, or human resource managers in the context of identifying possible hiring needs. As in decision making, numerous studies have highlighted the role of graphical displays in specialized problem-solving contexts. One focus of this research is the use of graphs by experts during problem solving. Experts more frequently than novices are able to make direct inferences from visual information rather than always converting information to verbal or propositional representations (e.g., Cheng et al., 2001; Tabachneck-Schijf et al., 1997; Trafton et al., 2000). Experts also tend to look for different kinds of information than novices; for example, experts tend to notice things that are anomalous or relevant to confirming or disconfirming ideas (Trafton & Trickett, 2001)

Although this chapter focuses on comprehension and use of graphs, people frequently choose and prefer graphic formats that are not necessarily the most optimal for communicating specific facts or relationships. For example, people prefer three-dimensional bars over two-dimensional bars, despite the fact that comprehension of three-dimensional bars is somewhat less accurate (Zacks et al., 1998) Presenters may decide to select graphs for impression management and especially self-promotion (e.g., during a job presentation) or when seeking to convince an audience. In one study, there was no difference in the preferences for graphical versus tabular formats when the presenter's goal was to facilitate decision making (Tractinsky & Meyer, 1999). However, for presentations in which the objective was to impress others, people preferred graphics, especially gratuitous graphics, to tables. Furthermore, they found there was a relatively greater likelihood of using graphics when the data were negative.

In summary, task demands can have a significant influence on graph comprehension and interact with other factors, such as the graph's format. Different cognitive processes are elicited in particular contexts. Furthermore, the appropriateness of a particular graphical format appears to be dependent on the task demands. However, significant additional research is necessary, especially in naturalistic contexts when goals are less defined and comprehension is embedded in problem-solving and decision-making contexts (Trafton & Trickett, 2001).

GRAPHICAL KNOWLEDGE, CONTENT KNOWLEDGE, AND ABILITY DIFFERENCES

Knowledge about graph comprehension and data interpretation, content knowledge, and visuospatial abilities and working memory influence viewers' interpretations of data and interact with the visual feature, data complexity, and task demands factors described earlier. The following anecdote from a cognitive psychology colloquium talk nicely illustrates the influence of data interpretation skill, content knowledge, and perhaps other abilities on data interpretation. About halfway through this talk, the speaker put up a line graph that depicted data to support his theory of object representation. The speaker had plotted the reaction time to recognize objects in different orientations, a relationship frequently plotted in line graphs and shown to cognitive psychology audiences. Almost instantly, ten expert faculty members in the audience raised their hands because they noticed nonlinear slopes that had not yet been explained by the speaker. In comprehending the reaction time graph in this example, some members of the audience were able to automatically associate a theory with particular quantitative relations and immediately recognized the graphic features that were consistent and inconsistent with those quantitative predictions. In this section, we describe how these factors influence the comprehension of graphs.

Data Interpretation and Graphical Literacy Skills

Graph readers differ in their data interpretation or graphical literacy skills. One important component of graphical literacy is knowing what graphic features imply about quantitative relationships. Pinker (1990) referred to this as one's *graph schema* that influences viewers' interpretation processes. As discussed in the section on models of graph comprehension, a number of theoretical approaches propose two kinds of graph interpretation processes (Cheng et al., 2001; Cleveland, 1993; Kosslyn, 1989, 1994; Larkin & Simon, 1987; Pinker, 1990; Shah et al., 1999; Stenning & Oberlander, 1995). One process involves relying on one's graph schema to retrieve automatically a conceptual interpretation of the data based on the visual features

in much the same way as the expert cognitive psychologists in the colloquium talk were able to retrieve the potential theoretical implications of a
slightly curved line. When viewers do not have graph schemas, an alternate, complex comprehension that is effortful and demanding is required
to make inferences from the information available (Larkin & Simon, 1987;
Pinker, 1990). Given the difficulty in interpreting data using these effortful
processes, viewers are more likely to provide superficial, inaccurate, or less
precise descriptions of data.

This conclusion is supported by a number of studies that demonstrate differences in expert (or high graph-skilled) and novice (or low
graph-skilled) viewers (Maichle, 1994; Preece & Janvier, 1992; Shah &
Shellhammer, 1999). When viewers interpreted line graphs with more than
one line, less-skilled graph viewers described the trends in the data whereas
the more-skilled graph subjects emphasized comparisons among trends
(Maichle, 1994). One possible interpretation of these data is that novice
graph viewers form representations that simplify the relations in the data.
In a similar study, we found that novice graph viewers were more likely to
provide superficial descriptions of each individual line in a line graph (Shah
& Shellhammer, 1999). By contrast, more knowledgeable graph viewers (as
determined by a pretest of graph skills; McKenzie & Padilla, 1986) were
more likely to make inferences about general quantitative trends (Shah &
Shellhammer, 1999). Finally, in a somewhat different type of study, Preece
and Janvier (1992) found a link between viewers' ability to sketch graphs
from memory and their ability to interpret those graphs. This study provides more direct support for the existence of graph schemas that allow
viewers to better remember information in a graph supporting comprehension processes.

Although graph schemas mediate graph comprehension, in many cases,
graph schemas can distort viewers' memory for graphs. One empirical
demonstration of the existence of graph schemas and their influence on
viewers memory for data was a series of studies in which participants drew
line graphs and maps from memory (Schiano & Tversky, 1992; Tversky &
Schiano, 1989). When told that a three-line figure depicted a graph, viewers'
drew the display as more symmetric and drew the middle line as being
closer to 45 degrees than the line was portrayed originally. When they were
told that the same display depicted a map, however, they drew the line so
that it was closer to 0 degrees or 90 degrees. Thus, viewers' memory for
data is distorted by general expectations about visually presented data. In
the case of graphs, viewers have a canonical graph schema that tends to
favor 45 degree lines rather than steeper or flatter lines.

Novice graph viewers also may have inaccurate graph schemas that can lead to systematic errors in interpretation. For example, viewers expect dependent variables to be plotted of the y–axis in a line graph, and causal or independent variables to be plotted of the x–axis. When the position of graphic labels is consistent with the viewers' expectations, or graph schema, the interpretation is easier than when the position of graphic variables is not consistent (Gattis & Holyoak, 1996). When the dependent variable is plotted on the y–axis as is typical, steeper slopes imply faster rates of change. If a graph that violates this constraint is presented to graph viewers, viewers often misinterpret the meaning of the slopes, incorrectly assuming that a steeper line represents a faster rate of change (Gattis & Holyoak, 1996). Thus, viewers' knowledge about the mapping between slope and rate of change can lead to errors in interpretation. In the similar *slope–height* error, children erroneously assume that a steeper slope implies higher value, rather than different rate of change (Bell & Janvier, 1981). In this error, viewers whose task is to report on which line represents a greater rate of change, represented in terms of the slope of two lines, focus instead on the relative heights of the two lines. Finally, in a recent study, Shah identified a third related error made by novice graph viewers (2001). In this study, she plotted three-variable data in line graphs such as the ones in Figure 11.10a and 11.10b. In Figure 11.10a, there is a systematic relationship between drunk drivers and car accidents, but in Figure 11.10b there is no systematic relationship between drunk drivers and car accidents (because for each value of drunk driving in the graph there are multiple values of car accidents and vice versa). However, novice graph viewers do not have the knowledge in their graph schemas to recognize that the variable along the x–axis and the variable that corresponds to multiple lines on the graph are independent. Therefore, they frequently included the statement, "As drunk drivers increase, car accidents increase" in their descriptions of the data in both graphs. Thus, viewers relied on their prior knowledge about the content rather than the information depicted in the graph.

In addition to graph schemas mediating visual feature and conceptual knowledge effects, more general scientific literacy skills influence viewers' data descriptions. In viewing data, for example, experts are more likely to identify anomalous information when it is relevant to explanations and interpretations of data (Trafton & Trickett, 2001). Similarly, we found that statistical-reasoning experts (graduate students in cognitive psychology) were more likely to spontaneously provide explanations and methodological evaluations for data, even for data representing information outside of

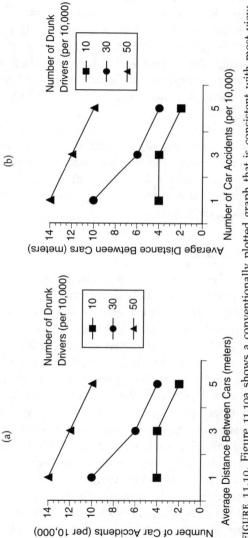

FIGURE 11.10. Figure 11.10a shows a conventionally plotted graph that is consistent with most view-ers' expectations of the causal relations between these variables. In Figure 11.10b, the x– and y–axes are reversed.

457

their expertise (Freedman & Shah, 2001). This result suggests that general knowledge influences viewers' goals in viewing data.

One task frequently performed by data analysis experts is making judgments of covariation by viewing scatterplots. However, these studies show little effect of expertise: Both statistically trained experts and novices were biased by slope and the existence of regression lines (Lane, Anderson, & Kellam, 1985; Meyer, Taieb, & Flascher, 1997). Thus, although scientific and statistical-reasoning expertise can influence data interpretation with experts sometimes minimizing the effects of visual features (Shah & Shellhammer, 1999), visual features continue to have a large influence on some tasks.

Although the influence of graph schemas has been studied more extensively, further research is necessary to examine the relationship between graph schemas and other scientific and statistical literacy factors that influence the comprehension of data. Understanding the processes by which skilled viewers comprehend graphs may suggest methods for improving novices' understanding of graphs.

Knowledge About Content

Domain knowledge reflects any mental representation of the content of the information. This knowledge may include underlying theories and models previous findings, and methodological techniques. The psychology colloquium anecdote also demonstrates that experts typically use extensive domain knowledge during the comprehension of graphical displays. As reviewed next, content knowledge has an influence on all graph viewers' interpretations of data, but it has a greater influence on novice graph viewers' interpretations. This aspect of graph comprehension is consistent with processing of other visuospatial information, specifically with how viewers' knowledge and expectations affect how they encode and remember pictures and diagrams (Carmichael, Hogan, & Walters, 1932). Similarly, viewers' expectations have long been known to affect their comprehension of data (not necessarily presented in graphs).

Few studies have examined the role of prior knowledge during graph comprehension. However, studies that examine how content knowledge affects the processing of experimental evidence and quantitative data have implications for the role of prior knowledge on graph comprehension. In a classic study, Lord, Ross, and Lepper (1979) gave people descriptions of studies that either supported or refuted their own prior beliefs about controversial topics like the death penalty. Overall, participants were more likely to notice problems in studies that were inconsistent with their beliefs than studies that were consistent with their beliefs. The influence of prior beliefs on data interpretation occurs not only for naïve undergraduate participants, but also for scientists. This bias is illustrated by a study in which psychologists distorted their memory for the findings from a classic expert memory study based on their schema of expert memory (Vicente & Brewer, 1993).

Research that has demonstrated the role of prior knowledge on viewers' interpretations of data has focused on viewers' estimations of correlations or covariation between variables (not necessarily presented graphically). Chapman and Chapman (1969) demonstrated that prior knowledge resulted in experts ignoring the objective relations in the data. In another study (Jennings, Amabile, & Ross, 1982), participants made judgments about the relationship among variables about which they had prior theories (e.g., height and weight) or they were shown data depicting the relationship between two variables about which they did not have prior theories (e.g., tone pairs of varying durations). Viewers typically overestimated the magnitude of the correlations that were presented for data for which they had prior expectations of relationships. Broniarczyk and Alba (1994) found that when raw data were presented in tabular form, perceivers' prior beliefs caused them to perceive relations where none were present. However, the data in these studies were not presented in graphical displays. Instead, viewers saw individual exemplars (e.g., different people of varying heights) and asked to judge from the set of exemplars what the relationship between the variables might be.

Only a handful of studies have examined the effects of prior theories on estimations of correlations for data presented graphically (Anderson, 1995; Anderson & Kellam, 1992; Freedman & Smith, 1996). In these studies, perceivers strike a compromise between their prior beliefs and the available data (Billman, Bornstein, & Richards, 1992; Freedman & Smith, 1996). One possibility is that theory-based covariation assessment depends on the relative strengths of the person's prior beliefs and the available information (Alloy & Tabachnik, 1984). Anderson (1983, 1995; Anderson & Kellam, 1992) has provided support for the idea that the strength of the prior beliefs may be important. These studies experimentally induced theories by providing explanations of the relations among behaviors (e.g., risk taking and career choice). Anderson and Kellam found that when these beliefs were relatively new, experimentally induced theories, these weak beliefs did not influence the perception of relations in unambiguous scatterplots. However, Anderson (1995) found that with relatively strong preexisting beliefs, the ratings of the degree of relation among the traits were significantly related to perceived correlation in the scatterplots.

It could be incorrectly concluded from the studies reviewed that prior knowledge immunizes graph perception from the true relations in the data. Indeed, Jennings et al. (1982) suggested that prior theories free subjects from the constraints imposed by the data. However, when scatterplots are completely incongruous with induced beliefs, participants make covariation assessments consistent with the correlations displayed in the scatterplots rather than entirely based on induced beliefs (Billman, Bornstein, & Richards, 1992). Thus, the available data portrayed in graphical displays exerts a powerful influence on graph comprehension above and beyond the influence of prior knowledge (Freedman & Smith, 1996).

Although the research reviewed here indicates that people can be biased by their content knowledge, content knowledge can also facilitate graph comprehension. Specifically, prior knowledge may make people more resistant to noise. In one study, participants were more likely to ignore noise in the data and provide better estimates of covariation when they had prior knowledge (Wright & Murphy, 1984). Not only does the type of data reduce the influence of noise on viewers' quantitative estimates, but also on their qualitative interpretations of data. In a recent study, participants described graphs that depicted familiar (e.g., number of car accidents, number of drunk drivers, and traffic density) and unfamiliar relationships (e.g., ice cream sales, fat content, and sugar content; Shah, 2001). Overall, viewers described general trends (main effects) more frequently and ignored idiosyncratic data when viewing graphs with familiar relationships, but described idiosyncratic data (noise) more frequently when viewing graphs with unfamiliar relationships.

Just as prior knowledge influences the comprehension of traditional graphs, prior knowledge also influences the comprehension of quantitative maps such as weather data. Using various tasks (e.g., map completion and reconstruction, sorting tasks), Lowe (1993, 1994, 1996) examined how meteorologists and nonmeteorologists interpreted weather maps. Meteorologists focused on the conceptual relations represented on the maps. Their extensive background knowledge enabled them to identify important map information, to extrapolate weather phenomena not represented on the maps, and to construct map representations that contained the depicted semantic relations. Novices relied on domain-general strategies (e.g., clustering based on perceptual similarity or spatial proximity), could not evaluate the significance of all the pieces of information, and drew inferences that were based solely on map elements. The nonmeteorologists' representations were more often based on the superficial features, that is, the visuospatial relationships of the map elements. In their work (they made the software) with educational earth science visualization software, Edelson, Gordin, and Pea (1999) reported that middle school students with low content knowledge made only superficial interpretations of thematic weather maps. Students focused on the extraction of individual data points and rarely explored weather patterns and relationships by integrating and comparing information about different geographic regions and times. Finally, Rittschof, Stock, Kulhavy, Verdi, and Johnson (1996) showed that readers performed poorly when they recalled map data using cartograms that depicted unfamiliar geographic regions. Thus, across various types of maps, the strategies readers use to interpret and learn from thematic maps and the quality and amount of information they can extract depends on their familiarity with the subject matter that is represented on the maps.

Although this brief review reveals a growing body of evidence focusing on the ways in which the display characteristics and viewers' knowledge interact during graph comprehension, the precise mechanisms by which prior knowledge is combined with the available data is not known (Billman et al., 1992; Freedman & Smith, 1996). Alloy and Tabachnik (1984) assumed that prior knowledge can lead to selective encoding of information into memory. Nevertheless, consistent with a construction–integration model of graph perception (Freedman & Shah, 2002; Shah, 2001), prior knowledge is a pervasive aspect of graphical information processing. Still, the integration of prior knowledge and display characteristics may require effortful construction of representations. Further research should address several important questions. First, what are the conditions under which prior knowledge facilitates or impairs graph comprehension? Second, what are the precise mechanisms by which prior knowledge and the display characteristics are integrated? Another open question is at what stage during the processing of graphical information does content knowledge influence comprehension. Specifically, does prior knowledge influence what information is perceived or encoded or does it influence the interpretation process? One way of resolving this question is to examine the impact of prior knowledge at different times during the interpretation and recall process (e.g., Freedman & Smith, 1996).

Development and Prior Knowledge

Young students are perhaps the most influenced by the content of information in a graph. Viewers commonly misinterpret abstract representations of data as an iconic representation of a real event (Bell & Janvier, 1981; Janvier, 1981; Leinhardt, Zaslavsky, & Stein, 1990; Preece & Janvier, 1992). For example, viewers might describe a graph representing the speed of a racecar in terms of the position of the racecar on a track (Janvier, 1981). This error is particularly common for contexts for which there is an obvious iconic interpretation, usually when the graph is meant to represent change (such as growth, speed) and the concrete interpretation is the value on some dimension (such as height instead of growth, location instead of speed). Although young graph readers (until around fifth grade) make this error frequently, minimal graphing instruction appears to help viewers overcome this error (Leinhardt et al., 1990).

These studies suggest that graph viewers appear to be better at understanding graphs with certain types of content compared to other types of content, such as those representing change. For example, students have the most difficulty with graphs depicting acceleration, followed by graphs depicting velocity; they have the easiest time comprehending graphs depicting distance or position (Clement, 1985). In addition, students are much better at dealing with data in which time is one of the dimensions, perhaps because the variables used in instructional contexts are frequently time-dependent (Leinhardt et al., 1990).

Tversky, Kuglelmas, and Winter (1991) compared the relative difficulty of graphically representing different types of quantitative information. They asked children (kindergarten through ninth grade, plus adults) about relative times for meals, quantities of sand and other objects, preferences for television shows, and heights. A sticker was placed on a blank piece of paper (representing a middle amount, event such as a midmorning snack, preference, etc.). The children placed the other stickers to represent the distance, along that dimension, of the other objects. For example, in the time example, the children placed a sticker representing breakfast, midmorning snack, and dinner. If children were able to represent, with greater distance, that dinner was farther away than breakfast (from midmorning snack), then their representation was considered to represent interval information. Children were more likely to represent temporal concepts with interval information than quantitative concepts. Similarly, quantitative concepts were easier for children to represent than preference concepts.

Together, these studies suggest that peoples' knowledge of the content in graphs has an influence on their interpretations of, and memory for, data. Furthermore, several studies suggest that this is especially true for novice graph viewers, who often did not have the graph schemas necessary to overcome the strong influence of their own content knowledge. This might be particularly problematic in the context of science and social science, in which a critical evaluation of the information in graphs, rather than mere fact retrieval, is often crucial (Hunter, Crismore, & Pearson, 1987; Lehrer & Romberg, 1996). Finally, nongraph or content-specific developmental factors may also influence the interpretations of graphs by children and adults.

Individual Differences in Visuospatial Abilities and Working Memory

In addition to prior content knowledge and graphical and scientific literacy skills, working memory, visuospatial ability (and development), and logical reasoning skills have all been shown to be correlated with performance on graph comprehension task. Working memory is necessary to help viewers keep track of and integrate graphically presented materials, especially when graphs become complex (Carpenter & Shah, 1998; Halford, Wilson, & Phillips, 1998; Lohse, 1997). A second individual differences factor correlated with performance on some graph tasks is spatial ability (Vessey, 1991). One reason given for children's difficulty in interpreting graphs is their level of spatial development (Blades & Spencer, 1989; Somerville & Bryant, 1985; Bryant & Somerville, 1986). Working memory and spatial ability interact with the nature of the display. Cues such as color and grid lines, which help people keep track of graphical information when reading graphs, are likely to be more beneficial for low-than for high-working memory individuals (Lohse, 1997). Also, thematic maps that integrate information about several variables may improve low-spatial ability viewers' performance, because these maps reduce the amount of spatial information that needs to be mentally integrated when the same data are presented in separate maps (Vekiri, 2001). Finally, some people have argued that logical reasoning skills also play a role. For example, Berg and Phillips (1994) found that line graph comprehension performance was correlated with performance on Piagetian tests of logical reasoning.

CONCLUSIONS

This chapter reviews cognitive research on graph comprehension. We describe the major models of graph comprehension and discuss the influence of display characteristics, data complexity, task demands, and prior knowledge on the comprehension of graphs. Prior reviews of graph comprehension have lamented that research has focused on perceptual processes, simple laboratory tasks, simple data, and novice viewers (Trafton & Trickett, 2001; Guthrie, Weber, & Kimmerly, 1993; Freedman & Shah, 2002; Lewandowsky & Behrens, 1999; Shah & Carpenter, 1995). The current review demonstrates that in recent years researchers have gone above and beyond these simple tasks and contexts to consider interpretation of complex data, often in realistic contexts. Research on graph comprehension also goes beyond examining simple pairwise effects such as comparing the effectiveness of bar graph and pie chart. This review demonstrates that display characteristics, data complexity, task demands, and prior knowledge interact with one another to influence interpretations viewers give to data (Gillan, 1995; Simkin & Hastie, 1986).

Research on graph comprehension shares several common themes with research on other kinds of visual display comprehension. One common theme in much of the research on external displays is the distinction between perception and cognition. Most cognitive approaches to display comprehension claim that displays are most effective when the major argument is perceptually obvious so that relevant information is automatically perceived rather than requiring complex, cognitively demanding inferential processes (Larkin & Simon, 1987). Another major theme is the correspondence between displays that use space to depict nonspatial (e.g., quantitative) or at least partially nonspatial information. One question relevant to all such displays is the extent to which the use of space allows people to exploit spatial thinking skills evolved for representing actual space (see for example, Tversky, Chapter 1). A third theme that is relevant to most external displays is the integration of prior propositional knowledge and textual information with the information depicted in the display. Finally, technological advances allowing the depiction of three-dimensional information, animation, and interactive display have relevance for external visuospatial representations of all kinds, including maps, navigational systems, and diagrams. In many cases, principles derived from research on graphs might be relevant to these other kinds of displays.

Practical Implications

In this chapter, we have highlighted some of the major implications of research on graph comprehension for data presentation. In particular, we have pointed out which graphic formats and display characteristics are best for the display of specific types of information, and to some extent, for different kinds of data, tasks, and users. Several other articles and books provide helpful guidelines based in large part on cognitive research on graph comprehension and more general research on visuospatial cognition, and the latest research adds to the possible body of recommendations (Kosslyn, 1994; Shah & Hoeffner, 2002; Tufte, 1983, 1990).

Although commercial graphing packages allow users to design graphs that follow cognitively based guidelines, one recent trend is to design software to automatically create displays that follow these principles, perhaps with some input about the goal of the graph designer and information about the prior knowledge of the graph user. Such automated data display systems are often designed by the information visualization community to depict extremely complex data for specialized applications and expert use. One successful example of an automatic data display system is Boz, which displays airline scheduling information (cost, time of flights, amount of layover, etc.; Casner, 1990; Casner & Larkin, 1989). Boz was designed to allow users to substitute simple perceptual inferences in place of more demanding cognitive inferences based on cognitive research on visual displays (Larkin & Simon, 1987), and experiments using Boz suggest that it helps viewers to schedule flights more accurately (Casner & Larkin, 1989). Further implementation of cognitively guided principles into commercial graphing packages and automated data display systems is likely to have benefits for users of such systems.

Directions for Future Research

This review suggests several directions for future research. At a theoretical level, an important need is an integration of very precise, perceptual-level models of graph comprehension with more general cognitive models into a more complete, process-oriented model of graph comprehension that incorporates the influence of display characteristics, task, data complexity, and prior knowledge. Such a model should specify the mechanisms through which prior knowledge and perceptual features interact with each other.

Current technological advances make two questions particularly salient for research on graph comprehension, and, more generally, data visualization. First, the quantity of data available to be communicated or comprehended is greater than and more complex than the kinds of data used in typical studies on graph comprehension. And data presented in the laboratory often involves random patterns with abstract variables but real-world graphs have meaning and structure (Meyer, Shamo, & Gopher, 1999). It is not clear that conclusions based on simple data sets without meaningful data can be applied to more meaningful, complex contexts. Second, technology allows us to animate and interact with data, but little research examines how these factors influence the comprehension of data.

Research on graph comprehension should continue to consider factors other than reaction time and accuracy. In many situations, graphs are used for purposes other than communication of specific quantitative facts (Tractinsky & Meyer, 1999). In other contexts, visual features may be less important than other factors such as the aesthetic value of a display or a viewer's emotional response. Increasing the aesthetic value of data may invite the individual to process the information more deeply, thereby improving their performance or comprehension of the data (Carswell, Frankenberger, & Bernhard, 1991). Viewers might also process, remember, or respond to certain displays differently because they have an emotional response (medical side effects illustrated by crossed-out people) or because data appear scientific or credible (e.g., a three-dimensional display or a scatterplot) or not (pictogram in the popular press). However, little research has considered these potentially important variables.

Finally, research on graph comprehension (and construction) needs to be done in the context of the scientific reasoning, decision-making, and communication contexts in which they occur. As mentioned in the introduction, there is a positive correlation between the hardness of a science and the use of graphics (Best, Smith, & Stubbs, 2001; Smith et al., 2000), and interpreting data is central to hypothesis testing and scientific discovery (Schunn & Anderson, 1999). Major life decisions, such as the type of car to purchase and the type of medical treatment to undergo are made by both experts and novices based on a large amount of quantitative data in the current information age. Graphical information is also frequently used for promoting arguments (Oestermeier & Hesse, 2000). However, at the present time much graph comprehension research is divorced from research on scientific thinking, decision making, and argumentation. Thus, research on graph comprehension should begin to incorporate how preferences, viewers' judgments of credibility, and other social cognitive factors also influence how viewers process and remember data presented graphically.

ACKNOWLEDGMENTS

Writing of this chapter was supported by the Office of Naval Research Grant No. N00014-02-1-0279. We would like to thank Hannah Chua and Barbara Tversky for their valuable comments on an earlier draft of this chapter.

Suggestions for Further Reading

We recommend a series of books by Edward Tufte for examples of excellent, creative graphics:

Tufte, E. R. (1983). *The visual display of quantitative information,* Cheshire, CT: Graphics Press.
Tufte, E. R. (1990). *Envisioning information.* Cheshire, CT: Graphics Press.
Tufte, E. R. (1997). *Visual explanations.* Cheshire, CT: Graphics Press.

For further reading about highly complex, interactive displays of data for data mining and visual data analysis, we recommend:

Card, S. K., MacKinlay, J. D., & Shneiderman, B. (Editors). (1999). *Readings in information visualization: Using vision to think.* San Francisco, CA: Morgan Kaufmann.
Cleveland, W. (1993). *Visualizing data.* Murray Hill, NJ: AT&T Bell Laboratories.

Finally, for psychologically based guidelines for presenting data, we recommend:
Kosslyn, S. (1994). *Elements of graph design.* New York: WH Freeman.

References

Aldrich, F. K., & Parkin, A. J. (1987). Tangible line graphs: An experimental investigation of three formats using capsule paper, *Human Factors, 29,* 301–309.
Alloy, L. B., & Tabachnik, N. (1984). Assessment of covariation by humans and animals: The joint influence of prior expectations and current situational information. *Psychological Review, 91,* 112–149.
Anderson, C. A. (1983). Abstract and concrete data in the theory perseverance of social beliefs: When weak data lead to unshakable beliefs. *Journal of Experimental Social Psychology, 19,* 93–108.
Anderson, C. A. (1995). Implicit personality theories and empirical data: Biased assimilation, belief perseverance and change, and covariation detection sensitivity, *Social Cognition, 13,* 25–48.
Anderson, C. A., & Kellam, K. L. (1992). Belief perseverance, biased assimilation, and covariation detection: The effects of social theories and new data. *Personality and Social Psychology Bulletin, 18,* 555–565.
Anderson, E. (1960). A semigraphical method for the analysis of complex problems. *Technometrics, 2,* 387–391.
Antes, J. R., & Chang, K.-T. (1990). An empirical analysis of the design principles for quantitative and qualitative area symbols. *Cartography and Geographic Information Systems, 17*(4), 271–277.
Attali, Y., & Goldschmidt, C. (1996). The effects of component variables on performance on graph comprehension tests. *Journal of Educational Measurement, 33,* 93–105.
Becker, R. A., Cleveland, W. S., & Wilks, A. R. (1988). Dynamic graphics for data analysis. In W. S. Cleveland & M. E. McGill (Eds.), *Dynamic graphics for statistics.* (pp. 1–49) Belmont, CA: Wadsworth.
Bell, A., & Janvier, C. (1981). The interpretation of graphs representing situations. *For the Learning of Mathematics, 2,* 34–42.

Bennett, B., & Flach, J. (1992). Graphical displays: Implications for divided attention, focused attention, and problem solving. *Human Factors, 34,* 513–533.

Berg, C. A., & Phillips, D. G. (1994). An investigation of the relationship between logical thinking structures and the ability to construct and interpret line graphs. *Journal of Research in Science Teaching, 31,* 323–244.

Bertin, J. (1983). *Semiology of graphics: Diagrams networks maps* (W. Berg, Trans.). Madison: University of Wisconsin Press.

Best, L. A., Smith, L. D., & Stubbs, D. A. (2001). Graph use in psychology and other sciences. *Behavioural Processes, 54,* 155–165.

Billman, D., Bornstein, B., & Richards, J. (1992). Effects of expectancy on assessing covariation in data: "Prior belief" versus "meaning." *Organizational Behavior and Human Decision Processes, 53,* 74–88.

Blades, M., & Spencer, C. (1989). Young children's ability to use coordinate references. *Journal of Genetic Psychology, 150,* 5–18.

Brockmann, R. J. (1991). The unbearable distraction of color. *IEEE Transactions on Professional Communication, 34,* 153–159.

Broniarczyk, S. M., & Alba, J. W. (1994). Theory versus data in prediction and correlation tasks. *Organizational Behavior and Human Decision Processes, 57,* 117–139.

Bryant, P. E., & Somerville, S. C. (1986). The spatial demands of graphs. *British Journal of Psychology, 77,* 187–197.

Card, S. K., Moran, T. P., & Newell, A. (1983). *The psychology of human-computer interaction.* HIllsdale, NJ: Lawrence Erlbaum Associates.

Carey, J. M., & White, E. M. (1991). The effects of graphical versus numerical responses on the accuracy of graph-based forecasts. *Journal of Management, 17,* 77–96.

Carmichael, L. C., Hogan, H. P., & Walters, A. A. (1932). An experimental study of the effect of language on the reproduction of visually perceived form. *Journal of Experimental Psychology, 15,* 73–86.

Carpenter, P. A., & Shah, P. (1998). A model of the perceptual and conceptual processes in graph comprehension. *Journal of Experimental Psychology: Applied, 4,* 75–100.

Carswell, C. M., & Ramsey, C. (1997). Graphing small data sets: Should we bother? *Behaviour and Information Technology, 16,* 61–71.

Carswell, C. M., & Wickens, C. D. (1987). Information integration and the object display: An interaction of task demands and display superiority. *Ergonomics, 30,* 511–527.

Carswell, C. M., Emery, C., & Lonon, A. M. (1993). Stimulus complexity and information integration in the spontaneous interpretation of line graphs. *Applied Cognitive Psychology, 7,* 341–357.

Carswell, C. M., Frankenberger, S., & Bernhard, D. (1991). Graphing in depth: Perspectives on the use of three-dimensional graphs to represent lower-dimensional data. *Behaviour and Information Technology, 10,* 459–474.

Casner, S. M. (1990). Task-analytic design of graphic presentations. Unpublished doctoral dissertation, University of Pittsburgh, PA.

Casner, S. M., & Larkin, J. H. (1989). Cognitive efficiency considerations for good graphic design. *Proceedings of the Cognitive Science Society* (pp. 275–282). Hillsdale, NJ: Lawrence Erlbaum Associates.

Chapman, L. J., & Chapman, J. P. (1969). Illusory correlation as an obstacle to the use of valid psychodiagnostic signs. *Journal of Abnormal Psychology, 74*, 271–280.

Cheng, P. C-H., Cupit, J., & Shadbolt, N. R. (2001). Supporting diagrammatic knowledge acquisition: An ontological analysis of Cartesian graphs. *International Journal of Human-Computer Studies, 54*, 457–494.

Chernoff, H. (1973). Using faces to represent points in k-dimensional space graphically. *Journal of the American Statistical Association, 68*, 361–368.

Clement, J. (1985). Misconceptions in graphing. In L. Streetfland (Ed.), *Proceedings of the Ninth International Conference of the International Group for the Psychology of Mathematics Education* (Vol. 1, pp. 369–375). Utrecht, The Netherlands: IGPME.

Cleveland, W. (1993). *Visualizing data.* Murray Hill, NJ: AT&T Bell Laboratories.

Cleveland, W. S., Diaconis, P., & McGill, R. (1982). Variables on scatterplots look more highly correlated when scales are increased. *Science, 216*, 1138–1141.

Cleveland W. S., & McGill, R. (1984). Graphical perception: Theory, experimentation, and application to the development of graphical methods. *Journal of the American Statistical Association, 77*, 541–547.

Cleveland, W. S., & McGill, R. (1985). Graphical perception and graphical methods for analyzing scientific data. *Science, 229*, 828–833.

Croxton, F. E., & Stryker, R. E. (1927). Bar charts versus circle diagrams. *Journal of the American Statistical Association, 22*, 473–482.

DeSanctis, G., & Jarvenpaa, S. L. (1989). Graphical presentation of accounting data for financial forecasting: An experimental investigation. *Accounting, Organizations and Society, 14*, 509–525.

Donoho, A. W., Donoho, D. L., & Gasko, M. (1988). MacSpin: Dynamic graphics on a desktop computer. In W. S. Cleveland & M. E. McGill (Eds.). *Dynamic graphics for statistics* (pp. 331–351). Monterey, CA: Wadsworth.

Dunn, R. (1988). Framed rectangle charts or statistical maps with shading. *The American Statistician, 33*, 165–178.

Edelson, D. C., Gordin, D. N., & Pea, R. D. (1999). Addressing the challenges of inquiry-based learning through technology and curriculum design. *The Journal of the Learning Sciences, 8*(3&4), 391–450.

Eley, M. G. (1981). Imagery processing in the verification of topographical cross-sections. *Educational Psychology, 1*, 38–48.

Eley, M. G. (1983). Representing the cross-sectional shapes of contour-mapped landforms. *Human Learning, 2*, 279–394.

Elting L. S., Martin C. G., Cantor S. B., & Rubenstein E. B. (1999). Influence of data display formats on physician investigators' decisions to stop clinical trials: Prospective trial with repeated measures. *Comment in BMJ, 319*, 1501–1502.

Fagerlin, A., Wang, C., & Ubel, P. A. (2003). Reducing the influence of anecdotal reasoning on people's health care decisions: Is a picture worth a thousand statistics? Manuscript submitted for publication.

Fienberg, S. E. (1979). Graphical methods in statistics. *The American Statistician, 33*, 165–178.

Fisher, H. T. (1982). *Mapping information.* Cambridge, MA: Abt Books.

Fischer, M. H. (2000). Do irrelevant depth cues affect the comprehension of bar graphs? *Applied Cognitive Psychology, 14*, 151–162.

Freedman, E. G., & Shah, P. S. (November, 2001). Individual differences in domain knowledge, graph reading skills, and explanatory skills during graph comprehension. Paper presented at the 42nd Annual Meeting of the Psychonomic Society, Orlando, FL.

Freedman, E. G., & Shah, P. S. (2002). Toward a model of knowledge-based graph comprehension. In M. Hegarty, B. Meyer, & N. Hari Narayanan (Eds.), *Diagrammatic representation and inference* (pp. 8–31). Berlin: Springer–Verlag.

Freedman, E. G., & Smith, L. D. (1996). The role of theory and data in covariation assessment: Implications for the theory-ladenness of observation. *Journal of Mind and Behavior, 17*, 321–343.

Gattis, M., & Holyoak, K. J. (1996). Mapping conceptual to spatial relations in visual reasoning. *Journal of Experimental Psychology: Learning, Memory, and Cognition, 22*, 231–239.

Gelman, A., Pasarica, C., & Dodhia, R. (2002). Let's practice what we preach: Turning tables into graphs. *American Statistician, 56*, 121–130.

Gillan, D. J. (1995). Visual arithmetic, computational graphics, and the spatial metaphor. *Human Factors, 37*, 766–780.

Goettl, B. P., Wickens, C. D., & Kramer, A. F. (1991). Integrated displays and the perception of graphical data. *Ergonomics, 34*, 1047–1063.

Gower, J. C., & Digby, P. G. N. (1981). Expressing complex relationships in two dimensions. In V. Barnett (Ed.), *Interpreting multivariate data*, New York: John Wiley & Sons.

Greaney, J., & MacRae, A. W. (1997). Visual search and the detection of abnormal readings in graphical displays. *Acta Psychologica, 95*, 165–179.

Guthrie, J. T., Weber, S., & Kimmerly, N. (1993). Searching documents: Cognitive process and deficits in understanding graphs, tables, and illustrations. *Contemporary Educational Psychology, 18*, 186–221.

Halford, G. S., Wilson, W. H., & Phillips, S. (1998). Processing capacity defined by relational complexity: Implications for comparative, developmental, and cognitive psychology. *Behavioral and Brain Sciences, 21*, 803–864.

Hastie, R., Hammerle, O., Kerwin, J., Croner, C. M., & Herrmann, D. J. (1996). Human performance reading statistical maps. *Journal of Experimental Psychology: Applied, 2*, 3–16.

Hegarty, M., Carpenter, P. A., & Just, M. A. (1991). Diagrams in the comprehension of scientific texts. In R. Barr, M. L. Kamil, P. Mosenthal, & P. D. Pearson (Eds.), *Handbook of reading research, Volume 2* (pp. 641–668). New York: Longman.

Hegarty, M., Quilici, J., Narayanan, N. H., Holmquist, S., & Moreno, R. (1999). Multimedia instruction: Lessons from evaluation of a theory-based design. *Journal of Educational Multimedia and Hypermedia, 8*, 119–150.

Heino, A. (1995). The presentation of data with graduated symbols. *Cartographica, 31*, 43–50.

Hoadley, E. D. (1990). Investigating the effects of color. *Communications of the ACM, 33*, 120–126.

Hoffman, R. R., Detweiler, M., & Lipton, K. S. (1993). General guidance for establishing color standards for meteorological displays. *Weather and Forecasting, 8*, 505–518.

Hollands, J. G., & Dyre, B. P. (2000). Bias in proportion judgments: The cyclical power model. *Psychological Review, 107*, 500–524.

Hollands, J. G., & Spence, I. (1998). Judging proportion with graphs: The summation model. *Applied Cognitive Psychology, 12*, 173–190.

Huber, P. J. (1987). Experiences with three-dimensional scatterplots. *Journal of the American Statistical Association, 82,* 448–453.

Hunter, B., Crismore, A., & Pearson, P. D. (1987). Visual displays in basal readers and social science textbooks. In D. Willows & H. A. Houghton (Eds.), *The psychology of illustration. Volume 2: Instructional issues.* (pp. 116–135). New York: Springer-Verlag.

Janvier, C. (1981). Use of situations in mathematics education. *Educational Studies in Mathematics, 12,* 113–122.

Jarvenpaa, S. L. (1989). The effect of task demands and graphical format on information-processing strategies. *Management Science, 35,* 285–303.

Jarvenpaa, S. L. (1990). Graphic displays in decision making: The visual salience effect. *Journal of Behavioral Decision Making, 3,* 247–262.

Jarvenpaa, S. L., Dickson, G. W., & DeSanctis, G. (1985). Methodological issues in experimental IS research: Experiences and recommendations. *MIS Quarterly, 9,* 141–156.

Jennings, D. L., Amabile, T., & Ross, L. (1982). Informal covariation assessment: Data-based versus theory-based judgments. In D. Kahneman, P. Slovic, & A. Tversky (Eds.), *Judgment under uncertainty: Heuristics and biases* (pp. 211–230) Cambridge: Cambridge University Press.

Jones, P. M., Wickens, C. D., & Deutsch, S. J. (1990). The display of multivariate information: An experimental study of an information integration task. *Human Performance, 3,* 1–17.

Katz, I. R., Xi, X., Kim, H-J., & Cheng, P. C-H. (2002). Graph structure supports graph description. *Proceedings of the 24th Annual Meeting of the Cognitive Science Society,* 530–535.

Kennedy, M., Te'eni, D., & Treleaven, J. B. (1998). Impacts of decision task data and display on strategies for extracting information. *International Journal of Human-Computer Studies, 48,* 159–180.

Kintsch, W. (1988). The role of knowledge in discourse comprehension: A construction-integration model. *Psychological Review, 95,* 163–182.

Kleiner, B., & Hartigan, J. A. (1981). Representing points in many dimensions by trees and castles. *Journal of the American Statistical Association, 76,* 499–512.

Kleinmuntz, D. N., & Schkade, D. A. (1993). Information displays and decision processes. *Psychological Science, 41,* 221–227.

Klimberg, R., & Cohen, R. M. (1999). Experimental evaluation of a graphical display system to visualizing multiple criteria solutions. *European Journal of Operational Research, 119,* 191–208.

Kosslyn, S. (1989). Understanding charts and graphs. *Applied Cognitive Psychology, 3,* 185–225.

Kosslyn, S. (1994). *Elements of graph design.* New York: WH Freeman.

Kubovy, M. (1981). Concurrent pitch segregation and the theory of indispensable attributes. In M. Kubovy & J. Pomerantz, (Eds.), *Perceptual organization.* Hillsdale, NJ: Lawrence Erlbaum Associates.

Kulhavy, R. W., Stock, W. A., & Kealy, W. A. (1993). How geographic maps increase recall of instructional text. *Educational Technology Research and Development, 41,* 47–62.

Lane, D. M., Anderson, C. A., & Kellam, K. L. (1985). Judging the relatedness of variables: The psychophysics of covariation detection. *Journal of Experimental Psychology: Human Perception and Performance, 11,* 640–649.

Larkin, J., & Simon, H. (1987). Why a diagram is (sometimes) worth ten thousand words. *Cognitive Science, 11,* 65–99.

Lauer, T. W., & Post, G. V. (1989). Density in scatterplots and the estimation of correlation, *Behaviour and Information Technology, 8,* 235–244.

Legge, G. E., Gu, Y., & Luebker, A. (1989). Efficiency of graphical perception. *Perception and Psychophysics, 46,* 365–374.

Lehrer, R., & Romberg, T. (1996). Exploring children's data modeling. *Cognition and Instruction, 14,* 69–108.

Leinhardt, G., Zaslavsky, O., & Stein, M. K. (1990). Functions, graphs, and graphing: Tasks, learning, and teaching. *Review of Educational Research, 60,* 1–64.

Levy, E., Zacks, J., Tversky, B., & Schiano, D. (1996). Gratuitous graphics: Putting preferences in perspective. *Human Factors in Computing Systems: Conference Proceedings* (pp. 42–49). New York: ACM.

Lewandowsky, S., & Behrens, J. T. (1999). Statistical graphs and maps. In F. T. Durso, R. S. Nickerson, R. W. Schvaneveldt, S. T. Dumais, D. S. Lindsay, & M. T. H. Chi (Eds.), *Handbook of applied cognition* (pp. 513–549). Chichester, UK: Wiley.

Lewandowsky, S., & Spence, I. (1989). Discriminating strata in scatterplots. *Journal of the American Statistical Association, 84,* 682–688.

Lewandowsky, S., Herrmann, D. J., Behrens, J. T., Li, S.-C., Pickle, L., & Jobe, J. B. (1993). Perception of clusters in statistical maps. *Applied Cognitive Psychology, 7,* 533–551.

Lohse, G. L. (1993). A cognitive model of understanding graphical perception. *Human-Computer Interaction, 8,* 353–388.

Lohse, G. L. (1997). The role of working memory on graphical information processing. *Behavior and Informational Technology, 16,* 297–308.

Lord, C. G., Ross, L., & Lepper, M. R. (1979). Biased assimilation and attitude polarization: The effects of prior theories on subsequent evidence. *Journal of Personality and Social Psychology, 37,* 2098–2110.

Lowe, R. K. (1993). Constructing a mental representation from an abstract technical diagram. *Learning and Instruction, 3,* 157–179.

Lowe, R. K. (1994). Selectivity in diagrams: Reading beyond the lines. *Educational Psychology, 14,* 467–491.

Lowe, R. K. (1996). Background knowledge and the construction of a situational representation from a diagram. *European Journal of Psychology of Education, 11,* 377–397.

MacEachren, A. (1994). *Some truth with maps: A primer on symbolization and design.* Washington, DC: Association of American Geographers.

Maichle, U. (1994). Cognitive processes in understanding line graphs. In W. Schnotz & R. W. Kulhavy (Eds.), *Comprehension of graphs* (pp. 207–226). Amsterdam, Netherlands: Elsevier Science.

Marchak, F. M., & Marchak, L. C. (1991). Interactive versus passive dynamics and the exploratory analysis of multivariate data. *Behavior Research Methods, Instruments, and Computers, 23,* 296–300.

Mersey, J. E. (1990). Color and thematic map design: The role of color scheme and map complexity in choropleth map communication. *Cartographica, 27,* Monograph No. 41, 1–82.

Merwin, D. H., Vincow, M., & Wickens, C. D. (1994). Visual analysis of scientific data: Comparison of 3-D-topographic, color and gray scale displays in a feature detection task. In *Proceedings of the 38th Annual Meeting of the Human Factors and Ergonomics Society.* Santa Monica, CA: Human Factors and Ergonomics Society.

Meyer, J. (1997). A new look at an old study on information display: Washburne (1927) reconsidered. *Human Factors, 39,* 333–340.

Meyer, J. (2000). Performance with tables and graphs: Effects of training and the visual search model. *Ergonomics, 43,* 1840–1865.

Meyer, J., Shamo, K., & Gopher, D. (1999). Information structure and the relative efficacy of tables and graphs. *Human Factors, 41,* 570–587.

Meyer, J., Shinar, D., & Leiser, D. (1997). Multiple factors that determine the performance with tables and graphs. *Human Factors, 39,* 268–286.

Meyer, J., Taieb, T., & Flascher, I. (1997). Correlation estimates as perceptual judgments. *Journal of Experimental Psychology: Applied, 3,* 3–20.

McKenzie, D. L., & Padilla, M. J. (1986). The construction and validation of the Test of Graphing in Science (TOGS). *Journal of Research in Science Teaching, 23,* 571–579.

Milroy, R., & Poulton, E. C. (1978). Labelling graphs for improved reading. *Ergonomics, 21,* 55–61.

Mittal, V. O., Roth, S., Moore, J. D., Mattis, J., & Carenini, G. (1995). Generating explanatory captions for information graphics. In *Proceedings of the Fourteenth International Joint Conference on Artificial Intelligence '95,* Montreal, Canada.

Morrison, J. B., Tversky, B., & Betrancourt, M. (2000, March). Animation: Does it facilitate learning? Paper presented at the AAAI Spring Symposium on Smart Graphics, Stanford, CA. AAAI Press.

Oestermeier, U., & Hesse, F. W. (2000). Verbal and visual causal arguments. *Cognition, 75,* 65–104.

Phillips, R. J. (1982). An experimental investigation of layer tints for relief maps in school atlases. *Ergonomics, 25,* 1143–1154.

Pinker, S. (1990). A theory of graph comprehension. In R. Freedle (Ed.), *Artificial intelligence and the future of testing* (pp. 73–126). Hillsdale, NJ: Lawrence Erlbaum Associates.

Preece, J., & Janvier, C. (1992). A study of the interpretation of trends in multiple curve graphs of ecological situations. *School Science and Mathematics, 92,* 299–306.

Rittschof, K. A., & Kulhavy, R. W. (1998). Learning and remembering from thematic maps of familiar regions. *Educational Technology Research and Development, 46,* 19–38.

Rittschof, K. A., Stock, W. A., Kulhavy, R. W., Verdi, M. P., & Doran, J. M. (1994). Thematic maps improve memory for facts and inferences: A test of the stimulus order hypothesis. *Contemporary Educational Psychology, 19,* 129–142.

Rittschof, K. A., Stock, W. A., Kulhavy, R. W., Verdi, M. P., & Johnson, J. T. (1996). Learning from cartograms: The effects of region familiarity. *Journal of Geography, 95,* 50–58.

Scaife, M., & Rogers, Y. (1996). External cognition: How do graphical representations work? *International Journal of Human-Computer Studies, 45,* 185–213.

Schaubroeck, J., & Muralidhar, K. (1991). A meta-analysis of the relative effects of tabular and graphic display formats on decision-making performance. *Human Performance, 4*, 127–145.

Schaubroeck, J., & Muralidhar, K. (1992). Does display format really affect decision quality? *Human Performance, 5*, 245–248.

Schiano, D. J., & Tversky, B. (1992). Structure and strategy in encoding simplified graphs. *Memory and Cognition, 20*, 12–20.

Schkade, D. A., & Kleinmuntz, D. N. (1994). Information displays and choice processes: Differential effects of organization, form, and sequence. *Organizational Behavior and Human Decision Processes, 57*, 319–337.

Schunn, C. D., & Anderson, J. R. (1999). The generality/specificity of expertise in scientific reasoning. *Cognitive Science, 23*, 337–370.

Shah, P. (2001). Graph comprehension: The role of format, content, and individual differences. In M. Anderson, B. Meyer, & P. Olivier (Eds.), *Diagrammatic Representation and Reasoning*. Berlin: Springer–Verlag.

Shah, P., & Carpenter, P. A. (1995). Conceptual limitations in comprehending line graphs. *Journal of Experimental Psychology: General, 124*, 43–61.

Shah, P., & Freedman, E. G. (2002). The role of prior knowledge in complex data comprehension. In J. G. Trafton (Chair), *The cognition of complex visualization*. Symposium presented at the 24th Annual Meeting of the Cognitive Science Society, Fairfax, VA.

Shah, P., Freedman, E. G., Watkins, P., Rahman, M., & Miyake, A. (2004). The comprehension of line graphs of multivariate data: The influence of legends, grouping cues, prior knowledge, and graphical literacy skills. Manuscript submitted for publication.

Shah, P., & Hoeffner, J. (2002). Review of graph comprehension research: Implications for instruction. *Educational Psychology Review, 14*, 47–69.

Shah, P., & Shellhammer, D. (1999, June). *The role of domain knowledge and graph reading skills in graph comprehension*. Paper presented at the 1999 Meeting of the Society for Applied Research in Memory and Cognition, Boulder, CO.

Shah, P., Hoeffner, J. H., Gergle, D., Shellhammer, D., & Anderson, N. (2000, November). *A construction-integration approach to graph comprehension*. Poster session presented at the 2000 meeting of the Psychonomic Society, New Orleans, LA.

Shah, P., Mayer, R. E., & Hegarty, M. (1999). Graphs as aids to knowledge construction: Signaling techniques for guiding the process of graph comprehension. *Journal of Educational Psychology, 91*, 690–702.

Simkin, D. K., & Hastie, R. (1986). An information–processing analysis of graph perception. *Journal of the American Statistical Association, 82*, 454–465.

Schmid, C. (1983). *Statistical graphics: Design principles and practices*. New York: Wiley.

Siegrist, M. (1996). The use or misuse of three-dimensional graphs to represent lower-dimensional data. *Behaviour and Information Technology, 15*, 96–100.

Smith, L. D., Best, L. A., Stubbs, D. A., Johnston, J., & Archibald, A. B. (2000). Scientific graphs and the hierarchy of the sciences: Latourian survey of inscription practices. *Social Studies of Science 30*, 1–22.

Somerville, S. C., & Bryant, P. E. (1985). Young children's use of spatial coordinates. *Child Development, 56*, 604–613.

Sparrow, J. A. (1989). Graphical displays in information systems: Some data properties influencing the effectiveness of alternative forms. *Behaviour and Information Technology, 8,* 43–56.

Spence, I. (1990). Visual psychophysics of simple graphical elements. *Journal of Experimental Psychology: Human Perception and Performance, 16,* 683–692.

Spence, I., & Krizel, P. (1994). Children's perception of proportion in graphs. *Child Development, 65,* 1193–1213.

Spence, I., Kutlesa, N., & Rose, D. L. (1999). Use of color to code quantity in spatial displays. *Journal of Experimental Psychology: Applied, 5,* 393–412.

Spence, I., & Lewandowsky, S. (1991). Displaying proportions and percentages. *Applied Cognitive Psychology, 5,* 61–77.

Stenning, K., & Oberlander, J. (1995). A cognitive theory of graphical and linguistic reasoning: Logic and implementation. *Cognitive Science, 19,* 97–140.

Stone, E. R., Yates, J. F., & Parker, A. M. (1997). Effects of numerical and graphical displays on professed risk-taking behavior. *Journal of Experimental Psychology: Applied, 3,* 243–256.

Stone, E. R., Sieck, W. R., Bull, B. E., Yates, J. F., Parks, S. C., & Rush, C. J. (2003). Forground: Background salience: Explaining the effects of graphical displays on risk avoidance. *Organizational Behavior and Human Decision Processes, 90,* 19–36.

Stuetzle, W. (1987). Plot windows. *Journal of the American Statistical Association, 82,* 466–475.

Tabachneck-Schijf, H. J. M., Leonardo, A. M., & Simon, H. A. (1997). CaMeRa: A computational model of multiple representations. *Cognitive Science, 21,* 305–350.

Tan, J. K. (1994). Human processing of two-dimensional graphics: Information-volume concepts and effects in graph-task fit anchoring frameworks. *International Journal of Human-Computer Interaction, 6,* 414–456.

Tan, J. K. H., & Benbesat, I. (1990). Processing of graphical information: A decomposition taxonomy to match data extraction tasks and graphical representations. *Information Systems Research, 1,* 416–439.

Te'eni, D. (1989). Determinants and consequences of perceived complexity in human-computer interaction. *Decision Sciences, 20,* 166–181.

Trafton, J. G., & Trickett, S. B. (2001). A new model of graph and visualization usage. *Proceedings of the 23rd Annual Meeting of the Cognitive Science Society* 1048–1053.

Trafton, J. G., Kirschenbaum, S. S., Tsui, T. L., Miyamoto, R. T., Ballas, J. A., & Raymond, P. D. (2000). Turning pictures into numbers: Extracting and generating information from complex visualizations. *International Journal of Human Computer Studies, 53,* 827–850.

Tractinsky, N., & Meyer, J. (1999). Chartjunk or goldgraph? Effects of presentation objectives and content desirability on *information* presentation. *MIS Quarterly, 23,* 397–420.

Tufte, E. R. (1983). *The visual display of quantitative information,* Cheshire, CT: Graphics Press.

Tufte, E. R. (1990). *Envisioning information.* Cheshire, CT: Graphics Press.

Tufte, E. R. (1997). *Visual explanations.* Cheshire, CT: Graphics Press.

Tuttle, B. M., & Kershaw, R. (1998). Information presentation and judgment strategy from a cognitive fit perspective. *Journal of Information Systems, 12,* 1–17.

Tversky, B. (2001). Spatial schemas in depictions. In M. Gattis (Ed.), *Spatial schemas and abstract thought* (pp. 79–112). Cambridge, MA: MIT Press.

Tversky, B., Morrison, J. B., & Betrancourt, M. (2002). Animation: Can it facilitate? *International Journal of Human-Computer Studies, 57,* 247–262.

Tversky, B., & Schiano, D. J. (1989). Perceptual and conceptual factors in distortions in memory for graphs and maps. *Journal of Experimental Psychology: General, 118,* 387–398.

Tversky, B., Kuglelmas, S., & Winter, A. (1991). Cross-cultural and developmental trends in graphic productions. *Cognitive Psychology, 23,* 515–557.

Umanath, N. S., Scamall, R. W., & Das, S. R. (1990). An examination of two screen/report design variables in an information recall context, *Decision Sciences, 21,* 216–240.

Umanath, N. S., & Vessey, I. (1994). Multiattribute data presentation and human judgment: A cognitive fit perspective. *Decision Sciences, 25,* 795–824.

Vekiri, I. (2001). An investigation of the role of graphical design and student characteristics in scientific reasoning with weather maps. Unpublished doctoral dissertation, University of Michigan, Ann Arbor.

Vessey, I., (1991). Cognitive fit: A theory-based analysis of the graphs versus tables literature. *Decision Sciences, 22,* 219–240.

Vicente K. J., & Brewer, W. F. (1993). Reconstructive remembering of the scientific literature. *Cognition, 46,* 101–128.

Ware, C., & Beatty, J. C. (1988). Using color dimensions to display data dimensions, *Human Factors, 30,* 127–142.

Wickens, C. D., & Carswell, C. M. (1995). The proximity compatibility principle: Its psychological foundation and relevance to display design. *Human Factors, 37,* 473–494.

Wickens, C. D., & Merwin, D. H. (1992, October). *Visualization of higher dimensional databases.* Paper presented at the IEEE Visualization '92 Workshop on Automated Design of Visualizations, Boston, MA.

Wickens, C. D., Merwin, D. H., & Lin, E. L. (1994). Implications of graphics enhancements for the visualization of scientific data: Dimensional integrality, stereopsis, motion, and mesh. *Human Factors, 36,* 44–61.

Winn, W. D. (1987). Charts, graphs, and diagrams in educational materials. In D. Willows & H. A. Houghton (Eds.), *The psychology of illustration.* New York: Springer-Verlag.

Wright, J. C., & Murphy, G. L. (1984). The utility of theories in intuitive statistics: The robustness of theory-based judgments. *Journal of Experimental Psychology: General, 113,* 301–322.

Zacks, J., & Tversky, B. (1999). Bars and lines: A study of graphic communication. *Memory and Cognition, 27,* 1073–1079.

Zacks, J., Levy, E., Tversky, B., & Schiano, D. J. (1998). Reading bar graphs: Effects of extraneous depth cues graphical context. *Journal of Experimental Psychology: Applied, 4,* 119–138.

12

Multimedia Learning: Guiding Visuospatial Thinking with Instructional Animation

Richard E. Mayer

ABSTRACT

Visuospatial thinking occurs when someone forms a mental image and manipulates it in a principled manner. Multimedia presentations – messages consisting of words and pictures – can be designed to prime appropriate visuospatial thinking during learning, which in turn leads to deeper understanding. This chapter examines the theoretical and empirical support for this assertion by describing a cognitive theory of multimedia learning, reviewing the history of attempts to use technology to support visuospatial thinking, summarizing research on eight design principles for fostering visuospatial thinking in multimedia learning, and briefly examining exemplary projects aimed at fostering visuospatial thinking in educational contexts.

INTRODUCTION

What Is Visuospatial Thinking?

Visuospatial thinking occurs when someone forms a mental image and manipulates it in a principled manner. This definition consists of two elements: (a) the content of visuospatial thinking consists of mental images, and (b) the process of visuospatial thinking consists of principled manipulation of mental images. For example, suppose you viewed an animation depicting the operation of a bicycle tire pump along with concurrent narration describing its operation, as summarized in Figure 12.1. Understanding this multimedia presentation requires visuospatial thinking because you must manipulate mental images based on nonarbitrary principles – that is, you must think about what happens when you pull up and push down the handle of a bicycle tire pump. Specifically, in viewing the pump

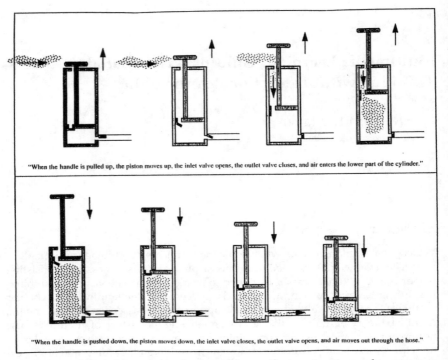

"When the handle is pulled up, the piston moves up, the inlet valve opens, the outlet valve closes, and air enters the lower part of the cylinder."

"When the handle is pushed down, the piston moves down, the inlet valve closes, the outlet valve opens, and air moves out through the hose."

FIGURE 12.1. Narration script and selected frames from animation on how a pump works. Reprinted with permission from Figure 1 in Mayer & Anderson (1991). American Psychological Association.

animation, you mentally construct a cause-and-effect chain in which one change (such as pulling up on the handle) is related to its effect (such as the inlet valve opening and air entering the cylinder) based on a principle (such as air moving from areas of higher pressure to areas of lower pressure). In contrast, an example of an arbitrary mental manipulation is visualizing various colors for the cylinder and handle of a bicycle tire pump.

What Is Multimedia Learning?

Multimedia messages consist of presentations using words and pictures (Mayer, 1997, 2001). The words may be printed or spoken text; the pictures may be static graphics (such as illustrations, photos, or graphs) or dynamic graphics (such as animation or video). The explanation of how a bicycle tire pump works (summarized in Figure 12.1) is a multimedia message because it involves words (in the form of narration) and pictures (in the form of animation). My premise in this chapter is that (a) appropriate visuospatial thinking during learning can enhance the learner's understanding, and (b) multimedia presentations can be designed to prime appropriate visuospatial thinking during learning.

What Is Learner Understanding?

How can we assess the learner's understanding? The classic way to measure learners' understanding is to ask them to use what they have learned to solve a new problem. For example, after receiving the narrated animation of how the pump works, we can ask learners to write answers to problem-solving transfer questions, such as "What could be done to make a pump more effective, that is, to move more air more rapidly?" or "Suppose you push down and pull up the handle of a pump several times but no air comes out. What could have gone wrong?" or "Why does air enter the pump? Why does air exit from a pump?" These questions involve redesigning the system, troubleshooting the system, and explaining the system, respectively. In scoring learners' answers, we tally the number of acceptable answers that they generated to each of four or five transfer questions.

COGNITIVE THEORY OF MULTIMEDIA LEARNING

How Do People Learn From Words and Pictures?

Figure 12.2 presents a cognitive theory of multimedia learning that is based on three basic ideas about the human mind: dual channels, limited capacity, and active processing. First, there are separate channels for processing auditory/verbal and visual/pictorial material (Baddeley, 1986, 1999; Paivio, 1986). Thus, pictures – such as illustrations, photos, graphs, video, and animation – are processed in one information-processing channel whereas spoken words – such as in a narration – are processed in another information-processing channel. Printed words may initially be processed in the visual/pictorial channel and later be processed in the auditory/verbal channel. Second, each channel has a limited capacity (Baddeley, 1986, 1999; Sweller, 1999). Thus, a learner can engage in a limited amount of auditory/verbal processing at any one time and a limited

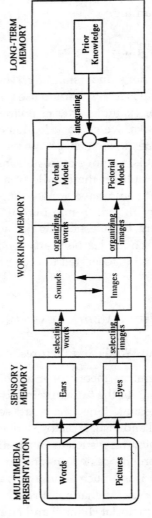

FIGURE 12.2. Cognitive theory of multimedia learning. Reprinted with permission from Figure 3-2 in Mayer (2001). Cambridge University Press.

amount of visual/pictorial processing at any one time. Third, meaningful learning occurs when learners engage in active processing within the channels including selecting relevant words and pictures, organizing them into coherent pictorial and verbal models, and integrating them with each other and appropriate prior knowledge (Mayer, 1999a, 2001; Wittrock, 1989). For deep understanding to occur, learners must engage in these five cognitive processes.

The top row of Figure 12.2 represents the auditory/verbal channel and the bottom row represents the visual/pictorial channel. Words may enter the cognitive system through the ears (if the words are spoken) and pictures enter through the eyes. In the cognitive process of *selecting words* the learner pays attention to some of the incoming words, yielding the construction of some word sounds in working memory. For example, if the narration says, "The negatively charged particles fall to the bottom of the cloud and most of the positively charged particles rise to the top," the learner might select the words "negatives go to bottom of cloud" for further processing in the auditory/verbal channel in working memory. In the cognitive process of *selecting images* the learner pays attention to some aspects of the pictures, yielding the construction of some images in working memory. For example, if the animation shows a cloud with negative signs within small circles moving toward the bottom of the cloud and positive signs within small circles moving to the top of the cloud, the learner may select the image of negatives on the bottom of the cloud for further processing in the visual/pictorial channel in working memory.

In the cognitive process of *organizing words* the learner mentally arranges the selected words into a coherent mental representation in working memory, which I call a verbal model. For example, with the lightning presentation, the learner might construct a causal chain such as "cool moist air is heated" leads to "heated moist air rises" leads to "moist air forms cloud" and so on. In the cognitive process of *organizing images* the learner mentally arranges the selected images into a coherent mental representation in working memory, which I call a pictorial model. For example, with the lightning passage, the learner might construct a causal chain such as an image of blue lines moving over the coast, which leads to an image of red lines moving upward, which leads to the red lines turning into a cloud, and so on. In the cognitive process of *integrating* the learner mentally connects the verbal and pictorial models as well as appropriate prior knowledge from long-term memory. Thus, the learner makes a one-to-one connection between each step in the verbal mental model (e.g., "negatives go to bottom of cloud") and each step in the pictorial mental model (e.g., an image of negative signs in small circles in the bottom of a cloud). In addition, the learner may retrieve and apply relevant information from long-term memory such as the idea that opposite charges attract or that hot air rises.

What Is the Role of Visuospatial Thinking in Multimedia Learning?

Visuospatial thinking is involved in this process of knowledge construction mainly through the processes of selecting images, organizing images, and integrating. Verbal thinking is involved through the processes of selecting words, organizing words, and integrating. According to the cognitive theory of multimedia learning, meaningful learning occurs when learners engage in appropriate verbal and visuospatial thinking as indicated by all five of the cognitive processes summarized in Figure 12.2.

In education, verbal modes of instruction have traditionally played a larger role than pictorial modes of instruction. Verbal modes of instruction are based on words and include spoken text (such as lectures and discussions) and printed text (such as the text portion of textbooks or on-screen text). Pictorial modes of instruction are based on pictures and include static graphics (such as photos, illustrations, figures, and charts) and dynamic graphics (such as animation and video). In spite of the disproportionate emphasis on verbal forms of instruction, advances in computer graphics and the proliferation of pictorial representations on the World Wide Web have led to an increasing interest in exploiting the potential of pictorial forms of instruction as aids to meaningful learning (Pailliotet & Mosenthal, 2000). In this chapter, my goal is to examine how adding visual modes of instruction to verbal ones can result in deeper understanding in learners. In particular, my goal is to explore the conditions under which multimedia explanations prime appropriate verbal and visuospatial thinking required for meaningful learning. A more detailed description of the cognitive theory of multimedia learning is presented in Mayer (2001). In addition, further information about specific kinds of displays such as maps and graphs can be found in Taylor, Chapter 8, and Shah, Freedman, and Vekiri, Chapter 11. Finally, related principles and guidelines for presenting information in external pictorial displays and animation are discussed in Tversky, Chapter 1 and Wickens, Vincow, and Yeh, Chapter 10.

THE ILLUSIVE SEARCH FOR TECHNOLOGY-BASED VISUOSPATIAL LEARNING

Computer-based technologies offer great potential for harnessing the potential power of visuospatial cognition in education. However, media research has a somewhat disappointing history partly because it sometimes focuses on unproductive questions, such as "How can we provide access to cutting-edge educational technology?" or "Which educational technologies are most effective?"

Technology-Centered Versus Learner-Centered Approaches to Educational Technology

First, it is useful to distinguish between technology-centered and learner-centered approaches to educational technology (Mayer, 1999b; Norman, 1993). In the technology-centered approach the focus is on the power of cutting-edge technology, and the major questions concern how best to ensure that students have access to technology. For example, someone who takes a technology-centered approach might be concerned with increasing the number of students who have access to the World Wide Web.

In contrast, the learner-centered approach focuses on how to promote human learning, and the major questions concern how to adapt technologies as aids to human learning. For example, someone who takes a learner-centered approach might be concerned with how to design multimedia presentations so that they foster active cognitive processing within the learner. A premise of this chapter is that media research will become more useful when it shifts from a technology-centered approach to a learner-centered approach (Lajoie, 2000; Lajoie & Derry, 1993; Mayer, 1999b; Norman, 1993).

Research on Media Versus Research on Methods

A related distinction should be made between research on the cognitive effects of different instructional media and research on the cognitive effects of different instructional methods (Clark, 1994; Kozma, 1991, 1994; Mayer, 1997, 2001; Salomon, 1994). Research on media focuses on determining which medium is most effective in promoting student learning, such as whether students learn better with animation than with still illustrations or whether students learn better from computers than from textbooks. Thus, media research is concerned with the devices used to present information and seeks to determine whether one delivery device is more effective than another.

In contrast, research on methods focuses on determining how various instructional methods affect student learning, such as whether a discovery approach is more effective than direct instruction (in both computer-based and teacher-led environments). Thus, methods research is concerned with instructional manipulations and seeks to determine whether one instructional method has a different effect on learning than another instructional method.

The consensus among media researchers is to avoid research questions aimed at determining which medium is most effective, and to instead focus on how instructional methods within each medium affect student learning (Clark, 1994; Kozma, 1991, 1994; Mayer, 1997, 2001; Salomon, 1994). In the debate on media effects, one side argues that media per se have little or no effect on learning (Clark, 1994), whereas the other side argues that certain media afford unique instructional methods that can improve learning (Kozma, 1994). However, all sides agree that it is not the medium that causes learning but rather the instructional method that causes learning. Thus, research is needed to determine how various computer-based instructional methods affect the learner's cognitive processing and learning outcomes.

DESIGN PRINCIPLES FOR FOSTERING VISUOSPATIAL THINKING IN MULTIMEDIA LEARNING

Multimedia Principle

Does adding pictures to a verbal explanation help learners to better understand the explanation? For example, a verbal explanation of how pumps work could consist of the narration given in Figure 12.1, whereas a multimedia explanation could consist of the narration along with the animation shown in Figure 12.1. In both cases, students hear the same verbal explanation, but the students who receive a multimedia explanation also see a concurrent animation depicting the steps in the operation of the pump.

According to a common senseview, the words and pictures both convey the same information so the information provided by adding the animation is redundant. Thus, students who receive the verbal explanation in the form of narration should perform as well on the transfer test as students who receive the multimedia explanation in the form of narration and concurrent animation.

Is there a problem with the commonsense view? The problem is that it conflicts with the cognitive theory of multimedia learning – and, in particular, with the idea that visuospatial thinking can enhance the learner's understanding of an explanation. The multimedia presentation encourages the learner to build a pictorial mental model of the pump system and to mentally connect it with a verbal mental model of the pump system. According to the cognitive theory of multimedia learning, deeper understanding occurs when students mentally connect pictorial and verbal representations of the explanation. This process is more likely to occur for multimedia presentations than for presentations in words alone.

Do students learn more deeply from a multimedia explanation than from a verbal explanation? We addressed this issue in a set of three studies in which students either viewed a narrated animation about pumps or brakes, or simply listened to a narration (Mayer & Anderson, 1991, Experiment 2a; Mayer & Anderson, 1992, Experiments 1 and 2). In each of the three studies, students scored substantially higher on the transfer test when they received a multimedia explanation rather than a verbal explanation. The median effect size was 1.90.

These results point to the importance of visuospatial thinking in understanding explanations, and allow us to offer the *multimedia principle*: Students learn more deeply from multimedia presentations involving words and pictures than from words alone. This principle is summarized on the first line of Table 12.1. The multimedia principle is also consistent with Rieber's (1990) finding that students learn better from computer-based science lessons when animated graphics are included.

The multimedia principle is consistent with the cognitive theory of multimedia learning, which holds that students understand more deeply when they engage in all five cognitive processes shown in Figure 12.2. When students learn solely from words they may be able to select and organize words, but they are less likely to be able to select images, organize images, and integrate (as they must generate the images on their own). However, when students learn from words and pictures that can select and organize words into a verbal model, they can select and organize images into a pictorial model, and therefore they are able to better integrate their visual and verbal models. Thus, students receiving multimedia messages are more likely to engage in all five cognitive processes than are students receiving words alone.

Contiguity Principle

How should words and pictures be coordinated in multimedia presentations? For example, consider a narrated animation that explains how brakes work, as summarized in Figure 12.3. In the narrated animation, corresponding words and pictures are presented simultaneously so that, for example, when the narration says, "The piston moves forward in the master cylinder," the animation depicts the piston moving forward in the master cylinder. In contrast, consider a situation in which the entire narration is

TABLE 12.1. *Principles of Multimedia Learning: How to Promote Visuospatial Thinking*

	Principle	Number of tests	Effect size
1.	Multimedia principle: Deeper learning from words and pictures than from words alone.	3 of 3	1.90
2.	Contiguity principle: Deeper learning from presenting words and pictures simultaneously rather than successively.	8 of 8	1.30
3.	Coherence principle: Deeper learning when extraneous words, sounds, or pictures are excluded rather than included.	4 of 4	0.82
4.	Modality principle: Deeper learning when words are presented as narration rather than as on-screen text.	4 of 4	1.17
5.	Redundancy principle: Deeper learning when words are presented as narration rather than as both narration and on-screen text.	2 of 2	1.24
6.	Personalization principle: Deeper learning when words are presented in conversational style rather than formal style.	2 of 2	0.82
7.	Interactivity principle: Deeper learning when learners are allowed to control the presentation rate than when they are not.	1 of 1	0.97
8.	Signaling principle: Deeper learning when key steps in the narration are signaled rather than nonsignaled.	1 of 1	0.74

presented before or after the entire animation, so the narration and animation are presented successively.

At first glance, it might appear that the successive presentation would promote learning as well or even better than simultaneous presentation. In both presentations, the learner receives exactly the same narration and animation, so you might expect both presentations to produce equivalent levels of learning. Learners exposed to the successive presentation spend twice as much time as students in the simultaneous presentation, so you might even expect the successive presentation to produce better learning than the simultaneous presentation.

What's wrong with this commonsense view? What's wrong is that it conflicts with our understanding of how people learn, as summarized in the cognitive theory of multimedia learning. According to the cognitive theory

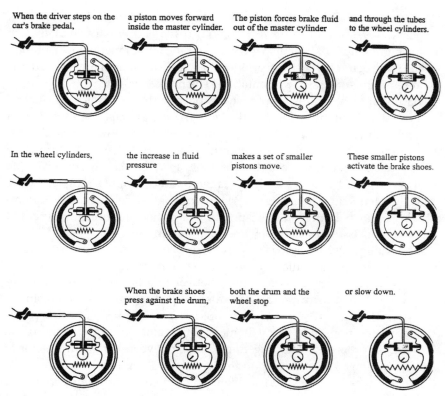

When the driver steps on the car's brake pedal,

a piston moves forward inside the master cylinder.

The piston forces brake fluid out of the master cylinder

and through the tubes to the wheel cylinders.

In the wheel cylinders,

the increase in fluid pressure

makes a set of smaller pistons move.

These smaller pistons activate the brake shoes.

When the brake shoes press against the drum,

both the drum and the wheel stop

or slow down.

FIGURE 12.3. Narration script and selected frames from animation on how brakes work. Reprinted with permission from Figure 2 in Mayer & Anderson (1992). American Psychological Association.

of multimedia learning, students are more likely to engage in productive cognitive processing when corresponding words and pictures are presented at the same time. Simultaneous presentation increases the chances that corresponding words and pictures will be in working memory at the same time, thereby enabling the learner to construct mental connections between them. This cognitive processing – which has visuospatial thinking at its core – should result in deeper understanding as reflected in measures of problem-solving transfer.

Does simultaneous presentation result in deeper learning than successive presentation? This question was addressed in a set of eight studies in which students viewed a narrated animation about lightning, brakes, pumps, or lungs in which the animation and narration were simultaneous or successive (Mayer & Anderson, Experiments 1 and 2a; Mayer &

Anderson, 1992, Experiments 1 and 2; Mayer & Sims, 1994, Experiments 1 and 2; Mayer, Moreno, Boire, & Vagge, 1999, Experiments 1 and 2). In each of the eight studies, students who received the simultaneous presentation performed better on tests of problem-solving transfer than did students who received successive presentation. The median effect size was 1.30.

Based on these results, I propose a condition that promotes productive visuospatial thinking, which I call the *contiguity principle*: Students learn more deeply from multimedia presentations in which animation and narration are presented simultaneously rather than successively. This principle is summarized in the second line of Table 12.1. The contiguity principle is also consistent with research by Baggett and colleagues (Baggett, 1984, 1989; Baggett & Ehrenfeucht, 1983) showing that students learn an assembly procedure better when corresponding narration and film are presented simultaneously than when they are separated in time.

The contiguity principle is consistent with the cognitive theory of multimedia learning, particularly its assertion that meaningful learning occurs when learners can make connections between verbal and pictorial representations. When corresponding words and pictures are presented simultaneously, learners are more likely to hold corresponding verbal and pictorial representations in working memory at the same time, thus enabling the integration process of building connections between verbal and pictorial representations. When corresponding words and pictures are presented at different times, learners are less likely to hold corresponding verbal and pictorial representations in working memory at the same time, and thus less likely to engage in the process of integration of verbal and pictorial representations. Thus, simultaneous presentation is more likely to enable the integration process than is successive presentation.

Coherence Principle

How can we make multimedia presentations more interesting? For example, consider a narrated animation that explains how lightning storms develop, as summarized in Figure 12.4. To spice up this lesson we could insert a few short video clips showing severe lightning storms or what happened when a golfer was struck by lightning. Alternatively, we could add background music and environmental sounds – such as the sound of wind blowing. We could even insert some additional narration such as a brief story about a football player's experience of being struck by lightning or what happens when lightning strikes an airplane in flight. The rationale

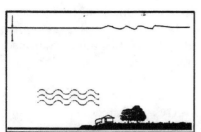

"Cool moist air moves over a warmer surface and becomes heated."

"Warmed moist air near the earth's surface rises rapidly."

"As the air in this updraft cools, water vapor condenses into water droplets and forms a cloud."

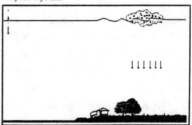

"The cloud's top extends above the freezing level, so the upper portion of the cloud is composed of tiny ice crystals."

"Eventually, the water droplets and ice crystals become too large to be suspended by the updrafts."

"As raindrops and ice crystals fall through the cloud, they drag some of the air in the cloud downward, producing downdrafts."

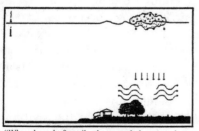

"When downdrafts strike the ground, they spread out in all directions, producing the gusts of cool wind people feel just before the start of the rain."

"Within the cloud, the rising and falling air currents cause electrical charges to build."

FIGURE 12.4. Portion of the narration script and selected frames from animation on how lightning forms. Reprinted with permission from Figure 1 in Mayer & Moreno (1998). American Psychological Association.

for adding these interesting adjuncts is that they will motivate the learner to exert more effort in understanding the narrated animation. This rationale is based on interest theory – the idea that adding interesting adjuncts arouses the learner and this arousal results in increased attention to the incoming material (Harp & Mayer, 1997, 1998).

What's wrong with this interest theory of learning, which posits that students learn more from an expanded version of a multimedia presentation (i.e., containing interesting adjuncts) than from a basic version (i.e., containing no interesting adjuncts)? Dewey (1913) was the first educational thinker to warn against viewing interest as some sort of flavoring that could be sprinkled on an otherwise boring lesson. Overall, research on *seductive details* shows that adding interesting but irrelevant text to a passage does not enhance learning of the passage and sometimes actually hinders learning (Renninger, Hidi, & Krapp, 1992). According to the cognitive theory of multimedia learning, adding interesting but irrelevant material to a multimedia presentation can overload one of the channels and thereby disrupt the process of making sense of the explanation in several ways. For example, adding video clips can cause the learner to pay attention to the sensational material in the video clips rather than to the causal explanation in the animation; inserting video clips can disrupt the process of building a causal chain because the video separates steps in the chain; and learners may use the content of the video clips as an assimilative context, encouraging them to relate all the material to the theme of lightning dangers.

Do students learn more deeply from a basic version than from an expanded version of a multimedia presentation? This question was addressed in a set of four studies in which students viewed a multimedia presentation about lightning or brakes that either did or did not include additional words, sounds, or video (Mayer, Heiser, & Lonn, 2001, Experiments 1 and 3; Moreno & Mayer, 2000a, Experiments 1 and 2). For example, in the presentation about lightning, additional words included descriptions of events in which a person was struck by lightning, additional sounds included background instrumental music or sounds of lightning storms, and additional video included short video clips of lightning storms. In each of the four studies, students who received the basic version (i.e., without added words, sounds, or video) performed better on tests of problem-solving transfer than did students who received the expanded version. The median effect size was 0.82.

Based on these results, I propose a condition that promotes productive visuospatial thinking, which I call the *coherence principle*: Students learn more deeply from multimedia presentations in which extraneous words, sounds, and video are excluded rather than included. This principle is summarized in the third line of Table 12.1. Supporting evidence comes from a study by Mayer, Heiser, and Lonn (2001, Experiment 4) in which presenting extraneous video clips and narration before a multimedia message resulted in poorer learning than presenting the same extraneous video clips and narration after the multimedia message. Our explanation is that when students receive the extraneous material before the presentation, this primes an inappropriate schema (e.g., stories about near-death experiences from lightning) that students use for assimilating and organizing the multimedia message about lightning formation. However, when the extraneous material comes at the end, students are more likely to assimilate and organize the multimedia message based on a cause-and-effect explanation of lightning. In related research, Kozma (1991) reports that audio portions of a television presentation can attract people's attention momentarily to various irrelevant features of the images on the screen.

The coherence principle is consistent with the cognitive theory of multimedia learning in several ways. First, a concise presentation fosters the processes of selecting words and selecting images because learners are more likely to select relevant material from a concise presentation than from one containing large amounts of extraneous material. Second, a concise presentation fosters the processes of organizing words and organizing images because learners are better able to build a step-by-step causal chain when there is no extraneous material between the steps. Third, a concise presentation can enable the process of integrating because fewer cognitive resources are used for other cognitive processes such as figuring out which material to attend to and figuring out how to organize the incoming material. In short, concise presentations are more likely than elaborated presentations to foster the cognitive processes needed for meaningful learning.

Modality Principle

So far, our research shows that visuospatial thinking is fostered by concise animated narrations. When sound is not readily available, it might make sense to present the narration as on-screen text. In this way, students receive both words (as on-screen text) and pictures (as animation) and the words are presented concurrently with the corresponding portions of the animation. Common sense tells us that words mean the same thing whether they are presented as narration or as on-screen text, so it is harmless to change narration to animation in multimedia explanations.

Is there a problem with this commonsense recommendation? There is a serious problem according to the cognitive theory of multimedia learning. The visual channel can become overloaded when learners must use their visual cognitive resources both to read the on-screen text and to watch the animation. In contrast, when words are presented as narration, the words are processed in the auditory channel. This frees the visual channel to focus on processing the animation. In short, presenting animation and narration makes more efficient use of cognitive resources than does on-screen text, thus allowing for more productive visuospatial thinking during learning.

Do students learn more deeply from presenting animation and narration than from animation and on-screen text? In each of the four studies involving multimedia explanations of lightning formation or how brakes work, students performed better on transfer tests when the multimedia presentation consisted of animation and narration instead of animation and on-screen text (Mayer & Moreno, 1998, Experiments 1 and 2; Moreno & Mayer, 1999, Experiments 1 and 2). The median effect size was 1.17.

These results pinpoint a condition that promotes productive visuospatial thinking, which I call the *modality principle*: Students learn more deeply from animation and narration than from animation and on-screen text. This principle is summarized in the fourth line in Table 12.1. The modality effect was first identified in a paper-based environment by Mousavi, Low, and Sweller (1995); students learned to solve geometry problems more productively from printed illustrations and concurrent narration than from printed illustrations and printed text.

The theoretical rationale for the modality principle can be explained within the context of the cognitive theory of multimedia learning. When learners must attend to animation and on-screen text, the visual channel can become overloaded because both pictures and words must be processed (at least initially) through the eyes. When learners receive animation and narration, the pictures can be processed in the visual channel and the words can be processed in the auditory channel. Thus, the visual channel is less likely to become overloaded and there is a greater chance that learners will be able to attend to relevant images and words (i.e., select images and select words).

Redundancy Principle

Another suggestion for improving a multimedia presentation is to present animation along with concurrent narration and on-screen text. The rationale for presenting the same words in two formats is that students will be able to choose the format that best suits their learning style. If students learn best from spoken words, they can pay attention to the narration; if they learn best from printed words, they can pay attention to the on-screen text. In short, adding on-screen text to a narrated animation can be justified on the grounds that it better accommodates individual learning styles.

What's wrong with this seemingly reasonable recommendation? According to the cognitive theory of multimedia learning, the added on-screen text will compete with the animation for cognitive resources in the visual channel – creating what Sweller (1999) calls a split-attention effect. In short, students will have to pay attention visually to both the printed words and the animation, resulting in a detriment to their processing of both the words and pictures. Thus, the cognitive theory of multimedia learning predicts that students learn more deeply from animation and narration than from animation, narration, and on-screen text.

In order to test this prediction, my colleagues and I conducted two comparisons in which students learned about lightning formation from animation and narration or from animation, narration, and on-screen text (Mayer, Heiser, & Lonn, 2001, Experiments 1 and 2). In both studies, students who received animation and narration performed better on transfer tests than did students who received animation, narration, and on-screen text. The median effect size was 1.24.

These results suggest another condition that promotes productive visuospatial thinking, which can be called the *redundancy principle*: Students learn more deeply from multimedia presentations consisting of animation and narration than from animation, narration, and on-screen text. This principle is summarized in the fifth line of Table 12.1. It is a somewhat more restricted version of the redundancy principle originally proposed by Kalyuga, Chandler, and Sweller (1999) and by Sweller (1999) based on research with printed diagrams, speech, and printed text. Specifically, Sweller and his colleagues use the term redundancy to refer to any situation in which "eliminating redundant material results in better performance than when redundant material is included" (Kalyuga, Chandler, & Sweller, 1998, p. 2). This may include a wide range of situations, including a situation in which a self-contained diagram is more effective than a self-contained diagram along with redundant narration. In contrast, I use the term redundancy to refer to a subset of such situations – namely, those in which students learn more deeply from animation and narration than from animation, narration, and on-screen text.

The theoretical rationale for the redundancy principle can be explained in the same way as the modality principle. When learners must attend to animation, on-screen text, and animation, the visual channel can become overloaded because the learner must process the animation and on-screen text (at least initially) through the eyes. In addition, learners may expend additional cognitive resources in trying to reconcile on-screen with concurrent narration, and thereby have an inadequate amount of cognitive resources to attend to relevant portions of the animation. When learners receive animation and narration (without redundant on-screen text), the pictures can be processed in the visual channel and the words can be processed in the auditory channel. Thus, the visual channel is less likely to be overloaded and there is a greater chance that learners will be able to attend to relevant images and words (i.e., select images and select words).

Personalization Principle

In the previous sections, our various attempts to improve on animated narrations failed: Learning was impaired when we increased the presentation time by presenting the animation and narration successively, added interesting adjunct material such as interspersed video clips, changed the narration to on-screen text, or added on-screen text. Undaunted, let's continue to search for improvements – but this time focus on improvements that are consistent with the cognitive theory of multimedia learning.

Let's return to the issue of how to increase students' interest and motivation so that they will try hard to make sense of the material. Adding interesting adjuncts did not improve learning, presumably because the adjuncts disrupted the processes of sensemaking in the learner. In contrast, students may try harder to understand a computer-based message when they feel that they are engaged in a social interaction (Reeves & Nass, 1996). Thus, a potentially useful recommendation is to add a conversational style to the narration in a multimedia explanation, such as adding personal comments and using first and second person rather third person constructions.

Do students learn more deeply from a personalized version than from a nonpersonalized version of a multimedia presentation? This question was addressed in a set of two studies in which students viewed a multimedia presentation about lightning that included either personalized or nonpersonalized prose (Moreno & Mayer, 2000b, Experiments 1 and 2). For example, the first segment in the personalized version included the addition, "Congratulations! You have just witnessed the birth of your own cloud." As another example, in the second segment the sentence, "The cloud's top extends above the freezing level, so the upper portion of the cloud is composed of tiny ice crystals," was changed to "Your cloud's top extends above the freezing level, so the upper portion of your cloud is composed of tiny ice crystals." Overall, in both studies, students performed better on transfer tests when the words were presented in conversational style rather than expository style. The median effect size was 1.30.

This result allows us to offer another condition that promotes productive visuospatial thinking, which can be called the *personalization effect*: Students learn more deeply when words are presented in a conversational style than in an expository style. This principle is listed in the sixth line of Table 12.1, and is consistent with related findings reported by Reeves and Nass (1996).

The theoretical explanation for the personalization effect is based on an elaboration of the cognitive theory of multimedia learning in which personalized text is assumed to prime a conversational schema in learners. The conversational schema includes a set of rules for how to communicate, including the idea that one tries hard to foster the comprehension process. When a learner accepts the computer as a conversational partner, the learner is more likely to try harder to understand what the computer is saying. By trying harder to understand, the learner is more likely to engage in the five cognitive processes underlying meaningful learning.

Interactivity Principle

Let's explore another theory-based recommendation for improving on narrated animations – allowing learners to have some control over the presentation rate. For example, the lightning passage consists of 16 segments; each segment lasts about 10 seconds and contains a sentence and animation clip that depicts one major change. To give learners more control, we added a button in the lower right corner that said "Click here to continue." When the learner clicked the button, the next segment was presented, consisting of about 10 seconds' worth of narrated animation. In this way, learners could receive the entire presentation, segment by segment, at their own rates.

According to the cognitive theory of multimedia learning, adding simple user interactivity can improve learning because it reduces the chances of cognitive overload and it encourages learners to engage in visuospatial thinking. At the end of each segment, learners can take all the time they need to build a visual image and coordinate it with the verbal explanation.

Do students learn more deeply from interactive versions of a multimedia explanation than from fixed versions? As predicted, in the one study where we tested this issue, students performed better on a transfer test when an explanation of lightning formation was presented in interactive form rather than fixed form (Mayer & Chandler, 2001, Experiment 2). The effect size was 0.97.

This research offers preliminary evidence consistent with a possible new condition for promoting visuospatial thinking that we call the *interactivity principle*: Students learn more deeply when they can control the presentation rate of multimedia explanations than when they cannot. This principle is summarized in the seventh line of Table 12.1. Prior research on learner control has led to inconclusive results, attributable to "the lack of theoretical foundations undergirding the experiments" (Williams, 1996, p. 963).

The theoretical rationale for the interactivity principle is based on the cognitive theory of multimedia learning because allowing learner control of the rate of presentation enables learners to better control their cognitive processing during learning. When learners can control the pace of presentation, they have adequate time to organize and integrate the relevant material in each segment. When learners cannot control the pace of presentation, they may not have adequate time to build connections between pieces of information that they attend to.

Signaling Principle

Finally, let's examine a final theory-based recommendation for improving on narrated animations – incorporating signals into the narration that help the learner determine the important ideas and how they are organized. For example, Figure 12.5 presents selected frames and script segments from a multimedia explanation of how airplanes achieve lift. The narration in this version is signaled because it contains: (a) an introductory outline of the main steps in lift (including the phrases beginning with "first," "second," and "third"), (b) headings spoken in a deeper voice and keyed to these steps (such as "Wing shape: Curved upper surface is longer" or "Air flow: Air moves faster across top of wing" or "Air pressure: Pressure on the top is less"), (c) pointer words aimed at showing the causal links among the steps such as "because it's curved ...," and (d) highlighted words spoken in a louder voice (such as emphasizing "top," "longer", and "bottom" in the sentence, "... the surface of the top of the wing is longer than on the bottom"). The signaling did not add any new content words to the passage,

"Airplane Flight: The Principles of Lift."

"What is needed to cause an aircraft, which is heavier than air, to climb into the air and stay there? An aerodynamic principle formulated by Daniel Bernouille in 1738 helps explain it."

"Bernouille's Principle explains how upward forces, called lift, act upon the plane when it moves through the air."

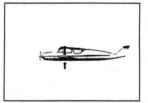

"To understand how lift works, you need to focus on differences between the top and bottom of an airplane's wing."

"First, how the top of the wing is *shaped* differently than the bottom."

"Second, how quickly *air flows* across the top surface, compared to across the bottom surface."

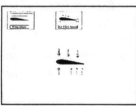

"and third, how the *air pressure* on the top of the wing compares to that on the bottom of the wing."

"Wing Shape: Curved upper surface is longer."

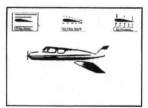

"A cross-section of a bird's wing, a boomerang, and a Stealth bomber all share a shape similar to that of an airplane wing."

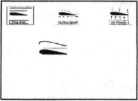

"The upper surface of the wing is curved more than the bottom surface."

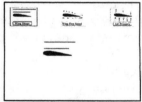

"Because it's curved, the surface of the top of the wing is *longer* than on the **bottom.** This is called an airfoil."

FIGURE 12.5. Portion of the narration script and selected frames from animation on how airplanes achieve lift. Reprinted with permission from Figure 1 in Mautone & Mayer (2001). American Psychological Association.

but rather emphasized the three key steps in achieving lift and the causal relations among them.

According to the cognitive theory of multimedia learning, signaling can help guide the process of making sense of the passage by directing the learner's attention toward key events and the causal relations among them. Even though the signaling is verbal, it can also guide visuospatial thinking by helping the learner construct mental images that correspond to the key ideas (such as the top of the wing being longer than the bottom).

Do students learn more deeply from signaled rather than nonsignaled presentations? In the one study in which we tested this issue, students who received a signaled presentation on how airplanes achieve lift performed better on a transfer test than did students who received a nonsignaled version (Mautone & Mayer, 2001, Experiment 3). The effect size was 0.74.

Based on these results we tentatively propose another condition that fosters visuospatial thinking, which we call the *signaling principle*: Students learn more deeply when multimedia explanations are signaled rather than nonsignaled. This principle is summarized in the bottom line of Table 12.1. Prior research has focused mainly on signaling of printed text (Lorch, 1989; Loman & Mayer, 1983).

The signaling principle is consistent with the cognitive theory of multimedia learning because signals may serve as cues to the learner about what material to attend to (i.e., selecting words) and how to organize the material into a coherent structure (i.e., organizing words). When learners receive an outline and headings, they are able to better select and organize the incoming material. Consistent with the cognitive theory of multimedia learning, signaling produces similar effects for printed text as for spoken text (Mautone & Mayer, 2001).

Finally, it should be noted that the principles are intended as general guides rather than universal prescriptions that must be rigidly applied. The utility of the principles depends on a number of factors including the characteristics of the learners and the nature of the instructional material. For example, our research (Mayer, 2001) has shown that using good design principles is more effective for low prior knowledge learners than for high prior knowledge learners and more effective for high-spatial learners than for low-spatial learners. Thus, the design of multimedia presentations should be based on theories of how people learn from words and pictures (such as the cognitive theory of multimedia learning) rather than on strict adherence to a set of design rules.

INNOVATIONS IN FOSTERING VISUOSPATIAL LEARNING
IN EDUCATIONAL CONTEXTS

Many scholars write about the educational potential of multiple representations – such as presenting material in words and pictures – but the development and evaluation of computer-based multimedia environments in authentic educational contexts remains a formidable challenge. In short, the principles summarized in Table 12.1 – as well as similar principles articulated by Najjar (1998), Narayanan, and Hegarty (1998), and Sweller (1999) – need to be tested within authentic educational contexts. Fortunately, there is a growing arsenal of computer-based multimedia environments for classroom use that are both well designed and well tested. In this section I examine several exemplary projects aimed at improving student learning by incorporating visual and verbal modes of presentation including multimedia programs in chemistry, physics, environmental science, mathematics, and history. Each relies heavily on visuospatial thinking – including various visual representations – as a key component in fostering deep understanding of the topic.

Multimedia Learning in Chemistry

Kozma and colleagues (Kozma, 2000; Kozma, Russell, Jones, Marx, & Davis, 1996; Russell, Kozma, Jones, Wykoff, Marx, & Davis, 1997) developed a computer-based multimedia program called "MultiMedia and Mental Models in Chemistry" (or 4M:Chem) to help students in a chemistry course understand basic principles in chemistry such as how chemical equilibrium is affected by changes in temperature, pressure, and concentration. For each of several experiments, students were asked to predict (i.e., state what they thought would happen in a given situation involving the mixing of two chemicals), observe (i.e., watch a multimedia presentation of the experiment), explain (i.e., state what the results mean), and draw conclusions (i.e., describe how chemical equilibrium works). During the observation phase some students received a narrated animation showing what was happening to the molecules in a mixture, some received a narrated video depicting the actual experiment, some received a narrated graph showing chemical changes over time, and some received all three treatments.

As you can see, the multimedia presentation is consistent with several of the principles listed in Table 12.1. The program is consistent with the multimedia principle because students receive both visual representations (that is, animation, video, or real-time graphs) and verbal representations (i.e., narration) rather than simply receiving words alone. The program is consistent with the contiguity principle because the corresponding parts of the visual and verbal representations were presented simultaneously, that is, "a voice narration directed the students' attention to key features in the representation and described what was occurring" (Kozma, 2000, p. 27). As expected, students who learned from these treatments showed significant improvements in their understanding of chemical equilibrium as measured by pretests and posttests. Although the results are generally consistent with the idea that instruction aimed at visuospatial thinking can improve classroom learning, it would be useful to compare the treatment groups against students who learned from words only (i.e., without the benefit of animations, video, or real-time graphics).

One of the treatments in 4M:Chem – in which students receive animation, video, graphics, and narration at the same time – appears to violate the coherence principle because the visual information-processing system may be overloaded. This problem is partially mitigated by the fact that the learner first receives each representation separately. Consistent with the coherence principle, the group that received three kinds of visualizations did not perform any better on tests of understanding of chemical equilibrium than did the groups that received only one kind of visualization. In this case, adding more information did not result in more learning, perhaps because the learner was unable to adequately process three concurrent visualizations. An important lesson of this research is that students need support in making connections among alternative visual representations.

Multimedia Learning in Physics

White and Frederiksen (1993, 1998, 2000) developed a computer-based physics game called ThinkerTools in which students learned about Newtonian principles of force and motion. Students worked with simulations consisting of objects (such as a circle called a "dot") and mazes (such as an L-shaped corridor). Students could use a joystick to apply a force to an object (called a "kick"). For example, to move the dot through the maze, the learner had to apply impulses in accord with Newtonian principles. According to White and Frederiksen (2000, p. 327), the visual format of the ThinkerTools simulation "allows students to create and experiment with models that are less abstract than algebraic laws." The use of an interactive visual format for helping students understand physics principles is consistent with the multimedia and interactivity principles listed in Table 12.1.

In addition, students were required to discuss and reflect on the principles they had learned, and to be able to state them in words. This reflective activity is consistent with the contiguity principle in Table 12.1 because students must actively connect that visually based experience with words.

Students who learned with the ThinkerTools curriculum performed better on tests of physics understanding than did students who were taught using traditional approaches. Importantly, the reflective activities were essential to improving student learning, that is, learning from computer-based graphics alone was not sufficient. Students also needed some scaffolding aimed at helping them relate their visually based experiences to verbal statements of the principles. This scaffolding was particularly helpful for low-achieving students who, presumably, would not normally engage in this kind of mental integrating process on their own.

Multimedia Learning in Environmental Science

In the Design-a-Plant simulation game (Moreno & Mayer, 2000a; Moreno, Mayer, Spires, & Lester, 2001), students take a virtual trip to another planet that has specified environmental conditions (such as heavy rainfall and lack of sunlight) and must design a plant that would survive there (by choosing appropriate roots, stem, and leaves). Students receive advice, feedback, and scientific explanations from an animated pedagogical agent named Herman the Bug who also provides narration for various animations. The goal of the program is to help students learn about environmental science by understanding the relation between plant structure and function. As you can see, the program is consistent with the multimedia principle because animation and graphics are added to words; the contiguity principle because narration is coordinated with animation; the interactivity principle because students make choices and receive explanative feedback; and the personalization principle because Herman speaks in a friendly, conversational style.

Students who learned from the Design-a-Plant program performed better on problem-solving transfer tests involving new problems than did students who received the identical factual material (including text and illustrations) presented in textbook-like form in formal writing style, without interaction, and without text being placed close to corresponding illustrations (Moreno, Mayer, Spires, & Lester, 2001). In other studies, (a) students learned more deeply when Herman spoke in a friendly, conversational style than in a formal style, consistent with the personalization principle (Moreno & Mayer, 2000a) and (b) students learned more deeply when Herman's words were spoken rather than printed on the screen, consistent with the modality principle (Moreno, Mayer, Spires, & Lester, 2001). Overall, the results suggest that visualizations can have positive effects on promoting scientific understanding but only when used in ways consistent with how people process information.

Multimedia Learning in Mathematics

Nathan, Kintsch, and Young (1992) investigated a computer-based learning environment called ANIMATE in which students build animations to represent the situation expressed in arithmetic word problems and to represent the equations needed to solve the problem. For example, in one problem a huge ant travels from San Francisco toward Detroit and an Army helicopter leaves Detroit traveling west to intercept it. The problem solver uses the ANIMATE system (a) to recreate an actual ant moving at a certain speed from west to east starting at a certain time and a helicopter moving at a certain speed from east to west starting at a certain time, and (b) to create a network diagram showing how the distance–rate–time equations fit together for this problem. Students are encouraged to link their animation to their network and to manipulate them until the animation matches their expectations. As you can see, the ANIMATE environment is consistent with the multimedia principle because students receive both visual and verbal material, the contiguity principle because they are encouraged to make connections between pictures and words, and the interactivity principle because students interact with the system. As expected, students who learn with the ANIMATE program showed greater improvements in their word problem-solving performance than did students who receive training on the same problems but without all the features of the ANIMATE program.

Moreno and Mayer (1999) taught elementary school children how to add and subtract signed numbers (such as $3 - -2 = \underline{\quad}$) by allowing them to interact with a computer-based system. The control version simply presented problems and provided feedback. In contrast, the BUNNY version allowed students to use a joystick to move a bunny along a number line in a way that simulated the problem and to receive feedback showing the correct movement, stating the moves in words, and highlighting the corresponding symbols in the problem. Like the ANIMATE program, the BUNNY program is consistent with the multimedia principle, contiguity principle, and the interactivity principle. High-achieving students in the BUNNY group showed much greater gains in problem-solving performance than did corresponding students who received practice on identical problems in the control group. Overall, the results encourage the effective use of visualizations to promote mathematical understanding.

Multimedia Learning in History

Wiley and Voss (1999) developed a short history lesson to help students learn and write an essay about an historical period, namely, Ireland between 1800 and 1850. One group learned by reading a textbook-like chapter presenting eight sources of information about Ireland from 1800 – 1850 such as a map; biographical accounts of political leaders such as King George III; brief descriptions of the Act of Union, Act of Emancipation, and the Great Famine; census population data; and economic statistics. Another group had access to the same eight pieces of information in a Weblike environment called the Sourcer's Apprentice (Britt & Aglinskas, 2002; Rouet, Britt, Mason, & Perfetti, 1996), in which each source is represented as a book with its title along the spine. Students could open one or two "books" at a time, and could return to the sources at any time while they were writing. Both groups received identical information.

As you can see, the Source's Apprentice program is consistent with several of principles listed in Table 12.1. The program is consistent with the multimedia principle because students have access to verbal modes of presentation (such as biographies and descriptions of laws) and visual modes of presentation (such as maps, figures, and tables) rather than simply verbal presentations. The program is also consistent with the interactivity principle in which students have control over the order and timing of presentation of the eight components in the multimedia presentation. The program is consistent with the spatial contiguity principle because two sources can be compared side by side, and it is consistent with the coherence principle – and the chance of overloading the cognitive system – because it does not allow students to open more than two sources at once. As expected, students who learned in the Weblike environment produced higher-quality essays and performed better on posttests involving problem-solving transfer than did students who learned in textbook-like environment.

Although the program appears to promote deep thinking in learners, some learners may need additional instructional support in how to coordinate multiple sources of information. In the present study, students were encouraged to make connections when they were charged with writing an essay, especially an essay that supports an argument or explanation. Wiley and Voss (1999, p. 310) note that "even without links between sources . . . a multiple source presentation can contribute to a more principled representation of the subject matter." However, additional research may be needed to determine ways to encourage students to integrate knowledge across multiple sources.

Overall, the principles of multimedia design summarized in Table 12.1 are consistent with the research results on computer-based instructional systems for teaching science, mathematics, and history as described in this section. Of course, it is not possible to attribute the effects of the instructional programs to just one or two features – such as the use of visualizations or interactivity – so findings on the effectiveness of these programs cannot be taken as conclusive tests of the design principles listed in Table 12.1. Further research is needed to explore the principles of multimedia learning that are most relevant to the design of computer-based multimedia learning environments. In particular, it is worthwhile to systematically alter the features of a successful program in order to pinpoint the specific features that contribute to learner understanding (as reported by Moreno, Mayer, Spires, & Lester, 2001).

CONCLUSION

Multimedia learning occurs when students are presented with words and pictures, such as a narrated animation. Based on the research summarized in this chapter, I conclude that multimedia learning offers a potentially powerful venue for fostering learner understanding, such as the construction of a coherent mental model. An important part of this process involves visuospatial thinking in which a learner builds and manipulates a mental image of the system.

Overall, our program of research has identified eight conditions that promote visuospatial thinking that leads to understanding of scientific explanations. These eight conditions are listed in Table 12.1 and are consistent with the cognitive theory of multimedia learning. Our work shows that (a) pictorial representations can play an important role in learners' understanding of scientific explanations, and (b) multimedia explanations can be designed in ways that promote productive forms of visuospatial thinking.

These principles can also be applied successfully to larger-scale studies of computer-based multimedia learning in science, mathematics, and history. In sum, the current state of research on multimedia learning highlights the potential of visuospatial forms of instruction for improving student learning.

ACKNOWLEDGMENTS

This chapter is an expanded version of a chapter in *New Directions in Teaching and Learning*, edited by Diane Halpern and Sheldon Zedeck, and published by Jossey-Bass. The author's address is: Richard E. Mayer, Department of Psychology, University of California, Santa Barbara, CA 93106.

Suggestions for Further Reading

This volume presents an in-depth description of the theory and research summarized in this chapter:
Mayer, R. E. (2001). *Multimedia learning.* New York: Cambridge University Press.

This article presents a brief review of research on multimedia learning with an emphasis on design principles:
Najjar, L. J. (1998). Principles of educational multimedia user interface design. *Human Factors, 40,* 311–323.

This volume shows how an important theory of multimedia learning – dual coding theory – applies in educational contexts:
Sadoski, M., & Paivio, A. (2001). *Imagery and text.* Mahwah, NJ: Erlbaum.

This volume describes cognitive load theory and summarizes an important program of research on multimedia learning in educational contexts:
Sweller, J. (1999). *Instructional design in technical areas.* Camberwell, Austrailia: ACER Press.

References

Baddeley, A. D. (1986). *Working memory.* Oxford: Oxford University Press.
Baddeley, A. D. (1999). *Human memory.* Boston: Allyn & Bacon.
Baggett, P. (1984). Role of temporal overlap of visual and auditory material in forming dual media associations. *Journal of Educational Psychology, 76,* 408–417.
Baggett, P. (1989). Understanding visual and verbal messages. In H. Mandl & J. R. Levin (Eds.), *Knowledge acquisition from text and pictures* (pp. 101–124). Amsterdam: Elsevier.
Baggett, P., & Ehrenfeucht, A. (1983). Encoding and retaining information in the visuals and verbals of an educational movie. *Educational Communications and Technology Journal, 31,* 23–32.
Britt, M. A., & Aglinskas, C. (2002). Improving students' ability to identify and use source information. *Cognition and Instruction, 20,* 485–522.
Clark, R. E. (1994). Media will never influence learning. *Educational Technology Research and Development, 42,* 21–30.

Dewey, J. (1913). *Interest and effort in education*. Cambridge, MA: Houghton Mifflin.

Harp, S. F., & Mayer, R. E. (1997). The role of interest in learning from scientific text and illustrations: On the distinction between emotional interest and cognitive interest. *Journal of Educational Psychology, 89*, 92–102.

Harp, S. F., & Mayer, R. E. (1998). How seductive details do their damage: A theory of cognitive interest in science learning. *Journal of Educational Psychology, 90*, 414–434.

Kalyuga, S., Chandler, P., & Sweller, P. (1998). Levels of expertise and instructional design. *Human Factors, 40*, 1–17.

Kalyuga, S., Chandler, P., & Sweller, J. (1999). Managing split-attention and redundancy in multimedia instruction. *Applied Cognitive Psychology, 13*, 351–372.

Kozma, R. B. (1991). Learning with media. *Review of Educational Research, 61*, 179–211.

Kozma, R. B. (1994). Will media influence learning? Reframing the debate. *Educational Technology Research and Development, 42*, 1–19.

Kozma, R. B. (2000). The use of multiple representations and the social construction of understanding in chemistry. In M. J. Jacobson & R. B. Kozma (Eds.), *Innovations in science and mathematics education* (pp. 11–46). Mahwah, NJ: Erlbaum.

Kozma, R. B., Russell, J., Jones, T., Marx, N., & Davis, J. (1996). The use of multiple linked representations to facilitate science understanding. In S. Vosniadou, R. Glaser, E. DeCorte, & H. Mandl (Eds.), *International perspectives on the psychological foundations of technology-supported learning environments* (pp. 41–60). Mahwah, NJ: Erlbaum.

Lajoie, S. P. (Editor). (2000). *Computers as cognitive tools* (Vol. 2). Mahwah, NJ: Erlbaum.

Lajoie, S. P., & Derry, S. J. (Editors). (1993). *Computers as cognitive tools*. Hillsdale, NJ: Erlbaum.

Loman, N. L., & Mayer, R. E. (1983). Signaling techniques that increase the understandability of expository prose. *Journal of Educational Psychology, 75*, 402–412.

Lorch, R. F. (1989). Text signaling devices and their effects on reading and memory processes. *Educational Psychology Review, 1*, 209–234.

Mautone, P. D., & Mayer, R. E. (2001). Signaling as a cognitive guide in multimedia learning. *Journal of Educational Psychology, 93*, 377–389.

Mayer, R. E. (1997). Multimedia learning: Are we asking the right questions? *Educational Psychologist, 32*, 1–19.

Mayer, R. E. (1999a). Multimedia aids to problem-solving transfer. *International Journal of Educational Research, 31*, 611–623.

Mayer, R. E. (1999b). Instructional technology. In F. T. Durso (Ed.), *Handbook of applied cognition* (pp. 551–569). New York: Wiley.

Mayer, R. E. (2001). *Multimedia learning*. New York: Cambridge University Press.

Mayer, R. E., & Anderson, R. B. (1991). Animations need narrations: An experimental test of a dual-coding hypothesis. *Journal of Educational Psychology, 83*, 484–490.

Mayer, R. E., & Anderson, R. B. (1992). The instructive animation: Helping students build connections between words and pictures in multimedia learning. *Journal of Educational Psychology, 84*, 444–452.

Mayer, R. E., & Chandler, P. (2001). When learning is just a click away: Does simple user interaction foster deeper understanding of multimedia messages? *Journal of Educational Psychology, 93,* 390–397.

Mayer, R. E., Heiser, J., & Lonn, S. (2001). Cognitive constraints on multimedia learning: When presenting more material results in less understanding. *Journal of Educational Psychology, 92,* 187–198.

Mayer, R. E., & Moreno, R. (1998). A split-attention effect in multimedia learning. *Journal of Educational Psychology, 90,* 312–320.

Mayer, R. E., Moreno, R., Boire, M., & Vagge, S. (1999). Maximizing constructivist learning from multimedia communications by minimizing cognitive load. *Journal of Educational Psychology, 91,* 638–643.

Mayer, R. E., & Sims, V. K. (1994). For whom is a picture worth a thousand words? Extensions of a dual-coding theory of multimedia learning. *Journal of Educational Psychology, 86,* 389–401.

Moreno, R., & Mayer, R. E. (1999). Cognitive principles of multimedia learning: The role of modality and contiguity. *Journal of Educational Psychology, 91,* 358–368.

Moreno, R., & Mayer, R. E. (1999). Multimedia-supported metaphors for meaning making in mathematics. *Cognition and Instruction, 17,* 215–248.

Moreno, R., & Mayer, R. E. (2000a). A coherence effect in multimedia learning: The case for minimizing irrelevant sounds in the design of multimedia instructional messages. *Journal of Educational Psychology, 92,* 117–125.

Moreno, R. E., & Mayer, R. E. (2000b). Engaging students in active learning: The case for personalized multimedia messages. *Journal of Educational Psychology, 92,* 724–733.

Moreno, R., Mayer, R. E., Spires, H., & Lester, J. (2001). The case for social agency in computer-based teaching: Do students learn more deeply when they interact with animated pedagogical agents? *Cognition and Instruction, 19,* 177–214.

Mousavi, S., Low, R., & Sweller, J. (1995). Reducing cognitive load by mixing auditory and visual presentation modes. *Journal of Educational Psychology, 87,* 319–334.

Nathan, M. J., Kintsch, W., & Young, E. (1992). A theory of algebra word problem comprehension and its implications for the design of learning environments. *Cognition and Instruction, 9,* 329–389.

Najjar, L. J. (1998). Principles of educational multimedia user interface design. *Human Factors, 40,* 311–323.

Narayanan, N. H., & Hegarty, M. (1998). On designing comprehensible interactive hypermedia manuals. *International Journal of Human-Computer Studies, 48,* 267–301.

Norman, D. A. (1993). *Things that make us smart.* Reading, MA: Addison-Wesley.

Pailliotet, A. W., & Mosenthal, P. B. (Editors). (2000). *Reconceptualizing literacy in the media age.* Stamford, CT: JAI Press.

Paivio, A. (1986). *Mental representations: A dual coding approach.* Oxford: Oxford University Press.

Reeves, B., & Nass, C. (1996). *The media equation.* New York: Cambridge University Press.

Renninger, K. A., Hidi, S., & Krapp, A. (Editors). (1992). *The role of interest in learning and development.* Hillsdale, NJ: Erlbaum.

Rieber, L. P. (1990). Animation in computer-based instruction. *Educational Technology Research and Development, 38,* 77–86.

Rouet, J. F., Britt, M. A., Mason, R., & Perfetti, C. (1996). Using multiple sources of evidence to reason about history. *Journal of Educational Psychology, 88,* 478–489.

Russell, J., Kozma, R., Jones, T., Wykoff, J., Marx, N., & Davis, J. (1997). Use of simultaneous synchronized macroscopic, and symbolic representations to enhance the teaching and learning of chemical concepts. *Journal of Chemical Education, 74,* 330–334.

Salomon, G. (1994). *Interaction of media, cognition, and learning.* Hillsdale, NJ: Erlbaum.

Sweller, J. (1999). *Instructional design in technical areas.* Camberwell, Australia: ACER Press.

White, B., & Frederiksen, J. (1993). ThinkerTools: Causal models, conceptual change, and science education. *Cognition and Instruction, 10,* 1–100.

White, B., & Frederiksen, J. (1998). Inquiry, modeling, and metacognition: Making science accessible to all students. *Cognition and Instruction, 16,* 3–118.

White, B., & Frederiksen, J. (2000). Technology tools and instructional approaches for making scientific inquiry accessible to all. In M. J. Jacobson & R. B. Kozma (Eds.), *Innovations in science and mathematics education* (pp. 321–359). Mahwah, NJ: Erlbaum.

Williams, M. D. (1996). Learner control and instructional technologies. In D. H. Jonassen (Ed.), *Handbook of research for educational communication and technology* (pp. 957–983). New York: Macmillan.

Wiley, J., & Voss, J. F. (1999). Constructing arguments from multiple sources: Tasks that promote understanding and not just memory for text. *Journal of Educational Psychology, 91,* 301–311.

Wittrock, M. C. (1989). Generative processes of comprehension. *Educational Psychologist, 24,* 345–376.

Author Index

Subject Index

abstract representations
  examples of, 356
acceleration, representation of, 267
accessibility
  measures of, 346
  spatial gradient of, 350
active locomotion, 259
active processing, learners engaging in, 481
actual navigation, 15
additive effects, of spatial and other
      variables, 353
additive factors methodology, 91
additive similarity tree analysis, 300, 301
ADI (aircraft attitude directional indicator),
      design of, 404
adjacent locations, 315, 317
adults
  guiding of children's map understanding
      by, 241
  navigation systems used by, 217
  spatial competence of, 231
aesthetic value of data, 466
age-associated dementias, incidence of, 194
age by gender interaction, for aides to map
      needing, 325
age factors, 195, 203
  and cognitive ability, 195
  and focus of attention, 362
  and gender differences, 201–203
  and map use, 325
  and reading ability, 362
  in visuospatial abilities, 203
aircraft
  operating in three dimensions, 388
  stalling of, 405

aircraft attitude directional indicator (ADI),
      design of, 404
alignment, 272
  of maps, 240, 273, 309
alignment errors, for reference objects, 13
alignment heuristic, 310
alignment relationship, depiction of, 38
allocentric coding of location, 215
allocentric maps, 279
  three-dimensional, 284
allocentric systems, 265
allothetic signals, for dead reckoning, 268
Alzheimer's disease, brain damage
      resulting from, 88
amodal representations, of spatial
      information, 356
analog, 337
  and display of mental images, 40
  metric "image," 356
  "perceptual symbol systems," 356
  spatial situation models in, 354
analogical mapping, 244
analytic strategies
  versus holistic/spatial strategies, 184
  for spatial visualization tests, 140
anaphor(s), 345
anaphora resolution, measuring, 350
anaphoric noun phrases, 349
anaphoric target sentences, 349
anaphor resolution, 345
anchors, 319, 431
androgens, 186, 187, 192
angular coordinate system, 383, 384
animals. *See also specific animal*
  navigation by, 286